THE
MAHABHARATA

Sabha Parva and Vana Parva (Part 1)

MW01156993

THE COMPLETE MAHABHARATA

MAHABHARATA

Sabha Parva and Vana Parva (Part 1)

RAMESH MENON

RUPA

Copyright © Ramesh Menon 2011

Published 2011 by
Rupa Publications India Pvt. Ltd.
7/16, Ansari Road, Daryaganj,
New Delhi 110 002

Sales Centres:

Allahabad Bengaluru Chandigarh Chennai
Hyderabad Jaipur Kathmandu
Kolkata Mumbai

All rights reserved.
No part of this publication may be reproduced, stored in a
retrieval system, or transmitted, in any form or by any means,
electronic, mechanical, photocopying, recording or otherwise,
without the prior permission of the publishers.

The author asserts the moral right to be identified
as the author of this work.

Typeset in Adobe Garamond by
Mindways Design
1410 Chiranjiv Tower
43 Nehru Place
New Delhi 110 019

Printed in India by
Replika Press Pvt. Ltd.

For Geetha Menon

CONTENTS

VANA PARVA (PART I)

A Brief Introduction

The last complete version of the Mahabharata to be written in India in English prose was the translation by Kisari Mohan Ganguli in the late 19th century. He wrote it between 1883 and 1896. To the best of my knowledge, it still remains the only full English prose rendering of the Epic by any Indian.

More than a hundred years have passed since Ganguli achieved his monumental task. Despite its closeness to the original Sanskrit and its undeniable power, in more than a hundred years the language and style of the Ganguli translation have inevitably become archaic.

It seemed a shame that this most magnificent of epics, a national treasure, an indisputable classic of world literature, believed by many to be the greatest of all books ever written, is not available in complete form to the Indian (or any) reader in modern, literary and easily accessible English: as retold by Indian writers.

So we, a group of Indian writers and editors, warmly and patiently supported by our publisher Rupa & Co, undertook a line-by-line retelling of the complete Mahabharata, for the contemporary and future reader. Our aim has not been to write a scholarly translation of the Great Epic, but an eminently readable one, without vitiating either the spirit or the poetry of the original, and without reducing its length.

This is not a translation from the Sanskrit but based almost entirely on the Ganguli text, and he himself did use more than one Sanskrit version for his work. However, as will be obvious, the style of this new rendering is very much our own, and our hope is to bring as much of the majesty and enchantment of this awesome epic to you as is possible in English.

Ramesh Menon
Series Editor

Acknowledgements

Jayashree Kumar and Kadambari Mishra edited and proofread this volume of the Mahabharata. I am most grateful to them for their fine, painstaking work.

Sabha Parva

CANTO 1

Sabhakriya Parva

AUM! I bow down to Narayana, and Nara, the most exalted Purusha, and also to the Devi Saraswati, and utter the word *Jaya*.

Vaisampayana said, "Then, in Vasudeva's presence, Mayaa Danava worships Arjuna and, hands folded, says repeatedly to him, and feelingly, 'Kaunteya, you have saved me from this Krishna in spate and from Agni Pavaka, who wanted to consume me. Say what I can do for you.'

Arjuna says, 'Great Asura, even by asking, you have already done everything. May you be blessed. Go wherever you please. Be kindly and well-disposed towards me, just as I am towards you!'

Mayaa says, 'Purusharishabha, what you say is worthy of you, exalted one. But Bhaarata, I am keen to do something for you, in joy. I am a great artist, a Viswakarman among the Danavas. Pandava, being so, I want to do something for you.'

Arjuna says, 'Sinless one, you think that I have saved you from death. Even if this is true, I cannot ask you to do anything for me. However,

I do not want to refuse what you ask. Do something for Krishna; that will be enough to requite what I did for you.'"

Vaisampayana said, "Then, Bharatarishabha, urged by Mayaa, Krishna thinks for a moment about what he should ask Mayaa to do for him. Having reflected, Krishna, Lord of the Universe, Creator of everything, says to Mayaa, 'Build a palatial sabha, as you choose, O son of Diti, O best among all artists, for Yudhishtira Dharmaputra. Indeed, build such a palace that no one in this world of men will be able to imitate it even after the closest inspection, within and without. O Mayaa, build a mansion in which we might see a blend of Deva, Asura and Manava styles.'

Mayaa becomes exceedingly pleased, and readily agrees to build a magnificent palace for the Pandava, one truly like a palace of the Devas. Returning, telling Yudhishtira everything that has transpired, Krishna and Arjuna bring Mayaa to him. Yudhishtira receives Mayaa respectfully, offering him the honour he deserves. Mayaa receives that honour, graciously, and holds it in high regard.

O King of the Bhaaratavamsa, that great son of Diti narrates for the Pandavas the legend of the Danava Vrishaparva. Then, after he rests awhile, that greatest of artists, after deep thought and careful planning, sets about building a great palace for the illustrious Pandavas.

In accordance with the wishes of both Krishna and Pritha's son, the Danava of untold prowess, on an auspicious day, performs the propitiatory rituals of laying the foundation. He also pleases thousands of learned Brahmanas with sweetened milk and rice, and with rich gifts of many kinds, then measures out a plot of land, five thousand cubits square, enchanting and beautiful, and suitable for building an edifice which would withstand every season's exigencies."

CANTO 2

SABHAKRIYA PARVA CONTINUED

Vaisampayana said, "One day, when he had lived in Khandavaprastha for a while, happily, looked after with great love and affection by the Pandavas, Krishna, who is worthy of all worship, wants to see his father. He of the large eyes, who is due the worship of the universe, folds his hands to Yudhishtira and to Kunti, and lays his head at the feet of Kunti, who is his father's sister. So adored by Krishna, Pritha sniffs the top of his head and embraces him. Krishna, illustrious Hrishikesa, his eyes now filling, goes to his sister Subhadra, lovingly, and speaks to her – words true and excellent, succinct and apposite, and laden with goodness. The sweetly-spoken Subhadra, in turn, worships him repeatedly, her head bowed, and gives him many messages for her kinsfolk in her father's home.

Bidding farewell to her, blessing her, now Vaarshaneya comes to Draupadi and Dhaumya. The Purushottama pays obeisance to Dhaumya and, comforting Panchali, takes leave of her to depart. Then, mighty, wise Krishna, with Arjuna beside him, goes to his cousins. Surrounded by the five brothers, he is as radiant as Indra among the Devas.

He who flies Garuda upon his banner now wants to perform the rituals undertaken before leaving on a journey and, purifying himself with a bath, puts on fine clothes and ornaments. The Yadavapungava, bull of the race of Yadu, worships the Devas and Brahmanas with garlands of flowers, mantras, prostrations, and with fine perfumes.

When these are done, he, that best of the good and the steadfast, actually thinks of setting out. Krishna now emerges from the inner apartment and, coming out to the outer apartments, he offers Brahmanas, worthy of worship, vessels of curd, fruit and aval, parched-grain, making them bless him copiously. He gives them rich gifts, and walks around them in pradakshina. Finally, climbing into his exceptional golden chariot, of blinding speed, which flies the flag of Tarkhya Garuda and is laden with his mace, discus, sword, his bow Saringa and other weapons, and is yoked to his horses Shaibya and Sugriva, the lotus-eyed one goes forth at a most auspicious moment, on a fine lunar day, during a propitious conjunction of the stars above.

Out of love, Yudhishtira climbs into that chariot after Krishna and, asking Daruka the sarathy to sit aside, takes the reins himself. Arjuna, also, of long arms, rides in that ratha; he walks around Krishna and fans him with a golden-handled, white, silken chamara whisk. Mighty Bhimasena, with the twins, Nakula and Sahadeva, and all the priests and the people of the city, follow behind Krishna's chariot. Kesava Krishna glows like a great Guru being followed by his favourite sishyas.

Then, Govinda embraces Arjuna tightly, speaks to him, pays homage to Yudhishtira and Bhima, and embraces the twins. He is embraced in return by the three older Pandavas, while the twins salute him reverently. When they have gone half a yojana, Krishna, subduer of hostile cities, respectfully asks Yudhishtira not to follow him anymore. Knower of every nuance of karma, Govinda now humbly worships Yudhishtira and clasps his feet. Yudhishtira quickly raises him up and sniffs the top of his head with love.

When he has raised up the lotus-eyed Krishna, Yudhishthira Dharmaraja, son of Pandu, gives him permission to leave, saying,

Svasti! Krishna bids them kind farewell, promising to return soon. With difficulty, he keeps them from following him any further on foot, and then sets out for his home, Dwaraka, with joy in his heart, even like Indra returning to Amaravati. From their intense love for him, the Pandavas stand gazing at Krishna's chariot for as long as they can see it; later their hearts follow him, unsatisfied, when he is out of sight. Finally, Pritha's sons, those bulls among men, minds still fixed on Krishna, turn back to their city, unwillingly.

Krishna swiftly reaches Dwaraka in his chariot, with the heroic Satyaki following him. Devaki's son, Sauri, with his charioteer Daruka, flies as swiftly as Garuda to Dwaraka.

Meanwhile, Yudhishthira, with his brothers and friends, re-enters his splendid capital. That tiger among men dismisses all his relatives, brothers and sons, and seeks to comfort himself in Draupadi's company. Krishna, received with worship by the greatest Yadavas, including Ugrasena, happily enters magnificent Dwaraka. He worships his father, who is old now, and his radiant and gracious mother. He salutes his brother Baladeva, and then the lotus-eyed one sits down. Finally, embracing Pradyumna, Shamba, Nishatha, Charudeshna, Gada, Aniruddha and Bhanu, his sons and grandsons, Krishna goes in to Rukmini's apartment."

CANTO 3

SABHAKRIYA PARVA CONTINUED

Vaisampayana said, "Mayaa Danava says to Arjuna, best of warriors, 'With your leave I must go now, but I will return soon. Upon the northern peak of Kailasa, near the Mainaka Mountains, once while the Danavas performed a great sacrifice on the banks of the Bindusaras, lake of waterdrops, I collected a treasure of varied jewels and gemstones, past compare. This I stored in the palace of Vrishaparva, ever devoted to dharma. If that treasure still exists, Bhaarata, I will bring it back, and then begin building the magnificent sabha of the Pandavas, which I will embellish with every manner of rare, precious jewel, so it shall be celebrated the world over.

Also, Kurunandana, I believe there is a great and fierce mace which the Danava king kept beneath the surface of the Bindusaras after slaughtering his enemies with it. It is mighty and heavy, studded with golden knobs, capable of savaging armies, and equal to a hundred thousand other maces. As the Gandiva for you, this mace is a worthy weapon for Bhima. Also, in the lake is a powerful conch-shell, the reverberant Devadatta, which was once Varuna's. I want to bring all these for you.'

So saying, to Partha, the Asura goes from Khandavaprastha towards the north-east. North of Kailasa, amidst the mountains of Mainaka, is a massive peak of gems and jewels called Hiranyashringa. Next to that sparkling massif is the enchanting lake called Bindu. Upon the banks of the Bindu, long ago, King Bhagiratha sat in intense penance, for countless years, wanting to invoke the Devi Ganga; indeed, she is called Bhagirathi in the world, after that king.

There, upon the banks of that sacred lake, Indra, irradiant lord of all created things, Bhaaratottama, once performed a hundred mahayagnas. He erected for their beauty, and not because it was ordained, yupastambhas, sacrificial stakes, made entirely of gold and encrusted with precious jewels. When he finished the hundred sacrifices, Indra, Lord of Sachi, had what he wanted.

There, too, the fierce Siva Mahadeva, eternal Lord of every creature, dwelt, when he had created all the worlds, and is worshipped by thousands of ganas. There, indeed, Nara and Narayana, Brahma and Yama and Sthanu, being the fifth, perform their profound sacrifices when a thousand yugas come to an end. There, to establish punya and dharma, Vasudeva devoutly performed his sacrifices which lasted countless years. Tens of thousands of stambhas, embellished with golden garlands and vedis, altars of shimmering splendour, Kesava set there.

Arriving in that place, Bhaarata, Mayaa retrieves the great sankha and the other crystalline and invaluable possessions of King Vrishaparva. The great Asura Mayaa takes Vrishaparva's entire hoard, guarded by Yakshas and Rakshasas, fetches it back to Khandavaprastha and there builds for the Pandavas a palace of incomparable loveliness, of unearthly craft, copiously encrusted with precious stones, which becomes renowned throughout the three worlds.

He gives Bhimasena that best of maces, and to Arjuna the exceptional conch, at whose sound all living creatures tremble. The palace which Mayaa builds has golden columns and is spread over full five thousand cubits of land. It shines for leagues around, so it seems to dim even the lustre of the Sun, and it is like the palace of Agni, Surya or Soma. Its radiance, which is a mixture of Heaven's light and this Earth's, is such that the edifice appears to be on fire.

Even like a bank of new clouds appearing in the sky, Mayaa's palace rises from the ground. The palace that Mayaa of untold genius built is fascinating; it is enchanting, built only with the rarest, most exquisite materials, with golden walls and arches, with the most beautiful paintings and hangings; why, it has been said that it excels the Sudharma of the race of Dasarhas, even the palace of Brahma himself.

Eight thousand Rakshasas, called Kinkaras, fierce, with powerful bodies, blessed with untold strength, red eyes, ears pointed like arrowheads, well-armed and who can fly through the air, guard the Mayaa sabha.

Inside the palace, Mayaa sets a lucid tank, in which he has lotuses, whose leaves are dark jewels and whose stalks are of clusters of bright gemstones, and other flowers with leaves of gold. Various waterbirds swim and frolic upon its water. Other resplendent lotuses adorn the tank, and golden fish and tortoises swim in it, and it is clear right to its bottom, where there is no trace of mud; its water is transparent like glass. A flight of crystal steps leads down to the water from its banks, which ripple in the gentle breezes that make the flowers quiver.

The banks of that tank are paved with slabs of priceless marble, set with pearls, and it is told that many a king who comes to the banks of the water mistakes it for solid ground and falls in.

Diverse lofty, great trees are planted all around the palace, verdant, their shade cool, and perennially in bloom, casting a spell of charm all around them. Mayaa creates artificial woods of scented trees, ever fragrant. Countless pools and tanks dot the great gardens, upon which chakravakas and karandavas swim. The breeze which wafts the fragrance of the lotuses that grow upon those waters, as well as of other flowers on land and tree, add to the joy of the Pandavas.

Mayaa builds the palatial sabha in fourteen months, and informs Yudhishtira that it is complete."

CANTO 4

SABHAKRIYA PARVA CONTINUED

Vaisampayana said, "Yudhishtira, best among men, feeds ten thousand Brahmanas payasa of sweetened milk and rice, mixed with ghee; honey mixed with fruit and roots; and with pork and venison. He pleases those holy ones, who have come from various lands, far and near, with delicacies seasoned with seasamum, prepared with rare vegetables called jivanti, rice mixed with clarified butter, and many different meat preparations, indeed with countless dishes, and every manner of fine drink.

He gives them the most excellent robes and other garments, and fine garlands of flowers. The king gives them each a thousand cows, O Bhaarata, and the voices of the gratified Brahmanas can be heard saying, 'What an auspicious day is this!' so loudly, all together, that what they say seems to resound even in heaven.

Finally, having worshipped the Gods, with music and song, with many kinds of rare and wonderful perfumes and incense, the Kuru king enters the great sabha, where athletes, mimes, wrestlers, bards and panegyrists begin to perform, in turns, to please Dharma's illustrious son, with their skills and art. Thus, celebrating their entry into the unparalleled edifice, Yudhishtira and his brothers take their delight within like Indra himself in Swarga.

Upon fine seats within that sabha, great Rishis and kings from other countries sit with the Pandavas. Asita and Devala are there; Satya, Sarpamali and Mahasira; Arvavasu, Sumitra, Maitreya, Sunaka and Bali; Baka, Dalvya, Sthulasira, Krishna Dwaipayana, and Suka Sumanta, Jaimini, Paila, and we the disciples of Vyasa – Tittiri, Yajnavalkya, and Lomaharshana with his son; Apsuhomya, Dhaumya; Animandavya, and Kausika are present, as are Damoshnisha and Traivali, Parnada, and Barayanaka, Maunjayana, Vayubhaksha, Parasarya, and Sarika; Balivaka, Silivaka, Satyapala, and Kritasrama; Jatukarna, and Sikhavat, Alamba and Parijataka; the lofty Parvata, and the great Muni Markandeya; Pavitrapani, Savarna, Bhaluki, and Galava; Janghabandhu, Raibhya, Kopavega, and Bhrigu; Haribabhru, Kaundinya, Babhrumali, and Sanatana, Kakshivat, and Ashija, Nachiketa, Aushija, and Gautama; Painga, Varaha, Sunaka, and Sandilya of great tapasya and punya; Kukkura, Venujangha, Kalapa and Katha – these learned and virtuous Sages, senses and minds completely controlled, and many others, as numerous as the above, all masters of the Vedas and Vedangas, knowers of the laws of dharma, pure, taintless in conduct, all attend upon Yudhishtira Dharmaputra and delight him with their sacred discourses.

So, too, many great Kshatriyas are present in the splendent Mayaa sabha – the illustrious and virtuous Munjaketu, Vivardhana, Sangramjit, Durmukha, the powerful Ugrasena; Kakshasena, great lord of the world, Kshemaka the invincible; Kamatha, the king of Kamboja, and the mighty Kampana who alone made the Yavanas to ever tremble, at mere mention of his name, even as the Vajradhari does the Asuras known as the Kalakeyas; Jatasura, and the king of the Madrakas, Kunti, Pulinda the king of the Kiratas, and the kings of Anga and Vanga, and Pandrya, and the king of Udhara, and Andhaka; Sumitra, and Shaibya Parantapa; Sumanas the king of the Kiratas, and Chanur king of the Yavanas, Devarata, Bhoja, and Bhimaratha, Srutayudha the king of Kalinga, Jayasena the king of Magadha; Sukarman, Chekitana, and Puru that scourge of his enemies; Ketumata, Vasudana, and Vaideha and Kritakshana; Sudharman, Aniruddha, Srutayu of vast strength; the invincible Anuparaja, the handsome Karmajit; Sisupala with his son, the king of Karusha; and the invincible princes of the Vrishni race, all as handsome as Devas – Ahuka, Viprithu, Gada, Sarana, Akrura, Kritavarman, Satyaka, the son of Sini; and Bhismaka, Ankriti, and the powerful Dyumatsena; those greatest of bowmen, the Kaikeyas; and Yagnasena of the Somaka race.

All these Kshatriyas of untold prowess and might, vastly wealthy and well-armed, as well as many others, wait upon Kunti's son Yudhishtira in that sabha, all of them keen to minister to his happiness.

Other great Kshatriya princes, who have put on deer-skin, and who learnt the astra shastra, the science of weapons under Arjuna, attend humbly on Yudhishtira. O Rajan, the princes of the house of Vrishni as well – Pradyumna and Samba, and Satyaki, Yuyudhana, Sudharman, Aniruddha and Saibya, best of men, and many other kings of the Earth, too, Lord of the World, wait upon Yudhishtira.

Dhananjaya's friend Tumburu the Gandharva, as well as Chitrasena, with his Gandharva ministers, and many other Gandharvas and Apsaras, all skilled at music, song and dance, as also Kinnaras, masters of music, sing unearthly songs, perfectly, in beautiful voices, playing on unworldly instruments, for the pleasure of Yudhishtira, his brothers and the Rishis who grace that sabha.

Truly, sitting in that great court, all these mighty heroes, Purusharishabhas of stern vows, men of unwavering dharma, wait upon Yudhishtira, even as the gods in heaven do upon Brahma."

CANTO 5

LOKAPALA SABHAKHYANA PARVA

Vaisampayana said, "While the splendid Pandavas sit in that sabha with the great Gandharvas, O Bhaarata, the Devarishi Narada arrives in that assembly, he who is a master of the Vedas and the Upanishads, he whom the Devas worship, he who knows the Itihasas and Puranas, why, who knows and is witness to all the Kalpas, who knows nyaya, logic, and the great and subtle truths of dharma, who knows exhaustively the six Angas.[1]

He is an unequalled master at reconciling apparently conflicting texts, and applying general principles to specific practical instances, as in interpreting contraries by reference to situational differences. Eloquent is Narada Muni, resolute, intelligent, and he has a powerful memory. He knows the science of morals and politics; he is profoundly learned, skilled at distinguishing inferior things from superior ones, at drawing unerring inference from evidence, competent to judge the correctness or fallaciousness of syllogisms consisting of five propositions.

---

[1]Pronunciation, grammar, prosody, the explanation of basic philosophical terms, description of religious rites, and astronomy.

Indeed, he can successfully debate with Brihaspati himself, with fine and decisive conclusions, accurately framed – about dharma, artha, kama and moksha; a Mahatman he is, and sees the entire universe, on every side, above and below and all around, even as if it is before his very eyes.

He is a master of both Sankhya and Yoga,[1] and he is always eager to humble both the Devas and the Asuras by stoking subtle dissention between them. He knows thoroughly the sciences of war and treaty, is a master at judging matters not within immediate ken, or obvious, as well as the six sciences of treaty, war, military campaigns, maintenance of posts against the enemy, and stratagems of ambuscades and reserves. Why, he is a perfect master of every branch of learning, fond of war and of music, would never shrink from any science or any deed; and possesses not just these but countless other accomplishments.

Having ranged many other worlds, Narada Muni arrives in Yudhishtira's sabha. And the Devarishi, his splendour incomparable, his tejas immeasurable, comes, O King, with Parijata, Raivata the brilliant, Saumya and Sumukha. Swifter than the wind does he arrive there, flying by Rishi patha, and is full of joy to see the Pandavas.

The Brahmana pays homage to Yudhishtira, by uttering blessings over him and wishing him success in every undertaking. Seeing the wise Narada, Yudhishtira, knower of every nuance of dharma, rises quickly from his throne, and his brothers as well. Bowing low, humbly, that king salutes the Muni, in delight, and offers him a lofty seat, with due ceremony. The Pandava king also offers him cows and arghya, honey and the other customary offerings. He adores Narada with gifts of gemstones and jewels, his heart full of joy. Receiving all this worship, appropriately, the Rishi is pleased.

When the Pandavas and the other Sages there have all worshipped him, Narada, who knows the Vedas perfectly, speaks thus to Yudhishtira about dharma, artha, kama and moksha.

Narada says, 'Is the wealth that you earn being spent righteously? Does your heart take pleasure in dharma? Do you also enjoy the pleasures

---

[1]Systems of philosophy.

of life? But does your mind sink under their weight? Lord of Men, do you continue the noble tradition of dharma and artha by which your sires lived and ruled the three kinds of subjects, the good, the middling and the evil? You must never wound dharma for the sake of artha, and never dharma and artha for the sake of kama, which so easily seduces.

Best of victorious men, always devoted to dharma, knower of the timeliness of all things, do you divide your time judiciously between dharma, artha, kama and the pursuit of moksha? Anagha, sinless, with the six gunas of kings,[1] do you attend to the seven ways which kings use to rule?[2] Do you, after carefully considering the strengths and weaknesses of yourself and your enemies, scrutinise the fourteen possessions of your foe – their country, forts, chariots, elephants, cavalry, foot-soldiers, the principal officials of state, the harem, store of food, their army's wealth, the religious beliefs of their soldiers, their accounts of state, their revenue, the wine-shops and other secret enemies?

Having examined, best of kings, your own resources and your enemy's, and having struck peace with him, then do you attend assiduously to the eight everyday occupations – agriculture, trade and the rest? I hope, Bharatarishabha, that your seven principal officers of state,[3] have not succumbed to the influence or blandishments of your enemies, or become idle and complacent because of their wealth? I trust they are all loyal and obedient to you?

I hope your secret counsels are never divulged by yourself or your ministers, or by your trusted spies who go disguised? I hope you are aware of what your friends and your enemies are engaged in? Do you strike peace and make war, each in its proper time? Are you neutral towards those who are neutral towards you? Kshatriya, have you made men like yourself, and old and sage, the restrained and continent, those

[1]Eloquence, generosity, adroitness in dealing with enemies, memory, knowledge of dharma, and knowledge of politics.
[2]Sowing dissension, chastisement, conciliation, gifts, mantras, medicine and magic.
[3]The governor of the citadel, the commander of forces, the chief judge, the general in interior command, the chief priest, the chief physician, and the chief astrologer.

who know what should and not be done, who are pure of blood and birth, and also devoted to you, your ministers?

Bhaarata, the victories of kings are attributed to sage counsel. Child, is your kingdom protected by ministers who know the Shastras, and who keep their counsel to you close? Are your enemies helpless to harm you? You have not, I hope, fallen victim to sleep? Do you wake up at the proper time? Knowing what yields artha, do you consider in the small hours what you should and should not do the next day?

I hope you neither take decisions by yourself nor consult with too many advisors. Do the secret decisions you take become known across the kingdom? Do you swiftly undertake such tasks, which are of great use and easy to accomplish? Are these measures never obstructed? You do not keep your farmers out of your sight? Do you achieve your purposes through agents who are experienced, incorruptible and trustworthy? Mighty King, I trust that the people only know about your undertakings that have already been accomplished, those that have been begun, and those that are partially completed, but nothing of those that are only being contemplated and have not been begun.

Have you appointed seasoned masters, men who can explain the roots of events, and who know dharma and every branch of knowledge, to instruct your princes and the commanders of your army? You must buy one learned man in place of a thousand fools. It is the learned man who provides comfort in times of distress.

Are your fortresses always stocked amply with gold, food, weapons, water, engines of war, arms and other tools, as with engineers and bowmen? Even one intelligent, brave minister, whose passions are under perfect control, and who has wisdom and judgement, can bring a king or the son of a king the highest prosperity. I ask you, do you have at least a single such minister?

Do you seek to know everything about the eighteen tirthas[1] of your enemy and the fifteen which are your own, through thirty and three

---

[1] Road; expedient; school of philosophy.

spies, all of whom who must not know one another? Parantapa, do you watch your enemies vigilantly, and without their knowledge?

Is the priest whom you worship humble, pure in blood, renowned, and without either envy or illiberality? Have you engaged a Brahmana of faultless conduct, intelligence, and guileless, as well as thorough in the laws, to perform your daily rituals before the sacred agni? Does he inform you at the proper time when a homa needs to be performed?

Is your astrologer skilled at reading physiognomy, interpreting omens, and competent to neutralise disturbances of nature? Have you engaged respectable servants to serve in respectable offices, indifferent ones in indifferent offices, and lowly ones in offices that are low? Have you appointed loyal, honest ministers, men born into bloodlines which are pure, superior and noble for generations?

You do not, surely, oppress your people with harsh and cruel punishments? Bharatarishabha, do your ministers rule the kingdom in accordance with your dictates? Do your ministers ever slight you like sacrificial priests slighting men who have fallen and can perform no more sacrifices, or like wives slighting husbands who are haughty and incontinent in their behaviour?

Is your Senapati confident, brave, intelligent, patient, of good conduct and noble birth, devoted to you, and able? Do you treat the chief commanders of your army with utmost consideration and regard? Are they men skilled in every kind of warfare, bold, well-behaved, and endowed with prowess? Do you give your soldiers their sanctioned rations and wages at the appointed time? You do not trouble them by withholding these? You do know that, when troops are plunged in misery by receiving irregular or insufficient wages and rations, they are driven to mutiny, which the wise regard as among the most dangerous harms in a kingdom?

Are all the main noblemen devoted to you, and ready to lay down their lives, cheerfully, in battle for you? I hope that you do not allow any one man, of unrestrained passions, to rule many aspects of military concern, pertaining to your army.

Do you have any excellent servants, especially accomplished and of exceptional ability, who are disgruntled about not receiving some extra remuneration from you, as well as some more regard? I hope that you reward men of learning, humility, and mastery over every branch of knowledge with gifts and honour appropriate to their merit? Bharatarishabha, I trust that you support the wives and children of men who have laid down their lives for you?

Son of Pritha, do you cherish with a father's affection the enemy whom you have weakened or vanquished in battle, and the one who has sought refuge in you? Lord of the Earth, are you equal to all men? Can anyone approach you without fear, even as if you were their mother and father?

O Bull of the race of Bhaarata, do you march against your enemy, immediately, having thought well about the three kinds of forces,[1] when you hear he is weak? Subduer of all your enemies, do you go forth, when the right time comes, having carefully considered all the omens you see, the resolutions you have made, and that final victory depends upon the twelve mandalas?[2] Parantapa, do you give gems and jewels to the main officers of the enemy, as they deserve, without your enemy's knowledge?

Son of Pritha, do you seek to conquer your inflamed enemies, slaves to passion, only after having first conquered your own mind and mastered your own senses? Before actually going to war against your enemy, do you correctly use the four arts of conciliation – with gifts, by creating dissent, with coercion, and only then with force? O King, do you march against your enemy only after first strengthening your own kingdom? And once having set out against them, do you then exert yourself to the utmost to triumph? Having conquered them, do you then protect them with every care?

Does your army comprise the four kinds of forces – the regular soldiers, allies, the irregulars and the mercenaries? Is each of these

---

[1] Infantry, chariots and horse, and elephants.
[2] Reserves, ambuscades, payment given to the troops in advance, etc.

furnished with the eight necessities for war – chariots, elephants, horses, officers, infantry, camp-followers, spies who have a thorough knowledge of the country, and ensigns led out against your enemies after being well trained by superior officers?

Parantapa, I hope you kill your enemies, Great King, without regard for their seasons of harvest or famine? Rajan, I hope your servants and agents, in your own kingdom and in those of your enemies, attend diligently to their duties and watch over one another.

O King, I hope you employ trusted servants to look after your food, the clothes you wear, and the perfumes you use. I hope your treasury, barns, stables, arsenals, and women's apartments are all protected by servants devoted to you, and always seeking your welfare. I trust that you first protect yourself from your domestic and public servants, and then from the servants of your relatives; and then your servants from the servants of these others.

Do your servants ever speak to you, in the forenoon, about your extravagant spending on wine, sport, food and women? Are your expenses always covered by a fourth, a third or at least half of your income? Do you look after your relatives, superiors, merchants, the old and other dependants, and those in distress with gold and with food?

Do your clerks and accountants come to you during the mornings, every day, and inform you of your daily income and expenditure? Do you ever dismiss, for no fault, servants who are good at their work, popular and devoted to you? Bhaarata, do you employ superior, average and lowly men, after examining them thoroughly, in offices they deserve?

Rajan, do you employ men who are thievish, or susceptible to temptation, who are hostile to you, or minors? Do you oppress your kingdom with thieves, greedy men, minors or with women?

Are the agriculturists in your kingdom contented? Have you caused large tanks and lakes to be created at fair intervals, throughout your lands, so that your farmers are never entirely dependent on the rains from heaven? Are the farmers in your kingdom wanting in seed or in food?

Do you give loans generously to the tillers of the land, taking from them just a fourth of their produce in excess of each hundred measure?

Child, are the four professions of agriculture, trade, cattle-rearing, and money-lending for interest conducted by honest men? For the happiness of your people depends on these. Rajan, do the five brave and wise men – those who watch over the city and the citadel, the merchants and the farmers, and those who punish criminals – always benefit your kingdom by working unitedly and closely with one another?

To protect your city, have your villages been made like towns, the hamlets and the outskirts of villages, like villages? Are all these entirely under your sway? If thieves and robbers sack a town, do your police hunt them through the flat and difficult parts of your kingdom?

Do you comfort the women in your kingdom and protect them? I hope that you never place any confidence in them, nor divulge any secret to them? O King, having heard of danger threatening, do you, after thinking deeply on it, still lie in your inner chambers enjoying every desirable object?

Having slept through the second and third yaamas of the night, do you lie awake during the fourth division of night, reflecting on dharma and artha? Pandava, do you rise from bed at the proper time, clothe yourself royally, show yourself to your people with ministers, who know which times are auspicious and which otherwise? Bane of all enemies, do men wearing red, armed with swords and adorned with ornaments stand beside you to guard your person?

Rajan, are you like Dharma Deva himself to those deserving chastisement, and to those that deserve worship, to those whom you love, as well as to those whom you do not care for? Son of Pritha, do you seek to cure yourself of bodily sickness with medicines and by fasting, and mental afflictions with the advice of the old and the wise? I trust that your personal physicians are well versed in the eight kinds of treatment and that all of them are attached and devoted to you.

Does it ever transpire, O King, that, from pride, folly or greed, you fail to decide between a plaintiff and a defendant who come to you?

From covetousness or neglect, do you ever deprive your dependants of their welfare or pensions, those who have sought refuge in you from love or in trust?

Do the people who live in your realm, having been bought by your enemies and uniting against you, ever seek to oppose or raise dispute with you? Do you suppress your weaker enemies with stronger troops and wise counsel? Are all the main chieftains in your lands loyal to you? Are they ready to lay down their lives for you, at your command?

Do you worship Brahmanas and Rishis according to their proficiency at the various branches of learning? I say to you, such reverence is of the highest benefit to you, beyond any doubt. Have you faith in the dharma based on the three Vedas, which was practised by men who lived before you? Do you meticulously follow the precepts by which they lived?

Do you entertain accomplished Brahmanas in your home, with fine food, and give them rich gifts when these feasts conclude? Passions perfectly controlled, with undivided mind, do you strive to perform the Vajapeya and Pundarika yagnas, with their entire complement of rituals? Do you worship your relatives and superiors, the elderly, the Devas, Rishis, Brahmanas, and the lofty nyagrodhas which stand in villages and bless the people in so many ways?

Sinless one, do you cause anger or grief to anyone? Do priests who are able to bestow auspicious fruit upon you always stand at your side? Anagha, are all your purposes and practices such as I have described, which inexorably increase the span of your life and spread your fame, and also further the cause of dharma, artha and kama? He who conducts himself thus, never finds his kingdom in distress or afflicted, and that king subdues the whole world and enjoys great felicity.

Rajan, I hope that no man of good conduct, who is pure and respected, is ever ruined or has his life taken, on a false charge or through theft, by your ministers, either because they are ignorant of the Shastras or out of their greed? Purusharishabha, I trust that your ministers, from greed, never free a real thief, having caught him red-handed with his booty? O Bhaarata,

I hope that your ministers can never be bought with bribes, and that they never decide unjustly in disputes between the rich and the poor?

Do you keep yourself free from the fourteen vices of kings – atheism, untruthfulness, anger, carelessness, procrastination, not visiting the wise, idleness, restlessness of mind, taking counsel with only one man, consulting men unacquainted with the craft of artha, abandoning a project decided upon, disclosure of secrets, not accomplishing beneficial projects, and acting without reflection? These ruin even the most well established sovereign.

Have your study of the Veda, your wealth, your knowledge of the Shastras, and your marriage proved fruitful?'

When the Rishi finishes, Yudhishtira asks, 'How, O Muni, do the Vedas, wealth, one's wife, and knowledge of the Shastras bear fruit?'

The Sage replies, 'The Vedas bear fruit when he who has studied them performs the Agnihotra and other sacrifices. Wealth is said to bear fruit when he who has it enjoys it himself and also gives it away in charity. A wife proves fruitful when she is useful and when she bears children. Knowledge of the Shastras bears fruit when it results in humility and good behaviour.'

Having thus answered Yudhishtira, Mahamuni Narada asks that righteous king, 'Do your officers of government, who are paid from the taxes levied on the people, take only their just dues from merchants who come from distant lands to your kingdom, impelled by the desire to make profit? Are these Vaisyas, O King, treated with kindness in your capital and kingdom? Are they able to bring their merchandise here without being cheated either by the buyers or the officials of your government?

O Monarch, do you always listen to the wise and righteous words of old men who know the profound doctrines of artha? Do you make the offerings of honey and clarified butter to Brahmanas, which make the harvest bounteous, swell the numbers of kine in the kingdom, yield an abundance of fruit and flowers, and increase virtue as well?

Do you always give the artists and artisans whom you engage, the materials they need and their wages, for not more than four months together? Do you inspect their work and praise them before good men, and also reward and honour them?

Bharatarishabha, do you live by the precepts and aphorisms of the Rishis, and particularly with regard to matters relating to elephants, horses and chariots? Are the sayings which relate to the science of arms, also those about the engines of war, so useful in towns and fortresses, studied in your court?

Sinless, do you know the arcane mantras and all about the poisons which can kill your enemies? Do you protect your kingdom from fear of fire, serpents and other feral creatures, from disease and rakshasas? Knowing every dharma as you do, do you care like a father for the blind, the dumb, the lame, the deformed, the friendless, and for ascetics who have no homes? Have you banished the six evils, O King – sleep, idleness, fear, anger, weakness of mind, and procrastination?'

The illustrious Kurupungava Yudhishtira listens to what that Brahmanottama says, then bows down and worships at Narada Muni's feet. Delighted by everything he hears, the king says to Narada of celestial form, 'I will do all that you say, for you have swelled my knowledge with your counsel.'

Indeed, Yudhishtira does as Narada asks him to and, in time, becomes sovereign of all the Earth with her girdle of seas.

Narada says, 'The king who protects the four varnas – Brahmana, Kshatriya, Vaisya and Sudra – passes his days in this world happily and then attains the realm of Indra.'"

CANTO 6

LOKAPALA SABHAKHYANA PARVA
CONTINUED

Vaisampayana said, "When Narada Muni finishes speaking, Yudhishtira Dharmaraja worships him appropriately and then, commanded by the Sage, he begins to answer, briefly, the questions the Rishi has asked.

Yudhishthira says, 'Holy One, the laws which you have enumerated are true and proper. As for me, I do observe those laws as best I can. For sure the karma done by kings of yore did bear fruit, and was undertaken from the purest motives to achieve the best possible objects. Master, we certainly wish to tread the same righteous path as those kings, who, besides, were men of perfect self-control.'

Pandu's son, Yudhishtira of great glory, having reverently listened to Narada Muni, and having answered the Sage's question, now falls into a moment's thought. Then, sensing a fine chance, sitting beside the Rishi, the king asks Narada, who sits at his ease, and who can journey into any world at will, in that sabha of kings, 'With the speed of the mind, you range through numberless worlds created by Brahma of yore, seeing all things. Tell me, O Brahmana, have you ever seen, anywhere, a sabha to equal this one of mine, or any superior to it.'

Narada replies, smilingly, sweetly, 'Child, O King, I have never seen or even heard before of a sabha among men built of jewels and gemstones like this one of yours. However, I will describe to you the courts of Yama, King of the Dead, of Varuna of vast intellect, of Indra, King of the Devas, and also of Kubera who has his home on Kailasa. I will also describe to you Brahma's celestial sabha, which dispels all unease.

All these sabhas reflect both divine and human design, and use every form that exists in the universe. The Devas, the Pitrs, the Sadhyas, the Ganas, self-controlled Rishis offering sacrifices, tranquil Munis always at Vedic sacrifice, all offer worship to these sacred courts. All of them I will describe for you, Bharatarishabha, if you have a mind to listen.'

Mahatman Yudhishtira, his brothers and the great Brahmanas present all fold their hands to beg Narada to do so.

Yudhishtira says, 'Describe all the sabhas for us, for we surely wish to listen to you. O Brahmana, of what is each one made? How big is each sabha, how long and how wide? Who attends upon the Pitamaha in his court, and who upon Indra, Lord of the Devas, and who upon Vivaswan's son Yama? Who waits upon Varuna and upon Kubera in their sabhas?

O Brahmarishi, tell us in detail, for all of us are agog to hear about them.'

Narada replies, 'Listen, O King, all of you, about these sabhas of heaven, one by one.'"

CANTO 7

LOKAPALA SABHAKHYANA PARVA
CONTINUED

"Narada said, 'Lustrous is the sabha of Indra, which he has got as the fruit of his punya. Splendid as the Sun, Sakra himself built his court. Indra's sabha can go anywhere at all, at his will; it is one hundred and fifty yojanas long, a hundred yojanas wide, and five yojanas high. It dispels the infirmities of age, grief, exhaustion and fear, and bestows great fortune. Fine and grand are its apartments, and beautiful the heavenly trees which surround it. Fine are its seats, and it is altogether delightful.

Son of Pritha, in that sabha upon a magnificent throne sits the Lord of the Devas with his wife Sachi of great beauty and fortune. He assumes a form which defies description, a crown upon his head, bright bracelets on his arms, wearing pure white robes, garlands with flowers of many colours, and sits there with Beauty, Fame and Glory beside him.

That illustrious Deva of a hundred sacrifices is waited upon in that sabha, O King, by the Maruts, who are all grihastas, the Siddhas, the Devarishis, the Sadhyas, the Devas, and by Marutas of shining skins, wearing golden garlands, with unearthly forms and shimmering ornaments. All these constantly attend upon Indra Parantapa.

Kaunteya, the celestial Sages, also, all pure-souled, washed of all sin, resplendent like Agni, tejasvins, free of any sorrow, free of anxiety's fever, all performers of the Soma yagna, wait upon and worship Indra.

Parasara and Parvata and Savarni and Galava; and Kankha, and the Muni Gaursiras, and Durvasa, and Krodhana and Swena and the Muni Dhirghatamas; and Pavitrapani, Savarni, Yagnavalkya and Bhaluki; and Udyalaka, Swetaketu and Tandya, and also Bhandayani; and Havishmat, and Garishta, and King Harischandra; and Hridya, Udarshanadilya, Parasarya and Krishibala; Vataskandha, Visakha, Vidhata and Kala; Karaladanta, Tvastri, and Vishwakarman, and Tumburu; and other Rishis, some born of women and others living on air, and others again living on fire – all these worship Indra, the Vajradhari, Lord of all the worlds.

And Sahadeva, and Sunitha, and Valmiki of great tapasya; and Samika of truthful speech, and Prachetas who always keeps his word, and Medhatithi, and Vamadeva, and Pulastya, Pulaha and Kratu; and Maruta, and Marichi, and Sthanu of vast tapasya; and Kakshivat, and Gautama, and Tarkhya, and also the Muni Vaishwanara; and the Muni Kalakavrikshiya, and Asravya, and also Hiranmaya, and Samvarta, and Devahavya, and Viswaksena of great tejas; and Kanva, and Katyayana, O King, and Gargya, and Kaushika – all dwell there, with the celestial waters and plants; and faith, and intelligence, and the Devi Saraswati; and artha, dharma and kama; and lightning, Pandava; and rain-bearing clouds, and the winds, and all the thunder of heaven; the eastern point, the twenty-seven fires which convey the sacrificial butter, Agni and Soma, and the agni of Indra, and Mitra, and Savitri, and Aryaman; Bhaga, Vishwa; the Sadhyas, Brihaspati the Guru, and also Sukra; and Vishwavasu and Chitrasena, and Sumanas; and also Taruna; the Yagnas; the gifts to Brahmanas, the planets, and the stars, O Bhaarata, and the mantras which are chanted during sacrifices – all these dwell there.

And, O King, many Apsaras and Gandharvas please the Lord of the Devas with various dances and music and songs; and with the performance of auspicious rites, and exhibitions of myriad feats of skill – they gratify Satakratu, the slayer of Bala and Vritra.

Besides these, many other Brahmanas and Rajarishis and Devarishis, all splendent as fire, adorned in bright garlands and precious ornaments, frequently visit and leave that sabha, riding in unearthly chariots of diverse kinds.

Brihaspati and Sukra are always present in Indra's sabha; and many other lustrous Rishis of stern vows, and Bhrigu and the Saptarishis, who are equal, O Rajan, to Brahma himself, come to and depart that sabha in vimanas as exquisite as the chariot of Soma, and themselves as brilliant as Soma himself.

This, O Mahabaho, is the sabha of Indra, of a hundred yagnas, which is called Pushkaramalini, which I have seen. Listen now to a description of Yama's sabha.'"

CANTO 8

LOKAPALA SABHAKHYANA PARVA
CONTINUED

Vaisampayana said, "Narada says, 'Yudhisthira, now I will tell you about the court of Yama, son of Vivaswat, which was built by Viswakarman. Listen.

Shining like burnished gold, that sabha sprawls across more than a hundred yojanas. Splendid as the Sun, it yields one's every wish. It is neither too warm nor too cold, and it enchants the heart. No grief, no weakness of age, neither hunger nor thirst enter that sabha. Nothing inauspicious finds any place there, or even any ill feeling.

Every object of desire, human or divine, can be found in that mansion – every manner of thing of delight. Sweet, succulent, delicious, pure things to eat, to drink and suck upon, are there in profusion, Parantapa. The vanamalas in that sabha are of unearthly fragrance, and the trees which surround the palatial court yield any fruit one wishes for.

Both hot and cold water are to be found here, sweet and enjoyable. In that sabha, numerous Rajarishis, all most holy, and Brahmarishis of immaculate purity, O Child, happily attend upon and worship Vivaswat's son Yama.

Yayati is there, Nahusha, Puru, Mandhatri, Somaka, Nriga; Rajarishi Trasadasyu, Kritavirya, Srutasravas; Arishtanemi, Siddha, Kritavega, Kriti, Nimi, Pratardana, Sibi, Matsya, Prithulaksha, Brihadratha, Varta, Marutta, Kusika, Sankasya, Sankriti, Dhruva, Chaturaswa, Sadaswormi and Kartavirya; Bhaarata and Suratha, Sunitha, Nishatha, Nala, Divodasa, and Sumanas, Ambarisha, Bhagiratha; Vyaswa, Sadaswa, Vadyaswa, Badhraswa, Prithuvega, Prithusravas, Prishadaswa, Vasumanas, Kshupa, and Sumahabala, Vrishadgu, Rusadru, Vrishasena, Purukutsa, Dhwajin and Rathin; Arshtisena, Dilipa, and the high-souled Ushinara; Ausinari, Pundarika, Saryati, Sarabha, and Suchi; Anga, Rishta, Vena, Dushyanta, Srinjaya and Jaya; Bhangasuri, Sunitha, and Nishadha, and Vahinara; Karandhama, Balhika, Sudyumna, and the mighty Madhu; Aila and the mighty king of the Earth Marutta; Kapota, Trinaka, and Sahadeva, and Arjuna also; Vyaswa; Saswa and Krishaswa and King Sasabindu; Rama, the son of Dasaratha, and Lakshmana, and Pratarddana; Alarka, and Kakshasena, Gaya, and Gauraswa; Jamadagnya's son Rama, Nabhaga, and Sagara; Bhuridyumna and Mahaswa, Prithaswa, and also Janaka; King Vainya, Varisena, Purujit, and Janamejaya; Brahmadatta, and Trigarta, and Uparichara also; Indradyumna, Bhimajanu, Gauraprishta, Nala, Gaya; Padma and Muchukunda, Bhuridyumna, Prasenajit; Aristanemi, Sudyumna, Prithulaswa, and Ashtaka also; a hundred kings of the Matsya race and hundred of the Nipa and a hundred of the Gaya races; a hundred kings all named Dhritarashtra; eighty kings named Janamejaya; a hundred sovereigns called Brahmadatta, and a hundred kings bearing the name Iri; more than two hundred Bhishmas, and also a hundred Bhimas; a hundred Prativindhyas, a hundred Nagas, a hundred Hayas, and a hundred Palasas, and a hundred called Kasa and Kusa; that king of kings Santanu, and your father Pandu, Usangava, Sataratha, Devaraja, Jayadratha; the most intelligent Rajarishi Vrishadarbha with his ministers; and a thousand other kings known by the name of Sasabindu, who have died, having performed many grand horse-sacrifices with munificent gifts to the Brahmanas – these holy Royal Sages of magnificent achievements and vast knowledge of the Shastras, O King, wait upon and worship the son of Vivaswat in that sabha.

And Agastya and Matanga, and Kala, and Mrityu, performers of sacrifices, the Siddhas, and many Yogins; the Pitrs,[1] as also others who have forms; the Kalachakra, wheel of time, and Agni, the burning conveyer of the sacrificial butter; all sinners among human beings, as also those that have died during the winter solstice; the helpers of Yama have been appointed to count the allotted days of everybody and everything; the Singsapa, Palasa, Kasa, and Kusa trees and plants, in their embodied forms – all these, Rajan, wait upon and worship the God of Justice in his sabha.

Many others, too, are present at the court of the king of the Pitrs. So numerous are they that I cannot tell you either all their names or their great deeds. This enchanting and vast sabha travels anywhere, at the will of its Lord. Viswakarman built it after a prolonged tapasya. And, O Bhaarata, brilliant with its own lustre, it stands beautiful, in all its glory.

Sannyasis of stern tapasya, grave vratas, of truthful speech, serene, pure and of sacred karma, their bodies radiant, wearing spotless robes, bracelets, garlands of flowers, golden earrings, and adorned by their own holy deeds as with the marks of their order constantly visit that sabha. Many bright Gandharvas and Apsaras fill every corner of the court with music and songs, with dance and with their unearthly laughter.

Fine perfumes, sweet sounds and garlands of celestial flowers make that an always supremely blest sabha. Hundreds of thousands of beings of dharma, of heavenly beauty and great wisdom, always attend upon and worship the illustrious Yama, Lord of the created, in that court.

Such, Rajan, is the sabha of the lustrous king of the manes. Now I will describe for you the sabha of Varuna, also called Pushkaramalini.'"

---

[1] Of the kinds known as called Agniswattas, Fenapa, Ushampa, Swadhavat, and Varhishada.

CANTO 9

LOKAPALA SABHAKHYANA PARVA
CONTINUED

"Narada says, 'Yudhishtira, the celestial sabha of Varuna is unequalled for its splendour. It is as large as Yama's hall, its walls and arches all pure white. Viswakarman built it in the waters. Countless unworldly trees made of gemstones and jewels, yielding excellent flowers and fruit, surround it, as well as numerous fine plants laden with blooms, blue and yellow, black and grey, white and red. Within their bowers lakhs of birds of myriad species, beautiful and variegated, constantly sing their sweet songs.

Salubrious is the air in and around that sabha, neither cold nor hot. Varuna's enchanting palace, blemishlessly white, contains numberless chambers, all furnished with fine seats. Within sits Varuna, wearing celestial raiment, ornaments and jewellery, with his queen, daubed with heavenly perfumes and smeared with sandalwood paste of unearthly redolence.

The Adityas wait upon and worship the illustrious Varuna, Lord of Waters; and Vasuki and Takshaka, and the Naga Airavana; Krishna and

Lohita; Padma and Chitra of great tejas; the Nagas called Kambala and Aswatara; and Dhritarashtra and Balahaka; Manimat and Kundadhara; and Karkotaka and Dhananjaya; Panimat and the mighty Kundaka, O Lord of the Earth; and Prahlada and Mushikada, and Janamejaya – all with auspicious marks, mandalas, and hoods extended. These and many other great snakes, Yudhishtira, without fear of any kind, wait upon and adore the illustrious Varuna.

And, O King, Bali the son of Virochana, and Naraka, subduer of the whole Earth; Sanghraha and Viprachitti, and the Danavas called Kalakhanjas; and Suhanu and Durmukha and Sankha and Sumanas and also Sumati; and Ghatodara, and Mahaparswa, and Karthana and, also, Pitara and Viswarupa, Swarupa and Virupa; Mahasiras and Dasagriva, Bali, and Meghavasas and Dasavara; Tittiva and Vitabhuta, and Sanghrada, and Indratapana – these Daityas and Danavas, all wearing earrings, crowns and draped in garlands, wearing unworldly robes, all blessed with great boons and possessed of untold valour, and immortal, and all of fine conduct and excellent vows, wait upon and worship the illustrious Varuna, the Deva whose weapon is the paasa, in that sabha.

And, O King, the four Oceans are there, the river Bhagirathi, the Kalindi, the Vidisa, the Vena, the swift-flowing Narmada; the Vipasa, the Satadu, the Chandrabhaga, the Saraswati; the Iravati, the Vitasta, the Sindhu, the Devanadi; the Godavari, the Krishnavena; and Kaveri, queen of rivers; the Kimpuna, the Visalya and the river Vaitarani, too; the Tritiya, the Jyeshtila, and the great Sona; the Charmanwati and the mighty Parnasa; the Sarayu, the Varavatya, and that river-queen, the Langali; the Karatoya, the Atreyi, the red Mahanada, the Laghanti, the Gomati, the Sandhya, and also the Tristrolasi – these and other rivers, all sacred and famed tirthas of pilgrimage, as well as other streams and holy waters, lakes and wells and springs, and tanks, large and small, all in their personified forms, O Bhaarata, wait upon and worship the Lord Varuna.

The cardinal points of the heavens, the Earth, and all the Mountains, as also every species of aquatic creature, all worship Varuna in his sabha.

Numerous tribes of Gandharvas and Apsaras, given to music and song, wait upon Varuna, singing hymns of praise to him.

All the mountains which are known for being beautiful and jewel-rich, come, embodied, to that sabha and enjoy sweet converse with one another. Varuna's foremost minister, Sunabha, surrounded by his sons and grandsons, also attends upon his master, along with a sacred body of water called Go, personified. All these worship that Deva.

Bharatarishabha, this is the sabha of Varuna, which I have seen during my wandering. Listen now to a description of the Hall of Kubera.'"

CANTO 10

LOKAPALA SABHAKHYANA PARVA
CONTINUED

"Narada says, 'The splendid court of Kubera Vaisravana, O Rajan, is a hundred yojanas long and seventy yojanas wide. Vaisravana himself built this sabha, using his tapasya shakti. As brilliant as the peaks of Kailasa, this edifice eclipses the very Moon with its radiance. Supported by Guhyakas, that palace appears to be fixed to the sky. Of unearthly contrivance, it is exquisite, with lofty golden chambers, of all delights, scented with heavenly perfumes, and encrusted with priceless jewels past counting.

It resembles the summits of massed white clouds, and truly seems to float on air. Painted in celestial gold, it appears to be adorned with streaks of lightning. Within that sabha, upon a beautiful throne bright as the Sun, covered with cloths of heaven, furnished with a peerless footstool, sits the Lord Vaisravana, handsome and pleasant, wearing fine robes, priceless ornaments, sparkling earrings, and surrounded by his thousand wives.

Cool, delightful breezes, which murmur through forests of tall Mandaras, bear the scents of great jungles of jasmines and also the fragrance of the lotuses which float upon the river Alaka and those of the divine gardens of Nandana, and these always minister to the pleasure of the King of the Yakshas.

Here the Devas, with the Gandharvas, and various troupes of Apsaras, sing in chorus, Rajan, songs of heavenly sweetness. Misrakesi and Rambha, and Chitrasenaa, and Suchismita; and Charunetra, and Ghritachi and Menaka, and Punjikasthala; and Viswachi, Sahajanya, and Pramlocha and Urvasi and Ira, and Varga and Saurabheyi, and Samichi, and Budbuda, and Lata – these and a thousand other Apsaras, and Gandharvas, all masters and mistresses of music and dance, attend on Kubera, Lord of Treasures.

That sabha, always brimming with notes from divine instruments and voices, as with the sounds of many Gandharva and Apsara tribes dancing, is full of charm and joy. The Gandharvas called Kinnaras, others known as Naras, and Manibhadra, and Dhanada, and Swetabhadra and Guhyaka; Kaseraka, Gandakandu, and the mighty Pradyota; Kustumburu, Pisacha, Gajakarna, and Viskalaka, Varahakarna, Tamroshta, Falakaksha, and Falodaka; Hansachuda, Sikhavarta, Hemanetra, Vibhishana, Pushpanana, Pingalaka, Sonitoda and Pravalaka; Vrikshavasyaniketa, and Chiravasas – these, O Bhaarata, and lakhs of other Yakshas always wait upon Kubera.

The Goddess Lakshmi ever remains there, also Kubera's son Nalakubara. I myself and many others like me, we go often to that Hall, as do many Brahmana Rishis and Devarishis. Numerous Rakshasas and Gandharvas, besides those I named, attend upon and worship, in that sabha, the illustrious Lord of all treasures.

O tiger among kings, the lustrous husband of Uma, Lord of created things, the three-eyed Mahadeva, wielder of the trident, the slayer of the Asura Bhaganetra, the mighty God of the fierce bow, surrounded by Ganasanghas, spirits in thousands, some dwarfish, some of fierce mien, some hunchbacked, some with blood-red eyes, some of frightful yells, some feeding upon fat and flesh, and some too terrible to look at, but all armed with diverse weapons and blessed with the speed of wind, along with the Devi Parvathi, who is always cheerful and who knows no tiredness, all come to the court of their dear friend Kubera, the Lord of Treasures.

Hundreds of Gandharva lords, with joyful hearts and wearing finery, and Viswavasu, and Haha and Huhu; and Tumburu and Parvarta, and Sailusha; and Chitrasena, musical genius, and also Chitraratha – these and countless other Gandharvas worship the Lord of Treasures.

Chakradharman, Lord of the Vidyadharas, with his followers, wait in that Hall, upon the Lord of Treasures; and Kinnaras, in their hundreds, and innumerable kings, Bhagadatta their lord; and Druma, Lord of the Kimpurushas; and Mahendra, Lord of the Rakshasas; and Gandhamadana accompanied by so very many Yakshas, Gandharvas and Rakshasas wait upon the Lord of Treasures.

Vibhishana of dharma, also, there worships his elder brother Kubera[1]. The Mountains Himavat, Pariyatra, Vindhya, Kailasa, Mandara, Malaya, Durdura, Mahendra, Gandhamadana, Indrakila, Sunabha, and the Sunrise and Sunset mountains – these and many other ranges, besides, all in their personified forms, with Meru standing before the rest, wait upon and worship the lambent Lord of Treasures.

The illustrious Nandiswara, and Mahakala, and many spirits with arrowy ears and sharp-pointed mouths, Kasta, Kutimukha, Danti, and Vijaya of great asceticism, with the mighty white bull of Siva roaring deep, all come to that sabha. Besides these, many other Rakshasas and Pisachas worship Kubera in that Grand Hall.

Kubera, son of Pulastya, once performed tapasya and worshipped Siva in all the known ways of adoration. He then sat by the very side of the Devadeva, God of Gods, creator of the three worlds, Mahadeva surrounded by his ganas. One day, Bhava, the most high, made Kubera his friend and then on, O King, Siva always dwells in the sabha of his friend, the Lord of Treasures.

---

[1]Ganguli says Croesus!

Those princes of all gemstones in the three worlds, Sankha and Padma, in their embodied forms, with all the jewels of the Earth, also personified, worship Kubera.

I have seen Kubera's sabha of fascination, which can cross the firmament, and it is, Rajan, as I have described. Now listen to what I say about the sabha of Brahma, the Grandsire.'"

CANTO 11

LOKAPALA SABHAKHYANA PARVA
CONTINUED

"Narada sas, 'Listen to me, Child, and I will tell you about the sabha of the Pitamaha, the House which none can describe adequately.

In the Krita Yuga, of old, the exalted Deva Aditya once came down from heaven into the world of men. He had seen the sabha of Brahma Svayambhuva, and now joyfully ranged the face of the Earth, to see what he could here. Pandava, it was then that I met him and that God told me, Bharatarishabha, about the unearthly Hall of the Grandsire, which is immeasurable, subtle, and indescribable, in form and shape, and which enchants and delights the hearts of all who see it with its splendour.

Bharatarishabha, when I heard about the glories of that sabha, Rajan, I wanted to see it. I asked Aditya, "Exalted one, I want to see the sacred sabha of the Pitamaha. Lord of Light, tell me, through what tapasya, karma, mantras or yagnas can I look upon that wondrous court, which washes every sin away?"

Aditya, God of Day, Deva of a thousand rays, replied, "With your mind restrained in dhyana, keep the Brahmavrata of a thousand years."

I went to the bosom of the Himavat and began that great vow. When I finished, the exalted and sinless Surya Deva of terrific tejas, who knows no tiredness, took me with him to the sabha of Brahma. Rajan, it is impossible to describe that sabha in words, for, in a moment it assumes a new and different form, which language cannot capture.

Bhaarata, I cannot tell you how vast it is or what its shape is. I had never seen anything like it before. It brings joy to those within it, and it is neither hot nor cold. Hunger, thirst and every manner of unease vanish as soon as one enters that Hall.

It appears to be made of scintillating jewels of countless kinds. No columns seem to support it, and being eternal, it knows no decay. It is self-refulgent, and with its numberless splendid lights it excels the Moon, the Sun and the Fire in lustre. Situated in Swarga, it blazes forth, as if it were chiding the illuminer of the day.

In that sabha, the Supreme Deity, the Grandsire of all created things, who has made them all through his maya shakti, abides ever. And Daksha, Prachetas, Pulaha, Marichi, Kashyapa the master, Bhrigu, Atri, and Vasishta and Gautama, and also Angiras, and Pulastya, Kratu, Prahlada, and Kardama, these Prajapatis, and Angirasa of the Atharvan Veda, the Balakhilyas, the Marichipas; Intelligence, Space, Knowledge, Air, Heat, Water, Earth, Sound, Touch, Form, Taste, Scent; Nature, and the Gunas of Nature, and the elemental and primal causes of the world — all dwell in that sabha beside the Lord Brahma.

And Agastya of great tejas, and Markandeya of great tapasya, and Jamadagni and Bharadwaja, and Samvarta, and Chyavana, and Durvasa the high, and the virtuous Rishyasringa, the illustrious Sanatkumara of great tapasya, master of all things regarding Yoga; Asita and Devala, and Jaigishavya who knows truth; Rishabha, Ajitasatru, and Mani of great vitality; and the science of healing with its eight branches — all in their personified forms, O Bhaarata; Soma with all the stars and the constellations; Aditya with all his rays; the Vayus; the Yagnas, the Declarations of intent in sacrifices, the vital principles – these luminous and vow-observing beings personified, and many others, too numerous to name, all attend upon Brahma in that sabha.

Wealth, Religion, Desire, Joy, Aversion, Asceticism and Tranquillity – all wait upon the Supreme Deity in that palace. The twenty tribes of the Gandharvas and Apsaras, as also their seven other tribes, all the Lokapalas, Sukra, Brihaspati, Budha, Angaraka, Sani, Rahu, and the other Planets; the Mantras, the secret Mantras of that Veda; the rites of Harimat and Vasumat; the Adityas with Indra, the two Agnis, Agnisoma and Indragni, the Marutas, Viswakarman, the Vasus, O Bhaarata; the Pitrs, and every sacrificial libation, the four Vedas, Rig, Sama, Yajuh, and Atharva; all the sciences and branches of learning; the Itihasas and all the minor branches of learning; the several Vedangas; the planets, the Sacrifices, the Soma, all the Devas; Savitri, who is Gayatri, the seven kinds of metre; Understanding, Patience, Memory, Wisdom, Intelligence, Fame, Forgiveness; the Hymns of the Sama Veda; the Science of all hymns, all the kinds of Verses and Songs; various Commentaries with arguments – all in personified forms, O King; and various Plays and Poems and Stories – these also, and countless others wait upon the Supreme Deity in that sabha.

Kshanas, Lavas, Muhurtas, Day, Night, Fortnights, Months, the six Seasons, O Bhaarata; Years, Yugas, the four kinds of Days and Nights, and that eternal, imperishable, undecaying, most excellent Kala Chakra, the Wheel of Time, and also the Wheel of Dharma, Virtue – these always wait there, O Yudhishtira; and Aditi, Diti, Danu, Surasa, Vinata, Ira, Kalika, Surabhi, Devi, Sarama, Gautami and the goddesses Prabha and Kadru – these mothers of the celestials; and Rudrani, Sree, Lakshmi, Bhadra, Shashthi, the Earth, Ganga, Hri, Swaha, Kriti, the goddess Sura, Sachi Pushti, Arundhati, Samvritti, Asa, Niyati, Srishti, Rati – these and many other Devis wait upon the Creator of all.

The Adityas, Vasus, Rudras, Marutas, Aswinas, the Viswadevas, Sadhyas, and the Pitrs blessed with the swiftness of the mind – these wait there upon the Grandsire. And, Bharatarishabha, know that there are seven classes of Pitrs, of which four have embodied forms and the remaining three dwell there without bodies or forms.

It is known that the illustrious Vairajas, Agniswattas and Garhapatyas, three classes of Pitrs, range in heaven. And those amongst the Pitrs that are called the Somapas, the Ekasringras, the Chaturvedas and the Kalas are ever worshipped amongst the four varnas of men. Gratified first with the Soma rasa, these later gratify Soma. All these tribes of Pitrs wait upon the Lord of Creation and joyfully worship the Supreme God of measureless tejas.

And Rakshasas, Pisachas, Danavas and Guhyakas; Nagas, Pakshis, and various beasts; and all the great beings, mobile and unmoving – all worship the Pitamaha. And Purandara, Lord of the Devas, and Varuna and Kubera and Yama, and Mahadeva with Uma, always go there. And, Rajadhiraja, Mahasena Kartikeya also adores the Grandsire there. Narayana himself, and the Devarishis, and the Rishis called Balakhilyas, and all beings born of female wombs and all those not womb-born, and whatever else there is in the three worlds, which moves and the immobile, I saw there, know, O King.

And eighty thousand celibate Rishis, their vital seed indrawn, and O Pandava, fifty thousand Rishis, with sons – I saw all these there. The dwellers in heaven go to that sabha look upon the Supreme God, when they like, and worshipping him by bowing their heads, return to their abodes.

King of men, the Grandsire of all created beings, the Soul of the Universe, the self-created Brahma of fathomless intellect and glory, equally merciful to all creatures, honours each as they deserve, and gratifies, with sweet speech and gifts of wealth and other things of enjoyment, the Devas, the Daityas, the Nagas, the Brahmanas, the Yakshas, the Pakshis, the Kaleyas, the Gandharvas, the Apsaras, and all the other lofty beings who come to him as his guests.

And that sabha of delight, O Child, always throngs with those who come and go. Brimming with every kind of tejas, worshipped by

Brahmarishis, that celestial Hall blazes forth with the divine and graceful possessions of Brahma and is enchanting to look at. Tiger among kings, even as this sabha of yours is unrivalled in the world of men, so is the sabha of Brahma, which I have seen, peerless in all in all the worlds.

These sabhas I have seen, O Bhaarata, in the realm of the celestials. This sabha of yours is unquestionably the best in the world of men!'"

CANTO 12

LOKAPALA SABHAKHYANA PARVA
CONTINUED

"Yudhishtira says, 'Best among all the eloquent, from your description of the different sabhas, it seems that almost all the kings of the Earth are to be found in the sabha of Yama. And, O Master, almost all the Nagas, the main Daityas, Rivers and Oceans are to be found in Varuna's sabha. So, too, the Yakshas, the Guhyakas, the Rakshasas, the Gandharvas and Apsaras and the God who has the Bull for his vahana are to be found in the sabha of the Lord of Treasures. You have said that in the sabha of the Grandsire, all the great Rishis, all the Devas, all the branches of learning are present. For the sabha of Sakra, you have named, O Muni, all the Devas, the Gandharvas, and various Rishis.

But, Mahamuni, you have named just a single king of the Earth as living in the sabha of the illustrious King of the Devas – the Rajarishi Harishchandra. What deed did that celebrated king do, or what great tapasya did he perform with what unwavering vratas, because of which he has become equal to Indra himself?

O Brahmana, how did you also meet my father, the noble Pandu, who now dwells in the realm of the Pitrs? Lofty one, of pure vratas, did he say anything to you? Ah, tell me everything; I am agog.'

Narada says, 'King of kings, I will tell you everything you want to know about Harishchandra, I will tell you of his matchless excellence. He was a powerful king, indeed, an emperor of all the kings of the Earth, and they obeyed him. Rajan, riding alone in a triumphal chariot, decked with gold, Harishchandra brought the whole world, with her seven dwipas, under his sway with the power of his arms.

Having subdued the entire Earth, with her mountains, forests and rivers, he prepared to perform the great Rajasuya yagna, the imperial sacrifice, and at his command all the kings of the world brought untold wealth to that sacrifice. All of them agreed to be distributors of food and gifts to the Brahmanas who were fed on the occasion.

During that sacrifice, King Harishchandra gave away to anyone that asked five times as much gold as they wanted. When the yagna was concluded, the king pleased the Brahmanas who came from many distant countries with bounteous gifts and wealth of many kinds. Delighted with the feasts of food and other gifts, given to their heart's content, and with the heaps of jewels, they began to say, "King Harischandra is greater than any king, ever, both in fame and splendour."

Know, O Rajan, this was why Harishchandra shone more brightly than thousands of other kings. The mighty Harishchandra concluded his great sacrifice and was installed as sovereign emperor of the Earth, and he was radiant upon his throne. Bharatarishabha, every king who performs the Rajasuya yagna attains to the kingdom of Indra and passes his time in felicity in Indra's company.

Those kings, too, who give up their lives on the field of battle, without ever turning their backs on the fight, find Indra's halls and live in joy with him. Those, again, who quit their bodies after stern tapasya, attain the same realm and shine there for many an age.

King of the Kurus, O son of Kunti, seeing the good fortune of Harischandra and wondering at it, your father did tell me something.

Knowing that I was coming to this world of men, he bowed to me and said, "O Rishi, you must tell Yudhishtira that, because his brothers all obey him, he can conquer the whole world. Once he does this, let him perform a Rajasuya yagna. He is my son; if he performs that sacrifice, like Harischandra I might also soon attain to Indraloka, and there in his sabha pass countless years in uninterrupted bliss."

I replied to him, "O King, I will tell your son all this if I go to the world of men."

Purushavyaghra, I have now told you what your father said to me. Pandava, fulfil your father's wishes. If you perform that sacrifice, you will then be able, along with your dead ancestors, to enter the realm of the king of the Devas. It is said that many obstacles and fears attend the performance of this great sacrifice. A race of Rakshasas called Brahma Rakshasas, whose task it is to obstruct every sacrifice, will do everything in their power to stop a Rajasuya yagna, once it has begun.

When such a sacrifice is undertaken, there might be a war which could destroy the Kshatriyas and create an occasion for the destruction of the very world. Even a slight mischance during a Rajasuya yagna may bring the whole world to ruin. Reflect upon all this, O King of kings, and do what is good for you.

Be vigilant in protecting the four varnas among your subjects. Grow in prosperity and enjoy every felicity. Please Brahmanas with gifts of wealth. I have now answered in detail everything which you asked. With your leave now, I will go to Dwaravati, city of the Dasarhas.'

O Janamejaya, having spoken thus to the son of Pritha, Narada goes away, accompanied by the Rishis with whom he had come. When Narada has left King Yudhishtira and his brothers begin to think about that greatest of sacrifices which is called the Rajasuya yagna."

CANTO 13

LOKAPALA SABHAKHYANA PARVA CONTINUED

Vaisampayana said, "After listening to Narada, Yudhishtira begins to sigh. O Bhaarata, plunged in thoughts of the Rajasuya, the king has no peace. Having heard about the glory of the illustrious kings of yore, knowing for certain now about attaining realms of grace through the performance of sacrifice and the resultant punya, and, especially, thinking of the Rajarishi Harischandra, who performed the great yagna, Yudhishtira wants to prepare to undertake a Rajasuya yagna.

Offering worship to his ministers and others in his sabha, and being worshipped by them in return, he initiates discussions about that sacrifice with them. After deep reflection, that King of kings, Bull among Kurus, turns his mind towards preparing for the Rajasuya. However, then, considering dharma, that prince of magnificent energy and prowess sets his heart again on discovering what would be good for all his people. For Yudhishtira, best of all good men, is unvaryingly kind to his subjects, and works for the weal of all, without distinctions.

Indeed, shaking off both anger and pride, Yudhishtira always says, 'Give each his due,' and the only words he likes to hear are, '*Blessed be Dharma! Blessed be Dharma!*'

Thus Yudhishtira rules and is like a father to all his people; there is no one in his kingdom that bears any hostility towards him. Hence, he comes to be known as Ajatasatru – he without an enemy. The king cherishes everyone as belonging to his family, and Bhima rules justly over all. Arjuna, the perfectly ambidextrous bowman, protects the kingdom from outside enemies, while the wise Sahadeva administers justice impartially. Nakula shows great humility towards everyone, and this was his nature.

Because of all this the kingdom is free from disputes and fear of every kind; and the people attend to their svadharma. The rain is plentiful, and none can ask for any more; the kingdom's prosperity grows. Because of the dharma and virtue of the king money-lenders, makers of articles needed for sacrifices, cattle-breeders, farmers and traders: why, all and everything, grow in prosperity.

During the reign of Yudhishtira there is no extortion in the kingdom, no stringent realisation of arrears of rent, no fear of disease, of fire, or of death by poisoning and mantras. It is never heard during that time that criminals, thieves, cheats or royal favourites ever enjoy any liberties – with the king, or the people, or even amongst one another.

Kshatriyas, kings conquered during the 'six occasions' wait on the king, to see to his welfare and to worship him always, while Vaishyas of the different classes come to pay him the taxes on their occupations. Thus during the reign of Yudhishtira Dharmaraja, his kingdom prospers. Why, the prosperity of the kingdom is swelled not only through these, but even by those who are addicted to voluptuousness and indulge in every luxury to their fill.

Yudhishtira, King of Kings, whose sway extends everywhere, is possessed of every accomplishment and treats all things with forbearance. Rajan, whichever countries that celebrated and splendid king conquers, their people, from Brahmanas to Sudras, become more attached to him than to their own fathers and mothers.

Now King Yudhishtira, most eloquent of men, calls together his ministers and his brothers and asks them repeatedly about the Rajasuya yagna.

All the ministers speak solemnly to the wise Yudhishtira, who wants to perform the imperial sacrifice, 'He who already owns a kingdom wishes to become an emperor through the yagna that confers all the attributes of Varuna on a king. O Prince of the Kurus, all your friends believe that you are worthy of becoming an emperor, indeed, that the time is ripe for you to perform the Rajasuya yagna.

Because of your possessions as a Kshatriya, we say the time has come for the performance of the sacrifice during which Rishis of austere vratas kindle six fires by chanting mantras from the Sama Veda. At the conclusion of the Rajasuya yagna, the sacrificer is installed as sovereign of the empire, and he is rewarded with the fruit of every other sacrifice, including the Agnihotra. For this, he is called the conqueror of all.

Mahabaho, you are more than capable of performing this yagna. All of us obey you, and very soon you will be able to undertake the Rajasuya. So, Maharajan, resolve to do it without further discussion.'

So say all his friends and ministers to the king, separately and together. Rajan, having heard these good, brave, agreeable and weighty words, Yudhishtira Parantapa, in his mind, is inclined to acquiesce. Having heard what his friends and counsellors say, and also knowing his own strength, O Bhaarata, yet the king reflects repeatedly on the matter.

After this, Yudhishtira, intelligent and virtuous, wise in counsel, consults again with his brothers, with the illustrious Ritvijas around him, with his ministers, and with Dhaumya and Dwaipayana, and others.

Yudhishtira says, 'How will this desire of mine to perform the Rajasuya yagna, which is worthy of an emperor, become fruitful through merely the consequence of my faith and speech?'

O you with eyes like lotus petals, asked this by the king, they reply then to Yudhishtira Dharmaraja, 'You well know the dictates of dharma,

O King, and so you are worthy of performing the awesome Rajasuya yagna.'

When the Ritvijas and the Rishis say these words to the king, his ministers and his brothers approve warmly of what they say. However, that most wise king, his mind perfectly controlled, wishing the weal of the world, yet again reflects on the matter and considers his own strength and his resources, all the circumstances of time and place, his income and expenditure. For, he knows that the wise never come to grief because they always act only after thorough deliberation.

Yudhishtira thinks that he should not begin the sacrifice only by his own resolve; carefully considering the gravity of the yagna, he thinks of Krishna, scourge of sinners, to be the best one to decide, because he knows that Krishna is the greatest of all persons, of measureless tejas, mighty-armed, un-born, yet born among men purely from his own will.

The Pandava thinks about Krishna's godlike deeds and decides that there is nothing unknown to him, nothing Krishna cannot achieve, nothing he cannot endure; and so concluding, Pritha's son Yudhishtira sends a messenger to that Master of all beings, sending through his man his blessings and greetings such as an older man does to one younger than himself.

Riding in a swift chariot, that messenger arrives in Dwaravati among the Yadavas and approaches Krishna. When Achyuta Krishna hears that Pritha's son wants to see him, he, too, becomes desirous of seeing his cousin. In his chariot drawn by fleet horses, flashing through many lands, Krishna, with Indrasena, arrives in Indraprastha.

Arriving in Indraprastha, Janardana comes directly to Yudhishtira. Yudhishtira receives Krishna with fatherly love, and Bhima also receives him likewise. Then Krishna comes in joy to greet his father's sister Kunti. When the twins have worshipped him, with reverence, he begins to speak in great delight with Arjuna, his friend, who is overjoyed to see him. When Krishna has rested awhile in a delightful apartment, and is refreshed, Yudhishtira comes to him at his leisure and tells him all about the Rajasuya yagna.

Yudhishtira says, 'I want to perform the Rajasuya, but that yagna cannot be undertaken just by my wishing to perform it. Krishna, you know everything about the royal sacrifice and what is needed for its performance. Only he can accomplish it in whom everything is possible, who is worshipped everywhere and who is the King of kings.

My friends and my ministers have come to me and said that I should undertake the yagna. But, Krishna, what you say about this will be my final guide. Some ministers do not see the true hazards of such an undertaking, out of their love; others from self-interest say only what is agreeable. Some, again, see what benefits them as being the course to follow. Thus, men give counsel of matters which await deciding.

But you, O Krishna, are above these motives. You are beyond both desire and anger. You must tell me what is truly most beneficial for the world.'"

CANTO 14

RAJASUYARAMBHA PARVA

"Krishna said, 'Maharajan, you are worthy and possess every quality needed to perform the Rajasuya yagna. You know everything, O Bhaarata, yet let me tell you something: those who now go in the world as Kshatriyas are inferior in every way to the Kshatriyas that Rama, the son of Jamadagnya, exterminated.

Mahipati, Lord of the Earth, Bharatarishabha, you know what kind of rule these Kshatriyas, guided by the laws and traditions handed down from generation to generation, have established amongst themselves, and how competent they are to perform the Rajasuya yagna.

Many royal lines, as well as other ordinary Kshatriyas, say that they are descendants of Aila and Ikshwaku. The descendants of Aila, O King, as also the kings of Ikshwaku's race are, know, each divided into a hundred separate dynasties. The descendants of Yayati and the Bhojas are great, both in extent and achievements. These last today are scattered all over the Earth, and all Kshatriyas worship the prosperity of these kings.

However, King Jarasandha has overwhelmed the power and prosperity enjoyed by their entire order and, overpowering them with his prowess, has set himself at the head of all these kings. Jarasandha enjoys sovereignty over the middle portion of the Earth, and he has resolved to create disunion amongst us.

Rajan, a king who is the paramount lord of all kings, and in whom alone the dominion of the world is vested, deserves to be called an emperor. Sisupala of Chedi, of great vitality, has placed himself under Jarasandha's protection and has become his Senapati, the Commander of all his forces. The mighty Baka, king of the Karushas, who can do battle using maya, waits upon Jarasandha as his sishya. Besides, two others, Hansa and Dimbhaka, of great tejas and atman, have sought shelter with the mighty Jarasandha.

There are others as well – Dantavakra, Karusa, Karava and Meghavahana, who serve Jarasandha. He, too, who wears upon his head the jewel known as the most wonderful on Earth, the king of the Yavanas, who has chastened Muru and Naraka, and whose power is unlimited, who rules the west like another Varuna, whose name is Bhagadatta, who is an old friend of your father, has bowed his head before Jarasandha, both by what he says and by what he does. However, in his heart he is bound by love for you, since he regarded your father as his son.

O King, that Lord of the Earth whose dominions extend in the west and the south, your maternal uncle Purujit, that fearless perpetuator of the race of Kunti, that slayer of all enemies, is the one king who has regard for you only out of love.

Then, he whom I did not kill, the vile wretch of the Chedis, who displays himself to the world as a divine one, and whom the world has also come to regard as such, who from his witlessness always carries the emblems of the Avatara, that king of Vanga, Pundra and the Kiratas, who is known in this world as Paundraka, and who also calls himself Vasudeva, has also allied himself with Jarasandha.

Bhishmaka, the mighty lord of the Bhojas, friend of Indra, slayer of hostile Kshatriyas, Bhishmaka who governs a fourth part of the world, who with his knowledge conquered the Pandyas and the Kratha-Kausikas, whose brother, the brave Akriti, was like Jamdagni's son Rama, also serves

Jarasandha, Master of Magadha. We are also Bhishmaka's relatives and so we do what is agreeable to him, but he does not respect us and always tries to do us harm. Rajan, he hardly seems aware of his own might or the honour of the great race to which he belongs; he is swayed just by Jarasandha's shining fame and has allied himself to the Magadhan.

Also, noble one, the eighteen tribes of Bhojas, fearing Jarasandha, have all fled west, as have the Surasenas, the Bhadrakas, the Bodhas, the Salwas, the Patachcharas, the Susthalas, the Sukuttas, and the Kulindas, along with the Kuntis. The king of the Salwayanas, his brothers and followers, the southern Panchalas and the eastern Kosalas have fled to the land of the Kuntis; so also the Matsyas and the Sannyastapadas, overcome by fear, leaving their dominions in the north, have fled south. Terrified by Jarasandha's power, the Panchalas fled in all directions.

Some time ago, the foolish Kamsa, who persecuted the Yadavas, married two of Jarasandha's daughters, Asti and Prapti, the sisters of his son, another Sahadeva. Strengthened by this alliance, the villainous Kamsa tyrannised his kinsmen and gained odium for himself. He also harried the old Bhoja kings, but they sought our help.

We gave Ahuka's beautiful daughter to be Akrura's wife, and then Balarama and I killed Kamsa and Sunamana, to do our relatives a service. However, even after the immediate cause of fear was removed, his father-in-law Jarasandha took up arms against us. We decided that if even we, the eighteen younger branches of the Yadava tribes, attacked our enemy concertedly with great weapons, we would still not be able to vanquish him, not in three hundred years.

Jarasandha had two friends who were like immortals and, in strength, the strongest among all men – they were called Hansa and Dimbhaka, both of whom no weapon could slay. With them for allies, the mighty Jarasandha, I believed, could not be killed even if the three worlds united against him. Most intelligent of men, this was not merely my opinion, but all the other kings also felt the same way.

However, there was another king, also called Hansa, and Balarama engaged him in battle and killed him after eighteen days of fight.

Bhaarata, when Dimbhaka heard the people saying that Hansa was slain, he felt could not bear to live without his friend and killed himself by throwing himself into the Yamuna. Later, when his friend Hansa, scourge of hostile armies, returned and heard that Dimbhaka had killed himself, he ran straight to the Yamuna and took his life by throwing himself into her waters.

Then, O Bharatarishabha, Jarasandha heard that both Hansa and Dimbhaka were dead and he turned back home with a broken heart. When he retreated, we were delighted and lived joyfully and in peace in Mathura.

Until Jarasandha's daughter, the lovely, lotus-eyed widow of Hansa, stricken by the death of her husband, went lamenting to her father and repeatedly begged him, that monarch of Magadha, "Parantapa, bane of all your enemies, kill the killer of my husband."

Then, great King, we again remembered what we had concluded long ago, and in alarm we fled Mathura. We divided our great wealth among many, into small portions, so each could be easily carried, and we fled with our cousins and kinsfolk, in fear of Jarasandha. Having thought carefully, we fled west.

In the west is a delightful city called Kusasthah, ringed by the Raivata Mountains; in that city, O King, we began living. We rebuilt its fort and made it so strong that even the gods cannot breach it; and from inside even our women can hold off any enemy, why speak of the Yadava heroes, who know no fear? Yes, Parantapa, we now live in that city, and because the great mountain is impregnable, the descendants of Madhu have become exceedingly glad, thinking that they have already passed beyond fearing Jarasandha.

Thus, though strong and powerful, we have been obliged to seek refuge in the Gomanta Mountains, which are three yojanas long, from fear of Jarasandha. In each yojana, we have established twenty-one outposts of armed soldiers; every yojana has a hundred gates, guarded by great Kshatriyas, all invincible, who belong to the younger strains of the Yadavas.

In our clan, O King, there are eighteen thousand brothers and cousins. Ahuka has a hundred sons, each like a god in strength. Charudeshna, his brother Chakradeva, Satyaki, myself, Rohini's son Baladeva, and my son Samba, who is my equal in battle – we seven, Rajan, are Atirathas. Besides, there are others, Rajan: Kritavarman, Anadhrishti, Samika, Samitinjaya, Kanka, Sanku and Kunti: these seven are Maharathas.

Maharathas, also, are the two sons of Andhaka-bhoja, as is the old king himself. Endowed with great prowess, all these are great Kshatriyas, each as mighty as Indra's thunderbolt. These Maharathas chose the middle country and now live among the Vrishnis. Bharatottama, only you are worthy of being an Emperor; it will become you to establish your empire over all the Kshatriyas.

However, in my judgement, you will not be able to perform the Rajasuya yagna as long as the powerful Jarasandha lives. As a lion keeps the carcasses of mighty elephants he has killed in his cave, Jarasandha has incarcerated many kings of the world inside his hill fortress. Parantapa, when they are a hundred in number he wants to sacrifice them to Umapati Siva, the illustrious Devadeva, whom he worships and who loves him for his fierce tapasya.

So it is that he has vanquished the kings of the Earth, and he now has the means to keep the vow he swore to sacrifice a hundred kings. He has made his city populous by conquering the kings and bringing them and their troops to his fortress, as his captives.

We, also, once fled Mathura to Dwaravati, from fear of Jarasandha. If, Maharajan, you want to perform this sacrifice, you must rescue the kings from Jarasandha and also bring about his death. Scion of the Kurus, otherwise you cannot undertake to perform a Rajasuya yagna: this is the only way you can succeed.

Rajan, this is my view; do, Sinless, as you see fit. The circumstances being what they are, reflect upon everything, consider all causes and effects, and then tell us what you think is proper to do.'"

CANTO 15

Rajasuyarambha Parva Continued

"Yudhishthira says, 'Being as intelligent as you are, you have said what no one else could; surely, no one but you can settle every doubt in this world. There are kings in every land, engaged in benefiting themselves, yet none amongst them has been able to become an emperor. Truly, the title is difficult of acquisition.

He who is aware of the strength and courage of others never praises himself. He alone is worthy of praise who conducts himself honourably while engaging his enemies. O Bearer of the dignity of the Vrishnis, even like the wide Earth is adorned with great many jewels, myriad and countless are the desires and propensities of man.

Even as experience can rarely be gained other than by journeying in lands far from one's home, so, too, salvation can never be gained other than by living by high principles, which are remote from one's desires and baser tendencies. I regard peace of mind as the highest goal here, for, from that alone comes true prosperity. In my view, if I undertake this sacrifice, I will never attain the highest goal.

O Janardana, blessed with vitality and wisdom, the Kshatriyas born into our race, also thought that some day one of them would become the greatest Kshatriya of all. But, noble one, we too were all touched by the fear of Jarasandha and, O Sinless, by his evil. Invincible one, the strength of your arms is my refuge. When you take fright at Jarasandha's power, how shall I dare think of myself as being stronger than him? Madhava, O Vrishni, I feel plunged in dejection to think that not you, or Balarama, not Bhimasena or Arjuna can kill Jarasandha.

But what shall I say, Krishna? You are my highest authority in all things.'

Hearing this, Bhima, skilled in speech, says, 'That king who, being torpid, or weak and without resources, engages in battle with a strong enemy, perishes like an anthill. However, it is observed that even a weak king, with vigilance and the use of stratagem, can vanquish a strong enemy and gain the fruit of his every wish.

In Krishna there is stratagem; in me, there is strength; and in Arjuna, victory. So, like the three fires which accomplish a sacrifice, we shall devise the death of the king of Magadha.'

Now Krishna says, 'One whose understanding is immature seeks the fruit of his desire, without looking to what might happen to him in the future. We observe that nobody forgives an enemy for his callowness, one who is self-serving! We have heard that, in the Krita Yuga, having subjugated the entire world, Yauvanaswin, through the abolition of all taxes, Bhagiratha, by his kindliness towards his subjects, Kartavirya, by the force of his asceticism, the Lord Bharata through his strength and valour, and Maruta by his prosperity – all these five became emperors.

But Yudhishthira, you, who wish for the imperial dignity deserve it not merely by one but by all these qualities: by victory, by the protection you give your people, by your virtue, your prosperity, and your policy. Know, O Bull of the Kurus, that Brihadratha's son Jarasandha is also, like you, one who wishes to and can become an emperor. A hundred dynasties of kings have not been able to subdue Jarasandha.

Surely, for his might he can be regarded an emperor. Kings who wear royal jewels make offerings of these to Jarasandha, but being evil since he was a child, he is not satisfied with their worship. He has become the most powerful king, yet he savagely attacks other kings who wear crowns upon their heads. There is no king from whom he does not take tribute, and so he has brought almost a hundred kings under his sway.

How, O son of Pritha, will any weak king dare confront him with hostile intentions? The kings whom he has locked up like so many animals in Siva's temple, to sacrifice them to that God, don't they experience abject misery? A Kshatriya who dies in battle is always honoured. So, why should we not combine to give battle to Jarasandha?

He has already taken eighty-six kings his captives; he needs only fourteen more to make them a hundred. As soon as he has them, he will perform his brutal sacrifice. He who impedes that savagery will surely win blazing fame, and he who vanquishes Jarasandha will become emperor of all the Kshatriyas.'"

CANTO 16

RAJASUYARAMBHA PARVA CONTINUED

"Yudhishtira says, 'Out of my selfish desire to perform the Rajasuya yagna, and relying on just blind courage, how can I in conscience send you, O Krishna, to Jarasandha? Bhima and Arjuna I think of as my very eyes, and you, Janardana as my heart. How will I live without my eyes and my heart?

Not Yama can conquer Jarasandha's awesome host in battle, his army endowed with dreadful valour, besides. What can you do against that force? I fear this will lead only to tragedy. I believe that we must not undertake this task. Listen, Krishna, to what I think. Janardana, desisting from this sacrifice seems to me to be best. Ah, today my heart is distressed; to me the Rajasuya appears hard to accomplish.'

Arjuna, who has received the Gandiva, best of bows, a pair of inexhaustible quivers, a chariot with Hanuman's banner, as also the great Mayaa sabha, now says to Yudhishtira, 'My lord, I have won a great bow, my quivers, astras, prowess, allies, dominions, fame and energy – all of which are difficult to gain, however one might wish for them.

Learned men always praise, in fine society, nobility of birth. But nothing is equal to might, and, O King, there is nothing I prefer to strength. He who is born into a race noted for its valour, but who himself has none, is hardly worthy of respect; while he who is born into an inferior race but is valiant, is superior to the first.

He, Rajan, is a Kshatriya in every way, who increases his fame and possessions by subjugating his enemies. He that is brave, even if he has no other merit, will conquer his enemies. However, he who has no courage, though he owns every other quality, can hardly achieve anything. Every other merit exists, latently, only beside valour.

A focus of attention, exertion and destiny are the three causes of victory. He that is valiant but acts rashly does not deserve success; this is why a powerful man is sometimes killed by his enemies. As meanness overtakes the weak, so does folly at times overtake the strong. So, a king who wants victory must avoid both these causes of ruin.

If we try to kill Jarasandha and rescue the kings incarcerated by him for a savage purpose, so that we might perform a Rajasuya yagna, there is nothing nobler that we could do. Equally, if we refrain from this task the world will forever think of us as being weak. We are surely capable, O King, so why should you think that we are not?

Those who become Munis, wishing to attain the peace of their souls, easily gain ochre robes. So, too, if we vanquish the enemy, we shall easily perform the Rajasuya yagna. We must, therefore, fight Jarasandha.'"

CANTO 17

Rajasuyarambha Parva Continued

"Krishna says, 'Arjuna has shown what the attitude should be of a prince born into the race of Bhaarata, especially a son of Kunti. We do not know when death will overtake us – by night, or by day; neither have we ever heard that we can become immortal by evading a battle. So, this is the dharma of men – to attack the enemy by principles laid down in the law. For this satisfies the heart.

With wise policy, any undertaking meets with success, unless destiny frustrates it. If two sides, both following precept, meet in battle, one must triumph for victory cannot belong to both. However, a battle influenced by bad policy, where one side is devoid of the renowned arts of war, must end in defeat or death. If, again, both sides are equal the outcome is in doubt. Yet both cannot win. When this is the case, why should we not confront the enemy, guided by wise policy, and destroy him as a river in spate uproots a tree?

If we disguise our own weaknesses while attacking those of the adversary, why should we not succeed? Surely the policy of wise men has always been never to engage in open warfare against the very powerful enemy at the head of his formidable forces. This is my view, as well. However, if we achieve our purpose by secretly entering the home of our foe and attacking just him, we shall not find disgrace.

That bull among men Jarasandha enjoys undimmed glory, indeed, even like him who is the atman in the heart of all the created. But I see his death. Wishing the welfare of our kinsmen, we will either kill him in a fight, or we will ascend into heaven being killed by him.'

Yudhishtira says, 'Krishna, who is this Jarasandha? What is the secret of his power and his energy, that even having touched you he has not been consumed like an insect by the touch of fire?'

Krishna says, 'Hear, O King, who Jarasandha is – what his tejas is, what his prowess; and also why I have spared him, despite his giving me repeated offence.

There was a mighty king called Brihadratha, Lord of the Magadhas. Invincible in battle, he had three Akshauhinis of men. Handsome he was and blessed with great vitality; he owned wealth and prowess beyond measure; always, upon his body, he bore the marks of having been installed as a sacrificer at countless yagnas. He was like a second Indra. In splendour he was like Surya, in forgiveness like the Earth, in wrath like Yama and in wealth like Vaisravana.

Bharatottama, the whole Earth was mantled by his great qualities, inherited from a long line of ancestors, covered as by rays from the sun. Endowed with great tejas, that king married the twin daughters of the king of Kasi, both blessed lavishly with the wealth of beauty. That bull among men made a secret pact with his wives that he would love them equally and would never show any preference for either.

And, with his two precious wives, both of whom were perfectly suited to him, the lord of the Earth spent his days in great joy, even like a mighty king elephant with two cow-elephants, or like the ocean, embodied, with Ganga and Yamuna. Yet, though the king's youth passed thus in delight, he had no son to continue his line, although he performed countless auspicious rites, homas and yagnas to that end.

One day, Brihadratha heard that the lofty-souled Chandakausika, son of Kakshivat of the illustrious race of Gautama, had ceased his tapasya and had come on his wanderings to the king's city, and now sat in the shade of a mango tree. Taking his wives with him, the king went to that Muni and worshipped him with offerings of jewels and other valuable gifts, which pleased the Sage greatly.

That best of Rishis, always truthful, indeed devoted to the truth, said to Brihadratha, "King of kings, I am pleased with you. Ask me for a boon, O you of excellent vratas."

Brihadratha and his wives prostrated before the Rishi and, his voice tearful from his despair at having no son, the king said, "Holy one, I am about to leave my kingdom and go into the forest to sit in tapasya. Ah, I am a most unfortunate man that I have no son. So what will I do, O Maharishi, with a kingdom?"

Hearing this, the Muni restrained his senses and entered into deep dhyana, where he sat in the shade of the mango tree. Into the Sage's lap there fell a juicy mango, untouched by the beak of a parrot, or any bird. That best of Munis took the mango and, breathing some silent mantras over it, gave the fruit to the king, so he could have a peerless child.

The Mahamuni, of exceptional wisdom, said to Brihadratha, "Go back, O King, for your wish is fulfilled. Do not leave your kingdom and go into the forest."

In joy, Brihadratha worshipped the feet of the Sage and returned to his palace. He remembered his old promise to his wives that he would never make any difference between them and, Bharatarishabha, the king gave that mango to them both. His exquisite queens divided that fruit in two halves and ate it.

Because of the Muni's power, because he could never utter a lie, both queens became pregnant after eating the mango, and Brihadratha's joy knew no bounds. When their time came both queens gave birth: each to a divided child. Each half had one eye, one arm, one leg, half a stomach, half a face and half an anus.

The mothers looked at what they had brought forth and shivered in fear. In great sorrow, the mothers decided to abandon the stillborn halves of a child. Their two midwives carefully swaddled the two lifeless pieces and, leaving the palace in stealth through a back door at dead of night, left the parcels outside at a crossing of streets and hurried back.

Purushvyaghra, a while later, a Rakshasi called Jara, a cannibal who lived on human flesh and blood, found the two halves of the abandoned child and picked them up to take them outside the city. She put them together so she could carry them more easily, when, O Bull among men, there was a flash of light and the two halves were united into a magnificent, now breathing child!

Now her eyes wide with amazement, the Rakshasi found that she could not make off with the human child, whose body was as hard and powerful as the Vajra, the thunderbolt of adamant. That infant clenched his hands into fists, red as copper, thrust them into his mouth and began to roar as dreadfully as rain-charged thunderheads. Alarmed by the sound, the king and others living in his palace came out.

The dejected and grieving queens emerged, as well, their breasts suddenly welling with milk to have back their child. The Rakshasi saw the queens who wanted their child back, she saw the king who was desperate for a son, she felt the strength of the child in her arms, and she thought, "I live in the domain of this king who is so anxious to have a son, and it does not become me to kill the infant of such a great and good king."

The Rakshasi held the child in her arms even as clouds enfold the sun and, quickly assuming a human form, came before the king and said to him, "Brihadratha, this is your child; I give him to you; here, take him. He has been born through the virtue of your wives and the blessing of the great Brahmana. The midwives abandoned him in the night, but I have given him refuge."

Receiving their son, the lovely daughters of the king of Kasi soon drenched him in mother's milk. When the king knew everything that had happened he was full of joy, and he spoke to the Rakshasi, who had assumed the form of a human woman with a golden complexion.

"O you who have the complexion of a lotus' filament, who are you that returns my son to me? Auspicious one, to me you seem like a goddess ranging the Earth at your whim!"'"

CANTO 18

RAJASUYARAMBHA PARVA CONTINUED

"Krishna continues, 'Hearing this, the Rakshasi answered, "May you be blessed, O King of kings! I am the Rakshasi Jara, who can take any form that I choose. I live contentedly in your realm and am revered by everyone: for I go from house to house, of men, and bring them fortune. The Svayambhuva Brahma created me of old, and I was called Grihadevi, the goddess of hearth and home.

I had celestial beauty, and I was sent to the world to destroy the Danavas. He who draws a likeness of me upon the walls of his house, a likeness full of youth and in the midst of children, shall indeed have prosperity in his home; otherwise, his household will suffer decay and ruin. O King, on a wall of your palace is a picture of me surrounded by children, which is worshipped daily with flowers and perfumes, with incense, offerings of food and other things of enjoyment.

Since I am so adored in your home, I think daily of doing you some great good in return. It happened, good king, that I saw the halves of your child born in two pieces. When I put them together, a living child was made. Great king, this transpired only because of your good fortune, and I was merely its instrument.

I can swallow Mount Meru if I choose; what then to say of this child? But you have gratified me with the worship, which you offer me in your home, and so I give you back your son."

With these words, Rajan, the Rakshasi vanished. Having received his son, Brihadratha returned to his palace, where he had all the rites of infancy performed. He ordered his people to observe an annual festival to honour the Rakshasi. Then, that king, who was as Brahma's equal, named his son Jarasandha – he who had been joined by Jara.

Jarasandha of Magadha grew in size and strength like a fire fed with libations of ghee. Growing, day by day, even like the moon waxing during the bright fortnight of the month, the child swelled his parents' joy.'"

CANTO 19

RAJASUYARAMBHA PARVA CONTINUED

"Krishna says, 'Some time later, the noble Maharishi Chandakausika came again to the land of the Magadhas. Joyful at his advent, King Brihadratha went out to welcome him, taking his ministers and priest and wives and son. O Bhaarata, he worshipped the Sage with padya and arghya, and then offered his entire kingdom to him, and also his son.

Receiving, graciously, the king's worship, and well pleased with it, that holy Rishi said to the sovereign of Magadaha, "I know everything that has happened with spiritual vision. But listen, O King of kings, to what this son of yours will become, and also what his beauty, excellence, strength and valour shall be.

Have no doubt that, blessed with fortune and growing in prowess, he will have all these. Just as other birds can never match the speed of Vinata's son Garuda, the other kings of the world will never be able to equal the tejas of your heroic son. All that stand in his way he will raze. Even as the force of a cataract makes no dent upon a mountain's breast of rock, weapons cast at him, even by the Devas, with cause him no injury or pain.

He will blaze forth over the heads of all that wear crowns. As the Sun dims the lustre of the stars, your prince will rob the glory of every other monarch. Even the mighty kings, who own great armies and countless chariots and beasts, will perish like moths in a flame when they confront your son.

This child will seize the burgeoning fortune of every other king, as the ocean receives the swollen waters of rivers during the monsoon. As the vast Earth bears all manner of thing, this child of inordinate strength will support the four varnas. Even as every creature born with a body depends on precious vayu, dear as their atman, to live, so will the kings of the world depend on your son.

This prince of Magadha, mightiest of all men in the world, will see with his human eyes the God of gods – Rudra, Hara destroyer of the Tripura."

Parantapa, with this, Chandkaushika dismissed King Brihadratha and turned back to his own ascetic pursuit. The lord of the Magadhas went back into his capital, and gathering all his friends and kinsfolk, installed Jarasandha upon his throne. Very soon, King Brihadratha began to feel a sharp aversion for all worldly pleasures. When he had made Jarasandha king, he and his two wives went away into the forest and began living in an asrama.

Rajan, once his father took sannyasa, Jarasandha, through his matchless valour, brought many kings under his sway.

King Brihadratha lived for some years in the forest, in tapasya, before finally rising into Swarga with his wives. King Jarasandha had all the boons that Chandakausika foretold, and ruled his people like a father. Some years later, when I, Krishna, killed Kamsa, enmity arose between Jarasandha and me. O Bhaarata, from his city, Girivraja, the king of Magadha whirled a great mace ninety-nine times over his head and flung it at Mathura.

I lived in Mathura then. The beautiful mace, which Jarasandha hurled all the way from Girivraja, flew ninety-nine yojanas and landed near Mathura. Seeing it, the people rushed to me to tell me about the fall of the mace. The place where that mace fell, next to Mathura, is called Gadavasan.

Jarasandha had two staunch supporters, Hansa and Dimbhaka, both invincible to all weapons. They were masters of politics and dharma, and in counsel they were the most intelligent among all men. I have already told you all about that awesome pair. The two of them and Jarasandha, together, I believe, were more than a match for the three worlds. This was why the powerful Kukkura, Andhaka and Vrishni tribes, out of discretion, did not consider it wise to fight Jarasandha.'"

CANTO 20

JARASANDHA-VADHA PARVA

"Krishna says, 'Hansa and Dimbhaka have both fallen; Kamsa and all his followers have been slain. So, the time has come to kill Jarasandha. But he cannot be killed in battle even by the Devas and the Asuras, even if they combine. However, I think that he can be vanquished in single combat. In me there is policy; in Bhima is strength, and in Arjuna there is victory; so, as prelude to your performing the Rajasuya yagna, we will surely destroy the king of Magadha.

We three shall go to him, secretly, and he will certainly fight one of us. Because he is proud and fears ignominy he will choose to fight Bhima. And like Death himself, who kills a man swollen with pride, the long-armed and mighty Bhima will kill the king of Magadha.

If you know my heart, and if you have any faith in me, then give me Arjuna and Bhima, without delay.'

Yudhishtira sees how cheerfully Bhima and Arjuna stand beside him, and cries, 'Achyuta, O Achyuta Parantapa, do not say this to me! You are the lord of the Pandavas, and we depend only on you. What you say, Govinda, is always wisdom. You never walk at the head of those whom Fortune has abandoned. I, who am yours to command, consider Jarasandha already dead and the kings he holds captive already set free, and that I have already performed the Rajasuya.

Lord of the Universe, Purushottama, go forth vigilantly so that this mission is accomplished. I cannot live without you – like a man stricken by disease and deprived of dharma, artha and kama.

Arjuna cannot live without Sauri, nor can Krishna live without Partha; neither is there anything in this world which these two cannot conquer. Then, this handsome Bhima is the strongest man in the world. Of great renown, what is there that he cannot achieve with the two of you?

When well led, troops excel in war; an army without a leader is lifeless, say the wise. So, armies must always be led by commanders of experience. The wise channel water into low-lying lands; even fishermen cause water to leak out through holes in the tank. We, too, shall attempt to achieve our purpose under the leadership of this Krishna, who knows politics, whose fame spreads through the world. Indeed, to succeed at any venture one should always set Krishna in the van, this Purushottama whose power consists of both wisdom and strategy, and who knows both methods and means.

So, to achieve our purpose, let Pritha's son Arjuna follow Krishna, best of the Yadavas, and let Bhima follow Arjuna. Through wise policy, good fortune and prowess, we will find success in this purpose which needs great valour.'

When Yudhishtira says this, Krishna, Arjuna and Bhima, all mighty tejasvins, set out for Magadha, their splendid bodies clothed in the garb of Snataka Brahmanas, and with the blessings and encouraging words of friends and kinsmen. Great is their splendour anyway; and their bodies, already like the Sun, the Moon and Fire, blaze brighter for being inflamed by wrath at the plight of the kings, their kin, imprisoned by Jarasandha.

The people see Krishna and Arjuna, neither of whom have ever been defeated in battle, with Bhima at their head, all three going forth to accomplish one mission, and they think of Jarasandha as being already dead. For the illustrious two are Masters, who direct everything that happens in all the worlds, as well as all things concerning the dharma, artha and kama of every creature.

Setting out from the land of the Kurus, they pass through Kurujangala and arrive at the charmed lake of lotuses. Crossing the hills of Kalakuta, they then passed over the Gandaki, the Sadanira, the Sarkaravarta and the other rivers, all of which spring from the same mountains. They then cross the lovely Sarayu and see the country of Eastern Kosala. Passing through that kingdom, they come to Mithila, then, crossing the Mala and Charamanwati, the three heroes ford the Ganga and the Sona, and continue eastwards.

Finally, those shuras, heroes of undimmed glory, arrive at Magadha at the heart of Kushamba. Coming to the hills of Goratha, they see below them the capital city of Magadha, always replete with cows, wealth, water and beautiful with the countless trees which grow there."

JARASANDHA-VADHA PARVA CONTINUED

"Krishna says, 'Look, Partha, at the great capital of Magadha in all its splendour. Rich are its flocks and herds, and inexhaustible its store of water. The finest mansions adorn its streets, free from all calamities and evil.

The five mountains Vaihara, Varaha, Vrishabha, Rishigiri, and the enchanting Chaitya, all with towering peaks, overgrown with great and lofty trees, intertwined and of cool shade: all these seem to protect this city of Girivraja together. The breasts of these hills are covered by delightful trees of Lodhra forests, fragrant, their branch ends profuse with flowers.

Here the lustrous Gautama, of stern vows, begot on Ausinari, the Sudra woman, Kakshivat and other sons of great renown. It only goes to reflect Gautama's mercy on human kings that the race sprung from him still lives under their mortal sway. Arjuna, it was here that, in elder days, the mighty sovereigns of Anga, Vanga and other lands came to the asrama of Gautama, and spent their days in joy.

Look, Partha, at these enchanting forests of Pippalas and lovely Lodhras, which surround the hermitage of Gautama Muni. Long ago, the Nagas Arbuda and Sakrapavain lived here, those Parantapas, as did the excellent Nagas Swastika and Mani. Manu himself had ordained that the land of the Magadhas would never feel the scourge of any drought; and Kaushika and Manimat also blessed this country.

Being master of this beautiful and impregnable city, Jarasandha, unlike other kings, is bent on fulfilling his vile purpose. But we will kill him, and crush his pride.'

With that, those mighty tejasvins, the Vrishni and the two Pandavas approach Girivraja, impregnable capital of Magadha, teeming with cheerful, well-fed people of all the four varnas: Girivraja of perennial festivities. Upon arriving at the city-gates, instead of entering peaceably, the cousins assault the sacred Chaityaka peak, which the race of Brihadratha as well as the people of Girivraja worship, and which gladdens the hearts of all Magadhans.

Once, Brihadratha killed the Rakshasa Rishabha upon that peak and made three great drums out of his hide, which he set up in Girivraja. Those drums, once struck, resound for a full month after! Krishna and the Pandavas tear down the peak of Chaityaka, the joy and pride of the Magadhas, and bring it down over those drums covered by the blooms of heaven, the drums which never stop reverberating. They, who have come to kill Jarasandha, it seems set their feet upon their enemy's head by what they do.

Having attacked that celebrated, ancient, immovable massif, always adored with perfumes and garlands, with awesome arms, breaking it down, the three heroes joyfully march into Girivraja. The Brahmanas inside the city see many evil omens, which they hasten to report to Jarasandha.

The chief priest makes the king mount an elephant and, blessed by lighted brands around him, Jarasandha of untold prowess, wanting to keep the evil omens signified at bay, enters into a yagna with every apposite vow; he fasts.

Meanwhile, Bhaarata, the brothers, unarmed, rather with their own bare arms their only weapons, enter the city disguised as Snataka

Brahmanas; they come seeking single combat with Jarasandha. They see how marvellously elegant are the shops, full of garlands and various delicacies to eat, indeed replete with everything that any man's heart could desire.

Looking at those affluent and excellent shops, the Purushottamas Krishna, Bhima and Dhananjaya walk along the public highway. Suddenly, they of untold strength begin to forcibly snatch the garlands that the flower-vendors have hung up for sale. Wearing colourful robes and earrings, putting on the garlands, the heroes walk into the abode of Jarasandha of lofty intellect, even like Himalayan lions eyeing cattle-folds.

Rajan, smeared with sandalwood paste, the arms of those Kshatriyas look like the trunks of Sala trees. The people of Magadha see those magnificent three, powerful as elephants, their necks thick as Sala trees, chests wide, and are wonderstruck. The Purusharishabhas pass through three crowded gates, where men throng, and in great heart and cheer approach Jarasandha, haughtily.

Jarasandha gets up in haste and receives them with padya, madhurpaka and other ingredients of arghya; he offers them gifts of kine, and shows them every reverence.

Says that great king to them, 'Be welcome!'

O Janamejaya, Partha and Bhima remain silent, while Krishna replies, 'King of kings, these two have sworn a vow of silence and they will not speak until midnight. After that hour, they will talk to you.'

Jarasandha houses his guests in the apartments of sacrifice and returns to his royal chambers. At the midnight hour, the king returns to his guests who wear the attire of Brahmanas. For, that invincible monarch keeps strictly his vow that, even if it be the midnight hour, he would grant audience to any Snataka Brahmanas who arrive in his court.

O Bhaarata, seeing the extraordinary attire of his guests, that best among kings is puzzled. Yet, he waits upon them patiently, respectfully, silently. Those Purusharishabhas, the three Parantapas, on the other hand, see Jarasandha and say, 'O King, may you attain moksha without any great effort!'

Tiger among kings, with that they fall silent, staring. Rajadhiraja, Jarasandha says to those Pandavas and the Yadava, all disguised as Brahmanas, 'Pray, be seated.'

Those Narapungavas sit themselves down, and they blaze with beauty like the three main priests of a great sacrifice.

Jarasandha, always devoted to truth, now softly censures his guests in disguise, saying, 'Well do I know that, throughout the world, Brahmanas who keep the Snataka vrata never deck their persons with garlands and fragrant paste, unseasonably.

So who are you, adorned with flowers, and your hands bearing the marks of the bowstring? Wearing coloured robes, wearing flowers and sandalwood paste, out of season, you tell me that you are Brahmanas although you have the bearing of Kshatriyas.

Tell me truly who you are. Truth embellishes even kings. Why, breaking the peak of the Chaityaka, have you come in here, disguised, and through an unlawful gate, without fear of my royal wrath? The Brahmana's tejas dwells in his speech; what you did is not suited to the varna to which you profess to belong.

Therefore, tell me what is your purpose? You have arrived here unlawfully; why do you disdain the worship that I offer you? What motive have you for coming here?'

Thus addressed by the king, Krishna Mahatman, that most eloquent one, replies calmly and gravely.

Krishna says, 'O King, know we are Snataka Brahmanas. Brahmanas, Kshatriyas and Vaishyas are all allowed to observe the Snataka vrata. Besides, this vow has numerous rules governing it, both general and particular. A Kshatriya who keeps this vow with special observances finds great prosperity. Therefore, we have decked ourselves in flowers.

Also, Kshatriyas sow their prowess not with words but deeds. That is why, O son of Brihadratha, a Kshatriya never speaks audaciously. Brahma has invested in the Kshatriya his own tejas, implanted it in the purpose of the warrior. If you wish to see it today, you shall.

This is the code of the Kshatriya: that the house of an enemy must be entered through the unlawful gate, and a friend's house through the proper one. Know, also, that having entered our enemy's house through the illegal gate to accomplish our purpose, we are sworn not to accept the worship offered us.'"

CANTO 22

JARASANDHA-VADHA PARVA CONTINUED

"Jarasandha says, 'I do not remember having ever done you an injury! Even after thinking carefully about it, I do not recall what harm I ever did you. When I have never wounded you, Brahmanas, why do you think of me as your enemy? Answer me honestly, for that is the way of the righteous.

The mind feels pain at any harm done to one's artha or dharma. The Kshatriya who injures an innocent man's pleasure or morality, let him not be a great warrior otherwise, and a master of every aspect of dharma, he, beyond doubt, finds the fate of sinners and falls away from fortune and grace.

The ways of the Kshatriyas are the noblest among all men of dharma in the three worlds. Indeed, all who know dharma acclaim the code of the Kshatriya. I follow the laws of my varna and never harm any who live under my rule. So, by bringing this charge against me, it seems that you speak in error.'

Krishna says, 'Mahabaho, there is one in this world who is sovereign of a certain royal line, and who upholds the honour of his race. We have come against you at his command. You have brought many Kshatriyas of the world here to your city as your prisoners. How can you still think of yourself as a man of dharma after what you have done? Best of kings, how can one king sin thus against other righteous kings?

But you treat other kings savagely and seek to offer them as human sacrifice to the Lord Rudra! O Son of Brihadratha, the sin you have committed touches me, as well, for I am with dharma and I can protect dharma. Killing human beings as a sacrifice to the gods is unheard of. So why do you wish to offer the lives of a hundred kings to the Lord Sankara?

You are treating noble men, who belong to your own varna, like animals. You are a fool, Jarasandha, for who else would behave in this wise? One always finds the fruit of whatever one does, under whatever circumstances. Therefore, since we are sworn to protect and help all those in distress, we have come here, for the weal of our kind, to kill you and prevent the slaughter of the captive kings, our kinsmen.

You believe that there is no man among the Kshatriyas who can match you; you are gravely mistaken in this. Rajan, there is no Kshatriya born who would not, thinking of his noble ancestry and birth, gladly ascend into heaven, which has no like anywhere on earth, by dying in battle.

Know, Purusharishabha, that Kshatriyas fight battles like men performing yagnas, with Swarga as their goal, and thus quell the whole world. Studying the Vedas, performing tapasya and dying in battle are all deeds which lead to heaven. Finding Swarga through the first two might not be certain, but for those who die in battle heaven is assured.

Death in battle inexorably brings triumph to equal Indra's. Countless gains accrue from dying in battle. It is through battle that Indra of the thousand yagnas became who he is; it is why he vanquishes the Asuras and rules the three worlds. You are so full of hubris about the untold might of your Magadha host; open hostility against you must surely lead only to heaven.

Do not underestimate other men, for valour dwells in everyone. Rajan, there are many whose valour might well equal or even exceed your own. It is only because they are not as renowned as you that your valour is noted. We can bear your strength. So, I say to you, King of Magadha, do not act like a superior: you are in the presence of your peers.

Do not tempt fate and go, along with your children, your ministers and your legions into Yama's land. Dambhodhbhava, Kartavirya, Uttara and Brihadratha were kings who met death, with all their forces, because they underestimated their superiors.

We who have come to liberate the kings you hold as captives, know, are surely not Brahmanas. I am Hrisikesa, also called Sauri, and these two heroes among men are the sons of Pandu. Lord of Magadha, we challenge you – stand before us and fight. Either free all the kings or go to Yamaloka!'

Jarasandha says, 'I never make a captive of a king without vanquishing him in battle. Who have I held here whom I have not first defeated in war? Krishna, it has been told that this is the dharma which every Kshatriya must follow: to bring others under his sway by force of arms, and then to treat them as his slaves.

I have collected these kings in order to sacrifice them to God. How will I now free them out of fear today, especially after I have told you what Kshatriya dharma is? With troops against troops, arrayed in battle formation, or alone against one of you, or alone against two or all three of you, simultaneously or separately, I am ready to fight!'

Saying this, and eager to have battle with those three warriors of dreadful achievements, Jarasandha has his son, another Sahadeva, installed upon his throne. Then, Bharatarishabha, on the brink of battle, that king remembers his two generals Kausika and Chitrasena. These two were once known through the world, reverentially, as Hansa and Dimbhaka.

And, Rajan, that tiger among men, the Lord Sauri, who is always devoted to the truth, that slayer of Madhu, Haladhara's[1] younger brother, Krishna greatest of men who have perfectly controlled their senses,

---

[1]Balarama's ploughshare weapon is the Halayudha, so he is Haladhara, bearer of the plough.

remembering Brahma's command and knowing that the lord of Magadha is destined to be killed in single combat by Bhima, and not by any Yadava, does not wish to himself kill Jarasandha, most powerful of men blessed with strength, that hero endowed with the strength of a tiger, that Kshatriya of terrible valour."

JARASANDHA-VADHA PARVA CONTINUED

Vaisampayana said, "Then, that best of orators, Krishna of the Yadava clan, says to Jarasandha who is resolved to fight, 'Rajan, which of us three will you fight? Which of us should prepare for combat with you?'

The splendid king of Magadha says that he will do battle with Bhima. Now, his priest fetches the yellow pigment got from the cow, garlands of flowers and every other auspicious thing, as well as the best specifics for restoring consciousness and relieving pain, to Jarasandha, eager for combat.

A celebrated Brahmana performs initiatory rites for Jarasandha, with all blessings, and, thinking of the dharma of a Kshatriya, the king readies himself for battle. He takes off his crown, ties up his hair and rises like an ocean which would burst apart its continents.

That sovereign of dreadful prowess says to Bhima, 'I will fight you, for it is honourable to be vanquished by a superior man.'

With that, Jarasandha rushes at Bhima even as the Asura Bala of old did at the king of the Devas. Krishna invokes the gods on behalf of the mighty Bhimasena, his cousin. Having taken counsel with Krishna, Bhima also advances upon Jarasandha, keen for battle. Then the two Purushavyaghras, those Kshatriyas of untold prowess, their bare arms their only weapons, joyfully lock in combat, each one eager to quell the other.

Grasping each other's arms, locking legs, at times slapping armpits in self-exhortation, they make the arena where they face each other tremble. Often they lay hold of each other's necks and push and heave violently, this way and that; they press every limb against a limb of the adversary; they continue to slap their own armpits in exultation and defiance.

At times extending their arms, at others withdrawing them, now lifting them high, now dropping them low, they circle and seize each other. Neck thrust against neck, brow striking brow, roughly, they make sparks fly from armour and headpieces, like flashes of lightning.

Grasping each other with many holds with their arms, lashing out with kicks violent enough to reach their inmost marmas, they also strike each other's chests with clenched fists. Roaring like thunderheads, they fight as two maddened elephants might with their trunks. Incensed by each other's blows, on they fight: hauling, pulling, dragging, ferociously, glaring like two angry lions.

Every limb of the other each one strikes, using arms, mighty legs; seizing one another by the waist, they fling each other far with awesome force. Accomplished wrestlers both, the two Kshatriyas pull and shove and clasp each other with violent force.

Then, those heroes perform the most difficult of all feats in wrestling: prishtabhanga, where they throw each other face down onto the ground and keep the fallen antagonist so for as long as possible. With their arms, they also perform the sampurna-murchcha and purna-kumbha.

At times, they wring each other's arms and other limbs as if these are vegetable fibres to be twisted into cords. At others, fists clenched, they strike thunderous blows upon other parts of their opponent's bodies than those at which they appear to aim.

So battle those heroes and the citizens, thousands of Brahmanas, Kshatriyas, Vaisyas and Sudras, and even women and the old, O Purushvyaghra, come out and gather around to watch the titanic duel. Quickly, the crowd swells, until it is great, and a single solid mass of humanity, no space between body and body.

The sounds the wrestlers make, while slapping their arms, seizing each other's necks to throw one another down, grabbing each other's legs also to fling the adversary to the ground – all these are so loud that they resemble the roar of thunder or of cliffs breaking and falling.

Both of them are the greatest among the strong and delight greatly in this encounter. Keen to prevail, each watches alert to take advantage of the slightest lapse by the other. And, O King, the awesome Bhima and Jarasandha fight ferociously in those lists, at times driving the crowd back by waving their hands; they fight even like Indra and Vritra did of old.

Dragging forward, thrusting back, and with sudden twists flinging each other down, onto face or side, they wound each other savagely. At times, they strike with bent and vicious knees, while roaring at each other: stinging taunts and insults. They strike each other with fists, the blows descending like the weight of rocks. With bull-like shoulders, long arms, and both masters of wrestling, they strike each other with those arms that are like maces of iron.

On the first day of the lunar month of Kartika begins that duel between the two heroes, and the lustrous Kshatriyas battle on, never pausing, not to eat; they battle on by night and day, until the thirteenth day of the Moon. However, on the night of the fourteenth day, the lord of Magadha calls a halt from fatigue.

And Krishna says bitingly to Bhima of terrible deeds, 'Kaunteya, an enemy who is tired must not be pressed, for if he is he might even die of exhaustion. So, Son of Kunti, you must not press this king while he is tired. Bhima, put forth only as much strength as he can now summon into his arms; fight him only with such strength as he has, Bull of the Bhaaratas.'

Bhima Parantapa understands at once what Krishna means, and he knows the time has come to kill Jarasandha. Bhima, strongest of all strong men, gathers himself, all his strength and valour, that prince of the Kurus, to bring down the hitherto unvanquished Jarasandha."

CANTO 24

JARASANDHA-VADHA PARVA CONTINUED

Vaisampayana said, "Deciding to kill Jarasandha, Bhima answers Krishna, 'Yaduvyaghra, O Krishna, I will not relent against this wretch among kings, who yet stands before me, strong enough and bent upon the fight; I will no show him mercy.'

Krishna, who wants to exhort that hero to kill Jarasandha swiftly, says, 'Bhima, today show some of the strength, which you have from your father Maruta Deva!'

Bhima Parantapa seizes Jarasandha, lifts him above his head and begins whirling that king round dizzily. Bharatarishabha, having whirled him round fully a hundred times, Bhima thrusts his knee into Jarasandha's spine and breaks his body in two. Killing the Magadhan thus, Vrikodara gives a dreadful roar, which mingles with Jarasandha's roars as his back snaps; at which there is a loud uproar which strikes fear into every creature's heart. The people of Magadha are speechless for fear, and many women even give birth prematurely.

Hearing those roars, the people think that either Himavat is crumbling or even the Earth herself is being rent asunder. Then, those scourges of all their enemies leave the lifeless body of Jarasandha at the palace gate, where he lies as one asleep, and they go out of the city. Krishna has Jarasandha's chariot, of the fine flagstaff, readied and makes Bhima and Arjuna ride in it. Together they go and set the imprisoned kings, their kinsmen, free.

Saved from certain death, those kings come to Krishna and offer him priceless gifts of jewels, every manner of gemstone. Having vanquished his enemy, Krishna, unscathed, bearing every kind of weapon, and accompanied by the kings he had freed, emerges from Girivraja riding in Jarasandha's unearthly chariot.

The ambidextrous Savyasachi, whom not all the kings of the world can contain, the extraordinarily handsome and inexorable Arjuna, with Bhima of untold strength, also comes out of the citadel of Magadha. Krishna drives the chariot in which the brothers ride, and it is splendid, for it is the very ratha in which, of old, Indra and Vishnu fought against the Asuras because of Brihaspati's wife Tara, and great blood was spilt.

Riding in that chariot, now Krishna comes out of the hill-fort. That ratha has the lustre of molten gold; it is lined with rows of tinkling, exquisite bells; and its wheels clatter as thunderclouds rumble; it is always triumphant, always vanquishes the enemy against which it is driven; it is the same chariot riding in which Indra slew ninety-nine great Asuras in the elder days.

The three Purushavyaghras are delighted to have that chariot. The people of Magadha see long-armed Krishna and the two brothers with him in the chariot and are wonderstruck. Bhaarata, that ratha is yoked to celestial steeds, which own the speed of the wind; and with Krishna driving it, it is indescribably beautiful.

Upon that best of all chariots is an uncanny flagstaff which stands without being physically or visibly attached: for it is a thing created with the art of heaven. It can be seen, glorious as a rainbow, from a yojana away. While emerging from Girivraja, Krishna thinks of Garuda; remembered by his master Garuda arrows down to him in a wink, and he is like a great tree of vast proportions standing in the heart of a village and being worshipped by all.

Garuda, of untold heaviness, who lives upon snakes, sits upon that finest of chariots, alongside numberless open-mouthed and frightfully roaring creatures, upon its flagstaff. At which, that greatest of chariots is even more resplendent, so brilliant that it is impossible to be looked upon by any being: even as is the midday Sun of a thousand rays.

And, O King, that best of flagstaffs, of unearthly creation, is such that never would it strike any tree, and nor could any weapon ever pierce it, even though all men see it plain. Achyuta, tiger among men, riding with the two sons of Pandu in that divine chariot, whose wheels sound like spring clouds rumbling, emerges from Girivraja.

The ratha which Krishna drives had once been received by King Vasu from Vasava, and from Vasu by Brihadratha, and from him by Jarasandha in course of time. Coming out of Girivraja, he of the long arms, eyes like lotus petals and luminous fame stops on a level plain outside the city. Then, all the people rush there, O Rajan, with the Brahmanas at their head, hurrying there to worship him with every religious ritual.

The kings who have been freed adore Madhusudana, reverently, and eulogising him, say, 'O Long-armed, we were plunged in the deep mire of grief in this land of Jarasandha, and you have saved us. Devakinandana, how extraordinary is this deed of yours, with Arjuna and Bhima to help you.

O Vishnu, we languished in the fell hill-fortress of Jarasandha; surely, it was only by our greatest good fortune that you rescued us, O Scion of the Yadavas, and swelled your fame by this deed. Purushavyaghra, we bow to you; your wish is our command. Say what you want us to do, and however difficult it might be, O Lord, we shall do it.'

When the kings speak thus to him, the Mahatman Hrishikesa reassures them and then says, 'Yudhishtira wishes to perform the Rajasuya yagna; that king who always walks the way of dharma, wants to acquire imperial dignity. I say to you, help him in his endeavour.'

Joyfully, those kings accept what Krishna says, crying, 'So be it!'

Saying this, those lords of the Earth give gifts of jewels to him of the Dasarha race. Moved by their kindness, Govinda takes but a portion of them.

Then, Jarasandha's son, the noble Sahadeva, accompanied by his kinsmen and main officers of state, and with his priest going before him, comes to that place. Bending low, offering lavish gifts of jewels and precious gems, he worships Krishna, god among men. Krishna gently reassures the weeping prince and accepts those priceless gifts. Joyfully, there and then, Krishna installs Sahadeva as king of Magadha.

Having been made king by the greatest of men and having gained Krishna's friendship, Jarasandha's mighty-armed and illustrious son is shown every kindness and respect by the two sons of Pritha; he re-renters his father's city. Laden with jewels, Krishna, the sons of Pandu with him and great fortune attending upon him, leaves the capital of Magadha.

And with the two Pandavas, Achyuta arrives in Indraprastha and, going to Yudhishtira, says in joy to that king, 'Rajottama, by good fortune Bhima has killed the mighty Jarasandha, and all the kings imprisoned in Girivraja have been freed. From good fortune, also, these two, Bhima and Dhananjaya, are well and have returned to their city, O Bhaarata, without injury.'

Yudhisthira worships Krishna, as he deserves, and embraces Bhima and Arjuna in joy. Ajatasatru, the king who has no enemy, has found victory because of his brothers and the death of Jarasandha, and he gives himself up to celebration in the company of all his brothers.

Pandu's eldest son, with his brothers, greets the kings who have come to Indraprastha, welcoming and honouring each according to his age. After the kings have been entertained duly, they depart immediately in fine chariots, with joyful hearts and the leave of Yudhishtira.

Thus does Janardana, tiger among men, of fathomless intellect, cause the death of his enemy Jarasandha at the hands of the Pandavas. O Bhaarata, having seen Jarasandha slain, that Parantapa, scourge of every foe, takes his leave of Yudhishtira and Pritha, Draupadi and Subhadra, Bhimasena and Arjuna, and the twins, Nakula and Sahadeva.

When he finally bids farewell to Dhananjaya, again, he sets out for his own city, Dwaraka, riding in that best of chariots, of unearthly craft, swift as the mind, given to him by Yudhishtira, the ratha which fills the ten points of the horizon with the rumble of its wheels.

O Bharatarishabha, just before Krishna goes forth, the Pandavas, with Yudhishtira at their head, walk around him in reverent pradakshina.

When Devaki's illustrious son leaves Indraprastha, after his magnificent triumph, and having dispelled the terror of the kings, that feat swells the renown of the Pandavas. Rajan, the sons of Pandu pass their days, always gladdening Draupadi's heart. And during that time, all that is just and in accordance with dharma, kama and artha are practised piously by Yudhishtira, while attending to his duty of protecting his people."

CANTO 25

DIGVIJAYA PARVA

Vaisampayana said, "Having acquired that highest of bows, the inexhaustible twin quivers, the chariot and flagstaff, as well as the great sabha, Arjuna says to Yudhishtira, 'A great bow, weapons, great energy, allies, territory, fame, a vast army – all these, which, O King, are difficult to gain, I have won.

I think that what we should now do is fill our treasury. Noblest of kings, I would like to make all the other kings of the world pay us tribute. I want to set out on an auspicious moment of a holy day of the Moon, when a favourable constellation is rising, to conquer the direction of the North, over which the Lord of Treasures, Kubera, reigns.'

When Yudhishtira Dharmaraja hears what Dhananjaya says, he replies in a grave and solemn tone, 'Bharatarishabha, make righteous Brahmanas chant blessings over you, to plunge your enemies in grief and to bring joy to your friends, then go forth. Partha, victory will surely be yours and your wishes will be fulfilled.'

When Yudhishtira has said this, Arjuna sets out in the unearthly chariot, which he got from Agni, and with a large host going with him.

Commanded by Yudhishtira lovingly, Bhimasena, also, as well as the twins set out, each at the head of a great army.

Arjuna, son of the chastiser of Paka, brings the North under his sway, the direction ruled by the Lord of Treasures. Bhimasena, with force, quells the East, while Sahadeva does the South, and Nakula, master of every weapon, conquers the West.

While his brothers are so engaged, the lofty Dharmaraja Yudhishtira remains in Khandavaprastha, enjoying great affluence, surrounded by friends and relatives."

CANTO 26

DIGVIJAYA PARVA CONTINUED

Vaisampayana continued, "In the North, Arjuna comes to Pragjyotishapura where Bhagadatta rules, and tells the king what he intends and asks for his fealty.

Bhagadatta says, 'O you who have Kunti for your mother, as you are to me, so is Yudhishtira. I will do all that you ask. Tell me, what else shall I do for you?'

Dhananjaya replies to Bhagadatta, 'If you give your word to do all this, you have done what I wish.'

Having thus subdued the king of Pragjyotishapura, Dhananjaya of the long arms, Kunti's son, marches further north – the direction ruled by Kubera. That Purusharishabha, the Kaunteya, conquers the mountainous regions and their hems, as also the realms of the hills and foothills. Having conquered all the mountains and the kings who reign there, bringing them under his sway, he takes tribute from them all.

Winning their affection, allying himself to them, O King, he next rides against Brihanta, the king of Uluka, making this Bhumi tremble with the sound of his drums, the rumble of his chariot-wheels, and the trumpeting of the elephants in his train. However, Brihanta swiftly emerges from his city with his army that comprises four kinds of troops, and gives battle to Falguna.

Fierce is the battle between the two, but Brihanta cannot bear the prowess of the Pandava. When that invincible king of the mountain realm realises that Kunti's son is irresistible, he yields and comes to Arjuna with great wealth. Arjuna takes his kingdom from Brihanta, but then, making peace with that king, marches with him at his side against Senabindu, whom he drives out of his kingdom without ado.

After this he quells Modapura, Vamadeva, Sudaman, Susankula, the Northern Ulukas, and all the kings of those countries and their peoples. Fettered by the command of Yudhishtira, O Rajan, Arjuna does not stir from the city of Senabindu, but only sends forth his legions to fetch those five realms under his sway.

Having arrived at Devaprastha, the capital of Senabindu, Arjuna stations himself there, along with his army consisting of four kinds of forces. Then, surrounded by the kings and the peoples he has subjugated, the Kshatriya marches against King Viswagaswa, that bull of the race of Puru. He defeats the bold mountain men, all great warriors, and the Pandava with his legions takes the city ruled by the Puru king.

Having vanquished the Puru king in battle, as also the robber tribes of the mountains, the Pandu brings under his sway the seven tribes known as Utsavasanketa.

The Kshatriyarishabha goes on to vanquish the heroic warriors of Kashmira, as well as the King Lohita and ten minor chieftains. Then, Rajan, the Trigartas, the Daravas, the Kokonadas, and many other Kshatriyas, together, advance against the Pandava.

The Kurunandana now takes the enchanting town of Abhisari and, later, defeats Rochamana who ruled in Uraga. Next, putting forth his great might, Indra's son Arjuna conquers the fine city of Singhapura, which is well guarded with every kind of weapon.

Arjuna leads his legions to fiercely attack the realms of Suhma and Sumala. Indra's son, of untold prowess, after pressing on direly, brings the Bahlikas, always so tameless, under his sway. Pandu's son Phalguna, with a small select force, vanquishes the Daradas and the Kambojas, and follows that by crushing the bandit tribes of the north-eastern frontier, and those that live in the forests.

Maharajan, Indra's son also subdues the allied tribes of the Lohas, the eastern Kambojas, and the northern Rishikas. The battle against the Rishikas is fierce in the extreme; why, the fight between Pritha's son and them is equal to that between the Devas and the Asuras, during which Brihaspati's wife Tara became the cause for so much slaughter.

Quelling the Rishikas, O King, on the field of battle, Arjuna takes from them as tribute eight horses which are the colour of the parrot's breast, and also other steeds of the hues of the peacock, born in northern climes, and endowed with great swiftness. Finally, having conquered all the Himalayas and the Nishkuta Mountains, that Purusharishabha, bull among men, arrives at the White Mountains, and camps upon its breast."

CANTO 27

DIGVIJAYA PARVA CONTINUED

Vaisampayana said, "That valiant Pandava, blessed with majestic force, crossed the White Mountains and subdues the land of the Kimpurushas, ruled by Durmaputra, after a great massacre of Kshatriyas, and brings the country under his control.

Having quelled that realm, Indra's son, with a calm mind, marches at the head of his legions to the country of Hataka, ruled by the Guhakas. He adopts a policy of conciliation with them and wins their alliance. In that realm, the Kuru prince sees the fine lake Manasa, and other sparkling water bodies, too, all sacred to Rishis.

Arriving at the Manasa sarovara, Arjuna conquers the lands ruled by the Gandharvas, which surround the Hataka territories. Here the conqueror takes, as tribute, countless superb horses called Tittiri, Kalmasha, and Manduka. At last, the son of the slayer of Paka comes to the country of North Harivarsha, and wants to conquer it. Thereupon, some formidable great-bodied frontier guardsmen come, with gallant hearts, to him.

They say, 'O son of Pritha, you can never conquer this land; if you seek your own good, go back from here. Any human who enters this country will die. We are pleased with you, Kshatriya; you have conquered enough and there is nothing here, Arjuna, for you to conquer.

The Northern Kurus live here, and there can be no war here. Even if you enter this land, you will see nothing; for there is nothing here which can be seen by human eyes. However, if you seek something else, anything, tell us, O Purushavyaghra, so that we can do your bidding.'

When they say this to him Arjuna replies, smiling, 'I seek that my brother Yudhishtira Dharmaraja, of great intellect, becomes emperor. If your land is shut to humans, I will not enter it. But pay some tribute to Yudhishtira.'

Hearing this from Arjuna, they give him many exquisite cloths and ornaments of unearthly make; silks of celestial texture and skins of unworldly origin.

So it is that tiger among men subjugates the realms of the North, fighting countless battles both against Kshatriyas and bandit tribes. Having vanquished those chieftains, bringing them under his sway, he takes great wealth from them, gems and jewels past counting, the horses known as Tittiri and Kalmasha, as also those of the colour of the parrot's breast and those coloured like peacocks, all endowed with the speed of the wind.

Surrounded, O King, by a huge army comprising the four kinds of forces, the hero returns to Sakraprastha, and Partha offers all that untold wealth and the animals he has brought to Yudhishtira Dharmaputra. Then, at his king's command, the Kshatriya retires to a private apartment in the palace to rest."

CANTO 28

DIGVIJAYA PARVA CONTINUED

Vaisampayana said, "Meanwhile, Bhimasena, also blessed with great tejas, marches east with Yudhishtira's leave. That Bharatavyaghra, of fathomless valour, always the bane of his enemies, goes with a vast host, with a full complement of elephants, horses and chariots; well-armed he goes forth, and he can crush any enemy kingdom.

Bhima comes first to the great land of the Panchalas, and begins to conciliate them with all the means at his disposal. Next, he effortlessly vanquishes the Gandakas and the Videhas.

The lofty one then subdues the Dasarnas. In the land of the Dasarnas, their King Sudharman fights a ferocious duel with bare hands against Bhimasena. Seeing how mighty Sudharman is, Bhima makes him the chief commander of all his legions.

Then, Bhima of terrible prowess marches east, making the very Earth tremble with the tread of the awesome host which follows him. Now that hero, who is the strongest of all strong men, defeats Rochamana, king of Aswamedha, who confronts him with his army. Having vanquished that king with feats of terrific ferocity, Kunti's son subdues the east.

The prince of the Kurus, blessed with great strength, enters the country of Pulinda in the south, and brings Sukumara and the king Sumitra under his sway. Next, O Janamejaya, that Bharatapungava, fettered by the command of Yudhishtira Dharmaraja, rides against Sisupala of great vitality. Hearing what the Pandava intends, the king of Chedi comes out of his city, and that Parantapa receives Pritha's son with respect.

Having met, those bulls of the lines of Kuru and Chedi enquire after each other's welfare.

Then, O Rajan, the king of Chedi offers his kingdom to Bhima, and says smilingly, 'Anagha, sinless, what is your purpose?'

At which Bhima tells him about the intention of Yudhishtira. For thirty nights, O King, Bhima stays there being entertained by Sisupala. Then he sets out again from Chedi with his troops and chariots."

CANTO 29

DIGVIJAYA PARVA CONTINUED

Vaisampayana said, "That punisher of all enemies then vanquishes King Shrenimat of the Kumara country, and then Brihadbala, King of Kosala. Now, the Panadavottama, with deeds of exceptional ferocity vanquishes the virtuous and mighty King Dirghayagna of Ayodhya; he then subdues the country of Gopalakaksha, the northern Kosalas and also the king of the Mallas.

Arriving next at the foot of the Himalaya, he quickly brings all that land under his sway. Thus, that Bharatarishabha conquers myriad countries. Endowed with great energy, and the strongest of all strong men, the son of Pandu next subdues the country of Bhallata, as also the Mountain Shuktimanta beside Bhallata.

Then Bhima of long arms and terrible prowess defeats the unretreating Subahu, the king of Kasi, and brings him under complete sway; after which, with awesome prowess he overwhelms the great King Kratha who reigned in the region which lies around Suparsa; he defeats the Matsyas and the powerful Maladas, and conquers the country called Pasubhumi, which has neither fear nor oppression of any kind.

The long-armed Kshatriya conquers Madhahara, Mahidhara, and the Somadheyas, and turns towards the north. With terrific force, the mighty Kaunteya subdues the kingdom of Vatsabhumi, and the king of the Bhargas, as also the ruler of the Nishadas, and Manimat and countless other kings.

Effortlessly, swiftly, Bhima overcomes the southern Mallas and the Bhogavanta mountains. Next, just through policy and conciliation, the hero vanquishes the Sharmakas and the Varmakas. With some ease, he defeats that Lord of the Earth, Janaka king of the Videhas.

With strategy, the Kshatriya then subdues the Sakas and the barbarians who live in that part of the country. Sending forth expeditions from Videha, where he remains, Bhima conquers the seven kings of the Kiratas who live around Indrakila, Indra's mountain. He vanquishes the Suhmas and the Prasuhmas. With them at his side, Kunti's son marches against Magadha.

On his way, he subdues the kings Danda and Dandadhara; taking them with him, he marches on Girivraja. Peacefully, he brings Jarasandha's son under his sway and takes tribute from him. Then, with the kings he has conquered going with him, Bhima marches against Karna, making the Earth tremble at the advance of his legions consisting of the four kinds of forces.

The Pandava faces Karna Parantapa and brings him under his power. O Bhaarata, having subdued Karna, he quells the powerful king of the mountain realms. Then, Pandu's son, with the strength of his arms, slays the king of Modagiri.

Next, the Pandava vanquishes those valiant and powerful Kshatriyas, Vasudeva king of Pundra and Mahaujah who rules in Kausika-kachcha, before attacking the king of Vanga. Defeating Samudrasena, the kings Chandrasena and Tamralipta, and also the sovereign of the Karvatas and the ruler of the Suhmas, as also the kings who live upon the sea-shore, that Bharatarishabha conquers all the Mlechcha tribes.

Having subjugated numerous kingdoms and countries, extracting tribute from them all, the son of Vayu advances towards Lohita. Now

Bhima makes all the Mlechcha kings who rule the marshlands of the coast pay him tribute, various kinds of wealth, sandalwood, aloe, fine clothes and gemstones, pearls and shawls, gold and silver, and priceless dark corals.

The Mlechcha kings shower untold wealth upon the son of Kunti, gold coins and precious stones counted in hundreds of millions, tens of crores.

Returning to Indraprastha, Bhimasena of dreadful prowess offers all those treasures to Yudhishtira Dharmaraja."

CANTO 30

DIGVIJAYA PARVA CONTINUED

Vaisampayana said, "Sahadeva, also commanded affectionately by Yudhishtira Dharmaputra, marches towards the south, taking a great host with him. That great prince of the Kurus first routs the Surasenas, bringing the king of Matsya under his sway.

Then he crushes Dantavakra, powerful king of the Adhirajas and, taking tribute from him, reinstates him on his throne. The Kshatriya then brings Sukumara and, then, King Sumitra under his sway, before vanquishing the other Matsyas and the Patacharas.

Blessed with great intelligence, the Kuru warrior now swiftly overruns the country of the Nishadas and also the lofty hill Gosringa, after which he subdues King Srenimat. He then subdues the country called Nararashtra, and the Kshatriya marches against Kuntibhoja who, with utmost willingness, accepts the sway of the conquering hero.

Marching to the banks of the Charmanwati, the Kuru warrior meets the son of King Jambaka who has, because of an old enmity, been defeated before by Krishna Vasudeva. O Bhaarata, Jambaka's son gives battle to Sahadeva, who overpowers that prince and presses on south.

The great warrior vanquishes the Sekas and others, and exacts tribute from them, many kinds of wealth and jewels. Making the vanquished tribes his allies, the Kshatriya marches on the countries that lie on the banks of the Narmada. There he defeats the two valiant kings of Avanti, Vinda and Anuvinda, who lead a teeming host, and the powerful son of the twin Devas takes great treasure from them.

After this, the Kshatriya comes to Bhojataka, and there, O King of unfading glory, is engaged in a fierce battle by the king of that city, which lasts two days. Madri's son vanquishes the invincible Bhismaka. He then overcomes the king of Kosala in battle, and the monarch of the lands which lie on the banks of the Vena, as also the Kantarakas and the kings of the eastern Kosalas.

Conquering both the Natakeyas and the Herambakas, quelling the kingdom of Marudha, he subdues Munjagrama by sheer strength. The Pandava overwhelms the mighty kings the Narhinas and the Arbukas and the myriad forest kings of that region of the country.

Endowed with huge prowess, Sahadeva makes a subject of King Vatadhipa. Defeating the Pulindas, he marches on south. Nakula's younger brother fights the Pandya king for an entire day; having quelled him, he goes south again, that long-armed Kshatriya.

Now he sees the celebrated caves of Kishkindha and there fights seven days against the monkey-kings Mainda and Dwivida. Those magnificent Vanaras, though not bested in battle, nor tired, are, however, delighted with Sahadeva.

Joyfully, they say to the Kuru prince, 'Tiger among Pandu's sons, go now, taking whatever tribute you desire from us, and may the purpose of Yudhishtira Dharmaraja, of great intelligence, be accomplished without obstacle.'

Taking precious gems and jewels from them, Sahadeva marches towards the city of Mahishmati, and there that Narapungava does battle with King Nila. Fierce and terrific is the encounter between the powerful Pandava, slayer of hostile heroes, and Nila. Exceedingly bloody it is, and with Agni Deva himself helping King Nila, Sahadeva's very life is in danger.

Suddenly, the chariots, horses, elephants, and soldiers in their coats of mail in Sahadeva's army all appear to be on fire. Seeing this, the Kuru prince becomes fearful, and O Janamejaya, he does not know what to do."

Janamejaya said, "Dvijottama, why did Agni Deva become inimical towards Sahadeva in battle when the Pandava was fighting to accomplish a yagna, which would gratify Agni himself?"

Vaisampayana said, "It is said, O Janamejaya, that while the Lord Agni lived in Mahishmati, he earned a reputation as a lover. King Nila had an exceptionally beautiful daughter. She always remained next to her father's sacrificial fire, stoking it vigorously, making it blaze up. Soon, King Nila's fire would not burn at all until it was fanned by the soft breath from that girl's lips.

It was told in Nila's palace and in the homes of all his subjects that Agni Deva wanted the exquisite princess for his bride. The girl accepted him, and one day, having assumed the form of a Brahmana, the Fire God was enjoying the princess when he was discovered by King Nila.

The king of dharma ordered the Brahmana be punished by law. At this, the lustrous deity flamed up in wrath; seeing which, the king was amazed and bent his head down and set it on the ground. Bowing low, in a while, Nila gave his daughter to Agni come in the guise of a Brahmana. The Deva Vibhavasu Agni took the fair-browed daughter of Nila, and turned kindly towards the king.

Agni, the shining gratifier of all desires told the king to ask him for a boon. Nila begged that his legions never become panic-stricken in battle. From that time, any king who dares attack Nila's city is struck by fear by Agni Hutasana.

From that time, also, the girls of the city of Mahishmati became unacceptable to marry, to men from outside the city. Then, Agni gave them sexual liberty so the women could roam at will, none bound to any single man. Bharatarishabha, indeed, from that time kings of other lands avoid Mahishmati from fear of Agni.

Virtuous Sahadeva sees his troops stricken with fear and surrounded by flames, but stands unmoved as a mountain. Purifying himself, touching holy water, the hero speaks to Agni, the Deva who sanctifies all things:

'I bow to you, whose trail is always marked by smoke. All these exertions of mine are for you, O sanctifier of everything. You are the mouth of all the gods; you are the sacrifice embodied. You are called Pavaka because you sanctify all things, and you are Havyavahana because you convey the clarified butter which is poured into you to the other Devas.

The Vedas have come to be to minister to you and so you are called Jataveda. Being great among the gods, you are called Chitrabhanu, Suresa, Anala, Vibhavasu, Hutasana, Jvalana, Sikhi, Vaiswanara, Pingesa, Plavanga, Bhuritejasa. You are he from whom Kumara had his origin; you are holy; you are called Rudragarbha and Hiranyakrit.

O Agni, you give me energy; let Vayu grant me life; let the Earth grant me nurture and strength, and let Water bless me with prosperity. O Agni who are the first cause of the waters, you who are of immaculate purity, you for ministering to whom the Vedas have come to be, you who are the foremost of the Devas, who are their mouth – O purify me with your truth.

Rishis and Brahmanas, Devas and Asuras pour clarified butter every day into you during their sacrifices, according to law. Let the rays of truth, which you exude while you show yourself at these yagnas, purify me. Smoke-bannered as you are, having many names, O great purifier of all sins, born of Vayu and ever present in all creatures, O purify me through the rays of your truth.

I have cleansed myself, lofty one, and happily do I worship you. O Agni, grant me contentment and prosperity, knowledge and joy.'

He who pours ghee into Agni chanting these mantras shall always be blessed with prosperity; having his spirit under perfect control, he will also be purified of all his sins.

Sahadeva addresses Agni again, 'O bearer of the sacrificial libations, it does not become you to obstruct a sacrifice!'

Saying this, that Purushavyaghra, Madri's son, spreads some kusa grass on the ground at the head of his terrified legions and calmly sits down to face the approaching fire.

And Agni, too, like the ocean which never transgresses its continents, does not sweep over him. Instead, approaching Sahadeva quietly, Agni, Lord of Men, reassures that Kuru prince, 'O Kuru, arise; I was only testing you. I know your purpose entirely, as also that of the Dharmaputra. But, O Bharatottama, as long as this city is ruled by a descendant of the line of King Nila, I will protect it. However, O Pandava I will fulfil your heart's desire.'

Hearing this, Madri's son arises cheerfully and, folding his hands, bowing his head, worships the Fire God, sanctifier of all creatures. When Agni has vanished King Nila comes there and, at the command of that Deva, worships Sahadeva, tiger among men, master of battle, with proper ritual, and pays him tribute.

Having thus brought Nila under his sway, the victorious son of Madri goes further south. The long-armed Kshatriya subdues the king of Tripura, of measureless tejas. He turns his forces against the Paurava kingdom, and makes a subject of the king of the land. After vanquishing that king, the prince, with some effort, brings Akriti, the king of Saurashtra and preceptor of the Kausikas under his sway. While staying in the kingdom of Saurashtra, the good prince sends an ambassador to King Rukmin, son of Bhishmaka, in the city of Bhojakata, who, wealthy and wise, is a friend of Indra himself.

Thinking of their relationship with Krishna, O Rajan, the king and his son gladly accept the sway of the Pandava. Taking jewels and wealth from King Rukmin, Sahadeva proceeds further south. Blessed with terrific tejas and awesome strength, he now reduces Shuparaka and Talakata, and the Dandakas also, to subjection.

The Kuru warrior subdues numberless kings of the Mleccha tribes, which live on the sea coast; and the Nishadas and the cannibals and even the Karnapravarnas, and also the tribes called the Kalamukhas who are a cross between humans and Rakshasas, and all the Kole Mountains; and also Surabhipatna, and the copper Island, and the Mountain Ramaka.

Having quelled King Timingila, the noble warrior conquers the wild tribe, the Keralas, who are men with one leg. Just through emissaries, the Pandava also conquers the town of Sanjayanti and the country of the Pakhandas and the Karahatakas, and makes them all pay tribute.

The Kshatriya also quells and exacts tribute from the Paundravas, the Dravidas, the Undrakeralas, the Andhras, the Talavanas, the Kalingas and the Ushtrakarnikas; he takes the enchanting city of Atavi, and also the cities of the Yavanas. And, O King of kings, arriving at the seashore, that Parantapa, Madri's most virtuous and brilliant son, slayer of all foes, confidently sends messengers to the illustrious Vibhishana, grandson of Pulastya. That sovereign willingly accepts the sway of the son of Pandu, because that sage and great-souled king thinks of it all as being providence.

He sends the Pandava a myriad of jewels, and sandalwood, many celestial ornaments, and reams of priceless apparel, as well as countless invaluable pearls. Taking all these, Sahadeva the intelligent returns to his own kingdom.

So it is, O King, that through conciliation and with battle, having subdued many kings and exacting tribute from them, Sahadeva comes home to Khandavaprastha. Giving all that wealth to Yudhishtira Dharmaraja, O Janamajeya, that bull of the Bhaaratas, Sahadeva, considers his purpose as being successful and is glad."

CANTO 31

DIGVIJAYA PARVA CONTINUED

Vaisampayana said, "I will now tell you about the adventures and triumphs of Nakula, and how he, exalted one, conquers the direction which Vasudeva once subjugated. At the head of a great host, making the Earth tremble with the shouts and lion's roars of his warriors and the rumbling of their chariot wheels, Nakula, the intelligent, sets out west.

First, that Kshatriya attacks the mountain country of Rohitaka, delightful, prosperous, rich with cattle, every other kind of wealth and produce, and dear to the Lord Kartikeya. Fierce is that encounter between the Pandava and the Mattamayurakas of that country.

Next, the illustrious Nakula overcomes the entire desert and the rest of the realm of Sarishaka, land of plenty, as also Mahetta. A savage battle the hero has with Rajarishi Akrosa. Having overwhelmed the Dasarnas, the Sibis, the Trigartas, the Ambashtas, the Malavas, the five tribes of the Karpatas, and the twice born Madhyamakas and Vatadhanas, the Pandava leaves that country.

Going circuitously through their territory, that Narapungava quells the Utsava-tanketa tribes. The luminous Kshatriya quickly conquers the mighty Gramaniya who dwells on the shore of the sea; and the Sudras and the Abhiras that live on the banks of the Saraswati; and all the tribes that lived by fishing, and also those who dwell upon the mountains; and all of the country named after the five rivers; and the Amara mountains; and the land called Uttarajyotisha; and the city Divyakata, and the tribe called Dwarapala.

Through sheer force, the Pandava reduces the Ramatas, the Harahunas and numerous kings of the west. While there, O Bhaarata, Nakula sends messengers to Vasudeva, and Vasudeva, along with all the Yadavas, accepts his sway.

The mighty Nakula goes on to Sakala, city of the Madras, and persuades his uncle Salya to accept, out of love, the Pandava sway. And, Rajan, his uncle lavishly entertains that noble and deserving prince. Nakula, master of war, receives a great quantity of jewels and gems from Salya, and leaves his kingdom.

Then the son of Pandu reduces the ferocious Mlechchas of that sea coast, as also the wild tribes of the Pahlavas, the Barbaras, the Kiratas, the Yavanas and the Sakas. Having conquered many kings, making them all pay him tribute, Nakula, Kurusthama, laden with wealth, turns back the way he came, homewards.

O King, so vast is the treasure Nakula brings that ten thousand camels carry it upon their backs with difficulty. Arriving in Indraprastha, the valiant and blessed son of Madri offers up all those treasures to Yudhishtira.

Thus, O Rajan, Nakula subdues the countries of the west, the direction over which Varuna Deva rules, which once Vasudeva himself had conquered."

CANTO 32

RAJASUYIKA PARVA

Vaisampayana said, "Because of the protection given them by Yudhishtira Dharmaputra, his unwavering righteousness, and because he always keeps his enemies at bay, his subjects cleave to the swadharma of their respective varnas. His rule is virtuous, the taxes he levies fair and kind; the clouds bring as much rain to his kingdom as the people want and prosperous indeed are his cities, towns and villages.

Truly, because of his dharma all in his kingdom prosper, especially the herds, the farms with their fields, and trade. O Rajan, even thieves and cheats never lie amongst themselves, nor do men who are the king's favourites. There are no droughts, floods, plagues or fires, and no one dies before their time in those days of Yudhishtira of dharma.

Never for battle or from enmity do other kings come to Yudhishtira but only to serve him, offer him worship or tribute which puts no strain upon them. The capacious treasury of that king becomes so full of every manner of virtuously obtained wealth that it cannot be emptied in a hundred years.

When he knows the extent of his possessions, the son of Kunti sets his heart upon the celebration of a sacrifice. Friends and officials, individually and together, come to him and say, 'Mahatman, the time has come for your yagna. Let arrangements be made without delay.'

Whilst they speak thus, that omniscient and ancient one, that soul of the Vedas, the one described by the wise as being invincible, that foremost of all lasting existences in the universe, that origin of all things, as also that in which all things come to be dissolved, that Lord of the past, the future and the present, Kesava slayer of Kesi, the strength of the Vrishnis, dispeller of every fear, smiter of all enemies, having made Vasudeva senapati of the Yadava army, and bringing with him great treasures for Yudhishtira – Krishna, Hari, enters Khandava, city of cities, bringing with him a mighty host and filling the air with the thunder of his chariot wheels.

With the ocean of invaluable gemstones that he brings, Madhava Purashavyaghra swells the Pandavas already limitless wealth; he enhances the sorrows of the enemies of the Pandavas. Even as a land of darkness is made joyful by the Sun, or a still place by a soft breeze, Krishna's presence gladdens the Bhaarata's city.

Welcoming him with delight, showing him every due reverence, Yudhishtira asks after his welfare. And when Krishna sits at his ease, the Pandava, bull among men, along with Dhaumya, Dwaipayana, the other sacrificial priests, with Bheema, Arjuna and the twins, speaks thus:

'O Krishna it is for you that I have brought the world under my sway. O Vrishni, it is through your grace that I have won vast wealth. O Devakinandana, O Madhava, I want to devote my wealth, by the law, to great Brahmanas and the bearer of the libations of the yagna.

And, O Dasarha, it becomes you, Mahabaho, to allow me to perform a sacrifice along with you and my brothers. So, O Govinda, if you permit my yagna, go and install yourself as the sacrificer, and I will be washed of all sin. Otherwise, Mahatman, give me leave to become the sacrificer myself, together with these my younger brothers: for with your blessing I will surely enjoy the fruit of an immaculate sacrifice.'

When Yudhishtira says this, Krishna replies, 'Rajavyaghra, you deserve the imperial dignity. So, you be the sacrificer. If you perform the yagna and gain the fruit thereof, I will think that I have done so myself and been triumphant.

I always seek your fortune, so perform the yagna which is close to your heart. Engage me, as well, in some task, for I will obey your every command.'

Yudhishtira replies, 'Krishna, I am already successful that you have come here, happily, at my wish.'

At Krishna's command, Yudhishtira and his brothers begin to collect whatever they need for the Rajasuya yagna. That Parantapa, the eldest Pandava, says to Sahadeva, best of warriors and ministers, 'Let us lose no time in gathering everything that the Brahmans have asked for to perform this sacrifice, and all that Dhaumya might want, all the auspicious materials, one by one, in their proper order.

Let Indrasena, Visoka and Puru, with Arjuna for his charioteer, gather the food we need, if they agree. Let these Kurusthamas also collect all such things of fine taste and scent, which will delight the hearts of the Brahmanas.'

Immediately as Yudhishtira Dharmaputra speaks, Sahadeva, foremost of warriors, goes forth to accomplish his tasks and, having done so, comes and informs the king. Now, O Rajan, Dwaipayana appoints pure and great Brahmanas, who are even like the Vedas embodied, to be sacrificial priests.

Satayavati's son himself becomes the Brahma of that yagna; Susama, bull of the race of Dhananjayas, becomes the chanter of the Sama hymns; Yagnavalkya, who is devoted always to Brahma, is the Adharyu, while Paila, son of Vasu and Dhaumya, becomes the Hotri.

Bharatarishabha, the sons of these Mahatmans, all masters of the Veda and the Vedangas, are the Hotragis.

Having chanted blessings and uttered the purpose of the yagna, they worship the large sacrificial arena, the yagnashala. At the Brahmanas' command, builders and artificers erect numerous edifices there, all capacious and perfumed like temples of the gods.

When all this has been done Yudhishtira, best of kings, commands his main advisor Sahadeva, 'Send forth messengers without delay to invite everyone to the sacrifice.'

Hearing this, Sahadeva dispatches the messengers, saying to them, 'Invite all the Brahmanas in the kingdom, all the Kshatriyas, who are landowners, all the Vaisya traders and merchants and every honourable Sudra, and bring them here yourselves.'

Thus commanded, and blessed with great speed, those messengers go abroad and invite everyone, as the Pandava told them, with no loss of time; and they all come accompanied by many friends and relatives, and strangers join them, as well.

Then, O Bhaarata, at the proper muhurta, the Brahmanas install Yudhishtira, the son of Kunti, as the sacrificer at the Rajasuya. After the ceremony of installation, Yudhishtira Dharmaraja, even like Dharma Deva himself in human frame, enters the yagnashala, surrounded by thousands of Brahmanas, his brothers, relatives, friends, counsellors, and by a large number of Kshatriya kings come from various countries, and by the officers of State.

Countless Brahmanas, skilled in all areas of gyana, versed in the Vedas and their many angas, begin pouring in from various countries. At the command of Yudhishtira, thousands of artisans create separate dwellings for those Brahmanas and their attendants, all well stocked with food, clothes and flowers and fruit of every season.

O King, having been duly worshipped, the Brahmanas start living in those dwellings, passing their time in spiritual and other converse, and watching the performances of actors and dancers. Without let or pause, the commotion of their cheery eating and talking together is heard there. 'Give' and 'Eat' are the words heard most often, incessantly, every day. And, O Bhaarata, Yudhishtira gives thousands of cows, bedsteads, gold coins and nubile young women to those Brahmanas.

Thus, on Earth commences the sacrifice of that peerless Kshatriya, Pandu's illustrious son, even like the yagna in Heaven of Sakra himself. Then, that Purusharishabha, Yudhishtira, sends Nakula, son of Pandu, to Hastinapura to fetch Bhishma and Drona, Dhritarashtra, Vidura, Kripa and those among his cousins who are affectionate towards him."

RAJASUYIKA PARVA CONTINUED

Vaisampayana said, "The always victorious Nakula arrives in Hastinapura and formally invites Bhishma and Dhritarashtra. Invited with due ceremony, the Kuru elders, with the Acharya at their head, come with joyful hearts to that yagna with Brahmanas walking before them.

Also, Bharatarishabha, hearing of Raja Yudhishtira's sacrifice, hundreds of other Kshatriyas, all of them knowing the nature of this yagna, come joyfully from numerous countries, wanting to behold Yudhishtira, the son of Pandu, and his yagnashala; they come bringing priceless jewels with them, of many kinds.

And Dhritarashtra and Bhishma and Vidura of the lofty intellect; and all the Kaurava brothers with Duryodhana at their head; and Subala the king of Gandhara, and Sakuni endowed with great strength; and Achala, and Vrishaka, and Karna greatest of all rathikas, and Salya of awesome might and Bahlika the strong; and Somadatta, and Bhuri of the Kurus, and Bhurisravas and Sala; and Aswatthama, Kripa and Drona; and Jayadratha, the king of Sindhu; and Yaksasena with his sons, and

Shalva, that lord of the world, and that Maharahika, King Bhagadatta of Pragjyotisha, and all Mlechcha tribes that dwell in the marshlands of the sea-shore; and many mountain kings, and King Brihadbala; and Vasudeva king of the Paundras, and the kings of Vanga and Kalinga; and Akarsa and Kuntala; and the kings of the Malavas and the Andhrakas; and the Dravidas and the Sinhalas and the king of Kashmira; and Raja Kuntibhoja of great tejas and King Gauravahana, and all the other heroic kings of Balhika; and Virata with his two sons, and Mavella endowed with great prowess; and many kings and princes ruling in various countries; and, O Bhaarata, King Sisupala blessed with terrific tejas and invincible in battle, accompanied by his son – all of these come to the sacrifice of the son of Pandu.

And Rama and Aniruddha and Kanka and Sahasarana; and Gada, Pradyumna, Samba, and Charudeshna of great energy; and Ulmuka and Nishata and the bold Angavaha; and innumerable other Vrishnis, all mighty Maharathikas, come there.

These and many other kings from the middle country come, O King, to that great Rajasuya yagna of the son of Pandu. Rajan, at the command of Yudhishtira Dharmaraja, mansions are assigned to all those monarchs, full of every kind of viand, set among tanks and tall trees. Dharma's son worships all those illustrious sovereigns, as they deserve; revered by him, they retire, each to the mansions given to them.

Those edifices are lofty like the cliffs of Kailasa, beautiful, lavishly and elegantly furnished. They are surrounded by lofty, strong white walls; their windows are covered by fine mesh of gold, and their interiors adorned with strings of pearls; gradual and easy to climb are the flights of steps inside, and the floors are covered with costly carpets.

Everywhere inside those palatial homes, garlands of fresh flowers hang, and the rooms are perfumed with fine aloe. White as snow or the moon, they appear enchanting even from a yojana away. Wide and high are their gates and doors, wide enough to admit a crowd. The mansions are embellished with every kind of invaluable jewel, fashioned with precious metals, and they look like the peaks of Himavat.

When they have rested a while in those palaces, the kings emerge to see Yudhishtira surrounded by numerous Sadasyas, and his sacrificial priests; they see him performing sacrifices distinguished by the munificent gifts he makes to Brahmanas.

O King, the yagnashala where the Kshatriyas, Brahmanas and Maharishis sit is as handsome as Swarga athrong with Devas!"

CANTO 34

RAJASUYIKA PARVA CONTINUED

Vaisampayana said, "Then, O King, Yudhishtira approaches and worships his Pitamaha and his Acharya, and he says to Bhishma, Drona, Kripa, Aswatthama, Duryodhana and Vivimsati, 'All of you must help me with this sacrifice. All the treasures which you see here belong to you. Consult with one another and guide me as you decide.'

Having been made the sacrificer, Pandu's eldest son says this and then appoints each of them to worthy and suitable offices.

He gives Dussasana charge of food and other items of enjoyment. Aswatthama is asked to look after the Brahmanas. Sanjaya is appointed to offer worship to the kings. Bhishma and Drona, both endowed with great intelligence, are given overall charge to decide what should be done and what should not.

The king appoints Kripa to look after the diamonds, gold, pearls and gemstones, as also the distribution of gifts to Brahmanas. So, too, are other tigers among men given various offices and tasks to discharge with honour.

Balhika and Dhritarashtra and Somadatta and Jayadratha, fetched by Nakula, move about, enjoying themselves as lords of the sacrifice. Vidura, also called Kshatta, knower of every nuance of dharma, becomes the disburser. Duryodhana is the receiver of the tributes brought by other kings. Krishna, focus of the worlds, around whom every living being turns, who wishes for the best karmaphala, at his own wish engages in washing the feet of the Brahmanas.

No one who comes to see the yagnashala or Yudhishtira Dharmaputra, does so without bringing tribute of less than a thousand, in number, weight or measure. All honour Yudhishtira with bounteous gifts of jewels. Each Kshatriya king comes with gifts in the conceit that his particular contribution would enable the Pandava, Kuru king, to complete his sacrifice.

O King, beautiful and magnificent indeed is the yagnashala of Kunti's son, with the plethora of palaces built to last for ever, thronging with guardsmen and warriors. So lofty are these that their tops touch the vimanas of the gods who come to witness the yagna. Wondrous are the chariots of the Devas, and wonderful the mansions created for the Brahmanas to stay in, which resemble those vimanas, and which are adorned with gems and filled with every kind of wealth.

Fine indeed are the crowds of kings who come here, all blessed with noble beauty and vast wealth. As if vying with Varuna himself in riches, Yudhishtira begins the sacrifice distinguished by six fires; he gives lavish gifts to Brahmanas. The king gratifies everyone with gifts of great value and, indeed, with every manner of object they can possibly desire.

An abundance of rice is served, as well as all other delicacies, then masses of jewels brought as tribute are distributed; that immense concourse consists only of those sated to surfeit. The Devas are worshipped at this yagna with the Ida, ghrita, homa and libations poured into the agni by the Maharishis, masters of mantras, their enunciation faultless.

Like the gods, the Brahmanas are also adored with sacrificial offerings, with food and wealth past calculation. The other varnas are also gratified at that yagna, and filled with joy."

CANTO 35

ARGHYAHARANA PARVA

Vaisampayana said, "On the last day of the sacrifice, when the king is to be sprinkled with holy water, the Brahmana Maharishis, who always deserve worship, enter the inner enclosure of the yagnashala all together. With Narada at their head, those lustrous Sages sit at their ease with the Rajarishis within the enclosure, and together they look like the Devas in Brahma's sabha, sitting with the Rishis of Heaven.

Endowed with boundless tejas, and at their ease now, those Rishis begin a host of discussions and arguments.

'This is so.'

'This is not so.'

'This is even so.'

'This cannot be otherwise.'

Thus, they speak animatedly among one another. Some of them, the skilled debaters, make the obviously weaker viewpoint seem stronger than the better one. Some, blessed with great intellects, fall upon the views urged by others like hawks darting at meat thrown up into the air, while those among them who are versed in the interpretations of religious treatises, and others of stern vratas, who know every commentary and glossary, engage themselves in sweet converse.

Rajan, that yagnashala, crowded with Devas, Brahmanas and Maharishis, is wonderful indeed, even like the wide sky studded with stars. O King, no Sudra approaches that yagnashala in Yudhishtira's palace, nor anyone who had not sworn severe vows.

Seeing the prosperity of Yudhishtira the fortunate, sprung from that sacrifice, Narada becomes exceedingly glad. Looking at that great assembly of Kshatriyas, the Muni Narada falls to thought. Purusharishabha, Narada recalls some words he heard of old in Brahma's Sabha, which prophesied the incarnation in amsa on Earth of every Deva. Knowing, Kurunanadana, that this is a concourse of Devas born as men, Narada, in his heart, thinks about Hari, whose eyes are like lotus petals.

The Sage knows that the creator of all things, that highest of Gods, Narayana, who once ordered the Devas, 'Be you born on Bhumi and kill one another before returning to Swarga,' that slayer of all the enemies of the Devas, that queller of all hostile towns has, in order to keep his own word, taken birth himself among the Kshatriyas.

Narada knows that the most holy and high Narayana, Lord of the Universe, having so commanded the Devas, has himself been born into the race of Yadava; that the greatest of all perpetuators of races has been born among the Andhaka Vrishnis on Bhumi and, graced by the highest fortune, now shines like the Moon herself among the stars.

Narada knows that Hari, Parantapa, whose might Indra and all the Devas always eulogise, is now living in the world in human form. Ah, Narada knows that the Svayambhu will himself remove from the Earth the great throng of Kshatriyas of such prowess.

Such is the vision of Narada, the omniscient, who knows Hari Narayana to be that Supreme Lord whom everybody worships with sacrifice. And Narada, blessed with vast intellect, best of all that know dharma, sits pondering this at the sacrifice of the wise Yudhishtira, and he is filled with awe.

Then, O King, Bhishma says to Yudhishtira, 'O Bhaarata, let arghya
be offered to each of these kings, exactly as each one deserves. Yudhishtira,
the master, the sacrificial priest, the relative, the Snataka, the friend and
the king, it has been told, are the six who deserve arghya.

The Sages have said that when any of these six live in one's house
for a year, he deserves to be worshipped with arghya. These kings have
been with us for a while, hence, O King, let arghya be procured to be
offered unto each of them. And let an arghya be given first of all to him
among all present who is the foremost of them all.'

Hearing these words of Bhishma, Yudhishtira says, 'O Pitamaha of
the Kurus, tell me who you deem to be foremost among all these, to
whom the first arghya should be offered.'

Then, O Bhaarata, Bhishma, son of Santanu, judges by his intellect
that on Earth Krishna is foremost of all. He says, 'As is the Sun among
all luminaries, so is this Krishna among us, because of his energy, his
strength, his majesty. This our yagnashala is illumined by him and filled
with joy by him, even as a sunless land is by the Sun, or a deathly still
realm by a breath of breeze.'

Thus commanded by Bhishma, Sahadeva of great prowess offers the
first arghya of most excellent ingredients to Krishna of the Vrishnis.
Krishna, too, receives it with grave propriety, by the law.

However, Sisupala cannot bear to see that worship being offered
to Vasudeva. That mighty king of Chedi censures both Bhishma and
Yudhishitra in the midst of that assembly."

CANTO 36

ARGHYAHARANA PARVA CONTINUED

"Sisupala says, 'O you of the House of Kuru, this Vrishni does not deserve royal worship, as if he were a king, in the midst of all these illustrious sovereigns. Pandava, it is not worthy of you to worship this lotus-eyed one like this; it is not becoming of the sons of Pandu.

Pandavas, you are children. You do not know what dharma is, for it is most subtle. This son of Ganga, this Bhishma, is also of small wit and transgresses dharma by giving you such counsel. O Bhishma, if one like you, virtuous and knowing dharma, behaves like this from self-interest, you surely deserve reprimand among the pious and the wise.

How does the Dasarha, who is not even a king, accept your arghya before all these kings, and how is it that you offer him this worship? O Bull of the race of Kuru, if you regard Krishna as being the eldest, here is Vasudeva, his father: how can his son be older than him?

Perhaps you think of Krishna as being your well-wisher, your supporter. But here is Drupada; how can Madhava deserve your worship before him? Or do you consider Krishna as being your Guru? But how can you worship the Vrishni first, when Drona is here?

Or, Kuru, do you regard Krishna as the Ritvija? How can you worship him first as such when old Dwaipayana is here? When this ancient Bhisma is present, the son of Santanu, foremost among men, he who cannot die except by his own wish, how, Rajan, have you offered Krishna arghya before him?

When the brave Aswatthama who knows all the angas of knowledge is here, why have you worshipped Krishna, O Kuru Raja? When that king of kings, Duryodhana Purushottama is here; when Kripa, Guru of the Bhaarata princes is here, how do you worship Krishna?

How, O Pandava, do you worship Krishna, while passing by Druma, Guru to the Kimpurushas? When the invincible Bhishmaka and King Pandya, who bears every auspicious sign upon his person, when Rukmi, best of kings, and Ekalavya and Salya, lord of the Madras, are here, how, O son of Pandu, have you offered Krishna the first worship?

Here, too, is Karna, always boasting of his strength among all the other kings, and who is endowed with immense prowess, who is the favourite disciple of the Brahmana Jamadagnya, the archer who vanquished everyone in battle by the strength of just his own arms. How, O Bhaarata, do you pass him over and offer Krishna first worship?

Madhusudana is neither a Ritvik, nor an Acharya, nor a king. That you adore him first, despite all these, could only be from some motive of gain. If, O Bhaarata, you always meant to offer the Purodasa to Krishna, why did you bring all these other kings here to be insulted?

We did not pay you tribute, illustrious Kaunteya, from fear, any desire for gain, or having been won over through conciliation. On the other hand, we paid you tribute because you wished to perform the Rajasuya yagna for the sake of dharma. But you have insulted us.

Rajan, it is only to insult us that you offered Krishna, who owns no insignia of royalty, the arghya in the midst of all these kings of the Earth. Surely, the renown you, Dharmaputra, have for your virtue is baseless, for who would offer such undeserved worship other than a man who has fallen away from dharma?

This Vrishni wretch treacherously killed the noble Jarasandha. Yudhishtira, you have abandoned dharma today; you have shown us baseness by offering Krishna the arghya.

If Kunti's helpless sons were afraid, disposed to baseness, should you, Madhava, not have enlightened them that you have no right or claim to this first worship? Janardana, why did you accept the arghya of which you are unworthy, even though it was offered you by these low-minded princes? But then you think highly of this worship of which you are not worthy: like a dog which laps up, by itself, some ghee it has chanced upon.

Krishna, in fact these Kurus have not insulted these assembled kings, but you. Indeed, as a wife is to an impotent man, a fine play to a blind man, so is this royal arghya to you who are not a king. We have seen what Yudhishtira is; what Bhishma is we have seen; and we have seen what this Krishna is. Yes, they have all been seen for what they really are.'

Saying this, Sisupala rises from his excellent seat and, accompanied by the rest of the kings, stalks out of the yagnashala."

CANTO 37

ARGHYAHARANA PARVA CONTINUED

Vaisampayana said, "Yudhishtira runs after Sisupala and speaks sweetly and conciliatingly to him:

'Lord of the Earth, what you have said hardly becomes you; it is needlessly cruel and sinful. Do not insult Bhishma, Rajan, by saying that he does not know what dharma is. Look, all these kings, who are older than you, approve of Krishna receiving the Purodasa. You, too, should bear it patiently, as they do. Lord of Chedi, Bhishma knows who Krishna really is. You do not know him as the Kuru patriarch does.'

Now Bhishma says, 'He who does not approve of the worship offered Krishna who is the eldest in the universe, deserves neither soft words nor conciliation. The greatest warrior among Kshatriyas is he who defeats his enemy in battle and then sets him free; he becomes a Guru to the one he frees. I do not see in this assembly even one king whom Krishna, son of the Satwatas, has not vanquished.

Krishna of untainted glory deserves to be worshipped not just by us; this mighty-armed one deserves the adoration of the three worlds. Numberless great Kshatriya warriors Krishna has quelled in battle. Why, all the universe is founded in this Vrishni. So it is that we worship Krishna before all the rest, all the eldest.

What you say does not become you, Sisupala, do not think like this. Rajan, I have waited upon many who are truly old in gyana. I have heard from all those men of wisdom about the countless transcendent and much honoured attributes of this Sauri.

How often I have listened to all the awesome deeds that Krishna of matchless intellect has performed since he was born. Also, O master of Chedi, it is not from caprice, neither thinking of our relationship to him or what gains he might bestow upon us, that we worship this Janardana, whom all the good on Earth worship and who is the source of the happiness of every creature.

We have offered the first arghya to him because of his fame, his heroism and his success. There is no one here, even of tender years, whom we have not considered before doing as we did. We have passed over many who are famed for their dharma, before deciding that Krishna alone deserves this worship.

Among Brahmanas he who excels in knowledge, among Kshatriyas he who has boundless strength, among Vaisyas he who has the most possessions and wealth, and the eldest among the Sudras deserve worship. We worshipped Govinda because no one knows the Vedas and Vedangas as he does, and no one is as strong as him.

Who in the world of men is as distinguished as him? Liberality, cleverness, knowledge of the Vedas, bravery, modesty, achievement, intelligence, humility, beauty, firmness, contentment and prosperity – all abide eternally in Achyuta. Hence, O Kings, it behoves you to endorse the worship which we have offered Krishna of great accomplishments, who, as the Acharya, the Father, the Guru, deserves everyone's worship.

Hrishikesa is the Ritvik, the Guru, worthy of being approached to give him one's daughter in marriage; he is the Snataka, the lord, the friend: so have we worshipped Achyuta. Krishna is the origin of the universe and that into which the universe will dissolve. Truly, this entire universe of creatures mobile and unmoving has sprung just from Krishna.

He is the unmanifest primal cause, the Avyakta Prakriti, the creator, the eternal, and beyond the ken of all creatures. Therefore does he of unfading glory deserve the highest worship. The intellect, the seat of sensibility, the five elements – air, heat, water, ether, earth – and the four species of beings are all founded in Krishna. The Sun, the Moon, the Constellations, the Planets, all the principal directions and the intermediate directions are all established in Krishna.

As the Agnihotra is foremost among all Vedic sacrifices, as the Gayatri is foremost among mantras, as the King is the first among men, as the Ocean is foremost among all rivers, as the Moon is foremost among planets, the Sun foremost among luminaries, as Meru is foremost among mountains, as Garuda is foremost among all birds, so, as long as the upward, downward and sideways course of the universe lasts, Kesava is foremost in all the worlds, including the realm of the gods.

This Sisupala is just a boy, and so he does not know Krishna and goes about everywhere disparaging Krishna. This king of Chedi will never see dharma in that light in which one who wants to gain great punya will. Who among the old and the young, or among these illustrious lords of the Earth does not regard Krishna as deserving worship, or does not worship Krishna?

If Sisupala considers this worship undeserved, he should do what he thinks is proper.'"

ARGHYAHARANA PARVA CONTINUED

Vaisampayana said, "Saying this, the mighty Bhishma stops.
Then Sahadeva answers Sisupala grimly, 'If there is any king
amongst you who cannot bear to see Krishna, of dark hue, the
slayer of Kesi, the possessor of immeasurable energy, whom I worship, I
set my foot on the head of that king and all others like him!

I wait for a reply from you. And let those kings who own intelligence
approve our worship of Krishna, who is the Acharya, the Father, the
Guru, and deserves the arghya and the worship.'

When Sahadeva shows his foot none of those intelligent, wise, proud
and mighty kings says anything. A shower of flowers falls on Sahadeva's
head, and an asariri, an incorporeal voice, says, 'Excellent, excellent!'

Then Narada, who wears black deer-skin, who speaks of both the
future and the dim past, dispeller of all doubts, who intimately knows
all the worlds, says in the midst of numberless creatures, these words of
the clearest import:

'Men who will not worship the lotus-eyed Krishna should be
considered dead though they move, and they should never be spoken
to on any occasion.'

Then that god among men, Sahadeva, who well knows the difference between a Brahmana and a Kshatriya, having worshipped those that deserved worship, completes the arghya ceremony.

But upon Krishna receiving the first worship, Sunitha Sisupala, Parantapa, his eyes red as copper with rage, says to those lords of men, 'Why do you sit thinking, still, when I am here to lead you all? Let us stand together in battle against the Vrishnis and the Pandavas!'

Thus stirring the kings, the Bull of the Chedis holds counsel with them how to obstruct the completion of the sacrifice. All the invited kings who had come for the yagna, now with Sisupala leading them, look angry and their faces become pale.

They all say, 'We must make certain that it is clear we have not acquiesced in Yudhishtira's sacrifice or to Krishna receiving the first arghya.'

Impelled by hubris and belief in their power, the kings, robbed of reason by anger, speak thus. Moved by arrogance, smarting under the insult offered them, the kings repeat this loudly. Though their friends seek to pacify them, their faces are suffused with rage, even like those of roaring lions driven away from their prey.

Krishna understands that the sea of kings, countless its waves of troops, is preparing for a terrific attack."

CANTO 39

SISUPALA-VADHA PARVA

Vaisampayana said, "Seeing that great assembly of kings agitated with wrath, like the tremendous Ocean by the winds that blow during the Pralaya, the universal dissolution, Yudhishtira says to the aged Bhishma, most intelligent of men and grandsire of the Kurus, even like Puruhuta Indra, slayer of foes, of boundless energy, addressing Brihaspati, 'This vast sea of kings is stirred by wrath. Tell me, Pitama, what shall I do that my sacrifice is not obstructed and my people are not harmed?'

When Yudhishtira, knower of dharma, says this, Bhishma, the Kuru grandsire, replies, 'Fear not, Kuruvyaghra. Can the dog kill the lion? I know of a solution which is both peaceable and easy.

These lords of the earth are barking all together even as a pack of dogs does at a sleeping lion. My child, truly like dogs at the lion, these are barks in anger at the sleeping Vrishni lion.

Yes, Krishna now is like a lion that is asleep. Until he wakes, this lord of the Chedis, this bull among men, makes these kings seem like lions. My child, best of all kings, this Sisupala of little wit wants to carry these kings with him, through the very will of Him that is the soul of the universe, to Yama's realm.

Surely, O Bhaarata, Vishnu wants to take back into himself the life that dwells in Sisupala. Wisest of men, O Kaunteya, the intelligence of this evil king of the Chedis, as also of all these Kshatriyas, has become perverted. Why, all these kings' minds have become as perverse as that of the Chedi.

Yudhishtira, Krishna is the progenitor as also the destroyer of all created beings – of the four species which exist in the three worlds.'

O Bhaarata, when Sisupala hears Bhishma, he retorts roughly, rudely."

SISUPALA-VADHA PARVA CONTINUED

"Sisupala says, 'Old and infamous wretch of your race, are you not ashamed of trying to frighten these kings with these false terrors? You are the foremost of the Kurus, and living as you do in the third state, of celibacy, does it become you to give counsel like this, which is so far removed from dharma?

Like one boat tied to another, or the blind following the blind, are the Kurus who have you for their guide. More than once you have pained us by eulogising the deeds of this Krishna – the slaying of Putana and all the rest. You are arrogant and ignorant, always praising this Yadava; why does your tongue not split into a hundred parts?

How can you, who have such superior gyana, want to extol this cow-boy, whom even men of little intelligence might berate? If in his childhood Krishna did kill a vulture, O Bhishma, what was so remarkable in that, or in his slaying later of Aswa and Vrishabha, both of whom were untutored in battle?

What is so wonderful in his bringing down a wooden cart with a kick? Bhishma, what is so remarkable in his holding Govardhana, which is like an anthill, aloft for a week?

"While he sported upon a mountain he ate a vast quantity of food" – listening to these words of yours, many have wondered. But, O you who knows dharma, is it not still more of a crime that Krishna killed the great one, Kamsa, whose food it was that he ate?

Ah base Kuru, you do not know dharma! Have you never heard from Sages who spoke to you the very things which I will now tell you? The wise and virtuous always teach the honest that weapons must never be made to use against women, cows and Brahmanas, nor against those whose food one has eaten, or whose shelter one has enjoyed.

Bhishma, it seems you have cast away all these teachings. Infamous Kuru, in your desire to praise Krishna you say to me that he is grand and has the highest knowledge and age, as if I know nothing at all. If at your word, O Bhishma, he who has killed a woman, Putana, must be worshipped, then what will become of this great teaching?

How can anyone like Krishna deserve such praise, Bhishma?

"This one is the foremost of all wise men; He is the Lord of the Universe".

Janardana listens to what you say and he believes it all to be true, while surely they are lies. The words of praise which a vabdhi, a chanter, sings, leave no impression upon him, however often he croons them. Every creature acts according to his nature, even like the bhulinga bird, which forever preaches against rashness and then picks shreds of meat from between the lion's teeth.

Your nature is low, Bhishma; it is mean, there is no doubt about it. So, too, it seems that the Pandavas, who consider Krishna as deserving of worship, who have you for their mentor, are also sinners by nature. Knowing dharma as you do, you have still fallen away from the way of the wise. And so, you are sinful.

Who, Bhishma, knowing himself to be virtuous and superior in knowledge, will do what you have done from motives of gain? If you know dharma's ways, if your mind is guided by dharma, then be you blessed. But then, why, Bhishma, did you carry the chaste Amba, who had already given her heart to another, forcibly from her swayamvara, if you are so full of virtue and wisdom?

Although you brought her forcibly, your honest and virtuous brother Vichitravirya did not marry her when he knew her condition. You boast of dharma, yet under your very eye, were sons not begotten upon your dead brother's wives by another; true, in accordance with dharma. Where, O Bhishma, is your own dharma?

I say that this great celibacy of yours, the brahmacharya that you observe either from foolishness or impotence, is in vain. O Bhishma of dharma, I do not see your wellbeing; you who preach virtue have never, as I see it, served the old, your ancestors.

Worship, charity, scriptural study, sacrifices distinguished by generous gifts to Brahmanas – all these together do not amount to a sixteenth part of the punya a man obtains by having a son. The punya acquired by fasts and vows beyond count are all fruitless to him who has no child. You are childless and old, and the dharma you preach is false.

Like the swan in the story, you will now die at the hands of your own kinsmen. Other men of knowledge have of old told this tale. I will now relate it in full for you to hear.

Of yore there lived a swan on the sea-coast. He always preached dharma to his feathered clan, while not following dharma in his life. *Practise dharma and abjure sin* – this was what all the other honest birds constantly heard him preach. And I have heard that the other birds that ranged the sea brought him food: for the sake of dharma.

O Bhishma, all those other sea-birds left their eggs with him and dived among the waves, and the sinful old swan would eat the eggs with which those other foolish avians trusted him. After a while, when the eggs decreased alarmingly, another wise bird became suspicious and one day actually saw what the old swan did.

Having witnessed the old swan's crime, the other bird spoke in great sorrow to his fellow birds. Then, all the other birds also saw the old swan at his sin and they descended on the evil wretch and killed him.

Your conduct, Bhishma, is just like the old swan's, and these kings of the Earth might kill you in anger even as the other birds did the sinful old swan. Men who know the Puranas have an old saying about the swan, and, Bhaarata – *O you that support yourself on your wings, though your heart is driven by lust, yet you preach dharma. But this your sin of eating the eggs transgresses what you preach.'"*

CANTO 41

Sisupala-vadha Parva Continued

"Sisupala says, 'That mighty king, Jarasandha, who had no wish ever to fight Krishna, saying *He is a slave*, deserved my deepest esteem. Who can commend what Kesava, Bhima and Arjuna with him, did when they killed Jarasandha?

Entering through the unlawful gate, disguised as a Brahmana: thus Krishna spied on the might of King Jarasandha. And when that great sovereign first offered this wretch padya to wash his feet, only then did he confess to not being a Brahmana, apparently from motives of dharma.

When Jarasandha, O Kuru, asked Bhima and Arjuna to take padya it was Krishna who refused for them. If this fellow is Lord of the Universe, as this other fool says he is, why does he disclaim being a Brahmana?

Ah, I am so surprised that, while you lead the Pandavas astray from the path of the wise, they regard you as being honest. Or, perhaps, it is hardly surprising from those who have you, O Bhishma, womanish in nature, bent with age, for their main counsellor in all things.'

Hearing these, Sisupala's words, harsh both in import and sound, Bhimasena, mightiest of strong men, of terrific energy, becomes enraged.

His eyes, large and expanded like lotus leaves, dilate still more; they grow red as copper. Upon his brow the assembled kings see three deep furrows, even like the Ganga of three paths upon the mountain of three peaks.

When Bhimasena begins to grind his teeth in rage the kings see that his face resembles that of Yama himself at the end of the Yuga, ready to devour every creature. Just as that furious Kshatriya is about to spring up, Bhishma Mahabaho catches hold of him even like Mahadeva seizing Mahasena, the divine Senapati.

O Bhaarata, Bhishma, Pitamaha of the Kurus, quickly pacifies the raging Bhima, with different kinds of gentle counsel. Bhima Parantapa cannot disobey Bhishma, even as the Ocean can never break his shores, not during the monsoon.

However, Rajan, even while Bhima rages, the bold Sisupala, depending just on his own manliness, does not tremble or grow afraid. Though Bhima leaps up every second moment in fury, Sisupala does not bestow a thought on him, just as a lion pays no heed to a small animal which is angry.

Seeing the dreadful Bhima in such frenzy, the powerful king of Chedi says with a laugh, 'Let him go, O Bhishma. Let all these kings watch me burn him with my prowess like a moth in a fire!'

Hearing this from the Chedi king, Bhishma, Kurusthama, best of all wise men, speaks thus to Bhima."

CANTO 42

SISUPALA-VADHA PARVA CONTINUED

"Bhishma says, 'This Sisupala was born in the line of the kings of Chedi; he was born with three eyes and four arms. As soon as he was born he screamed, and brayed like a little donkey. His father and mother, and all his kinsfolk were terrified.

Seeing the extraordinary child and these ominous signs, his parents decided to abandon him, but then an asariri, a disembodied voice, spoke to the king, his wife, their ministers and their priest, who stood stricken with anxiety:

"O King, this son of yours will be both fortunate and of superior strength. You have nothing to fear from him; indeed cherish him, nurture him without fear. His time has not come and he will not die yet. Besides, the one who will kill him with a weapon has also been born."

When the mother heard this, she cried anxiously to the invisible being, "I bow with folded hands to him that spoke these words! Be he a lofty god or any other, let him tell me one more thing – I want to know who will be my son's killer."

The invisible one then said, "When this child is placed upon the lap of his killer to be, his superfluous arms will fall onto the ground like a pair of five-headed snakes and his third eye on his forehead will vanish tracelessly."

When the kings of the Earth heard about the child's three eyes and four arms and what the unseen being had said about him, they all went to Chedi to see the infant. Worshipping each one as he deserved, the king of Chedi gave his son to be placed upon the laps of each of those kings. Though that child was set upon the laps of a thousand kings, one after the other, yet what the asariri foretold did not come to pass.

Hearing about all this in Dwaravati, the mighty Yadava heroes Sankarshana and Janardana also went to the capital of the Chedis to see their father's sister – the Chedi queen was a daughter of the Yadavas. When they had greeted everyone present according to his rank, and the king and queen, too, and asked after their welfare, Rama and Krishna sat upon fine seats.

After those heroes had been worshipped, the queen, with great joy, herself brought her child and set him in Damodara Krishna's lap. As soon as the child was placed on his lap, his extra arms fell off and the third eye in his brow disappeared.

When the queen saw this, she anxiously begged Krishna for a boon. She cried, "Krishna, fear afflicts me and I want a boon from you! You reassure all who are afraid; you dispel their fears."

Krishna, scion of the Yadavas, said, "Revered one, fear not! You know dharma and you need have no fear of me. What boon shall I give you? What shall I do, Matuli, O my aunt? I will do what you ask, why, whether I can or not!"

The queen Srutakirti said, "Mighty, mighty Krishna, for my sake you must pardon every offence of my child Sisupala, O Yaduvyaghra. O Lord, this is the boon I ask of you."

Krishna said, "Aunt, even when he deserves to be killed, I will pardon a hundred offences of his, so do not grieve.'"

Bhishma continues, 'It is thus, O Bhima, that this wretched king, this evil-hearted Sisupala, haughty with the boon which Krishna granted his mother, dares summon you to battle.'"

SISUPALA-VADHA PARVA CONTINUED

"Bhishma says, 'The will which moves the lord of Chedi to call you to fight, though he knows how strong you are, of strength which knows no exhaustion, that will is not his own but surely the purpose of Krishna himself, of Jagannatha. O Bhima, which king on Earth would dare abuse me as this wretch of his race, already in death's clasp, has done today?

There is no doubt that this mighty-armed one is an amsa of Hari's tejas, and I am certain that the Lord wants to take back unto himself that energy of his. That is why, O Kuruvyaghra, this tiger-like Chedi king, so vile his heart, roars as he does, caring nothing for all of us.'

The Chedi king hears what Bhishma says and can bear no more. In fury he responds, 'May our enemies, O Bhishma, be endowed with whatever prowess this Kesava has, whom you praise like a hymn chanter, rising repeatedly from your seat.

If, Bhishma, you find such delight in giving praise, then praise these kings, not Krishna. Praise this Darada, most excellent ruler of Balhika, who rent this very Earth as soon as he was born. Praise, O Bhishma, this Karna, king of Anga and Vanga, who is equal in strength to him of a thousand eyes; who draws a great bow; this mighty-armed one who wears celestial kundalas with which he was born, and this coat of mail splendid as the rising sun; who vanquished Jarasandha, Vasava's equal, at wrestling, almost mangling that king.

Bhishma, praise Drona and Aswatthama, father and son, mighty warriors, worthy of praise and the best of Brahmanas, either of whom, I am certain, if angered could destroy this Earth with all its mobile and unmoving beings. I do not see any Kshatriya who is the equal in battle of Drona or Aswatthama.

Why don't you want to praise them? You pass over Duryodhana, most mighty-armed king, unequalled in this whole sea-girt world, and King Jayadratha master of weapons, blessed with great prowess, and Druma, Guru of the Kimpurushas, renowned for his untold might, and old Kripa, Acharyar of the Bhaarata princes, also endowed with vast prowess: you ignore all these and praise Krishna?

You pass over that best of bowmen, Rukmin of blazing energy, and praise Kesava? You ignore Bhishmaka of prodigious might, and King Dantavakra, and Bhagadatta famed for his numberless sacrificial stakes, and Jayatsena king of the Magadha, and Virata and Drupada, and Sakuni and Brihadbala, and Vinda and Anuvinda of Avanti; Pandya, Sweta, Uttama and Sankha of great prosperity, the proud Vrishasena, the powerful Ekalavya, and the great warrior Kalinga of abundant energy, and praise just Krishna?

And, Bhishma, if your mind is always inclined to sing the praises of others why do you not praise Salya and the other kings of the Earth? What can I do when it seems that you have not heard anything before from virtuous old men about teaching dharma? Have you never heard that both the reproach and glorification of either oneself or others are not practised by honourable men?

There is no one who approves of what you do, when you ceaselessly praise, with such adoration, and out of sheer ignorance, this Krishna so unworthy of praise. How do you, from your mere wish, establish the entire universe in the servant of the Bhojas, this cowherd?

O Bhaarata, this is not your true nature as a man, but more like that of the bhulinga bird, of whom I already spoke. On the far side of Himavat there lives a bird called bhulinga, who never utters a word of evil import. *Never do anything rash* – this is what she always cries, but never understanding that, she herself always acts rashly.

Having little intelligence, this birds pecks out the shreds of meat sticking between the lion's teeth, and at that always while the lion is eating. Assuredly, that bird lives at the lion's pleasure. O wretched Bhishma, O sinner, you always speak like that bird, just as surely as you are alive only at the pleasure of these kings.

Yet, there is no one like you to serve the worst interests of these same kings!' Hearing these harsh words from the king of Chedi, O Rajan, Bhishma says to him, 'Truly I am alive at the pleasure of these lords of the Earth, but I do not consider these kings as being even equal to a straw.'

No sooner does Bhishma say this than the kings become inflamed! The hairs on the bodies of some stand on end, and some begin to reproach Bhishma. Some, who wield large bows, cry, 'The wretched Bhishma is old but he is boastful and does not deserve our forgiveness. Kings, mad with anger as this patriarch is, it is just that we kill him like an animal. Let us together burn him in a fire of grass or straw!'

Bhishma hears this, and the Kuru grandsire, great his intelligence, says to those lords of the world, 'I see no end to our talk, for words can always be answered with more words. So, O lords of the Earth, listen to what I have to say, all of you. Whether you kill me like an animal or burn me in a fire of grass or straw, I set my foot on all your heads!

Here is Krishna, Govinda who knows no decay. We have worshipped him with the first arghya. Let him who wishes for a swift death call the dark Madhava, the Chakra-bearer, the Gadadhari, to a fight, and dying at his hands, enter into and become one with the being of this Devadeva, this God of gods.'"

SISUPALA-VADHA PARVA CONTINUED

Vaisampayana said, "Hearing these words of Bhishma, the Chedi king, endowed with great prowess, says to Krishna, 'Janardana, I challenge you! Come fight me and I will kill you and all these Pandavas, too. For, O Krishna, the sons of Pandu have dishonoured all these kings by worshipping you who are no king, and they also deserve to die.

Yes, I am convinced that these who have adored you, who are a slave, a wretch and no king, surely deserve death at my hands.'

Saying this, that tiger among kings stands there roaring in anger. After Sisupala has stopped ranting, Krishna speaks in the mildest voice to all the assembled kings and the Pandavas, 'O Kings, this evil one is the son of a daughter of the Satwatas, yet he is a terrible enemy to all of us Satwatas.

Although we never seek to harm him, he always seeks our ill. When this ruthless fellow heard that we had gone to Pragjyotishapura, though he is my father's sister's son, this villain came and burnt Dwaraka.

While King Bhoja sported upon the Raivataka hill, this vile Chedi attacked the attendants of that king, slew many and led many others away to his city in chains.

His every motive sinful, this wretch stole my father's sacrificial horse, which had been loosed across the lands with an armed guard: so that he could obstruct my father's yagna.

This sinner ravished the wife of the pure Akrura, while she was on her way from Dwaraka to the Sauvira country. This injurer of his uncle disguised himself as the king of Karusha and ravished the chaste Bhadra, princess of Visala, whom Karusha was meant to marry.

Patiently have I borne all these sorrows for the sake of my father's sister. It is fortunate that today this has happened before all of you kings. You have all seen the hatred and enmity this Sisupala bears me. You also know everything that he has done to me behind my back.

For the arrogance he has shown me in the presence of you lords of the Earth, he deserves to be killed by me, and today I find myself ill able to forgive him. Wishing for a swift death this fool dared desire Rukmini for himself. But like a Sudra failing to hear the Vedas being recited, he did not get her.'

Listening to Krishna, all the gathered kings begin to reprove the king of Chedi. But the mighty Sisupala laughs aloud and says, 'Krishna, are you not ashamed to say in this sabha, especially before all these kings, that I desired your wife Rukmini? Madhusudana, who other than you, calling himself a man, would declare in the midst of honourable men that his wife was intended for someone else?

Krishna, pardon me if you please, or do not. But angry or friendly, what can you do to me anyway?'

While Sisupala says this, Kirshna thinks of the Chakra which humbles the hubris of the Asuras. As soon as the discus appears in his hands, the eloquent and illustrious one says loudly, 'Lords of the Earth, hear why I have always forgiven this Sisupala in the past. It is because of the boon I gave his mother that I would pardon a hundred offences of his. This was the boon she asked me for and this was the boon that I granted her.

But today, O Kings, that number has become full, and now in your presence I will kill him.'

With that, and a growl, the Lord of the Yadus sloughs off Sisupala's head with the Chakra, and the mighty-armed king of Chedi falls like a cliff struck by thunder. Rajan, the gathered kings see a fierce light, pulsing, bright as the Sun in the sky, issue from the body of Sisupala. The spirit light worships Krishna of the lotus-leaf eyes, whom all the worlds worship, and melts into the Lord's body.

The kings are wonderstruck to see that light entering Krishna Purushottama. When Krishna kills the Chedi king the cloudless vacant sky pours down showers of rain; peals of thunder echo; the Earth herself trembles.

Some kings never say a word during those dreadful moments but merely sit gazing at Janardana; others rub their palms in fury with their forefingers; yet others are beside themselves with rage and bite their lips; while some in their hearts approve entirely of what Krishna does. Some are there who are moved by anger, while others turn pacifiers.

The great Rishis are profoundly pleased; they praise Krishna warmly before departing. Indeed, all the high-souled Brahmanas and many of the mighty Kshatriyas, too, who are there, are overjoyed to witness the prowess of the Vrishni. They eulogise him.

Yudhishtira now commands his brothers to perform the funeral rites for Sisupala, bold son of Damaghosha, without delay and with proper honour. The sons of Pandu obey the behest of their brother, and then Yudhishtira, along with all the others kings, makes Sisupala's son king of the Chedis.

Then, O Rajan, the yagna of the Kuru king of great tejas, Yudhishtira blessed with every kind of prosperity, becomes exceptionally beautiful and pleases all the young men there. Begun auspiciously, every obstacle removed, replete with an abundance of wealth and corn, with rice and every other kind of food, Kesava watches over the sacrifice.

In due course, Yudhishtira completes the yagna, while Janardana Mahabaho, the lofty Sauri, guards it until the end, armed with his bow the Saringa, his Chakra and Gada.

When the good Yudhishtira has had his ritual bath after the sacrifice, all the Kshatriyas come to him and say, 'Through good fortune you have gained imperial dignity. O you of the race of Ajamida, you have spread the fame of your entire race.

King of kings, you have gained profound religious merit by what you have done. You have worshipped us all to our hearts' content, and we now say to you that we wish to return to our own kingdoms. It becomes you to give us leave.'

The just Yudhishtira hears what the kings say, worships each one as he deserves, then commands his brothers, 'All these kings came to us at their pleasure. These Parantapas now wish to return to their own kingdoms, and to bid me farewell. Be blessed, my brothers, escort them to the frontiers of our kingdom.'

Listening to their brother, the other Pandavas follow the kings, one after the other, as each deserves. Without delay, the powerful Dhrishtadyumna escorts King Virata; Dhananjaya follows the illustrious Maharatha Yagnasena; the mighty Bhimasena goes with Bhishma and Dhritarashtra; Sahadeva, master of battle, follows the brave Drona and his son; Nakula, O King, follows Subala and his son; the sons of Draupadi along with the son of Subhadra follow the mighty warriors-kings of the mountain countries.

Other Kshatriyarishabhas escort other Kshatriyas, while the Brahmanas in their thousands also depart, duly worshipped.

When all the Kshatriyas and Brahmanas have left, Krishna says to Yudhishtira, 'O son of the Kurus, with your leave, I, too, wish to return to Dwaraka. Through great good fortune, you have performed the greatest of all sacrifices, the Rajasuya yagna!'

Yudhishtira replies, 'By your grace, Govinda, I have accomplished this. Because of your grace alone all the world of Kshatriyas is now under my sway, and all the kings came here with tribute.

Lord, without you my heart never feels any joy. So how can I, O Anagha, give you leave to go? Yet, I know that you must go home to Dwaraka.'

The great Hari, his fame worldwide, now goes with his cousin to his aunt Kunti, and says cheerfully, 'Matuli, your sons have performed the Rajasuya yagna and gained imperial dignity. Vast wealth they have obtained, and their endeavours have all been crowned with success. Be pleased with all this, and now, with your leave, I wish to return to Dwaraka.'

After this, Krishna bids farewell to Draupadi and Subhadra. Coming out of the inner apartments accompanied by Yudhishtira, he performs his ablutions and goes through the daily rites of worship, and then has the Brahmanas utter their blessings.

Now the mighty-armed Daruka arrives in a chariot of wondrous design, its body like clouds. Krishna Mahatman, his eyes like lotus leaves, looks at that Garuda-bannered chariot, walks around it in reverent pradakshina before climbing into it and setting out for Dwaraka.

Yudhishtira Dharmaraja, blessed with prosperity, along with his brothers, follows the mighty Krishna on foot. Then Hari of the eyes like lotus leaves stops that best of rathas for a moment, and speaks to the son of Kunti.

'King of kings, cherish your subjects with indefatigable vigilance and patience. As the clouds are to all creatures, as the great tree of spreading boughs is to birds, as he of a thousand eyes is to the immortals, you be the refuge and support of your kin.'

With this, Krishna and Yudhishtira take leave of each other and return to their respective homes. Rajan, after the lord of the Satwatas has gone back to Dwaravati, only King Duryodhana, with King Subala's son Sakuni, bulls among men, continue staying in that unearthly sabha."

CANTO 45

DYUTA PARVA

Vaisampayana said, "When that greatest of sacrifices, the Rajasuya, so difficult of accomplishment, was completed Vyasa, surrounded by his disciples, presents himself before Yudhishtira. Upon seeing him, Yudhishtira rises quickly from his throne, and surrounded by his brothers, worships his grandfather, the Rishi, with water to wash his feet and offers him a fine place to sit.

Having sat on a costly carpet inlaid with gold, the illustrious one says to Yudhishtira Dharmaraja, 'Sit yourself down.'

When the king and his brothers sit, the illustrious Vyasa, always truthful in speech, says, 'Son of Kunti, your fortune swells and you with it. You have gained empire, so difficult to acquire. And, O furtherer of the race of Kuru, the Kauravas have all prospered because of you.

O Chakravartin, I have been duly worshipped, and with your leave I now wish to go.'

Yudhishtira salutes the dark Rishi, his grandfather, touches his feet and says, 'Greatest of men, a doubt has arisen in my mind, hard to dispel. O Bull among the regenerate, none but you can remove it.

The illumined Narada said that, in consequence of the Rajasuya yagna, three kinds of omens, celestial, atmospheric and terrestrial, occurred. Grandsire, has the death of Sisupala caused evil fortune?'

The exalted son of Parasara, the island-born Vyasa of dark hue, says, 'For thirteen years, O King, those omens will bear momentous consequences, ending in the absolute destruction, Rajadhiraja, of all Kshatriya kind. At that time, with you as sole cause, O Bharatarishabha, all the Kshatriyas of the Earth shall be annihilated: because of the sins of Duryodhana and through the prowess of Bhima and Arjuna.

Towards the end of this night, in your dream you will see the blue-throated Bhava, annihilator of Tripura, always absorbed in dhyana, the Bull his emblem, drinking from a human skull, and fierce and terrible, Lord of all creatures, God of Gods, Umapati, called Hara and Sarva also, and Vrisha, armed with the trident and the bow Pinaka, and wearing tiger skin.

You will see Siva, tall and white as the Kailasa cliff, seated upon his Bull, gazing unwinkingly towards the south, the direction presided over by the king of the Pitrs. King of kings, this shall be your dream tonight. Do not grieve for dreaming such a dream, for no one can escape time.

Be you blessed! I now will go towards Kailasa. You must rule the Earth with vigilance and steadfastness, patiently bearing every privation!'

Saying this, the illustrious Krishna Dwaipayana, accompanied by his disciples, who always follows the dictates of the Vedas, goes away towards Kailasa. When his grandfather has gone, the king is gripped by anxiety and grief and thinks ceaselessly of what the Sage said.

He tells himself, 'Surely, what the Rishi foretold must come to pass. Who can keep Fate at bay by effort alone?'

Then Yudhishtira, endowed with great energy, says to his brothers, 'Tigers among men, you have heard what the Dwaipayana said to me. Having heard him, I have resolved that I must die, since I alone, otherwise, am ordained to be the cause of the death of all Kshatriya kind.

Ah, my precious brothers, if this is what time has in store for me what need is there for me to live?'

Hearing the king, Arjuna replies, 'Rajan, do not yield to this manic dejection, which destroys reason. Summon your courage and do what would truly be good for us all.'

Yudhishtira, resolute in truth, thinking all the while of what Vyasa Muni said, replies to his brothers, 'Be blessed and listen to the vow I swear from this day. For thirteen years, what ever be the purpose for which I must live, I will never speak a harsh word to you my brothers or to any king of the Earth.

Commanded by my kinsmen, I will observe dharma and exemplify my vratas. If I live thus, making no distinction between my own children and others, there cannot be any disagreement between me and anyone. Disputation causes war in this world. If I keep war at bay, always doing what is agreeable to everyone, infamy shall never be mine, O Purusharishabhas.'

The other Pandavas listen to what their brother says, and being ever engaged in doing his will, they approve. Having sworn this oath, Yudhishtira Dharmaraja, together with his brothers, gratifies his priests as also the Gods with due ceremonies, in that sabha.

Bharatarishabha, when all the kings have gone Yudhishtira performs the customary rituals and then returns to his palace with his ministers. King of men, Duryodhana and Sakuni, son of Subala, continue to stay in the Mayaa sabha of fascination."

CANTO 46

DYUTA PARVA CONTINUED

Vaisampayana said, "That bull among men, Duryodhana, continues to live in the Mayaa Sabha. With Sakuni, the Kuru prince slowly examines the entire edifice, and sees many an unearthly design in it, which he has never seen in Hastinapura, the city named after the elephant.

One day, while walking through the mansion, Raja Duryodhana comes upon a crystal surface. Mistaking it for a pool of water, he draws up his clothes, only to find it is solid floor; he continues in some shame and sorrow.

Sometime after, mistaking a lake of crystalline water adorned with lotuses of crystal petals for solid ground, he falls into it with his clothes on, drawing peals of laughter from the mighty Bhima, as also from the servants of the palace.

At Yudhishtira's command, the servants quickly bring Duryodhana fine fresh clothes. Yet, seeing Duryodhana like that, Bhima, Arjuna and the twins all laugh out loud. Unused to being insulted, Duryodhana cannot bear that laughter. He hides his feelings and does not even look at them.

Yet again, he draws up his clothes to cross some dry ground which he once more mistakes for water and again they all laugh. Soon, Duryodhana mistakes a solid crystal door for being open space, walks straight into it and stands stunned, his head reeling. Then, he thinks an open door is shut and cautiously reaches out his hands to feel empty space, and tripping, falls down.

Coming to yet another door, which is ajar, but thinking it closed, he turns away from it. Finally, O King, having seen the staggering wealth of the Pandavas during the Rajasuya yagna, and having humiliated himself repeatedly inside the Mayaa Sabha, Duryodhana takes his leave of the Pandavas and returns to Hastinapura.

Dwelling darkly in his mind on everything that he has seen, which has made him burn with envy, and all that has happened to shame him, his heart turns to dire thoughts of sin even while riding home.

He has seen the Pandavas full of joy, with all the kings of the Earth paying them homage; he has seen young and old serving the sons of Pandu; he has seen the splendour and prosperity of his illustrious cousins, and Duryodhana, son of Dhritarashtra, is pale with jealousy.

While riding home, his heart sorely afflicted, Duryodhana thinks of little other than the grand sabha, and the unmatched prosperity of the wise Yudhishtira. Dhritarashtra is so absorbed by these thoughts that he says not a word to Subala's son, even when Sakuni repeatedly addresses him.

Seeing him plunged in dejection, Sakuni asks, 'Duryodhana what afflicts you like this?'

Duryodhana replies, 'Uncle, seeing all the world under the sway of Yudhishtira from the power of the weapons of the illustrious Arjuna, seeing the glory of the yagna of Pritha's son being equal to that of the sacrifice of Sakra himself, I am filled with flaming envy, burning me night and day, drying me up like a shallow tank in summer.

When Sisupala was killed by the lord of the Satwatas, there was no man to take the side of Sisupala. Consumed by the fire of the Pandava, they all forgave that crime; else, who could ever condone such a thing? Because of the power of the son of Pandu, Krishna got away with his heinous offence.

And so many kings brought myriad and untold wealth for Kunti's son: even like tribute-paying Vaisyas! Seeing Yudhishtira's fortune, his resplendent prosperity, my heart burns with envy, although this does not become me.'

Truly as if flames burn him, Duryodhana says again to the Gandhara king, 'I will cast myself into a fire, swallow poison or drown myself. I cannot live. Which man of vigour in the world can bear to see his enemies prosper, while he himself is destitute?

I who watch my enemy prosper am neither a woman, nor yet not a woman; neither am I a man, nor one who is not a man. Seeing the Pandavas' sovereignty over the Earth, their vast affluence, ah, watching that Rajasuya yagna of theirs, who is there in the world who would not be aggrieved?

By myself I can never hope to gain such empire or wealth, and I see no allies who would help me acquire them. This is why I think of killing myself. I see the unparalleled and serene prosperity of Kunti's son, and I know that Fate is supreme and all effort pointless.

Son of Subala, once I strove ceaselessly to effect his death. But he baffled all my attempts and look at him now bloomed fully like a lotus from a pool of water. Surely, Fate is supreme and effort in vain: behold, day by day, the sons of Dhritarashtra decay and the sons of Pritha wax.

Ah, my heart burns as if it were on fire to look at the fortune of the Pandavas, that sabha of theirs, to think of their servants laughing at me. O Uncle, know that I am grief-stricken and fit to burst with envy, and I will speak of it to Dhritarashtra.'"

CANTO 47

DYUTA PARVA CONTINUED

"Sakuni says 'Duryodhana, you must not be jealous of Yudhishtira. Through their own good fortune the sons of Pandu are only enjoying what they deserve. Parantapa, O great King, with all the numberless plots you hatched to do away with them you could not. Providence saw the Purushavyaghras escape all your machinations and plots.

They have Draupadi for their wife, and Drupada, his sons and Vasudeva Krishna of immense prowess are their allies, with whose help they can subdue the very world. They inherited their patrimony and have grown immeasurably through their own vitality.

Why should you be aggrieved at this? Gratifying Agni Hutasana, Dhananjaya has got the bow Gandiva, the pair of inexhaustible quivers and many celestial astras. With that peerless bow and the strength of his arms, as well, he brought all the kings of the world under his sway. Why should you grieve over this?

Arjuna Parantapa, Savyasachin, saved the Asura Mayaa form the forest fire and Mayaa built that grand sabha out of gratitude. Commanded by

Mayaa, the grim Rakshasas, the Kinkaras, support the sabha. What is there in this to cause you grief?

You said, O King, that you have no allies. Bhaarata, this is not true. These brothers of yours are obedient to you. Drona of great prowess, who wields a great bow, his son Aswatthama, Radha's son Karna, the Maharatha Kripa Gautama, I with my brothers and King Saumadatti – these are your allies. Unite yourself with these, and conquer all the Earth.'

Duryodhana says, 'O King, if it pleases you, with your help and that of the other great warriors you mention, I will defeat the Pandavas. If I can subdue them now, the world will be mine and all her kings, and that sabha so replete with wealth.'

Sakuni replies, 'Dhananjaya and Krishna, Bhimasena and Yudhishtira, Nakula and Sahadeva, and Drupada with his sons – these cannot be vanquished in battle even by the Devas, such great warriors are they, wielding the greatest bows, masters of astras, and delighting in battle.

However, I know how Yudhishtira himself can be vanquished. Listen to me and do as I say.'

Duryodhana says, 'Uncle, tell me if there is any way by which I can quell Yudhishtira without endangering our friends and these other illustrious Kurus.'

Sakuni says, 'The son of Kunti loves dice-play although he does not know the art of the game. If that king is asked to play dice, he cannot refuse. I am a master of dice, why there is no one in the world to match me at rolling the dice, why, no one in the three worlds, O son of Kuru.

Therefore, ask him to play dice. With my skills at dice, I will win his kingdom and all his vast fortunes for you. Duryodhana, tell all this to your father the king. If he commands me, I will definitely win all of Yudhishtira's kingdom and possessions for you.'

Duryodhana says, 'Son of Subala, you tell all this yourself to Dhritarashtra, king of the Kurus. I will not be able to.'"

CANTO 48

DYUTA PARVA CONTINUED

Vaisampayana said, "Rajan, impressed by the great Rajasuya yagna of Yudhishtira, and knowing Duryodhana's heart during their journey home from the Mayaa Sabha, and wanting to gratify the Kuru prince's desire, Sakuni, son of Subala, goes to Dhritarashtra, of great wisdom, and finding the blind king seated upon his throne, speaks these words to him.

'Know, Maharajan, Bharatarishabha, that Duryodhana has grown pale, emaciated, dejected and fallen prey to great anxiety. Why don't you, through due inquiry, discover the grief which is in the heart of your eldest son, the sorrow caused by the enemy?'

Dhritarashtra says, 'Duryodhana, what is the cause of your great sorrow, Kurunandana? If it is fit for me to hear, tell me the reason for your affliction. Sakuni here says that you have lost colour, become pale and thin, and fallen prey to anxiety. I do not know what the reason for this sorrow can be. All my vast wealth and power are yours to control. Your brothers and all our kinsmen never do anything disagreeable to you.

You wear the finest clothes; eat the best food, all the most excellent meats. The best horses carry you. So what is it that makes you pale and thin? Rich beds, beautiful damsels, mansions with the costliest furniture, every sport to delight you – all these are at your disposal, even as with the gods themselves. Proud one, O my son, why do you grieve as if you are destitute?'

Duryodhana says, 'I eat and dress myself like a wretch, and I spend my time burning with savage envy. He is indeed a man who cannot bear the fortune and pride of his enemy, and lives only after vanquishing his enemy and liberating his own subjects from the tyranny of his enemy.

Contentment and pride, O Bhaarata, destroy prosperity, and also those other two: compassion and fear. He that acts under the influence of these never achieves anything great.

Having seen Yudhishtira's prosperity, whatever I enjoy brings me no joy. So splendid is the prosperity of Kunti's son that what I have is as nothing before it. Knowing the affluence of my enemy and my own relative poverty, even though that affluence is not before me, yet I see it constantly. This is why I am pale and lean, why the colour has drained from me and I am melancholy.

Yudhishtira supports eighty-eight thousand Snataka Brahmanas, giving thirty slave-girls to each one. Besides these, a thousand other Brahmanas eat daily at his palace: the best food on golden plates.

The king of Kamboja sent him innumerable skins, black, dark, and red, of the kadali deer, as also countless shawls of the softest texture, as tribute. Hundreds of thousands of she-elephants and thirty thousand she-camels wander within the palace: the kings of the Earth brought them all as tribute to the capital of the Pandavas.

Lord of the world, the kings also brought to this greatest of yagnas piles and piles of jewels and great gemstones for the son of Kunti. Never before did I see or even hear of such immense wealth as was brought to the sacrifice of the intelligent sons of Pandu.

Rajan, after seeing that treasure past imagining, which belongs to my enemy, I have no peace of mind. Hundreds of Brahmanas supported by the wealth which Yudhishtira gave them, and now owning great wealth of kine, waited with tribute of thirty crores of gold coins, but the dwarapalakas at his palace gates did not allow them to enter. Bringing with them the finest ghee in handsome kamanadalus made of gold, yet they could not gain admission into the palace.

The Ocean himself brought, in vessels of white copper, the nectar that is created within his waters, which is far superior to what flowers and plants produce for Sakra.

And at the end of the sacrifice, Vaasudeva bathed Pritha's son with sea water fetched in a thousand bejewelled jars of gold, which he poured over Yudhishtira from his own rarest conch shell.

Ah, seeing all this I became feverish with envy. Those golden urns had gone to the Eastern and the Southern Oceans upon the shoulders of men, and to the Western Ocean, O Bull among men. O Father, though none but birds only can go to the Northern realms, Arjuna went there and brought back untold wealth which he extracted as tribute.

Let me tell you about another wonderful thing which happened; listen to me. It was arranged that when a hundred thousand Brahmanas were fed, each day, conches would be blown in unison. O Bhaarata, I heard conches sounding there almost ceaselessly, and my hair stood on end to listen to their bass.

Maharajan, how can I describe how magnificent was that palatial compound, filled with countless kings come to witness the yagna, except to say that it was like a cloudless sky with stars? Each of the kings came to the sacrifice bringing untold and variegated wealth as tribute for the wise son of Pandu.

The kings who came, besides, became like Vaisyas, distributing food to the Brahmanas who were fed. The prosperity I saw of Yudhishtira was such that neither Indra himself, nor Yama or Varuna, nor Kubera, Lord of the Guhyakas, owns.

Oh, my father, my heart burns after seeing the awesome treasures of the son of Pandu, and I have no peace.'

When Duryodhana has spoken thus, Sakuni says, 'O you who have truth as your strength, listen to how you can have for yourself the unmatched prosperity which you saw with the son of Pandu.

O Bhaarata, I am a master of dice, the best player in the world. I know beforehand the success or failure of every throw of the dice, and when to wager and when to refrain. I have special, occult knowledge of the game. The son of Kunti is also fond of playing dice, but he has small skill at the game.

If you summon him either to battle or to a game, he will certainly accept. If he and I play dice I will beat him again and again, with sleight of hand, with subtle deception in my fingers.

I swear that I will win all his wealth and kingdom for you, Duryodhana, and you will enjoy everything the Pandava has.'

When Sakuni says this, without a moment's lapse, Duryodhana says to Dhritarashtra, 'Sakuni, master of dice, is ready to win all the fortune of the Pandavas at the game. You must give him leave to do this for me.'

Dhritarashtra replies, 'I always follow the advice of Kshatta, Vidura my minister of deep wisdom. Let me consult with him, and I will tell you what I decide about this matter. He has great foresight, and he will keep dharma squarely before him and tell us what is best for both parties, and what should be done.'

Duryodhana says, 'If you consult Kshatta he will persuade you to desist, and if you do not allow this, O King, I will surely kill myself. When I am dead, Rajan, you can be happy with your Vidura. You will enjoy the whole world, what need will you have of me?'

Dhritarashtra hears this dire threat from his son and, indeed, being in his own heart quite prepared to do what Duryodhana asks, calls a servitor and commands him, 'Let artisans be engaged immediately to build a capacious and beautiful palace of a thousand columns and a hundred doors. Fetch the finest masons, carpenters and joiners and encrust the edifice's walls with precious stones, all over.

Let it be grand and handsome; make it easy of access. When it is completed come and inform me.'

After King Dhritarashtra resolves to please his Duryodhana, he sends messengers to Vidura to summon him. For it is true that the king never takes a decision without first consulting Vidura. However, in this matter, although he well knows the evils of gambling, Dhritarashtra is drawn irresistibly to the plot.

However, as soon as the wise Vidura hears of it, he knows that the Kali Yuga is at hand. Seeing the gates to perdition about to open, Vidura rushes to Dhritarashtra. Bowing at his elder brother's feet, Vidura says, 'Great King, I cannot endorse this resolve of yours. It becomes you to act in a manner by which no dispute arises between your children caused by this gambling.'

Dhritarashtra replies, 'O Kshatta, if the gods are kind to us no dispute will ever arise between our children. So, auspicious or not, good or otherwise, let the friendly dice game be played, for beyond doubt this is what fate has ordained for us.

Besides, when I am present, and Drona, Bhishma and you, as well, no evil which even fate has decreed is likely to occur. So, take a chariot yoked to horses swift as the wind, so that you will reach Khandavaprastha even today and bring Yudhishtira back with you.

Vidura, this is my final decision. Say nothing to me, for I believe that supreme fate brings this upon us.'

Listening to Dhritarashtra, Vidura feels certain that his race is doomed. In great sorrow, he goes to Bhishma of profound wisdom."

CANTO 49

DYUTA PARVA CONTINUED

'Janamejaya says, "O best among all those who know the Veda, how was that game of dice played? It was always fraught with such evil and brought heartbreak to the cousins, and because of it my grandsires, the sons of Pandu, were plunged into grief.

Tell me which Kshatriyas were present in that sabha, and which of them approved of the gambling and which would have forbidden it. Anagha, Sinless, best among the twice-born, I want to hear you narrate all this in detail: that which indeed brought about the ruin of the very world."'

Sauti says, 'Thus addressed by the king, the disciple of Vyasa, blessed with great tejas and a master of the entire Veda, related everything that had happened.

Vaisampayana said, "O Bharatottama, Maharajan, if you wish to hear it all, listen while I tell it to you in detail.

Having confirmed the opinion of Vidura, Ambika's son Dhritarashtra calls Duryodhana to him again, in private.

'Son of Gandhari, I say to you, do not have anything to do with this game of dice. Vidura does not speak well of it. He is wise beyond all common measure, and he would never counsel me against my best interest. I, too, think that what Vidura says is true and best for me. Do as I say, my son, for I am convinced that it is in your best interest also.

Vidura knows dharma, all its mysteries, even as the illustrious, learned and wise Brihaspati, the Devarishi who is Indra's preceptor, unfolded dharma to the king of the Devas. My son, I never fail to take Vidura's advice. Suyodhana, even as the wise Uddhava is revered among the Vrishnis, so is Vidura among the Kurus: as the most intelligent of us.

So, my son, have nothing to do with dice; for it is plain that gambling sows dissension, and discord is the ruin of the kingdom. Duryodhna, abandon this very thought of playing dice.

My child, you have received everything from us, which a father and mother should give their son. You have rank and you have possessions. You are learned and astute in every branch of gyana. You have been raised with love in your father's house. You are the eldest among all your brothers; you live in your own kingdom: why are you unhappy?

Mahabaho, you eat such food and wear such clothes that common men cannot even dream of. Why, still, do you grieve? My son, O mighty-armed, yours is a great ancestral kingdom, brimming with people and with wealth, and you shine forth as gloriously as the king of the Devas in Swarga.

You have wisdom. Tell me what lies at the root of this despondency of yours, the terrible melancholy.'

Duryodhana replies, 'I am a wretch and a sinner, O King, for I can neither eat not clothe myself regally, having seen the prosperity of my enemy. Indeed, it has been said that the man who is not filled with envy at seeing the good fortune of his enemy is truly a wretch.

Exalted, the wealth and power which I have mean nothing to me, for I have seen the resplendent glory of Kunti's son and I am full of pain. Why, I say to you that I must be strong, indeed, that I continue to live when all the world is under the sway of Yudhishtira.

The Nipas, the Chitrakas, the Kukkuras, the Karaskaras, and the Lohajanghas all live like bondsmen in the Pandava's palace. Himavat, the Ocean, the rich realms upon the shores of the sea, the countless other lands which yield precious jewels and gems have all admitted that Yudhishtira's palace is superior to them in the treasures it houses.

Rajan, welcoming with honour me as the eldest among my brothers, Yudhishtira gave me charge of receiving the jewels which came as tribute. Bhaarata, nowhere have such treasures, without limit, been seen; my hands grew tired receiving that incalculable wealth. And when I was tired they who brought those treasures from distant lands would wait until I could resume my task.

Fetching jewels from the Bindusaras, the Asura architect Mayaa created a lake-like surface of crystal for the sons of Pandu. Looking at the artificial lotuses which adorned it, I mistook it, O King, for water. I drew up my clothes to cross it and seeing this Vrikodara laughed at me: surely, thinking that I have no jewels myself and that I had been deranged by the sight of the affluence of my enemy.

If I could, my father, I would immediately kill Bhima for that laughter. But if we try to kill Bhima now I have no doubt that we will meet the same fate as Sisupala did. Yet, that insult scathes me.

Then again, O King, I saw a similar looking water body, and now I felt certain that this was crystal again, solid ground. I stepped forward and fell into water. Bhima and Arjuna laughed mockingly, as did Draupadi and the other women of their palace. Ah, how that sears my heart.

My clothes were drenched, and at Yudhishtira's command his servants brought me fresh clothes. Even that humiliated me. Rajan listen to yet another blunder of mine. I tried to pass through what I was certain was an open door, but there was no passage beyond, and I struck my head painfully against strange stone and injured myself. Nakula and Sahadeva saw me from a distance and, full of apparent solicitude, came to lend me arms of support.

Smiling, Sahadeva said again and again to me, "Rajan, this is the door, come this way."

Bhimasena laughed aloud and said, "Dhritarashtraputra, the door is here."

Also, my lord, I had not even heard the names of many of the gemstones which I saw sparkling in that sabha. Ah, these are the reasons for the anguish which rends my heart.'"

CANTO 50

DYUTA PARVA CONTINUED

"Duryodhana says, 'Listen, O Bhaarata, to everything about the most priceless treasures that I saw, brought to the Pandavas by the kings of the world. Oh, seeing that wealth of the enemy I lost my reason and hardly knew myself. Let me describe for you those treasures, both man-made and produce of the earth.

The Kamboja king gave countless skins of the rarest quality, shawls made of wool, of the soft fur of rodents and other burrowers, of silky hair of cats, all inlaid with golden threads. He gave three hundred Tittiri and Kalmasha horses, with snouts like parrots. Three hundred camels he gave and as many she-asses, all fattened with the olives and the pilusha.

Numberless Brahmanas, rearing cattle and performing lowly tasks for the illustrious Yudhishtira Dharmaraja, waited at the gates with three hundred millions worth of tribute, but they were denied admission into the palace.

Hundreds and hundreds of Brahmanas, wealthy in kine and living on lands which Yudhishtira had given them, came there with their beautiful golden kamandalus full of ghrita. Although they brought such tribute, they were refused admission into the palace.

The Sudra kings, who live along the sea-coast, brought lakhs of serving girls of the Karpasika country, all beautiful, slender-waisted, with luxuriant tresses, decked in golden ornaments. They also brought many skins of the ranku deer, worthy even for Brahmanas, as tribute to King Yudhishtira.

The Vairama, Parada, Abhira and Kitava tribes, who live on crops that depend on rain, water from rivers, as well as those born beside the sea, in woodlands, or countries beyond the Ocean, all waited at the gate, bringing goats, kine, asses, camels and vegetables, honey, blankets, jewels and gemstones of diverse kinds, but were refused entry.

That mighty Kshatriya king, Bhagadatta, the valiant sovereign of Pragjyotisha, the powerful monarch of the Mlechchas, at the head of a vast horde of Yavanas, waited at the gate, unable to enter, though bringing considerable tribute of horses of the best breed, swift as the wind. Bhagadatta was forced to leave the gates after making over a number of swords with handles of the purest ivory and richly inlaid and adorned with diamonds and every kind of jewel.

Many strange tribesmen came from diverse realms: some had two eyes, some three and some with one eye on their foreheads; those called the Aushmikas came, Nishadas and Romakas, and some cannibals with just one leg. I say to you, my father, they all stood at the gates and were refused entry.

Their extraordinary rulers brought tribute of ten thousand varicoloured asses, with black necks, huge bodies, great speed, all very docile, these animals being famed the world over. All of them, indeed, were large and their colouring attractive, and they were all bred on the coast of Vankhu.

So many kings gave Yudhishtira much gold and silver, and giving thus they gained entry into the palace of the Pandava.

The one-legged tribesmen brought innumerable wild horses for him, some red as cochineal, some white, some rainbow-hued, some like evening clouds, and some of many colours besides all these. All these had the swiftness of the mind.

The kings also brought the purest gold for the son of Pandu, vast quantities of it. I also saw countless Chins and Sakas and Uddras and many barbarian tribesmen who live in forests, and many Vrishnis and Harahunas, and the dark tribes of the Himavat, and many Nipas and folk who live on the sea-coast, all waiting at the gates for leave to enter.

And the people of Balhika gave Yudhishtira ten thousand asses as tribute, all of goodly size and black necks, which could run a hundred yojanas in a day. These beasts were of myriad shapes, well-trained and famed the world over. Superbly built they were, their colours resonant and their skins velvet to the touch.

The Balhikas also gifted many, many woollen blankets woven in Chin, and skins of the ranku deer past counting, and clothes made from jute, and others made from the threads spun by insects. They also gave thousands of other garments, none cotton, but all the colour of the lotus, and all so smooth. They gave soft sheep-skins by the thousands.

Many sharp and great swords and scimitars, hatchets and fine-edged battle-axes fashioned in the western countries they gave. Having sent in rare perfumes, diverse glittering jewels and gems in thousands as tribute, they waited at the gates, being refused admission into the palace.

The Sakas and Tusharas and Kankas and Romasas and men with horns on their heads brought very many great elephants as tribute, and ten thousand horses, and hundreds and hundreds of millions of gold coins, and waited at the gates, being refused permission to enter.

The kings of the eastern countries brought uncountable costly carpets, and fine bedsteads, and armour of many colours adorned with jewels, gold and ivory, and weapons of different kinds, and chariots of different shapes, elegant and chased with gold, drawn by superbly trained horses of handsome make and adorned with gold, drawn by well-trained horses, tiger-skins upon their backs, and rich and varied cloths to caparison elephants, and again a myriad manner of jewels and gems, arrows long and short and many other weapons, and they received permission to enter the sacrificial palace of the illustrious Pandava!'"

CANTO 51

DYUTA PARVA CONTINUED

"Duryodhana says, 'Anagha, listen to me describe the vast mass of wealth, the many kinds of tribute given to Yudhishtira by the kings of the Earth. They who live beside the River Sailoda, which flows between the Mountains Meru and Mandara, who enjoy the delightful shade of the groves of the kichaka bamboo, they who are called the Khashas, Ekasanas, Arhas, Pradaras, Dirghavenus, Paradas, Kulindas, Tanganas, and the other Tanganas brought as tribute mounds of gold sealed in great dranas, which are raised from under the earth by ants and are hence named after those creatures.

The mountain tribes of great strength brought tribute of countless soft chamara whisks, some black, others white as moonrays; sweet honey they brought, distilled from flowers which grow upon the Himavat, as well as from the mishali champaka; they brought masses of garlands of flowers from the lands of the northern Kurus, and diverse plants from the north, even from Kailasa, and waited with their heads bent at the gates of Dharmaraja Yudhishtira, and were refused permission to enter.

I also saw there numberless Kirata chieftains, armed with cruel weapons and always engaged in savage deeds, who eat fruit and root and wear skins and live on the northern slopes of the Himavat and upon the Udaya Mountain from behind which the Sun rises, and also in the realm of Karusha on the sea-coast and on both sides of the Lohitya Mountains.

My King, they brought as tribute load upon load of sandalwood, aloe, also black aloe, and heap upon heap of valuable skins and perfumes, and ten thousand serving-girls of their race, and many exotic animals and birds of remote countries, and so much gold of shining splendour, and the Kiratas waited at the gate, being refused permission to enter.

The Kairatas, the Daradas, the Darvas, the Suras, the Vaiyamakas, the Audumbaras, the Durvibhagas, the Kumaras, the Paradas along with the Bahlikas, the Kashmiras, the Ghorakas, the Hansakayanas, the Sibis, the Trigartas, the Yauddheyas, the ruler of the Madias and the Kaikeyas, the Ambashtas, the Kaukuras, the Tarkshyas, the Vastrapas along with the Palhavas, the Vashatalas, the Mauleyas along with the Kshudrakas, and the Malavas, the Paundryas, the Saundikas, the Kukkuras, the Sakas, the Angas, the Vangas, the Punras, the Sanavatyas, and the Gayas, all good men and wellborn, divided into their respective clans, all proficient at arms, brought tribute to Yudhishtira, all of it countable in lakhs.

The Vangas, the Kalingas, the Magadhas, the Tamraliptas, the Supundrakas, the Dauvalikas, the Sagarakas, the Patrornas, the Saisavas, and innumerable Karnapravaranas, who presented themselves at the gate, were told by the gate-keepers, at the command of the king, that if they brought proper tribute and waited at the gates, they could possibly gain entrance.

Then the kings of those nations each gave a thousand elephants with tusks like the shafts of ploughs, adorned with golden girdles, covered with fine cloths and so resembling the lotus in complexion, while they were all dark as rocks and always in musth, captured from around the Kamyaka lake, and covered in armour, too. Of the highest breed were these, and exceptionally patient.

When they had made these gifts those kings were allowed to enter. Rajan, these and many others, hailing from diverse lands, and numberless other illustrious sovereigns brought jewels and gems to the sacrifice.

Chitraratha, king of Gandharvas, friend of Indra, gave four hundred horses blessed with the speed of the wind. The Gandharva Tumburu joyfully gave a hundred horses, the colour of the mango leaf and decked in gold.

O Kurusthama, the celebrated king of the Mlechcha tribe, the Sukaras, gave hundreds of the finest elephants; Virata, king of Matsya, gave two thousand elephants decked in gold, while King Vasudana of the Pansu kingdom gifted the son of Pandu with twenty-six elephants and two thousand horses, all decked in gold and endowed with speed and strength and in the full vigour of youth, as well as many other kinds of wealth.

Drupada Yagnasena gave the Pandavas fourteen thousand serving-girls and ten thousand serving-men with their wives for the sacrifice, hundreds of magnificent elephants, twenty-six chariots with elephants yoked, and also his entire kingdom.

To enhance the dignity of Arjuna, Vaasudeva of the Vrishnis gave fourteen thousand fine elephants. Surely, Krishna is the soul of Arjuna as Arjuna is the soul of Krishna, and whatever Arjuna asks Krishna is certain to do. Why, Krishna will forsake Swarga for Arjuna, just as Arjuna will gladly give his life for Krishna.

The Chola and Pandya kings, though they brought numberless golden jars filled with fragrant sandalwood juice from the hills of Malaya, and heaps of sandal and aloe wood from the Dardura hills, and many gemstones of great brilliance and fine cloths chased with gold, did not gain entry into the palace.

The Sinhala king brought those best of sea-born jewels, the lapis lazuli, and heaps of pearls, also, and hundreds of coverlets for elephants, and uncountable dark-skinned men, the tails of whose eyes were red as copper, wearing bejewelled clothes, and waiting at the gates with these gifts.

Countless Brahmanas, and Kshatriyas who had been vanquished, and Vaisyas and serving Sudras, brought tribute to the son of Pandu out of love for Yudhishtira; even the Mlechchas, all of them came to Yudhishtira out of love and respect. All orders of men – good, indifferent and base, belonging to numberless races, coming from diverse lands – made Yudhishtira's city the focus of the world.

Seeing the kings of the world bring such fabulous and invaluable gifts to my enemies, I wished for death from anguish.

O King, I will now tell you about the servants of the Pandavas, for whom Yudhishtira supplies food, cooked and uncooked. There are a hundred thousand crores of mounted elephants and cavalry, and a hundred million chariots and foot soldiers past counting. In one place, raw provisions were being measured out; at another they were being cooked; at another the food was being distributed.

Everywhere, one heard the sounds of festivity. Among men of all the varnas, I did not see a single one in the palace of Yudhishtira who had not food and drink and rich ornaments.

Eighty-eight thousand Snataka Brahmanas, grihastas all, Yudhishtira supports, with thirty serving-girls given to each, and gratified by the king, these always pray with tranquil hearts for the destruction of his enemies. Ten thousand other ascetics, brahmacharins, their vital seed indrawn, eat daily from golden plates in Yudhishtira's palace.

Rajan, without eating herself, every day Draupadi Yagnaseni first sees to it that everyone else, why even the deformed and dwarfs, has eaten. O Bhaarata, only two peoples do not pay tribute to the son of Kunti: the Panchalas because of their being related through marriage, and the Vrishnis in consequence of their friendship.'"

CANTO 52

DYUTA PARVA CONTINUED

Duryodhana says, "Every king on Earth who is respected the world over, devoted to dharma, sworn to unflinching vratas, deeply learned and eloquent, who knows the Vedas and their Angas as well as all about yagnas, who is pious and modest, who is a dharmatma, who owns great fame, and who has been anointed with the majestic rites of coronation, waits upon and worships Yudhishtira.

Rajan, I saw thousands of wild cows, and as many white copper vessels into which to milk them, brought there by those kings of the world as sacrificial gifts for Yudhishtira to gift to the Brahmanas. For Yudhishtira's ceremonial bath at the conclusion of the sacrifice, a hundred kings rushed to purify themselves and fetched the finest urns full of holy water.

King Bahlika brought a chariot made of pure gold, while King Sudakshina with his hands yoked four white Kamboja horses to it, and the mighty Sunitha fitted the lower shaft and the king of Chedi, also with his own hands, fixed the flagstaff. The Dravida king stood with the Pandava's kavacha; the sovereign of Magadha held the garlands of flowers and the helmet; the great Kshatriya Vasudana stood by with a sixty year old elephant; the Matsya had the side-fittings of the chariot, all sheathed in gold; King Ekalavya of the Nishadas held the sandals for his feet; the king of Avanti fetched different kinds of water for the final ablution; King Chekitana held Yudhishtira's quiver; the king of Kasi, held his bow; Salya had his sword whose hilt and straps were adorned with gold.

Then, Dhaumya and Vyasa, of great tapasya, with Narada and Asita's son Devala performed the ceremony of sprinkling sacred water over the king. Joyfully sat the greatest Rishis where the sprinkling ceremony was performed. Other illustrious Munis, knowers of the Vedas, Jamadagni's son among them, approached Yudhishtira, the munificent giver of sacrificial gifts, chanting mantras all the while, even as the Saptarishis approach Indra in Devaloka.

Satyaki of untold prowess held the royal white parasol over the king's head. Dhananjaya and Bhima fanned him, while the twins held silken chamaras in their hands.

In a sling, the Ocean himself brought Varuna's great conch, which the heavenly artificer Viswakarman created with a thousand nishkas of gold, and which Prajapati gave to Indra in a previous Kalpa. It was with that conch that Krishna bathed Yudhishtira when the yagna was concluded, and seeing that, I swooned.

Men travel to the Eastern, the Western and also to the Southern Seas, but Father, only birds can ever go to the Northern one. But the Pandavas have extended their dominion even there, for I heard hundreds of conches, which had been brought from those waters, being sounded at that sacrifice, celebrant and auspicious.

While those exceptional conches blew all together, my hair stood on end, and the weaker kings there fell down from the reverberation. Seeing me turn pale and the other kings faint, Dhrishtadyumna, Satyaki, the Pandavas and Krishna – those eight, all mighty and handsome, laughed aloud.

Then, O Bhaarata, Arjuna Vibhatsu joyfully gave the main Brahmanas five hundred bullocks each, their horns plated with gold. Having completed the Rajasuya yagna, Yudhishtira, the son of Kunti, gained such wealth and fortune, even like the great Harischandra: such prosperity that not Rantideva, Nabhaga, Yauvanaswa, not Manu, nor Vena's son King Prithu, not Bhagiratha, Yayati or Nahusha had seen its like.

And seeing this fortune of Pritha's son, equal to what Harischandra had, I do not see the least point in continuing to live! King of men, a yoke tied by a blind man comes loose. So it is with us: the younger ones are growing while the elder are diminishing. Seeing all this, O Lord of the Kurus, I can find no peace, not even after deep thought.

This is why, Rajan, I am plunged in grief and have become pale and wasted.'"

CANTO 53

DYUTA PARVA CONTINUED

" Dhritarashtra says, 'You are my eldest son and also born to my first wife. My child, do not envy the Pandavas. The jealous man is always unhappy and suffers pangs even like those of death.

Bharatarishabha, Yudhishtira is not deceitful, he owns wealth equal to yours, his friends are your friends, and he feels no envy towards you. So why should you be envious of him? My son, you have as many friends and allies as Yudhishtira does. So, why, from folly, must you covet the wealth of your brother?

Do not be like this; abandon your envy. Do not grieve, O Bull of the Bhaaratas, if you wish for the honour attached to the performance of a sacrifice, let our priests arrange to perform the Saptatantu mahayagna for you, and then the kings of the Earth will happily and with respect bring you great wealth, jewels and ornaments.

My child, it is lowly to covet another's possessions. On the other hand, he who is content with what he has, and engages in his svadharma diligently, he is the happy man. Never attempting to gain what others own, persevering in one's own affairs and protecting what one has earned – these are the signs of true greatness.

He who is unmoved in calamity, skilled in his own work, always at work, vigilant and humble: he always finds prosperity. The Pandavas are like your very arms; do not seek to cut off those arms. No, nor create internal strife for the sake of your brothers' wealth.

Do not envy the sons of Pandu; you are as rich as they are. There is great sin in falling out with friends. They who are your grandsires are also theirs. Give charity during sacrifices, satisfy every desire which is dear to your heart, disport freely in the company of women, and be at peace, Duryodhana.'"

CANTO 54

DYUTA PARVA CONTINUED

"Duryodhana says, 'He who has no intelligence himself but has merely heard many things can hardly understand the true meaning of the scriptures, even like a spoon which does not know the taste of the soup it touches. You know everything, yet you confound me.

Like boats fastened, one to the other, you and I are bound to each other. Are you mindful of your own interests, or are you hostile towards me? Having you for their king, your sons and your allies are condemned to be destroyed, for you speak of having in the future what can be had even now!

The man who acts under the counsel of others, frequently trips and falls. Then how can his followers expect to tread the right path? Rajan, you have maturity and wisdom; you have heard the ancient truths, and you have restrained your senses. It does not become you to confound us who are eager to seek our own interest.

Brihaspati himself has said the ways of kings differ from those of commoners, and so kings must always vigilantly attend to their own interests. Finding success must be the only criterion which guides the way of the Kshatriya. So, what does it matter if the means are virtuous or sinful, what place for scruples in performing one's svadharma?

He who wants to snatch the blazing prosperity of his enemy, O Bharatarishabha, must tame all the directions, even as the sarathy does his horses with his whip. Those who wield weapons always say that a weapon is not merely a sharp instrument, but a means to vanquish an enemy, whether covertly or openly.

Who is an enemy and who a friend does not depend on one's size or strength. He who causes pain is an enemy to the one whom he hurts. Discontent is the root of prosperity; and so, O King, I want to be discontented.

The truly politic man is he who strives after property. None should be attached to property or wealth, for both these, once having been acquired and hoarded, can be plundered. This is the way of kings.

Sakra cut off Namuchi's head after pledging peace with him, and this was because he endorsed this eternal way with an enemy. Like a snake swallowing frogs and other creatures which live in holes, the Earth swallows kings who are peaceful and Brahmanas who do not stir from their homes.

Rajan, merely by nature no one is anybody's enemy; only he who has common purposes as oneself is one's foe. He who is foolish enough to neglect an infected toenail has his vitals excoriated by a disease that he himself nurtured without treatment. If an enemy, however insignificant, is allowed to grow in might, he swallows one like termites at the roots of a tree, felling the tree itself.

O Bhaarata, O Ajamida, never acquiesce in your enemy's prosperity: this is a policy that the wise must always bear upon their heads even like a load. He who always desires and seeks his own prosperity grows among his kinsmen even as the body does, naturally, from the moment of its birth.

Prowess confers rapid growth. I covet the wealth of the Pandavas, but I have not yet made it my own. So, I doubt myself, my ability, and I am determined to lay my doubt at rest. I will either have what belongs to them or die in battle trying to have it.

When this is my state of mind, what do I care anymore for my life, as the Pandavas' fortunes swell daily while ours know no increase?'"

CANTO 55

DYUTA PARVA CONTINUED

"Sakuni says, 'Best of men of victory, I will take this great wealth of Pandu's son Yudhishtira from him, the sight of which aggrieves you so much, and give it to you. Therefore, O Rajan, let Kunti's son Yudhishtira be summoned here. By throwing dice a man of skill can vanquish an unskilled opponent, while remaining uninjured himself. O Bhaarata, know that wagering is my bow, the dice are my arrows, the marks on them is my bow-string, and the dice-board my chariot.'

Duryodhana says, 'Rajan, this Sakuni, master of dice, is ready to take the wealth of the Pandavas from them at a game. It becomes you to give him leave to do so.'

Dhritarashtra says, 'I follow the advice of my wise brother Vidura. I will consult him and then tell you what to do.'

Duryodhana says, 'Vidura always has the welfare of the sons of Pandu at heart, while, O Kaurava, his feelings towards us are different. I have no doubt that he will turn your mind from what we propose. No man must let another man decide for him what he must do, for, O Kurusthama, two minds rarely agree upon any enterprise.

The fool who lives his life avoiding any fear wastes himself like an insect during the rains. Neither sickness nor death waits for prosperity to visit one of its own accord. So, as long as we have life and health, we must strive to accomplish our purpose.'

Dhritarashtra says, 'My son, I never see wisdom in seeking hostility of any kind with those who are powerful. Hostility changes the heart and is a weapon by itself, if not made of steel. O Prince, you think of as a great blessing what will bring dreadful war in its wake, while in fact what you wish to do is fraught with danger. If you set yourself on this course, it will inexorably fetch out keen swords and sharp arrows.'

Duryodhana replies, 'The most ancient men invented the game of dice precisely because there is no bloodshed in it or any striking with weapons. So, listen to what Sakuni says, and quickly order the sabha to be built. The gambling will open the door of heaven, the way to great happiness for us. Why, those who gamble for such stakes deserve the fortune which comes to them.

The Pandavas, who are now your superiors, will become your equals; so play dice with them, O King.'

Dhritarashtra says, 'Your words do not find favour with me. Do as you please, ruler of men, but you will repent choosing this path, for a way of such adharma can never fetch enduring prosperity, only disaster.

Vidura, who has profound wisdom, who always lives in dharma, has already foreseen the calamity which will destroy Kshatriya kind itself, coming towards us brought by fate.'

Saying this, the weak-minded Dhritarashtra yields to Fate as being supreme and inexorable. Indeed, his reason taken from him by Fate, submitting to his son's wish, the king commands his men in stentorian tones, 'With every care, with no delay, immediately build a magnificent sabha. Call it the palace of crystal arches and a thousand columns; let it be adorned with gold and lapis lazuli; let it have a hundred gates, and be full two miles in length and width.'

At his command, thousands of brilliant artificers swiftly raise that edifice, and having built it, furnish it with every manner of exquisite artefact. When they finish, they come in joy to the king to inform him that the grand sabha is complete and that it is beautiful and lavish and adorned with everything that he might wish it to have: priceless jewels upon the walls, invaluable carpets in every hue, gold-chased, upon its floors.

Now Dhritarashtra, the learned, summons Vidura and says, 'Go to Khandavaprastha and fetch Yudhishtira here immediately. Let him come with his brothers to see my grand sabha of gemstones past counting, priceless beds and carpets. And let a friendly game of dice be played in our city.'"

CANTO 56

DYUTA PARVA CONTINUED

Vaisampayana said, "Knowing that Fate is ineluctable and what his son's heart is set upon, Dhritarashtra does as I have said.

However, the most intelligent Vidura does not approve of what his brother intends and says, 'My King, I do not like this command which you give me. Do not do this thing, for I fear it will end in the annihilation of our very race. Terrible dissension will result from this game of dice and lead inevitably to great tragedy.'

Dhritarashtra says, 'If Fate is not hostile to us, such a falling out will not grieve me. All the Universe moves at its Creator's will, and through Fate. It is not free. Therefore, Vidura, I command you, go to Yudhishtira and fetch Kunti's invincible son here quickly.'"

CANTO 57

DYUTA PARVA CONTINUED

Vaisampayana said, "Against his will, ordered by Dhritarashtra, Vidura sets out, taking the finest, swiftest and strongest horses, steeds that are quiet and patient as well, for the home of Pandu's wise sons.

Vidura of lofty intellect rides to Khandavaprastha and, arriving in Yudhishtira's city, enters it and goes straight towards the palace, being worshipped by many Brahmanas on the way. Coming to that palace, which is even like that sabha of Kubera himself, the virtuous Vidura approaches Yudhishtira Dharmaputra.

The illustrious Yudhishtira Ajamida, devoted to dharma, who is without an enemy in the world, reverently salutes Vidura, and asks after Dhritarashtra and his sons. Then Yudhishtira says, 'O Kshatta, your mind seems cheerless. Do you come here in peace and happiness? I hope Dhritarashtra's sons are obedient to their old father. I hope the people also are obedient to Dhritarashtra's rule?'

Vidura says, 'The illustrious king and his sons are well and happy, and surrounded by his kinsmen, Dhritarashtra rules even like Indra.

The king is happy with his sons, who are all obedient to him, and he has no grief.

That great sovereign is bent upon his own aggrandisement. The king of the Kurus commands me to enquire after your peace and prosperity, and he asks you to come to Hastinapura with your brothers to inspect the new palace he has built there and then say if it is equal to your own.

Coming to the city of elephants with your brothers, O son of Pritha, enjoy a friendly game of dice in the new sabha. The other Kurus have all arrived there already, and we shall be glad if you come at once. And there you will see the gamblers and cheats that the illustrious King Dhritarashtra has brought to his home.

It is for this, O Rajan, that I have come here. May you heed my king's command.'

Yudhishtira says, 'O Kshatta, if we sit down to a game of dice, we might well quarrel amongst ourselves. Well knowing this, what man will agree to gamble? What do you think we should do? We all are obedient to your counsel.'

Vidura says, 'I know that gambling is a root of misery, and I strove to dissuade the king. However, he has sent me to you. Knowing Yudhishtira, keep this in mind and do what you think best.'

Yudhishtira says, 'Besides Dhritarashtra's sons what other gamblers are there, prepared to play, who cheat? Who are they, Vidura, whom we will have to contend with, wagering our wealth in hundreds and thousands?'

Vidura says, 'Sakuni, king of Gandhara, who is a master of dice, whose sleight of hand is legend and whose stakes are extreme; Vivimsati, King Chitrasena, Satyavrata, Purumitra and Jaya – these, Yudhishtira, are there.'

Yudhishtira says, 'Ah, it seems that some of the most crooked, skilled and wild gamblers are there! But by the will of its Maker, the universe is under Fate's control. It is not free.

Most learned Vidura, I do not wish to gamble at Dhritarashtra's command, for he always wants to benefit only his son. You are our master,

O Vidura; you say what I should do. I am loath to gamble, and unless the vile Sakuni does not call me to the sabha I will not do so. However, if he challenges me, I will never decline, for I am so sworn, eternally.'

Having said this, Dharmaraja Yudhishtira orders preparations to be made immediately for his long journey. The next day, with his relatives and attendants, and also taking with him the women of his household, with Draupadi among them, he sets out for the capital of the Kurus.

Yudhishtira says, 'Fate deprives us of reason, like some brilliant body falling before our eyes, and man, as if bound with a cord, submits to providence,' and that Parantapa, chastiser of his enemies, goes forth with Kshatta, without even reflecting upon Dhritarashtra's cunning summons. With his brothers, that slayer of hostile heroes, the son of Pandu and Pritha, riding in the chariot given him by the king of Balhika, he goes forth.

He wears royal robes; he is, as it were, ablaze with regal splendour; Brahmanas walk before him, as Yudhishtira sets out from his city: summoned by Dhritarashtra and impelled by what Time has ordained.

Arriving in Hastinapura, he goes to Dhritarashtra's palace. He approaches Bhishma, Drona, Karna, Kripa, Drona's son, and embraces and is embraced by them all. The Mahabaho, endowed with immense prowess, comes to Somadatta, then to Duryodhana and Salya, and to the son of Subala, and also to those other kings who have arrived there before him.

The Pandava emperor approaches the bold Dussasana, then all his brothers, then Jayadratha, and then all the Kurus, one after another. Then, surrounded by his brothers, the mighty-armed one enters the apartment of the wise Dhritarashtra. There Yudhishtira see the revered Gandhari, always obedient to her lord, and surrounded by her daughters-in-law, like Rohini by the nakshatras. Saluting Gandhari, being blessed by her in return, Pandu's great son sees his old uncle, that illustrious king whose wisdom is his eye. Dhritarashtra sniffs the top of his head, as also the heads of his brothers, the other Kuru princes, Bhimasena's first among them.

Rajan, all the Kuru Purushavyaghras are delighted to see the handsome Pandavas. Then, at the king's command, the sons of Pandu retire to the lavish chambers given to them, all furnished with jewels and gems.

When they are ensconced, the women of Dhritarashtra's household, Dussala leading them, visit the Pandavas. When the daughters-in-law of Dhritarashtra see the blazing, awesome beauty of Draupadi Yagnaseni, and her incomparable attire and ornaments, jealousy attacks them and they lose their cheer.

The Pandavas speak gently to those women. They go through their daily regimen of physical exercise and then perform their daily religious rites, their nitya karma. Finishing their devotions, they anoint their bodies with the most fragrant sandalwood paste, and the Brahmanas chant blessings over them for their good fortune.

They now partake of the finest delicacies prepared in the palace, then retire again to their apartments, where they are entertained with music by beautiful women and by other diversions. Happily those subduers of hostile cities pass that night, until they fall asleep.

At dawn, bards wake them with sweet music again; they rise from their beds and perform their morning rituals, before coming into the sabha, where they are greeted by those who have already gathered there for the gambling."

CANTO 58

DYUTA PARVA CONTINUED

Vaisampayana said, "Yudhishtira leads his brothers into the sabha, where they approach the other kings present. Worshipping their elders who deserve to be worshipped, saluting the others as each deserves, by age, they seat themselves on fine thrones covered with costly cloths.

When they have sat, and also the other kings, Subala's son Sakuni says to Yudhishtira, 'Rajan, the sabha is full; we have all been waiting for you. Let the rules of play be decided upon and the dice be cast, Yudhishtira.'

Yudhishtira replies, 'Deceitful gambling is a sin; there is no Kshatriya prowess in it. There is surely no dharma in it. Why, then, do you favour gambling so? The wise never approve of the pride that gamblers take in cheating. Sakuni, do not vanquish us like a wretch, with deceit.'

Sakuni says, 'The noble player, who knows the secrets of winning and losing, who is skilled enough to confound his adversaries' deceit, who indeed knows all the subtleties of gambling, he is the true player, and he endures everything which results from gaming. Son of Pritha, it is the stakes at dice, which might be lost or won, that could injure us, and this is why gambling is regarded as a sin. But let us play, O King. And do not fear, for let the stakes be fixed. Let us play now!'

Yudhishtira says, 'Devala, best of Munis, the son of Asita, who always teaches us all what deeds lead us to heaven, to hell, or to other realms, has declared that it is a sin to play dice with a gambler, for there is deceit in it. To have victory in open battle, with neither cunning nor stratagem: that is a noble sport. But gambling is not.

Honourable men never use the language of the Mlechchas, nor do they use deceit. War waged without crookedness and treachery is the way of the honest man. Sakuni, playing with cunning, do not take from us the wealth with which we seek to support Brahmanas. Even enemies must not be vanquished by wild stakes in a game of cheating. I have no wish either to earn wealth or to gain pleasure through vile means.

Besides, the way of the gambler, even if he does not cheat, is never lauded.'

Sakuni says, 'Yudhishtira, impelled by the desire for victory, which is not an honest motive, one Kshatriya confronts another. So, too, from a desire to prove superiority in learning, does one scholar face another in a debate. But these are hardly regarded as being adharma.

A skilled dice player confronts one who is less skilled than himself from the desire to vanquish him even as a superior warrior does one of lesser prowess, or a superior man of knowledge does an inferior. At dice too the strong confront the weak. So how is the dice player's motive any more or less dishonest?

The motive is the same: victory, and in any contention this is so. However, if you still regard dice as being more dishonest than other contests, or if you are afraid, then do not play.'

Yudhishtira says, 'I never retreat from a challenge, this is my dharma. Besides, O King, Fate is all powerful and we are all controlled by destiny. Whom shall I play against in this sabha? Who is here who can match my stakes? Let play begin.'

Duryodhana says, 'Rajan, I will stake every manner of jewel and gemstone, and gold. And this Sakuni, my uncle, will play for me.'

Yudhishtira says, 'I believe that it is unlawful for one man to play for another, and you also, learned cousin, will grant this. However, if you still wish it, let play begin.'"

CANTO 59

DYUTA PARVA CONTINUED

Vaisampayana said, "When play begins all the kings present, Dhritarashtra at their head, take their places in that sabha. O Bhaarata, Bhishma and Drona and Kripa and the Vidura Mahatman sit at the back with forlorn hearts.

The other kings, their necks like those of lions, endowed with mighty power, sit singly or in pairs upon lofty seats of wonderful make and hue. Rajan, that assembly is as splendid as Heaven with a conclave of the Devas of great fortune. And they all know the Vedas; they are valiant and radiant of countenance. And, O great King, the friendly match at dice then begins.

Yudhishtira says, 'Here is my stake: this string of invaluable pearls set in gold, and exquisite, which was once churned up from the Ocean of old. What is your stake with which you will match mine and play against me?'

Duryodhana says, 'I have many jewels and great wealth, but I am not vain because of them.' He tells Sakuni, 'Win these pearls, Uncle.'

Then Sakuni, master of the game, takes up the dice and, casting them perfectly, says to Yudhishtira, 'I have won!'"

CANTO 60

DYUTA PARVA CONTINUED

Yudhishtira says, 'You have won this wager unfairly, but do not preen Sakuni. Let us raise the stakes to thousands upon thousands. I have many beautiful jars in my treasury, each one full of a thousand nishkas; I have gold past exhausting, and silver and other precious metals. O King, I will wager all this wealth with you!'

Sakuni says to the eldest Pandava, Yudhishtira, whose glory can sustain no diminution, 'Look, I have won!'

Yudhishtira says, 'My sacred and triumphant royal chariot, which delights the heart and has borne us here, which is equal to a thousand chariots, which is perfectly wrought, covered with tiger-skin, which has immaculate wheels and flagstaffs, which is beautiful, decked with strings of little bells, whose sound clatters like the roar of thunderheads or the ocean, which is drawn by eight noble steeds renowned through the land, white as moonbeams, whose hooves no earthly creature can escape – this, O Rajan, is my next wager with you!'

Sakuni throws the dice, deceitfully, with sure sleight of hand and says to Yudhishtira, 'Lo, I have won!'

Yudhishtira says, 'I have a hundred thousand serving-girls, all young, and adorned with golden bracelets on their wrists and arms, with necklaces of nishkas around their necks, and other ornaments, wearing priceless garlands, rich robes, anointed with sandalwood paste, wearing jewels and golden ornaments, skilled in the sixty-four elegant arts, especially versed in singing and dancing, who wait upon and, at my command, serve the Devas, the Snataka Brahmanas, and kings: this wealth my next stake!'

Sakuni hears this, and ready with his crafty dice, rolls and says to Yudhishtira, 'I have won!'

Yudhishtira says, 'I have thousands of serving-men, skilled at waiting upon guests, always wearing silken robes, blessed with wisdom and intelligence, young but their senses restrained, and decked in golden earrings, who serve all my guests night and day with plates and dishes in hand. This wealth I wager!'

Sakuni, ready with his loaded dice, says to Yudhishtira, 'I have won!'

Yudhishtira says, 'Son of Subala, I own one thousand elephants with golden girdles and other ornaments, with the mark of the lotus upon their temples, necks and other parts, adorned with golden garlands, with white tusks long and thick as plough-shafts, worthy of bearing kings on their backs, which can bear every dread sound of battle, their bodies huge, which can batter down the walls of enemy cities, their colour of freshly formed clouds, and each possessing eight cow-elephants.

This wealth I wager, O King.'

Subala's son Sakuni, rolling the dice, laughs, 'Yudhishtira, I have won your elephants!'

Yudhishtira says, 'I have as many chariots as elephants, all fitted with golden poles and flagstaffs, trained horses and warriors who fight magnificently, each receiving a thousand coins as his monthly wage, whether he fights or not.

This wealth I wager, Rajan!'

When these words have been said, the vile Sakuni, sworn to enmity, rolls the ivory dice, and says to Yudhisthira, 'Ah, I win!'

Yudhishtira says, 'When Arjuna vanquished him in battle, Chitraratha joyfully gifted my brother who wields the Gandiva horses of the Tittiri, Kalmasha and Gandharva breeds, all decked in unearthly ornaments.

This wealth, Rajan, I wager.'

Sakuni, master cheat, says to Yudhishtira, 'I have won!'

Yudhishtira says, 'I have ten thousand chariots and carriages yoked to the finest draught animals. I have sixty thousand broad-chested warriors, all valiant and heroic, handpicked from the rest of my forces, all fed on milk and fine rice.

This wealth, O King, is my stake.'

Sakuni, ready, always cheating, says to Yudhishtira, 'I have won!'

Yudhishtira says, 'I have four hundred nidhis, jewels of incomparable value, in caskets of copper and iron. Each one is worth five draunikas of the most pure and expensive leaf gold of the jatarupa variety.

This wealth, O King, shall be my wager.'

Sakuni, ready with his cunning dice, always cheating at the roll, says to Yudhishtira, 'I have won!'"

CANTO 61

DYUTA PARVA CONTINUED

Vaisampayana said, "While the ruinous gambling is underway, Vidura, dispeller of doubts, says to Dhritarashtra, 'Great king of the race of Bhaarata, listen to what I have to say, though my words might not be agreeable to you even like bitter medicine to a man who is ill and dying.

When this evil-minded Duryodhana howled abysmally like a jackal soon after he was born, we knew that he would fetch destruction upon the race of Bhaarata. Rajan, know that he will be the cause of the death of all of you. A jackal lives in your house and he has the form of Duryodhana, but in your dotage you do not realise it, you do not know what the consequences of your folly will be.

Listen to what Sukra Kavi said. They who gather honey on mountains, take what they desire but do not notice that they are about to fall. Climbing perilous heights, distracted by their avid pursuit, they fall and die.

Like the honey gatherer, this Duryodhana, also, is maddened by this game of dice and is not mindful of the dire consequences that will visit him. Making enemies of these great Kshatriyas, he does not notice the certain fall to death which lies before him.

You well know, O King of much wisdom, that the Bhojas abandoned an unworthy son for the sake of their people. The Andhakas, the Yadavas, and the Bhojas, uniting, abandoned Kamsa. Later, when, at their very command, Krishna Parantapa killed Kamsa, all the men of those tribes became joyful for a full hundred years.

Even so, at your command, let Arjuna kill this Suyodhana. And let the Kurus rejoice at the death of this sinful wretch and pass their days in joy. In exchange for a crow, O great King, buy these peacocks: the Pandavas; in exchange for a jackal, buy these tigers.

For the sake of a family, one of its members can be sacrificed; for the sake of a village, a family may be sacrificed; for the sake of a province, a village may be sacrificed, and for the sake of one's own soul, the whole earth can be sacrificed.

This is what the omniscient Sukra himself, who knows the thoughts of ever creature, who is a terror to all his enemies, said to the great Asuras to persuade them to abandon Jambha at the moment of his birth.

I have heard that once a king kept a flock of wild birds in his house because they vomited gold from their beaks, and later, killed them. O Parantapa, blinded by temptation and the lust for pleasure, for the sake of gold that king destroyed both his present and future gains.

Rajan, do not, like the king in the tale, persecute the Pandavas from your lust for wealth. For, this blind folly will make your repent sorely later, just like the one who killed the birds.

Like a flower-seller who, over long years, plucks countless flowers from the trees in his garden which he nurtures carefully, you also pluck flowers gently from the Pandavas, daily, O Bhaarata.

Do not burn them at their roots like a fiery wind which makes black char of all things. O King, do not go to the realm of Yama with your sons and all your soldiers, for who is there in this world who can defeat the sons of Pritha in battle? Why speak of the rest, can the king of the Devas himself contain them?'"

CANTO 62

DYUTA PARVA CONTINUED

"Vidura says, 'Gambling is the root of dissension; it fetches deep rifts. Its consequences are dreadful. Yet, Duryodhana creates terrible enmity for himself with what he is doing.

The descendants of Pratipa and Santanu, with all their valiant troops and their allies, the Bahlikas, will be destroyed for Duryodhana's sins. Duryodhana is drunk with avarice and he will force fortune and prosperity out of this kingdom, like an angry bull breaking its own horns.

The brave and learned man who ignores his own foresight and follows the bent of another's dark heart is plunged into dreadful calamity, rather as a man who goes out to sea in a boat guided by a child.

Duryodhana is gambling with the son of Pandu, and you are in raptures that he is winning. And it is such success, which begets war and ends in the death of men. This gambling which you have so cunningly abetted can only lead to dire disaster. Your heart is dark and sick, Rajan, and it is death that you court.

Yudhishtira is so closely related to you, and even if you do not foresee the extent of the damage which would be done, you are still an accomplice in it: it has your approval.

O listen, you sons of Santanu, you scions of Pratipa who now sit in the sabha of the Kauravas, to these words of wisdom. Do not walk into these dreadful flames which blaze forth, following this vile wretch Suyodhana.

When Ajatasatru, the son of Pandu, now intoxicated with dice, gives in to his anger, when Vrikodara and Arjuna and the twins do, who will be your refuge in that terrible hour?

Great King, you are already a mine of wealth yourself, and you can earn as much more as you want to by this gambling. What will you gain by taking the immense wealth of the Pandavas from them, when you can win over the sons of Pandu themselves, who will be far more valuable to you than all that they own?

We all know the mastery of Subala's son at dice, for this hill-king knows numberless ways to cheat at gambling. Let Sakuni go back to where he came from. O Bhaarata, do not seek enmity with Pandu's sons.'"

CANTO 63

DYUTA PARVA CONTINUED

"Duryodhana says, 'Kshatta, you are always praising our enemies, and disparaging the sons of Dhritarashtra. We know, O Vidura, of whom you are truly fond, for you never think of us as your own children.

A man wishes for the success of those that are dear to him and the defeat of those whom he does not love. His praise and blame are accordingly given. Your tongue and your mind betray your heart, yet the hostility which you show with your words is even greater than what is in your heart.

We have nurtured and cherished you like a serpent in our lap. Like a cat, you wish evil upon those that keep you. The wise have said that there is no graver sin than harming one's master. How is it, O Kshatta, that you do not fear this sin?

By vanquishing these enemies of ours, we have gained great advantage. Speak not harshly of us, and always be so willing to make peace with the enemy. A man becomes an enemy by speaking inexcusably of another, and this is how you have come to detest us, always.

Also, while praising an enemy one must never divulge the secrets of those that are one's own. But you willingly break this law. Why do you come in our way, O parasite? You say whatever you like. Do not insult us; we know your heart.

Go sit at the feet of the old and the sage and learn more wisdom. Maintain the great repute which you have won for yourself. Do not meddle in the affairs of other men. Do not imagine that you are our lord. Do not dare speak cruelly to us always, O Vidura, for we do not ask you what is good for us.

Stop now. Do not annoy those who have already borne too much from you. There is only one Lord, no second. He controls even the child that is in its mother's womb. I am ruled by Him. Like water, which always flows downwards, I am doing precisely what he wants me to.

He who breaks his head against a stone wall and he who feeds a serpent are moved by their own minds. He becomes an enemy who seeks to control others through force. When advice is offered in the spirit of friendship, the wise listen and tolerate it.

Who sets camphor alight does not even see its ashes, not if he runs to put it out. One should never shelter a man who is a friend to one's enemies, or a man who is always envious of his protector and whose mind is thus full of evil.

So, Vidura, go wherever you please. However well treated in her duties, an unchaste wife will abandon her husband.'

Vidura says to Dhritarashtra, 'O King, tell us, as an impartial witness, what you think of those who abandon their servants so for giving them counsel. Truly, the hearts of kings are fickle. They first give you protection then finally strike you down with a bludgeon.

Duryodhana, you think that you have a mature intellect, and, evil prince, you think that I am a child. But know that he is the child who first accepts a man for his friend and then finds fault with him. An evil-hearted man can never be brought to the path of dharma, just like an unchaste wife in the house of a wellborn husband.

Surely, being advised is as disagreeable to this Bharatarishbaha as a husband of sixty years is to a young woman. After this, O King, if you want to hear what is pleasing to you at all times, regardless of what you do, good or bad, go and ask women, idiots, cripples or similar folk to speak to you.

A sinful man speaking agreeable words is easy to find in this world, but the man who speaks the truth, whether it be pleasing or distasteful, and the man who listens to him are both rare indeed. A king's true ally is his man who will speak dharma to his master, regardless of whether what he says pleases him or no.

Great King, drink the drink called humility, which honest men imbibe and evil ones shun, which is like bitter medicine, pungent, burning, distasteful, revolting, on which you cannot get drunk. Drinking it, regain your sobriety.

I always wish Dhritarashtra and his sons prosperity and fame. Whatever now happens to you, I bow to you. Let the Brahmanas here wish me well. O Son of Kuru, this is the lesson that I teach with care: the wise should never anger snakes like cobras, which have venom in their very glances!'"

CANTO 64

DYUTA PARVA CONTINUED

"Sakuni says, 'Yudhishtira, you have lost a lot of the wealth of the Pandavas. If you still own anything which you have not lost, Kaunteya, tell us what it is.'

Yudhishtira says, 'Son of Subala, I own untold wealth. Why do you speak to me of wealth, Sakuni? Wager lakhs and crores and crores of crores of crores and arabs, and arabs of arabs, and I will match your stake. I have as much.

With that wealth, King, I will play with you.'

Sakuni, ready with his loaded dice, always cheating, says to Yudhishtira, 'I have won!'

Yudhishtira says, 'Son of Subala, I have uncountable cattle and horses, and milch cows with calves, and goats and sheep in the lands that extend from the Parnasa to the eastern bank of the Sindu.

With this wealth, O King, I will play.'

Sakuni, ready with his loaded dice, always cheating, says to Yudhishtira, 'I have won!'

Yudhishtira says, 'I have my city, my country, land, the wealth of all who live there other than the Brahmanas, and all those people themselves except the Brahmanas, who will remain with me.

With this wealth, O King, I will play with you.'

Sakuni, ready with his loaded dice, always cheating, says to Yudhishtira, 'I have won!'

Yudhishtira says, 'King, these princes here, resplendent in their royal ornaments, earrings and nishkas are now my wealth. This wealth, Rajan, I will wager with you.'

Sakuni, ready with his loaded dice, always cheating, says to Yudhishtira, 'I have won them already. Play!'

Yudhishtira says, 'This Nakula, mighty-armed, his neck a lion's, his eyes red, youthful, I wager. Know him to be my wealth.'

Sakuni says, 'O Yudhishtira, Nakula is dear to you. He is already our subject. Who will you wager next?'

Saying this, Sakuni casts his dice, and says to Yudhishtira, 'We have won him!'

Yudhishtira says, 'This Sahadeva administers justice. He has gained great renown through the world for his learning. He does not deserve to be my wager, yet with such a dear one I will play you, though I fervently wish that I did not!'

Sakuni, ready with his loaded dice, always cheating, says to Yudhishtira, 'I have won him! O King, I have won both Madri's sons, so dear to you. It seems that Bhimasena and Dhananjaya are too dear for you to wager.'

Yudhishtira cries, 'Wretch! You want to make dissension among those that are one at heart? You ignore dharma, serpent.'

Sakuni says, 'He who is drunk falls into a pit and stays there unable to move. Yudhishtira, you are older than the Kauravas and have the highest accomplishments. O Bharatarishabha, I bow to you. You know, Yudhishtira, that while in the grip of the game, gamblers rave as they never do otherwise, awake or even in their dreams.'

Yudhishtira says, 'He who bears us like a boat across the sea of battle, he who always triumphs over enemies, this prince of mighty vigour, this greatest Kshatriya in the world: this Phalguna, who does not deserve this, I wager against you.'

Sakuni, ready with his loaded dice, always cheating, says to Yudhishtira, 'I have won! This greatest bowman, this son of Pandu who is perfectly ambidextrous in his archery I have won. Now, Pandava, stake your remaining wealth, your beloved brother Bhima.'

Yudhishtira says, 'King, however undeserving he is of becoming my wager, I will play against you with Bhimasena as my stake: this prince who is our leader, who is the mightiest warrior, who is even like the Vajradhari, the single enemy of the Danavas, himself, this high-souled one of leonine neck, his brows arched, his eyes looking askance, who brooks no insult ever, who has no equal on Earth for strength, who is the greatest among all mace-wielders, this grinder of his enemies.'

Sakuni, ready with his loaded dice, always cheating, says to Yudhishtira, 'I have won. Kaunteya, you have lost great wealth, horses, elephants and your brothers as well. Tell us if you have anything which you have not lost yet.'

Yudhishtira says, 'I alone, eldest of all my brothers and precious to them, remain unwon. If you win me, I will do whatever I must.'

Sakuni, ready with his dice, cheating, casts them and says to Yudhishtira, 'I have won. You have let yourself be won and that is a sin, for you still have wealth left to lose, O Rajan.'

Sakuni, master of dice, boasts to the kings gathered there of how he has won all the Pandavas. Subala's son then says to Yudhishtira, 'O King, there remains one possession dear to you, which is still unwon. Stake Krishnaa, princess of Panchala, and through her win yourself back!'

Yudhishtira says, 'Draupadi is neither too short nor tall, not lean or fat, and her tresses are blue and wavy. Her eyes are like the leaves of the autumn lotus, and she is fragrant, also, as the autumn lotus, and her beauty equal to Lakshmi who delights in the lotuses of autumn. Her form is as perfect as that of Sri herself, as is her grace.

She is a woman that any man would want for his wife, for the softness of her heart, the wealth of her beauty and her virtues. She owns every accomplishment; she is compassionate and sweetly-spoken; truly, she is a woman whom a man might want for his wife, for with her he could indeed have great dharma, artha and kama.

She goes to bed last of all and wakes first. She cares for everyone, down to the shepherds and cowherds. Ah, when her face is filmed with sweat she looks like the lotus or the jasmine. Her waist is as slender as a wasp's, her locks long and flowing, her lips red, and her body without so much as down: this is the Princess Panchali.

I wager this slender-waisted Draupadi to play against you, son of Subala!'

When Yudhishtira Dharmaputra says this, cries of 'Fie!' are heard from all the elders in that sabha. The entire conclave grows distraught, and the kings there yield to grief. Bhishma, Drona and Kripa are bathed in perspiration. Vidura holds his head between his hands and sits like one who has lost his reason. He sits face turned down, plunged in despair, sighing like a snake.

But Dhritarashtra is glad and asks repeatedly, 'Has the stake been won? Has the stake been won?' and he cannot hide his excitement.

Karna, Dussasana and some others laugh aloud, while tears flow down the faces of everyone else in the sabha.

And Subala's son, flushed with success, cries again and again, 'I have won! I have won your precious stake.'

He picks up the dice and flings them into the air in evil excitement."

CANTO 65

DYUTA PARVA CONTINUED

"Duryodhana says, 'Kshatta, go and fetch the Pandavas' most beloved wife Draupadi here. Let her sweep the chambers, force her to, and let the unfortunate woman live among our serving women.'

Vidura cries, 'Don't you know, O wretch, that with these words you are tying a noose around your neck? Don't you realise that you are hanging over the edge of a cliff? Being a deer yourself, dare you provoke so many tigers to anger? Snakes of deadly venom, stirred to fury, are upon your head! Vile Duryodhana, do not provoke them further lest you go straight to Yama's land.

I say that no slavery attaches to Krishnaa because Yudhishtira staked her after he lost himself and ceased to be his own master. Dhritarashtra's son wins treasure at dice even like the bamboo which fruits only when it is about to die. Intoxicated, he does not see in his final moments the enmity and terrors that this gambling brings.

No man should speak so viciously and pierce the hearts of others. No man should subdue his enemies through dice and other contemptible methods. No one should speak such harsh words, of which the Vedas disapprove and which wound others and lead one straight to hell. One speaks cruelly, and stung by his words, another burns day and night, for such words pierce the very heart. So, the wise man never lets fly these barbs from his lips, aiming them at anyone.

Once a goat swallowed a hook, and when the hook pierced it the hunter set the animal's head upon the ground and tore the hook out rending its throat fearfully. Duryodhana the Pandavas' wealth is a similar hook: do not swallow it and imperil yourself. Do not make enemies of them.

Pritha's sons never speak such savage words. Only base men, who are like dogs, use such speech, and towards all classes of men: vanaprasthas, grihasthas, sannyasins and muktas. Alas that Dhritarashtra's son does not know that dishonesty is one of the dreadful doors which leads into hell. Alas that so many of the Kurus, Dussasana among them, followed him eagerly down the path of adharma in this game of dice.

Gourds may sink and stones float, boats might also sink in water, always, but this foolish king, Dhritarashtra's son, will not listen to what I say, which might save him. I have no doubt that he will cause the destruction of the Kurus.

When friends and well-wishers speak words of wisdom and these go unheeded, and when, rather, only temptation waxes, devastation is bound to overtake all the heirs of Kuru.'"

DYUTA PARVA CONTINUED

Vaisampayana said, "Drunk with pride, Dhritarashtra's son hisses, 'Fie on you, Kshatta!' and his gaze moving to the Pratikamin in attendance, in the midst of all those revered elders, commands that man, 'Go Pratikamin, and fetch Draupadi here. You have no fear of the sons of the Pandavas. Vidura raves because he is afraid. Besides, he never wishes for our prosperity.'

The Pratikamin, a man of the Suta caste, hears the words of the king and hurries to the apartments of the Pandavas, and entering like a dog a lion's den, approaches the queen of the sons of Pandu.

He says, 'Yudhishtira became intoxicated with dice play, O Draupadi, and Duryodhana has won you. So come now to Dhritarashtra's palace. I will take you there and put you to some menial task.'

Draupadi says, 'Pratikamin, what are you saying? Which Kshatriya will wager his wife at dice? Surely Yudhishtira was drunk with the play; could he find nothing else to stake?'

The Pratikamin says, 'When he had nothing else to stake, Pandu's son Ajatasatru staked you. He first wagered his brothers, then himself, and at last you, O Queen.'

Draupadi says, 'O Sutaputra, go and ask that gambler in the sabha if he lost himself first or me. After that come back here and I will go with you.'

The messenger returns to the court and repeats what Draupadi said for all to hear. He says to Yudhishtira, sitting among the kings, 'Draupadi asks you, "Whose lord were you when you lost me at dice? Did you lose yourself first or me?"'

But Yudhishtira sits like a man demented, one who has lost his reason, and makes no reply to the Suta, good or ill.

Then Duryodhana says, 'Let the Panchala princess come here and ask her question. Let all in this sabha listen to the exchange between Yudhishtira and her.'

Obedient to Duryodhana's command, though himself distrait, the messenger returns to the palace and says to Draupadi, 'Princess, they summon you to the sabha. It seems the end of the Kurus has drawn near. When Duryodhana orders you to appear in the court how will that witless king save his fortunes?'

Draupadi says, 'The Great Ordainer of the world has decreed that joy and misery attend on both the wise and the witless, equally. Yet, it is told that dharma is the one highest thing in this life, which if cherished will surely bless us. Let the Kauravas not abandon dharma now.

Go back to the sabha and tell them what I have said about dharma. I am prepared to do what the wise elders of the court, men that know dharma well, tell me to.'

The Suta returns to the court and repeats Yagnaseni's words. But no one says anything; they all sit with their faces turned down for they know the lust and resolve of Dhritarashtra's son.

However, O Bharatarishabha, Yudhishtira sends his own trusted messenger to Draupadi, ordering her to appear, even if crying bitterly, before her father-in-law Dhritarashtra, though she wore but a single piece of cloth upon her body and her navel was exposed, for she has her period. That intelligent messenger, O Rajan, goes quickly to Draupadi's chambers and gives her Yudhishtira's message.

Meanwhile, the stricken Pandavas cannot decide what they should do. Duryodhana, his heart bursting with joy, lets his eyes range over them, and says to the Suta, 'Pratikamin, fetch her here. Let the Kauravas answer her question to her face.'

Bound by his master's command, yet terrified of Draupadi's wrath, the Suta musters the courage to address the sabha again, 'What shall I say to Krishnaa?'

Duryodhana says, 'Dussasana, this son of my Suta, of little intelligence, fears Bhima. So, my brother, go yourself and bring Panchali here, by force if need be. Our enemies now depend on our will, they belong to us. What can they do to you?'

Dussasana rises, his eyes blood-red, stalks into the apartments of the Pandavas and says to Draupadi, 'Come, come, O Krishnaa, princess of Panchala, we have won you. O you whose eyes are as big as lotus leaves, you must now accept the Kurus for your new lords. You have been won fairly, come now to the sabha.'

Hearing him, Draupadi, trembling, jumps up in anguish, covres her face gone pale with her hands in distress and runs towards Dhritarashtra's antahpura, where the women of his household are. Roaring, Dussasana runs after her and seizes that queen by her tresses, so long and blue and wavy. Alas! Those locks that had been sprinkled with holy water during the great Rajasuya, and sanctified with mantras, Dhritarashtra's feral son now seizes, forgetting the prowess of the Pandavas; by her hair he drags Krishnaa into the sabha, while she shakes like a banana plant during a storm.

Hauled along by him, she cries, 'Wretch, it degrades you to take me like this before the sabha! I have my period and I am wearing just a single cloth.'

But Dussasana drags Panchali mercilessly, while she prays in despair to Krishna and Jishnu, who are Nara Narayana upon the Earth.

He roars at her, 'Whether you have your period or not, whether you wear a single cloth or are naked, you have been won at dice and you will live among our serving women!'

Her hair in disarray, half her single cloth come loose, modest Panchali, dragged into the sabha, consumed by rage, protests weakly, 'In this sabha are great men, all equal to Indra, men who know all the Shastras, who devotedly perform yagnas, some of whom are truly my superiors and others who deserve to be revered as such. I cannot stay before them in this state.

Vile, cruel wretch, do not drag me like this! Do not uncover me so. My husbands will not forgive you, not if Indra and all the Devas be your allies. Dharma Deva's son is bound now by the dictates of dharma. But dharma is subtle, and only men who have great clearness of vision can know it.

I will not blame my lord with a word to say that he has broken dharma by an atom. O you have dragged me before these Kuru heroes when I am in my season, and this is surely a great sin. Yet no one here rebukes you. Surely, they are of the same mind as you.

O, truly, truly, the dharma of the Bhaaratas is lost! Truly, the dharma of the Kshatriya is gone! Else these Kurus in this sabha would never silently look on at this vile thing which you have done.

Oh, Drona and Bhishma have lost their tejas, and so also has the renowned Kshatta, and this king. Otherwise why do these greatest of Kuru elders look silently on this great crime?'

So does Krishnaa of the slender waist wail out her anguish in that sabha. She looks at her already angry lords with her teary eyes, and inflames them further with that glance of hers. They are not so distressed at having been robbed of their kingdom, their wealth, of their costliest jewels, as by that look from Krishnaa moved by modesty and rage.

Dussasana sees her gaze at her husbands and drags her more roughly still, crying, 'Slave! Slave!' while he laughs aloud. Karna hears him and laughs loudly as well. And Subala's son Sakuni, Gandhara king, applauds Dussasana. But all else in that sabha, other than these three and Duryodhana are filled with sorrow at seeing Krishnaa dragged around coarsely in sight of everyone.

Bhishma says, 'Blessed one, dharma is subtle and I find myself unable to answer your question with any certitude, for though it is true that he who has lost himself owns nothing anymore, yet a wife is always at the disposal of her husband. Yudhishtira will renounce the whole world with all the wealth in it but he will never abandon dharma. The son of Pandu said, "I am lost" and so I cannot decide this thing. Sakuni has no equal among men at dice play, still Kunti's son played willingly against him. Yudhishtira himself does not think that Sakuni cheated. No, I cannot decide this matter.'

Draupadi says, 'My king was summoned to this sabha, and though he has no skill at dice, he was made to play against a masterly, base, deceitful and desperate gambler. How can you say that he played willingly? Acting in cohort, these wretched, sinful ones deprived Pandu's eldest son of his reason and then vanquished him. At first, he did not suspect their motives but now he has understood.

Here in this sabha are Kuru elders who are lords of both their sons and their daughters-in-law. Let them all think about what I say and then answer my question of dharma.'

Krishnaa sobs piteously, looking from time to time at her helpless husbands, while Dussasana says many cruel, vile things to her. Seeing her dragged thus into that sabha during her period, with her single cloth come loose, seeing her in that state which she little deserves, Bhima is stirred beyond endurance and, looking straight at Yudhishtira, gives way to fury."'

CANTO 67

DYUTA PARVA CONTINUED

"Bhima says, 'Yudhishtira, gamblers keep many loose women in their homes, but even they do not wager their women, good or shameless, at gambling. Our enemies won all the wealth, all the precious things, which the king of Kasi gave us, jewels and animals, gold, coats of fine mail; they won all the excellent weapons which other kings of the world gave us; they won our kingdom, your brothers and yourself.

Not all this stirred my anger, for you are our lord. But this, the wagering of Draupadi, is a dreadful sin; our innocent wife does not deserve this. The Pandavas are her lords, yet just because of you these villainous Kauravas are tormenting her. For her sake, O King, my anger falls on you and I mean to burn those hands of yours which wagered Panchali. Sahadeva, bring me fire!'

Arjuna says quickly, 'Bhimasena, you have never spoken like this before! For sure these vile enemies have destroyed your high dharma. You must not fulfil the wishes of the enemy. Remain with dharma; do not cross our virtuous elder brother.

The enemy summoned the king, and remembering Kshatriya dharma, he played dice against his will. That can only add greatly to our honour and fame.'

Bhima relents and says, 'Dhananjaya, if you did not remind me that our brother acted in accordance with Kshatriya dharma, I would have taken his hands by force and burnt them in a fire.'

Seeing the Pandavas distraught and Panchali in anguish, Dhritarashtra's son Vikarna says, 'O Kings, answer Yagnaseni's question, for if we do not, all of us will surely go to hell. How is it that Bhishma and Dhritarashtra, the eldest of the Kurus, and also Mahatma Vidura do not say anything? Bharadwaja's son, Acharya to us all, and Kripa are here. Why do these Brahmanottamas not answer the question?

And the other kings gathered here, from all parts of the land, give a reply to Draupadi, each according to his judgement and with no thought towards anger or gain. Kings, answer the question asked of you by Drupada's blessed daughter, declare which side each of you takes.'

Vikarna repeatedly appeals to those present in that sabha, but none of the kings says a word to answer him, good or ill. Vikarna begins to rub his hands together loudly and to sigh like a snake.

Finally, the prince says, 'You kings of the Earth, you Kauravas, you may or not answer Draupadi but I will say what I think is just. Purushottamas, it is said that hunting, drinking, gambling and over indulgence in women are the four vices of kings. The king who is addicted to these lives without dharma, and men do not take what such a king says or does seriously.

Urged on by deceitful gamblers, Pandu's son Yudhishtira was absorbed in one of these vices when he made Draupadi his stake. Besides, innocent Draupadi is also the common wife of all the sons of Pandu. Then, Yudhishtira had already lost himself when he wagered her. Finally, Sakuni persuaded him to wager the queen. Considering all these, I believe that Draupadi has not been won.'

The sabha roars its approval to hear what Vikarna says; all the kings praise him and censure Sakuni. But Karna jumps up in a froth, and waving his mighty arms, cries, 'Vikarna, it seems this sabha is full of contradictions! As for your anger, it is like fire kindled from a faggot, which consumes the faggot itself.

These great personages here have not said a word, though repeatedly asked by Krishnaa. They all regard Drupada's daughter to have been fairly won. You, O son of Dhritarashtra, are immature and bursting with outrage. You are just a boy but you speak in this sabha as if you were an old man. You do not know what dharma truly is, and like a fool you insist that Krishnaa who has been fairly won has not been won at all.

Dhaartarashtra, how do you say she is not won when the eldest Pandava staked all he owned in this sabha? Bharatarishabha, Draupadi is part of what Yudhishtira owns. So how do you say that what has been justly won has not been won at all? Yes, Sakuni asked for her to be wagered and the Pandava agreed. Then how do you say she was not won?

And if you think that her being fetched here wearing a single cloth is a crime, let me dispel your callowness. Kurunandana, the Gods have ordained only one husband for every woman, but Draupadi has many. It is certain that she is far from chaste. To bring her in this sabha wearing one cloth, or even to strip her naked here is no crime at all, for she is already such a woman.

Whatever wealth the Pandavas had – she herself and these sons of Pandu, too – have all been justly won by Sakuni.

Dussasana, this Vikarna who seems to speak like a wise man is only a boy. I say strip the Pandavas of their robes and strip Draupadi of her cloth, as well!'

Hearing this, O Bhaarata, the Pandavas take off their upper garments and throw them down. Then, O Rajan, Dussasana lays hold of Draupadi's cloth and begins to pull it away from her body roughly, before all the sabha.

Draupadi, in despair, thinks of Hari, and cries aloud, 'Govinda, you who dwell in Dwaraka, O Krishna, lover of the gopis! Kesava, don't you see how the Kauravas shame me? Lord, Lakshmipathe, Lord of Vraja, destroyer of sorrow, Janardana, save me from drowning in the Kaurava sea. Krishna, Krishna, Mahayogin, Soul of the Universe, Creator of all things, save me, I am in dire trouble and losing my mind here among these Kurus!'

Covering her face, still so stunningly beautiful, thinking of Krishna, of Hari, Lord of the three worlds, Draupadi's cries these words out to him. Krishna hears her and is moved.

At which, while Yagnaseni still wails out to him, as also to Vishnu and Hari and to Nara for protection, invisible Dharma Deva covers her in fine cloths of many colours. Each layer of cloth which Dussasana tears from her reveals another below it, as exquisite and lustrous. Quickly, hundreds and hundreds of robes of many hues lie piled on the floor.

A deep roar of many voices rises from the sabha, and all the kings begin to applaud the amazing spectacle, to applaud Draupadi and to censure Dussasana. Then Bhima, clenching his great fists, his lips quivering in anger, swears a terrible oath in the midst of all those kings, an oath in a loud and echoing voice.

Bhima cries, 'Hear me, you Kshatriyas of the world! Words that I will speak now have never been spoken by another man, nor will anyone in the future ever speak them. Lords of earth, if after what I say I do not do what I swear I will, let me find the realm of my dead ancestors.

I swear that I will tear this beast Dussasana's breast open with my hands and drink his blood. If I do not let me die!'

Hearing Bhima's dreadful oath, their hair stands on end and everyone in that sabha applauds him and curses Dussasana. Masses of bright coloured cloth, all dragged from Draupadi's body, are piled on the floor of the sabha, and finally, exhausted and defeated, Dussasana gives up and sits down in shame, while again those gods among men gathered in that court cry 'Fie!' at him, to see the plight and disgrace of the sons of Pandu.

So loudly do those Kshatriyas roar that anybody who hears them trembles. Now every honest man in that sabha begins to say, 'Alas! The Kauravas still do not answer the question which Draupadi asked.'

Now they blame Dhritarashtra, all together, making a loud clamour. Then Vidura, master of dharma, waves his hands, silencing them, and says, 'O you who sit in this sabha, Draupadi sobs helplessly having asked her question. Yet you do not answer her and you betray virtue and dharma with your silence.

Like one being burnt by fire does a woman in distress seek the mercy of a conclave of righteous men. With truth and dharma does such an assembly quench that fire. The aggrieved woman asks the sabha what her rights are, according to dharma, and those in the sabha must answer, without prejudice or self-interest.

O Kings, Vikarna has answered Panchali, as he knows dharma, and you must also answer her. He who knows dharma and attends a sabha incurs the sin of lying if he fails to do so, just as he who replies falsely, or with prejudice, gains the same sin. The knowing tell the ancient tale of Prahlada and Angiras's son to illustrate this.

Long ago, there was a king of the Daityas called Prahlada. He had a son named Virochana. To marry a wife, Virochana quarrelled with Angiras' son Sudhanwan. Each staked his life, saying "I am superior to you!" for the sake of the woman, and they made Prahlada their arbiter to decide between them.

They said to him, "Which of us is superior? Answer this without falsehood."

Prahlada was afraid and looked at Sudhanwan, who, blazing in anger even like Yama's danda, said, "If you answer falsely or do not answer, your head will be split in a hundred pieces by Indra's thunderbolt!"

Trembling like a leaf of a fig tree, Prahlada went to Kasyapa of great tejas. The Daitya said to the Sage, "Most illustrious and exalted one, you know dharma entirely and you guide the Devas, the Brahmanas and the Asuras, too.

I find myself on the horns of a great dilemma regarding dharma. I ask you, what realms are found by one who does not answer a question or answers it falsely?"

Kasyapa replied, "He who knows but does not answer a question, from temptation, anger or fear, casts a thousand nooses of Varuna upon himself, just as he does who answers falsely. At the end of each year one paasa shall be loosened. So, he who knows should answer truthfully and not hide anything.

If virtue, struck by sin, comes to a sabha for help, it is the duty of everyone in that assembly to remove the barb, else they themselves shall be pierced by it. In a sabha where a truly censurable act is not rebuked, half the sin of that omission attaches to the head of the sabha, a fourth to the one who has sinned and another fourth to those who held their peace and did not speak out against the crime.

However, in a sabha where the sinner is reprimanded, the lord of the sabha is freed from all his sins and the others also incur none. Then, only the sinner finds sin for himself and pays alone for it.

Prahlada, they who answer falsely those who ask them about dharma, destroy the punya of seven generations before and after them.

The grief of one who loses all his wealth, one who loses a son, one who is in debt, one who is separated from his friends, that of a woman who has lost her husband, of one who loses his all through the king's demand, of a sterile woman, of one who is being eaten by a tiger, a woman who is one of two wives, and of one who is deprived of his wealth by false witnesses: all these the Devas have declared to be equal.

All these combined accrue to one who speaks falsely. A man becomes a witness by his having seen, heard, and understood a thing. So, a witness must always tell the truth. A witness who speaks truly never loses his punya or his worldly possessions."

Hearing Kasyapa, Prahlada told his son, "Sudhanwan is superior to you, just as his father Angiras is my superior. Sudhanwan's mother is also superior to your mother. So, O Virochana, this Sudhanwan is now the lord of your life."

Sudhanwan said, "Because you have kept dharma, unmoved by love for your child, I say let your son live for a hundred years.'"

Vidura continues, 'So, let all those in this sabha think carefully, deeply on what answer they should make to Draupadi's question.'

The other kings do not say a word. But Karna says loudly to Dussasana, 'Take this serving woman away into the antahpura.'

Dussasana begins to haul away the helpless and chaste Draupadi, who is trembling and crying piteously to her lords, the Pandavas."

CANTO 68

DYUTA PARVA CONTINUED

"Draupadi cries, 'Wait a little, O worst of men, evil-hearted Dussasana. I have something to do, a dharma which I have not yet done because I was hardly in my senses after this wretch dragged me from my chambers. I fold my hands and salute these venerable elders in the Kuru sabha. That I could not do this before cannot be my fault.'

Dussasana hauls her more savagely than before, and Draupadi falls to the ground and wails in that great sabha, 'Only once in my life, during my swayamvara, did such a gathering of kings ever see me, never before or after, until today when I have been dragged here. She whom even the winds and the Sun never saw before, even in her palace, is today exposed to the gaze of this host of men.

Alas, in my palace, the sons of Pandu could not suffer me to be touched even by the wind, and today they can stand my being seized by this dog. Alas, these Kauravas also suffer their daughter-in-law, who is unworthy of such treatment, to be tormented before them. Surely, it seems that the age has grown dark.

I am high-born and chaste. What can wound me more than being forced to come into this public court? Where is that dharma for which these kings were noted? We all know that the kings of old never brought their wives into their courts. Oh, that ancient custom has vanished from among the Kurus, or how has the wife of the Pandavas, the sister of Prihasta's son, she who is Krishna's sakhi, been dragged into this sabha?

O you Kauravas, I am the wife of Yudhishtira Dharmaputra, who hails from the same line as your king. Now tell me if I am your serving maid or not, and I will cheerfully accept your answer. This vile destroyer of the honour of the Kurus, hurts me sorely and, O Kauravas, I cannot bear it anymore.

You Kings, I want to hear your answer to my question: am I won or not? Whatever you say, I will accept your verdict.'

Bhishma answers her, 'Blessed child, I have already said that the course of dharma is subtle, and even the most enlightened in this world cannot always fathom it.

In this world, whatever a strong man calls dharma others accept as being so, even if the truth is very different. But what a weak man calls dharma is hardly regarded, even if it is indeed the highest virtue. What you ask is deep and grave, intricate and subtle, and I find myself unable to answer with any certainty.

However, there is no doubt that all the Kurus have become slaves to greed and folly, and our race shall very soon find its destruction. Blessed child, the family into which you have come as a daughter-in-law never abandons dharma, whatever calamities it faces. Panchali, you are plunged in grief, yet you also keep your eyes on dharma.

These elders here, Drona and the others, of mature years and knowers of dharma, sit with their heads bent down even like dead men, from whose bodies life has gone. I feel that Yudhishtira is the one best suited to answer your question. Let him say if you have been won or not.'"

CANTO 69

DYUTA PARVA CONTINUED

Vaisampayana said, "From fear of Duryodhana, the kings present in that sabha do not say a word, good or ill, although they see Draupadi crying piteously, like a female osprey, and hear her appealing to them repeatedly. Duryodhana sees those kings, their sons and grandsons all keeping quiet, and smiles.

He says to Draupadi, 'Yagnaseni, let your husbands Bhima of mighty strength, Arjuna, Nakula and Sahadeva answer your question. Panchali, for your sake let them declare in the midst of these honourable men that Yudhishtira is not their lord, and let them thus make great Yudhishtira a common liar. If they do, you will be free from the bondage of slavery.

Let the illustrious son of Dharma, who always keeps dharma, who is like Indra himself, declare whether or not he is your lord. And at what he says, accept either the Pandavas or ourselves. Indeed, all the Kauravas in this sabha float upon the sea of your distress. They are kind and generous and, looking at your pitiable husbands, cannot answer your question.'

Everyone in that court applauds loudly, while surreptitiously making signs to one another through movements of their eyes and lips. Some cry, 'Oh!' and 'Alas!' The Kauravas hear what their brother says and are overjoyed, and the other kings look sidelong at Yudhishtira, waiting to hear what he will say. All are curious to hear what Arjuna, Pandu's son never defeated in battle will say, and Bhimasena, and the twins.

When the hum of many voices ceases, waving his mighty arms smeared with sandalwood paste, Bhima says, 'If this Mahatman Yudhishtira Dharmaraja, our eldest brother, had not been our lord, we would never have forgiven the Kurus. He is the lord of all our dharma and punya, the lord of our lives. If he regards himself as won, all of us have also been won. If this were not so, which creature whose feet touches this Earth and is mortal would escape me alive after touching Panchali's precious tresses?

Look at these arms of mine, like iron maces. Even he of a hundred sacrifices could not escape their clasp. Bound by the ties of dharma and bhakti owed to our eldest brother, and urged repeatedly by Arjuna to be silent, I restrain myself from doing terrible things. But if Yudhishtira commanded me, I would kill these vile sons of Dhritarashtra, making blows do the work of swords, why, like a lion killing a herd of small animals.'

When Bhima says this, Bhishma, Drona and Vidura say to him, 'Forbear, O Bhima, for you can do anything.'"

CANTO 70

DYUTA PARVA CONTINUED

"Karna says, 'Among all in this sabha, three – Bhishma, Vidura, and Drona – seem to be independent indeed, for they speak ill of their master, censure him and never wish for his prosperity.

Excellent Panchali, the slave, the son and the wife are always dependent. They cannot earn wealth, for whatever they earn belongs to their master. You are the wife of a slave, who cannot own anything. Go now to Dhritarashtra's antahpura and serve the king's relatives. That is now your proper place, for O Princess, all the sons of Dhritarashtra and not the sons of Pritha are now your masters.

Beautiful one, choose another husband for yourself, one who will not gamble you away to become a slave. It is known that women, especially slaves, are not to be censured if they freely choose husbands for themselves. So, you do so now.

Nakula has been won, as have Bhimasena, Yudhishtira, Sahadeva and Arjuna. And, Yagnaseni, you are now a slave, and your husbands who are also slaves cannot be your husbands anymore.

Ah, does Pritha's son think of life, prowess and manhood as being useless that he offers this daughter of Drupada, the king of Panchala, in the presence of this entire sabha, as a stake at dice?'

Bhima, a picture of misery, breathed hard, but obedient to his king and bound by dharma, he can only blaze at everything around with his eyes, and say, 'Rajan, I cannot even be angry at what this son of a Suta says, for we have truly become slaves. But Yudhishtira, could our enemies dare say this to me if you had not wagered Draupadi?'

Duryodhana says to Yudhishtira who is silent, as if he has lost his mind, 'O King, Bhima and Arjuna, and the twins also, are under your sway. You answer the question. Say if you think that Krishnaa has been won or not.'

Saying this to Kunti's son, and wanting to encourage Karna and taunt Bhima, Duryodhana suddenly bares his left thigh, his thigh like the stem of a plantain tree or the trunk of an elephant, his thigh graced with every auspicious sign and endowed with the strength of thunder, and shows it to Draupadi.

Bhima's red eyes bulge, and he says to Duryodhana in the midst of all those kings, words like arrows, 'Let not Bhima Vrikodara never attain the realms gained by his sires if he does not break that thigh of yours during the Great War!'

And sparks of fire come forth from Bhima's wrathful body, like those which fly from every crack in a tree on fire.

Vidura now says, addressing the entire sabha, 'You kings of Pratipa's race, behold the great danger which rises from Bhimasena. Know for certain that this great calamity that threatens to overtake the Bhaaratas has been sent by Destiny itself.

Dhritarashtra's sons have gambled, ignoring every tenet of dharma. Even now they insist that a queen of our royal house is their slave, and here will the good fortune of your kingdom end. Look, how they consult evilly among themselves. Kauravas, take into your hearts what I am saying. If you corrupt dharma here, this sabha will be ruined.

If Yudhishtira staked Yagnaseni before he lost himself, he would then certainly have been her master. However, if man who is himself lost and cannot own any possession wagers something, it is like wealth won or lost in a dream. Do not, all of you, listen to this Gandhara king and fall away from the indubitable truth.'

Duryodhana says, 'I am content to abide by what Bhima, Arjuna and the twins say. Let them declare that Yudhishtira is not their master, and Yagnaseni will be free from bondage.'

Arjuna says, 'This illustrious Kaunteya, Yudhishtira Dharmatma, was certainly our master before he began to play. But when he had lost himself, let all the Kauravas judge whose master he could be after that.'

Just then, a jackal begins to howl dismally in the very homa-chamber of King Dhritarashtra's palace. Rajan, donkeys bray in response to the jackal's ululating howls. Then dreadful birds also join the cacophony from every side with their various screeches and cries.

Vidura, who knows all things, and Subala's daughter Gandhari, also, understand what those terrible sounds portended. Bhishma, Drona and the wise Gautama cry, '*Swashti! Swashti!*'[1] Gandhari and Vidura anxiously explain the wild omens to the king.

Dhritarashtra says, 'Evil-hearted Duryodhana, ruin has already come to us when you speak in such vile language to a wife of these Kururishabhas, especially to Draupadi herself.'

The wise Dhritarashtra, wanting to save his kin from disaster, begins to console Krishnaa. He says to her, 'Ask me for any boon you want, O Panchali. So chaste and devoted to virtue, you are the first among all my daughters-in-law.'

Draupadi says, 'O Bharatarishabha, if you will grant me a boon, I ask that the handsome Yudhishtira Dharmatma be freed from slavery, for let no thoughtless child call my son Prativindhya, of great tejas of mind, the son of a slave, for my prince is a superior boy and has been raised by kings.'

---

[1] A blessing.

Dhritarashtra says to her, 'Auspicious Panchali, let it be as you want. Excellent princess, ask for another boon for my heart is inclined to grant you a second wish. You deserve more than one.'

Draupadi says, 'O Rajan, let Bhimasena, Dhananjaya and the twins have their liberty back, and their chariots and bows.'

Dhritarashtra says, 'Blessed daughter, let it be as you wish. Ask me for a third boon, for just two boons do not sufficiently honour you. You are virtuous, the best of all my daughters-in-law.'

Draupadi says, 'Best of kings, most illustrious one, greed always fetches the loss of dharma. I do not deserve a third boon, and so I dare not ask for one. O King of kings, it is said that a Vaisya may ask one boon, a Kshatriya woman two boons, a Kshatriya man three, and a Brahmana a hundred.

Maharajan, now that my husbands are free from ignominious bondage, they can achieve their own prosperity through their dharma and deeds.'"

CANTO 71

DYUTA PARVA CONTINUED

"Karna says caustically, 'Never have we heard of such a wonderful thing being accomplished by any woman famed through the world for her beauty. When both the sons of Pandu and Dhritarashtra's princes were stirred by anger, this Draupadi has become the Pandavas' salvation. The sons of Pandu were drowning in a sea of distress and Panchali became a boat to them and has brought them safely ashore.'

Hearing this in the midst of all the Kurus, the angry Bhimasena says desperately to Arjuna, 'Devala Maharishi has said that three lights live in every person, their children, their deeds and their knowledge, for from these three all creation springs.

When life comes to an end and the body decays and a man is cast off by his relatives, these three become useful. But the light in us has been dimmed by the humiliation of our wife. How, Arjuna, can a son born from this shamed queen ever be useful to us?'

Arjuna replies, 'Bhima, superior men never react to the harsh words with which inferior men might pierce them. Men who have earned honour for themselves, even if they can retaliate, forget the hostility shown them by their enemies and only treasure their good deeds.'

Bhima says, 'Yudhishtira, shall I kill all these enemies, even here in this sabha, or shall I tear them up by their life-roots outside the palace? Ah, what need have I for words or your command? I will kill them at once and then you will rule over the whole world, without a rival.'

Saying this Bhima and the twins, like lions in the midst of a herd of lesser beasts, glare angrily around them. However, Arjuna Swetakarma, he of white deeds, tries to pacify his older brother with appealing looks. But Bhima Mahabaho blazes again in wrath. Rajan, fire issues from Vrikodara's ears and nostrils with flames, sparks and smoke.

His brow is knit and furrowed, his face is terrible, and he is like Yama himself during the Pralaya. Then Yudhishtira puts his arms around Bhima and forbids him, saying 'Do not be like this. Be silent and peaceful.'

Having restrained red-eyed Bhima, Yudhishtira, with folded hands, approaches his uncle Dhritarashtra."

DYUTA PARVA CONTINUED

"Yudhishtira says, 'O King, you are our master. Command us what we should do. O Bhaarata, we want to always remain obedient to you.'

Dhritarashtra replies, 'Be blessed, O Ajatasatru. Go in peace and safety. I command you to go and rule your own kingdom with your wealth. And, my child, I have another command for you which, I beg you, take to your heart. It is the plea of an old man and will provide nurture to you.

Yudhishtira, child, you know the subtle path of dharma. You own great wisdom, yet you are humble and you wait upon your elders. Where there is intelligence, there is forbearance; so, O Bhaarata, follow the counsels of peace.

The axe sinks into wood but not stone, and you will listen while Duryodhana will not. The best of men never remember the hostile actions of their enemies, they see only the good and not the evil even in those that harm them. And they never seek enmity or revenge.

Also, the good do good without expecting anything in return. Yudhishtira, only the worst men speak harshly during a quarrel; while mediocre men reply in kind when spoken to harshly. But the good and the wise never pay heed to or retort in kind to harshness.

The good know themselves and understand the feelings of others; hence, they think only of the goodness in other men not the darkness. You have always been honourable, never breaking the bounds of dharma, artha, kama and moksha. My son, forget Duryodhana's harshness.

Look at your mother Gandhari and at me, if you wish to remember only what is good. O Bhaarata, look at me, who am a father to you, and am old and blind, and still alive. It was only to see our friends and also to examine the strengths and weaknesses of my children that I allowed the game of dice.

Rajan, those among the Kurus who have you for their king and the wise Vidura, who knows every Shastra deeply, for their minister, surely have nothing to grieve over. In you is virtue, in Arjuna patience, in Bhimasena might, and in the twins, those best of men, is pure reverence for their elders.

Be you blessed, O Yudhishira! Return to Khandavaprastha, and let there be brotherly love between you and your cousins. Let your heart always be fixed on dharma.'

When his uncle speaks thus to him, Yudhishtira Dharmaraja then pays every homage and courtesy to his elders, and sets out for Khandavaprastha with his brothers. Their hearts glad now, and Draupadi with them, they climb into their chariots, which are all the colour of clouds, and ride towards the city called Indraprastha."

CANTO 73

DYUTA PARVA CONTINUED

Janamejaya says, "How did Dhritarashtra's sons feel when they learnt that, with Dhritarashtra's leave, the Pandavas had left Hastinapura with their kingdom, all their wealth and jewels returned to them?"

Vaisampayana says, "O King, when he learns that wise Dhritarashtra has given the Pandavas leave to return to their capital, Dussasana hurries to his brother. O Bharatarishabha, arriving in Duryodhana's presence, the stricken prince cries, 'Great Kshatriyas, the old man has thrown away what we won with so much trouble! He has given back everything to our enemies, all their kingdom and wealth.'

Duryodhana, Karna and Subala's son Sakuni, all of them ruled by hubris, come together in some haste, and privately, to Vichitravirya's son Dhritarashtra. They speak sweetly and artfully to him.

Duryodhana says, 'O King, have you not heard what Brihaspati the Devaguru said to Indra about mortals and politics? Parantapa, these were Guru's words: "Enemies who harm you by stratagem or by force must be killed."

If we used the Pandavas' wealth to please the kings of the earth and then fight the sons of Pandu, how could we lose? Ah, but if a man wraps angry poisonous serpents around his neck and back, how can he take them off? My father, in their chariots and armed, the angry sons of Pandu are like venomous snakes and they will certainly kill us.

Even now Arjuna rides in his chariot, wearing mail, his twin quivers strapped on, often picking up the Gandiva, while he breathes hard and casts blazing looks around him. Bhima rides in wrath, whirling his mace in his great hands. Nakula rides with his sword and his half-moon shield in his hands, and Sahadeva and Yudhishtira also have made clear what they mean to do.

Whipping their horses, they go like five winds in their chariots towards Khandavaprastha to muster their forces. They will never forgive us for humiliating them. Which of them will forget what we did to Draupadi?

Be you blest, my father, we must gamble again with the Pandavas, this time to send them into exile. Purusharishabha, only thus can we conquer them again. The wager shall be that either we or they will live in the forest for twelve years wearing deerskin, and a further thirteenth year in some city, in ajnatavasa, undiscovered, unrecognised. Either we or they will live so.

Let us cast the dice immediately, let the sons of Pandu play against us once more. Bull of the race of Bhaarata, O King, this is our highest dharma and Sakuni is a master of the rolling dice. Even if the Pandavas survive their exile, during those thirteen years we will take deep root in the kingdom and, making many allies, collect a vast and invincible army, so if the sons of Pandu reappear we will vanquish them.

Let this plan recommend itself to you, O Parantapa.'

Dhritarashtra says, 'Bring the Pandavas back even if they have gone a good way. Let them come back at once to cast the dice again.'

Drona, Somadatta and Balhika, Gautama, Vidura, the son of Drona, Dhritarashtra's great son by his Vaisya wife, and Bhurisravas, Bhishma and the mighty Vikarna all say, 'Let there be no more dice, let there be peace.'

But Dhritarashtra is partial to his sons. He ignores the counsel of his wise friends and kinsmen and summons the Pandavas back."

CANTO 74

DYUTA PARVA CONTINUED

Vaisampayana said, "Rajan, now Gandhari, in great distress for her sons, says to Dhritarashtra, 'When Duryodhana was born the wise Vidura said, "It would be well for us to send this disgrace to our race to the next world. Look how he howls again and again like a jackal; it is certain that he will cause the destruction of the Kurus."

Take what Vidura said to heart, O King of the Kurus. O Bhaarata, do not drown, from your own fault, in a sea of calamities. My lord, do not listen to these evil and foolish princes. Do not become the instrument of the brutal end of this noble House.

Who can break an embankment once it has been built, or rekindle a forest fire which has been extinguished? O Bharatarishabha, who lives that will provoke the peaceful sons of Pritha?

Ajamida, you remember all things, but still let me remind you that no scripture can restrain those that have evil hearts from doing evil. An immature man will never do as one of mature years will. Let your sons follow you, and not the other way. Let death not take them from you for ever.

I say to you today, my husband, abandon this vile prince of mine, this evil Duryodhana. From fatherly love you could not do it before, but now you must, for the time is here when, if you do not, our very race will be annihiliated.

Do not err in this, my lord, let your mind be guided by counsels of peace, virtue and true policy, and be what it naturally is. The fortune won through evil means is quickly lost, while that acquired gently takes root and swells and goes down from generation to generation.'

The king replies to Gandhari who pointed out the path of dharma to him, 'If the destruction of our race has come, let it takes its course freely, for I cannot prevent it. Let my sons' wish be granted and the Pandavas return to play another game of dice.'"

CANTO 75

DYUTA PARVA CONTINUED

Vaisampayana said, "A royal messenger, sent by Dhritarashtra, rides like the wind to Pritha's Yudhishtira, who by then has come a good way from Hastinapura. The messenger says, 'Your uncle, who is like a father to you, says, "The sabha is ready, O Pandava, come and cast the dice!"'

Yudhishtira says, 'All creatures find fruit, good and ill, by the will of the Creator. They are inevitable, if I play or not. This is a summons to dice; it is, besides, the command of the old king. Although I know that it will prove ruinous to me, I cannot refuse.'

Although a golden living animal could not exist, Rama allowed himself to be tempted by a golden deer. Truly, minds of men over whom calamities hang, become unhinged. So, Yudhishtira returns to Hastinapura with his brothers. Knowing full well how Sakuni cheated, the son of Pritha comes back to sit at dice with him again.

Those mighty Kshatriyas enter that sabha once more, while their friends grieve for them. Compelled by fate, they sit down again to gamble and, indeed, to ruin themselves.

Sakuni says, 'The aged king has given you back all your wealth. That is well. But, Bharatarishabha, listen to me, here is a stake of great value: either defeated by you at dice, we will enter the forest, wearing deerskin, and live there for twelve years, and then spend a thirteenth in a place of men, undiscovered. And if we are discovered during the thirteenth year, we will spend another twelve years in exile. However, if you lose, you, along with Krishnaa, will spend twelve years in the vana and pass the thirteenth in a place of men, in ajnatavasa. If you are found during the thirteenth year, you will go back into exile for another twelve years.

When the thirteenth year is over each one will give his kingdom back to the other. Yudhishtira, for this stake, play with us, O Bhaarata. Cast the dice.'

The other noble ones in the sabha raise their arms up in alarm and cry anxiously, and feelingly, 'Alas, Duryodhana's friends do not warn him of his great danger. Dhritarashtra, whether he understands the peril or not, it is your duty to tell him plainly.'

Yudhishtira hears this, but from a sense of shame and dharma, sits again to play dice. Though he is most intelligent and knows the consequences well, he begins to play, as if he knows that the end of the Kurus is near and it is ineluctable.

Yudhishtira says, 'Sakuni, how can a king like me, who always observes Kshatriya dharma, refuse to play when he has been summoned to dice? And so I will play with you.'

Sakuni replies, 'We have many horses and milch cows, an infinite number of goats and sheep, and elephants and treasuries and gold, and slaves both male and female. We staked all these before but now let this be our one stake: exile into the forest. If you beat us we will live in the vana for twelve years and the thirteenth in ajnatavasa. Purusharishabhas, with this determination, will we play.'

O Bhaarata, only once does he speak about the exile in the jungle. Yudhishtira accepts it and Sakuni takes up the dice. Casting them, he says to Pritha's son, 'I have won!'"

CANTO 72

DYUTA PARVA CONTINUED

Vaisampayana said, "The vanquished Pandavas prepare for their exile in the forest. One after another, in order of age, they cast off their royal robes and clothe themselves in deerskin.

Seeing those Parantapas wearing deerskin, their kingdom taken from them and ready to go into exile, Dussasana cries, 'The absolute sovereignty of the illustrious King Duryodhana has begun. The sons of Pandu have been vanquished, and plunged into ruin.

We have achieved our goal, be it by the broad or the narrow way. Today, we have more wealth and kingdom than our enemies, and we have become worthy of the praise of men, while Pritha's sons are plunged in everlasting hell. For ever, they have lost their kingdom and their happiness.

Arrogant of their wealth, they once laughed derisively at Duryodhana. Now, beaten by us and their wealth lost, they must go into the vana and exile. Let them take off their armour, their resplendent robes of celestial make; let them put on deerskins, according to the stake of Sakuni, which they accepted.

These who always boasted that they had no equals in the world will now see themselves like grains of sesame without a kernel. Though in this new garb, Pandu's sons seem like wise and powerful men installed in a sacrifice, yet they do not look men entitled to perform yagnas.

When the wise Yagnasena of the Somakas gave his daughter Panchali to the Pandavas he made a great mistake, for these sons of Pritha are like eunuchs. Yagnaseni, what joy will you have in the forest seeing your husbands wearing deerskin and threadbare valkala, impoverished, all their wealth lost?

Choose a husband for yourself from this sabha. The Kurus here are all great and self-restrained, and all of them are vastly wealthy. Choose one of them for your lord, so that the calamity which has overtaken you does not drag you into wretchedness. The Pandavas are now like sesame seeds without a kernel, like stuffed animals, or grains of rice without a husk. When they have fallen, why should you wait on them anymore? Ah, vain is the labour which seeks to press the sesame without a kernel!'

So does Dussasana, the son of Dhritarashtra, speak viciously again in the hearing of the Pandavas. At which, Bhima suddenly rushes at him in fury, like a Himalayan lion at a jackal, and roars, 'Villain, do you rave like this as only sinners do? Dare you brag in this sabha of kings after your cause has been advanced by the cheating skill of Sakuni?

As you pierce our hearts with your words like arrows, I will remember these words and pierce your heart and shed your blood in battle. And I will also send to Yamaloka those who stand behind you today, from their anger or their greed, as your protectors. Yes, them and all their sons and kin!'

But Dussasana begins to dance rudely around Bhima, clad in deerskin, who is restrained by dharma from doing him any harm, crying, 'Cow! O you cow!'

Bhima fumes, 'Dare you, wretched Dussasana? Dare you preen and brag after winning our wealth by the basest means? I say to you that if this Vrikodara, son of Pritha, does not tear open your breast and drink your blood, may he never find heaven for himself.

I say to you all that, before a great host of Kshatriyas, I will kill all these sons of Dhritarashtra and quench my wrath!'

As the Pandavas leave the sabha, the joyful Duryodhana mimics Bhima's leonine gait with mincing steps.

Vrikodara turns to that king and says, 'Fool, you think to put me down with these vile tricks? I will kill you and all who follow you soon enough, and that will be my answer to your strutting.'

With that, controlling the great anger which surges in him, the mighty and proud Bhima turns to follow Yudhishtira from the Kaurava court again. Going, he says, 'I will kill Duryodhana, and Dhananjaya will slay Karna. Sahadeva will kill Sakuni the gambler.

And hear again, all of you in this sabha, the oath I swear, and the Gods will surely make my oath come true. If we ever meet the Kurus in battle, I will kill this dog Duryodhana with my mace, and laying him on the ground I will stamp on his head with my foot. As for this other evil one, so brave with his words, I will drink his blood like a lion!'

Arjuna says, 'Bhima, the resolutions of superior men are not known only by their words. On the fourteenth year from this day, these will see what happens.'

Bhima says, 'The earth will drink the blood of Duryodhana, Karna and the evil Sakuni, and Dussasana will be the fourth.'

Arjuna says, 'Bhima, as you have sworn, I will kill this malicious, envious, harsh-tongued and vain Karna. To please Bhima, Arjuna vows that he will kill Karna and all his followers with arrows in battle. Yes, and I will send to Yama's realm all the other foolish kings who dare face me in war.

The Mountains of Himavat might move from where they are, the Sun who makes the day might lose his lustre, the Moon his coldness, but I will keep my vow. All that I have sworn will happen if, on the fourteenth year from today, Duryodhana does not return our kingdom to us with proper respect.'

After Arjuna, Madri's handsome son Sahadeva, of great tejas, eager to kill Sakuni, waves his arms and, red-eyed and sighing like a snake, cries, 'O you disgrace of the Gandhara kings, those whom you think of as defeated are not really so. You have risked death by arrows in battle, and I will do as Bhima has sworn by killing you and all your followers in war.

So, if there is anything at all that you wish to do, do it before that day comes, for then I will kill you if you keep Kshatriya dharma and do not flee the field like a dog, O son of Subala!'

Now Nakula, handsomest of all men, says, 'I will kill all these sons of Dhritarashtra, who have dared insult Draupadi in this sabha. They have wished for death and are moved by Fate and the desire to please Duryodhana. I will remember what they have said today and they will find death at Yudhishtira's command. The Earth will be devoid of Dhritarashtra's sons.'

Having sworn these oaths, those Purushavyaghras, tigers among men, all blessed with long arms, approach King Dhritarashtra."

CANTO 77

Dyuta Parva Continued

"Yudhishtira says, 'I bid farewell to all the Bhaaratas, to my Pitama, to King Somadatta, the great Bahlika, Drona, Kripa, all the other kings, Aswatthama, Vidura, Dhritarashtra, all the sons of Dhritarashtra, to Yuyutsu, Sanjaya and all the courtiers. I bid you all farewell, and returning, I will see you again.'

Overcome by shame, none of those men can make any reply to him. In their hearts, though, they pray for the welfare of that good and wise prince.

Vidura now says, 'Pritha is a princess by birth. It does not become her to go into the forest. She is old, delicate and used to luxury. She will live in my home. Know this, O sons of Pandu, and let safety always be yours.'

The Pandavas say, 'Anagha, sinless one, let it be as you say. You are our uncle and so even like our own father. We are all obedient to you, and you are, O learned one, our most revered elder. We must always obey you and, Mahatman, command us, what else shall we do?'

Vidura replies, 'Yudhishtira, in my opinion a man vanquished by foul means need feel no pain at his defeat. You know every law of dharma; Arjuna is ever victorious in battle; Bhimasena is the slayer of enemies; Nakula is the gatherer of wealth; Sahadeva is a great administrator; Dhaumya is the foremost of all who know the Vedas; and Draupadi knows both virtue and frugality well.

You are devoted to one another, feel delight in each other's company, enemies cannot divide you and you are contented. Who is there that will not envy you? O Bhaarata, this patient abstraction from the possession of the world will be of great benefit to you. No enemy, even if he were equal to Indra himself, will be able to withstand it.

Once, on the mountains of Himavat, beside Meru, Savarni taught you; in the town of Varanavata, Krishna Dwaipayana did; upon the cliff of Bhrigu, Rama; and on the banks of the Dhrishadwati, Siva himself. Maharishi Asita gave you instruction on the hills of Anjana; and you became a disciple of Bhrigu on the banks of the Kalmashi.

Narada and your priest Dhaumya will now become your Gurus. In the matter of the next world, never abandon these profound lessons you have had from the Munis. O Pandava, your intelligence is greater than even that of Ila's son Pururavas; in might, you exceed all other kings, and in virtue, even the Rishis.

Therefore, resolve earnestly to win victory, which belongs to Indra; to control your wrath, which belongs to Yama; to give charity, which belongs to Kubera; and to restrain all passions, which belong to Varuna. O Bhaarata, from the Moon take the power to please; the power to sustain from Water; patience from the Earth; energy from the Sun; strength from the Wind, and affluence from the other elements.

May welfare and immunity from disease be yours; I hope to see you return. Yudhishtira, act righteously and duly in all seasons: those of distress, those of difficulty, indeed, in all things.

O Son of Kunti, go forth with our leave. O Bhaarata, my blessings be upon you. No one can say that you have sinned, and so we do earnestly want to see you return, crowned with success.'

Bowing low to Bhishma and Drona, Yudhishtira, the son of Pandu, of prowess incapable of being baffled, says, 'Tathastu, so be it!' and departs."

CANTO 78

DYUTA PARVA CONTINUED

Vaisampayana said, "When Draupadi is about to set out she goes to the illustrious Kunti and solicits her leave. She takes her leave of the other ladies of the household, all of them plunged in grief. Saluting and embracing every one of them, as each deserves, she asks them to permit her to go away.

Then, within the inner apartments of the Pandavas, a loud wail of grief arises. Kunti, in terrible distress to see Draupadi about to go, says, her voice choking, 'My child, do not grieve that this calamity has overtaken you. You know well the dharma of women, and your behaviour and conduct are as they should be. O my princess of sweet smiles, I need not teach you your duty towards your husbands.

You are chaste and accomplished, and your qualities have adorned the race of your birth, as also the House into which you have come through marriage. Ah, the Kauravas are fortunate that your wrath has not burnt them to ashes. My daughter, go safely, blessed by my prayers. Good women never allow their hearts to come unstrung at what is inevitable. Protected by dharma, which is superior to everything, you will soon find good fortune again.

While living in the vana, keep your eye on my child Sahadeva. See that his heart does not sink under the weight of this tragedy.'

Bathed in tears, still wearing her single cloth stained with her woman's blood, her hair in disarray, saying, 'Tathastu,' Draupadi leaves her mother-in-law. As she goes, sobbing, Pritha follows her in grief. Kunti does not go far, when she sees her sons, shorn of their ornaments and royal robes, clad in deerskin, and their heads bent down with shame. She sees them surrounded by rejoicing enemies and pitying friends.

Filled by a tide of mother's love, Kunti approaches her sons. Embracing them, tears in her eyes and voice, she says, 'You are virtuous and decorous; you own every noble quality, and you are respectful towards all. You are all high-minded and serve your elders, and you are also devoted to the Gods and the performance of yagnas. Ah, then why has such disaster overtaken you?

From where this sudden reversal of fortune? I do not see through whose villainy this sin has come over you. Alas, I gave birth to you, this must be my ill luck visited on your innocent lives, for you are all blessed with the finest virtues, great vitality and prowess, strength, fortitude and power.

Oh, how will you now live in penury in the pathless forest? If I knew that one day this would be your fate, I would never have left the mountains of Satasringa to come to Hastinapura when Pandu died.

Your father was a fortunate man, as I see now, and reaped every fruit of his asceticism. He was gifted with foresight, and he rose into Swarga without feeling any pain on his sons' account. Fortunate, too, was Madri, as I look at it today. She, also, it seems, knew what the future held and chose the high path of freedom from this life, and every blessing which comes with it. Ah, Madri looked on me as her support, and her heart and her love were always fixed upon me.

I curse my desire to live, which makes me suffer like this today. My children, all of you are exceptionally worthy and dear to me. I had you all after long suffering. Oh, I cannot leave you. I will also go with you!

Oh Panchali, why do you leave me? All that lives is sure to die. Has Brahma forgotten to ordain this Kunti's death? Perhaps it is so, and that is why life does not quit me.

Krishna! O you who dwell in Dwaraka, O Sankarshana's younger brother, where are you? Why don't you deliver me and these Purushottamas from such misery? They say that you, who are without beginning and without end, save those that think of you. Why is this being proved false?

These sons of mine have always cloven to virtue, nobility, honour and prowess. They do not deserve this suffering. Oh, show them mercy! When there are such elders in our race like Bhishma and Drona and Kripa, all of whom know dharma and the world well, how does this tragedy overtake us?

O Pandu, where are you? How do you countenance your good princes to be sent into exile, defeated at dice? Sahadeva, do not go! You are my dearest child, dearer to me, O Son of Madri, than my body. Do not forsake me. You must show me some kindness. Let dharma bind your brothers to go into the vana, but you stay with me, my child, and earn your punya through serving me.'

The Pandavas console their weeping mother and, also plunged in grief, set out for the forest. Though grief-stricken himself, Vidura consoles Kunti as best he can and slowly leads her back into his home.

The women of Dhritarashtra's household hear about all that happened, about Draupadi being dragged into the sabha, about the exile of the Pandavas, and they weep and blame the Kauravas openly. Then they sit sunk in gloom, many with their lotus-like faces buried in their fair hands.

Dhritarashtra begins to think of the danger, which his sons now face, and he has no peace of mind but is a prey to constant anxiety. Utterly distraught, he sends a messenger to Vidura, saying, 'Let Kshatta come to me without a moment's delay.'

Vidura comes immediately to Dhritarashtra's palace. As soon as he arrives, the king questions him about how the Pandavas left Hastinapura."

CANTO 79

Dyuta Parva Continued

Vaisampayana said, "As soon as Vidura of great foresight enters his presence, Ambika's son, the King Dhritarashtra, asks his brother nervously, 'How did Dharmaputra Yudhishtira leave? And how Bhima and Arjuna? And how Madri's twins? How, O Kshatta, did Dhaumya proceed? And the lustrous Draupadi? I want to hear everything, Vidura, tell me everything they did.'

Vidura replies, 'Kunti's son Yudhishtira went forth covering his face with a cloth. Bhima, O King, went staring at his own mighty arms. Arjuna threw pieces of earth around him as he followed Yudhishtira. Madri's son smeared his face darkly when he went, and Nakula, also, covered his handsome face with dirt, and he was full of sorrow.

The large-eyed and beautiful Krishnaa's hair was loose and dishevelled, and she covered her face as well, following the king, and she wept ceaselessly. Rajan, Dhaumya walked with kusa grass in his hands, and he chanted the ominous mantras from the Sama Veda which are for Yama, the God of Death.'

Dhritarashtra asks, 'Tell me, O Vidura, what does all this mean, the manner of the Pandavas' going forth?'

Vidura replies, 'Although your sons persecuted him, robbed him of his kingdom and wealth, the mind of Yudhishtira Dharmatma has not yet deviated from the way of dharma. O Bhaarata, Yudhishtira is always kindly towards your sons.

Though he has been deprived of his kingdom and possessions by vile means, and wrath fills his heart, he does not open his eyes. Thinking, "I will not burn the people by looking at them with angry eyes," Pandu's royal son went forth covering his face.

Let me tell you now why Bhima went forth as he did.

"I have no equal in the strength of my arms": this is what Bhima thought, as he repeatedly flexed his mighty arms. He is proud of his strength, Vrikodara, and he flexed and stretched them to show what he would like to do to his enemies with those arms.

And Kunti's son Arjuna Savyasachin, who is perfectly ambidextrous, followed Yudhishtira, scattering bits of earth which shall be as the arrows he will loose in battle. Bhaarata, he showed the ease with which he will despatch his arrows by what he did.

Sahadeva had darkened his face, thinking that none should recognise him on this dreadful day.

Exalted one, Nakula had smeared himself with dirt, for he thought, "I must not steal the heart of any woman who sees me". So handsome is he.

Draupadi wore one piece of stained cloth, with her hair loose and crying. She meant that the wives of those who had reduced her to this will lose their husbands, their sons and all their kinsmen when thirteen years have passed. And they shall enter Hastinapura, during their periods, smeared with blood, their hair loose and forced to offer tarpana to their dead.

O Bhaarata, the learned Dhaumya, his passions restrained, held the kusa grass in his hand, its blades pointing to the south-west, and walked before the sons of Pandu, singing the mantras of the Sama Veda, which belong to Yama.

What that Brahmana meant is that, when the Kurus are slain their priests will sing the Sama mantras for their dead as he was doing.

As for the people, they are grief-stricken and repeatedly they cried out, "Alas, alas, our lords are going away! Fie on the Kuru elders that, from base greed, they acted like foolish children by banishing the heirs of Pandu. Alas, we shall all be masterless without Pandu's eldest son.

What love can we ever have for the avaricious and evil Kurus?"

Thus, O King, did the sons of Kunti, of great tejas leave, showing by their manner and with signs the resolutions that are in their hearts. As those Purushottamas left Hastinapura, gashes of lightning crackled in a cloudless sky and the Earth herself trembled. Rahu came to devour the Sun, although it was not the day of the eclipse. Meteors fell, keeping the city to their right. Jackals, vultures, crows and other carnivorous beasts and birds shrieked and cried aloud from the temples of the Gods and from the tops of sacred trees and walls and from house-tops.

All these awful omens we saw, O King, portending the destruction of the Kurus as a result of your evil counsels.'

While Dhritarashtra and Vidura speak thus together in the Kaurava sabha, before the eyes of all appears Narada, best of all Devarishis.

He says direly, 'Because of Duryodhana's sins, fourteen years from now the mighty Arjuna and Bhima will kill all the Kauravas.'

Saying this, that greatest of divine Sages, adorned with transcendent Vedic grace, rises straight into the air and vanishes.

Then, Duryodhana, Karna and Sakuni think of Drona as their only hope and refuge and offer him the kingdom. Drona says to the envious and choleric Duryodhana, Dussasana, Karna and indeed all the Bhaaratas, 'The Brahmanas all say that the Pandavas are born of the Devas and they cannot be killed. Yet, since Dhritarashtra's sons and all these kings seek my protection with reverence, I will protect them to the best of my power. Destiny is supreme, and I cannot abandon the Kauravas.

Beaten at dice, the sons of Pandu have gone into exile in the forest for twelve years. They will practise brahmacharya during these years, return in anger and take revenge on their enemies.

Once, I took his kingdom from Drupada, and he performed a yagna to have a son who would kill me. Helped by the Rishis Yaja and Upayaja, Drupada did have a son, Dhrishtadyumna, born from the sacrificial fire, and also a faultless daughter, Krishnaa. Dhrishtadyumna is now the brother-in-law of the Pandavas and dear to them. It is him that I fear.

No mortal woman bore him; he is resplendent, born with a bow and arrows and clad in armour. I am a mortal, and I do fear him. That Parantapa has taken the side of the Pandavas, and I will lose my life if I ever encounter him in battle.

O Kauravas, the world says, "Dhrishtadyumna is destined to kill Drona". What can be more painful to me? Because of you, Duryodhana, the dread time of war and death has almost come. You must prepare yourself for every exigency.

Do not think that you have achieved everything you wanted by sending the Pandavas into exile. This happiness will last just a moment, for as long as in winter a palm tree's shadow rests at its base. Perform every yagna that you can, Bhaarata, enjoy your life while you are still able and give generous charity. When thirteen years have passed great tragedy will overwhelm you.'

Dhritarashtra says, 'Kshatta, the Acharya speaks the truth. Go and bring back the Pandavas. If they do not come back, let them go with our respect and affection. They are like my sons, let them be given weapons, chariots, footsoldiers and the means to enjoy every luxury in the wilderness.'"

CANTO 80

DYUTA PARVA CONTINUED

Vaisampayana said, "When, beaten at dice, the Pandavas leave for the forest Dhiratarashtra is overcome by anxiety. While he sits restless and sighing in sorrow, Sanjaya approaches him and says, 'Lord of the earth, you have gained the whole world with all its wealth, and you have sent Pandu's sons into exile. Why, O King, are you grieving now?'

Dhritarashtra says, 'Who are they that would not grieve who must face those Kshatriyarishabhas in battle? Fighting from their great chariots, with their allies around them!'

Sanjaya says, 'Rajan, this terrible enmity is because of what you did, and it will surely fetch the destruction of the world as we know it. Although Bhishma, Drona and Vidura forbade him, your evil, shameless Duryodhana sent his Suta messenger to bring the chaste Draupadi into court.

The gods first deprive the man of his reason, to whom they wish to send defeat and disgrace. Then, that man sees everything in strange light. When doom is near, evil appears as good to his mind corrupted by sin, and he clings firmly to it. Adharma appears to be dharma and dharma as adharma to the doomed man, and invariably he chooses to tread the path of sin, for it attracts him inexorably.

The time of doom does not arrive with a cudgel upraised to smash a man's head. No, the mark of impending doom is that it makes a man see good in evil, and evil in good.

The wretches have brought unthinkable nemesis upon us all by dragging the helpless Panchali into our sabha. Who but Duryodhana, cheating at dice, could even think of bringing chaste, beautiful and intelligent Draupadi, born from no woman's womb but from the sacred fire, she who knows dharma, and shaming her in this court?

In her period, wearing only a single cloth, when the lovely Krishnaa was dragged here she looked at the Pandavas. She saw them robbed of their kingdom, their wealth, even stripped of their robes; she saw them as slaves. Bound by dharma, they could do nothing to protect her, and before these assembled kings Duryodhana and Karna spoke vile, savage words to her, while she wept in grief and anger.

All this surely portends fearful consequences.'

Dhritarashtra says, 'Sanjaya, the angry look of Drupada's daughter could consume the world. Will even a single son of mine escape death?

The wives of the Bhaaratas and Gandhari set up a great lament, wailing in grief to see the young, virtuous and beautiful Krishnaa dragged into our court. Even now, they and all my subjects weep every day.

Enraged by what was done to Draupadi, the Brahmanas, in a body, did not perform their Agnihotra that evening. The winds blew in awesome gusts even as they do at the time of the Pralaya, and there was a fearsome thunderstorm. Meteors fell from the sky, and Rahu swallowed the Sun unseasonably, terrifying the people.

Suddenly war-chariots took fire and their flagstaffs fell down, foreboding evil to the Bhaaratas. Jackals began to howl frightfully from Duryodhana's sacred fire-chamber, and asses brayed in response from all directions. Bhishma, Drona, Kripa, Somadatta and Mahatama Bahlika all left the sabha.

It was then that, at Vidura's advice, I said to Draupadi, "I will grant you boons, O Krishnaa, whatever you ask."

Panchali begged me to set the Pandavas free, and I did, commanding them to return to their capital in their chariots with their bows and arrows.

Vidura told me, "This will prove to be the end of the race of Bhaarata. This Panchali is the faultless Sri Lakshmi herself. She is divinely born and the wife of the sons of Pandu. The angry Pandavas will never forgive this insult to her, nor will the mighty Vrishni bowmen or the dauntless Panchala warriors suffer this.

With Krishna of invincible prowess to support him, Arjuna will assuredly return, surrounded by the Panchala host. Prodigious Bhimasenaa of unequalled strength will come back, whirling his mace like Yama himself with his cudgel. These kings will never be able to bear the force of Bhima's mace.

Therefore, Rajan, to me not hostility but peace for ever with the sons of Pandu seems the best course. The Pandavas have always been mightier than the Kauravas. You know that Bhima killed the great Jarasandha with his bare hands. O Bhartarishabha, make peace with the sons of Pandu.

Without any scruple or favour, unite the cousins. If you do that, you will surely find good fortune."

So Vidura said to me, speaking words of both dharma and artha. But, moved by love for my son, I did not listen to him!'"

So said Vaisampayana to Janamejaya.

End of Sabha Parva

VANA PARVA
(Part 1)

CANTO 1

ARANYAKA PARVA

AUM! I bow down to Narayana, and Nara, foremost of Purushas, and the Devi Saraswati, and utter the word Jaya!

Janamejaya said, "O Dvijottama, having been beaten at dice by Dhritarashtra's sons and their counsellors, incensed by those evil ones who so created a fierce enmity, having been spoken to so harshly, what did my ancestors, Pritha's sons, do?

Equal to Sakra in prowess, deprived suddenly of their wealth and plunged into misery, how did the Pandavas pass their days in the forest? Who followed them? How did those Mahatmas bear themselves, how did they sustain themselves and where did they live? Most illustrious Brahmanottama, how did those Kshatriyas pass twelve years in the vana, those Parantapas?

How did the princess, best among women, devoted to her husbands, so virtuous, always speaking the truth, and surely deserving no such trial, endure the exile? Tell me all this in detail, O Brahmana, for I want to hear the story of those heroes of abundant prowess and lustre. Ah, great is my curiosity."

Vaisampayana said, "Defeated at dice and incensed by Dhritarashtra's evil sons and their counsellors, Pritha's princes set out from Hastinapura through the Vardhamana gate of the city, bearing their weapons and accompanied by Draupadi; they go in a northerly direction. Indrasena and others, with their wives and servants, all together fourteen, follow them in swift chariots.

When the people hear of their leaving, they are grief-stricken and censure Bhishma and Vidura, Drona and Gautama. Gathering, they speak fearlessly to one another, 'Alas, our families, we ourselves, and our homes are all lost, when the malignant Duryodhana, supported by Sakuni, Karna and Dussasana, aspires to this kingdom.

Oh, our families, our customs, our virtue and prosperity, are all doomed, where this sinner, supported by wretches as sinful as him, aspires to the throne. And where can there be happiness, where these are gone? Duryodhana bears malice towards all his superiors; he has left dharma, and fights with his own kin.

Covetous, vain and mean, his nature is cruel. The very Earth is doomed, when Duryodhana rules. So let us go with the kind and noble Pandavas, who are self-controlled, victorious over their enemies, who are humble, honourable, and devoted to dharma!'

The people follow the Pandavas, and with folded hands say to the sons of Kunti and Madri:

'Be you blest! Where are you going, leaving us in sorrow? Wherever you go, we will follow you. We are distraught to hear how ruthless enemies vanquished you with deceit. We are your loving subjects, your devoted friends who always serve and wish you well, and it does not become you to forsake us.

We do not want to be plunged into ruin, living under the rule of the Kuru king. Purusharishabhas, listen while we describe the punya and paapa which accrue from associating with the good and the evil. As cloth, water, the ground, and sesame seeds are perfumed by contact with flowers, so are the qualities of men always produced through their associations.

Associating with fools creates illusions which entangle the mind, just as keeping company with good men, daily, leads to the practice of virtue. They who wish for moksha must associate with the wise, the old, the honest and the pure – ascetic men. They must serve such men, for the knowledge, the birth and the deeds of such men are all pure, and associating with them is superior even to studying the scriptures.

Though we have no religious merit ourselves, we will find punya if we keep the company of the good, just as we will find sin by serving sinners. The very sight and touch of the dishonest, conversation with them and their company, all cause diminution of dharma, and such men never find purity of mind.

Associating with the base impairs the understanding, and with the mediocre makes the mind mediocre, while communion with the good exalts the heart. All the attributes which are spoken of as sources of dharma, artha and kama, and which men esteem and which the Vedas extol, dwell in you, individually and jointly.

So, for our own welfare, we want to live amongst you, who possess those qualities!'

Yudhishtira says, 'We are blessed that the people, led by the Brahmanas, moved by kindness and love, credit us with merits which we do not have. But my brothers and I ask all of you to do just one thing, and you must not do otherwise, because of your affection or your pity for us.

Our grandfather Bhishma, King Dhritarashtra, Vidura, my mother and most of my well-wishers are all in Hastinapura. So, if you seek our welfare, unite together, and care for them, for they are plunged in sorrow.

Grieved by our leaving, you have come far! Go back, and let your hearts be directed with tenderness towards the relatives I entrust to you as pledges. This is the one thing upon which my heart is set, and by doing this you will do me great service and give me much satisfaction.'

When Yudhishtira Dharmatma says this the people set up a loud lament, crying, 'Alas, O king!'

Sorrowing deeply when they think of the virtues of Pritha's son, reluctantly they take leave of the Pandavas and turn back towards the city.

When the people followed them no longer, the Pandavas climb into their chariots, and riding, reach the mighty banyan tree called Pramana on the banks of the Ganga. It is dusk and Pandu's heroic sons purify themselves, touching the river's holy water, and pass the night in that place. They spend that night, only drinking water.

Some Brahmanas, both those that kept the sacred fire and those who did not, with their disciples and kin, have followed the Pandavas out of love; they, too, spend the night there with them. Surrounded by those Brahmavadis, the king shines resplendent in their midst.

And that evening, at once beautiful and terrible, those Brahmanas, having lit their sacred fires, begin to chant the Vedas and they speak among themselves. Those Brahmanottamas with swan-sweet voices spend the night comforting that best of the Kurus, the king."

CANTO 2

ARANYAKA PARVA CONTINUED

Vaisampayana said, "When night passes and day breaks, the mendicant Brahmanas stand before the Pandavas of lofty deeds, who are about to enter the forest.

King Yudhishtira, the son of Kunti, says to them, 'We have been robbed of our kingdom and wealth, robbed of everything, and we are about to enter the deep vana in sorrow. We will eat fruit and roots, and what the hunt fetches. The forest is full of danger, abounding in snakes and beasts of prey.

You will suffer privation and misery there. The sufferings of Brahmanas can overpower even the gods. That they will overwhelm me is certain. Therefore, O Brahmanas, turn back, go wherever you will.'

The Brahmanas reply, 'O King, our path is yours. We are your devotees, you who practise true dharma; do not forsake us. The very gods are compassionate to their worshippers, especially Brahmanas of self-restraint!'

Yudhishtira says, 'Regenerate ones, I am also devoted to Brahmanas. But destitution has overtaken me, and I am confused. My brothers who will gather fruit and roots and hunt deer are stupefied with the shock of losing our kingdom and the grief of Draupadi. I cannot employ them in painful or demanding tasks.'

The Brahmanas say, 'Dharmaraja, have no care about supporting us. We will follow you, providing for our own food. Through our dhyana and our prayers we will care for you, and cheer you and ourselves with pleasant conversation.'

Yudhishtira says, 'Indeed nothing pleases me more than the company of good Brahmanas. Yet, in my fall I see myself as deserving reproach. How then will I bear to look at all of you feeding yourselves, while you follow me out of your love? Ah, I curse Dhritarashtra's evil sons!'

Sobbing, the king sits upon the ground. Then a learned Brahmana, Saunaka versed in the knowledge of the Atman and skilled in Sankhya yoga, says to him, 'Day after day, causes of grief in thousands, and causes of fear in hundreds overwhelm the ignorant, but not the wise. Surely, sensible men like you never allow themselves to be deluded by actions which are contrary to true knowledge, which are fraught with every kind of evil, and which destroy moksha.

In you there dwells the understanding furnished with the eight attributes, the gyana which comes from studying the Sruti[1] and the Shastras, which knowledge provides against all evils. And men like you are never confounded, not upon finding themselves impoverished or at the affliction of their friends, either through mental or bodily unease.

Listen, and I will repeat the slokas told of old by Janaka, which deal with the subject of controlling the self. This world is afflicted with both bodily and mental suffering. Hear now the means of allaying the twin torments, both in brief and in some detail.

Disease, contact with things of pain, toil and being deprived of objects of desire cause bodily suffering. Disease is allayed with medicines, ailments of the mind through yoga and meditation. Good physicians first seek to allay the mental sufferings of their patients with pleasant conversation and offering them desirable objects.

---

[1]The Vedas.

Even as a hot iron rod immersed into a jar heats the water inside, even so mental grief brings bodily agony; and as water quenches fire, so does true knowledge allay mental disquiet. When the mind finds ease, the body finds ease also.

Affection seems to be the root of all sorrow; affection makes every creature miserable and brings on every kind of woe. Affection is the root of misery and of all fear, of joy and grief of every kind, of pain. From affection spring all motives to action, and the love of worldly goods. Both these are sources of evil, though the first is worse than the second.

As a spark fire lit in the hollow of a tree consumes the tree to its very roots, even so affection, be it ever so little, destroys both dharma and artha. A man who has merely withdrawn from worldly life cannot be said to have renounced the world. However, he who, while in active contact with the world, clearly sees its flaws, may be said to have truly renounced the world. Freed from every evil passion, his soul dependent on nothing, such a man has indeed renounced the world.

No one should seek to attach his affections either on friends or the wealth he has earned. So, also, must attachment and affection for one's own person be extinguished through knowledge. Like the lotus-leaf, which is never wetted by water, are the souls of men who can distinguish between the ephemeral and the everlasting.

Men devoted to the pursuit of the eternal, who know the scriptures and are purified by knowledge, can never be moved by affection. The man influenced by affection is tortured by desire; from the desire that springs up in his heart, his thirst for worldly possessions increases. This thirst is sinful and is the source of all anxiety. This terrible thirst, fraught with sin, leads men to sin.

Those who can renounce this thirst, never the wicked, find the happiness which does not decay with the decay of the body, which is truly the fatal disease. That joy has neither beginning nor end.

Abiding in the heart, desire destroys creatures, like an incorporeal fire. As a faggot of wood is consumed by the fire that it feeds, even so an impure person finds death from the covetousness born in his heart.

As all living creatures always have a dread of death, wealthy men live in constant dread of the king and the thief, of water and fire and even of their relatives.

A morsel of meat, if in the air, can be devoured by birds; if on the ground, by beasts of prey; if in water, by fish: even so a man of wealth is exposed to danger wherever he is. To many the wealth they own is their bane, and he who sees happiness in wealth and becomes wedded to it, never knows true happiness.

So, the accession of wealth is seen as what increases covetousness and folly; wealth alone is the root of niggardliness and boastfulness, pride, anxiety and fear. These are the miseries of men that the wise see in owning riches. Men undergo infinite miseries in the acquisition and the retention of wealth. Its expenditure is also fraught with grief. Why, sometimes life itself is lost for the sake of wealth.

Loss of wealth brings misery, and even those whom a man nurtured with his wealth become enemies for the sake of that wealth. When owning wealth is fraught with such sorrow, one should not mind its loss.

Only the ignorant are discontented; the wise are always content. The thirst for wealth can never be slaked. Contentment is the highest happiness; so it is that the wise regard contentment as the highest goal worth striving for.

The wise know the evanescence of youth and beauty, of life and treasure, of prosperity and the company of loved ones, and never covet these. A man must refrain from acquiring overmuch wealth, for none who is rich is free from trouble; this is why the virtuous laud those who are free from the desire for wealth.

And for those that pursue wealth for dharma, it is better for them to desist, since, surely, it is better not to touch dirt at all than to wash it off after having been besmirched by it. Yudhishtira, do not covet anything, and if you seek dharma, free yourself from the desire for possessions.'

Yudhishtira says, 'Dvija, my desire for wealth is not for enjoying it, but only to support you Brahmanas. I am not driven by greed. Why, O Brahmana, do I lead the life of a grihasta, if I cannot cherish and support those who follow me? All creatures divide the food they procure amongst those that depend on them.

A grihasta should share his food with yatis and brahmacharins who have renounced cooking for themselves. The houses of good men must never want for grass, beds, food, water and, fifthly, sweet words. For the standing a seat of grass, for the weary a bed, water for the thirsty, and food for the hungry.

Kind looks, a cheerful heart and sweet words are always due to a guest. Rising, the host must go up to welcome a guest, offer him a seat, and worship him. This is Sanatana Dharma. They who do not perform the Agnihotra,[1] do not care for their cows and bulls, cherish their kinsmen, guests, friends, sons, wives and servants, are consumed by sin for their neglect.

None should cook food just for himself; none should slay an animal without dedicating it to the gods, the manes, and guests. Nor should one eat food which has not been duly offered to the Devas and the Pitrs. One must set food on the earth, morning and evening, for dogs and Chandalas, scatter grain for birds, and then perform the Viswadeva sacrifice.[2]

He who eats the vighasa, what has first been offered during a sacrifice to the gods and the manes, eats ambrosia; what remains after feeding a guest is vighasa and equal to amrita. Feeding a guest is equal to a sacrifice, and the pleasant looks the host casts upon the guest, the attention he pays him, the sweet words in which he addresses him, the respect he pays by following him, and the food and drink which he serves him are the five dakshinas of that sacrifice.[3]

---

[1]A form of sacrifice which consists of pouring oblations of clarified butter accompanied by prayers into a blazing fire. It is obligatory for Brahmanas and Kshatriyas, except those that take certain vows of great austerity.

[2]The Viswadeva sacrifice is the offering of food to all creatures of the Earth.

[3]A gift. It may be of various kinds. The fees paid to Brahmanas assisting at sacrifices and religious rites, such as offering oblations to the dead, are dakshinas; as also gifts to Brahmanas on other occasions particularly when they are fed, it being to this day the custom never to fete a Brahmana without paying him a pecuniary fee. There can

He who gives food, unstintingly, to a tired wayfarer whom he has never seen before, finds great punya.

The grihasta who follows these practices, I have heard, gains great religious merit. O Brahmana, what do you say about this?'

Saunaka says, 'Alas, this world is full of contradictions! He who blames the good pleases the evil. Moved by ignorance and passion, and being slaves to their senses, even fools perform many acts of apparent punya, but only to gratify their appetites in the after-life!

With eyes open, their seducing senses lead these men astray, rather like a charioteer who has fallen, by having restive and wicked horses. When any of the six senses finds its particular object, desire springs up in the heart to enjoy that particular object. When the heart begins to enjoy the object of a sense, it entertains a wish, which then spawns a resolve.

Finally, pierced by the shafts of the objects of enjoyment set loose by the desire which constitutes the seed of the resolve, like an insect falling into a flame from its love of light, the man falls into the fire of temptation. Thereon, blinded by sensual pleasure which he seeks without stint, steeped in dark ignorance and folly, which he mistakes for joy, for he does not know himself.

Like a wheel which incessantly rolls, every creature, from avidya, karma and kama, falls into various states in this world, wandering from one birth to another, and ranges the entire range of existences from Brahma to the point of a blade of grass, now in water, now on land, and again in the air!

This is the careen of those who are without knowledge. Listen now to the course of the wise, they who are intent on dharma, artha, and who wish for moksha. The Vedas enjoin that we act but renounce action's fruit. You must perform karma, but without ahamkara, ego.

The performance of sacrifices, study of the Vedas, gifts, penance, truth in both speech and act, forgiveness, subduing the senses, and renunciation

---

be no sacrifice, no religious rite, without dakshina.

of desire – these have been declared to be the eight cardinal duties which make up the true path.

Of these, the four first pave the way to the world of the Pitrs, and these must be practised without abhimana, pride. The last four are observed by the pious, to attain the heaven of the Devas. The pure in spirit must always follow these eight paths. Those who wish to subdue the world for moksha, must engage in karma, entirely renouncing motives, subduing their senses, unswervingly observing some vratas, devotedly serving their Gurus, austerely regulating their food, diligently studying the Vedas, relinquishing action as mean and restraining their hearts.

By renouncing desire and aversion, have the gods attained prosperity. Through the wealth of Yoga, the Rudras, the Sadhyas, the Adityas, the Vasus, and the Aswin twins rule other creatures. Therefore, Kaunteya, like them, O Bhaarata, you also refrain from karma with motive; strive towards attaining Yoga through austerities.

Already, you have paid your debts to your ancestors, both male and female; you have successfully performed yagnas and good karma; now in order to serve the Brahmanas, strive to attain success in tapasya. For those who find success at penance can do whatever they like. So, through tapasya gain whatever you wish.'"

CANTO 3

ARANYAKA PARVA CONTINUED

Vaisampayana said, "Thus addressed by Saunaka, Yudhishtira approaches his priest, and in the presence of his brothers says, 'The Brahmanas versed in the Vedas mean to follow me into the forest. I am beset by misfortune and cannot support them. I cannot abandon them either, but I have no power to offer them sustenance. Holy One, tell me what I should do.'

Dhaumya uses his yogic powers to reflect a moment, then that Dvijottama says to Yudhishtira, 'Once, long ago, all living creatures were sorely afflicted by hunger, and Savita the Sun took pity upon them, even like a father. First, he went north and drew up water through his rays; returning south, he remained above the world, with his heat indrawn.

While the Sun remained thus poised, the Moon made the vapour within the solar orb into clouds, poured them down as rain and created plants. Thus, it is the Sun himself who, drenched by the Moon's influence, is transformed, upon the sprouting of seeds, into holy vegetables furnished with the six tastes. And these constitute the food of all creatures upon the Earth.

So, the food which supports the lives of creatures is infused with solar energy, and hence the Sun is the father of all creatures. Yudhishtira, you must also seek refuge in Surya.

Many illustrious and high-born kings, of mighty deeds, delivered their people through tapasya. The great Kartavirya, Vainya and Nahusha, all, saved their people from calamities by practising dhyana after swearing stern vratas. Virtuous Bhaarata, you also purify yourself with dhyana and vigorously support the Brahmanas.'"

Janamejaya said, "How did that Bull among the Kurus, Yudhishtira Dharmaraja, adore the lustrous Sun for the sake of the Brahmanas?"

Vaisampayana said, "Listen carefully, O King, purify yourself and withdraw your mind from every other thought. King of kings, appoint an hour for it and I will tell you everything in detail.

Listen to the one hundred and eight names of the Sun as Dhaumya disclosed them of old to Pritha's son, the Mahatman.

Dhaumya spoke these names, 'Surya, Aryaman, Bhaga, Twastri, Pusha, Arka, Savitri, Ravi, Gabhastimat, Aja, Kala, Mrityu, Dhatri, Prabhakara, Prithivi, Apa, Teja, Kha, Vayu, Parayana, Soma, Brihaspati, Sukra, Budha, Angaraka, Indra, Vivaswat, Diptanshu, Suchi, Sauri, Sanaischara, Brahma, Vishnu, Rudra, Skanda, Vaisravana, Yama, Vaidyuta, Jatharagni, Agni, Aindhna, Tejasampati, Dharmadhwaja, Vedakarta, Vedanga, Vedavahana, Krita, Treta, Dwapara, Kali, full of every impurity, Kala, Kashta, Muhurta, Kshapa, Yama, and Kshana; Samvatsarakara, Aswattha, Kalachakra, Vibhavasu, Purusha, Saswata, Yogin, Vyaktavyakta, Sanatana, Kaladhyaksha, Prajadhyaksha, Viswakarma, Tamounda, Varuna, Sagara, Ansu, Jimuta, Jivana, Arihan, Bhutasraya, Bhutapati, Srastri, Samvartaka, Vahni, Sarvasyadi, Alolupa, Ananta, Kapila, Bhanu, Kamada, Sarvatomukha, Jaya, Visala, Varada, Manas, Suparna, Bhutadi, Sighraga, Prandharaka, Dhanvantari, Dhumaketu, Adideva, Aditisuta, Dwadasatman, Aravindaksha, Pita, Mata, Pitamaha, Swargadwara, Prajadwara, Mokshadwara, Trivishtapa, Dehakarta, Prasantatman,

Viswatman, Viswatomukha, Characharatman, Sukhsmatman, the merciful Maitreya.[1]

These are the hundred and eight names of Surya of measureless energy, as told by the Swayambhuva.

For prosperity I bow down to you, O Bhaskara, who blaze like gold or fire, who is worshipped by the Devas, the Pitrs and the Yakshas, who is adored by Asuras, Nisacharas, and Siddhas.

He who with fixed attention recites this hymn at sunrise, gains a wife and children, riches and the remembrance of his former life; by reciting this hymn a person attains patience and memory. Concentrating his mind, let a man recite this hymn, for he shall become proof against grief, forest-fire and ocean; and every object of desire shall be his.'

Hearing this from Dhaumya, Yudhishtira absorbs himself in dhyana, so he can support the Brahmanas. Worshipping the maker of day with flowers and other offerings, the king performs his ablutions. Standing in the river, he turns his face towards the god of day. Touching the water of the Ganga, the virtuous Yudhishtira, his senses perfectly controlled, the air his only sustenance, stands there, his soul rapt, his breath regulated in pranayama. Having purified himself and restrained his speech, he begins to sing the hymn of praise to the Sun.

Yudhishtira says, 'You are, O Surya, the eye of the universe. You are the soul of all corporeal existences. You are the origin of all things. You are the embodiment of the deeds of all religious men. You are the refuge of the Sankhyas and the support of the Yogins.

You are a door without bolts. You are the sanctuary of those who seek moksha. You sustain and light the world, sanctify and support it out of pure compassion. Appearing before you, Brahmanas versed in the Vedas worship you with hymns from the Vedas.

The Rishis adore you. Wanting boons from you, the Siddhas, the Charanas, the Gandharvas, the Yakshas, the Guhyakas and the Nagas follow your chariot coursing through the sky. The thirty-three Devas,

[1]Not exactly 108 names in the KMG text!

with Upendra and Mahendra, and the order of Vaimanikas, have attained success by worshipping you.

By offering you garlands of the celestial mandaras, the best of the Vidyadharas have had all their wishes fulfilled. The Guhyas and the seven orders of the Pitrs—both divine and human—became superior only by adoring you. The Vasus, the Marutas, the Rudras, the Sadhyas, the Marichipas, the Balakhilyas, and the Siddhas became pre-eminent by bowing down to you.

I know there is nothing in all the seven worlds, including that of Brahma, which is beyond you. There are other beings both great and endowed with tejas; but none of them has your lustre and energy. All light is in you, indeed, you are the lord of all light.

In you are the five elements and all intelligence, knowledge, asceticism and the ascetic qualities. The Chakra with which the wielder of the Saranga humbles the pride of Asuras, the disc with the beautiful nave, was forged by Viswakarman from your tejas.

In summer, through your rays, you draw moisture from all corporeal beings, from plants and fluid things, and pour it down during the monsoon. Your rays warm and scorch, and, becoming clouds, roar and flash with lightning and pour down showers when each season comes. Not fire, shelter, or woollen cloths give greater comfort against the cold than your rays.

With your rays you illumine all the Earth, with her thirteen Dwipas. You alone engage yourself constantly in the welfare of the three worlds. If you do not rise, the universe becomes blind and the wise cannot strive to attain dharma, artha and kama. Through your grace the three varnas, the Brahmanas, the Kshatriyas and the Vaisyas, perform their various duties and sacrifices.

Those who fathom time say that you are the beginning and the end of a day of Brahma, which lasts a full thousand Yugas. You are the lord of Manus and the sons of the Manus, of the Universe and of man, of the Manvantaras, and their lords.

When the time of Pralaya comes, the fire Samvartaka, born of your wrath, consumes the three worlds and exists alone. Born of your rays, clouds of many hues, along with Airavata and the Vajra, bring the appointed deluges, and dividing yourself into twelve parts, becoming as many Suns, you drink up the ocean once more with your rays.

You are called Indra, you are Vishnu, you are Brahma, you are Prajapati. You are fire and you are the subtle mind. You are the Lord and the eternal Brahman. You are Hansa, you are Savitri; you are Bhanu, Ansumalin, and Vrishakapi. You are Vivaswan, Mihira, Pusha, Mitra, and Dharma. You are thousand-rayed; you are Aditya, Tapana, and the lord of rays.

You are Martanda, Arka, Ravi, Surya, Saranya and the maker of day. You are Divakara, Saptasaspti, Dhamakesin and Virochana. They say you are swift as light and the destroyer of darkness, the owner of golden steeds.

He who reverentially adores you on the sixth or the seventh lunar day, humbly and with tranquillity of mind, finds the grace of Lakshmi. They that single-mindedly worship you are delivered from all dangers, agonies and afflictions. They who hold that you are everywhere, being the soul of all things, live long, are freed from sin and are immune to all disease.

O Lord of all food, it becomes you to grant abundant food to me, for I wish to feed my atithis, my guests, with every reverence.

I bow also to all your followers, who have taken refuge at your feet—Matara, Aruna, Danda, Asani, Kshubha and the others. And I bow to the celestial mothers of all creatures: Kshubha, Maitri and the rest.

O let them deliver me, their supplicant!'

Thus, O Maharajan, Yudhishtira adores the Sun, purifier of the world. Pleased with the hymn, the maker of day, self-luminous, and blazing like fire shows himself to the son of Pandu.

Vivaswan says, 'You will have everything that you want. I will provide you with food for five and seven years. O King, take this copper vessel from me, and as long as Panchali holds this vessel, without partaking of its contents, or fruit, roots, and meat and vegetables cooked in your kitchen, these four kinds of food shall well inexhaustibly from it from today.

On the fourteenth year from this, you will regain your kingdom.'

Saying this, the Deva vanishes. He who wants a boon and recites this hymn with his mind absorbed in dhyana, will have whatever he wishes for from the Sun, however difficult of acquisition what he asks for might be.

And the one who hears or chants this stotra, day after day, wanting a son, he or she gets one; and if riches, gets those; and if learning, acquires that too. And the man or woman who chants this hymn every day, during the two sandhyas, is delivered from all danger and bonds.

Brahma himself taught this hymn to the illustrious Sakra; Narada had it from Sakra, and Dhaumya from Narada. Dhaumya gave it to Yudhishtira, and the Pandava got whatever he wished for. Through this hymn a man can always be victorious at war and acquire immense wealth, too. It leads the one who recites it from all sins, to the realm of the Sun.

With the Sun's boon – the copper vessel – Yudhishtira comes out of the water, clasps Dhaumya's feet and embraces his brothers. Going into their kitchen with Panchali, then, Pandu's son begins to cook the day's food. That food, though minuscule in quantity, clean and furnished with the four tastes, increases and becomes inexhaustible.

With it, Yudhishtira begins to feed the Brahmanas; and when they have eaten, he feeds his brothers and eats what remains himself, the portion called vighasa. After Yudhishtira has eaten, Prihasta's daughter Draupadi eats what remains. And when she has eaten, the food for that day is exhausted and the copper vessel empty.

Thus, with his boon from the maker of day, the son of Pandu, himself as splendid as that Deva, begins to feed his Brahmanas the finest fare.

Obedient to their priest, Pritha's sons, on auspicious lunar days, constellations and conjunctions, perform sacrifices according to the ordinance, the scriptures, and the mantras. After the sacrifices, the Pandavas, blessed by the auspicious rites which Dhaumya performs, and accompanied by him, and surrounded also by the Brahmanas, set out for the Kamyaka vana."

CANTO 4

ARANYAKA PARVA CONTINUED

Vaisampayana said, "After the Pandavas have entered the forest, Ambika's son Dhritarashtra, whose knowledge was his eye,[1] grows exceedingly sorrowful. Sitting at his ease, the king says to the virtuous Vidura of profound intelligence, 'Your understanding is as clear as Bhargava's. You know all the nuances of dharma, and you look at all the Kauravas equally.

Tell me what is right for them and for me, as well. Vidura, things having this course, what should we do now? How can I secure the goodwill of the people so that they do not uproot us? Tell us all, for you know every excellent expedient.'

Vidura says, 'My King, artha, kama and moksha are all founded in dharma, and the Sages say that a kingdom also stands if it is based on dharma. So, Rajan, cherish your son and Pandu's son equally, in dharma.

---

[1]Being blind, Dhritarashtra is described as *Pragnachakshu,* having knowledge for his eye. It may also mean, 'Of the prophetic eye'.

Evil souls, with Subala's son Sakuni leading them, subverted that dharma when your son called the righteous Yudhishtira here and vanquished him at dice. I see one expiation for this base act, by which your son can be freed from his sin and win back his place among good men. Give back to the Pandavas what you first returned to them; give Indraprastha back to them. For, a king's highest dharma is that he must remain content with his own possessions and never covet another's. Thus your honour will remain and nor will dissension arise in your family, and nor any sin attach to you. Your first duty now is to disgrace Sakuni and to satisfy the Pandavas. If you want to restore your sons to the good fortune that they have lost, do this immediately.

If you do not, the Kurus will surely be destroyed because neither Bhimasena nor Arjuna, if angry, will leave any of their foes unslain. What is there in this world that they cannot attain, who have Savyasachin among their warriors, the Gandiva, most potent of weapons his bow, and also the inexorable Bhimasena?

Once, as soon as your son was born, I said to you, Abandon this inauspicious child, for in that lies the good of your clan. But you did not do as I said then. Now, also, I am showing you the way to your salvation. If you do as I say, you will not have to repent later.

If your son agrees to rule jointly with the sons of Pandu, and in peace, you will pass your days in joy. If he will not, forsake Duryodhana for the sake of your own happiness. Cast him aside and crown Yudhishtira Ajatasatru, who is free from passion, king of all the Kurus, and let him rule the Earth with dharma. And then all the kings of the world will quickly pay homage to us, even like Vaisyas. Let Duryodhana, Sakuni and Karna wait upon the Pandavas; let Dussasana, in the open sabha, ask Bhimasena's forgiveness and the forgiveness of Draupadi also; and pacify Yudhishtira by setting him upon the throne with every show of respect.

You have asked me, and what other counsel can I give you? By doing this, O King, you will do what is right, and keep dharma.'

Dhritarashtra says, 'You said the same thing in this sabha, Vidura, but what you say is only beneficial to the Pandavas, not to me. My heart does not like what you say.

How have you decided all this in your mind? You speak only for the good of the Pandavas and I see that you are not friendly towards me. How can I abandon my son for the sake of the sons of Pandu? Doubtless they, too, are my sons, but Duryodhana has sprung from my body. Who, speaking impartially, will ever advise me to renounce my own body for the sake of another's?

Vidura, though I hold you in high esteem, everything that you say is crooked. Stay here or go as you please. However much he might humour and please her, an unchaste wife will always forsake her husband!'

Saying this, Dhritarashtra rises abruptly and goes into his antahpura.

Vidura says, 'This race is doomed', and he goes away to where the sons of Pritha are.'"

CANTO 5

ARANYAKA PARVA CONTINUED

Vaisampayana said, "Wanting to live in the forest, those bulls of the race of Bhaarata, the Pandavas, with their followers, set out from the banks of the Ganga and journey to the field of Kurukshetra. Performing their ablutions in the Saraswati, the Drisadwati and the Yamuna, they go from one forest to another, travelling in a westerly direction.

Finally, they see the Kamyaka vana before them, favourite haunt of Munis, looming beside a level and wild plain on the banks of the Saraswati. In that forest, abounding in birds and deer, those heroes begin to dwell, entertained and comforted by the Munis. Always yearning to see the Pandavas, Vidura rides in a single chariot to the Kamyaka aranya, abundant with all things good and auspicious.

Arriving in the Kamyaka in his chariot drawn by swift steeds, he sees Yudhishtira Dharmatma, sitting with Draupadi in a secluded spot, surrounded by his brothers and the Brahmanas. Seeing Vidura approach from a distance with swift steps, the king says to his brother Bhimasena, 'With what message does Kshatta come to us now? Does he come sent by Sakuni to invite us to another game of dice? Does the vile Sakuni intend to win back our weapons by gambling?

O Bhima, I cannot refuse anyone who asks me for anything. And if we lose the Gandiva at dice, how will we regain our kingdom?'

The Pandavas rise to welcome Vidura, and he, descendant of Ajamida, sits down among them and makes the customary enquiries after their welfare. When Vidura has rested awhile, those bulls among men ask him the reason for his coming, and he tells them in detail everything that transpired with Ambika's son Dhritarashtra.

Vidura says, 'Ajatasatru, Dhritarashtra called me, his dependant, to him and honouring me duly, said, "Things have taken their course, Vidura. Now tell me what I should do which will benefit both the Pandavas and myself."

I told him what was dharma and also good for both yourselves and him. But Dhritarashtra did not relish what I said to him, and I could not see what other counsel to offer.

What I advised, O Pandavas, was truly beneficial, but Ambika's son would not listen to me. My words failed to please him, even as good medicine does not recommend itself to one that is ill. And, O Yudhishtira, as an unchaste wife in the family of a man of pure descent cannot be brought back to the path of virtue, so did I fail to bring Dhritarashtra back to dharma.

Indeed, as a young woman does not like a husband of three score years, even so Dhritarashtra did not like what I said. Surely, doom will overtake the Kuru race; surely Dhritarashtra will never find good fortune. For, as water dropped on a lotus-leaf does not remain there, my counsels will have no effect upon my brother.

The incensed Dhritarashtra told me, O Bhaarata, "Go where you like! I will never again seek your help in ruling the earth or my capital."

Best of kings, forsaken by Dhritarashtra, I have come to you. What I said in the open court, I will now repeat. Listen, and bear my words in mind:

The wise man who bears all the gross wrongs heaped upon him by his enemies, who patiently bides his time, and multiplies his resources even as men turn a small fire into a large one by degrees, will rule the whole world. He who shares his substance with his followers in prosperity will find in them sharers of his adversity. This is the best means of securing followers, and he who has followers wins the sovereignty of the world.

O Pandava, divide your prosperity with your followers, be honest with them, and speak to them agreeably. Share your food with them, and never boast in their presence. Such conduct increases the prosperity of kings!'

Yudhishtira says, 'You have such a lofty intelligence, undisturbed by passion, and I will do as you say. Whatever else you advise, in time and place, I will follow carefully and entirely.'"

CANTO 6

ARANYAKA PARVA CONTINUED

Vaisampayana said, "O King, after Vidura leaves Hastinapura and goes to the Pandavas, Dhritarashtra repents. Thinking of Vidura's great intelligence in matters of both war and peace, and also of the rise of the Pandavas in the future, Dhritarashtra, grieving for Vidura, comes to the door of the great sabha and falls senseless in the presence of the waiting kings.

Regaining consciousness, the king rises from the ground and says to Sanjaya standing by, 'My brother is even like Dharma Deva himself. I think of him today and my heart burns in grief. Go Sanjaya, fetch my brother to me, my Vidura master of dharma.'

And the king weeps. Scalded by remorse, overwhelmed with sorrow to think of Vidura, Dhritarashtra, full of brotherly love, says again, 'Sanjaya, go and find out if my brother, whom I so cruelly cast out in my anger, is still alive! He is wise, immeasurably intelligent, and he has never been guilty of the slightest transgression; yet it is him that I have wronged so grievously.

Seek him, wise Sanjaya, and bring him back here. Otherwise, I will kill myself.'

Sanjaya hears the king and approves heartily. Saying, 'Tathastu!' he sets out for the Kamyaka forest. Arriving swiftly in the vana where the Pandavas dwell, Sanjaya sees Yudhishtira clad in deerskin, sitting with Vidura, in the midst of thousands of Brahmanas – Yudhishtira guarded by his brothers, even like Purandara amongst the celestials!

Approaching Yudhishtira, Sanjaya duly worships him and is received with respect by Bhima and Arjuna and the twins. Yudhishtira makes the customary inquiries after his welfare. When he has been seated at his ease, Sanjaya discloses the reason for his visit, 'O Kshatta, Ambika's son Dhritarashtra remembers you, he grieves terribly for you! Return to him immediately, and restore the king's spirits.

O best of men, I say that, with the leave of the Kuru princes, these Purushottamas, it becomes you to return to that lion among kings, your brother, at his command.'

The wise Vidura, always loving towards his kin, hears what Sanjaya says, and with Yudhishtira's leave, he goes back to the city named for the elephant. He comes into the king's presence and Ambika's son, Dhritarashtra of bright tejas, says to him, 'Ah Vidura, it is my great fortune that you, sinless one, knower of dharma, have come back, thinking of me! Bharatarishabha, while you were away I could not sleep by day or night, like one who had been lost in the world.'

The king takes his brother onto his lap and sniffs the top of his head in love, saying, 'Forgive me, Anagha, sinless one, for what I said to you!'

Vidura says, 'My King, I have already forgiven you. You are my superior, worthy of the highest reverence. Here I am, and I came back eager to see you. Purusharishabha, all men of dharma are naturally partial towards those in distress and this is hardly because of any deliberation. Your sons are as dear to me as the sons of Pandu, but the Pandavas are in trouble and that is why my heart goes out to them.'

Thus conciliating each other, the two illustrious brothers, Vidura and Dhritarashtra, feel happy.'"

CANTO 7

ARANYAKA PARVA CONTINUED

Vaisampayana said, "Hearing that Vidura had returned, and that the king had consoled him, Dhritarashtra's evil son burns with grief. His mind clouded with ignorance, he summons Sakuni, Karna and Dussasana, and says to them, 'The learned Vidura, the minister of the wise Dhritarashtra, has returned! He is partial to the Pandavas, and always seeks to favour them.

I hope he does not persuade the king to bring them back. If ever I see Pritha's sons return to this city, I will starve myself to death, take poison, hang myself, immolate myself or kill myself with my own weapons. But I can never see the sons of Pandu prosper again!'

Sakuni says, 'Lord of the earth, what folly takes hold of you? The Pandavas have gone into the forest, having sworn an oath not to return for thirteen years, so what you fear will never happen. Bharatarishabha, the Pandavas always keep dharma and their word. Even if your father calls them back they will not return.

Yet, if they do, perchance, come back at the king's command, breaking their vow, we must remain calm, keep our own counsel, and be seemingly obedient to the king's wishes, while we watch the sons of Pandu carefully.'

Dussasana says, 'I agree with you, O most intelligent uncle. You always speak words of wisdom which recommend themselves to me!'

Karna says, 'Duryodhana, all of us seek to do your will, O King, and I see that we are unanimous in this thing. The self-controlled sons of Pandu will not return during their time of their exile, and thereby break their solemn word. But if they do, from foolishness, I say beat them again at another game of dice!'

But Duryodhana is cheerless and turns his face away from his confederates. Karna marks this, expands his beautiful eyes, gesticulates angrily, and says vehemently, haughtily, to Duryodhana, Dussasana and Subala's son, 'Kshatriyas, know my mind! We are all servants of Duryodhana, and wait upon him with folded hands. We must always do what pleases him, yet we are not always able to please him promptly because of his father Dhritarashtra.

I say let us put on our armour, take our weapons, mount our chariots and ride at once to kill the Pandavas in the forest. When Pandu's sons have been silenced and sent on the unknown journey, both Dhritarashtra and we will find peace. As long as they are in distress, as long as they are plunged in sorrow, as long as they are without help, we are a match for them. This is my mind!'

They loudly applaud what the Sutaputra says, and finally cry all together, 'Yes, let us do what you say!'

Each of them mounts his chariot, and confident of success, rush forth in a body to kill the sons of Pandu. However, Krishna-Dwaipayana, of pure soul, divines their intention, appears before them and sternly commands them to desist. Sending them back, the holy one, worshipped by all the worlds, quickly appears before the king, whose sight is his knowledge, sitting upon his throne.

The Maharishi Vyasa speaks thus to that sovereign."

CANTO 8

ARANYAKA PARVA CONTINUED

"Vyasa says, 'Dhritarashtra, listen to what I have to say, for I will tell you what is good for all the Kauravas. Mahabaho, I am not pleased that, deceitfully beaten at dice by Duryodhana and the others, the Pandavas have gone into exile. O Bhaarata, at the end of thirteen years, recollecting all their travail, they may well shower astras of death, even like virulent poison, upon the Kauravas.

Why does your sinful son, always inflamed by anger, seek to kill the sons of Pandu for the sake of their kingdom? Let the fool be restrained; let your son remain quiet. If he tries to kill the Pandavas in exile, he will only lose his own life.

You are as honest as the wise Vidura, Bhishma, or I, as Kripa or Drona. O you of profound wisdom, dissension within one's family is forbidden, sinful and reprehensible. O King, you must refrain from such folly.

Bhaarata, Duryodhana looks upon the Pandavas with such envy that great harm will come of it, if you do not interfere. Otherwise, let this evil son of yours go, alone and unaccompanied, to the forest and live with the sons of Pandu. For then, if the Pandavas, from association, begin to feel attachment for Duryodhana, then good fortune may be yours.

Ah, but this cannot be, for it is said that a man's congenital nature does not leave him, not until his death. But what do Bhishma and Drona and Vidura think? What do you think?

You must do what is beneficial while there is time, or all your purposes will remain unrealised.'"

CANTO 9

ARANYAKA PARVA CONTINUED

"Dhritarashtra says, 'Holy one, I did not favour the gambling, but, O Muni, I believe that fate made me consent to it. Neither Bhishma nor Drona, Vidura nor Gandhari, liked the game of dice. No doubt, it was folly. And, illustrious one, you who delight in keeping vratas, I know this is folly, yet I am ruled by fatherly love and I am unable to cast off my senseless son Duryodhana.'

Vyasa says, 'Son of Vichitravirya, what you say is true! I well know that a son is the best of all things and there is nothing as good as a son. Taught by Surabhi's tears, Indra learnt that a son surpasses every other possession, however valuable, in worth.

Rajan, let me tell you that best of stories, which deals with a conversation between Indra and Surabhi. In elder days, Surabhi, the mother of cows, was once crying in Devaloka. Indra felt compassion for her, and asked her, "Auspicious one, why are you crying? Is everything well with the Devas? Has any misfortune, ever so little, befallen the world of the Manavas or Nagas?"

Surabhi replied, "No evil which I perceive has befallen you. But I am aggrieved because of my son, and that is why I weep! Look, O Lord of the Devas, where yonder cruel farmer belabours my weak son with a wooden stick, and oppresses him with a plough, so my son is in agony and falls onto the ground.

At this sight, O Devendra, pity fills me and my mind is agitated. The stronger of the pair bears his burden easily, but the weaker, O Vasava, is lean, a mass of skin and bones, with veins and arteries showing. He bears his load with great hardship and it is for him that I grieve.

Look where lashes of the whip mark his hide and he staggers. It is for him I am grief-stricken and these tears flow from my eyes."

Sakra said, "Fair one, when thousands of your sons are daily oppressed, why do you grieve for one?"

Surabhi replied, "Although I have a thousand offspring, my affections flow equally towards them all! But, O Indra, I feel great love and pity for one who is weak and innocent."'

Vyasa continues, 'Indra was greatly surprised to hear these words of Surabhi; he became convinced that a son is dearer than one's life. The illustrious chastiser of Paka suddenly poured a heavy rain and obstructed the farmer's work. As Surabhi said, your affections, O King, flow equally towards all your sons. Let them be greater towards those that are weak!

As my son Pandu is to me, so are you, my child, and so also Vidura of profound wisdom. I say all this to you out of my love. Bhaarata, you have a hundred and one sons, but Pandu has only five. And they are in a sad plight and pass their days in sorrow.

How can they save their lives, how will they thrive – such thoughts about Pritha's sons constantly agitate my soul. King of the earth, if you want all the Kauravas to live, let your son Duryodhana make peace with the Pandavas!'"

CANTO 10

ARANYAKA PARVA CONTINUED

"Dhritarashtra says, 'Muni of profound wisdom, it is even as you say. I know it well as do all these kings. Indeed, what you consider beneficial for the Kurus was pointed out to me by Vidura, Bhishma and Drona. And, if I deserve your favour, and if you bear kindness for the Kurus, I beg you speak to my sinful son Duryodhana.'

Vyasa says, 'The holy Rishi Maitreya comes here, after visiting the Pandavas. This mighty Rishi will admonish your son for the weal of this race. Kauravya, what he says must be followed implicitly, for if it is not, the Sage will curse your son in anger.'

Saying this, Vyasa leaves and Maitreya makes his appearance. Dhritarashtra and his son receive that travel-worn lord of Munis reverentially, with offerings of arghya and other rituals.

Ambika's son Dhritarashtra says respectfully to the Sage, 'Holy one, has your journey from Kurujangala been a pleasant one? Are those heroes, the five Pandavas, living happily there? Do those bulls of the Kuru race intend to serve their exile in full? Will the brotherly affection of the Kauravas be impaired?'

Maitreya says, 'Setting out on a pilgrimage to the different tirthas, I arrived at Kurujangala, and there, to my surprise, I saw Yudhishtira Dharmaputra in the Kamyaka vana. Many other Munis had come there to see Yudhishtira, living in an ascetic asrama, clad in deer-skin and wearing matted jata.

There, King of kings, I heard of the grave sin which your sons committed, and the disaster and danger they have brought upon themselves through the game of dice. So, I have come to you for the good of the Kauravas, because my affection for you is great and I am pleased with you.

O King, it is not fit that your princes should fall out amongst one another for any cause, while Bhishma and you are alive. You, Rajan, are the stake to which all these bulls are tied, and you have the power to reward and to punish. Why do you ignore this great evil that is about to overtake all of you?

The Rishis do not think well of you for the crimes that were committed in your court, sins which are like the deeds of vile chandalas!'

Then, turning to the choleric Duryodhana, the lustrous Rishi Maitreya says softly to him, 'Duryodhana Mahabaho, most eloquent of men, illustrious one, pay heed to what I say, for I speak for your good. Do not seek enmity with the Pandavas!

Purusharishabha, think of your own weal, as also the good of the Pandavas, of all the Kurus, and of the world. All those tigers among men are Kshatriyas of invincible prowess in war, strong each one as ten thousand elephants, their bodies hard as the adamantine Vajra, who never swerve from their vows, and who are proud of their manliness!

They have killed Rakshasas who could assume any form at will, demons like Hidimba and Kirmira. When the noble sons of Pandu went forth from here, the fierce Rakshasa Kirmira stood in their way at night like a hill. As a tiger kills a little deer, Bhima, strongest of all the strong, always delighting in battle, killed that monster.

Do not forget how Bhima killed the mighty Jarasandha, who was himself as strong as ten thousand elephants. The Pandavas are related to Krishna; Drupada's sons are their brothers-in-law; who among mortals will dare face Pandu's sons in battle?

O Bull of the Bhaaratas, let there be peace between you and the Pandavas. Do not yield to envy and anger, listen to what I say.'

Even as Maitreya admonishes him, Duryodhana slaps his own thigh which is like the trunk of an elephant, and, smiling insolently, scratches the ground with his foot, as if he cares nothing for what the Sage says. The vile prince does not say a word but looks down, away from the Rishi.

Rajan, when Maitreya sees Duryodhana slighting him, he becomes angry. As if urged by fate, that best of Munis decides to curse Duryodhana. His eyes red, Maitreya touches holy water and curses Dhritarashtra's evil son.

'You dare slight me, and pay no mind to what I say? You will swiftly reap the fruit of your insolence! During the Great War which will spring from your sins, the mighty Bhima will smash that thigh of yours with a stroke of his mace!'

When the Muni curses Duryodhana, Dhritarashtra hastily tries to placate the Sage, so that his curse does not come true.

Maitreya says, 'If your son makes peace with the Pandavas, my curse will not take effect. Otherwise it must be as I have said!'

Wanting to gauge the strength of Bhima, that foremost of kings, Duryodhana's father asks, 'How did Bhima kill Kirmira?'

Maitreya says, 'I will say no more to you, for your son disregards my words. When I have left, Vidura will tell you everything.'

Saying this, Maitreya leaves and returns to where he had come from. Duryodhana is shaken to hear about the slaying of Kirmira and he also leaves the sabha."

CANTO 11

ARANYAKA PARVA CONTINUED

"Dhritarashtra says, 'O Kshatta, I want to hear about the death of Kirmira. Tell me about the encounter between Bhima and the Rakshasa.'

Vidura says, 'Listen, then, to the tale of that feat of Bhimasena of superhuman achievements. I heard it often during my stay with the Pandavas.

Beaten at dice the Pandavas went from here, and, after journeying for three days and nights, they arrived in the forest known as Kamyaka. Rajan, after the midnight hour, when nature sleeps, terrible man-eating Rakshasas range that vana, and no ascetic, cowherd or other forester dares go near the Kamyaka aranya for fear of the fiends.

At that very hour, as the Pandavas entered that jungle, a fearsome Rakshasa, a lit brand in his hand and his eyes aflame, appeared in their path. His face terrible, his arms outstretched, he stood barring their way. Eight fangs bared on his face, his eyes coppery, his hair like flames standing erect, he seemed like a great cloud mass reflecting the Sun's rays, or streaked with lightning gashes with flights of cranes below them.

With frightful yells and roaring like a mass of thunderheads charged with rain, the monster began to the use the maya which is typical of his kind. Crying out in fear, birds and other little creatures dropped senseless or dead when they heard that terrible roar. Deer, leopard, bison and bear fled in every direction, so it seemed the whole forest was in motion.

Swayed by the wind raised by the Rakshasa's great sighs, creepers growing leagues away seemed to fling their arms of auburn leaves around the trees and embrace them. At that moment, a violent wind began to blow, and the sky was dark with dust covering it. Even like grief, the worst enemy of the five senses, that unknown enemy appeared before the five Pandavas.

Seeing from a distance the sons of Pandu clad in black deer-skins, the Rakshasa blocked their path through the forest even like the Mainaka Mountain. The lotus-eyed Krishnaa looked at him and shut her eyes in fright. Standing among the five Pandavas, she whose tresses had been dishevelled by the hand of Dussasana looked like stream chafing among five hills.

Even as the five senses cling to their objects of desire, the sons of Pandu supported the shaking Draupadi. Dhaumya of great tejas dispelled the wild illusions created by the Rakshasa's maya; he chanted powerful mantras to kill the devil.

Seeing his illusion dispelled, the mighty Kirmira, who could assume any form he chose, dilated his eyes in wrath and seemed like Death himself.

Yudhishtira said to him, "Who are you, and whose son? Tell us what we can do for you."

The Rakshasa replied, "I am the brother of Baka, I am the renowned Kirmira. I live at my ease in this empty Kamyaka vana, and daily I eat by defeating men in fight. Who are you that have come to me as my food? I will crush you all and feast on your flesh."

Yudhishtira announced his own name and lineage, saying, "I am Yudhishtira, the son of Pandu, of whom you might have heard. Losing my kingdom, I have come with my brothers Bhimasena, Arjuna and the others into this dread jungle, your domain, intending to spend my exile here.'"

Vidura continues, 'Kirmira said to Yudhishtira, "Ah, great fortune! Today fate has accomplished my long-cherished desire. With weapons raised, I have ranged the world with the single purpose of killing Bhima. But I did not find him.

But today, it is my great good fortune that my brother's killer, whom I have sought so long, has appeared before me. Bhima, disguised as a Brahmana, slew my brother Baka in the Vetrakiya forest through some sorcery. He has no real strength!

This evil one is he who also once slew my precious friend Hidimba, and ravished his sister. And the fool has now come into this deep forest of mine, when the night is half spent, even at the time when our kind is abroad. Tonight, at last, I will have vengeance on him, and gratify Baka with his blood in plenty.

By killing this enemy of the Rakshasas, tonight I will free myself from the debt I owe my friend and my brother, and thereby find supreme happiness. Baka once let Bhimasena escape, but tonight, O Yudhishtira, I will devour him in your sight. Even as Agastya ate and digested the mighty Asura Vatapi, will I this Bhima!"

Yudhishtira said angrily, "You cannot!"

Bhima tore up a tree ten vyamas long, and stripped it of its leaves. In a flash, Arjuna strung the Gandiva, powerful as a thunderbolt. O Bhaarata, Bhima stopped Arjuna and strode towards the Rakshasa, who still roared like thunderclouds, crying, "Stop! Stop!"

Bhima tightened his waistcloth, rubbed his hands together, bit his lower lip, and tree in hand rushed at the demon. Even like Indra casting his Vajra, Bhima crashed that tree, which was like Yama's danda, down on the fiend's head. The Rakshasa was unmoved by the blow, and hurled his flaming brand at Bhima like a streak of lightning.

But the Kshatriya deftly struck it with his left foot and the burning thing flew back at Kirmira. Now Kirmira drew up a tree and rushed into the fray like Yama himself with his mace. Quickly, the forest around them was denuded of trees and looked like the place where once, ages by, the Vanara brothers Vali and Sugriva fought for possession of a woman.

Striking the adversaries' heads, the trees broke into slivers, and were like lotus stalks flung at the temples of mating elephants. All around, numberless trees lay strewn like so many crushed reeds. However, the duel between that greatest of Rakshasas and Bhima did not last long, O Bharatarishabha.

The raging Kirmira snatched up a great rock from the ground and flung it squarely at Bhima standing before him, but the Pandava did not flinch. Then, like Rahu flying to devour the Sun, the Rakshasa, arms outstretched, flew at Bhima and they locked together, grappling and pulling and dragging, like two infuriated bulls; or like two mighty tigers, fighting tooth and claw – the encounter between them waxed fierce and hard.

Bhima thought of the humiliation by Duryodhana, he thought of Draupadi watching him, and Vrikodara found the true strength of his arms, strength which swelled in tide. Bhima seized the Rakshasa by his arms, as one elephant in rut seizes another. The powerful Rakshasa also clasped his antagonist, but Bhimasena, strongest of all strong men, flung the monster down violently.

The sounds that the interlocked fingers of the two made echoed like splitting bamboos. Bhima hurled the Rakshasa down, seized him by the waist, and began to whirl him around, like some ferocious hurricane shakes a tree. The Rakshasa was tired, he felt faint; yet, trembling all over, he still pressed the Pandava with all his strength.

Seeing that Kirmira was tiring, Vrikodara twined his great arms around him, even as one binds an animal with rope. The monster began to roar frightfully, like some dissonant trumpet. Bhima whirled him round until the Rakshasa seemed to lose consciousness and then threw him on the ground, where his body shook in convulsions. Bhima swiftly seized him again and killed him like an animal. He planted his great knee on Kirmira's belly and wrung his neck. As the fiend's eyelids closed, Bhima hauled his bruised body savagely across the earth roaring, "Sinful wretch, you will not have to wipe your tears for Hidimba and Baka because you are also bound for Yama's halls!"

Bhima saw the Rakshasa naked, his ornaments torn from his great body; he saw that Kirmira was dead and left him there. When the Rakshasa of the hue of clouds died, Yudhishtira embraced Bhima and praised him joyfully.'

Vidura says, 'So it was, O lord of men, that at Yudhishtira's command, Bhima killed Kirmira the Rakshasa.

Having rid the jungle of its menace, the Pandavas entered the now peaceful vana, and comforting the frightened Draupadi, began living there. In some joy, the Bharatarishabhas often praised Bhima's magnificent deed.

When I passed through the Kamyaka vana, I saw Kirmira's huge corpse lying there, and when I reached the Pandavas' asrama I heard about Bhima's prowess and how he killed the Rakshasa from the Brahmans who live there with the sons of Pandu.'

Dhritarashtra hears about the slaying of Kirmira, he sighs and plunges into deeper gloom."

CANTO 12

ARANYAKA PARVA CONTINUED

Vaisampayana said, "Hearing that the Pandavas have been banished, the Bhojas, the Vrishnis, and the Andhakas come to those heroes living in sorrow in the great forest. The Panchalas, Dhrishtaketu the king of Chedi, and those celebrated and powerful brothers, the Kaikeyas, their hearts fired by anger, come to the forest to see the sons of Pritha.

They reproach the sons of Dhritarashtra, and say, 'What shall we do?'

With Vasudeva Krishna at their head, those Kshatriyarishabhas sit around Yudhishtira.

Krishna reverently salutes that Kurusthama and says in some rage, 'The Earth shall drink the blood of Duryodhana and Karna, of Dussasana and the vile Sakuni! We will kill all these and all who are their allies and follow them and set Dharmaraja Yudhishtira upon the throne of Hastinapura. The evil deserve killing – this is Sanatana Dharma.'"

Seeing Krishna wrathful, why, even bent upon consuming all created things, Arjuna attempts to pacify him by reciting the Lord's own great feats of his past lives, what He, Vishnu of fathomless wisdom, immeasurable one, eternal one, Soul of all things, his tejas infinite, the Lord of Prajapati himself, final sovereign of all the worlds had done in lives and ages gone by.

Arjuna says, 'In olden days, you, O Krishna, wandered upon the Gandhamadana Mountains for ten thousand years as a Muni, whose home was wherever he found himself at dusk. Living on just water, Krishna, you also lived beside the Pushkara Lake for another eleven thousand years!

Madhusudana, your arms upraised and standing on one leg, you passed a hundred years on the high hills of Badari, imbibing just air! Your body bare, emaciated, a mass of veins, you lived on the banks of the Saraswati, engaged in a yagna which lasted twelve years.

And, Krishna of boundless tejas, keeping a vrata you stood upon one leg for a thousand years of the Devas, on the plains of Prabhasa which virtuous men visit in pilgrimage.

Vyasa has told me that you are the cause of the creation and its course. O Kesava, as the Lord of Kshetra,[1] you are the mover of all minds, and the beginning and end of all things. All tapasya rests in you, and you are also the embodiment of all sacrifices, and the eternal one.

Killing Narakasura, son of Bhumi, your first begotten, you took his earrings and performed the first aswamedha, offering the Asura as the sacrificial horse. Lokarishabha, O Bull of all the worlds, with that Yagna you triumphed over all things.

Killing all the Daityas and Danavas mustered in battle, you gave Sachi's Lord Indra sovereignty over the universe, and you have now, O Mahabaho, been born into this world of men.

Parantapa, who once floated upon the primal waters, you later became Hari, Brahma, Surya, Dharma, Dhatri, Yama, Anala, Vasu, Vaisravana,

---

[1]Nilakantha explains *kshetra* as including Mahabhuta, consciousness, intellect, the unmanifest (primordial elements), the ten senses, the five objects of the senses, desire, aversion, pleasure, pain, the combinations of elements, and chaitanya.

Rudra, Kala, Akasa, Bhumi and the ten directions. Un-born yourself, you are the lord of all the moving and unmoving universe, O First of all existences.

Slayer of Madhu, O you of boundless energy, in the forest of Chitraratha, Krishna, you worshipped the God of gods with your yagnas. Janardana, at each sacrifice you offered gold, in measures of hundreds of thousands.

Yadava, being born as Aditi's son, you became Indra's younger brother. Parantapa, even a child, you traversed with just three strides Swarga, Bhumi and Patala. When you were thus transformed, you entered into the body of the Sun and paled his splendour with your light.

Highest, during a thousand incarnations you slew Asuras past count. You killed the Mauravas and the Paashas, Nisunda and Naraka, and the road to Pragjyotishapura was safe again. You killed Ahvriti at Jaruthi; Kratha and Sisupala and his followers, Jarasandha, Saibya and Satadhanwan!

Riding your chariot, roaring like thunderheads and brilliant as the Sun, you took Bhoja's daughter Rukmini for your wife, vanquishing her brother Rukmi in battle. In anger, you slew Indradyumna and the Yavana called Kaseruman. You killed Salva, the lord of Saubha, and destroyed his city.

All these you killed in battle; let me tell of others you despatched. At Iravati, you slew King Bhoja equal to Kartavirya in battle; and both Gopati and Talaketu you killed! Janardana, you have taken for yourself sacred Dwaraka, of measureless wealth and which the Rishis all adore, and finally you will submerge Dwaravati in the Sea!

Madhusudana, how can any crookedness dwell in you, when, Dasarha, you have no anger, envy, untruth or cruelty? O You without decay, all the Rishis come to you, seated in glory upon sacrificial ground, and seek your protection. You alone remain at the end of the Yuga, contracting all things and withdrawing this universe into yourself, Parantapa!

O Vrishni, at the beginning of the Yuga, Brahma himself sprang from your lotus-like navel, Brahma lord of all mobile and immobile things, to whom this entire universe belongs.

When the dreadful Danavas, Madhu and Kaitabha, were bent on killing you, you were infuriated and from your forehead, O Hari, sprang Sambhu, Trilochana. Thus these two greatest of Gods issued from your body, to do your work. Narada told me this.

Narayana, in the Chaitraratha vana, you performed a multitude of yagnas, marked by a plenitude of gifts. Lord, you with eyes like lotus leaves, what you have done while still a mere boy, along with Baladeva, no one else has ever done, nor will in the future.

Why, you went and stayed on Kailasa with some Brahmanas!'

Saying all this to Krishna, Arjuna who was Krishna's soul, falls quiet.

Janardana says to him, 'You are mine as I am yours, and he who hates you hates me as well, as he that follows you follows me, too. Irrepressible one, you are Nara and I, Narayana; we are those two Rishis born into the world of men for a great purpose. Partha, you are of me, and I of you. Bharatarishabha, who can fathom any difference which exists between us?'

When the illustrious Kesava says as much in that conclave of valiant kings, all excited with anger, Panchali, along with Dhrishtadyumna and her other heroic brothers, approaches him of eyes like lotus leaves, seated with his cousins, and, wanting his protection speaks angrily to that Sanctuary of all beings.

'Asita and Devala have said that in the creation of all things, you are the only Prajapati, Creator of all the worlds. Irrepressible one, Jamadagnya says that you are Vishnu, O Madhusudana, and that you embody the sacrifice, the sacrificer and He for whom the sacrifice is performed.

Purushottama, the Rishis say that you are Forgiveness and Truth. Kasyapa has said you are Sacrifice sprung from Truth. Exalted one, Narada calls you the God of the Sadhyas, and of the Sivas, the only final Creator and the Lord of all things.

Purushavyaghra, you sport repeatedly with all the Gods, including Brahma, Sankara and Sakra even as children play with their toys. Loftiest, your head covers Swarga, your feet Bhumi, and all these worlds are as your womb, O Eternal!

For Rishis sanctified by the Vedas and by tapasya, their souls purified through penance, who are contented with visions of the soul, you are the best of all things. Purushottama, you are the refuge of Rajarishis of dharma who never turn their backs on the field of battle, men possessed of every accomplishment.

You are the Lord of all, you are Omnipresent, you are the Soul of all things, and you are the active power pervading everything. The rulers of all the worlds, the worlds themselves, the stellar conjunctions, the ten points of the horizon, the firmament, the Moon and the Sun are all founded in you.

Mahabaho, the dharma of mortal creatures and the immortality of the universe are established in you. You are the Supreme Lord of all creatures, celestial or human.

And so, O Madhusudana, impelled by the love you bear for me, will I tell you of my sorrows! Krishna, how could I, the wife of Pritha's sons, the sister of Dhrishtadyumna, and your sakhi, your friend, be dragged into the Kuru sabha as I was? Ah, during my period, bleeding, wearing just a single cloth, trembling and weeping, I was dragged into the court of the Kurus.

Seeing me, stained with blood in the presence of those kings in the sabha, the vicious sons of Dhritarashtra laughed at me. While the Pandavas, the Panchalas and the Vrishnis lived, Dhritarashtra's sons dared say they wanted me to be their slave.

By law, Krishna, I am both Dhritarashtra and Bhishma's daughter-in-law, yet they wanted to forcibly make me a slave. I accuse the Pandavas, who are the greatest warriors in the world, because they watched their wife being treated so savagely and did not stir.

Fie on the might of Bhimasena, fie on Arjuna and his Gandiva, for both, O Janardana, suffered me to be shamed by small men. Men of dharma, regardless of however weak they might be, have always protected their wives. By protecting his wife a man protects his children, and that is to protect oneself.

A man begets himself upon his wife, as his children, and that is why she is called Jaya. A wife also must protect her lord, remembering that he takes birth in her womb. The Pandavas never forsake anyone who seeks their protection, yet they forsook me when I turned to them in my dire need.

Through my five husbands five sons of exceptional tejas I have borne: Prativindhya by Yudhishtira, Sutasoma by Vrikodara, Srutakirti by Arjuna, Satanika by Nakula and Srutakarman by the youngest – all of them dauntless, invincible. For their sake, Janardana, my husbands should have protected me!

My sons are all mighty Kshatriyas, even like your own Pradyumna. My husbands are the greatest archers, and no enemy can defeat them in battle. Why do they bear what Dhritarashtra's sons made me endure, those princes of such negligible prowess?

Deprived of their kingdom through deception, the Pandavas were made bondsmen and I was dragged to the sabha while in my season, and wearing just one cloth!

Fie on the Gandiva, which none else can string save Arjuna, Bhima and you. Fie on the strength of Bhima, and fie on the prowess of Arjuna, because, Krishna, after what he dared do Duryodhana has drawn breath even for a moment!

He once drove the guileless Pandavas and their mother from the kingdom, while my lords were boys, students still, and young brahmacharins. That sinner mixed poison into Bhima's food, but Bhima ate the poison with the food and came to no harm, for his days in the world had not ended.

Krishna, Duryodhana bound the unconscious Bhima hand and foot and, below the house at Pramana, rolled him into the Ganga. But Bhima Mahabaho awoke, tore off his bonds and rose from the river. Duryodhana was responsible for black cobras biting Bhima all over his body, but this Parantapa did not die. Waking, Kunti's son killed all the snakes with his left hand, and he also killed Duryodhana's favourite sarathy, who was the agent for the dastardly crime.

Again, while the Pandavas slept at Varanavata with their mother, Duryodhana had that house set on fire, intending to immolate them inside. Who else could do such an evil thing? Kunti, surrounded by flames, cried out in terror to her sons, "Ah, I am undone! How will we escape? Alas, my children and I will die today."

Then Bhima Mahabaho, mighty as the wind, comforted his mother and his brothers, "I will leap into the air even like Vinata's son Garuda, king of birds. We have no fear from this fire."

Taking up his mother onto his left side, Yudhishtira on his right, the twins on each shoulder, and Arjuna on his back, the mighty Vrikodara cleared the towering flames with one leap. Setting out that night, they came to the Hidimba vana, and while Kunti and her sons slept the Rakshasi Hidimbi approached them.

She looked at Bhima and desired him. She took Bhima's feet onto her lap and began to press them with soft hands. Bhima tejasvin awoke and asked her, "Faultless featured, what do you want?"

The Rakshasi, who was beautiful, and could also assume any form she chose, replied to the Mahatman Bhima, "Fly from this place. My mighty brother will come to kill you. Do not tarry, fly!"

Bhima said haughtily, "I do not fear him. If he comes here, I will slay him."

Hearing this conversation, her brother Hidimba, vilest of Rakshasas, arrived there. He was terrible to behold, and came roaring. The Rakshasa said, "Hidimbi, who are you talking to? Bring him to me, let me eat him. Quickly, Hidimbi, do not delay."

But moved by compassion, the Rakshasi, whose heart was pure, made no reply. Then the monster, man-eater, rushed roaring at Bhima. He seized Bhima's hand and clenching his own hand into a fist as hard as Indra's thunderbolt, struck Bhima a blow like lightning.

Vrikodara flew into a rage, and a fearful fight erupted between Bhimasena and Hidimba. Both were skilled in the use of weapons, and their duel was even like the one between Indra and Vritra, of old.

Sinless Krishna, Bhima toyed with the mighty Rakshasa, wearing him down, and when Hidimba was exhausted Bhima Mahabaho killed him. Then, setting Hidimbi before them, Bhima, his brothers and Kunti

Devi left that forest. Later, Hidimbi would give birth by Bhima to Ghatotkacha.

After that, surrounded by Brahmanas, these Parantapas went towards Ekachakra with their mother. Meanwhile, Vyasa met them and became their counsellor. At Ekachakra, the Pandavas of stern vratas killed another mighty Rakshasa called Baka, as savage as Hidimba.

When he had killed Baka, Bhima went with his brothers to the capital of Drupada. And there, O Krishna, even as you won Bhishmaka's daughter Rukmini, Arjuna Savyasachin won me! Arjuna won me during my swayamvara, first performing an incredibly difficult feat of archery and then defeating all the other kings gathered there.

O Krishna, innumerable griefs afflict me now and we live here, with Dhaumya for our priest and guide, but separated from our beloved Kunti. Why do these, who are gifted with such strength, who have the prowess of lions, sit here indifferent, doing nothing, after they have seen me humiliated by vile and despicable enemies?

Am I born to suffer such searing indignity at the hands of base sinners, men of little strength beside? Am I to burn endlessly with grief? I was born into a great race, and came into this world in an extraordinary manner. Besides, I am the beloved wife of the Pandavas, and the daughter-in-law of the illustrious Pandu.

I, who am called the best of women, I who am devoted to my husbands, even I, O Krishna, was seized by my hair, and in the sight of the Pandavas, each of whom is like an Indra!'

Draupadi hides her face in her soft hands like lotus buds and sobs. Her tears flow down and wash her deep, full and graceful breasts, which bear every auspicious mark.

Wiping her eyes, sighing frequently, her voice choked, she says, 'No, I have no sons, husbands, friends, brothers or father, I have no one! I do not even have you, Krishna, for all of you see me having been savaged by vile men and you sit here and do nothing.

How will my grief at Karna's ridicule ever be assuaged? Krishna, I say to you that I deserve your protection always: because of our being related, because of your respect for me, because of our friendship and because you are the Lord!'

In that gathering of Kshatriyas in the forest, Krishna says to the weeping Panchali, 'Beautiful One, the wives of those who have angered you will weep even as you do, seeing their husbands lying dead on the ground, covered in blood and pierced by Arjuna's arrows.

Do not cry, for I will do everything in my power to help the sons of Pandu. I swear to you that you will again be a queen of kings. The Heavens may fall, or Himavat split open, the Earth might be rent, or the waters of the Ocean dry up, but my words shall never prove to be in vain!'

Draupadi listens to what Krishna says and looks sidelong at Arjuna. Mighty king, Arjuna says to her, 'You with the lovely copper eyes, do not grieve, it will be even as Krishna has said! Beautiful Panchali, it can never be otherwise.'

Dhrishtadyumna says, 'I will kill Drona, Sikhandin will kill the Pitama, Bhimasena will kill Duryodhana, and Dhananjaya will kill Karna. My sister, with Balarama and Krishna on our side, even Indra himself could not vanquish us in battle, then what are these sons of Dhritarashtra?'

Now, all the Kshatriyas there turn to Krishna, who then speaks to them."

CANTO 13

ARANYAKA PARVA CONTINUED

"Krishna says, 'Yudhishtira, lord of the earth, if I had been in Dwaraka, this evil would not have befallen you. Irrepressible one, I would have come to the game of dice, even if Ambika's sons had not asked me, or the other Kauravas. I would have called upon Bhishma, Drona, Kripa and Bahlika to help me, and prevented the game from being played.

Noble one, for your sake I would have said to Dhritarashtra, "Best of kings, let your sons have nothing to do with dice!" Yes, I would have spoken at length on all the evils of gambling, through which once Virasena's son lost his kingdom and through which you have now fallen into such distress.

Rajan, unthought-of evils befall a man from playing dice. I would have told how a man plays in compulsion, even if he wishes to stop. Women, dice, hunting and drinking, to which men become addicted from temptation, are regarded as the four evils that deprive a man of his prosperity. Those who know the Shastras say that evil attends upon all these.

Those who are addicted to dice also know all its evils. Mahabaho, appearing before the son of Ambika, I would have told him that through dice men lose all their possessions in a day and exchange harsh words. I would have named innumerable other ills which attend on dice.

If Dhritarashtra had accepted what I said, both the weal of the Kurus and dharma itself would have been secured. If he had rejected my gentle counsel, offered like a specific, then, Bharatasreshta, I would have compelled him with force. If those who sit in his sabha, professing to be his friends but who are actually his enemies, had supported him, I would have slain them all, along with the gamblers.

Kauravya, it is because I was away from Anarta[1] then that you played dice and have fallen into woe. Kurusthama, when I returned to Dwaraka, Yuyudhana told me about the disaster. As soon as I heard, my heart pierced by grief, I came here to you.

Alas, Pandava, such dire distress has overtaken you and I see you brothers and you plunged in misfortune.'"

---

[1]Krishna's country, of which Dwaraka is the capital.

CANTO 14

ARANYAKA PARVA CONTINUED

"Yudhishtira says, 'Krishna, where were you, away from Dwaraka? What did you do while you were away?'

Krishna says, 'Bharatarishabha, I went forth to raze the city of Salva. Best of the Kurus, listen to why I did this.

At your Rajasuya yagna, I slew Damaghosha's son Sisupala, mighty-armed and of great energy, because that evil one could not bear to see me being given the purodasa.

Hearing that Sisupala was slain, Salva, burning with anger, went to Dwaraka while I was away in Indraprastha with you. Arriving in a chariot made of precious metals, the Saubha, he engaged the young Vrishni princes, bulls of our line. Without mercy he slaughtered many young Vrishni heroes, and devastated all the gardens of our city.

Mahabaho, he roared, "Where is Krishna, that wretch of the Vrishni race, Vasudeva's evil son? I mean to humble his pride in battle. Tell me, O Anartas, where he is. I will go and kill him who slew Kamsa and Kesin, and then return.

By my weapons I swear I will not return without slaying him!"

Roaring again and again, "Where is he? Where is he?" the lord of the Saubha dashed here and there, wanting battle with me. Salva also raged, "He has dared kill Sisupala, and I will send him to Yama's halls today! I must kill Janardana for he slew my brother who was just a boy of tender years, and not on a field of battle, but while my brother was unprepared!"

Raging and howling thus, abusing me vilely, he flew up into the sky in his magical chariot, the Saubha which could fly anywhere at his very will. I returned to Dwaraka and heard what the evil king of Martika had said about me. I grew angry, O King, and considering his attack on Anarta, his abuse of me and his intolerable arrogance, I decided to kill him.

I set out from Dwaravati to slay the lord of the Saubha. I looked for him and found him on an island in the sea. I blew on my Panchajanya, challenging Salva to battle. However, at that moment, a host of Danavas attacked me and I slew them all.

Mahabaho, it was because of this that I could not come to you then. As soon as I heard about the game of dice at Hastinapura, I have come to see you and comfort you in your distress.'"

CANTO 15

ARANYAKA PARVA CONTINUED

"Yudhishtira says, 'Krishna, tell us in detail about the death of the lord of the Saubha. You have whetted my curiosity!'

Krishna says, 'When Salva heard that I had killed Sisupala, he came to Dwaravati, and with his army besieged that city from above and around. Keeping himself in the sky, he began his assault with a heavy shower of weapons of every kind.

Bharatarishabha, Dwaraka was fortified on all sides with pennons, arches, soldiers, walls, turrets, miners; her streets were barricaded with spikes; she had towers, storehouses full of provisions, engines for hurling burning brands and other fiery missiles, and vats of scalding oil and water; there were skins for carrying water to drink; trumpets, tabors we had, drums by thousands, lances and pitchforks, sataghnis, halayudhas, rockets, balls of stone, battle-axes, iron shields, and other engines for flinging iron balls, bullets and steaming fluids.

Many chariots defended Dwaraka, Kuruvyaghra, with maharathas like Gada, Samba, Uddhava and other great heroes, all nobly born, tried in battle, and who could resist any enemy. All these positioned themselves at their commanding posts, with horsemen and standard-bearers, and began to defend the city.

Ugrasena, Uddhava and others ordered that no one should drink throughout the city, to prevent any folly or carelessness. Knowing that Salva would destroy them if they were in the least careless, all the Vrishnis and Andhakas remained sober and watchful.

The soldiers made all the mimes, singers and dancers of Anarta leave Dwaraka, and they sank the bridges leading to the Sea city; boats were forbidden to ply, and long spikes raised upright in the moats which ring Dwaravati. The land around the city, for two yojanas, is always dug up, in pits and holes, in which explosives are hidden.

Anagha, our city-fortress is naturally protected, and well-defended and stocked with all kinds of weapons. Because of all this, Dwaraka was well prepared to counter any attack; why, she resembled Indra's own Amaravati. When Salva came, no one could enter or leave the city of the Vrishnis and Andhakas without giving a pre-arranged secret signal.

All the streets of the town and the open spaces, too, were filled with numberless elephants and horses. Mahabaho, all our soldiers were paid handsomely and given plentiful rations, weapons and clothes. All of them were paid in gold; all of them were in some way obliged to us, and all were of tried valour.

Yudhishtira of eyes like lotus-leaves, so, comprehensively, did Ugrasena defend Dwaraka!'"

CANTO 16

ARANYAKA PARVA CONTINUED

"Krishna continues, 'King of kings, Salva, master of the Saubha, great chariot and city of the air, came towards our city with an immense force of infantry, cavalry and elephants. His army, led by four other kings of great power, occupied a level ground commanding a plentiful water-supply.

Apart from cemeteries, temples dedicated to the gods, sacred groves of trees, and grounds covered by ant-hills, that host occupied every other place around Dwaraka. Divisions of that army barred all the roads into our city, and the secret entrances also were all blocked by the enemy.

O Kauravya, even like Garuda, Salva flew towards Dwaraka, with his host bearing all kinds of arms, skilled at all weapons, a dense array of chariots, elephants and cavalry, flying a sea of banners – well-paid and well-fed warriors, of great strength, bearing every mark of heroism, riding those wonderful chariots, armed with magnificent bows.

The young Vrishni princes saw Salva's army and sallied forth from our gates to face it. Charudeshna, Samba, the mighty Pradyumna, all put on mail, mounted their chariots, and decked with ornaments, their colours flying, rode to fight Salva's teeming legions.

Fiercely, Samba attacked Kshemavriddhi, the Senapati of Salva's forces, and struck his chief counsellor too with gusts of arrows. Why, Jambavati's son showered arrows upon the enemy in a river even as Indra does the rain. Kshemavriddhi stood unmoved as Himavan in that deadly storm.

Using maya, Kshemavriddhi discharged an even mightier tide of shafts at Samba. Samba dispelled the sorcery with his own maya and loosed a thousand arrows at his adversary's chariot. Now, pierced by Samba's barbs, overwhelmed, Kshemavriddhi fled in his fleet chariot.

When Salva's evil general left the field, a mighty Daitya called Vegavat rushed at my son. Samba stood his ground calmly. Kaunteya, Samba whirled a flashing mace and cast it at Vegavat, who fell on the ground like a mighty, faded patriarch of the forest whose roots have rotted away.

Upon the death of that ferocious Asura, Samba was at the enemy, spilling blood all around.

Another renowned Danava, Vivindhya, mighty warrior wielding a menacing bow, faced Charudeshna. And, O monarch, the encounter between Charudeshna and Vivindhya was as fierce as the one in olden days between Vritra and Vasava.

In fury, roaring like two great lions, they struck each other with arrows. Rukmini's son fitted a mighty astra, splendid as fire and the sun, to his bowstring; he chanted mantras over it and it could raze every enemy. Yudhishtira, my son loosed that weapon at Vivindhya, and the Danava fell dead.

Seeing Vivindhya slain, and his entire army wavering, Salva advanced again in his beautiful chariot, which could go anywhere. Mahabaho, seeing Salva in his chariot the fighters of Dwaraka trembled and began to retreat.

Then Pradyumna sallied forth, crying to the Anartas, "Do not fear! Watch me, I will drive back Salva in his chariot. Yadavas, today my astras will be like serpents and consume this entire host of the lord of the Saubha. I will kill Salva today and smash his fine Saubha."

Pandava, when Pradyumna spoke to them, fear left the Yadavas and they stayed to fight.'"

CANTO 17

ARANYAKA PARVA CONTINUED

"Krishna continued, 'Bharatarishabha, Pradyumna climbed into his golden chariot, drawn by the finest steeds covered in mail. Over it flew a standard bearing a Makara, a fierce crocodile with jaws agape and dreadful as Yama. His horses more flying than running on the ground, he charged the enemy.

Pradyumna bore quiver and sword, his fingers were encased in leather, and switching his bow, brilliant as lightning, from hand to hand, he twanged its string resoundingly, laughing in the enemy's face, spreading panic through their ranks.

He slew them all around him, contemptuously, and no one could mark any interval between the shafts he loosed. No colour rose into his face, his limbs did not so much as quiver; only his leonine roars rang across the field, while the sea monster's image on his golden flagstaff struck terror in his enemies' hearts.

Pradyumna, destroyer of his enemies, flew at Salva, himself eager for an encounter. But Salva could not bear Pradyumna's assault; he leapt down from his beautiful chariot of untold speed. Those watching, the people, saw the duel between Salva and the Vrishni hero which was even like that between Bali and Vasava, of old.

Kshatriya, Salva, mighty and lustrous, climbed back into his chariot and beset Pradyumna with a storm of arrows. Pradyumna fought back, briefly overwhelming Salva, who now shot arrows of blazing fire at my son. But Pradyumna easily parried that burning shower. Salva rained more shafts afire over him.

Best of kings, wounded by Salva's arrows, Pradyumna loosed an astra which could pierce the entrails of any enemy. That winged shaft pierced Salva's armour and entered his heart, at which he fell in a swoon. Seeing their lord fall, the Danava chieftains all fled the field.

Lord of the earth, cries of Oh! and Alas! arose from Salva's army. But Salva regained his senses, jumped up and suddenly loosed a clutch of savage barbs at Pradyumna. Pierced about his throat, Pradyumna staggered in his ratha. Wounding Rukmini's son, Salva roared like a lion, filling the world with that great sound. O Bhaarata, when my son fell senseless, Salva did not lose a moment but shot him with more deadly arrows. Pierced by numberless arrows, Pradyumna became motionless on the field of battle.'"

CANTO 18

ARANYAKA PARVA CONTINUED

"Krishna continues, 'Seeing Pradyumna felled by Salva, the Vrishnis all grew disheartened and stricken. Their fighters broke into loud cries of *Oh*! and *Alas*! while joy swept through the enemy ranks. Daruka's son, his sarathy, bore him swiftly from the field.

The chariot had not gone far when Pradyumna regained his senses, picked up his bow and said to his charioteer, "Sutaputra, what have you done? Why do you leave the battlefield? This is not the custom of the Vrishni heroes in battle!

Were you confounded by the sight of Salva? Or frightened by our duel? Tell me truly, I must know your mind."

The charioteer answered, "O son of Janardana, I am not confounded or afraid. On the other hand, I saw that it was difficult for you to vanquish Salva, and so I left the field. The wretch is stronger than you, and besides a sarathy must protect his warriors, especially when his Kshatriya faints.

Long-lived, I must always protect you even as you must always watch over me. Besides, you are alone while the Danavas are legion. I felt, O

Rukminiputra, that you are not equal to them in this fight and began to leave the field.'"

Krishna continued, 'When the charioteer said this, he who bears the Makara on his banner, retorted, "Turn the chariot around! O son of Daruka, never do this again, never flee the field, not while I am alive. No son of the House of Vrishni ever forsakes battle or kills an enemy fallen at his feet, crying I am yours! No Vrishni ever kills a woman, a boy, an old man, or a warrior in distress, who has lost his chariot or has had his weapons broken.

You are born a Suta and are well trained in your craft. O son of Daruka, you know the customs of the Vrishnis in battle. Never again fly from the field as you have done today. What will the irrepressible Krishna say to me when he hears that I left the field in bewilderment or that I was struck in the back, as I fled from battle?

What will Krishna's elder, the mighty-armed Baladeva, wearing blue and drunk on wine, say when he returns? What, O Suta, will that lion among men, Sini's grandson Satyaki, that great warrior, say when he hears I abandoned the fight?

Sarathy, what will the ever-victorious Samba, the invincible Charudeshna, Durdarsha, Gada, and Sarana, and Akrura of mighty arms say to me? What will the wives of the Vrishni heroes say to one another of me, who have so far been considered brave of noble conduct, honourable and manly?

They will even say, This Pradyumna is a coward who leaves the battle and comes here. Fie on him! They will never say, Well done! Ridicule, O Suta, is worse than death to someone like me. So never again leave the field of battle!

Leaving Dwaraka in my charge, Krishna has gone to the yagna of the Bhaarata lion. I cannot be a bystander now. Suta, when the brave Kritavarman was sallying out to face Salva, I stopped him, saying, You stay, I will fight Salva. And to honour me, Hridika's son desisted. If I leave the field of battle, what will I say to that mighty warrior when I meet him?

When Krishna, wielder of the sankha, chakra and gada, returns, what will I tell him of the eyes like lotus leaves? Satyaki, Baladeva and all the other Vrishnis and Andhakas always boast about me. What will I say to them?

Having left the field of battle and with wounds of arrows on my back, as you bore me away, I will not be able to live! O son of Daruka, turn the chariot around at once, and never flee again during battle, for I do not consider the life worth living which was gained by fleeing the field like a coward.

Sutaputra, have you ever seen me fly in fear from an enemy? It does not become you to leave the battle while my desire to fight on remains unquenched. Hurry, turn back!'"

CANTO 19

ARANYAKA PARVA CONTINUE

"Krishna continues, 'His charioteer replied hastily to Pradyumna, in sweet tones, "O son of Rukmini, I am not afraid to guide your horses on the field, and I know well the customs of the Vrishnis in war. But, O long-lived, the sarathy is taught that his warrior's life is always to be safeguarded by his charioteer.

You were sorely wounded by Salva's arrows, you fell unconscious, O Kshatriya. Only then did I leave the field. But, O lord of the Satwatas, now that you have regained consciousness, watch my skill in driving your horses! Daruka is my father and he has taught me chariotry. Watch me pierce Salva's army, O Hero!"

Saying this, that sarathy snapped his reins and turned back to the field of battle. Struck by his whip, deftly manoeuvred, those fine steeds seemed to fly through the air; beautifully they ran, in circles, now to the left then to the right, in even paths, then uneven. Truly, so light, so deft was the artistry of Daruka's son, his horses blazed along, and it seemed their hooves did not touch the ground, it seemed they read the sarathy's very thoughts.

So effortlessly and swiftly did that chariot dart through and wheel around Salva's force that they who watched were wonderstruck. Salva could not bear this and shot three arrows at Pradyumna's charioteer. But he sped on to the right, taking no notice of the shafts which pierced him.

Salva again loosed a shower of every kind of missile at Pradyumna. But that Parantapa, Rukmini's son, smiled, and with breathtaking lightness of hand cut them all down in flight. Salva used maya now and attacked Pradyumna more savagely still. Using the Brahmastra, Pradyumna again stopped those fell and powerful weapons, all the while shooting a stream of winged arrows at Salva.

And delighting in blood, these shafts truncated Salva's missiles, and flashed on to pierce his head, breast and his face. Salva fell senseless, and Pradyumna aimed another arrow at him, one which could kill any enemy.

Seeing that great astra, which all the Dasarhas worship, burning like fire and deadly as a serpent, fitted to Pradyumna's bowstring, the air was filled with cries of Oh! and Alas!

Now, the Devas, led by Indra and the Lord of treasures, Kubera, sent Narada down, and Vayu, the Wind God, whose speed is that of the mind. Coming to Pradyumna, they gave him this message: "Kshatriya, you must not kill Salva. Do not draw your astra, for you cannot kill him.

There is no man whom that arrow will not kill, but, Mahabaho, Brahma has ordained his death at the hands of Devaki's son Krishna. Do not let what Brahma has ordained be proved false."

Happily, Pradyumna withdrew that best of astras and thrust it back into his quiver. Then, best of kings, wounded sorely by Pradyumna's arrows, the mighty Salva rose, disheartened, and sped away. Afflicted by the Vrishnis, Salva mounted his magical chariot and, leaving Dwaraka, flashed away into the sky."

CANTO 20

ARANYAKA PARVA CONTINUED

"Krishna said, 'When Salva had left Dwaravati, I returned to it, O King, upon the completion of your great Rajasuya yagna. On my arrival, I found Dwaraka shorn of its splendour, and there were no sounds of Vedic chanting or sacrificial offering.

All the lovely young women wore no ornaments, and the gardens were desolated, no longer beautiful. Alarmed, I asked Hridika's son, "Why are the men and women of the city woebegone, O tiger among men?"

Kritavarman then told me in detail about Salva's invasion of Dwaraka, and also how he fled. Bharatottama, I decided to kill Salva. Cheerfully, I said to King Ahuka and Anakadundubhi, and the other great Vrishni heroes, 'Yadavarishabhas, stay in the city, taking every care, for I now go forth to kill Salva and I will not return to Dwaravati until I have.

I will come to you again when I have destroyed both Salva and his precious Saubha. Now strike up the sharp, middle and flat notes of the Dundubhi, which so terrifies our enemies!"

O Bharatarishabha, those Kshatriyas cried joyfully to me, "Go and slay the enemy!"

Taking their blessings and having the Brahmanas chant auspicious mantras, while I bowed down to those Dvijottamas, and to Siva also, I set out in my chariot, yoked to my great steeds Saibya and Sugriva, filling all the world with the clatter of my wheels and blowing on the Panchajanya, best of all sankhas!

I set out accompanied by my redoubtable and ever victorious army, consisting of the four kinds of forces and steadfast in battle. Passing over many countries, mountains crowned with trees, and water bodies, lakes, rivers and streams, I arrived at last in the country of Matrikavata.

There, Purushavyaghra, I heard that Salva flew in his aerial chariot, which was also his township, his city, near the sea and I pursued him there. Parantapa, I found him right in the midst of the billowing, heaving waves. Seeing me from a distance, Yudhishtira, that evil one challenged me repeatedly to fight. I loosed many arrows at him, great missiles, but they did not penetrate his Saubha.

I grew angry, and the evil, powerful son of a Daitya began to shoot thousands of arrows at me in a torrent. He covered my warriors, my sarathy and my horses with arrows, but we fought on.

Salva's legions loosed more arrows, again in thousands, over me. They mantled my ratha, my horses and Daruka with astras which could pierce one's very entrails. Then, I could no longer see my chariot, horses or even Daruka; my army and I were both shrouded in arrows.

Kaunteya, I chanted mantras to summon astras, and loosed tens of thousands of them at the enemy. But the Saubha was far away, two yojanas, and my warriors could not see it. They could only stand below on the battlefield and, like spectators in an arena, cheer me with lions' roars and loud handclapping.

My tinted arrows, meanwhile, pierced Danava bodies like fierce insects, and there arose cries from within the Saubha of those who died by them, and fell into the sea below. Arm and necks cut off, Danavas looking like dismembered kabandhas fell, roaring horribly. Carnivores of the deep devoured them hungrily.

I blew an echoing blast on the Panchajanya, which once rose from those waters, and which is as graceful as a lotus-stalk, and white as milk, the kunda flower, the moon, or as silver. Seeing his soldiers die, Salva began to fight using maya, illusion.

He cast a tirade of maces, ploughshares, winged darts and lances, javelins, battle-axes, daggers, arrows blazing like thunderbolts, nooses, swords, bullets from barrels, other strange shafts, and missiles. I allowed them to fly towards me, then dispelled the sorcery of which they were made.

Salva now cast mountain peaks of maya at me. Then he created uncanny weather changes – darkness and light, alternately, the day was now fair, and now gloomy, now hot, and now cold. He caused a fierce shower of live coals, hot ash and arrows to pour down over me.

With these illusions, he duelled with me; and I dispelled all his maya with my own power, and also continued to loose thousands of shafts at the Saubha. Suddenly, the dome of heaven blazed as with a hundred suns and with a hundred moons, too, and millions of stars; and no one could tell if this was day or night; no one could distinguish the points of the horizon.

Perplexed myself, I fitted the Pragnastra to my bowstring. That weapon blew away Salva's sorcery in the sky even as the wind does wisps of cotton wool. Now we had light again, and we fought fiercely once more, so those who watched had their hair stand on end.'"

CANTO 21

ARANYAKA PARVA CONTINUED

"Krishna says, 'Tiger among men, Salva flew high into the sky again and cast down blazing sataghnis, and mighty maces, and flaming lances, and thick cudgels. I shot them all down as they flew at me, and the sky echoed.

Salva covered Daruka, my horses and ratha with hundreds of straight, deadly shafts. Daruka seemed about to faint and said to me, "Ah Krishna, I am sorely wounded. I have not left the field only because it is my dharma to stay. But my limbs turn weak and I cannot continue."

Hearing his piteous voice, I looked at him and saw he was wounded by countless arrows. There was no place on his chest, his head, his arms or the rest of his body from which fell arrows did not protrude. Blood flowed profusely from his wounds, and he looked like a mountain of red chalk after heavy rain.

Mahabaho, seeing Daruka wounded, I tried to embolden him and make him cheerful.

Just then, a man from Dwaraka came running to my chariot with a message from Ahuka. He seemed to be one of Ahuka's followers, and said in a voice choking with sorrow, "Ahuka, the lord of Dwaraka, sends you this message. Krishna, listen to what your father's friend says. O Vrishni, irrepressible one, while you were away today, Salva came to Dwaraka, seized your father Vasudeva by main force and killed him. No need for you to fight anymore. Cease, Janardana, you must return to Dwaraka now; to defend her is your only dharma."

My heart grew heavy, and I could not decide what to do. Inwardly I blamed Satyaki, Baladeva, and the mighty Pradyumna, for when I left to attack Salva I had given them charge of protecting Dwaraka and Vasudeva.

In grief I asked myself, "Does the mighty-armed Baladeva live, and Satyaki, and Rukmini's son and Charudeshna of great prowess, and Samba and the others? For, if they did, even Indra himself could not kill Vasudeva. Ah, if Vasudeva is dead, surely all these others and Balarama, too, must also be dead."

Yudhishtira, I was overwhelmed by grief, and in that condition I encountered Salva again. And now I saw Vasudeva himself falling from the Saubha! Oh, my father seemed like Yayati himself falling down to the earth when he lost his punya; I saw my father fall like a luminary whose punya was exhausted, his clothes in disarray, his helmet loose and his hair flowing free and wild, and I swooned away.

The bow Saranga dropped from my hand and I had to sit down abruptly in my chariot. My legions saw me thus, and their cries rent the air. Ah, my father fell like a dead bird, and Salva's soldiers on the ground hewed savagely at him with sword and axe.

At this my heart shook violently and I regained consciousness. O Kshatriya, nowhere did I see my father or Salva or his Saubha made of precious metals. I knew that it had all just been maya, the enemy's illusion, and recovering quickly, I began to loose my arrows again, in hundreds.'"

CANTO 22

ARANYAKA PARVA CONTINUED

"Krishna continues, 'Seizing up my beautiful bow, I began to decapitate the Danavas who rode in the Saubha. My Saranga streamed arrows formed like serpents, of intense energy and which could fly up to great heights.

Then, I did not see the Saubha anymore, for it had vanished through maya. I was filled with wonder. However, the frightful Danava host set up a loud and joyful howling. I fitted an astra to my bowstring, a missile which would bury itself in an invisible enemy if only his voice was audible. Immediately, their shouting stopped. However, those who had howled were already slain by my arrows blazing like the sun.

When the shouts and yells stopped in one place, they broke out in another, and there too I loosed my arrows. Bhaarata, the Asuras roared from the ten directions, as well as from above and below, and all those who did roar I slew: those that were in the sky and invisible, all with arrows of diverse forms, and astras summoned with mantras.

Suddenly, the Saubha reappeared, of all places at Pragjyotishapura, dazzling my eyes. The monstrous Danavas showered a lashing rain of great rocks over me, covering me entirely, even like some vast anthill. Mighty crags covered my horses, my charioteer and flagstaffs, and I could not be seen anymore.

The Vrishni army panicked and fled in every direction. Seeing me covered over with the massive stones, heaven and earth resounded with shocked cries; all my kinsmen and comrades began to weep and wail aloud, while grief tore at their hearts.

My enemies were delighted, so I heard after I had defeated the enemy! Then, I wielded the Vajra, Indra's thunderbolt, which can rive the hardest stone, and smashed the mountain of rocks. However, my horses could hardly bear the weight of the rocks, and seemed on the point of death. They trembled.

When my warriors saw me again they rejoiced as men do when the Sun breaks out from behind dark clouds, dispelling darkness. Seeing my horses almost at last gasp, sorely wounded by the mass of stones, my sarathy Daruka said to me, "O Vrishni, look where Salva sits in his Saubha. Kill him, Krishna! Abandon your mercy and mildness, Mahabaho, do not let him live.

Parantapa, you must do everything in your power to kill your inveterate enemies. A strong man should not disregard even a weak enemy who is under his foot, then what to say of someone like Salva, who dares us to fight? Tiger among men, Lord, exert yourself and kill him!

Do not delay any longer, this one cannot be vanquished with milder methods. And surely, he that is fighting you so savagely, he who has devastated Dwaraka, cannot be your friend!"

Kaunteya, listening to Daruka and knowing that what he said was true, I turned my attention back to the battle, now meaning to kill Salva and destroy his Saubha.

I said to Daruka, "Stay here a moment!", and I summoned my favourite weapon, of fire, chakra of blazing energy, irresistible and splendid disc. I cried to that great wheel, "Consume the Saubha and all the enemies inside it!"

In anger, chanting mantras of power, I loosed the inexorable Sudarsana Chakra, which makes ashes of Yakshas, Rakshasas, Danavas and kings born into fell tribes, the disc sharp as a razor, stainless, which is even like Yama the destroyer, and incomparable.

Spuming up into the sky, it seemed like another Sun of the blinding fulgurance with which the yuga ends. Flashing at the airborne township, the marvellous Saubha, whose glory vanished in a moment, the Chakra scythed right through it, even as a saw divides a tree.

Cut in two by the Sudarsana, the Saubha fell like the city of Tripura cloven by the shafts of Maheswara. When the Saubha fell, the Chakra flew back into my hands. I cast it again, crying, "Go now to Salva!"

Salva was about to hurl a sorcerer's mace at me, when the Sudarsana struck him, cut him in half and set him ablaze. When that fierce and valiant Danava died, Asura women lamented everywhere, and were led away sobbing.

I brought my chariot before the townlike vimana Saubha and joyfully blew my conch, gladdening the hearts of my friends. Seeing their city, lofty as the peak of Meru, with its palaces and gateways ruined, and all ablaze, the Danavas fled in fear. Having thus destroyed the Saubha and slain Salva, I returned to the Anartas and my kin and friends were delighted.

Rajan, this is why I could not come to Hastinapura. If I had come, Suyodhana would not be alive nor would the game of dice have been played. What can I do now? It is hard to confine the waters after a dam is breached!'"

Vaisampayana continued, "Having addressed the Kaurava thus, Krishna Purushottama, Mahabaho, Madhusudana, owner of all grace, salutes the Pandavas, and prepares to depart.

Reverently, he salutes Dharmaraja Yudhishtira, and in return the king and Bhima, also, sniff the crown of his head affectionately. Arjuna embraces Krishna, and the twins salute him with reverence. Dhaumya duly honours Krishna, and Draupadi, in tears, worships him.

Making Subhadra and Abhimanyu climb into his golden chariot, Krishna mounts it himself. After consoling Yudhishtira, Krishna sets out for Dwaraka in his ratha resplendent as the Sun, chariot to which the horses Saibya and Sugriva are yoked.

After the Dasarha has left, Dhrishtadyumna also sets out for his own city, taking Draupadi's sons with him. Bidding farewell to the Pandavas, Dhrishtaketu, king of Chedi, sets out for his beautiful city Suktimati, taking his sister with him. The Kaikeyas, too, with leave from Yudhishtira of immeasurable tejas, reverentially salute all the Pandavas, and depart.

But the Brahmanas, the Vaisyas and the other people of Yudhishtira's kingdom will not leave the Pandavas, though asked repeatedly to do so. Best of kings, extraordinary is the multitude that surrounds those Mahatmans in the Kamyaka vana.

Yudhishtira honours those high-minded Brahmanas, then commands his men, 'Prepare my chariot!'"

CANTO 23

ARANYAKA PARVA CONTINUED

Vaisampayana continued, "After Krishna leaves, Yudhishtira, Bhima, Arjuna, and the twins, each of them as magnificent as Siva, with Draupadi and their priest, climb into fine chariots yoked to pedigreed horses, and drive into the jungle together.

As they go, they distribute nishkas of gold, clothes and cows to Brahmanas versed in siksha, akshara and mantras, and twenty attendants follow them, all carrying bows, more gleaming weapons, astras and other engines of war. With the princess's clothes and ornaments, her maids and her sakhis, Indrasena follows speedily in another chariot.

Approaching the best of Kurus, the noble-minded citizens walk around him. The principal Brahmanas of Kurujangala cheerfully salute him, and Dharmaraja Yudhishtira and his brothers salute them back in joy. The illustrious king stops there a while, looking at the concourse of the inhabitants of Kurujangala.

Yudhishtira feels for them as a father for his sons, and they also feel for him what sons feel for their father. Coming up to the great Kuru, they stand around him.

Taken with shyness, tears in their eyes, they all exclaim, "Alas, O Lord! O Dharma!" And they say, "You are the lord of the Kurus, our king, and we are your subjects. Where are you going, O king of dharma, leaving all these your people, like a father leaving his sons?

Fie on the cruel son of Dhritarashtra! Fie on the evil-minded son of Subala! Fie on Karna! For, O best of kings, who are steadfast in dharma, these wretches always wish you ill.

Having established the unrivalled city of Indraprastha, splendid as Kailasa itself, where do you go leaving it? O illustrious and just king, O Dharmaptura, where do you go, leaving the peerless Mayaa Sabha, as resplendent as the palace of the Devas, which is even like some divine illusion, always guarded by the gods?"

Arjuna, who knows the ways of dharma, artha and kama, says to them in a loud voice, "By living in the forest, the king means to take away the honour of his enemies. O you with these Brahamans at your head, who know dharma and artha, ask them privately what they believe will fetch us supreme felicity."

When the Brahmanas and the other varnas hear what Arjuna says, they salute Yudhishtira, that best of men. Walking reverently around the king—Bhima, Arjuna, Yagnaseni, and the twins—and commanded by Yudhishtira, they return to their homes in the kingdom with heavy hearts."

ARANYAKA PARVA CONTINUED

Vaisampayana said, "After they have gone, Yudhishtira says to his brothers, 'We must live in the forest for twelve years. So, search this mighty vana for some spot which abounds in birds, deer, flowers and fruit, a place that is beautiful, auspicious, and also where Sages dwell, so we might live there pleasantly all those years.'

Arjuna says to his elder brother, as reverently as to a Guru, 'You have worshipfully served all the great and old Rishis, and there is nothing in the world of men that you do not know. Bharatarishabha, with the utmost respect, you have waited upon great Brahmanas, Dwaipayana and others, and Narada of great punya, who with their senses perfectly controlled, journey freely from the gates of this world to those of the realms of the Devas, the Gandharvas and the Apsaras, and even to Brahmaloka.

Beyond doubt, you know the mind of the Maharishis, as well as their power. You also know, O King, what is best for us. We will live wherever you say. Here in this forest called Dwaitavana is a lake full of holy water, enchanting to look at, with its profusion of flowers and every kind of bird.

Rajan, if this place pleases you, shall we remain there for twelve years? Or are you of a different mind?"

Yudhishtira replies, "Partha, what you say recommends itself to me. Let us go the famed, great and sacred Dwaitavana."

Pandu's son goes towards the sacred lake known as Dwaitavana. Yudhishtira is surrounded by many Brahmanas, some of whom sacrifice with fire and some without it; some are devoted to the study of the Vedas, living on alms and they are Vanaprasthas, forest-dwellers. The king is also surrounded by hundreds of Mahatmans, of stern vows, their tapasya crowned with success.

Those Bharatarishabhas, the Pandavs, and their Brahmanas, enter the sacred and enchanting vana of Dwaita. At summer's end, Yudhishtira sees the great jungle full of salas, palms, mango trees, madhukas, nipas, kadambas, sarjas, arjunas and karnikaras, many of them covered with flowers.

Flocks of peacocks, datyuhas, chakoras, varhins and kokilas sit on the tops of the tallest trees, pouring down mellifluous songs. Mighty herds of gigantic elephants, big as the hills, he sees, with the juice of rut trickling down their temples, accompanied by herds of cow-elephants.

Approaching the beautiful Saraswati, the king sees many Sannyasins, and other ascetics, within that vana, all wearing valkala, with matted jata upon their heads.

Alighting from his chariot, Yudhishtira enters the forest even like Indra entering Devaloka. Hosts of Charanas and Siddhas, wanting to see that king of dharma, come towards him. Quickly, the dwellers of the Dwaita throng around that lion among kings, of the great intellect.

Saluting all the Siddhas, and saluted by them in return as a king or a god should be, that best of men walks into the forest with folded hands, along with those Dvijottamas. Yudhishtira sits down in the midst of those good ascetics, at the foot of a magnificent tree, adorned with flowers, even as his father Pandu had once.

All of them tired, Bhima, Dhananjaya, the twins, Panchali and their followers, leave their chariots and sit around their king. And that mighty tree, bent with the weight of thick creepers, with those five illustrious bowmen sitting beneath it, looks like a mountain with five noble elephants resting upon its side."

CANTO 25

ARANYAKA PARVA CONTINUED

Vaisampayana said, "In their distress, the exiled princes find a
pleasant place to live in the vana. And there in that jungle of
plentiful Sala trees, forest washed by the Saraswati, they who
are like five Indras begin to besport themselves.

The king devotes himself to befriending, serving and pleasing all the
Yatis, Munis and the main Brahmanas in that forest, with offerings of
fine fruit and roots. Dhaumya, their priest of tremendous tejas, and like
a father to the princes, begins to perform the sacrificial rites of Ishti and
Paitreya for the Pandavas in that great forest.

One day, the ancient Rishi Markandeya, of intense and abundant
tejas, arrives as a guest in the Pandavas' asrama. Yudhishtira pays devout
homage to the great Muni, revered by the devas, by Rishis and by men,
and who is as splendid as blazing fire.

Seeing Draupadi, Yudhishtira, Bhima and Arjuna living amongst
ascetics of the vana, the lustrous and all-knowing Sage smiles. Yudhishtira
asks, 'Muni, all these hermits feel sad to see us here in the wilderness,
but you smile as if in joy. Why is it that you alone seem pleased?'

Markandeya replies, 'My child, I too feel sad and do not smile in any joy, nor do I feel any satisfaction to see you here. But seeing you today I am reminded of Dasaratha's son Rama, who lived in the forest at his father's command.

Son of Pritha, I saw him in those olden days, ranging through the jungle, his bow in his hand and Lakshmana beside him. I saw him on the hill of Rishyamooka. Rama was like Indra, the lord of Yama himself, and the slayer of Namuchi. Yet, that sinless one had to live in the forest at his father's command, and he accepted that as his dharma.

Yes, Rama was Sakra's equal in prowess; he was invincible in battle. Yet, abandoning all luxury and pleasure he went to live in the vana. So no one should sin, or leave dharma thinking *I am mighty!*

The king Nabhaga, Bhagiratha and others, too, subdued the Earth bounded by seas, only through dharma, and finally gained the realms beyond. Child, no one should leave dharma, thinking *I am mighty!*

Noblest of men, the virtuous and honest king of Kasi and Karusha was called a mad dog for relinquishing his kingdom and his wealth. No one should sin, saying *I am mighty!*

Best of men, O son of Pritha, the Saptarishis blaze in the sky for having followed the eternal dharma which the Creator has laid down in the Vedas. Ah, no one should leave dharma, thinking *I am mighty!*

Behold, O King, mighty elephants, tusked and great as mountain cliffs do not transgress the laws of the Creator. So, too, no man should break dharma thinking *Might is mine!* Best of kings, look how every creature and species follows its own nature and law, as created by God. Surely, no one should break dharma saying *Might is mine!*

Prithaputra, in truth, in virtue, in righteous conduct and in humility you have surpassed all creatures, and your fame and brilliance are as those of Agni or Surya. You are steadfast in keeping your word, and when you have passed your painful exile in the forest you will take back your lambent fortune from the Kauravas, through your own might!'

Saying this much to Yudhishtira, who sits among his friends and the ascetics of the forest, the Maharishi Markandeya salutes Dhaumya and the Pandavas and walks away towards the north."

CANTO 26

ARANYAKA PARVA CONTINUED

Vaisampayana said, "While the Pandavas live in the forest, the Dwaitavana teems with Brahmanas. The lake always resounds with Vedic chanting, and is like a second holy Brahmaloka, as the very air thrills to the sounds of the Yajus, the Riks, the Samas, and other incantations. These chants mingle with the twanging of the bowstrings of the sons of Pandu, creating a union of Brahmana and Kshatriya customs, noble and beautiful.

One evening, the Rishi Baka of the Dalbhya clan says to Yudhishtira who sits among the Brahmanas, 'Look, lord of the Kurus, it is the time of the homa and the sacred fires have been lit. All these Brahmanas of stern vows sanctify this place with their rituals.

The descendants of Bhrigu and Angiras, along with those of Vasishta and Kasyapa, the illustrious sons of Agastya, the offspring of Atri, indeed all the foremost Brahmanas of the world are here with you! Listen, O Kaunteya, you and your brothers, to what I have to say to you.

As fire helped by the wind consumes a forest, so will Brahmana tejas combining with Kshatriya might consume all enemies. My child, he who wants to subdue this world and the next must never be without Brahmanas beside him. A king vanquishes his enemies only when he has for his priest a Brahmana who knows dharma, worldly affairs, and is free from passion and folly.

King Bali, who loved his subjects, performed his dharma, which led to moksha, knowing of no other means to achieve his ends other than the Brahmanas. For this alone all the wishes of Virochana's son, the Asura, were always gratified, and his wealth was inexhaustible.

He gained the whole world with the help of Brahmanas, and found destruction when he wronged them. This Earth, with her treasures, never for long adores as her lord a Kshatriya who lives without a Brahmana. The same sea-girt Bhumi, however, bows to him who is ruled by a Brahmana and taught his dharma by a Brahmana. Like an elephant in battle without his mahout, a Kshatriya destitute of Brahmanas decreases in power.

The Brahmana's vision is without compare, and the Kshatriya's might is also unparalleled. When these combine, the whole world joyfully yields to the twain. As fire becomes stronger blown by the wind, and consumes straw and wood, so do kings with Brahmanas consume all foes.

To gain what he has not, and to increase what he has, a Kshatriya should take the counsel of Brahmanas. Therefore, O son of Kunti, you also keep a Brahmana of repute with you, one who knows the Vedas, a man of wisdom and experience. Yudhishtira, you have always had the highest regard for the Brahmanas. It is because of this that your fame is great and blazes through the three worlds.'

All the Brahmanas there are delighted to hear Baka of the Dalbhya clan praise Yudhishtira and they, in turn, worship Baka. Dwaipayana, Narada, Jamadagnya and Prithusravas; Indradyumna and Bhaluki and Kritachetas and Sahasrapat; and Karnasravas and Munja and Lavanaswa and Kasyapa; and Harita and Sthunakarna and Agnivesya and Saunaka; and Kritavak and Suvaka, Brihadaswa and Vibhavasu; and Urdhvaretas and Vrishamitra and Suhotra and Hotravahana – these and many other Brahmanas, too, then adore Yudhishtira even like Rishis adoring Purandara in heaven!"

CANTO 27

ARANYAKA PARVA CONTINUED

Vaisampayana said, "Exiled to the forest, one evening as they sit together, in some sorrow, the sons of Pritha and Draupadi speak to one another.

Beautiful, knowing, beloved of her lords and devoted to them, Panchali says to Yudhishtira, 'Ah, when Dhritarashtra's cruel, sinful son could send us into the vana wearing deerskin, surely the evil one feels no twinge of remorse. His heart is made of iron, that he could speak to you, his elder brother, as harshly as he did.

No, causing you, who deserve every happiness, such distress, the evil one rejoices with his friends. O Bhaarata, when you were sent into exile only four men did not shed a tear: Duryodhana, Karna, the vile Sakuni and the beast Dussasana. All the other Kurus grieved and they wept.

Seeing this harsh bed on which you sleep, I think of what you had before and I grieve for you, O King who were raised in every luxury and do not deserve the least hardship. I think of the jewelled ivory throne in your court, and now I see you on this seat of kusa grass, and grief devours me.

Rajan, I saw you surrounded by kings in your sabha. What peace can my heart know seeing you like this today? I have seen your body anointed with sandalwood paste, and now I see you smeared with dust and mud. I saw you clad in royal silken robes, and now I see you wearing rags.

Once, the purest, finest food was carried from your palace in golden plates to thousands of Brahmanas, and you fed delicacies to ascetics, both homeless and grihastas. You lived in your palace once and worshipped the Brahmanas of the earth, satisfying their every wish.

Yudhishtira, what peace can my heart now have, seeing all this? These brothers of yours, young and wearing the costliest ornaments, were once clad in the most expensive clothes and fed by the greatest cooks. Alas, I see them all now, none deserving sorrow, living in the wild, upon what the wilderness yields.

O King, my heart knows no peace! Thinking of this Bhimasena living in sorrow in the vana, does your anger not blaze up? Why are you not wrathful seeing Bhima, who always did everything for us all, now plunged in grief, though it is every happiness that he deserves? Why does your fury not blaze seeing Bhima, who once lived amidst every luxury, with countless chariots and wearing the most superior clothes, like this today, in this jungle?

This noble one is ready to kill all the Kurus, but he contains his rage and his grief to keep your solemn word.

Arjuna, O Rajan, has but two hands, but he is equal to Kartaviryarjuna of a thousand arms in his prodigious archery. To his enemies, he is even like Yama himself. Was it not through his prowess that all the kings of the Earth waited upon the Brahmanas at your Rajasuya yagna?

How is it that seeing Arjuna, tiger among men, whom both men and the gods worship, in this wretchedness, you anger does not blaze up? I grieve, O Bhaarata, that you are not wrathful at seeing this son of Pritha in exile – Arjuna who deserves no such misery, who had been raised in the lap of every luxury.

Why are you not furious, seeing Arjuna in exile, Arjuna who in a single chariot vanquished the Devas, the Manavas and the Nagas, all? Why are you not furious seeing Arjuna in exile, Arjuna who was honoured with offerings of chariots, horses and elephants, who forcibly took from the kings of the Earth their treasures, who is the conqueror of all foes, who with one motion can loose five hundred arrows? Why are you not furious seeing Nakula in exile, Nakula so fair, able-bodied and young, who is foremost among swordsmen? How can you pardon your enemy, O Yudhishtira, seeing Madri's son, the handsome and brave Sahadeva, in exile? Why are you not furious seeing both Nakula and Sahadeva overwhelmed by grief, though so undeserving of it?

How can you pardon your enemy while seeing me in exile, I who am Drupada's daughter, Dhrishtadyumna's sister, illustrious Pandu's daughter-in-law and the devoted wife of the Pandavas? Truly, O Bhaarata, you are incapable of anger, for how else is it that you are not moved seeing your brothers' and distress and mine? It is said that there is no Kshatriya in the world who is free of anger, that the Kshatriya who does not find his anger when the need arises is forever disrespected by all creatures.

O King, you should not forgive your enemies. With your power, you can defeat them all. Know also that the Kshatriya who does not forgive when the time for forgiveness comes is cursed by every creature and meets with destruction both in this world and the next.'"

CANTO 28

ARANYAKA PARVA CONTINUED

"Draupadi continues, 'Once, Vali, son of Virochana, questioned his grandfather Prahlada, the chief of the Asuras and the Danavas, possessed of great wisdom and versed in the subtleties of dharma, saying, "Sire, is forgiveness greater, or strength and anger? I am unsure, Pitama, enlighten me! Tell me, since you know dharma so well, which is better? I will do whatever you command."

Prahlada said, "Know this truth with certainty – neither anger nor forgiveness is invariably greater! He that forgives suffers many ills. Servants and strangers and enemies disrespect him. No creature bows down to him. So it is that the learned do not approve constant forgiveness.

The servants of an ever-forgiving person will seek to deprive him of his wealth and belongings. They do not give others the things that they are directed to by their master, nor do they give their master the respect that is his due. Dishonour is worse than death. My child, sons, servants, attendants, and even strangers speak harshly to the man who always forgives.

Disregarding this man, people even desire his wife, and his wife also behaves as she pleases. Servants who are not punished by their master acquire all sorts of vices, and some even injure such a master. These and many other ills afflict the ever forgiving.

Listen now, O son of Virochana, to the troubles of those that never forgive. The man of wrath who, surrounded by darkness, uses his strength to constantly inflict punishment on others, whether deserved or not, is separated from his friends. Such a man is hated by both relatives and strangers. Such a man, because he insults others, loses his wealth and reaps disregard, sorrow, hatred, bewilderment and enemies.

Because of his ire, the man of wrath listens to harsh words, is parted from his friends, relatives, prosperity and his very life. He who uses his strength against both his friend and his foe, is an object of alarm to the world, as a snake who has taken shelter in a house is to its residents. What prosperity can he have who alarms the world? People will hurt him whenever they have an opportunity.

So, men should never use strength in excess, nor forgiveness on all occasions. One should use might and show forgiveness when appropriate. He who forgives at the proper time and is angry at the proper time finds happiness both in this world and the next.

I will now tell you in detail about the occasions prescribed by the Sages for forgiveness, which everyone should observe. Listen carefully. If someone who has once done you a service wrongs you, even grievously, he must be forgiven in remembrance of the old service. Those who offend because they are ignorant or callow should be forgiven because not all men are learned or wise.

However, those who wrong you knowingly, even if their offence be trivial and they plead ignorance, must be punished. Such false, crooked men should never be pardoned. Although every man's first offence should be forgiven, the second you must punish, even if it is trivial.

But if a man offends you unwittingly, and his plea of ignorance is found to be true after a judicious and thorough enquiry, he should be pardoned. Humility will vanquish might; humility will also vanquish weakness; there is nothing which humility cannot accomplish. Truly, humility is fiercer than it seems!

One must act in accordance with place and time, taking note of his own strength or weakness. No undertaking which does not take place and time into account can succeed; always wait upon place and time. Sometimes, offenders should be forgiven from fear of the people. These have been declared to be times for forgiveness, while on other occasions force should be put forth against offenders.'"

"Draupadi continues, 'O King, I believe that this is the time to use your strength and force. Dhritarashtra's greedy sons always seek to harm us, and this is no time to forgive them but to use your power against them.

The ever humble and forgiving person is disregarded; while those that are always fierce and persecute others are despised. But he is indeed a king, who takes recourse to both, each at their proper time.'"

CANTO 29

ARANYAKA PARVA CONTINUED

"Yudhishtira says, 'Anger is the slayer of men and is again their prosperor. Wise one, know that anger is the root of all prosperity and all adversity. Beautiful one, he who restrains his anger prospers, while he who gives in always to his rage reaps adversity.

In this world, anger is the cause of the destruction of every being; then how can one like me indulge my anger, when it can destroy the very world. The angry man commits sin. The angry man kills even his Gurus. The angry man insults even his elders with harsh words.

The man who is angry cannot distinguish between what he should and should not say. There is nothing that an angry man will not do, no vile word that an angry man will not utter. In anger a man might kill someone who does not deserve killing, and he might worship another who deserves to die.

The angry man might even send his own soul to the land of Yama. Seeing all this clearly, the wise control their anger, wishing for great prosperity both in this world and the next. This is why serene souls banish anger, then how can I indulge in wrath?

Draupadi, I reflect on this, and do not allow my anger to be excited. He who does not respond to an angry man saves himself and others from great fear. Indeed, he can be regarded as the physician of both himself and the angry man.

If a weak man is persecuted by men who are stronger than himself, and foolishly turns his anger on them, he causes his own downfall. Such a one who deliberately throws away his life gains no realms of felicity in the hereafter. So, Draupadi, a weak man should always suppress his anger. And the wise man who, even though wronged, does not allow his anger to be roused, passing over his persecutor in indifference, enjoys great happiness in the next world.

This is why it has been said that, be he strong or weak, the wise man forgives his enemy. Panchali, this is why the good applaud those who have conquered their wrath. Sage men believe that the honest and forgiving man is always victorious.

Truth is ever more beneficial than falsehood, and gentleness than cruelty. Then how can one like me show anger even to kill Duryodhana, when anger has so many faults, anger which men of dharma banish from their souls? The wise surely regard those who only outwardly show anger as being men of character. Men of learning and true insight call him who can control his provoked anger, through his wisdom, a man of character.

O you of the fair hips, the angry man does not see things in their true light. He does not see his way or respect anyone. The angry man kills even those that do not deserve killing. The man of wrath kills even his preceptors. So, the man of character must always banish wrath to a distance.

The man who is overwhelmed by anger does not easily acquire generosity, dignity, courage, skill, and the other qualities which belong with true character. By forsaking anger a man can show his strength and energy at the proper time, while this is very difficult for the angry man to do.

Fools regard anger as being equivalent to strength, but wrath has been given to man for the destruction of the world. So, the man who wishes to live in dharma must always forsake anger. For sure, those who abandon the virtues of their svadharma indulge anger.

Faultless one, if fools, their minds full of darkness, trangresss dharma in every way, should I be like them and do the same? If there were none among men equal to the Earth in forgiveness, there would be no peace in the world, but ceaseless strife caused by wrath.

If the injured return their injuries, if one chastised by his superior were to chastise his superior in return, the consequence would be the destruction of every creature, and sin would prevail throughout the world.

If the man who is spoken harshly to speaks back savagely in turn, if fathers kill sons and sons their fathers, if husbands kill wives, and wives husbands, Draupadi, how can there be any births into such a world where anger held such sway? For, lovely one, know that men are born because there is peace.

Panchali, if kings yield to wrath, their subjects quickly find death. The consequence of anger is distress and destruction for the people. It is because there are men who are as forgiving as the Earth that all beings live and prosper. One should forgive every injury, for every species and race continues because man is forgiving.

Truly, the wise and excellent man, who has conquered his anger, is he who forgives even when he is insulted, persecuted and infuriated by a strong enemy. The man of power who controls his anger enjoys countless everlasting realms, while the angry man is known to be a fool and finds destruction both in this and the other world.

O Krishnaa, the illustrious and forgiving sang this of men who are always forgiving:

"Forgiveness is virtue; forgiveness is sacrifice; forgiveness is the Vedas, forgiveness is the Sruti. He who knows this can forgive anything. Forgiveness is Brahman; forgiveness is truth; forgiveness is punya; forgiveness protects the punya of the future; forgiveness is sannyasa; forgiveness is holiness; and by forgiveness the universe is held together.

Men of forgiveness attain the realms gained by those who perform great tapasya, or those who are masters of the Vedas, or those that have great ascetic merit. Those who perform Vedic yagnas, as also those who perform other sacred karma obtain lesser realms, while men of forgiveness find the adored realms which are in Brahmaloka. Forgiveness is the might of the mighty; forgiveness is sacrifice; forgiveness is quiet of mind."

How, Krishnaa, can someone like me abandon forgiveness, in which Brahman, truth, wisdom and the worlds are founded? Kasyapa said, "The man of wisdom should always forgive, for when he is capable of forgiving everything, he attains Brahman.

This world belongs to those that are forgiving; the other world is also theirs. The forgiving find honour here, and a state of blessedness hereafter. Men who subdue even their anger through forgiveness gain the loftiest realms. So has it been said that forgiveness is the highest virtue."

So did Kasyapa sing of those who are ever forgiving. Panchali, having heard what he said, content yourself. Do not give way to your anger!

Our Pitama, Santanu's son Bhishma, will worship peace; Krishna, the son of Devaki, will worship peace; Acharya Drona and Vidura will both speak of peace; Kripa and Sanjaya also will preach peace; and Somadatta and Yuyutsu and Drona's son and our grandsire Vyasa, every one of them always speaks of peace.

Urged constantly by these towards peace, I believe that Dhritarashtra will return our kingdom to us. However, if he yields to temptation, he will meet with destruction. Panchali, a crisis has entered the history of the Bhaaratas to plunge them into doom. For some time now, I have been convinced of this.

Suyodhana does not deserve the kingdom, and that is why he has not discovered forgiveness; I, however, do, and for that, forgiveness has possessed me. Forgiveness and gentleness are the qualities of the reposed man. They represent eternal virtue, and I will embrace these gunas.'"

CANTO 30

ARANYAKA PARVA CONTINUED

"Draupadi says, 'I bow down to Dhatri and Vidhatri who have so clouded your good sense! You think differently from your sires and grandsires about the burden you bear. Influenced by karma, men find themselves in various circumstances of life. Karma produces inevitable consequences; we wish for emancipation from mere folly.

It seems that man can never attain prosperity in this world through virtue, gentleness, forgiveness, honesty and fear of censure. If this were not so, O Bhaarata, this intolerable calamity would never have overtaken you, who are so undeserving of it, and your brothers of great tejas.

Neither in your days of prosperity nor in these of adversity, O Bhaarata, have you held anything as dear as dharma, which you hold even dearer than life. The Brahmanas, your elders, even the Devas know that your kingdom and your life are for dharma alone.

You will abandon Bhimasena, Arjuna, these twin sons of Madri and me, but you cannot leave dharma. I have heard that the king protects dharma, and dharma protects him in return. But I do not see that dharma protects you.

Like his shadow pursues a man, your heart, O Purushavyaghra, single-mindedly always seeks dharma. Never have you disregarded your equals, your inferiors or superiors. Even gaining the whole world, pride never touched you.

O son of Pritha, you always adore the Brahmanas, the Devas and the Pitrs, with swadhas, and other forms of worship. Kaunteya, you gratify Brahmanas by fulfilling their every wish. Yatis, Sannyasins and Grihastas have always been fed in your house from plates of gold, and I served their food.

You always give gold and food to Vanaprasthas. Why, there was nothing in your house which you would not give away to Brahmanas. During the Viswadeva sacrifice, conducted for your peace, in your palace, the consecrated offerings were always first given to sadasyas and every other living being, while you contented yourself with whatever was leftover.

Ishti Pasubandhas, sacrifices for obtaining fruition of desires, the religious rites of domesticity, Paka sacrifices, and sacrifices of other kinds were constantly performed in your royal house.

Even in this great forest so solitary and haunted by robbers, living in exile, divested of your kingdom, your dharma has sustained no diminution. You performed the Aswamedha, the Rajasuya, the Pundarika, and Gosava, the grandest yagnas which demand prodigious gifts and charity.

Rajan, yet during the dire game of dice, perversity moved you to wager me as a stake? You lost your kingdom, your wealth, your weapons, your brothers, and me! You are simple, gentle, liberal, modest and truthful; how, Rajan, could your mind be attracted to the vice of gambling?

Ah, grief overwhelms my heart and I am losing my mind to see this distress of yours, this calamity. Surely, it is true that men are subject to the will of God and never to their own wishes. The Supreme Lord and

Ordainer of all things ordains every joy and sorrow, all the happiness and misery of all creatures, even before they are born, in accordance with their karma which is like a seed destined to sprout into this tree of life.

O Kshatriya, God moves men as a puppeteer does his wooden puppets with his wires. Even as akasa covers everything, God pervades every creature, and ordains its weal or woe. As a bird tied with a string, every creature depends on God. Everyone is subject to God and none else. No one can decide his own fate.

Like a pearl on its string, or a bull held by the rope through its nose, or a tree fallen from the bank into the river, every creature follows God's command because they are imbued with His Spirit and because they are established in Him.

Dependent on the Universal Soul, man cannot pass a moment independently. Enveloped in darkness, creatures are not masters of their own joy or sorrow. They go to heaven or hell urged by God Himself.

Like light straws fly on strong winds, all creatures, O Bhaarata, fly on God's will. And God pervades all creatures, engaged in deeds right and wrong; He moves in the universe, but none can say This is God.

This body is only the means through which God causes every creature to reap fruits of karma, good and bad. Ah, look at God's maya which confounds men and makes them kill their fellows.

Truth-knowing Munis see these bodies differently, as rays of the Sun, which is the Lord, while ordinary men see the things of the Earth otherwise. God creates them all, each one uniquely born and destroyed. O Yudhishtira, Brahma the Pitamaha spreads his maya and kills his creatures through the agency of other creatures, even as one might split a piece of wood with another, crack a stone with another stone or break a piece of iron with an iron rod.

Lord sports with his creatures, creating and destroying them at his pleasure, like a child with his toy. O King, it does not seem to me that God treats his creatures as a father or a mother does their children. Rather, like a vicious man, he seems to treat them with anger, maliciously.

Ah, I am deeply troubled seeing good, superior men persecuted, while sinners thrive and are happy. I cannot think or speak well of the Great Ordainer seeing your distress and Suyodhana's prosperity. How can God suffer such iniquity?

What does He gain by allowing Duryodhana, who breaks every sacred law, who is greedy and crooked, who grievously harms dharma, to prosper? If a deed done pursues the doer and none else, then certainly it is God himself who is stained with the sin of every act. If however, the sin of an action does not attach to the doer, then might and not God is the true cause of whatever happens, and I grieve for those who are weak and have no prowess!'"

CANTO 31

ARANYAKA PARVA CONTINUED

"Yudhishtira says, 'You speak beautifully, Yagnaseni, your words smooth, your phrases delightful. I have listened carefully to what you say, but you speak the language of atheism.

Princess, I never do anything for the fruits of what I do. I give because it is my duty to give; I sacrifice because it is my duty to sacrifice. Krishnaa, I do to the best of my ability whatever a grihasta should do, regardless of whether what I do benefits me or not.

Fair-hipped one, I act virtuously not from the desire to reap the fruits of virtue, but so that I do not break the ordinances of the Veda, and also with an eye on the conduct of the good and wise. Krishnaa, my heart is drawn naturally towards virtue.

The man who wishes to reap the fruit of virtue is a trader in virtue. His nature is base, and he can never be counted among the virtuous; nor does he ever gain the fruit of his actions.

The man of sinful heart, who does a virtuous thing, but doubts dharma in his mind0 – he, too, does not obtain the fruits of his deed, because of his scepticism. I speak to you by the authority of the Vedas, which constitute the highest proof in these matters – you must never doubt dharma.

The man who doubts dharma is destined to be born into bestial species. The man of weak understanding who doubts religion, virtue or the words of the Rishis, is excluded from the realms of immortality and bliss, even as are Sudras from the Vedas!

Intelligent one, if a young child born into a noble race studies the Vedas and conducts himself virtuously, great Rajarishis regard him as a mature Sage, notwithstanding his years. But the sinner that doubts dharma and transgresses the scriptures, is regarded as even lower than Sudras and robbers.

With your own eyes, you have seen the Maharishi Markandeya of immeasurable soul come to us. Through dharma alone did he acquire immortality in his very body.

Vyasa, Vasishta, Maitreya, Narada, Lomasa, Suka and other Rishis have all been purified through dharma alone. You see them with your own eyes as having the power of divine asceticism, able to curse or bless, and superior to the Devas themselves.

Anagha, sinless one, all these, equal to the Devas, look at what is written in the Vedas and describe virtue as the foremost dharma. Sweet Queen, so it does not become you to either doubt or censure God, or to act rashly.

The fool that doubts religion and disregards virtue, being proud of his own reasoning, does not regard other great reasons, and thinks of the Rishis, who see into past, present and the future, as being madmen.

The fool regards only the external world as being capable of gratifying his senses, and is blind to everything else. He who doubts religion finds no expiation. The miserable one is full of anxiety and gains no realms of bliss hereafter. A heretic, a slanderer of the Veda, a sinner moved by lust and greed, he goes to hell.

On the other hand, he who always cherishes dharma with faith finds eternal bliss in the other world; while the fool who not does keep dharma, disregarding all the proofs which the Rishis offer, does not prosper in any life. Have no doubt, lovely one, that he who pays no heed to what the Rishis say, and to their lives as living proof, he finds no joy in this world or the next.

Draupadi, do not doubt the ancient dharma which good men live by, the religion framed by Sages of universal knowledge, who can see all things. Dharma is the only raft for those who want to find heaven, even as a ship is to merchants who want to cross the sea.

Faultless one, if the dharma by which men of dharma live were fruitless, all the universe would be shrouded in infamous darkness. No one would then pursue moksha; no one would seek to acquire knowledge or even wealth, but men would live like beasts. If sannyasa, the austerities of brahmacharya, sacrifices, study of the Vedas, charity, honesty were all fruitless, men would not have practised dharma and virtue, generation after generation.

If all karma was fruitless, dreadful chaos would prevail. Think, why do Rishis and Devas and Gandharvas and Rakshasas, all of whom are not human, treasure dharma with such love? Knowing for certain that God rewards the practise of dharma, they all observe dharma. Dharma, Panchali, is eternal prosperity.

While we see the fruit of both gyana and tapasya, dharma and adharma, virtue and sin, cannot be without their fruit. Krishnaa, just think of the circumstances of your own birth, as you have heard of it, and the birth of the mighty Dhrishtadyumna. O you of the sweet smiles, what better proof of the value of dharma?

They that have their minds under control reap the fruit of their actions, and are content with little. The ignorant are not content with what they receive here, however much it might be, because they have no joy born of virtue to inherit in the hereafter.

When dharma and adharma appear to prove fruitless, and the very origin of all karma – why, my beautiful one, these are mysterious even to the gods. Not everyone knows these things, certainly not ordinary men. The Devas preserve the mystery, for the maya which obscures what the gods do is inscrutable.

Those regenerate ones who have destroyed all desire, who have founded their aspirations on vratas, sannyasa and tapasya, who have burnt up all their sins, and in whose minds and hearts quietness, peace and holiness dwell – they understand all these.

So, though you might not see the fruits of dharma, you must never doubt dharma or the gods. You must perform sacrifices with a will, and practise charity without insolence. All karma in this world has its fruit, and dharma is eternal. Brahma himself told this to his sons, as Kasyapa has said. So, let your doubts be dispelled like mist, Draupadi. Reflecting on all this; let your scepticism give way to faith.

Do not slander God, who is the lord of all creatures. Learn how to know him. Bow down to him. Do not let your mind be sad, and never disregard the Supreme Being through whose grace mortal men, with piety, find immortality!'"

CANTO 32

ARANYAKA PARVA CONTINUED

"Draupadi says, 'Son of Pritha, I never disregard or slander dharma. Why would I disregard God, the lord of all creatures? O Bhaarata, I am griefstricken and ranting. Yet, I will lament again, and you must listen to me.

O Parantapa, every conscious creature must certainly perform karma in this world. Only the immobile, not other beings, may live without doing. Immediately after its birth the calf sucks its mother's teat. Why, men feel pain when fell mantras are chanted using their statues.

So, O Yudhishtira, it seems that beings derive the character of their lives from their karma of past births. Among the mobile, man differs from the rest in that he aspires to affect the course of his life in this and the other world through his deeds.

All creatures visibly reap the fruit of their karma of past lives. Indeed, all creatures exist because of past karma, even Brahma, the Creator and the Ordainer of the Universe, even as a crane lives, untaught, in water. If a creature does nothing, it cannot live; all beings must act.

You must also act, and not incur censure by abandoning karma. Cover yourself with deeds, as with armour. Among a thousand men, there is perhaps one who truly knows the worth of karma, of action. One must act to protect oneself, and to increase one's wealth, for if a man only spends without earning, even if he owns a hoard as great as Himavan, it will quickly be exhausted.

But for karma, doing, all the creatures of this world would have become extinct. If karma bore no fruit, the created would never have multiplied. We see that at times men perform karma even though it bears no fruit, for without doing, life's course itself would be impossible.

Those in this world who believe in destiny, and those again who believe in chance, are both the worst among men. Only those that believe in the efficacy of karma are laudable. He who does nothing, believing just in destiny is soon destroyed, even like an unburnt earthen pot in water. Also, he that believes in chance and sits idle though he can act, does not live long, for his life is one of weakness and helplessness.

If a man gains wealth without effort, it is told that he does so by chance; if he acquires fortune through religious rites, it is deemed providential. But the fruit gained through his own actions is proof of his own ability.

Best of men, wealth gained through chance is called spontaneous acquisition; wealth thus gained is through the karma of a previous life. God dispenses the fruit of the karma of past lives to men in this world – good and bad.

This body is only the instrument in God's hands for the performance of karma; inert of itself, it does what God urges it to. Kaunteya, it is the Supreme Lord of all who makes every creature do what it does. The creatures themselves are inert.

O Kshatriya, deciding upon some purpose in his mind, man accomplishes it, working with his intelligence. Thus we say that man himself is the cause of what he does. Purusharishabha, it is impossible to count the deeds of men, for mansions and cities are the result of man's deeds.

Intelligent men know that oil may be had from sesame, curds from milk, and that food can be cooked by igniting fuel. They also know the means for accomplishing all these; and knowing them, they use the required appliances to accomplish them. Through what they do, men support their lives.

If a skilled workman does something, it is well executed; and the opposite happens if a thing is done by an unskilful hand. In karma, if a man was not himself his own karma's doer and cause, then no sacrifice would bear any fruit for him, and nor would anyone be a Guru or a sishya.

It is because a man himself is the cause of his work that he is applauded when he achieves success; and he is censured when he fails. If this were not so, how would praise and blame be justified?

Some say that everything is the result of Providence; others, that this is not so, but that everything is the result of the karma, good and bad, of past lives. Chance fetches possessions, as also does destiny; some things are gained through exertion; there is no fourth cause — so say those who know the truth, men of gyana.

However, if God himself did not dispense good and bad fruit, then there would be no misery among the created. If the effects of past karma are a myth, then a man would achieve everything for which he strives. So, those who believe that chance, destiny and effort are the only causes of success, and who deny the effects of karma from past lives, are dull, why, inert as the body itself.

Yet, a man must act; Manu himself has said so. He who does not act, surely succumbs, O Yudhishtira. While the man of action usually finds success in this world, the idle never succeed. If success becomes impossible, one seeks to remove the obstacles in one's path to it.

Rajan, if a man works, his debts of karma are paid, whether he succeeds or not. Adversity overtakes the idle man, while the active, skilful one will certainly prosper. Intelligent men, who engage confidently in karma, regard others as being faithless and failures. They think of the confident and the faithful as being men of success.

Misery has found us now, but if you act against it, it will surely be removed. If you fail, it will prove that Bhima, Arjuna and the twins cannot take the kingdom back. But since the efforts of most men meet with success, it is likely that we shall also have what we strive for.

How can anyone predict whether we shall win or lose? Only if you act will you know what fruit your action will bring. The tiller tills the soil with his plough and sows seeds. He then sits quiet, for only the clouds can bring the rain which will make his seeds grow into plants. If the clouds do not favour him, he is absolved from blame.

He says to himself, "I have done what others do. If despite this I have failed, the fault is not mine," and he does not reproach himself.

O Bhaarata, no one should despair saying, "Oh, I am doing what I should yet success is not mine!"

For there are two other causes, besides exertion, for success. One should never despair about the success or failure of any undertaking because both depend upon the concatenation of many circumstances. If one important element is wanting, success does not come immediately, sometimes not at all. But without exertion there can never be any success.

Nor is there anything to applaud in abstaining from action. The intelligent put forth all their might, bringing together time, place, means and auspicious rites to acquire prosperity. With care and vigilance a man must set himself to his task, his main strength being his prowess. In the union of qualities needed to succeed in any undertaking prowess, ability, seems to be the main.

When the intelligent man sees that his enemy is superior to himself in many ways, he should seek success through conciliation. But he must wish his enemy ill and seek his banishment. Why speak of mortal men, even if his enemy were the ocean or the mountains, these motives should guide him.

A man who seeks to strike at his enemy's weaknesses discharges his dharma to himself and his own. No man should ever disparage himself, for he who does, never finds great prosperity. O Bhaarata, only through such endeavour can success be found in this world. Indeed, success in the world depends on acting when the time and circumstances are ripe.

My father used to keep a learned Brahmana with him. Bharatarishabha, he said all this to my father. My brothers first heard these tenets of dharma, uttered by Brihaspati himself. It was from them that I heard these, later, in my father's house. Yudhishtira, whenever I had time, I would go and sit on my father's lap, and that knowing Brahmana would recite these truths to me, sweetly consoling me by what he said!'"

CANTO 33

ARANYAKA PARVA CONTINUED

Vaisampayana said, "Bhimasena listens to Draupadi, and sighing in anger, approaches the king and says to him, 'Walk, O Rajan, in the ancient path trodden by great kings who went before you! What do we gain by living in an asrama of Sannyasins, deprived of our own dharma, kama and artha?

Duryodhana took our kingdom not by dharma, nor by might, but through a game of dice at which he cheated. Like a weak, offal-eating jackal snatching their prey from mighty lions, he has taken our kingdom from us. Why, Rajan, just for the trite merit of keeping your given word, do you suffer such distress, abandoning our wealth, the source of both dharma and kama?

He who wields the Gandiva protected our kingdom, and not Indra himself could take it by force; yet taken it was, because of your carelessness. Because of you our kingdom was taken like some fruit from a man who has no arms, or cattle from one who has no legs.

You are faithful in dharma. To please you, Bhaarata, we allowed ourselves to be overwhelmed by such a calamity. It is because we are obedient to you that today we rend the hearts of our friends and gratify our enemies.

Ah, how it grieves me that, just to obey you, we did not kill Dhritarashtra's son even then. This is your home in the forest, where you live like a wild animal. Only a weak man would bear this, surely no strong one would ever lead such a life.

Not Krishna, Arjuna, Abhimanyu, the Srinjayas, Madri's sons or I myself, approve of this life you have chosen. Bound by your vows, you always cry Dharma! Dharma! Has despair deprived you of your manliness? Only cowards, who cannot win back their lost wealth, cherish despair – vain despair which destroys one's purposes.

You have ability and eyes; you see that manliness dwells in us. But you have accepted a life of peace, and feel no distress. The Dhartarashtras think of us, who are in truth forgiving, as being weak, inept. This hurts me more than dying in battle.

Even if we all die in fair fight, without showing our backs to our enemies, that would be better than this shameful exile, for then we would find realms of bliss in the next world. Or if we slay them and gain the whole world, that would be wealth well won, and worth the attempt.

We always keep Kshatriya dharma; we always seek grand achievements; we always avenge injustice; it is our bounden duty to win our kingdom back with battle. Then our fame would mantle the world, not our shame.

Rajan, the dharma which torments oneself and one's near and dear ones is no dharma at all; rather, it is evil, fetching calamities. Sometimes, dharma becomes the weakness of a man; and though such a man might always cleave to dharma, yet both dharma and artha forsake him even like pleasure and pain forsaking a dead man.

He who clings to dharma for dharma's sake always suffers. He can hardly be called a wise man, for he does not know the very ends of dharma, like a blind man who cannot see the light of the Sun. He who uses his wealth only for himself does not understand the meaning or purpose of artha. He is really like a servant who tends cows in a forest.

Again, he who hankers only after artha, ignoring dharma and kama deserves censure and killing. He who pursues only pleasure, without seeking dharma and artha, quickly loses his friends and also his virtue and wealth. Without dharma and artha, only indulging indiscriminately in kama, a man exhausts his pleasures and finds death, like a fish when the water in which it lives runs dry.

For these reasons, the wise always cherish both dharma and artha, because a union of these is essential to pleasure, even as fuel is to fire. The root of kama is dharma, and dharma, too, is not apart from pleasure. The two depend on each other as the ocean and the clouds, the ocean causing the clouds and the clouds filling the ocean.

Pleasure, kama, is the joy that one feels from contact with the objects of the senses or from the possession of wealth. It exists in the mind, having no corporeal existence which one can see.

He who desires wealth, first seeks a large share of dharma to have his desire fulfilled. He who wishes for kama, first seeks artha, wealth. But pleasure, in its turn, yields nothing. One pleasure cannot lead to another, being its own fruit – as ashes may be had from wood, but nothing from those ashes in their turn.

As a fowler kills the birds we see, so does sin slay the creatures of the world. So, he who is misled by pleasure or covetousness, and does not see the true nature of dharma becomes wretched both here and hereafter, and deserves killing.

Rajan, you know that pleasure is to be had from possessing the various objects of enjoyment. You also know well the changes these objects of desire and enjoyment undergo. At their loss or disappearance, occasioned by decrepitude or death, there arises distress. That distress has now overtaken us.

The joy which comes from the five senses, the intellect and the heart, all being directed to the objects proper to each, is called kama, pleasure. I believe that pleasure is one of the best fruits of our karma, our actions.

So one must respect dharma, artha and kama, one after the other. One should not devote oneself just to dharma, or think of wealth as the highest object of one's wishes, nor pleasure; one should always pursue all three.

The Shastras ordain that one should seek dharma in the morning, artha at noon, and kama in the evening. The scriptures also say that one should seek pleasure in the first part of life, wealth in the second, and virtue in the last. And the wise pursue all three, dividing their time equally.

Kurunandana, you must think carfeully whether these three should be independent or interwoven, for those that seek happiness. Then you must unhesitatingly act either to acquire them, or abandon them all. For he who lives wavering in doubt between two paths, leads a wretched life.

The world knows that you always live by dharma. Knowing this, still your friends tell you to act. Charity, sacrifice, respect for the wise, study of the Vedas, and honesty – these constitute the highest dharma, and are efficacious both here and hereafter. Yet, these virtues cannot be attained by one who has no wealth, not, O Purushavyaghra, if his other accomplishments are infinite.

All the universe depends upon dharma; there is nothing higher than virtue. And he who has great wealth can attain to virtue. Wealth cannot be earned by leading a mendicant life, nor by a life of feebleness. Wealth can be earned by using intelligence, directed by dharma.

For you, begging alms, which is allowed Brahmanas, is forbidden. So strive to acquire wealth by exerting your might and energy. Neither mendicancy nor the life of a Sudra is proper for you. Might and energy constitute the special dharma of the Kshatriya. So, adopt your swadharma and kill your enemies.

Destroy the power of Dhritarashtra's sons, with my prowess and Arjuna's. The learned and the wise say that sovereignty is virtue. So acquire sovereignty, for it does not become you to live in this wretched condition. Awake, O King, and understand the Sanatana Dharma. By birth you belong to a varna whose deeds are violent and cause pain to men.

Cherish your subjects and reap the fruit thereof; for that you can never be reproached. This is the dharma ordained by God himself for the Kshatriya! If you fall away from it, you will make yourself ridiculous. There is no praise for leaving the path of one's swadharma. Therefore, set your heart where it ought to be, in concord with the varna to which you belong, cast away this course of feebleness, summon your energy, and bear your burden manfully, as you should.

No king ever gained sovereignty of the earth, prosperity or affluence through dharma alone. As a fowler snares small game by offering them food, so does an intelligent man acquire a kingdom by offering bribes to base and greedy enemies. The Asuras, though elder to the Devas and more powerful and wealthy, were vanquished through stratagem by the gods.

Everything belongs to the mighty. Mahabaho, kill your enemies who used vile strategy to vanquish us. No one can equal Arjuna at wielding a bow in battle; none is my equal with a mace. Depending on their own prowess, strong men fight battles; they care little for the numbers ranged against them, or on information gleaned from spies.

O Pandava, exert your might. Might is the only root of wealth; whatever else is said to be its root is not really so. As in winter the shade of a tree counts for nothing, so also without might everything else becomes fruitless. A man who wants to increase his wealth should spend it, O Kaunteya, in the manner of scattering seeds on the ground.

Have no doubt about this. However, unless the returns from what you spend are not more than or at least equal to what you spend, you must not invest your wealth. For the man who spends wealth unreasonably is like the ass scratching itself – pleasurable at first but painful afterwards.

So, too, the man who scatters a little of his seeds of dharma to gain greater dharma is considered wise. Have no doubt, it is as I say.

The wise man alienates his enemies' friends by scattering seeds of wealth; once the enemy's friends abandon him, the intelligent man brings him to subjection. Even the strong engage in battle depending on their courage. Without courage, neither ceaseless efforts nor the arts of conciliation can always win a kingdom.

Sometimes weak men, uniting in great numbers, kill even a powerful enemy, like bees killing a honey-gatherer through the sheer power of numbers. Yudhishtira, adopt the ways of the Sun – who nurtures as well as kills through his rays – to protect our kingdom and the people, as our ancestors did; Rajan, I have heard that this is a sannyasa which even the Veda speaks about.

A Kshatriya cannot acquire the realms of blessedness through asceticism as he can by honourable battle, regardless of whether he wins or loses. Seeing you in this condition, the world has concluded that light may well forsake the Sun and the Moon; good men come and go from here, singly or in groups, and all of them praise you and blame our enemies.

Moreover, the Kurus and the Brahmanas, together, always speak of your absolute truthfulness, how you have never told a lie, from ignorance, from meanness, from greed, or from fear.

Whatever sins a king commits to gain kingdom he later consumes them through sacrifices distinguished by bountiful charity. Like the Moon emerging from behind clouds, a king is purified from all sins by gifting villages to Brahmanas, and cows by thousands.

Almost all the people of the country, young or old, praise you, Yudhishtira. They also say that sovereignty vested in Duryodhana is as milk in a bag of dog-hide, as the Vedas in a Sudra, as truth in a robber, as strength in a woman. Even women and children say this repeatedly, as if it were a lesson they seek to commit to memory.

Parantapa, you have not fallen by yourself; all of us are also lost with you. So, climb into your chariot laden with every weapon, make superior Brahmanas utter benedictions over you, and fly, this very day, at Hastinapura, so that you can give the spoils of victory to your Brahmanas.

Surrounded by your brothers who are great archers, and by other Kshatriya heroes who are like snakes of virulent poison, set out even like

Vritra's slayer surrounded by the Marutas. Kaunteya, you are powerful; decimate your weakling enemies, crush them like Indra did the Asuras; and snatch the prosperity he enjoys from Dhritarashtra's son.

There is no mortal who can even bear the touch of the vulture-feathered arrows, like vicious serpents, loosed from the Gandiva. Bhaarata, there is no warrior, no horse or elephant which can withstand the blows of my mace when I am enraged in battle.

With the Srinjayas, the Kaikeyas, and the Vrishni Bull fighting for us, why should we fail to wrest the kingdom from the enemy? How will we not take back the Earth, with our allies, if only we put forth our might?'"

CANTO 34

ARANYAKA PARVA CONTINUED

Vaisampayana said, "Yudhishtira is silent for a few moments after listening to Bhimasena; he gathers his patience.

Then he says, 'Bhaarata, all this is no doubt true. I cannot reproach you for savaging me with your arrow-like words. This disaster has overtaken you solely through my fault. I cast the dice wanting to take Dhritarashtra's son's kingdom from him. But Subala's son, that expert gambler, played against me on Suyodhana's behalf.

Sakuni is fom the hill country, and is exceptionally artful, while I am innocent of any artifice; and he routed me in the presence of all the sabha. Bhimasena, this is why distress and calamity have overtaken us.

I saw how the dice rolled invariably, odds and evens, as Sakuni wished. I could have controlled myself, and stopped playing. But anger drives away a man's patience. Child, when the mind is influenced by arrogance or vanity, it cannot be restrained. I do not reprimand you for what you say to me, or for the harsh words you use.

I believe that what has happened to us is fate, and pre-ordained. When for his greed for our kingdom, Dhritarashtra's son Duryodhana made slaves of us at first; then, O Bhima, it was Draupadi who rescued us. When we were summoned again to the sabha to play dice again, you know, as Arjuna does, what Dhritarashtra's son told me, before all the Bhaaratas, what stakes we would play for.

He said, "Ajatasatru, if you lose, you and all your brothers must live in the forest of your choice for twelve years, then spend a thirteenth year in ajnatavasa. If my spies discover you in the final year, you must live another twelve years in the vana and yet another in ajnatavasa, without being discovered.

Think about this and pledge yourself to it. As for me, I, Duryodhana, swear solemnly in this august sabha that if my agents cannot find you during the thirteenth year, this kingdom of the five rivers shall once again become yours.

And if we lose the game of dice, instead, we will abandon all our wealth and pass the same years in the wilderness, the same rules applying to us."

I replied to him, in the midst of all the Kurus, "So be it!"

The wretched game began; we were beaten and have been exiled. This is why we range in misery and discomfort through these forests. But Suyodhana was not satisfied and, giving himself up to anger, made the Kurus and everyone one else whose allegiance he enjoys express joy at our misfortune.

Having entered into such an agreement in the presence of good men, who dares break his word for the sake of a kingdom on Earth? I think, for an honourable man, death is preferable to gaining a kingdom after breaking one's word.

During the game of dice you wanted to burn my hands, but Arjuna stopped you and you only wrung your own hands. If you had done what you wanted, would this calamity have overtaken us? You well knew your prowess, Bhimasena, then why did you not object to the second game of dice?

Now it is too late and we are plunged in distress by the word we gave; what use is it for you to berate me now? Bhima, my greatest grief lies in the fact that we saw Draupadi shamed and could do nothing to stop her humiliation. My heart burns as if I have drunk poison.

But having given my word in the midst of the Kuru heroes, I cannot break it now. Bhima, wait for better days to return to us, like the scatterer of seeds waiting for the harvest. When he who has been done an injury succeeds in avenging himself when his enemy's designs have borne flowers and fruit, that man accomplishes a great thing through his prowess. That brave man earns undying fame; he finds immense fortune and prosperity. His enemies bow down to him, and his friends gather round him, like the Devas do around Indra for protection.

But Bhima, know that I will never break my word. I consider dharma as being superior to life itself, I think of it as a divine condition. Kingdom, sons, fame, wealth – all these together do not equal even a sixteenth part of truth.'"

CANTO 35

Aranyaka Parva Continued

"Bhima says, 'O King, being insubstantial as froth, impermanent as a fruit falling from a tree, dependent on time, mortal, you have given your word on a matter of time, which is infinite, immeasurable, quick as an arrow, or flowing like a stream, carrying all before it as Death. How can you consider time to which you are subject to be available for you to keep your word?

Kaunteya, how can a mortal man whose life is shortened with each moment, even as some collyrium is reduced each time a grain of it is taken up by a needle, wait for the future? Only an immortal, or he who knows how long he will live, who knows the future as if it were before his eyes, can wait for time, for an exact period of time to arrive.

If we wait thirteen years we will be thirteen years closer to death, which takes us all. We must strive to recover our kingdom before we die. He who does not achieve fame by punishing his enemy is an unclean thing. He is a useless burden upon the Earth, like a castrated bull, and he dies ingloriously. He who has no strength and courage, who does not chastise his enemy, lives in vain; I think of such a man as lowborn.

Your hand can rain gold; your fame can cover the whole world. So kill your enemies in battle and enjoy the wealth won through the might of your arms. Parantapa, if a man kills his enemy who has done him injury and goes that same day to hell, hell turns into heaven for him.

The pain I feel from having to suppress my anger is worse than burning fire; I cannot sleep for it, day or night. This Partha, this Arjuna, is the greatest archer; he, also, surely burns with grief although he lives here like a lion in his den. Like some mighty tusker, he who wants to kill every other bowman in the world single-handedly, represses his wrath.

Nakula, Sahadeva are all silent, to please you; as are all our friends, including the Srinjayas. Only I and Prativindhya's mother burn so much that we speak to you in grief. The rest agree with everything that I say to you, for they are all plunged in sorrow and eagerly wish for battle.

What more wretched catastrophe can overtake us than that our kingdom should be taken from us by weak and contemptible enemies, and enjoyed by them? You have a weak nature and you feel ashamed to violate your given pledge. But no one lauds you for suffering like this out of your kindliness.

Rajan, your mind does not seem to see the truth – like that of a highborn but foolish man, who commits the hymns of the Veda to memory but does not understand their meaning.

You are kind, like a Brahmana; how have you been born a Kshatriya? Kshatriyas have devious hearts. You have heard the dharma of kings, as taught by Manu, full of crookedness, unfairness and everything opposed to peace and virtue. Then why do you forgive Dhritarashtra's sons?

You have intelligence, prowess, learning and are nobly born. Why are you like a great snake which cannot move? Kaunteya, whoever wishes to hide us will be like one trying to conceal the mountains of Himavat with a handful of grass.

All the world knows you, O son of Pritha; you will no more be able to live undiscovered than the Sun can course through the sky unseen. Like a great tree in a well-watered land, with spreading branches and flowers and leaves, or like Indra's elephant – how will Arjuna live unknown?

How, also, will these children, Nakula and Sahadeva, who are like a pair of young lions, both live undiscovered? How will Drupada's daughter Krishnaa, our princess and mother of heroes, of great virtue and famed throughout the world, live unnoticed?

All the world knows me, as well, from my boyhood; I do not see how I can live unknown anymore than the mountains of Meru can seek concealment.

Then, we expelled many kings from their kingdom; these Kshatriyas will all become the evil Duryodhana's followers and allies, for we robbed them of their wealth and drove them into exile. How will they ever be our friends?

They will join Dhritarashtra and wish to do us harm. They will certainly send countless spies to seek us out. If these find us, great danger will come to us. We have already spent thirteen months in these forests. Rajan, consider them to be thirteen years, for the wise have said that a month is a substitute for a year even as a pot-herb is for Soma.

Otherwise, Rajan, free yourself from the fetter of your pledge by offering savoury food to a quiet bull which bears sacred burdens. Thus, decide to kill your enemies – for the Kshatriya has no higher dharma than battle!'"

CANTO 36

ARANYAKA PARVA CONTINUED

Vaisampayana said, "Listening to Bhima, Yudhishtira Purushavyaghra, Parantapa, begins to sigh, and to reflect silently.

Within himself, he thinks, 'I have heard the dharma of kings recited, and also the dharmas of the other varnas. Only he who always keeps these tenets before his eyes can regulate his conduct both in the present and the future.

I know the true way of dharma, so difficult to know; then how can I use force to try to grind it down, even like trying to crush Meru?'

Thinking thus for a moment, deciding what he should do, he replies firmly to Bhima, without allowing his brother to say another word.

Yudhishtira says, 'Mahabaho, what you say is true, but, my eloquent brother, listen once more to me. Bhima, whatever sin one seeks to commit, rashly, depending purely on one's strength and courage, invariably end up as a source of failure and pain; while whatever is begun with deliberation, with well-directed prowess, after much thought, inevitably succeeds – the gods themselves favour such designs.

Bhima, you are proud of your strength, and restless, but listen to what I think of what you think we should do immediately. Bhurisravas, Sala, Bhishma, Drona, Karna, the mighty son of Drona, Dhritarashtra's powerful, invincible sons are all great warriors and even now prepare for battle against us.

The kings and chieftains of the Earth, also, whom we have injured, are all on the side of the Kauravas, bound to them by ties of affection. O Bhaarata, they seek Duryodhana's good, not ours. With full treasuries and allied to great forces, they will all surely give their all in battle.

Also, Duryodhana has given much largesse, wealth and every luxury, to the warriors of the Kuru army, their sons and relatives. He honours those heroes and holds them in high regard. I am certain that they will give their lives for him in battle.

Although Bhishma, Drona, and the illustrious Kripa love us as much as we do them, I am also certain they, too, will sacrifice their very lives, than which there is nothing dearer, in return for the royal favours they enjoy in Hastinapura. All of them are masters of the devastras, and devoted to dharma. Why, I believe even the Devas led by Vasava himself cannot vanquish these three.

Then they have Karna with them, the impetuous, always angry Karna, master of astras, invincible, he who wears impentrable armour.

Without first killing all these awesome warriors, Bhima, how will you kill Duryodhana? Ah, Vrikodara, I cannot sleep when I think of the swiftness of the Sutaputra's hand; to me he is the greatest of all archers!'

Bhima hears what Yudhishtira says and, slightly taken aback, falls silent.

While the Pandavas speak thus among themselves, Satyavati's son, the Maharishi Vyasa arrives there. The sons of Pandu receive him with due worship.

Then Vyasa, most eloquent among all speakers, says to Yudhishtira, 'Yudhishtira Mahabaho, with spiritual vision I saw what was passing through your heart, and I have come to you, Purusharishabha.

I will dispel this fear in your heart of Bhishma, Drona, Kripa, Karna, Drona's son, Duryodhana, and Dussasana. I will dissolve your fear through a secret enjoined in the Veda. Parantapa, hear it from me, acquire it patiently, and having done so, O King, quell this fever of yours quickly.'

Parasara's son, the Muni, takes Yudhishtira apart and speaks words of deep import to him.

Vyasa says, 'Best of the Bhaaratas, when the time of your fortune arrives, Arjuna will kill all your enemies in battle. Now learn this arcane Pratismriti from me, for you are worthy and capable of receiving it. You must then teach it to Arjuna, and with it he will be able to accomplish what needs to be done.

Pandava, let Arjuna go to Mahendra and Rudra, and to Varuna, and Kubera, and to Yama, and from them receive their astras. For his asceticism and prowess, he is fit to look upon the gods. Why, this Arjuna is in truth a Rishi of immense tejas, he is Narayana's friend Nara, the ancient, a god himself, invincible, always attended on by success, knowing no decay.

He will perform mighty deeds, once he receives their weapons from Indra, Rudra and the Lokapalas.

Also, think of leaving here and going to another forest in which to live. It is hardly pleasant to live in one place for too long a time. In your case, it might also cause the hermits here some anxiety. And as you maintain so many Brahmanas, knowers of the Vedas and their angas, for you to live here too long might deplete the forest of its deer, and its creepers and plants.'

Now, Yudhishtira purifies himself, and Vyasa, of great wisdom, who knows the mysteries of the world, teaches him the Pratismriti, best of hermetic mantras. Then, quickly bidding farewell to Kunti's son, Vyasa vanishes before his eyes.

Having received the Pratismriti, the virtuous Yudhishtira treasures it carefully in his mind and always chants it at the proper times. Glad of

Vyasa's advice, the son of Kunti now leaves the Dwaitavana and goes to the Kamyaka forest on the banks of the Saraswati.

Rajan, numberless ascetic Brahmanas follow him as Rishis do Indra. Arriving in the Kamyaka, those illustrious Bharatarishabhas begin living in that vana, along with their friends and attendants. Listening all the while to the Vedas being chanted, devoting themselves to the practice of archery, those mighty Kshatriyas live in that forest for some length of time.

Every day, armed with pure arrows, they go deep into the jungle in seach of deer. And they dutifully perform all the rites in honour of the Pitrs, the Devas and the Brahmanas."

CANTO 37

ARJUNABHIGAMANA PARVA

Vaisampayana said, "After some time, Yudhishtira rememebers the command of Muni Vyasa and calls Arjuna, bull among men, possessed of great wisdom, to him privately.

Taking Arjuna's hands, with a smile, Yudhishtira appears lost in thought for a moment, before saying gently to Arjuna, 'Bhaarata, all of the astra shastra, the sciene of warfare, dwells in Bhishma, Drona, Kripa, Karna and Aswatthama. They are masters of every sort of Brahmastra, Devastra, Manavastra and Vayavyastra, as well as the means to loose and repel them.

Dhritarashtra's son conciliates, honours and pleases all of them; he treats them all as a sishya his gurus. Why, Duryodhana treats all his warriors with great affection; all his allied chieftains he honours and gratifies, and in turn they seek his weal. They will not fail to put forth their might on his behalf.

Besides, remember, the whole world, all its cities, towns and villages, all its seas, forests and mountains, are now under Duryodhana's sway.

Arjuna, you are our only refuge and a great burden rests on you. Parantapa, I want you to do something for me now.

Vyasa Muni taught me a secret science. If you use it, the very universe will lie revealed before you. Child, receive that Pratismriti from me, and through it, in due course, find the grace of the gods. Bharatarishabha, first you must devote yourself to a fierce tapasya.

Taking your bow and your sword, wearing mail, keeping stern vows, travel north without giving way to anybody. Arjuna, Indra has all the Devastras because, when they feared Vritrasura, the other gods all invested their might in Sakra. Indra has all the weapons of heaven; go to him and he will give them to you.

Take your bow, and set out even today to see Indra Purandara.'

Yudhishtira Dharmatma teaches Arjuna the Pratismriti, with all the proper rituals. Having communicated the secret gyana to his heroic younger brother, restrained in speech, action and mind, Yudhishtira commands him to go forth. Arjuna takes up the Gandiva and his inexhaustible twin quivers, puts on his kavacha, and his finger guards made of the skin of the iguana.

Pouring oblations into a sacred fire and giving gifts to the Brahmanas and having them utter blessings over him, Arjuna sets out from the Kamyaka vana to find Indra. As he goes, bow in hand, that Kshatriya heaves a sigh and casts a look heavenwards so that he might kill Dhritarashtra's sons.

Seeing Kunti's son, armed and about to go forth, Siddhas and invisible spirits say to him, 'Kaunteya, may you get what your hearts desires.'

The Brahmanas also bless him, 'Achieve your purpose, let victory truly be yours!'

And seeing heroic Arjuna, his thighs like trunks of Sala trees, about to set out, and taking with him the hearts of all, Draupadi says fervently, 'Mahabaho, let everything that Kunti wished for when you were born, and everything that you wish for be yours, Dhananjaya!

Let none among us ever be born again into Kshatriya kind. I always bow down to Brahmanas, who live through mendicancy.

Ah, my great sorrow is that, seeing me in the sabha of Kshatriyas, the wretched Duryodhana called me a cow! Many other savage things he said to me in that assembly of princes, and they are raw wounds. But the grief and pain that I experience at parting from you makes all those insults seem as nothing.

Surely, while you are gone your brothers will spend their days recounting your deeds. Certainly, in your absence, your brothers will while away their waking hours in recalling your heroic deeds, over and over. But Arjuna, if you stay away for long, we will have no pleasure or any joy in our lives. Why, our very lives will become despicable.

Partha, our weal and woe, life and death, our kingdom and prosperity all depend on you. Bhaarata, I bless you, let success be yours! Sinless one, you will accomplish your mission even against the most powerful enemies. Mahabaho, go swiftly and win success. Let no danger be yours.

I bow to Dhatri and Vidhatri! I bless you, let prosperity be yours.

Dhananjaya, let Hri, Sri, Kirti, Dhriti, Pushti, Urna, Lakshmi and Saraswati, all protect you on your way, for you always worship your elder brother and always obey his commands.

I pray to the Vasus, the Rudras and Adityas, the Marutas, the Viswadevas, and the Sadhyas, for your welfare. O Bhaarata, be safe from all evil spirits of earth, sky and heaven, and from all evil spirits in general!'

Crying out these blessings, Yagnasena's daughter Krishnaa stops. Arjuna walks in pradakshina around his brothers, and around Dhaumya, and again taking up his beautiful bow, sets out.

Every creature moves hastily out of the path which the Pandava takes, on his way to meet Indra. Many mountains, homes to countless sannyasis, the bane of his enemies passes over and arrives at the sacred Himavat, resort of the Devas. The Mahatman reaches the holy mountain in a single day, for like the wind he is gifted with the mind's very speed due to his asceticism and the Pratismriti he received from his brother.

Having crossed Himavat, as also Gandhamadana, he passes through diverse uneven and dangerous places, walking night and day without fatigue. And reaching Indrakila, Dhananjaya halts, for he hears a voice in the sky, saying, 'Stop!'

The Pandava looks around him and Arjuna Savyasachin sees a hermit sitting under a tree, an ascetic quite ablaze with Brahmic lustre, his skin tawny, his hair matted into jata, an emaciated sannyasi.

Seeing Arjuna, the ascetic says to him, 'Who are you, child, come here with a bow and arrows, wearing kavacha, a sword, and obviously a Kshatriya? There is no need of weapons here. This is the abode of peaceful Brahmanas devoted to tapasya, who have no anger or pleasure.

There is no use for your bow here, for here there is no dispute of any kind. Child, throw away that bow of yours. You have found grace by coming here, Kshatriya, for truly no man is your equal in energy and prowess.'

Smiling, that Brahmana says this repeatedly to Arjuna. But Arjuna, set firmly on his course, is unmoved.

Then, smiling even more, the Brahmana says, 'Parantapa, be you blest! I am Indra, ask for the boon you want.'

Arjuna bends his head, folds his hands, and replies to him of a thousand eyes, 'Illustrious, give me all your astras, that is the boon I want.'

The king of the Devas, still smiling, says, 'Dhananjaya, when you have come to this blessed place what need have you of astras? You have already found beatitude. Ask me for any realms of bliss that you want.'

Arjuna replies to the thousand-eyed Sakra, 'I want no realms of bliss, nor even to become a god, then why speak of joy? Lord of the Devas, I do not wish for the prosperity of even all the gods.

For if I leave my brothers in the forest, and not avenge myself on our enemies, I will earn infamy forever throughout the world, through all the ages.'

Now, the slayer of Vritra, whom the worlds worship, says gently to the Pandava, 'Child, I will give you all the devastras when you can see the three-eyed Trisulin, Siva, Lord of all creatures. So, seek a vision of Mahadeva, greatest of Gods, because it is only after you have seen him, Kaunteya, that you will have everything you wish for.'

Saying this to Phalguna, Indra vanishes and Arjuna sets himself to tapasya, staying in that very place."

CANTO 38

KAIRATA PARVA

Janemejaya said, "Illustrious one, tell me every detail of how the taintless Arjuna acquired the devastras. Tell me how Arjuna, Purushavyaghra, the mighty-armed, entered that solitary forest without fear. Also, Best among those who know the Veda, what did he do whilst he lived in that forest?

How did he gratify Siva Sthanu and Indra, as well? Dvijottama, bless me by telling me all this. You are omniscient; you know all about the gods and about men. O Brahmana, I have heard that the battle that look place of old between Arjuna and Bhava was most extraordinary and without parallel.

I have heard it makes one's hair stand on end to listen to it. Even the hearts of those lions among men—the valiant sons of Pritha—trembled to hear about it, in wonder, joy, and a sense of their own inferiority.

O tell me everything else that Arjuna did. I do not see even the most trivial thing about Jishnu which is censurable. So, narrate in full the legend of that Kshatriya, that hero."

Vaisampayana said, "Tiger among Kurus, I will narrate the story of that peerless Kshatriya to you, a tale excellent, extensive and unrivalled. Sinless one, hear in detail about Arjuna's meeting with the three-eyed God of gods, and his contact with the illustrious God's person!

At Yudhishtira's command, Dhananjaya of immeasurable prowess sets out from the Kamyaka to see Sakra, lord of the Devas; and Sankara, the God of gods. Arjuna Mahabaho sets out armed with his unearthly bow, his golden-hafted sword; north he goes towards the summit of the Himavat.

Rajan, the best of all warriors in the three worlds, Indra's son, firmly committed to his mission, calms his mind and losing no time devotes himself to fervid tapasya. All alone, he enters that terrible forest full of thorny plants and trees, dense with flowers and fruit of every kind, swarming with wild animals and birds of many species, a vana where Siddhas and Charanas went.

When Arjuna enters that forest, where no human being goes, heaven resounds with conches and drumrolls, and a rain of flowers falls upon the earth, while clouds spread across the sky darkening the earth below. Passing through the dense jungles at the foot of the great mountains, Arjuna soon reaches the breast of the Himavat; staying there for some time at penance, he shines forth with his dhyana.

He sees great trees, their branches alive with the songs of countless birds. He sees rivers flowing like fluid lapis lazuli, their currents broken by fierce eddies here and there, and echoing with the calls of swan, duck and crane. The banks of those rivers echo with the mellifluous songs of the male kokila and the cries of peacocks.

Seeing those sacred rivers, their waters, pure and sweet, their banks enchanting, the mighty warrior is filled with delight. Arjuna of fierce energy and high soul then performs a stern tapasya in that charmed place.

Wearing valkala and a black deerskin, he holds a stick in his hand and eats only dry leaves fallen onto the ground. The first month, he also eats some fruit once every three nights; the second month he eats fruit once every six nights; and the third month, only once a fortnight.

When the fourth month comes, that Bharatottama, Pandu's mightiest son, does not eat at all but subsists on just the air he breathes. His arms raised up, standing on tiptoe, he continues his penance. Because he bathes frequently, his hair assumes the sheen of lightning, or of the lotus.

Now all the great Rishis go together to the God of the Pinaka, Siva, to inform him of Arjuna's tapasya.

Bowing to the God of gods, they say, 'Pritha's son, of great tejas, performs the most difficult penance upon the breast of the Himavat. Heated by his tapasya, the Earth issues smoke all around, O Devadeva. We do not know what his tapasya is for, but he causes us distress. You must make him stop, Lord!'

Pasupati, Umapati, Siva listens to those Munis of perfect self-restraint, and says, 'It does not become you to grieve over Phalguna's tapasya. Return, all of you, to where you came from; go in peace. I know the desire that is in Arjuna's heart. He does not want heaven, wealth or a long life. I will give him, even today, everything he wishes for!'

The Rishis of truth hear what Mahadeva says and go back to their respective asramas and dwellings."

CANTO 39

KAIRATA PARVA CONTINUED

Vaisampayana said, "When the illustrious Munis have left, Siva, who cleanses all sins, the lustrous Hara, assumes the form of a Kirata, a huntsman as resplendent as a golden tree, with a great and stalwart form like a second Meru, and taking up a handsome bow and arrows resembling snakes of virulent poison, and looking like an embodiment of fire, comes quickly down onto the breast of Himavat.

The beautiful Lord comes with Uma in the guise of a Kirata woman, and also with a motley swarm of merry spirits, his ganas, of various forms and attire, and thousands of women also in the form and garb of Kiratas.

Rajan, all that forest suddenly blazes up in splendour, at the arrival of Siva and his company; soon enough, a solemn stillness pervades the place. The sounds of springs, and rivers and birds all suddenly cease.

As Mahadeva approaches Pritha's irreproachable son, he sees an extraordinary thing – the Danava Muka, taking the form of an enormous boar, has come to kill Arjuna. Seeing the demon, Arjuna picks up the Gandiva and some arrows like serpents.

Stringing his bow and filling the air with its twang, he says to the boar, 'I have come here but done you no harm. But you want to kill me, so I will send you to Yama.'

Seeing Phalguna about to kill the boar, Siva disguised as the Kirata suddenly says, 'Stop! I aimed first at the beast the colour of the Indrakila mountain.'

Ignoring him, Arjuna shoots the boar; at the same moment the splendid Kirata also lets fly an arrow like fire at the boar. Both shafts strike Muka's massive body, hard as adamant, at the same instant.

The two astras strike Muka with a sound like Indra's Vajra and the thunder of clouds falling together upon a mountain. Each astra emits countless arrows like snakes with mouths ablaze, and Muka dies, and assumes again his dreadful Rakshasa form in death.

Arjuna now sees the Kirata before him, the mountain hunter whose form blazes like a God's, surrounded by many women. His heart strangely joyful, Kunti's son says smilingly, 'Who are you that wander in this solitary forest, surrounded by women? O you of the splendour of gold, are you not afraid of this terrible forest?

Why did you shoot the boar? This Rakshasa came here to kill me and I aimed at him first. You will not escape with your life. You have flouted the law of the hunt, and so, O Kirata, I will take your life.'

The Kirata says to the Pandava, softly, 'Kshatriya do not fear for me in this forest, which is our home. But why are you here amidst its danger? Yogi, we live here amongst all the wild creatures, but why are you, who are delicate, raised in luxury, and splendid as agni, here in this lonely place?'

Arjuna says, 'Depending on this Gandiva and arrows which are like fire, I live here like a second Indra. You saw how I despatched the monstrous Rakshasa who came as a boar.'

The Kirata replies, 'I shot the Rakshasa first. I killed him and sent him to Yama. It was my arrow which slew him. You are arrogant of your strength, and blame others for your own faults. Wretch, you are the guilty one and shall not escape with your life today.

Come, I will loose my arrows at you. You do the same!'

Arjuna becomes angry and attacks the Kirata with fierce arrows. However, the Kirata cheerfully receives those deadly shafts upon his breast, saying all the while, 'Wretch, come shoot your most terrible astras at me, shafts which can consume a man's very entrails!'

Arjuna looses a rain of missiles at him. Now the Kirata also shoots back fiercely at Arjuna, storms of barbs, each one like a virulent serpent. Arjuna looses a perfect volley which falls out of the sky over the huntsman, who stands unmoved, unharmed, like some invincible mountain.

Seeing this, Arjuna is full of awe and thinks, 'Wonderful! Wonderful! Ah, a delicate-limbed mountaineer who lives on the heights of Himavat calmly bears arrows shot from the Gandiva. Who is he? Is he Rudra himself, or some other Deva, or a Yaksha, or an Asura?

The Devas do sometimes come down to the summits of Himavat, but only he that wields the Pinaka can stand a thousand arrows shot from the Gandiva. Let him be a Deva or a Yaksha; unless he is Rudra himself, I will send him to Yamaloka!'

Arjuna looses hundres of arrows, resplendent as sunrays. The lustrous Creator of the worlds, the Trisulin, calmly bears those shafts as a mountain might a shower of stones. Suddenly, Arjuna finds he has no arrows left! In some alarm, now, he thinks of Agni who gave him his inexhaustible quivers when the Khandava vana burned.

Arjuna thinks, 'My arrows are exhausted. Now what shall I shoot from my bow? Who is this who consumes all my astras? But I will kill him with the tip of my bow, as elephants are killed with spears, and send him to land of the mace-wielding Yama!'

Arjuna rushes at the Kirata, and strikes him some thunderous blows with the Gandiva, at which the mountaineer deftly snatches the divine bow out of the Pandava's hands. Arjuna draws his sword and with all his might, wanting to end this duel, brings it down squarely on the Kirata's head. That blade cuts the hardest rocks like pats of butter, but that best of swords shatters into bits when it touches the Kirata's crown.

The desperate Arjuna now attacks the Kirata with trees and stones; the mountain huntsman bears these rough weapons as calmly as he had arrows, bow and sword. Frothing at the mouth, Arjuna strikes the Kirata some dreadful blows with his fists, blows like thunderclaps. Now the Kirata strikes Phalguna back, and the sounds they make are truly fearsome.

That battery of blows exchanged, which resembles the fight of old between Vritra and Vasava, lasts only moments. The mighty Jishnu clasps the Kirata to him and presses him hard with powerful arms, while the huntsman presses back, so their bodies burn like charcoals in fire, and smoke.

Abruptly, Mahadeva strikes the already beaten Pandava and makes him unconscious, and the bruised and battered Arjuna falls down as one dead. However, he regains consciousness, and rising, his body covered in blood, he is filled with despair.

He prostrates in his mind before Siva, and fashioning an earthen linga of that God, he worships it with a vanamala, a wildflower garland. But he sees the garland he offered the linga of clay decking the crown of the Kirata! Joy surges through the Pandava and he prostrates at the feet of the Kirata. Siva becomes pleased with Arjuna.

Seeing the wonder of Pandu's son, seeing his body emaciated by long austerities, Rudra says to him in a voice deep as rumbling clouds, 'Phalguna, I am pleased with you, for what you just did is without parallel. No Kshatriya is your equal in courage, and patience; and, sinless, why your strength and valour are almost equal to mine!

Mahabaho, I am pleased with you. Behold me, O Bharatarishabha! I will give you sight to see my true form. You were a Rishi before. You will vanquish all your enemies, even those that dwell in heaven. Since I am pleased with you, I will give you an inexorable astra, my own astra. You shall have it soon.'

Then Arjuna sees Siva, God of ineffable splendour in his true form – Mahadeva, who wields the Pinaka, who dwells on Kailasa, with Uma at his side. Falling onto his kness, bowing his head, that conqueror of hostile cities, Pritha's son worships the Lord Hara.

Arjuna says, 'O Kapardin, O Devadeva, O You who put out Bhaga's eyes, Nilakanta, O You with matted jata, I know you are the Cause of all causes, O Three-eyed, O Lord of all!

You are the sanctuary of all the gods; this universe has sprung from you! Not the three worlds of Devas, Asuras and Manavas together can vanquish you. You are Siva in the form of Vishnu and Vishnu as Siva.

Of old, you razed Daksha's great yagna. O Hari, O Rudra, I bow to you! You have a third eye on your brow. O Sarva, who shower the objects of desire, O Trisulin, O Pinakin, O Surya, O You of the pure body, O Creator of all, I bow to you!

Lord of all creatures, I crave your grace with my worship. You are the Lord of the Ganas, the Source of every blessing in the universe, the Cause of the causes of the universe. You are beyond the greatest Purusha, you are the highest, you are the subtlest, O Hara!

Lustrous Sankara, I beg you to forgive my offence. I came to this great mountain, so dear to you, home of Yogis, to have a vision of you, whom all the worlds worship.

Lord, I worship you to have your grace. Rashly and in ignorance did I dare to fight you. O Sankara, I seek your protection, forgive me for what I did!'

Mighty Siva, whose emblem is the Bull, takes Arjuna's handsome hands into his own, and says smilingly to him, 'I have already forgiven you!'

Brilliant Hara clasps Arjuna lovingly in his arms and consoles him again."

KAIRATA PARVA CONTINUED

"Mahadeva says, 'You were Narayana's friend Nara in your past life. You sat in fierce tapasya in Badarikasrama for many thousands of years. In you dwells great might, even as it does in Vishnu, that Purushottama. You both, through your might, are the holders of the universe.

During Indra's coronation, with your great bow whose twanging is like the roar of thunderheads, you and Krishna, as well, chastened the Danavas. The Gandiva is that bow, O Partha, it belongs in your hands. I took it from you with my maya, and your twin quivers shall again be inexhaustible!

Partha, Kurunandana, the bruises will leave your body, and it shall be free forever from pain and disease. Your prowess shall be invincible. I am pleased with you, ask me, best among all men, for the boon you want.

Parantapa, you who worships me, not in heaven is there anyone who is your equal, nor any Kshatriya who is your superior.'

Arjuna says, 'Illustrious Vrishabhdhvaja, if you would grant my wish, Lord, give me your own Pasupatastra of dreadful power, which destroys all the universe at the end of the Yuga; that weapon through which, Devadeva, with your grace, I can be victorious over Karna the vile-tongued, Bhishma, Kripa and Drona; with which I can kill Danavas, Rakshasas, Pisachas, Gandharvas and Nagas; the astra which when loosed with the proper mantras emits thousands of arrows, fierce maces, narachas like serpents.

O Destroyer of the eyes of Bhaga, this is my first wish so that I can prevail over our powerful enemies.'

Siva replies, 'Mighty one, I will give you my favourite astra, the Pasupata. Pandava, you are capable of bearing, loosing and withdrawing it. Not Indra, Yama, Kubera king of the Yakshas, Varuna, or Vayu know it – then how could man know anything of it?

But, Partha, this astra must not be loosed without adequate cause, because if it is cast against an enemy of small might it can consume the very universe. In the three worlds, with all their mobile and immobile creatures, there is no one whom this astra cannot consume. You can cast it with your mind, your eye, through words and with your bow.'

Arjuna now purifies himself, comes to the Lord of the universe and says with rapt attention, 'Instruct me!'

Mahadeva gives that best of Pandu's sons the knowledge of that weapon, which looks like an embodiment of Yama, together with all the mysteries about casting and withdrawing it. Now that astra begins to wait upon Arjuna as it does on Sankara. Gladly, too, does Arjuna receive it.

At that moment all the Earth trembles – its mountains, forests, trees, seas, villages, towns, cities, mines. Thousands of conches, drums and trumpets resound. Whirlwinds and hurricanes sweep land and sea.

The Devas and the Danavas see that terrible weapon stay beside Arjuna of measureless tejas, in its embodied form. Whatever evil there had been in the body of Phalguna is all dispelled by the touch of the three-eyed God.

Three-eyed Siva commands Arjuna, 'Go into Swarga!'

Bending his head, Arjuna worships the God, then gazes at him with folded hands. The Lord of all who dwells in heaven, He who dwells upon mountains, Uma's lord, the Mahayogin whose passions are under perfect control, the source of all blessings, gives Arjuna, best of men, back the Gandiva, bane of Danavas and Pisachas.

As Arjuna watches, Siva, Uma beside him, ascends into the sky, vanishing from that blessed mountain with snowy tablelands, valleys and caves, favourite haunt of sky-ranging Maharishis."

CANTO 41

KAIRATA PARVA CONTINUED**

Vaisampayana said, "Siva, whose emblem is the Bull, who wields the Pinaka, vanishes from Arjuna's sight even as the Sun sets on the world.

Arjuna Parantapa is full of awe. He exults, 'Ah, I have seen the God of gods. Fortunate indeed am I, and greatly favoured, for I have both seen and touched with my hands the three-eyed Hara, in his boon-giving form.

I will win success. I am already great. My enemies have already been vanquished by me. My purposes have already been achieved!'

As he stands thinking all this, suddenly Varuna, Lord of waters, appears before Arjuna, handsome and splendid beyond belief and of the hue of lapis lazuli, surrounded by all manner of aquatic beings, and filling all the points of the horizon with blazing effulgence.

Varuna Deva, lord of all creatures of water, comes with the Rivers—male and female—and Nagas, and Daityas and Sadhyas and lesser deities.

Then Kubera, whose body is like the purest gold, arrives in his splendent vimana, numerous Yakshas coming with him. The most beautiful Lord of treasures, also illumining the sky with his lustre, comes to see Arjuna.

Yama himself, also magnificently beautiful, mighty destroyer of all the worlds, comes to that place, and with him those lords of creation, the Pitrs, both embodied and disembodied. Yama of inconceivable soul, dispenser of justice, destroyer of all enemies, the son of Surya, also flies here in his vimana, mace in hand, lighting up the three worlds, and the realms of the Guhyakas, the Gandharvas and the Nagas even like a second Sun, rising at Yuganta.

Arriving there, upon three refulgent summits of the great mountain, those Lokapalas see Arjuna at his tapasya.

Next moment, the blindingly bright Indra also arrives, with his queen Sachi, upon his mount Airavata, and with all the Devas around him. With the sovereign white parasol unfurled over his head, he looks like the full moon among fleecy clouds.

Eulogised by Gandharvas, and Rishis endowed with a wealth of tapasya, the king of the Devas alights upon a peak of that mountain, like another Sun.

Now Yama of fathomless intelligence, who knows the depths of dharma, says from his peak in a cloud-deep voice, these auspicious words, 'Arjuna, look, we the Lokapalas have come here! We will grant you spiritual vision, for you deserve to behold us.

In a past life you were the Rishi Nara of immeasurable soul, of plumbless might. Child, at Brahma's command, you have been born among men. Anagha, sinless, you will vanquish that most righteous grandsire of the Kurus in war, Bhishma of tameless energy, born of the Vasus.

You will also defeat all the ferocious Kshatriyas commanded by the son of Bharadwaja. Besides, you will quell all the terrible Danavas who have incarnated as men, as well as the Danavas on high called the Nivatakavachas.

Dhananjaya, Kurunandana, you will also kill the mighty Karna, who is an amsa of my father Surya, his tejas celebrated throughout the worlds. Kaunteya, Parantapa, you will also kill all the amsavataras of the Danavas and Rakshasas who have been born into the world as men; and slain by you, these will attain the realms they have earned through their karma.

And, O Phalguna, the legend and fame of your achievements will last for ever in the world, for you have pleased Siva himself with your prowess. With Krishna, you will lighten the burden of the Earth.

Here, take this mace, this inexorable danda of mine. With this weapon you will accomplish great things.'

Pritha's son receives that weapon from Yama, and the secret mantras for casting and withdrawing it.

Now Varuna, Lord of all water beings, blue as seas, says from a peak on which he has perched towards the west, 'Son of Pritha, you are the greatest Kshatriya, and you engage in Kshatriya dharma.

Look at me, O you with the large coppery eyes! I am Varuna, the lord of waters. No one can resist my fluid pasas, my weapons that are deadly nooses. Kaunteya, receive these Varunastras and the secrets of casting and withdrawing them. During the Devasura yuddha of old, which began because of Brihaspati's wife Tara, these pasas seized and bound thousands of mighty Daityas.

Here, take them from me. With these in your hands, even if Yama himself is your adversary, he will not escape you. When you range over the field of war with my pasas, be certain that the land will become destitute of Kshatriyas.'

When Varuna and Yama have given Arjuna their weapons, Kubera, lord of treasures, who dwells on the heights of Kailasa, says, 'O mighty and wise Pandava, I am also pleased with you, and this meeting with you gives me as much pleasure as a meeting with Krishna.

Savyasachin, Mahabaho, once you were a Deva, eternal and immortal. On ancient Kailasa, you performed tapasya with the rest of us. Best of men, I grant you celestial vision. Mighty-armed, you will vanquish even invincible Daityas and Danavas.

Here, take from me, also, a great weapon with which you will consume the legions of Dhritarashtra. Take then this favourite weapon of mine, the Antardhana of awesome energy, power and splendour. It will make your enemies sleep.

When the illustrious Sankara razed Tripura, he loosed this astra and consumed countless great Asuras. Magnificent Arjuna, as dignified as Meru, you are capable of wielding this weapon.'

Arjuna the Kuru prince duly receives that celestial weapon from Kubera.

Now the king of the Devas himself, great Indra, speaks to Pritha's son sweetly, in a voice deep as thunderheads rumbling or a battery of great bass drums. 'Kaunteya, Mahabaho, you are an ancient God. Already, you have achieved the highest success, and acquired the status of a Deva. But, O Parantapa, scourge of your enemies, you have yet to accomplish a mission for the Devas.

You must ascend into Devaloka. So, prepare yourself, splendid Kshatriya! My own chariot, with Matali its sarathy, will soon fly down to the earth. I will bring you to Devaloka in it, and there give you all my Devastras.'

Arjuna is wonderstruck to see the four Lokapalas together upon the summits of Himavat. He worships them with japa, water, and fruit. The Devas return his worship, then vanish, going back to their abodes.

Arjuna, Bull among men, is full of joy to have received the astras of Varuna, Yama and Kubera. He considers himself one whose tapasya has been fulfilled and crowned with success."

CANTO 42

INDRALOKABHIGAMANA PARVA

Vaisampayana said, "After the Lokapalas leave, Arjuna Parantapa begins to think of the chariot of Indra. Even as he does, that vimana of tremendous resplendence, Matali its sarathy, comes, dividing the clouds and illumining the sky, and filling all the firmament with a roar deeper than those of massed thunderclouds. Across its form are gleaming swords, astras with dreadful forms, maces too frightful to be described, winged arrows of unearthly splendour, streaks of dazzling lightning, thunderbolts, whirling propellors and jets, all creating that deafening sound.

Also in that chariot are fierce and immense Nagas with flaming mouths, with precious gemstones on their hoods white as fleecy clouds. Tens of thousands of golden coloured horses, swift as the wind, draw that chariot. Endowed with maya, so swift is that chariot that the eye can hardly mark its flight.

Arjuna sees the flagstaff Vaijayanta, effulgent, of the hue of the emerald or the deep blue lotus, decked with golden ornaments and straight as a bamboo stalk. Seeing a charioteer wearing gold sitting in that ratha, the mighty Partha knows this is a chariot of the Devas.

As he stands thinking about this, the sarathy Matali descends from the ratha, and bending down, says, 'Most fortunate son of Sakra! Sakra himself wishes to see you. Come now, Indra has sent this chariot.

Your father, the God of a hundred yagnas, king of the Devas, said to me, "Fetch Kunti's son here, and let the Devas see him."

Sakra himself, surrounded by the Devas, Devarishis, Gandharvas and Apsaras, waits to see you. At the command of the chastiser of Paka, therefore, come with me to Devaloka. You will return after receiving the astras of Indra.'

Arjuna replies, 'O Matali, lose no time but mount your wondrous ratha, which cannot be attained even after hundreds of Rajasuya and Aswamedha yagnas. Even kings of great wealth who performed Mahayagnas distinguished by vast gifts to Brahmanas, why, even the Devas and Danavas do not ride in this vimana.

He who does not have the wealth of tapasya cannot see or even touch this chariot, far less ride in it. Blessed Matali, after you have climbed into it and the horses have become still, I will follow you like a virtuous man stepping onto the high path of dharma.'

Indra's sarathy climbs back into the marvellous ratha and makes his horses still. His heart full of joy, Arjuna purifies himself with a bath in the Ganga; Kunti's son silently says his daily prayers and makes water offerings, tarpana, to the Pitrs.

Finally, he prays to Mandara, that king of mountains, 'O you who are the sanctuary of holy, heaven-seeking Sages, it is through your grace, O Mountain, that Brahmanas and Kshatriyas and Vaisyas attain Swarga, and then, their anxieties gone, sport with the gods.

O King of mountains, you are the refuge of Munis, and bear many most sacred shrines upon your breast. Happily have I dwelt upon your heights. I leave you now, bidding you farewell. How long my eyes have dwelt on your tablelands and bowers, your sparkling springs and brooks, and your sacred shrines.

I have eaten the delicious fruit which grow upon your trees, and slaked my thrist with the scented, nectarine water of your streams, sweet as amrita. O Mandara, as a child sleeps happily on the lap of his father, so have I, King of mountains, dwelt and slept upon you, in woods that ring with the songs of Apsaras and the chanting of the Vedas.

O Mountain, every day I have spent upon you I have spent in joy!'

Thus bidding farewell to the mountain, Arjuna, slayer of foes, bright as the Sun himself, climbs into the celestial chariot. Joyfully, then, he courses through the sky in that divine and extraordinary vimana, brilliant as a star.

Once he has vanished from the sight of mortals of the Earth, Arjuna sees thousands of sky ships of extraordinary beauty. And in that realm, there is no Sun, Moon or Fire to give light, but it is lustrous of itself, lit by tapasya! The Pandava sees that the stars, which appear like minuscule lamps from the Earth are in fact great and huge, of exceptional beauty and brilliance.

There he sees Rajarishis, in hundreds upon hundreds, whose lives had been crowned by ascetic success; he sees them ablaze, and also heroes who had given their lives in battle; and men who had gained Swarga through tapasya.

And there are also Gandharvas, illustrious as suns, thousands and thousands of them, as also Guhyakas, Rishis and numerous tribes of Apsaras. Arjuna is wonderstruck, exhilarated, seeing these self-luminous realms and beings, and asks Matali about them.

And Matali answers gladly, 'These, O son of Pritha, are virtuous beings stationed in their places. It is these whom you have seen, great one, as stars from the Earth.'

Now Arjuna sees the gates to Indra's own realm, and standing there, the magnificent, always triumphant elephant Airavata, four-tusked, and resembling the Mountain Kailasa with its peaks. Coursing along that path of the Siddhas, that best the Kurus, that son of Pandu, sits in beauty even like Mandhata, greatest of the kings of old.

He of the eyes like lotus leaves passes through that realm set apart for kings of dharma. Thus flying through many regions of Swarga, Arjuna of great renown finally sees Amaravati, the city of Indra."

CANTO 43

INDRALOKABHIGAMANA PARVA CONTINUED

Vaisampayana said, "Indra's city, resort of Siddhas and Charanas, is beautiful past describing. Flowers of every season adorn it, and sacred trees of all kinds. Arjuna sees the divine garden Nandana, favourite haunt of Apsaras. Fanned by fragrant breezes charged with the scents of unearthly flowers, the trees of that garden and their lord of celestial blossoms seem to welcome him among them.

This is a realm that none can see who has not performed tapasya or poured libations on sacred fire. Only the virtuous ever come here, and none that ever turn their backs on the field of battle. None who have not performed sacrifices, kept stern vows, or who are not knowers of the Veda, or who have not bathed in sacred waters, or who are not distinguished for sacrifices and gifts can ever see this realm.

None can ever see this place who ever disturbed a yagna, or who are base, or who drink intoxicating liquor, or who violate their Guru's bed, or who eat unsanctified meat, or who are evil can ever come to the enchanted Nandana.

Having seen those celestial gardens full of soft divine music, the strong-armed son of Pandu enters Indra's city. He sees vimanas here, in thousands, which can fly anywhere at all at will, each kept in its place; he also sees tens of thousands of more such craft flying in every dircetion.

Fanned by flower-scented breezes, Apsaras and Gandharvas sing the Pandava's praises. Along with the Siddhas and Maharishis, the Devas joyfully welcome Pritha's son of white deeds, pouring blessings over him, while divine music plays.

Arjuna hears conches and drums, and eulogised all round, at Indra's behest, the Pandava goes to the great starry way known as Suravithi, where he meets with the Sadhyas, the Viswas, the Marutas, the twin Aswins, the Adityas, the Vasus, the Rudras, the Brahmarishis of great splendour, and numerous Rajarishis with Dilipa at their head, and Tumburu and Narada, and that pair of master Gandharvas known as Haha and Huhu.

Having met and duly worshipped all these, the Kuru prince finally sees before him the king of the Devas, Indra of a hundred yagnas. Arjuna alights from the chariot and approaches the Deva king—his father—the chastiser of Paka.

A great and beautiful white parasol, with a golden staff, is unfurled over Devendra's head; he is fanned by a chamara whisk scented with the perfumes of heaven. Many Gandharvas, led by Viswavasu and others, hymn Indra, as do bards and singers, while the loftiest Brahmanas chant Rik and Yajur mantras.

Kunti's son approaches Indra and bends his head down to the ground before him. Whereupon, Indra embraces him with round, mighty arms. Taking Arjuna's hand, Sakra makes him sit beside him on a part of his own throne, that sacred throne which the Devas and Rishis worship.

Indra, Parantapa, sniffed the top of his son's head in affection, and even took him onto his lap. Sitting on Sakra's throne, at the command of that God of a thousand eyes, Pritha's son of immeasurable tejas begins to blaze in splendour, like a second Indra.

Moved again by love, Indra, slayer of Vritra, comforts Arjuna, touching his handsome face with his scented, beautiful hands. Repeatedly patting and stroking with his hands, which bear the sign of the thunderbolt, Arjuna's mighty arms, which are like two golden columns, hardened by years of a bowstring being drawn across them, Indra and his son appear like the Sun and the Moon illumining the beauty of that divine sabha, as they do the sky on the fourteenth day of the dark fortnight.

A band of Gandharvas headed by Tumburu, masters of music both sacred and profane, sing many rapturously melodious songs. Ghritachi and Menaka and Rambha and Purvachitti and Swayamprabha and Urvasi and Misrakesi and Dandagauri and Varuthini and Gopali and Sahajanya and Kumbhayoni and Prajagara and Chitrasena and Chitralekha and Saha and Madhuraswara – these and thousands of others, all with eyes like lotus leaves, who engage in seducing the hearts of men at tapasya, dance there.

Slim are their waists and ample and fair their hips, as they dance, their bodies twisting sinuously, with astonishing suppleness and agility, and deep bosoms shaking, casting their alluring glances around, and otherwise enticing those that watch them."

CANTO 44

INDRALOKABHIGAMANA PARVA CONTINUED

Vaisampayana said, "Knowing Indra's wishes, the Devas and the Gandharvas procure a most excellent arghya and worship the son of Pritha. Giving him water to wash his feet and his face, they bring the Kshatriya into Indra's palace.

Thus worshipped, Jishnu begins to live in his father's home, and while he is there, he acquires the Devastras, and the secrets of loosing and withdrawing them. From Sakra's hands he receives Indra's favourite weapon, the inexorable Vajra, and other astras too, all awesome – heaven's very gashes of lightning, vari-coloured as clouds and dancing peacocks' fans.

When he has all these astras, Arjuna remembers his brothers and misses them. However, at Indra's command he spends full five years in Devaloka, ensconced amidst every comfort and luxury.

After some time, Indra says to him, "Kaunteya, learn music and dancing from Chitrasena. Learn the instrumental music of the gods, which does not exist in the world of men, for, O son of Kunti, it will benefit you."

And Purandara gives Chitrasena as a friend to Arjuna, who lives happily and in peace with that Gandharva. All the while, Chitrasena teaches Arjuna music, both singing and the instruments; he teaches him dancing.

However, Arjuna is restless and has no peace, because thoughts of Subala's son Sakuni, the game of dice, angry thoughts of Dussasana and of killing him, roil the Pandava. But his friendship with Chitrasena ripens and he does learn the unrivalled dance and music of the Gandharvas.

Finally, even after having learned all the various forms of song and instruments, and dance as well, that Parantapa still finds no peace of mind, thinking constantly of his brothers and his mother Kunti."

INDRALOKABHIGAMANA PARVA CONTINUED

Vaisampayana said, "One day, knowing that Arjuna's glances turn repeatedly to the Apsara Urvasi, Indra calls Chitrasena to him privately and says, 'King of Gandharvas, go as my messenger to that best of Apsaras, Urvasi, and let her wait upon my son Arjuna, tiger among men.

Tell her that I said, "Even as I have caused Arjuna to learn the secrets of all the astras, as well as all the arts, worshipped by everyone, so should you make him conversant with the arts of disporting himself in feminine company!"'

Chitrasena goes at once to Urvasi, most beautiful among Apsaras. She honours and delights him with her welcome and the worship she offers him.

When he sits at his ease, he says to Urvasi, who sits relaxed in his company, 'O You of the fair hips, know that I come here at the word of the only Lord of Swarga, who asks a favour of you.

You do know Arjuna, who is known among the gods and men for his many natural virtues, for his grace, his conduct, the beauty of his person, his vows and self-control; who is noted for might and prowess, and respected by the virtuous, and quick-witted; who is endowed with genius and splendid energy, is of a forgiving temper and without malice of any kind; who has studied the four Vedas with their angas, the Upanishads, and the Puranas, also; who is blessed with devotion to his preceptors and with an intellect possessed of the eight attributes; who by his abstinence, ability, origins and age, is by himself capable of protecting the Devaloka like Maghavat himself; who is never boastful; who shows proper respect to all; who sees the minutest things as clearly as if those were gross and large; who is sweet-spoken; who showers diverse kinds of food and drink on his friends and dependants; who is truthful, worshipped by all, eloquent, handsome, and without pride; who is kind to those devoted to him, and universally pleasing and dear; who is firm in keeping his promises; who is equal even to Mahendra and Varuna for owning every worthwhile quality and attribute.

Know, Urvasi, that Kshatriya is to taste the joys of heaven! Commanded by Indra, let him today find your favours. Do this, O sweet one, for Dhananjaya is inclined towards you, he desires you.'

Urvasi of faultless features smiles; her heart glad to hear the Gandharva's words, she says, 'I would bestow my favours on anyone who owns such qualities. Then why should I not choose Arjuna for a lover? Indeed, at Indra's command, for the sake of my friendship with you, and stirred by Arjuna's numerous virtues, I am already under the spell of the god of love.

O Chitrasena, go where you will now, and I will go to Arjuna.'

CANTO 46

INDRALOKABHIGAMANA PARVA CONTINUED

Vaisampayana said, "Having thus sent away the Gandharva, who has succeeded in his mission, Urvasi of the luminous smiles, moved by the desire of possessing Arjuna, bathes luxuriantly. She decks herself in wonderful ornaments and garlands of heaven's fragrances. Inflamed by the god of love, her heart pierced through by Kama's flowery shafts to think of Arjuna's beauty, her mind entirely absorbed in thoughts of him, she already makes love to him in her imagination, on a wide and fine bed covered with celestial linen.

When twilight deepens and the moon rises, that Apsara of the high hips sets out for Arjuna's palace. In that mood and her soft long tresses adorned with flowers, she is exquisite, absolutely graceful. The movements of her eyebrows, her soft accents are full of enchantment. Her own face like a full glowing moon, she goes forth as if challenging the moon for beauty.

As she goes, her deep, finely pointed breasts, smeared with unworldly unguents and sandalwood paste, covered by a golden chain, begin to tremble. So heavy are they that with each step she takes she seems to bend forward slightly at her lovely waist with three folds.

Faultless are her loins, ah, elegant abode of Kama Deva; her hips are fair, round and wide at their base. Wearing the sheerest clothes, decked in golden ornaments, she could shake the sainthood of any yogi.

Fine are her ankles, flat the soles of her feet, straight her toes the hue of burnished copper, and dorsum high and curved like the back of the tortoise; she wears anklets with little bells tinkling.

She has drunk some wine, she is flushed with desire; soft anticipation and delight course through her; she sways slightly from all these and is more beautiful than ever. And though Devaloka abounds in wonders of every kind, when Urvasi goes to Arjuna as she does, the Siddhas and Charanas and Gandharvas think that she is the most beautiful thing on which they ever laid eyes.

Dressed exquisitely in a fine, cloud-coloured garment, she is surely as lambent as a digit of the moon in the sky with fleecy clouds across his face. Swiftly as the wind or the mind goes she of the luminous smiles, and soon arrives at Arjuna the Pandava's mansion.

Purushottama, at the gates Urvasi sends word in through the dwarapalaka, and quickly she is inside the splendid and elegant palace. O Rajan, when Arjuna sees her in his palace at night he feels anxiety grip him, but then he comes forward to welcome her respectfully. However, when he sees her as she is, the Pandava shuts his eyes out of modesty.

Saluting her, he offers the Apsara worship that is given to an elder, a superior.

Arjuna says, 'O best of the Apsaras, I bend my head down before you. Command me, for I am your servant.'

Hearing this, and his reverential tone, Urvasi is distraught. She tells Arjuna how Chitrasena the Gandharva came to see her, and of their meeting.

She says, 'Best of men, I will tell you everything which passed between Chitrasena and me, and why I have come here.

Arjuna, because of your coming to this realm, Mahendra called together a large and charming sabha, where celestial festivities were held. The Rudras, the Adityas, the Aswins and the Vasus came to that gathering, as did a number of Devarishis, Rajarishis, Siddhas, Charanas, Yakshas and great Nagas.

O large eyes, when the members of that gathering, all splendid as fire, the Sun or the Moon, all sat according to rank, honour, and prowess, O son of Sakra, the Gandharvas began to play on their vinas and sing songs of divine enchantment. And, Kurupravira, the main Apsaras also began to dance.

Then, O son of Pritha, you looked at me, gazed at me, why, stared only at me. When that assembly of the celestials broke, at your father's command, the gods went away to their respective abodes. The Apsaras also went away to their homes, and the others also, O Parantapa, with your father's leave.

It was then Sakra sent Chitrasena to me, and arriving in my home, O you of the eyes like lotus leaves, he said to me, "Fairest, the king of the Devas has sent me to you. Do something which would please Mahendra, and me, and yourself as well.

O fair hipped, go and please Arjuna, who is as brave in battle as Sakra himself, and is always magnanimous and great-hearted."

Even these, Partha, were his words to me. So, Anagha, commanded by Chitrasena and by your father I have come to serve you, Parantapa. My heart has been attracted by your virtues, and I am already under the influence of the god of love.

Kshatriya, this is also my own fervent wish, and I have cherished it since I first saw you.'"

Vaisampayana continued, "Listening to this, Arjuna is overcome by bashfulness. He stops his ears with his hands, and says, 'Devi, I curse my hearing that you speak to me like this! For, O beautiful one, I think of you as the wife of an elder. Auspicious one, you are even like Kunti to me, or Indra's queen Sachi.

This is the only way I have always thought of you, and that is why I gazed at you and no one else, most blessed one. I have my particular reason for this and I will tell you what it is, O you of luminous smiles.

I stared at you in Indra's sabha, my eyes wide with delight, thinking, "This most exquisite woman is the mother of the race of Kuru!" O Apsara, it does not become you to have other feelings for me, because you are superior to all my superiors – you are the mother of my race!'

Urvasi says, 'O son of Indra, we Apsaras are free and bound to no one; we choose whom we will. You must not think of me as your elder or suprior. The sons and grandsons of Puru's race who came here through their punya have all sported freely with us, without incurring any sin.

So, relent, Kshatriya, it does not become you to send me away. I am afire with desire for you. I am devoted to you. Accept me, take me if you would properly adore me.'

Arjuna replies, 'Listen to me, O you of fautless, perfect features. I speak truly, and let the four directions and the gods hear me as well. Sinless one, as Kunti, Madri or Sachi is to me, so are you, the mother of my race, an object of reverence to me. Return, O fairest, I bend my head down to you and prostrate at your feet. You deserve my worship as a son, and I your love as a mother.'

Hearing this, Urvasi is beside herself with rage. Trembling with it, knitting her brows, she curses Arjuna, 'Since you spurn a woman come to your palace at your father's command and of her own will, a woman, besides, who is pierced by the shafts of Kama, O Partha, you will spend your time among women as a dancer, your manhood gone and scorned as a eunuch!'

With this curse, her lips still pale and quivering, her breasts still heaving in wrath, Urvasi walks out of Arjuna's palace and returns home. Arjuna, Parantapa, desparate, immediately seeks out Chitrasena, and finding him, tells him everything that passed between Urvasi and himself in the night, anguishing repeatedly over the Apsara's curse.

Chitrasena goes to Sakra and tells him everything. Indra calls Arjuna to him privately, and consoles him.

Indra says gently, 'O greatest of all men, today Pritha has truly become a blessed mother for having you as her son. Mahabaho, you have excelled even the Rishis in your self-control.

Do not fear, the curse of Urvasi will benefit you, it will prove a blessing. Anagha, back on Earth you must spend the thirteenth year of your exile in ajnatavasa, unrecognised, undiscovered. That is when you will suffer the curse of Urvasi, and when you have spent one year exactly as a eunuch and a dancer, you will have your manhood back.'

When Indra says this to him, great relief and delight wash over Arjuna; he no longer anguishes over the curse. Pandu's son Dhananjaya spends his time pleasantly in Devaloka in the company of the celebrated Gandharva Chitrasena.'

The desires of the man that listens to this story of Arjuna never turn towards blind lust. The best men who listen to this tale of the awesome purity of Phalguna, son of the lord of the Devas, become devoid of pride, arrogance, anger and every other fault, and ascending into Swarga, sport there in bliss."

CANTO 47

INDRALOKABHIGAMANA PARVA CONTINUED

Vaisampayana said, "One day, during his wanderings, the great Rishi Lomasa comes to Indra's abode, wanting to meet the king of the Devas. The Mahamuni approaches the Lord of the gods and bows reverentially to him. He sees Pandu's son occupying half of Vasava's throne.

Having been worshipped by the Devarishis, that Dvijottama, invited by Indra, sits in a most excellent seat. He wonders how Arjuna, who was a Kshatriya, has attained to the throne of Sakra himself. What great deeds of punya has he performed, what lofty realms has he conquered, that he sits upon the throne which the gods themselves worship?

As these thoughts engage the Rishi, Sakra, slayer of Vritra, reads the Muni's heart. With a smile, Indra says to Lomasa, 'Brahmarishi, I see what you are thinking – this one is no mortal though he has been born among men. Mahamuni, this mighty-armed Kshatriya is my own son born to Kunti.

He has come here to acquire astras, for a great purpose. Alas! Don't you recognise him as an ancient Rishi of the highest punya? Listen to me, O Brahamana, I will tell you who he is and why he has come to me.

Know, those magnificent Rishis of antiquity, Nara and Narayana, are none other than Dhananjaya and Hrishikesa. Nara and Narayana, celebrated throughout the three worlds, have been born on Earth for the sake of dharma.

That sacred asrama, which even Devas and Maharishis never see, which is known through the world as Badari, which nestles by the source of the Ganga, which is worshipped by the Siddhas and the Charanas, was the hermitage, O Lomasa, of Vishnu and Jishnu.

Brahmarishi, at my wish, the two Sages of blazing splendour have been born into the world of men, and endowed with awesome tejas, they will lighten the burden of Bhumi Devi.

Besides this, the Asuras known as Nivatakavachas, arrogant of the boon they have, are constantly engaged in doing us harm. They boast of their power, and are even now plotting to destroy the Devas, for with their boon they no longer fear us. They are fierce and mighty Danavas, who live in the Patalas, and not all the Devas together can withstand their might.

The blessed Vishnu, slayer of Madhu, Kapila who made ashes of the sons of Sagara with just his look when they attacked him roaring in the bowels of the Earth, can indeed quell the Nivatakavachas. Either Hari or Partha, or both, can slay those Asuras.

Just as he subdued the Nagas in the great lake, the lustrous Hari can surely consume the Nivatakavachas and all their followers, with just his look. But the task is too insignificant for Madhusudana himself, for being the awesome mass of energy which he is, if incensed, his wrath might consume the very universe.

This Arjuna can also kill our enemies, and having killed them he will return to the world of men. Now you must go to the Earth, for my sake. You will find the brave Yudhishtira living in the Kamyaka vana. For me, you must tell Yudhishtira of unbaffled prowess in battle that he should not be anxious about Arjuna, because this hero will return as a great master of astras, for without being a complete and perfect master he will not be able to face Bhishma, Drona and the others in battle.

You must also tell Yudhishtira that the mighty Arjuna has not only acquired the devastras, he has also mastered the arts of celestial music, both singing and of instruments, and dancing as well.

You will also tell Yudhishtira that, taking all his brothers with him, and yourself, O Muni, he should set out on a pilgrimage and visit all the sacred tirthas of the holy land. Bathing in the various sacred waters, he will be washed of all his sins, and the fever in his heart will abate. Then, he will be able to enjoy his kingdom, in the knowledge that his sins are gone.

Dvijottama, you must protect Yudhishtira during his wandering over the Earth. Fierce Rakshasas live in mountain fastnesses and rugged plains. Protect the king from those eaters of men.'

When Mahendra has said this much to Lomasa, Arjuna also speaks reverently to that Rishi. 'O, always bless and protect the son of Pandu, and with your protection, Maharishi, the king will undertake his tirtha yatra and give charity to Brahmanas across the land.'

The mighty Sage Lomasa says to them both, 'So be it,' and sets out for the Earth and the Kamyaka aranya. Arriving in that jungle, he sees that Parantapa, Kunti's son Dharmaraja Yudhishtira, surrounded by Rishis and his younger brothers."

CANTO 48

INDRALOKABHIGAMANA PARVA CONTINUED

Janamejaya said, "Surely, the feats of Partha of measureless energy were certainly marvellous. O Brahmana, what did Dhritarashtra of great wisdom say, when he heard about these?"

Vaisampayana said, "When Ambika's son Dhritarashtra hears about Arjuna's arrival and stay in Indra's realm from Dwaipayana, first among Rishis, he says to Sanjaya, "O Sarathy, do you know everything about what Arjuna did, from beginning to end, all that I have just heard?

Sanjaya, my wretched, sinful son even now pursues the most base and vulgar policy. Ah, his soul is evil and he will surely unpeople this very Earth. The illustrious man, who speaks the truth even when he speaks in jest, and who has Arjuna to fight for him, is certain to win the three worlds.

Who that is even beyond the influence of death and decay will be able to stay before Arjuna, when he looses his barbed arrows whetted on stone? My wretched sons, who must fight the invincible Pandavas are all doomed. I think about it night and day but do not see the warrior amongst us who can withstand the wielder of the Gandiva.

If Drona, Karna or even Bhishma advance against him in battle, a great calamity is likely to befall the Earth. Even then, I do not see the way to our victory. Karna is kind and forgiving. Acharya Drona is old, and besides he is Arjuna's teacher.

But Arjuna is wrathful, strong, proud, and of firm and steady prowess. All these warriors are invincible and a terrible battle will take place between them. All of them are heroes skilled in weapons and of great repute. They would not wish for the sovereignty of the world, if it was to be bought by defeat. Indeed, peace will be restored only after the death either of these or of Phalguna.

But there is no one who can kill Phalguna, no one who can vanquish him. Oh, now I am the object of his anger; how will that rage be quenched? Equal to the king of the Devas, that Kshatriya gratified Agni at Khandava; he subdued all the monarchs of the Earth during the occasion of the great Rajasuya.

O Sanjaya, the thunderbolt falling on the mountain top leaves a portion unconsumed; but, child, the shafts shot by Kiriti leave no rack behind. As the rays of the Sun heat this mobile and immobile universe, so will Arjuna's shafts scorch my sons. It seems to me that the legions of the Bhaaratas, terrified by the clatter of Arjuna's chariot wheels, are already broken through on all sides.

Vidhatri has created Arjuna as an all-consuming Destroyer. He stays in battle as an enemy, spewing swarms of arrows. Who will defeat him?'"

INDRALOKABHIGAMANA PARVA CONTINUED

" Sanjaya says, 'All that you say about Duryodhana is entirely true. Nothing that you have said is untrue, O Lord of the Earth.

The sight of their pure wife Krishnaa dragged into the sabha has filled the Pandavas with rage. They have been so incensed to hear the cruel words of Dussasana and Karna that they will never forgive the Kurus.

I have heard how Arjuna pleased the God of Gods in battle with his bow – Sthanu of eleven forms. Wanting to test Phalguna, the illustrious Kapardin assumed the guise of a Kirata and fought him.

And there it was that the Lokapalas revealed themselves to that Kururishabha, and gave him their weapons. What other man on earth, except Phalguna, would strive to see these gods in their own forms? Rajan, who will weaken Arjuna in battle, when the eight-formed Maheswara could not do so?

By coarsely dragging Draupadi into this sabha and shaming her, and enraging the Pandavas, your sons have brought this terrifying calamity upon themselves. When Bhima saw Duryodhana bare both his thighs to

Panchali, with quivering lips Vrikodara said, "Wretch! I will smash those thighs of yours with my mace when thirteen years have passed."

All the sons of Pandu are the greatest warriors; all of them have immeasurable energy; all of them are masters of every kind of weapon; not the gods can vanquish them. Incensed at the insult to their wife, Pritha's sons will kill all your sons in battle.'

Dhritarashtra says, 'O Sarathy, what mischief Karna did by speaking savage words to the sons of Pandu! Was not enough enmity provoked by bringing Krishnaa into the sabha?

How can my evil sons live, whose eldest brother and preceptor does not walk the way of dharma? Seeing me blind, Sanjaya, and incapable of exerting myself actively, my son believes me to be a fool, and does not listen to what I say. The wretches who are his counsellors, Karna, Sakuni and the others, always pander to his vices, because he does not see light.

Arjuna's arrows, even if he shoots them lightly, can consume all my princes; what then when he looses them in anger? Why, arrows shot by Arjuna's mighty arms, from his great bow, with mantras spoken over them, can turn themselves into astras which can punish the Devas themselves.

He who has for his counsellor, protector and friend that scourge of sinners, the lord of the three worlds, Hari himself, encounters nothing that he cannot conquer. O Sanjaya, we have heard that the Lord Siva himself clasped Arjuna in his arms.

All the world knows what Phalguna did, with Krishna beside him, to help Agni in the Khandava vana. So, when Bhima, Partha and Vaasudeva of the Satwatas are enraged, surely my sons, with their allies and the Subalas are no match for them in battle.'"

INDRALOKABHIGAMANA PARVA CONTINUED

Janamejaya said, "O Muni, surely, after sending Pandu's heroic sons into exile, these lamentations of Dhritarashtra were perfectly futile. Why did the king allow his foolish son Duryodhana to incense the mighty Pandavas?

O Brahmana, tell us now what did the sons of Pritha eat while they lived in the forest? Was it produce of the wilderness or of cultivation?"

Vaisampayana said, "Those bulls among men gather fruit and roots and also hunt deer with purified arrows. They first dedicate a portion of the food to the Brahmanas, and then eat the rest themselves.

For, O King, while those heroes with great bows live in the forest, Brahmanas of both classes follow them, those that worship with fire and those that do not. Ten thousand illustrious Snataka Brahmanas, all knowers of the means to moksha, Yudhishtira supports in the vana.

Killing Rurus and the black deer with arrows, as well as other clean animals of the wild, fit for eating, he gives them to those Brahmanas. None who stays with Yudhishtira looks pale or ill, or is lean or weak, or melancholy or afraid. Yudhishtira, lord of the Kurus, looks after his brothers as if they are his sons, and his other kinsmen as if they are his brothers.

The chaste Draupadi feeds the Brahmanas and her husbands, even as if she is their mother, and only after they have eaten, does she herself eat.

Daily, bows in hand, the king himself goes east, Bhima to the south, and the twins west and north, and kill deer for meat. Thus do the Pandavas spend five years in the Kamyaka vana, in some anxiety at the absence of Arjuna, and engage all the while in study, prayers and sacrifices."

INDRALOKABHIGAMANA PRAV CONTINUED

Vaisampayana said, "Ambika's son, Dhritarashtra Purusharishabha listens to this account of how the Pandavas live in exile, and is filled with grief and dread. Overwhelmed by dejection, sighing heavily and sweating, that king says to Sanjaya, 'Sarathy, I have not a moment's peace, day or night, thinking of my son's terrible conduct during the gambling, and also thinking of the heroism, the patience, the high intelligence, the unbearable prowess, and the extraordinary love for one another of the sons of Pandu.

Among the Pandavas, the lustrous Nakula and Sahadeva, born of Devas and as splendid as the king of the Devas himself, are invincible in battle. They wield their weapons powerfully, loose their arrows over great distances, are resolute in battle, of remarkable lightness of hand, of quenchless wrath, possessed of great steadiness, and blessed with terrific energy. They have the strength of lions and are as inexorable as the Aswins themselves.

When they take the field with Bhima and Arjuna before them, I see, Sanjaya, that my soldiers will all be slain without a remnant. Those mighty warriors, all Devas' sons, unrivalled in battle by anybody, filled with anger at the memory of Draupadi's humiliation, will show no mercy.

The awesome Vrishni warriors, also, the Panchalas of tameless tejas, and the sons of Pritha, led by Krishna of unbaffled prowess, will raze my legions. All the warriors on my side together cannot bear the might of just the Vrishnis, for Balarama and Krishna command them.

Then, Bhima of dreadful prowess, his iron mace raised, he who can kill any Kshatriya, will prowl among my soldiers like Death himself. High above the din of the field, the twang of the Gandiva will resound, loud as heaven's thunder. No king who is with us can withstand the force of Bhima's mace and the mere sound of the Gandiva's bowstring.

And then, Sanjaya, obedient as I have been to the voice of Duryodhana, I will have to recall all the rejected counsels of those who were truly my friends and well-wishers, counsels which I should have attended to more timely.'

Sanjaya says, 'This was your grievous mistake, O King, that although you could have stopped your son from doing what he did, you did not, out of your love for him.

Hearing that the Pandavas had been defeated at dice, Krishna of unfading glory went to the Kamyaka vana and consoled them there. Draupadi's sons, too, led by Dhrishtadyumna arrived in that vana, as did Virata, Dhrishtaketu and the mighty Kekayas.

Through our spies, I learnt everything those Kshatriyas said there, when they saw the Pandavas after they were beaten at dice. I have told you everything I know. When Krishna met the Pandavas, they asked him to be Arjuna's charioteer in battle. Hari replied, "So be it."

Seeing Pritha's sons clad in deer-skins, Krishna was full of rage, and said to Yudhishtira, "During the Rajasuya yagna, in Indraprastha, I saw the prosperity you sons of Pritha had, which no other king of the world could acquire. I saw all the other kings, even those of the Vangas, Angas, Paundras, Odras, Cholas, Dravidas and Andhakas subservient to you at the great sacrifice, as were the chieftains of many islands and countries on the sea-board as also of frontier kingdoms, including the rulers of the Sinhalas, the barbarous Mlecchas, the natives of Lanka, and all the kings of the West, by hundreds, and the kings of the Pahlavas and the Daradas, and the many tribes of the Kiratas, Yavanas and Sakas; and the Harahunas and Chinas; the Tusharas and the Saindhavas and the Jagudas; and the Ramatas and the Mundas and the inhabitants of the kingdom of women; and the Tanganas and the Kekayas and the Malavas and the inhabitants of Kasmira – all officiated as your vassals at the Rajasuya yagna, obedient to your summons, afraid of your prowess.

O King, I will restore that prosperity to you, which is so unstable now and waits upon the enemy! I will take your enemies' lives from them. Lord of the Kurus, with Rama and Bhima and Arjuna and the twins and Akrura and Gada and Samba and Pradyumna and Ahuka and the heroic Dhrishtadyumna and the son of Sisupala, I will kill Duryodhana and Karna and Dussasana and Subala's son and any others who face us in battle, in a single day!

And, O Bhaarata, you will rule from Hastinapura, with your brothers; taking from Dhritarashtra's sons and their allies the prosperity they are enjoying, you will rule this Earth."

Rajan, these were Krishna's words to Yudhishtira. When Krishna had finished, Yudhishtira spoke to him in that conclave of heroes, within hearing of all those valiant Kshatriyas led by Dhrishtadyumna, saying, "O Janardana, I accept what you say as truth. But, Mahabaho, kill my enemies and all that follow them when thirteen years have passed. Kesava, promise me this much, because I gave my word in the presence of the king that I would spend thirteen years in exile, in the wilderness."

Consenting to these words of Yudhishtira Dharmaraja, his counsellors led by Dhrishtadyumna and the others pacified the furious Krishnaa with sweet words. Within Krishna's hearing, they said to Draupadi, "Because of your anger, Duryodhana will lose his life. We swear it, most beautiful one, so grieve no more.

Panchali, those that mocked you will reap the fruit of what they dared do. Beasts of prey and birds of carrion shall eat their flesh, and thus mock them. Jackals and vultures will drink their blood. And, Panchali, you will see the corpses of the wretches who dared drag you into the sabha lying on the ground, being dragged about and devoured by wild carnivores.

They also that gave you pain and ignored you will lie headless upon the Earth and the Earth herself will drink their blood."

Those bulls of the Bhaaratas said all this and more in that place, O King – all of them endowed with boundless prowess and valour, all of them marked with the scars of battle. At the end of thirteen years, those mighty Kshatriyas, chosen by Yudhishtira, led by Krishna, will come to the field of battle.

Rama and Krishna, Dhananjaya and Pradyumna, Samba and Yuyudhana, Bhima and the sons of Madri, the Kekaya and the Panchala princes, with their Matsya kinsmen – all these, illustrious, celebrated and invincible heroes, with their allies and their troops, will come. Who is there, who wishes to live, that will encounter these in battle, these like angry lions with manes erect?'

Dhritarashtra says, 'What Vidura told me during the game of dice is about to be realised. He said, "O King, if you try to vanquish the Pandavas at dice, it will end in great bloodshed, a war which will destroy all the Kurus." It is true what he said, a terrible war will be fought as soon as the thirteen years of the Pandavas' exile is over.'

CANTO 52

NALOPAKHYANA PARVA

Janamejaya said, "What did Yudhishtira and the other Pandavas do when Arjuna went into Indra's realm to acquire the astras?"

Vaisampayana said, "When Partha goes to Devaloka, those other Bharatarishabhas continue to live in the Kamyaka, with Draupadi. One day, those best of men, full of sorrow, sit with Panchali upon a clean and solitary rock; they grieve for Arjuna, they weep for him, all of them equally afflicted by his absence.

Full of anguish at both Arjuna being away and at losing their kingdom, the mighty Bhima says to Yudhishtira, 'At your command, great King, Arjuna, on whom our lives depend, as well as those of our son, and the Panchalas, and Satyaki and Krishna, has gone away.

What can be sadder than this, that he has gone bearing so much grief in his heart? Depending upon the might of his arms, think of our enemies as being already dead and the whole world as belonging to us again.

Why, it was for his sake that I restrained myself from despatching all the Dhartarashtras and the Saubalas, there in that sabha. We are mighty, we have Krishna's support, yet we must perforce suppress the wrath which has been kindled in our hearts because you are the root of that anger.

With Krishna's help, slaying our enemies we can even today rule the world, conquering it through the might of our arms. Manliness we possess, yet we are overwhelmed by calamity, because of your vice of gambling, while the foolish sons of Dhritarashtra grow stronger every day with the tribute they receive from other kings.

Great King, you should keep Kshatriya dharma in your sight. It is not the dharma of a Kshatriya to live in the forest; the first dharma of a Kshatriya is to rule. You know Kshatriya dharma, so do not leave the path of your duty.

Turn away from the forest and let us summon Partha and Krishna, and kill the sons of Dhritarashtra, even before twelve years are over. Illustrious king of kings, even if the Dhartarashtras are surrounded by soldiers in battle array, I will send them to the next world with just my own strength.

I will kill all the sons of Dhritarashtra, along with the Saubalas, Duryodhana, Karna, and anyone else who fights me. After I have killed all our enemies, you can return to the vana, and so no sin will attach to you. And Parantapa, even if any sin does cling to you, we will wash it away through great yagnas and find a lofty heaven for ourselves.

Yes, we might have such a consummation if our king is not unwise or procrastinating. But you are too virtuous, and the deceitful must be destroyed with deceit. O Bhaarata, there is no sin in killing the deceitful with deceit. Also, those who know dharma all say, great Kshatriya, that one day and one night are equal to a full year.

The Veda also frequently declares that a day passed in keeping difficult vratas equals a year. Glorious brother, if the Vedas are an authority for you, think of the time we have spent in the wilderness as being equal to thirteen years, more.

Parantapa, this is the time to kill Duryodhana and his followers, otherwise he will soon bring the whole world under his sway. Ah Yudhishtira, all this is the result of your addiction to gambling.

Already we live in grave peril because of your word given – to go undiscovered during the thirteenth year. I can think of no land where the evil Suyodhana's spies will not track us down. Once we are found, the evil one will send us into exile for another thirteen years.

Or if, perchance, we pass the ajnatavasa undiscovered, the sinner will challenge you to play dice again, and once more you will lose everything. You are no dice-player, and once you sit down to play you will lose control of yourself again, and yet again you will find exile for yourself.

If you do not want to ruin all our lives, follow what the Veda says – that the deceitful must be killed with deceit. If you only command me, I will go straightaway to Hastinapura, and as fire falling upon a heap of dry grass consumes it, I will put forth my strength and kill Duryodhana. It becomes you, my lord, to give me leave.'

Thus addressed by Bhima, Dharmaraja Yudhishtira sniffs the top of his brother's head affectionately, and pacifying him, says, 'Mahabaho, beyond doubt, along with Arjuna who wields the Gandiva, you will kill Suyodhana, when thirteen years have passed.

But, O son of Pritha, as for your assertion that the time is complete, I will not dare tell a lie, for falsehood is not in me. Kaunteya, you must kill the evil and powerful Duryodhana, and his confederates, but without using deceit.'

While Yudhishthira is speaking to Bhima, the great and illustrious Rishi Brihadaswa appears before them. Seeing the virtuous Sage, the king worships him with the offering of madhuparka. When the Muni is seated and refreshed, the mighty Yudhishtira sits at his feet, and looking up at Brihadaswa, speaks to him in a piteous tone.

'Holy one, challenged by cunning gamblers skilled at dice, I have lost all my wealth and kingdom at gambling. I am no adept at dice, and am unacquainted with deceit. Sinful men vanquished me at dice, by cheating. They even brought my wife, dearer to me than life, into the public sabha.

Defeating me a second time, they have sent me into exile in this great forest, clad in deer-skin, and I live here with my heart heavy, full of grief. The harsh and cruel words they pierced me with, and what my friends and kin later said about the game of dice are all fresh in my memory.

Thinking of these, I cannot sleep at nights but lie awake in anxiety. I am also without Arjuna, upon whom all our lives depend, and that is like being dead. Oh, when will I see the sweet-spoken and large-hearted Vibhatsu, so full of kindness and vitality, return to us, having acquired all the astras?

Is there a king on this Earth who is more unfortunate than me? Have you ever seen or heard of one? To my mind, there is no man more wretched than I am.'

Brihadaswa says, 'Great king, O Pandava, you say that there is no man more miserable than you are. Sinless monarch, if you will listen, I will tell you the tale of a king more wretched than yourself.'

Yudhishtira says to the Rishi, 'Illustrious one, tell me, I want to hear the story of the king who fell into such misery.'

Brihadaswa says, 'O King who has never fallen, listen attentively, with your brothers. I will narrate the story of a Kshatriya more miserable than yourself. There was a celebrated king among the Nishadhas, named Virasena. He had a son called Nala, versed in ways of dharma and artha. I have heard that Nala was vanquished through deceit by his brother Pushkara, and overtaken by calamity, lived in the forest with his wife.

While he lived in the vana, he had neither servants nor chariots, neither brothers nor friends with him. But you are surrounded by your heroic brothers, who are like Devas, and also by magnificent Brahmanas who are like Brahma himself. Therefore, it does not become you to complain.'

Yudhishtira says, 'I am anxious to hear in detail, O foremost of eloquent men, the tale of Nala. You must tell me his story.'

NALOPAKHYANA PARVA CONTINUED

Brihadaswa says, 'There was a king named Nala, the son of Virasena. He was strong, and handsome, a master of horses, and possessed of every accomplishment. A king of kings, he was even like the lord of the Devas. Exalted above all others, he resembled the Sun in glory.

And he was the king of the Nishadhas, intent on the welfare of Brahmanas, versed in the Vedas, and possessed of heroism. He always told the truth, he was master of a mighty army, and he was fond of dice. Men and women loved him; he was a great soul, his passions subdued. He was the greatest bowman, protector of his people, and like Manu himself.

And among the Vidarbhas, there was another king like him called Bhima, of terrible prowess, heroic, kindly towards his subjects and possessed of every virtue. However, he had no children. Single-mindedly, he did his best to have a child.

O Bhaarata, one day a Brahmarishi named Damana came to Bhima. Desperate to have children, Bhima, versed in dharma, and his queen received the lustrous Rishi with every reverence. Well pleased, Damana granted the king and his consort a boon in the form of a jewel of a daughter, and also three sons of lofty soul and great fame.

These were named Damayanti, Dama, Danta, and Damana after the Sage. The three sons were accomplished in every way; they were fierce to behold and fierce in prowess. The slender-waisted Damayanti became celebrated the world over for her beauty and radiance, her good nature, her grace and fortune. Upon her coming of age, hundreds of sakhis and female slaves, all decked in precious ornaments, waited upon her as if she were Sachi herself, while Bhima's daughter shone amongst them like the luminous lightning of the clouds.

Damayanti of large eyes was as beautiful as Sri; not among the Devas, the Yakshas or among men had such beauty ever been seen or heard of before. She filled even the Devas' hearts with joy.

So also, Nala was peerless in the three worlds, for he was as handsome as Kandarpa himself. Admiring heralds sang Nala's praises before Damayanati and Damayanati's praises before the king of the Nishadhas. Hearing over and over about each other's virtues the two conceived an attachment towards each other, though neither had seen the other.

That affection grew, and then Nala could not contain the love which was in his heart. He began to pass much of his time alone, in the wooded gardens which adjoined his royal apartments in his palace. There he saw a flock of golden-winged swans, wandering among the trees, and one he caught in his hands.

The sky ranging avian said to Nala, "I do not deserve to be killed by you, O King. Let me do something for you instead – lord of the Nishadas, I will speak to Damayanti about you in such a way that she will never want any other man for her husband."

The king let the swan go, and the flock rose in flight and winged its way to the land of the Vidarbhas. Arriving, the birds alighted before Damayanti and her sakhis, and seeing the extraordinary swans, she was full of delight and, along with her maids, tried to catch the sky-coursers.

The swans fled in all directions pursued by that bevy of beautiful young women, while each maiden ran after one bird. The one that Damayanti chased led her to a secluded place, and then spoke to her in human speech.

"Damayanti, there is a king of the Nishadhas called Nala. He is equal to the Aswins in beauty, and has no remote peer among men. Indeed, he is as handsome as Kama Deva. Fair one, slender-waisted one, if you become his wife, your own beauty and your life will become fruitful.

We have seen Devas and Gandharvas, Nagas and Rakshasas, and the best among men, but never have we seen anyone like Nala. You, also, are an incomparable jewel among women, even as Nala is among men. Happy is a union between the best and the best!"

Damayanti said to the swan, "Go and say the same thing to Nala!"

The swan replied, "So be it," and flew back to the land of the Nishadhas, and told Nala everything.'

CANTO 54

NALOPAKHYANA PARVA CONTINUED

Brihadaswa says, 'O Bhaarata, after hearing what the swan said about Nala, Damayanti lost all peace of mind. Sighing repeatedly to think of him, she became full of anxiety and melancholy, she was pale and grew lean. Kama, god of love, seized her heart; she grew paler by the day, and her gaze turned skywards; her mood always abstracted, she seemed to be quite deranged.

She lost all her taste for fine beds and seats, and every object of enjoyment. Night and day, she would not lie down, but always wept, with soft and loud exclamations of despair.

Seeing her like that, her sakhis went and hinted about her condition to her father, the king of the Vidarbhas. King Bhima realised that Damayanti's condition was serious and he asked himself, "Why does my daughter seem to be so ill now?"

Reflecting by himself, the king thought that his daughter had attained puberty and decided that he should hold a swayamvara for Damayanti. That monarch invited all the lords of the Earth, saying, "Kshatriyas, know that Damayanti's swayamvara is at hand!"

When they heard this, all the kings came to Bhima, filling earth and sky with the clatter of their chariot wheels, the trumpeting of their elephants, and the whinnying of their horses, and bringing their magnificent legions decked in ornaments and beautiful garlands. The mighty-armed Bhima paid due homage to those illustrious sovereigns, and honoured by him, they began living in his city.

At this time, those best of Devarishis, Narada and Parvata, both of untold splendour, wisdom and stern vows, arrived during their wanderings in Indra's realm and entered the palace of the Deva king, where they were received with reverence. Indra Maghavat worshipped the two, and asked after their welfare and peace.

Narada said, "Divine one, peace attends on us in every way, and, O Maghavat, peace attends also upon the kings of the whole world."

Indra, slayer of Vritra, said, "Those righteous kings of the Earth who fight leaving all desire to live, and who die by weapons when their time comes, never fleeing the field of battle – theirs is this Swarga, everlasting for them and granting all desires, even as it is for me.

Where are those Kshatriya heroes? I do not see those kings coming here to me. Where are my favourite guests?"

Narada replied, "O Maghavat, I will tell you why you do not see those Kshatriyas now. The king of the Vidarbhas has a daughter, the renowned Damayanti. In beauty she excels all the women of the Earth. O Sakra, her swayamvara is to take place shortly and every king and prince from every direction and land is going to that swayamvara.

All the lords of the Earth desire that pearl of the Earth for themselves, O slayer of Bala and Vritra."

While they sat talking together, those greatest of the Devas, the Lokapalas, and Agni with them, appeared before the lord of the celestials, and they all heard that Narada said, which was of grave import. As soon as they heard him, they exclaimed in excitement, "We will also go there!"

Mounting their various vahanas and vimanas, taking their attendants with them, the gods set out for the land of the Vidarbhas where all the Kshatriyas of the world had gone.

Kaunteya, meanwhile, Nala also heard of the swayamvara and set out for it, his heart full of joy and love for Damayanti. On his way, the gods saw Nala, as handsome as Kama Deva. Seeing him splendid as the Sun, the Lokapalas were astonished at his wealth of beauty.

Leaving their chariots in the sky, the gods flew down to Nala, king of the Nishadhas, and said to him, "Greatest of the Nishadha kings, O Nala, you are devoted to dharma. You must help us. Best of men, be you our messenger.'"

NALOPAKHYANA PARVA CONTINUED

Brihadaswa continues, 'O Bhaarata, Nala pledged his word to the gods saying, "I will do what you ask."

Then, approaching them with folded hands, he asked, "Who are you? And who is he that wants me to be his messenger? And what must I do for you? Tell me!"

Maghavat said, "We are the Devas come here for Damayanti's sake. I am Indra; this one is Agni; this the Lord of waters, and this, O King, is even Yama, destroyer of the bodies of men.

You must inform Damayanti of our coming, saying, 'The Guardians of the world, great Indra and the others, are coming to your swayamvara. The Devas Sakra and Agni and Varuna and Yama want to have you for their wife, so choose one of them for your lord.'"

Nala said with joined hands, "I too have come here for the same reason. It does not become you to send me on this errand. How can a man who is himself smitten by love bring the suit of another to the woman that he loves? So, spare me, O Devas!"

But the gods said, "King of the Nishadhas, having sworn that you will do what we ask, will you now break your word? Tell us quickly, O Nala!"

The Nishadha king said, "Those palaces are well guarded, how can I hope to enter them?"

Indra replied, "You will be able to enter."

Saying, "So be it," Nala went to Damayanti's palace. Arriving there, he saw, surrounded by her sakhis, the daughter of the king of Vidarbha ablaze with beauty, her form of exquisite symmetry, her limbs so delicate, her waist slender, and her eyes lage and lovely. And she seemed to rebuke the light of the moon with her own luminosity.

As he gazed upon that young woman of the sweet smiles, Nala's love grew, but wanting to keep his dharma, he suppressed his passion. And when they saw the Naishadha, all those finest among women were overpowered by his radiance and rose to their feet in amazement. Full of wonder, they praised Nala in joy, silently in their minds.

"Oh, what beauty, what gentleness belongs to this Mahatman! Who is he? Is he some Deva or Yaksha or Gandharva?"

Quite confounded by Nala's splendour, and full of bashfulness, those best among women did not speak to him at all. But, although stricken by amazement herself, Damayanti spoke smilingly to Nala, who also gently smiled at her.

"What are you, O you of faultless features, who have come here awakening my love? O Sinless, O Hero of celestial form, I am anxious to know who you are, and why you have come here. And how have you come undiscovered into my apartments, when the king's mandates are stern?"

Nala replied, "Beautiful one, my name is Nala, and I come here as a messenger of the gods. The Devas Sakra, Agni, Varuna and Yama want you, lovely one, choose one of them for your lord. It is through their power that I have entered here unobserved, and unobstructed. Gentle one, the gods have sent me here on this mission. I have given you their message, most fortunate one, now do as you please.'"

CANTO 56

NALOPAKHYANA PARVA CONTINUED

Brihadaswa says, 'Damayanti bowed to the Devas, then said to Nala with a smile, "O King, love me with proper regard, and command me what I should do for you. I myself and everything precious which I own are yours. Magnificent one, grant me your love in complete trust, for what the swan said burns in my heart.

Kshatriya, it is for your sake that I called this swayamvara, and for your sake I, who adore you, will take my life with poison, immolate myself in fire, drown or hang myself."

Nala replied, "When the Lokapalas ask for you, you would choose a man? Turn your heart to those great gods, I am not equal to the dust on their feet. If a mortal displeases the gods he certainly finds death. Save me, O you of faultless limbs! Choose the all-excelling Devas. By accepting the gods, enjoy wearing incomparable garments, unearthly garlands of myriad hues, and divine ornaments.

What woman would not choose Hutasana for her lord, he who devours the Earth? What woman would not choose Yama for her lord, from dread of whose danda all creatures tread the way of dharma? What woman would not choose for her lord the virtuous and high-souled Mahendra, the king of the Devas, the scourge of Daityas and Danavas? Or, if you choose Varuna in your heart among the Lokapalas, do so without hesitation.

Lovely one, I beg you, accept my friendly advice!"

Her eyes by now swimming with tears, Damayanti said to Nala, "Lord of the earth, bowing to all the gods, I choose you for my husband. Truly do I tell you this."

The king, who had come as the messenger of the gods, replied to the trembling Damayanti standing before him folded hands, "Sweet one, do as you please. Having pledged my word to the very Devas, how can I dare seek my own interest? If seeking my own interest coincides with dharma, I will seek it, and beautiful one you must also do the same."

Her voice choked with tears, Damayanti of luminous smiles said slowly to Nala, "Lord of men, I see a blameless way, by which no sin whatever will attach to you. Best among men, come to the swayamvara with all the Devas led by Indra. There, O Kshatriya, in the presence of the Lokapalas I will, tiger among men, choose you, and then no blame will be yours."

Having heard this from Damayanti, Nala returned to where the Devas were. Seeing him, the gods asked him eagerly about what had happened.

"Kshatriya, have you seen Damayanti of the sweet smiles? What did she say to us? Sinless king, tell us all."

Nala replied, "At your command I entered Damayanti's palace of lofty portals, guraded by veteran guardsmen with wands in their hands. By your power, no one saw me as I went in, other than the princess. I saw her hand-maidens, and they also saw me. Most exalted Devas, they saw me and were filled with wonder.

And even as I pressed your suit to her, O you best among gods, that beautiful princess said she had her heart set on me and chose me for her husband. She said to me, 'Purushavyaghra, let the Devas come with you to the swayamvara, and in their presence I will choose you for my lord. At this, Mahabaho, no blame will attach to you.'

O Devas, this is all that transpired, and now everything depends upon you."

CANTO 57

NALOPAKHYANA PARVA CONTINUED

Brihadaswa continues, 'At the sacred hour of the holy lunar day of the auspicious season, King Bhima summoned the kings to the Swayamvara. All the lords of the Earth came with alacrity to his city, all of them keen to have Damayanti. The Kshatriyas entered the great hall decorated with golden pillars and a lofty portal arch, like mighty lions entering the mountain wilds.

Wearing fragrant garlands and polished earrings hung with jewels, the kings and princes sat down on the fine seats provided. And that sacred assembly of kings, graced by those tigers among men, resembled the Bhogavati swarming with Nagas, or a mountain cave with tigers.

They were mighty, resembling iron maces, and well-shaped, and graceful, and looked like five-headed snakes. With lustrous locks, fine noses, eyes and brows, the faces of the kings shone like the stars in the sky.

And when the muhurta arrived, the exquisite Damayanti entered that great hall, dazzling the Kshatriyas, stealing their gazes and hearts. The gazes of those illustrious kings were riveted to those parts of her person where they had chanced to fall first, and never moved.

O Bhaarata, when the names of the monarchs were proclaimed, Bhima's daughter saw five men all identical in appearance. Seeing them sitting there, no difference whatever between the five, doubt filled her mind for she could not tell which one was Nala. All five looked exactly the same and all of them seemed to be the king of the Nishadhas.

Anxiety sweeping through her, the princess thought, "How will I know which are the Devas and which my love?"

Grief had its way with her. She thought of the signs and marks attributed to each of the Devas but saw none of these upon the five who sat before her. Long she thought, and hard, and then decided to seek the help of the Lokapalas themselves.

She folded her hands, and bowing down to them, mind and body, the trembling Damayanti said piteously, "Since I heard what the swan said, I chose the king of the Nishadhas as my lord. For the sake of dharma, and as I have never swerved from my love in my heart or speech – for that truth, let the Devas themselves reveal him to me. The gods have decided that Nala will be my lord; for that truth, let them show him to me.

Since I have taken this vow to pay homage to Nala, for that truth let the gods reveal him to me. O, let the exalted Guardians of the worlds assume their own forms, so that I may know the good king."

When the Lokapalas saw how firm her resolve was, how fervent her love for Nala, how pure her heart, the gods reassumed their natural forms which they had hidden. She saw the awesome ones, skins untouched by human sweat, eyes winkless, garlands unfading, no speck of dust upon them, feet never touching the ground. Nala Naishadha stood revealed mortal, his garlands fading, himself stained with dust and sweat, feet resting on the ground, and his eyes blinking from time to time.

O Bhaarata, when she saw which of the five were the gods and which Nala, Bhima's chaste daughter chose Nala for her lord. Bashfully, she seized the hem of his robes and draped a bright and graceful garland of flowers around his neck. A great outcry of regret arose from the other Kshatriyas, while the Devas and Rishis cried out in wonder and approval.

O Kauravya, the royal son of Virasena, Nala, his heart filled with joy, said to the beautiful Damayanti, "You have chosen a mortal while you could have had a god. From this day you shall have a husband obedient to your every wish and command. And, O you of sweet smiles, I swear that as long as there is life in this body, I will be yours and yours alone."

Damayanti, also, with folded hands, paid homage to Nala in similar words. Seeing Agni and the other Devas, the happy couple sought their protection, in their minds. When the daughter of Bhima had chosen Naishadha for her husband, the Lokapalas, of blinding effulgence, their hearts pleased, bestowed eight boons on Nala.

Sakra, the lord of Sachi, blessed Nala with the boon that he would be able to see his Deity during sacrifices and that he would attain blessed realms after this life; Agni Hutasana blessed him with the boon of his own presence whenever Naishadha wished, and realms, also, bright as himself; Yama granted him subtle taste in food as well as pre-eminence in dharma; and Varuna, the lord of waters, granted Nala his own presence whenever the Naishadha desired, and also garlands of heavenly fragrance. Thus, each Lokapala blessed Nala with two boons each, and having blessed him the gods returned to Swarga.

Having witnessed, with wonder and delight, Damayanti's choosing of Nala, the kings of the world also returned to their kingdoms. When they had gone, Bhima, well pleased, celebrated the wedding of Nala and Damayanti. Nala remained in the Vidarbha city for some while, to please Bhima, and then returned to his own home.

Having married that pearl of a woman, Nala now passed his days in joy with Damayanti, even as Indra does with Sachi. Like the Sun in glory, that king ruled with dharma and his people were all satisfied and happy. Like Nahusha's son Yayati, the brilliant Nala performed the Aswamedha yagna and many other great sacrifices, and gave abundant gifts to Brahmanas.

Truly like a Deva, Nala dallied with Damayanti in romantic woods and charmed groves, and he begot on his lovely wife a son named Indrasena, and a daughter named Indraseni. Thus, performing countless sacrifices, and making love with Damayanti, Nala ruled the world, and it was a time of grace and plenitude.'

CANTO 58

NALOPAKHYANA PARVA CONTINUED

Brihadaswa says, 'When the blazing guardians of the worlds were returning to their homes after the swayamvara, they saw Dwapara and Kali approaching them. Seeing Kali, Sakra said, "O Kali, say where you are going with Dwapara."

Kali replied, "Sakra, I am going to Damayanti's swayamvara, and I will have her for my wife, for my heart is fixed upon that young woman."

Hearing this, Indra said with a smile, "That swayamvara is already over, and she has chosen Nala for her husband."

Kali, vilest of the celestials, was filled with wrath, and said to the gods, "Since she dared chose a mortal when the Devas were present, she must suffer a heavy consequence."

The Devas replied, "It is with our sanction that Damayanti chose Nala. What young woman would not choose Nala, who is blessed with every virtue? He knows his dharma, always conducts himself with rectitude, he has studied the four Vedas together with the Puranas that are regarded as the fifth. He harms no living creature, speaks only the truth, keeps his vows faithfully, and worships the gods with sacrifices in his house.

In that tiger among men, that king who is like a Lokapala, dwell truth, forbearance, knowledge, asceticism, purity, self-control and perfect tranquillity of spirit. O Kali, the fool that wants to curse Nala, who has such character, curses only himself and destroys himself by what he does. Kali, he who seeks to curse Nala of such immaculate virtue sinks into the wide, bottomless pit of hell, rife with torments."

Saying this to Kali and Dwapara, the Devas went to their heavens. And when the gods had gone, Kali said to Dwapara, "Dwapara, I cannot contain my anger. I will possess Nala, deprive him of his kingdom, and he shall not sport anymore with Bhima's daughter. Enter into the gambling dice; you must help me."

CANTO 59

NALOPAKHYANA PARVA CONTINUED

Brihadaswa says, 'Having made this compact with Dwapara, Kali came to the city of the king of the Nishadhas. Always watching for an opening, the slightest lapse from Nala, he continued to dwell in the country of the Nishadhas for a long lime. In the twelfth year, Kali saw his chance.

One day, after answering the call of nature, Naishadha touched water and said his twilight prayers, but without having washed his feet. Through this ritual lapse, Kali entered into him, and having possessed Nala, he appeared before Pushkara, and said to him, "Come and play dice with Nala. I will help you and you will certainly win. Defeat Nala and, winning his kingdom, rule the Nishadhas!"

Exhorted by Kali, Pushkara went to Nala; and Dwapara also came to Pushkara and became the main dice called vrisha. Appearing before the warlike Nala, that slayer of hostile heroes, Pushkara repeatedly said, "Let us play dice together."

Thus challenged in the presence of Damayanti, the lofty-minded Naishadha could not refuse for long. He fixed a time for the game.

Possessed as he was by Kali, Nala began to lose all his stakes – in gold, silver, chariots with their teams of horses, costly garments. And maddened by the dice, none amongst his friends could make him stop playing.

O Bhaarata, the citizens in a body, with the chief councillors, came to see the king and make him stop. The charioteer came to Damayanti and said, "O Queen, the people and the officers of the state are waiting at the gate. You must tell the king that they cannot bear the calamity which has overtaken him."

Overwhelmed by grief, almost mad from it, Bhima's daughter spoke in a choked voice to Nala, "Rajan, the loyal people and the councillors are at the gates, waiting to see you. You must grant them audience."

But possessed by Kali, the king did not reply to his desperate wife. At this, the people and the officials returned to their homes, in shame and sorrowing, saying among themselves, "He does not live!"

Yudhishtira, for many months Nala and Pushkara gambled, and the viruous Nala always lost.'

CANTO 60

NALOPAKHYANA PARVA CONTINUED

Brihadaswa says, 'Bhima's daughter, the calm Damayanti, saw her husband maddened by the dice, and she was full of alarm; she saw how ciritical the situation was, for he had lost almost everything. She said to her nurse and maid-servant Brihatsena, "Go and summon the councillors in the name of Nala, and tell them also what wealth has been lost and what remains."

The councillors heard Nala's summons and said, "This is fortunate for us". They came to the king, along with all the people, for the second time. Damayanti informed Nala of their coming, but he ignored her and she returned in shame to her apartments.

Hearing that the dice rolled constantly against Nala, and that he had lost everything, she said again to her nurse, "Brihatsena, go again in Nala's name and fetch the charioteer Varshneya. For this is a crisis."

Brihatsena had Varshneya summoned by trusted servants, and the blameless Damayanti said softly to the sarathy, "You know how good the king has always been to you. He is in trouble now, and you must help him. The more the king loses to Pushkara, the more ardently he wants to play on. The dice fall obedient to Pushkara, and roll against Nala.

He is so possessed by the game that he does not listen to his friends and family, not even to me. O Sarathy, I seek your protection; my heart is weak within me and I fear the king will come to grief. I beg you, yoke Nala's favourite horses, swift as the mind, and take these twins, my son and daughter, in the royal chariot to Kundina. Leave them there with my kin, Sarathy, and then do as you will – either remain there yourself or go anywhere else that you please."

Nala's cahrioteer reported what Damayanti said to the chief officers of the king. With their assent, he then set out for Vidarbha, taking the children in his ratha. Leaving the boy Indrasena and the girl Indraseni, and also that best of chariots and those finest of horses with Bhima, and his heart full of sorrow for Nala, Varshneya the sarathy wandered here and there for some time, then arrived in Ayodhya and entered the service of King Rituparna, as his charioteer.'

CANTO 61

NALOPAKHYANA PARVA CONTINUED

Brihadaswa says, 'After Varshneya left, Pushkara won Nala's kingdom and what remained of his wealth. Then, laughing, he said to Nala, "Let us play on! But what will you stake now? You have lost everything you own except Damayanati. I am prepared to accept her as a wager, if you will put her up."

Nala listened to Pushkara and felt his heart would burst in anger, but he did not say a word. Only gazing at his adversary in anguish, Nala stripped all the precious ornaments from every part of his body. Wearing just a single piece of cloth, his body uncovered, all his wealth lost, having brought great grief to all his friends, the king set out from his city. Damayanti, also clad in one piece of cloth, followed him. Coming to the outskirts of the city, Nala stayed there for three nights with his wife. But Pushkara had it proclaimed that anyone who gave shelter to Nala or paid him the least attention would be put to death. No citizen, O Yudhishtira, dared show Nala any regard or hospitality.

Nala passed three nights upon the city's hem, living just on water. Roiled by hunger, the king went in search of fruit and roots, Damayanti following him. After many days, in agony from starving, Nala saw some birds of golden plumage and the mighty lord of the Nishadhas thought, "These will be my banquet today and also my wealth."

He covered them with the single cloth which he wore, but in a flash the birds rose up into the sky with that last garment. They looked down at Nala, now standing naked and stricken, his face turned down in shame, and those rangers of the sky said to him, "O you of small sense, we are the dice with which you played. We came here to take away your cloth, for we wanted to see you go naked from here!"

Nala now said to Damayanti, "They whose anger took my kingdom from me, they who have ravaged me with hunger, they who keep me from finding food, who kept the Nishadhas from offering me any hospitality have now come as birds and taken away my last cloth.

Ah, I have plunged into disaster, and my mind and senses reel with grief. I am your lord still, so listen to what I say and do as I ask; it is for your own good. These many roads lead to the southern country, passing by the city of Avanti and the Rikshavat Mountains. This is the mighty Vindhya; yonder, the river Payasvini runs seawards, and there are the asramas of the Rishis, where many roots and fruit grow.

This road leads to the country of the Vidarbhas, and beyond that is the land of the Kosalas. Beyond these roads, to the south, is the Dravida country. Leave me and go there."

Over and over, the almost deranged Nala repeated these words to Damayanti. At which, in grief, her voice full of tears, Damayanti said piteously to the Naishadha, "O King, my heart trembles and my limbs turn weak to think of your purpose. How can I go, leaving you alone in this forest, having lost your kingdom and wealth, naked, worn with hunger and exhausted?

When you think of your old felicity in this deep vana and grieve, I will soothe your sorrow, great king. All the physicians say that in every sorrow there is no physic equal to a wife. It is the truth, O Nala, that I speak."

Nala replied, "Slender-waisted Damayanti, it is even as you say. To a man in distress, there is no friend or medicine that is equal to his wife. But I do not seek to renounce you, so why are you in dread? Faultless one, I can forsake myself but you I can never leave."

Damayanti said, "Mighty King, if you do not intend to forsake me, then why do you point out the way to the country of the Vidarbhas? I know, my lord, that you would not desert me. But, Lord of the Earth, your mind is sorely disturbed and you might desert me. Best of men, repeatedly you point out the road which leads out of here, and you swell my sorrow, O godlike.

If you intend that I go to the country of my kin, then let us both go the land of the Vidarbhas. The king of the Vidarbhas will receive you with honour, and you will live happily in our home.'"

CANTO 62

NALOPAKHYANA PARVA CONTINUED

'Nala said, "Surely, your father's kingdom is as my own. But I will not go there in this condition. Once I appeared there in glory, increasing your joy. How can I go there now in misery, augmenting your grief?"

Saying this again and again to Damayanti, King Nala, wrapped in half a garment now, comforted his wife. Both of them sharing her single cloth, weary with hunger and thirst, they wandered on weakly, and at last came to a wayside shelter for travellers, a meagre shed.

Arriving there, the king of the Nishadhas sat down on the bare earth with the princess of Vidarbha. Sharing the same piece of cloth, dirty and haggard, stained with dust, exhausted, they fell on the ground. Plunged so abruptly in distress, the delicate and innocent Damayanti, every mark of fortune upon her body, fell into a deep slumber.

But Nala, his heart and mind distraught, could not sleep as he used to. He thought about losing his kingdom, the desertion by his friends, and his distress in the wilds.

He thought to himself, "To what avail my living on? Is death better for me now? But can I desert my wife, who is so devoted to me and suffers this hardship for my sake? But if I leave her, she might find her way to her relatives.

She is absolutely loyal and if she stays with me distress can be her only lot; while, if I leave her, she might find fortune and even happiness again someday."

Reflecting upon this repeatedly, he concluded that he should leave Damayanti. He also thought, "She has lofty fame, auspicious fortune; she is devoted to me, her husband, and no one will harm her on her way, such is her tejas."

It was the evil Kali influencing his mind to desert Damayanti. Nala then thought that they were sharing her single cloth, and he wanted to cut half of it away for himself. He thought, "How shall I divide this garment, so that my beloved does not awaken?"

Thinking of this, he paced that shelter and, O Bhaarata, he found a handsome sword lying nearby, unsheathed. That Parantapa used the blade to shear away one half of the cloth, then throwing the weapon aside, he left the daughter of Vidharbha asleep and walked away.

But his heart failed him, and he returned to the shelter, and seeing Damayanti again, burst into tears. He said, "Alas! My beloved, whom not the Wind or the Sun has seen before, lies forsaken and wretched on bare ground, wearing a single cloth. Ah, what will she of the luminous smiles do when she awakens alone? How will Bhima's beautiful daughter find her way through this forest full of wild animals and snakes?

O blessed one, may the Adityas and the Vasus, and the twin Aswins together with the Marutas protect you, your virtue being your best guard."

Saying this softly to his wife, whose beauty was unmatched in the world, Nala, deranged by Kali, tried to leave again. He came back again and again, helplessly, hauled away by Kali but pulled back by love; and it seemed as if the heart of the wretched king was torn in two, and like a swing, he kept going out from the shelter and coming back into it.

At length, after lamenting long and piteously, Nala, entirely stupefied by Kali, went away, forsaking his sleeping wife. Bereft of reason through Kali's touch, the king left in sorrow leaving Damayanti alone in that solitary forest.'

NALOPAKHYANA PARVA CONTINUED

Brihadaswa says, 'O King, some time after Nala had left, the exquisite and timorous Damayanti awoke in that lonely forest. Not finding her lord Naishadha, she screamed in fright, "My husband, have you abandoned me? I am lost, undone, oh, I am terrified in this dreadful jungle. Illustrious Kshatriya, you are always truthful and you know dharma well. Then how have you deserted me while I slept in this wilderness? Oh, why have you left your wife, who is devoted to you, who has never wronged you, even when everyone else has abandoned you?

King of men, you said in the presence of the Lokapalas that you would always be true to me. Purusharishabha, it is only because mortals die when their time comes that I am alive for even a moment after you have left me.

Ah, Bull among men, enough of this joke! Irrepressible one, I am terribly afraid. Lord, show yourself to me. I see you! I see you hiding in the bushes, why don't you answer me? You are being cruel, Nala, that you see me in this plight but do not come to comfort me.

I do not grieve for myself, nor anything else. I only grieve to think how you will pass your days alone. In the evening, savaged by hunger, thirst and tiredness under the trees, how will you live without seeing me, without having my comfort?"

The anguished Damayanti began to dash here and there, sobbing and wailing. Now the helpless princess would spring up, then sink down to the ground again; now she shrank in terror, and then she wept aloud. Sighing, burning with grief, Bhima's daughter sobbed, "He through whose curse Nala suffers this grief will suffer torment worse than ours! May the evil one who has reduced the sinless Nala to this lead a life of greater misery than ours, bearing greater ills."

So lamenting, the crowned queen of Nala began to seek her husband in that forest, which teemed with predators. Crying bitterly, the daughter of Bhima wandered here and there, like a madwoman, exclaiming, "Alas! O King!"

As she wailed loudly like a female osprey, and grieved unceasingly and lamented piteously, she came near a gigantic serpent. The huge and hungry snake suddenly seized Bhima's daughter, who had come within its striking range. Folded in serpent's coils, in pain, she still wept not for herself but for Naishadha.

She cried, "O Nala, why don't you rush to me now that this snake has seized me in this wild place? Naishadha, how will you bear it when you think of me? O lord, why have you gone away, abandoning me in this jungle? When you are freed from your curse and regain your mind and your wealth, what will you do when you remember me?

Sinless one, who will comfort you when you are tired, hungry and feel faint, O tiger among kings?"

As she cried all this aloud, a hunter ranging through the deep vana heard her and ran to the place. Seeing the doe-eyed beauty in the coils of the snake, he cut off the serpent's head and freed Damayanti. He sprinkled water over her, fed and consoled her, O Bhaarata.

Then the vetala asked her, "Who are you, O gazelle-eyed, and why have you come into the jungle? Beautiful one, how did you fall into this extreme misery?"

Damayanti told him everything. Looking at her wearing half a cloth, her breasts deep and her hips round, her limbs flawless and delicate, her face like the full moon, her long lashes curved, her speech as sweet as honey, the hunter became inflamed. In the grip of Kama Deva, he began to console her in a soft voice, with smooth words.

The chaste Damayanti immediately understood his intentions; she blazed up in anger. The wild fellow, in the grip of lust, also grew angry and tried to force himself on her who was fierce as a flame. Already stricken past endurance, Damayanti cursed in fury, "I have never even thought of another man other than Naishadha, so let this wretch who subsists on the hunt fall dead!"

As soon as she said this, the hunter fell lifeless on the ground, like a tree consumed by fire.'

CANTO 64

NALOPAKHYANA PARVA CONTINUED

Brihadaswa continues, 'Having killed the hunter, Damayanti of eyes like lotus leaves walked on through that fearful and solitary forest, which rang with the chirping of crickets. The vana abounded with lion, leopard, ruru, tiger, bison, bear and deer. It swarmed with birds of various species, and was, besides, infested by thieves and mlechcha tribes.

Sala trees grew there, bamboo, Dhavas and Aswatthas, Tindukas and Ingudas, Kinsukas and Arjunas, Arishtas, Sanchanas, Nimbas and Tinisas, Syandana, Salmalas and Jambus, and mango trees, and Lodhras, and Khadiras, and the cane, and Padyakas, and Amalakas, and Plakshas, and Kadambas, and Udumvaras and Badaris, and Bilvas, and banians, and Priyalas, and palms, and date-trees, Haritakas and Vibhitakas.

The princess of Vidarbha saw many mountains with lodes of precious minerals of diverse kinds, and groves resounding with the music of winged choirs, and many glades of great beauty, and many rivers and lakes and tanks and all manner of birds and beasts. She saw numberless

Nagas and Pisachas and Rakshasas of grim visage, and pools and rillets and hillocks, and brooks and fountains of wonder.

Herds of bison Damayanti saw, sounders of boar and solitary bears and snakes in that pristine wilderness. Safe in her virtue, glory, good fortune and patience, Damayanti wandered through those forests alone, in search of Nala. Bhima's royal daughter was not frightened by anything—feral creature or sight—in the fearsome vana; she only grieved at being apart from Nala.

O King, she sat down upon a flat stone, full of sorrow, her every limb trembling, and she lamented, "O King of the Nishadhas, you with the mighty arms and broad chest, where have you gone, leaving me in this lone forest? O Kshatriya, you performed the Aswamedha and other sacrifices, gave profuse gifts, then why have you betrayed me, Purushavyaghra?

Best of men, O you of great splendour, O auspicious one, don't you remember what you swore to me, Rajarishabha? Remember what the swan said to both of us! Tiger among men, all the four Vedas together, with the Angas and the Upangas, mastered, are only equal to a single truth spoken and honoured. So, Parantapa, honour the oath you swore to me.

Alas, O Kshatriya! O Nala! Sinless one, being yours, I am about to die alone in this dreadful forest. Oh! Why don't you answer me? This terrible lord of the forest, of grim face and gaping jaws, and famished with hunger, fills me with fear. Should you not deliver me?

You would always say, 'Other than you there is no one that I love.'

O blessed king, keep your word to me now. Nala, why don't you come back to your wife, who is demented with grief, and wailing here, she that you love and who loves you in return? Lord of the earth, O large-eyed, honoured one, bane of your enemies, don't you see me here, emaciated, distraught and pale, wearing a half piece of cloth, alone, crying, desolate, and like a solitary doe separated from the herd?

Nala, it is I, Damayanti, devoted to you, who, alone in this great forest, that speaks to you. Why don't you reply? Oh, I do not see you today upon this mountain, lord of men, you of noble birth and character, your every limb so full of grace! Whom shall I ask in this terrible forest, full of lions and tigers, O King of the Nishadhas, foremost of men, enhancer of my sorrows, if you are lying down, sitting or standing nearby, or gone?

Griefstricken as I am, whom shall I ask, 'Have you seen Nala in this jungle? Do you know where the noble and handsome Nala, scourge of his enemies, has gone?'

From whom shall I hear the sweet words, 'The royal Nala is here!'

Look, here comes the king of the jungle, the lordly tiger, his cheeks high and four fangs showing. I will accost even him fearlessly, and say, 'You are the lord of all beasts, and king of this vana. I am Damayanti, daughter of the king of the Vidarbhas, and the wife of Nala, Parantapa, king of the Nishadhas. I am distrait and griefstricken, seeking my husband alone in this forest. King of beasts, comfort me with news of Nala, if you can, or best of animals, free me from my misery by devouring me.'

Alas, he stalks away without responding.

Look! This king of mountains, this lofty and sacred hill crested with countless peaks hears my piteous appeal and seems to loll towards the sea. Let me, then, ask the mountain king for tidings of my Nala, this lord of mountains with so many heaven-kissing and many-hued and beautiful peaks, abounding in precious ores, decked with gemstones of diverse kinds, and rising like a banner over this great forest, the mountain upon whom lions and tigers and elephants and boars and bears and stags roam, the mountain which echoes with the songs of birds of every kind, mountain adorned with Kinsukas and Asokas and Bakulas and Punnagas, with blossoming Karnikaras, and Dhavas and Plakshas, and with streams teeming with waterfowl of every kind.

O sacred one! O best of mountains! O you wondrous spectacle! O celebrated massif! O refuge of the distressed! O most auspicious one! I bow to you, O pillar of the earth! Approaching, I bow to you.

Know me for a king's daughter, and a king's daughter-in-law, and a king's wife. I am Damayanti, daughter of Bhima, mighty warrior king of the Vidarbhas, protector of the four varnas. That best of kings performed the Rajasuya and Aswamedha yagnas, with bountiful gifts to Brahmanas. Bhima of the beautiful and large eyes, distinguished for his devotion to the Vedas, of blemishless character, always truthful, devoid of guile, gentle, powerful, lord of immense wealth, versed in dharma, and pure, has vanquished all his enemies and protects all the people of Vidarbha. Holy Mountain, I am that Bhima's daughter, come to you in dire straits.

That best of men, the renowned king of the Nishadhas, Virasena of towering fame, was my father-in-law. His heroic and beautiful son, of invincible prowess, who rules well the kingdom he inherited from his father, is called Nala. Know, O Mountain, that I am the wife of that golden-complexioned slayer of foes, devoted to Brahmanas, versed in the Vedas, gifted with eloquence, that righteous and Soma-drinking and fire-adoring king, who performed great sacrifices and is both liberal and warlike, who punishes evil men – I am his innocent queen who stands before you.

Having lost all that we owned and also my husband now, I have no one to protect me anymore, and I have come before you in deep distress. I have come seeking my husband. O foremost of mountains, with your hundreds of peaks towering into the sky, have you seen Nala in this fearful jungle? Have you seen my husband, that king of the Nishadhas, the lustrous Nala with the tread of a mighty elephant, blessed with great intelligence, long-armed, and of fiery tejas, possessed of prowess and patience and courage and high fame?

Ah, best of mountains, you see me lamenting alone, overwhelmed by sorrow, then why don't you comfort me with your voice, as your own daughter in distress?

O mighty Kshatriya, O warrior of truth and prowess, O you who know every particular of dharma, O lord of the earth – if you are in this forest, O King, show yourself to me. Ah, when will I hear the voice of Nala again, gentle, and deep as that of the clouds, that voice sweet as amrita, of my illustrious king calling me Vidarbha's daughter, in accents clear, rich and holy, and musical as the chanting of the Vedas, and soothing all my sorrows? Nala, I am frightened. Virtuous one, comfort me."

Having said all this to that greatest of mountains, Damayanti walked towards the north, and having gone three days and nights, she came to an incomparable tapovana of Rishis, as beautiful as a grove in heaven. She saw great Sages that adorned that asrama— Valmiki, Bhrigu and Atri—all holy men, at stern tapasya, their senses and minds restrained, some living on water, some on air, and some on fallen leaves, passions in check, eminently blessed, clad in barks of trees and deer-skins, seeking the way to salvation.

Damayanti's spirits revived seeing that charmed hermitage of Munis, where herds of deer grazed and monkeys frolicked in the trees. That best of women, her eyes large and black, her brows graceful, her tresses long, her hips wide, her bosom deep, her face perfect, her teeth like pearls, her form lustrous and noble, entered the hermitage. She saluted those ascetics, grown old practising their austerities, and stood humbly before them.

They said to her, "Welcome! Sit down and tell us what we can do for you."

Damayanti said, "Sinless and most blessed Munis, is all well with your tapasya, your sacrificial fire, religious observances, and your svadharma? And is all well with the beasts and birds of this asrama?"

They answered, "Beautiful, illustrious woman, prosperity attends us in every way. But O you of faultless limbs, tell us who you are, and what you seek. Seeing your lovely form and your bright splendour, we are amazed. Do not grieve. Blameless, blessed one, tell us, are you the Devi of this forest, or of this mountain, or of this river?"

Damayanti replied, "Brahmanas, I am not the goddess of this forest, or of this mountain, or of this stream. O Rishis of ascetic wealth, I am a human woman. I will tell you about my life in detail. I beg you, listen to me.

There is a king called Bhima, the mighty ruler of the Vidarbhas, and O Dvijottamas, I am his daughter. Nala, wise ruler of the Nishadhas, heroic, of great renown, always victorious in battle, and learned, is my husband, the large-eyed Nala, his face like the full moon, who always worships the gods, who is devoted to Brahmanas, guardian of the line of the Nishadhas, of mighty energy, of great strength, truthful, conversant with dharma, wise, unwavering in keeping his word, crusher of his foes, devout, graceful, conqueror of hostile towns, foremost of kings, equal in splendour to the king of the Devas.

He performs great sacrifices, knows the Vedas well, and their Angas, destroys his enemies in battle, is as splendid as the Sun and the Moon. That king devoted to truth and dharma was summoned to play dice by some deceitful and evil ones, skilled at gambling, and he had his kingdom and his wealth taken from him.

Munis, I am the wife of that Rajarishabha, and my name is Damayanti. My lord has gone missing and I am desperate to find him. I am wandering through forests and among mountains, lakes, rivers and tanks, in sorrow, in search of my husband – Nala, skilled in battle, high-souled, and a master of weapons.

O Rishis, has Nala, lord of the Nishadhas, come to this beautiful asrama of yours? It is for him, O Brahmanas, that I have come to this forest full of terror, haunted by tigers and other beasts. If I do not see King Nala in a few days, I will seek my weal by leaving this body. Of what use is my life without that bull among men? How will I live tormented by grief at being without him?"

The Rishis said to the forlorn Damayanti, "Blessed and beautiful child, with our mystic powers, we see that the future holds joy for you and that you will soon find Nala. O daughter of Bhima, you will see the lord of the Nishadhas, slayer of his enemies, foremost of the virtuous, freed from distress. You will see the king, your husband, freed from all sin, wearing precious jewels, again ruling his own city, punishing his enemies, striking terror into their hearts, and gladdening the hearts of friends, while all success and every blessing crown him."

When they had said this to the princess, Nala's beloved queen, those Sages and all that asrama vanished before her eyes! Damayanti of faultless limbs stood wonderstruck. She asked herself, "Was it a dream that I saw? Ah, what a marvel! Where are all those Brahmanas? Where is that asrama? Where is that sparkling river of sacred water, on which so many kinds of waterbirds swam? Where are those enchanted trees laden with flowers and fruit?"

After wandering for some time, Damayanti was melancholy again and the colour drained from her face from grief for Nala. She went to another part of the forest and saw a great asoka tree. Going up to that first of trees, blossom-laden and full of leaves, resounding with birdsong in its branches, Damayanti, with tears in her eyes and her voice choking, said, "Oh, this graceful tree in the heart of the forest, decked in flowers, is so beautiful, like some charming king of hills. O beautiful Asoka, quickly set me free from sorrow!

Have you seen King Nala, Parantapa, the beloved husband of Damayanti? Have you seen my precious husband, the king of the Nishadhas, clad in half a piece of cloth, his skin delicate, hero plunged in woe who came into this wilderness? O Asoka, free me from my grief! Vindicate your name, for Asoka means destroyer of grief."

Thrice she walked around that tree, then entered an even denser part of the jungle. Wandering in quest of her lord, Bhima's daughter saw many unusual, majestic trees, lovely rills, towering mountains, and beasts and birds, and caves, and cliffs, many rivers of wonderful beauty.

As she went, she came upon a wide path where, in some amazement, she saw a mighty group of merchants, with their horses and elephants, on the banks of a river full of clear and cool water, and lovely to behold, and wide, the banks overgrown with bamboo clumps, echoing with the cries of cranes and ospreys and chakravakas, the river itself full of tortoises, crocodiles and fish, and studded with innumerable islets.

As soon as she saw that caravan, Damayanti, dishevelled, lean, her hair tangled and filthy, wearing half a cloth, went towards the merchants like some madwoman, that lovely queen. Seeing her some of the Vaisyas fled in fear, some grew anxious, while some cried out, and others laughed at her, and yet others despised the very sight of her.

However, some felt pity, O Bhaarata, and asked her, "Blessed one, who are you, and whose? What do you seek in this forest? We are frightened of you, tell us truly are you human or the Devi of this jungle, or this mountain, or of the points of the sky? We seek your protection. Are you a Yakshi or a Rakshasi, or a Devastri? Anyway, bless us, O you of faultless features, and protect us so our caravan passes through this place safely, with ourselves and our goods secure."

Damayanti said, "O leader of the caravan, merchants, youths, old men, children, I am a human woman. I am the daughter of a king, the daughter in-law of a king, and the consort, also, of a king, eager for the sight of my lord. The king of the Vidarbhas is my father; my husband Nala is the lord of the Nishadhas, and even now I am looking for him.

If you have seen my beloved Nala, tiger among men, razer of hostile armies, tell me quickly!"

At which the leader of that great caravan, Suchi, said to Damayanti of faultless limbs, "Blessed one, you of sweet smiles, I am a Vaisya and the leader of this caravan. Lovely lady, I have not seen any man called Nala. In this great forest, where no men live, there are only elephants, leopards, bison, tigers, bears and other beasts. Other than you I have met no human in this vana, may Manibhadra, king of the Yakshas, help us now!"

She asked, "Tell me where this caravan is bound."

The leader of the band said, "O daughter of a great king, we are bound for the city of Subahu, the honest sovereign of the Chedis, to make some profit from our goods.'"

NALOPAKHYANA PARVA CONTINUED

Brihadaswa said, 'Damayanti went with that caravan, and she was anxious to see her Nala. After travelling for many days, the merchants saw a large lake fragrant with lotuses in the midst of that dense and terrible forest. Its banks adorned with velvet grasses, with plenty of wood to burn as fuel, and with flowers and fruit, it was a charmed place indeed.

The shimmering water abounded with birds of many kinds; it was cool, clear and sweet, and captivated the heart. Worn with their long journey, the merchants of the caravan decided to halt there and spread themselves through the fine woods surrounding the lake. It was dusk.

At midnight, when all was still and quiet, when the tired caravan had fallen asleep, a herd of wild elephants, the juice of rut flowing down their temples, and going to drink from a mountain stream, saw the caravan of sleeping Vaisyas, and also the many tame elephants which went with the merchants. Seeing the domesticated elephants, the wild herd, maddened by musth, rushed at them, meaning to kill them; they came like great boulders loosed down a mountain slope.

The charging wild elephants found their way to the lake of lotuses and the elephants of the caravan barred by sleeping merchants and they trampled the Vaisyas. Many died, while others awoke and fled screaming in all directions, into the deeper forest. Some were gored to death, others scooped up in massive trunks and dashed on the ground, while more were crushed under massive feet.

The wild elephants killed many camels and horses, as well, while in panic the fleeing merchants with weapons drawn even killed one another in the dark. Some fell on the ground, others scrambled up trees, while yet others jumped down into deep pits. O King, great losses that caravan suffered when the wild herd attacked it.

An uproar broke out, for precious jewels the Vaisyas were carrying scattered on the ground.

"Save us!" they screamed.

"Pick up the jewels!"

"Leave them. What do the jewels matter when our lives are in danger?"

"Fly!"

"Where to fly?"

And they dashed about blindly in complete terror. Damayanti awoke in fear, while the slaughter held sway around her; she awoke trembling and panting.

Finally, the elephants lumbered away and those merchants who had escaped with their lives met together, and they asked "What have we done that this disaster has overtaken us?"

"Surely, we did not worship the Manibhadras, and the exalted and graceful Vaisravana, the king of the Yakshas."

"Perhaps, we have not worshipped the gods who fetch calamities, or perhaps we did not pay them the first homage. Maybe, this evil follows the birds we saw on our way."

"Our stars are not unpropitious. From what other cause, then, has disaster come?"

Some, who had lost their wealth and relatives, and were distraught, cried, "This mad looking woman came among us and she was strange and hardly human. Surely she has brought this on us. She must be a Rakshasi, a Yakshi or as Pisachi! Beyond doubt, this evil is her doing.

"If we see that evil creature again, we will kill her!"

Damayanti heard what they said and fled into the forest. She said desperately to herself, "Alas! Fierce and great is the wrath of God upon me. Peace does not follow my paths. What have I done to deserve this? I do not remember that I ever harmed anyone in the least, in thought, word or deed. Then why such terrible consequences?

Surely, some great sins from a past life are being visited on me that my husband has lost his kingdom, and his own kinsmen turned against him and vanquished him. I have been separated from my son and daughter, and my lord, and find myself alone in this dreadful jungle full of savage beasts."

O King, the next day, what remained of the once mighty caravan of merchants left that place, loudly lamenting their lost wealth and their dead brothers, fathers, sons and friends.

And the princess of Vidarbha also lamented, "Ah, what have I done? Surely, it is my misfortune which has devastated the company of men with whom I took refuge. Now, surely, I will have to suffer for a long time. I have heard wise old men say that no one dies before their time; surely, that is why the elephants did not trample me while I slept.

Everything which has happened to me is only because of something I did in a past life, for not even as a child did I commit any such sin in thought, word, or deed, which could bring such tragedy as this one as its consequence. Oh, I do believe that I have been parted from my Nala because I chose him over the all-powerful Lokapalas who came to my swayamvara. It is their power which has brought calamity into my life."

Thus grieving, pale as the autumn moon, Damayanti now attached herself to the Brahmanas, knowers of the Vedas, who had survived the night's massacre. Travelling briskly, towards evening she came to the mighty city of Subahu, king of the Chedis. Wearing half a garment, she entered that magnificent city.

The citizens saw her, full of fear, lean, melancholy, her hair dishevelled and soiled with dirt, and altogether like a madwoman. In curiosity, the boys of that city began following her. Surrounded by them, she came to the palace of the king.

The queen-mother saw her from a terrace, surrounded by the crowd of youths. She said to her nursemaid, "Go and bring that woman to me. She is forlorn and the crowd troubles her. She is in distress and in need of succour. I find her beauty such that it illumines my house. Though she looks like a madwoman, with her large eyes, the fair one is as lovely as the Devi Sri herself."

The woman went out and, dispersing the crowd, brought Damayanti to that fine terrace. O King, wonderstruck, that nursemaid asked Damayanti, "You are plunged in misfortune, yet you are so very beautiful. You shine like lightning in the clouds. Tell me who you are, and whose. Your lustre is celestial; surely you are not merely human. You wear no ornaments, and although you are helpless, you are unmoved by the coarseness of these men."

Damayanti said, "I am a human woman, devoted to my husband. I am a serving woman from good stock. I live wherever I like, eating fruit and roots, and without a companion, and sleep where night overtakes me. My husband is a man of countless virtues and was always devoted to me. I was also deeply attached to him, following him like his shadow.

Once he became involved in a desperate game of dice. Beaten, losing everything, he came into the wilderness. I came with him into the forest, comforting that hero clad in a single piece of cloth, who was demented by his sudden adversity. Afflicted by hunger, thirst and grief, he was forced to relinquish even his last cloth.

Naked and deranged as he was, I still followed him, myself in a single garment. For nights together, I did not sleep. Many days passed, until, once while I slept, he cut away one half of my garment and abandoned me, who had done him no wrong.

I am seeking my husband but cannot find him, who has the complexion of the filaments of a lotus. Without seeing him who delights my heart, my beloved lord who owns my heart, for he is like a Deva to look at, I am consumed by grief by night and day."

Now the queen-mother herself said to the tearful Damayanti, "Blessed one, you stay with me. I am well pleased with you. Lovely one, my men will search for your husband, or he might come here on his wanderings. Remain here with me and you will have your lost lord back."

Damayanti replied, "Mother of heroes, I can only stay with you on some conditions. I will not eat the leavings of any food, nor will I wash anyone's feet, nor must I have to speak to any other man. If anyone tries to make me his wife or mistress, he must submit to my punishment; more, if he solicits me repeatedly, he must be punished with death.

This is the vow I have sworn. I also want to speak to the Brahmanas who will go forth to seek out my husband. If you can do all this for me, I will certainly live with you. But if you cannot, I also cannot remain here with you."

The queen-mother answered her gladly, "I will do all this. I approve of the vow you have taken."

O Bhaarata, the queen-mother now said to her daughter Sunanda, "Sunanda, take this woman who is like a goddess to be your Sairandhri. She is the same age as you are, let her be your companion, and enjoy her company."

Sunanda cheerfully accepted Damayanti and led her to her own apartments, along with her sakhis. Treated with respect, Damayanti was satisfied and she lived there without any anxiety, for all her wishes were met.'

NALOPAKHYANA PARVA CONTINUED

Brihadaswa says, 'Rajan, after deserting Damayanti, Nala saw a mighty conflagration that raged in that dense forest. From the great fire, he heard some creature crying repeatedly to him, "O righteous Nala, come here!"

Answering, "Fear not!" he ran into the fire and saw a mighty Naga king in coils. Trembling, with folded hands, the Naga said to Nala, "O King, I am a snake and Karkotaka is my name. I once deceived the Maharishi Narada and he cursed me in anger: 'Stay here immobile as if graven of stone, until one Nala takes you out from this place. And at the very place to which he bears you, you will be free from my curse.

For that curse, I canot move. I will tell you how to save me, and I will be your friend. There is no Naga to equal me, but I will be light in your hands. Pick me up, Nala, and hurry from here!"

Saying this that prince of snakes became as small as a man's thumb. Picking him up, Nala took him out of the forest fire. Coming to an open glade, Nala meant to set the Naga down, when Karkotaka said again to him, "King of the Nishadhas, go on a little further, a few steps more. Mahabaho, I will do you great good."

As Nala walked on, the snake bit him at the tenth step. As soon as he was bitten, Nala found himself transformed; he saw the snake also resume his own massive form.

Karkotaka comforted Nala, "I have taken your beauty from you so that people will not recognise you. And, Nala, he who has deceived you and plunged you in despair will continue to dwell inside you, but now tortured by my venom. As long as he does not leave you, he will be in agony in your body, its every limb filled with my venom. O King, I have saved you from the one who has destroyed you out of anger and hatred, though you are perfectly innocent and undeserving of wrong.

Also, tiger among men, from now through my grace you will feel no fear from any fanged creature, from other enemies as well as Brahmanas who know the Vedas. Nor will you feel any pain from my poison. Kshatriya, you will always be victorious in battle.

Lord of Nishadhas, go to the wondrous city of Ayodhya even today and present yourself before King Rituparna, who is a master of gambling, and say to him, 'I am Bahuka, a charioteer.' In return for your knowledge of horses, he will teach you the skills of dice. He is of the line of Ikshvaku, and prosperous; he will be your friend.

When you are an adept at dice you will have your fortune back. You will find your wife and children and have your kingdom again. I say this to you in truth, so do not let sorrow cloud your mind.

Lord of men, when you want to have back your own form, think of me and put on this garment."

That Naga gave Nala two pieces of celestial cloth, and the king of snakes vanished.'

CANTO 67

NALOPAKHYANA PARVA CONTINUED

Brihadaswa says, 'After the snake disappeared, Nala made his way towards Ayodhya and entered Rituparna's city on the tenth day.

He went to the king and said, "My name is Bahuka. There is no one in this world to equal me in tending to horses. My counsel is also valued in all difficult problems, and I have many other skills besides. I am also a most excellent cook. Why, for you I will excel at every art which exists in this world, and accomplish everything difficult. O Rituparna, keep me in your palace."

Rituparna replied warmly, "Bahuka, stay with me! May fortune befall you, for I believe what you say. I have always particularly wanted to be driven fast; I leave it to you to make my horses swift. I give you charge of my stables, and I will pay you ten thousand coins for that.

Varshneya and Jivala will always be under your direction, and you will spend your time pleasantly with them. So, Bahuka, do stay with me!"

Nala began to live in Rituparna's city, and was treated with respect, while Varshneya and Jivala were his companions. Living there, he thought of Damayanti and every morning and evening he would sing aloud to himself, even like a sloka, "Where is that helpless one, afflicted by hunger and thirst, worn with toil, thinking of that wretch. Ah, on whom does she now wait?"

Once as the king was chanting this in the night, Jivala asked him, "Bahuka, for whom do you so lament daily? I am curious. O you who are blessed with a long life, whose wife is she for whom you so grieve?"

Nala replied, "There is a certain foolish man who had a wife known to all. However, the wretch proved false in his vows to her. He was separated from her and wandered the earth, tormented by sorrow, without rest by day or night. At nights, he remembers her, and he sings this verse. Having wandered over all the world, he has finally found a refuge, and undeserving of the suffering which has overtaken him, he passes his days thinking of his wife.

When calamity overtook this man, his wife followed him into the jungle. Deserted by him of small virtue, her very life is in danger. Alone, with no knowledge of the ways of the world, ill able to bear grief, faint with hunger and thirst, she can hardly protect herself. And, O friend, that man of small sense and little fortune has abandoned her in that terrible forest, teeming with predators."

Thus always remembering Damayanti, Nala, king of the Nishadhas, continued to live, unknown, in the palace of Rituparna of Ayodhya.'"

CANTO 68

NALOPAKHYANA PARVA CONTINUED

Vaisampayana said, "Brihadaswa says, "After Nala lost his kingdom and became a bondsman, while Damayanti entered the service of a queen-mother, Bhima wanted to see Nala and he sent out Brahmanas to search for him. Giving them profuse wealth, Bhima said, "Seek out Nala and also Damayanti. He who finds the Naishadha and my daughter, and brings them to me, shall have a thousand cows from me, and fields and a village as big as a town. Even if he does not fetch Damayanti and Nala here, he that discovers where they are will have wealth equal to a thousand cows."

The Brahmanas happily went forth in every direction, combing cities and provinces. But nowhere did they find Nala or his queen, until, at last a Brahmana called Sudeva came to the city of the Chedis, and there, during the time of the king's prayers, saw Damayanti in the king's palace, sitting with Sunanda. Lean and soiled as she was, her incomparable beauty glowed like fire hidden in curls of smoke, and he felt certain she was the princess of Vidarbha.

Sudeva said to himself, "I am blessed, that my eyes behold the princess who is like Sri herself, delighting the worlds! Her face is like the full moon; she is in the fullness of her youth, her breasts round and high, illumining this place with her lustre like moonrays, her eyes like lotus petals, fascinating as Kama's Rati herself, although, alas, she seems like a lotus stalk transplanted by ill fortune from the Vidarbha lake, and covered with mire in the process.

Grieving for her husband, she looks like the paurnima night when Rahu swallows the Moon, or like a river which has run dry. Ah, she is like a lake of lotuses, whose blooms have been ravaged by the trunks of elephants, a lake whose birds are terrified by the rampaging herd. Surely, this delicate girl of exquisite limbs, who deserves to dwell in a jewelled palace is indeed like a lotus uprooted and scorched by the sun.

She is beautiful past compare, she is generous; she should wear ornaments but has none, and is like the moon covered by black clouds. Deprived of every comfort and luxury, torn away from her friends, she is in distress, supported only by the hope of seeing her lord, for truly her husband is the best ornament of a woman, even if she has no other. Without her husband beside her, this lady, though beautiful, does not shine forth as she should.

As for Nala, how does he remain alive separated from such a wife? Why, I look at her, black-haired, her eyes like lotus leaves, unhappy though she deserves to be joyful, and even my heart is pained. When will this girl, graced by every auspicious mark and devoted to her husband, cross this ocean of woe, and be with her lord again, even like Rohini regaining the Moon?

For sure, when Nala finds her again, he will experience the delight of a king regaining his lost kingdom. He is her equal in nature, in age and lineage; Nala deserves Damayanti and this black-eyed beauty deserves the Naishadha. I see how she pines for him, and I should comfort the queen of that hero of immeasurable prowess, energy and might. Let me console this distraught girl, her face like the full moon, and suffering as she never has before, and always thinking only of her husband."

The Brahmana Sudeva approached Damayanti, and said, "Princess of Vidarbha, I am Sudeva the Brahmana, your brother's dear friend. I have come here seeking you at the behest of King Bhima. Your father is well, and also your mother, and your brothers. Your son and daughter, blessed with length of days, live in peace. However, your kinsfolk, though living are almost as dead on your account, and hundreds of Brahmanas range the world in search of you."

Damayanti recognised Sudeva, and asked about all her family, one after the other. O King, then, overwhelmed, the princess began to sob bitterly at unexpectedly seeing that best of Brahmanas, her brother's friend. Sunanda saw Damayanti crying, and speaking privately to Sudeva, and went in some distress to her mother and said, "Sairandhri is sobbing in the presence of a Brahmana. Come and see."

The mother of the king of the Chedis came out of the inner apartments of the palace, to where Damayanti was with the Brahmana. Calling Sudeva, the queen-mother asked him, "Whose wife is this fair one, and whose daughter? How has she of beautiful eyes lost the company of her relatives and of her husband as well? How do you know her? Tell me all this in detail, about this girl of unearthly beauty."

Then, O Bhaarata, Sudeva, that best of Brahmanas, sat at his ease and began to tell the story of Damayanti.'

NALOPAKHYANA PARVA CONTINUED

'Sudeva said, "There is a virtuous and illustrious king of the Vidarbhas called Bhima. This young woman is his daughter Damayanti. She is also the wife of the wise and righteous Nala, king of the Nishadhas, the son of Virasena. Defeated at dice by his brother, and deprived of his kingdom, that king, taking Damayanti with him, left his city.

We have been ranging the earth in search of Damayanti, and at last we have found her in the palace of your son. No woman exists who can rival her beauty. From her infancy she has had a fine birthmark between her eye-brows, a mark like a lotus. It now seems to have all but vanished, for her face is covered by dust, even as clouds hide the moon. Put there by Brahma himself, to be a mark of fortune and wealth, that lotus is still faintly visible, like the cloud-covered crescent moon of the first day of the bright fortnight.

And though her body, too, is covered with dirt, her beauty has not disappeared. Though she is careless of her person, her beauty still shines through like gold. Ah, by her birthmark and her mole I have recognised her, even as one discovers a covered fire by its heat!"

O King, hearing what Sudeva said, Sunanda washed away the dust that covered the mark between Damayanti's eye-brows, whereupon it became clear like the moon appearing from behind clouds. When they saw the lotus mark, Sunanda and the queen-mother began to cry; they embraced Damayanti and stood silent for a time.

Still shedding tears, the queen-mother said gently, "Through this mark I know that you are my sister's daughter! Lovely one, your mother and I are both daughters of the high-souled Sudaman, king of the Dasarnas. She was given to King Bhima, and I to Virabahu. I witnessed your birth in our father's palace in the kingdom of the Dasarnas. My beautiful child, my house is as your own father's house to you; all my wealth, Damayanti, is yours as much as mine."

At this, Damayanti, her heart glad, bowed down to her mother's sister and said, "Even before you knew me, you took me in and cared for me. I have already been happy in your house, and now I am sure I will be still happier. But, mother, I have long been an exile and so, I beg you, give me leave to go.

My son and daughter live in my father's palace. Deprived of both their father and mother, they must pass their time in great sorrow. If you want to please me, give me an escort even now and let me go to the Vidarbhas."

Rajan, Damayanti's aunt agreed happily, "So be it."

And with her son's permission, she sent Damayanti in a handsome palanquin, carried by sturdy servitors, protected by a large escort and provided with food and drink and the finest garments. Soon enough, she reached the country of the Vidarbhas, where all her family received her in great joy, while she worhipped the Gods and Brahmanas and gave thanks at seeing her relatives, her children, both her parents, and all her old sakhis well.

King Bhima gave Sudeva a thousand cows and much wealth and a whole village.

Having slept the night in her father's palace, and having recovered somewhat from her exhaustion, Damayanti said to her mother, "O mother, if you want me to live, you must find Nala and bring him to me."

At which, the queen, her mother, began to cry but could give her daughter no reply. Seeing her like that all the women of the harem began to lament and weep loudly. Then the queen went to the mighty Bhima and said, "Your daughter Damayanti grieves heartbroken for Nala. She told me so herself. Let all your men do their utmost to find the Naishadha."

Bhima sent his Brahmanas in all directions, saying, "Do everything you can to find Nala!"

Before going forth, those Brahmanas came to Damayanti and told her of their mission. Bhima's daughter said to them, "Go and cry out in every realm, 'Beloved gambler, where have you gone cutting away half my garment, and abandoning your devoted wife while she slept in the jungle? That girl waits for you, consumed by grief. Relent, O King, O Kshatriya, and answer her, for she weeps incessantly for you!'

Say all this and more so that he is moved by pity. Say, 'Helped by the wind, fire consumed the forest. A husband must always protect and provide for his wife. Why then, good as you are and acquainted with every duty, have you neglected to do both? You have fame, wisdom, lineage, and kindness; why have you been unkind?

I fear that all this is because of my good fortune being lost! O tiger among men, take pity on me, O bull among men! You always said to me that kindness is the highest virtue, why are you not kind now?'

If anyone answers you when you say all this, find out who he is and where he lives. Dvijottamas, come and tell me what that man says who answers you. You must be careful that no one knows that the words you speak are at my behest, nor that you will come back to me. You must discover everything about him who answers you – if he is rich or poor, powerful or powerless, everything about him."

With these instructions from Damayanti, the Brahmanas set out in all directions in search of Nala overtaken by misfortune. They looked for him in kingdoms, cities and villages, in Rishis' asramas and cowherd settlements. Wherever they went they repeated aloud what Damayanti had told them to say.'

CANTO 70

NALOPAKHYANA PARVA CONTINUED

Brihadaswa says, 'After a long time, a Brahmana named Parnada returned to the city of the Vidarbhas, and said to the daughter of Bhima, "Damayanti, seeking Nala, king of Nishadhas, I went to the city of Ayodhya, and appeared before the son of Bhangasura, where I repeated your words in the presence of the blessed Rituparna. However, neither that king of men nor any of his courtiers said anything in reply, although I uttered them over and over.

Then, after I had been dismissed by the king, a man in Rituparna's service, a certain Bahuka, accosted me. Bahuka is that king's charioteer, of unseemly appearance and short arms. He is skilled at driving chariots and riding horses very fast, and is also a master cook.

I found that he sighed often, and wept, as he asked about my welfare. Then he said, 'Although they might fall into great distress, chaste women protect themselves and so secure heaven. Although their lords might abandon them, yet they do not become angry, for women that are chaste lead their lives encased in the armour of virtue. It becomes her not to be angry since he that abandoned her was overcome by calamity, and deprived of everything.

A beautiful and virtuous woman should not be angry with one whom birds deprived of his single cloth, while he went looking for food, with one who, besides, is being consumed by grief. Regardless of whether she is treated well or ill, a chaste wife should never succumb to anger, seeing her husband in such a plight, having lost his kingdom, destitute of prosperity, ravaged by hunger and overwhelmed by disaster.'

After hearing what he said, I returned quickly to you, and now I have told you what transpired. Tell your father the king about it and then do as you see fit."

Tears in her eyes, Damayanti went to her mother and spoke to her in private, "Mother, you must not under any circumstances tell my father King Bhima of what I intend. In your presence, I will send Sudeva, that best of Brahmanas, to Ayodhya immediately, to fetch Nala here just as he did me."

When Parnada had refreshed himself and recovered from his tiredness, the princess of Vidarbha worshipped him with profuse wealth. She also said, "When Nala comes here, O Brahmana, I will give you abundant wealth again, for you have done me a great service by which I hope to see my lord again quickly."

That high-minded Brahmana uttered blessings over her, auspicious mantras, and went home, regarding his mission as accomplished. When he had left, Damayanti, still in the clutches of grief, called Sudeva and, in her mother's presence, said to him, "O Sudeva, go to the city of Ayodhya, straight as a bird, and say there to King Rituparna, 'Bhima's daughter Damayanti will hold another swayamvara. All the kings and princes are going to it. Calculating the time, I find that the ceremony will take place tomorrow. O Parantapa, if it is possible for you, go there without delay.

Tomorrow, after the Sun rises, she will choose a second husband, since she does not know whether King Nala still lives or not.'"

Sudeva went to Ayodhya and declared what Damayanti had told him to King Rituparna.'

CANTO 71

NALOPAKHYANA PARVA CONTINUED

Brihadaswa continues, 'When he heard what Sudeva said, King Rituparna called Bahuka and said gently to him, "O Bahuka, you are a master of horses. I want you to take me to Damayanti's Swayamvara in a single day."

When he heard this, Nala thought his heart would burst with grief that seared his very entrails.

He thought to himself, "Perhaps Damayanti is deranged by sorrow that she is doing this; or, perhaps, she has conceived this wonderful plan for my sake? Alas, I senselessly abandoned the innocent princess of Vidarbha and this is a cruel thing that she plans. The world knows that the nature of women is fickle. Besides, I have wronged her grievously, and she might well be doing this because she has no love for me anymore.

But then, how will the slender-waisted one do this thing when she is the mother of my children? The only way to discover the truth is by going there, and I will go, to accomplish both Rituparna's purpose and my own."

Bahuka folded his hands to Rituparna and, though his heart was full of sadness, said, "Purushavyaghra, I will take you to the city of the Vidarbhas in a single day!"

At the command of Bhangasura's son, Nala went to the stables to choose his horses. Rituparna called repeatedly to him to hurry, and after some scrutiny and carfeul deliberation. Bahuka chose some lean steeds, of high pedigree, docile, strong and which could go a great distance. They had wide nostrils, outthrust cheeks, no inauspicious marks, or ten curls which are considered unfortunate; they were all born in the land of Sindhu and were fleet as the wind.

But when Rituparna saw those horses, he cired, "What are you doing? This is no time for jesting. How can such weak horses bear us to the Vidarbha city in a day?"

Bahuka replied, "Each of these horses has one curl on his forehead, two on his temples, four on his sides, four on his chest, and one on his back. Have no doubt they will go to the country of the Vidarbhas. If, O King, you want to choose some others, point them out and I will yoke them for you."

Rituparna replied, "Bahuka, you know about horses and are a master of driving them. Quickly yoke the ones you think best."

Nala yoked the four fine steeds he had chosen to the king's chariot. Rituparna climbed into the chariot and at once all the horses fell down on their knees! Then, O King, Nala began to soothe those beasts endowed with speed and energy. He lifted them again to their feet by their reins and made the charioteer Varshneya sit beside him at the chariot head; Nala prepared to ride at great speed.

Now, urged by Bahuka, those horses rose into the sky! The king of Ayodhya and his sarathy were dumbstruck; they went at the speed of the wind.

The astonished Varshneya thought, "Is this Matali, the charioteer of Deva king? For the magnificent Bahuka's skills are no less than his. Or, has Salihotra taken human shape? Or is this King Nala who has come here? Or it may be that this Bahuka knows whatever Nala does about horses.

Bahuka and Nala are of the same age; yet, this might not be Nala, only someone who knows as much about horses as he does. However, when misfortune strikes them, the most illustrious men walk this earth in disguise, as ordained by the scriptures. True, he is ugly, but then Nala might even have changed his features. Bahuka and Nala are of similar age, but they are unlike in appearance.

Yet, Bahuka is as accomplished, in every way, as Nala and I feel certain that he is indeed the Naishadha."

Thus, long thought Varshneya, who was once Nala's own sarathy. King Rituparna delighted in the marvellous skills of Bahuka. He looked at how Bahuka held his reins and how he made his horses fly and he was full of joy.'

NALOPAKHYANA PARVA CONTINUED

Brihadaswa says, 'Like a bird coursing through the sky, Nala crossed rivers and mountains, forests and lakes. Suddenly, Rituparna's upper garment peeled away from his body and fell to the earth below.

Rituparna said to Nala, "I must have my royal garment back. Restrain your steeds, most intelligent one, and let Varshneya bring my cloth back."

Nala replied, "The cloth has fallen far down, and we have come a yojana since. We cannot recover it now."

When Nala said this to him, Rituparna saw a Vibhitaka tree laden with fruit, in a forest. The king said quickly to Bahuka, "Sarathy, observe my extraordinary skill at counting. There is no one who is a master of every art or science. Knowledge in its entirety is not found in any one person. O Bahuka, the leaves and fruit of this tree which are lying on the ground exceed those that are still upon it by one hundred and one. The two branches of the tree have fifty million leaves, and two thousand and ninety-five fruit. Examine the two branches and all their boughs."

Bahuka stopped his chariot and said to the king, "Parantapa, you take credit for yourself in a matter that is beyond my perception. But, O King, I will cut down the Vibhitaka and count the leaves and fruit. Let Varshneya hold the reins of the horses for a while."

The king replied, "We have no time to lose."

But Bahuka replied humbly, "Stay awhile, otherwise make Varshneya your charioteer. The road lies straight and even."

Rituparna said, "Bahuka, you are the only charioteer, there is no other in this world like you. I place myself in your hands, only you can take me to the Vidarbhas. If you make me see the Sun rise in the land of the Vidarbhas, I will give you anything you wish for."

Bahuka said, "Let me count the leaves and fruit of the Vibhitaka and then I will take you to the Vidarbha country."

Reluctantly the king said, "Count, and upon counting the leaves and fruits of a portion of this branch, you will be satisfied with what I said."

Bahuka quickly got down from the chariot and felled the tree. He was amazed to find the fruit to be exactly as many as the king had said. He said to Rituparna, "This power of yours is extraordinary. O King, I want to learn this art from you."

Wanting to ride on swiftly, the king said, "Know that apart from the art of reckoning, I am also a master of dice."

And Bahuka said to him, "Bull among men, teach me that art and in return receive my knowledge of horses and kine."

Knowing that he depended on Bahuka's goodwill to arrive in the Vidarbha land, and also tempted by the horse-lore that his charioteer possessed, Rituparna said, "So be it. Receive the art of dice from me, O Bahuka, and let the equine science remain with you in trust."

Rituparna imparted that art to Nala, and immediately Kali came out of his body incessantly vomiting the virulent poison of Karkotaka. As soon as he left Nala, the fire of that curse left Kali.

Nala, who had been possessed and tormented for so long, wanted to curse Kali, when terrified and trembling, Kali said with folded hands,

"Control your anger, O King! I will make you lustrous. When you abandoned her, Indrasena's mother cursed me and, ever since, I have lived in your body in torment. Unconquered one, miserable and scalded night and day by the venom of the snake prince, I lived inside you.

I seek your protection. If you do not curse me, who am frightened and seek refuge in you, then anyone who attentively recites your story will never have to fear me."

Nala controlled his wrath, and Kali swiftly entered into the Vibhitaka tree. All the while that Kali spoke with Nala, he remained invisible to the others. Delivered from his travail, and having counted the fruits of that tree, Naishadha, filled with great joy and of terrific energy, climbed back into the chariot and urged his fleet horses on.

From that hour, the Vibhitaka tree fell into disrepute because of the touch of Kali.

Nala's horses flew up again into the air even like winged creatures, and he drove them in the direction of the Vidarbha country. When he had gone far, Kali crept out of the tree and returned to his own abode.

O King, when Kali left Nala, that lord of the earth was free again from calamity, though he did not yet assume his natural form.'

Nalopakhyana Parva Continued

Brihadaswa says, 'Rituparna arrived that same evening at the gates of the city of the Vidarbhas; the people brought news of his coming to King Bhima. And at the invitation of Bhima, the king of Ayodhya entered the city of Kundina, filling the ten cardinal points with the sound of his chariot wheels.

The horses of Nala who were in that city heard that sound and were as delighted as they used to become in the presence of Nala himself. Damayanti also heard the sound of that chariot driven by Nala, like the deep roar of clouds during the monsoon. Bhima and Nala's horses inside Bhima's city felt they were hearing the chariot wheels of Nala himself, as of old.

Like the horses, the peacocks on the terraces and the elephants in their stables heard the rumble of Rituparna's chariot, like that of thunderheads, and they all began to cry out and trumpet, full of joy such as they experience when they hear the actual roar of clouds.

Damayanti said, "The rumble of this chariot fills all the world and gladdens my heart, so it must be Nala. If I do not see Nala, his face bright as the moon, the Kshatriya of countless virtues, I will surely die. If today I am not clasped in that hero's arms, his thrilling embrace, I shall cease to be.

If Naishadha, whose voice is as deep as that of the clouds, does not come to me today, I will walk into a pyre of golden brilliance. If that best of kings, strong as a lion, mighty as a bull elephant in musth, does not appear before me, I will not live anymore. I do not remember a single untruth in him, or a single wrong done by him to anyone. He has never told a lie even in jest.

Ah, my Nala is noble, forgiving, heroic, magnificent, superior to all other kings, faithful to his marriage vow and like a eunuch to other females. Night and day my heart is full of him, and if I do not see him quickly, my heart will burst."

So she spoke to herself, as one devoid of sense, and climbed up to her terrace to catch a glimpse of the righteous Nala. In the central courtyard of the main palace she saw Rituparna in the chariot with Varshneya and Bahuka. Varshneya and Bahuka climbed down from that fine ratha and unyoked the horses, then left the chariot itself in a proper place.

Rituparna climbed down and presented himself before King Bhima of terrible prowess. Bhima received him with great respect, for without a due occasion, a great man cannot be received as a guest. Honoured by Bhima, Rituparna looked around him again and again, but saw no sign of any swayamvara.

O Bhaarata, the Vidarbha king approached Rituparna, and said, "Welcome! What is the occasion for this visit of yours?"

Bhima asked this without knowing that Rituparna had come to obtain the hand of his daughter. Rituparna saw that there were no other kings or princes here; nor did he hear anything of the swaymvara; nor did he see any concourse of Brahmanas.

The most intelligent Kosala king thought for a while, then said, "I have come here to pay my respects to you."

Bhima was astonished and tried to fathom why Rituparna had come a hundred yojanas. He thought, "It is unlikely that he has passed through so many kingdoms and by countless kings just to pay his respects to me. But I will learn the truth by and by."

Bhima said to Rituparna summarily, "Rest now, you are tired."

Honoured thus by the pleased Bhima, King Rituparna, his heart glad, went to his appointed quarters, followed by the servants of the royal household.

When Rituparna had gone with Varshneya, Bahuka took the chariot to the stables. He freed his horses there, rubbed them down, soothed them with his own hands, and sat down at one end of the ratha.

Meanwhile, having seen the royal son of Bhangasura, and Varshneya of the Suta race, and also Bahuka as a Suta, Damayanti was forlorn and asked herself, "Whose is this chariot-rumble? It was as loud as Nala's, but I do not see the lord of the Nishadhas.

Varshneya has learnt the art from Nala, and that is why this chariot rumbled as Nala's did. Or is Rituparna as skilled as Nala so the sound of his chariot wheels is as that of Nala's?"

Thinking all this, that blessed and beautiful woman sent a female messenger in search of the Naishada.'

NALOPAKHYANA PARVA CONTINUED

'Damayanti said, "O Kesini, go and find out who that ugly and short-armed sarathy is, sitting beside the chariot. Faultless one, approach him cautiously, with sweet words, showing him courtesy and discover everything about him. Ah, from what my mind feels and the joy in my heart, I fear that he is King Nala.

Kesini, after asking about his welfare, say the words of Parnada to him and, my beautiful one, listen carefully to his reply."

While Damayanti watched from the terrace, Kesini softly approached Bahuka and said, "Best of men, you are welcome here. I wish you happiness. O bull among men, now listen to what Damayanti says. When did you all set out, and with what object have you come here? Tell us truly, for the princess of Vidarbha wishes to know."

Bahuka replied, "The king of Kosala heard from a Brahmana that Damayanti will hold a second swayamvara, and Rituparna flew here in this chariot yoked to horses swift as the wind, steeds which could fly a hundred yojanas. I am his sarathy."

Kesini then asked, "Who is the third among you, whose son? And whose son are you, and how have you become a charioteer?"

Bahuka replied, "The third one was the charioteer of Nala, and his name is Varshneya. Beautful one, after Nala left his kingdom, Varshneya came to the son of Bhangasura. I am skilled in horse-lore, and so I have been made charioteer. Indeed, King Rituparna himself chose me as his charioteer and cook."

Kesini said, "Perhaps Varshneya knows where King Nala has gone, and, O Bahuka, he may also have spoken to you about his master."

Bahuka said, "Varshneya brought the children of Nala here and then left. He does not know where Naishadha is, nor does anybody else know Nala's whereabouts, for the king wanders over the world in disguise and despoiled of his natural beauty. Only Nala knows who Nala is, for he does not seem like himself anymore, not in the least particular."

Kesini said, "The Brahmana who went to Ayodhya repeated these words suitable to female lips, 'O beloved gambler, where have you gone tearing off half my piece of cloth, and abandoning me, your devoted wife, asleep in the woods? Your wife waits for you in half a garment still, burning with grief day and night.

'O Kshatriya, relent towards her that weeps ceaselessly for you and give her a reply. Illustrious one, send her a soothing message, for she hungers for your words.'

When you heard what the Brahmana said in Ayodhya, you made a reply. The princess of Vidarbha wants to hear again the words you then spoke."

Hearing Kesini, Nala's heart ached and his eyes filled with tears. Steadying his voice that choked, restraining his grief, that king repeated what he had said to the Brahmana, "Though overtaken by calamity, chaste women still protect themselves, and thereby secure heaven. Even when deserted by their lords, chaste women never become angry, but continue to live sheathed in virtue's mail. Deserted by one fallen into calamity; bereft of sense, and deprived of bliss, it still does not become her to grow angry.

A virtuous woman must not be angry with one that had his garment taken by birds, as he strove to find food, one who, besides, burns in misery. The chaste woman would never be angry, after seeing her husband in that plight, despoiled of his kingdom, bereft of prosperity, oppressed by hunger, and overwhelmed by catastrophe."

Nala could not contain his grief anymore and began to cry. Kesini went back to Damayanti, and told her everything, also about the outburst of sorrow.

CANTO 75

NALOPAKHYANA PARVA CONTINUED

Brihadaswa says, 'Damayanti heard everything and sorrow overwhelmed her, too. She suspected the man beside the chariot was Nala.

She said, "O Kesini, go again and study Bahuka; staying silent beside him, mark his conduct. Lovely one, whenever he does anything skilful, mark it well, how he does it. And, Kesini, whenever he asks for water or fire, be in no hurry to give it to him. Study him carefully and come and tell me how he is and what he does, all that is human and also whatever is superhuman. Everything."

Kesini went to Bahuka and having observed him, that master of horses, with great care, she returned to Damayanti. She told Damayanti all that had happened, everything both human and superhuman that she had seen in Bahuka.

Kesini said, "Damayanti, I have never seen or even heard of a person of such control over the elements. Whenever he comes to a low passage, he never stoops down, but seeing him, the passage itself grows in height so that he may pass through it easily. At his approach, impassable narrow openings open wide.

King Bhima sent diverse kinds of meals, of various meats, for Rituparna's food. Many vessels have been set down there for washing the meat. As Bahuka looked at them, the vessels were full of water. Having washed the meat, he set himself to cook. He took up a handful of grass and held it in the sun, and fire blazed up all on a sudden.

I saw this marvel and came here amazed. Further, I witnessed other great wonders in him. Most beautiful one, he put his hand into the fire and was not burnt. And at his will, falling water flows in a stream.

Another still greater wonder I saw. He took some flowers and kneaded them slowly with his hands; they were not crushed but became brighter and more fragrant.

All these I saw and hurried back to you."

Damayanti heard all this and knew this was Nala and felt she already had him back. Suspecting that Bahuka was her husband, tears in her eyes, she said to Kesini softly, "My beautiful one, go out again and, without Bahuka knowing, fetch some meat that he has cooked."

Always eager to please Damayanti, Kesini went to where Bahuka was, and without him noticing, took some hot meat which he had prepared and took it back to Damayanti, who immediately tasted it. Having eaten meat cooked by Nala before, she felt even surer that Bahuka was her husband, and wept.

O Bhaarata, overwhelmed by grief, she then washed her face and sent her two children with Kesini, to Bahuka. Recognising Indrasena and her brother, he ran to them, embraced the children and took them onto his lap even as if they were children of the Devas. Shaken by deep sorrow, he wept aloud.

Naishadha then suddenly put them down and said to Kesini, "Fair maiden, these twins are so like my own children that seeing them suddenly made me cry. If you come often to me like this, people may think evil thoughts, for we are guests from another land. Therefore, blessed one, go at your ease.'"

CANTO 76

NALOPAKHYANA PARVA CONTINUED

Brihadaswa says, 'Seeing the agitation of the virtuous and wise Nala, Kesini went back to Damayanti and told her everything.

Sorrowing, eager to see Nala, Damayanti sent Kesini now to her mother, with this message: "I suspect that Bahuka is Nala and I have tested him in various ways. The only doubt which remains with me is his appearance, and I mean to examine him myself. Mother, either let him into the palace, or give me leave to go to him. Arrange this either with the knowledge of my father or without."

Her mother told Bhima of Damayanti's intention and he gave his consent. Bharatarishabha, with both her parents' consent, Damayanti had Nala fetched to her apartments. When he saw her, suddenly before him, Nala was overwhelmed and he sobbed and tears streamed down his face. Damayanti, best among women, saw him like that and she was also griefstricken.

O King, wearing a strip of red cloth and her hair matted in jata, covered with dust and dirt, Damayanti said, "O Bahuka, have you ever seen a man that knows dharma abandoning his sleeping wife in the heart of a jungle? Who but the virtuous Nala could desert his exhausted wife in the vana?

Of what offence was I guilty in his eyes, that my lord since my early youth should leave me like that and go away while I slept? Why did he whom I chose over the Devas abandon his devoted and always loving wife, and the mother of his children besides?

Before the sacred fire, and in presence of the gods, he took my hand, vowing, '*I will be yours.*' Oh, Parantapa, what happeed to that vow when he left me?'

As she spoke, tears flowed down her face. Nala also shed tears, black as of those of the gazelle with extremities of red.

He said, "Soft, gentle one, neither losing the kingdom nor abandoning you was my doing, but both were because of Kali. Best of chaste women, you cursed Kali in the forest and he possessed me, and began dwelling in my body. Burning with your curse, he lived in me like fire within fire.

Through vratas and tapasya, blessed one, I have vanquished that wretch so that our grief might end. The sinful spirit has left me and that is how I have come here. I have come here only for you and nothing else.

But, gentle one, will any other woman forsake her loving, devoted husband and seek a second lord as you have? At the command of the king, messengers are ranging this earth, crying, '*Bhima's daughter will choose a second husband worthy of her.*'

Immediately on hearing this, the son of Bhangasura has arrived here."

When she heard Nala lament thus, Damayanti, frightened and trembling, said with folded hands, "It does not become you, blessed one, to suspect any fault in me. King of the Nishadhas, I ignored the Devas themselves and chose you as my husband. It was to bring you here that the Brahmanas went forth in all directions, to every horizon, singing my words, as ballads.

Rajan, at last a learned Brahmana called Parnada found you in Kosala, in the palace of Rituparna. When you answered the message he carried, O Naishadha, I devised this plan to get you back.

Lord of the earth, there is no one in the world who can cover a hundred yojanas in a day with horses. O King, touching your feet, I can swear that I have never sinned, not even in thought.

May the all-witnessing Air that courses through this world take my life, if I have sinned. May the Sun that courses through the sky take my life, if I have sinned. May the Moon, that dwells within every creature as a witness, take my life, if I have sinned.

May these three Gods who sustain the three worlds in their entirety, declare that I speak the truth, or let them forsake me today."

The Wind-god said from the sky, "O Nala, I tell you truly, she has done no wrong. O King, Damayanti has protected your family honour, she has enhanced it. Of this we are the witnesses, as we have been her protectors for these three years. It is for your sake alone that she devised this unrivalled scheme, for, other than you, none on earth can travel a hundred yojans in a single day.

O Naishadha, you have found Bhima's daughter, and she has found you. You have no cause to be suspicious but be united with your wife."

When the Wind-god had spoken, flowers fell from the sky and drums of heaven sounded and auspicious breezes blew. Seeing those wonders, Nala Parantapa cast away all his doubts about Damayanti. He remembered the serpent king, put on the pure garment and regained his native form.

Seeing him back to himself, Bhima's daughter of faultless limbs embraced him and wept. Nala also clasped her, his devoted wife, and his children, and knew great joy. Burying her face in his chest, the lovely doe-eyed Damayanti began to sigh heavily, remembering her griefs. Overwhelmed, that tiger among men stood for some time, clasping the dust-covered Damayanti of sweet smiles.

Rajan, the queen-mother joyfully told Bhima everything that had passed between Nala and Damayanti. That mighty monarch said, "Let Nala pass this day in peace. I will see him tomorrow, after his bath and prayers, with Damayanti by his side."

Pleasantly the couple passed that night, also telling each other all about what had chanced with them in the forest. So, their hearts full of joy, Nala and the princess of Vidarbha passed their days in the palace of King Bhima, intent upon making each other happy.

It was four years after losing his kingdom that Nala was reunited with his wife and, all his desires gratified, once more experienced the highest bliss. Damayanti rejoiced at having recovered her lord even as fields of tender plants on receiving a shower of fine rain. Having Nala back, Bhima's daughter blazed forth in beauty, her weariness gone, her anxieties dispelled and welling over with joy, even like a night that is lit by the bright disc of the full moon!'"

NALOPAKHYANA PARVA CONTINUED

"Brihadaswa says, 'Having passed that night, Nala, wearing royal ornaments and with a radiant Damayanti by his side, presented himself before the king. Nala saluted his father-in-law with becoming humility; after him, the fair Damayanti paid her respects to her father.

With untold joy, the noble Bhima received him as a son, and honoured him duly with his devoted wife, and comforted them. Accepting the homage paid to him, Nala in return offered Bhima his services, as became him.

When the people saw Nala, they were overjoyed; an uproar of delight arose in the city. The citizens decorated the city with flags and standards and garlands of flowers; the streets were watered and decked in garlands. The people piled flowers at their gates, and all the shrines and temples were adorned with flowers.

Rituparna heard that Bahuka was united with Damayanti, and he was glad. He called Nala and begged his forgiveness. The intelligent Nala also asked Rituparna's forgiveness, for diverse reasons. After being honoured by Nala, Rituparna said to the Naishada, "Through good fortune you have been re-united with your own wife and you have found happiness. O Naishadha, while you lived in my house I hope I did not wrong you in any way, O lord of the earth! If I did knowingly do you any wrong, forgive me!"

Nala replied, "O King, you have never done me the slightest injury, and even if you did, you did not rouse my anger because you deserve to be forgiven. You were my friend and also, ruler of men, you are related to me. Now on, I will find greater delight in you because I lived so happily in your house, all my desires satisfied, indeed, more happily than in my own home.

This Aswa shastra, knowledge of horses, is something I have. If you wish, I will give it to you."

Saying this, Naishadha gave Rituparna that secret science and the latter took it with the ordained rites. Bhangasura's son thus received the mysteries of horses and taught Nala those of dice play; then, taking another charioteer, he returned to his own city.

Rajan, after Rituparna had gone, Nala did not stay long in the city of Kundina.'

CANTO 78

Nalopakhyana Parva Continued

Brihadaswa says, 'Kaunteya, Nala lived in Bhima's city for a month, then, with Bhima's leave, he set out from Kundina taking just a few men with him. With a single white chariot, sixteen elephants, fifty horses, and six hundred infantry, that illustrious king swiftly entered the Nishadha kingdom, his anger swollen and making the earth tremble.

Virasena's mighty son went to his brother Pushkara and said to him, "Let us play again, for I have earned vast wealth. Let Damayanti and everything else that I own be my stake, Pushkara, and let the kingdom be yours.

Let the play begin; I am determined. Let us stake everthing that we own along with our lives. Having won another's wealth or kingdom, it is high dharma to wager it again when the owner demands.

If you do not care to play with dice, let us contend with weapons instead. O King, let one of us, either you or I, find peace through single combat. The Rishis have all said that a lost ancestral kingdom must be recovered under all circumstances and by any means.

Pushkara, choose one of the two – gambling with dice or bending the bow in battle!"

The arrogant Pushkara answered laughingly, "Naishadha, it is good fortune that you have earned wealth enough to gamble, good fortune also that Damayanti's ill-luck has at last come to an end. O King, it is good fortune that you are still alive with your wife, Mahabaho.

I will win all your newfound wealth, and your Damayanti will wait upon me as an Apsara does upon Indra in heaven. O Naishadha, I think of you every day and have been waiting for you, for I find no pleasure in gambling with anyone not related to me by blood.

Today, I will win the exquisite Damayanti of faultless features and consider myself fortunate indeed, for she has always dwelt in my heart!"

Nala's eyes turned red with anger and he wanted to cut off Pushkara's head. However, instead, he said with a smile, "Let us play. You have vanquished me and you can say what you like. But come, let us play."

The game began between Pushkara and Nala, and in a single throw Nala won back everything that he had lost, along with the life of his brother, which had also been wagered.

Smiling, Nala said to Pushkara, "This whole kingdom is now mine, and, worst of men, you cannot even dare look at the princess of Vidarbha now. Fool, you and all your family shall now be her slaves.

But, though you did not know it, whatever you did was never your own doing, but Kali did it all. So, I shall not impute another's crime to you. Live happily, as you choose, I spare your life.

I also grant you your share in the kingdom and its wealth. Kshatriya, have no doubt that my affection for you is as before, undiminished, as is my brotherly love. You are my brother, Pushkara, live in peace and joy for a hundred years!"

Nala embraced Pushkara repeatedly and gave him leave to return to his own city. And Pushkara saluted his brother of dharma and said to him with folded hands, "O King who grant me both life and refuge, let your fame be immortal and may you live happily for ten thousand years!"

Entertained by the king, Pushkara lived there for a month and then went home to his own city, taking his kindred with him, as well as many obedient servants and a large force of soldiers; his heart was full of joy and that bull among men blazed forth in splendour like a second Surya.

Thus establishing Pushkara, giving him wealth and freeing him from his debt, Nala entered his own magnficent palace. The king of the Nishadhas now comforted his people; citizens and people from the countryside were awash with joy. Led by the officers of state, the people said with folded hands, "O King, throughout the city and the rest of the country your people rejoice today that we have our sovereign back, even like the Devas their Lord of a hundred yagnas!"'

CANTO 79

NALOPAKHYANA PARVA CONTINUED

Brihadaswa says, 'Fear of every kind left the city; it welled with joy. Nala took a large force with him and fetched Damayanti from her father's home. Bhima of awesome prowess, slayer of enemies, of immeasurable soul, sent his daughter back after honouring her duly.

When the princess of Vidarbha arrived, with her son and daughter, King Nala began to pass his days in delight even like the king of the Devas in the gardens of Nandana. Having regained his kingdom and shining forth among the kings of Jambu Dwipa, Nala ruled again. Numerous sacrifices he performed, with abundant gifts to Brahmanas.

Maharajan, Yudhishtira, you also will soon blaze forth in glory with your brothers and your kin. For, O best of men, it was through dice that great Nala and his wife fell into distress. Lord of the earth, Nala suffered direly, and all alone, before he recovered his prosperity, while you, Pandava, your heart set on dharma, sport in joy in this great forest, not alone but with your brothers and Krishnaa.

You keep the company of blessed Brahmanas who know the Vedas and their angas – you have small cause for sorrow. Besides, this itihasa of the Naga Karkotaka, of Damayanti, of Nala and of that Rajarishi Rituparna destroys evil. This tale of unfading glory banishes the influence of Kali, and it comforts those like you who listen to it.

Reflect upon the uncertainty of all human endeavour; it does not become you to exult or grieve at prosperity or adversity. Having listened to this tale, be comforted, O King, and do not yield to sorrow. A great king like you should not succumb to calamity.

Men of self-possession reflect upon the caprice of destiny and the futility of labour, and they never allow themselves to be dejected. Adversity will never lay its hand upon those who repeat the noble history of Nala, as well as those who listen to it.

He that listens to this old and excellent itihasa has his purposes crowned with success and, without doubt, finds fame, besides sons, grandsons, a high position among men, wealth and animals, health and happiness.

Also, Rajan, let me dispel forever the fear you keep in your heart that someone might summon you to another game of dice. Invincible Yudhishtira, I know the science of dice-play in its entirety. I am pleased with you, Kaunteya, take the arcane science from me.'"

Vaisampayana continued, "Gladly, then, Yudhishtira says to Brihadaswa, 'Illustrious one, I want to learn the science of dice play from you.'

The Rishi imparts that art to the high-souled son of Pandu, and having done so, the great Sage leaves for the sacred waters of Hayasirsha for his ablutions.

After Brihadaswa has gone, some Brahmanas and asetics, who come to him from various parts, from holy tirthas of pilgrimage, from mountains and forests, tell Yudhishtira Dridavrata that Arjuna of lofty intelligence, Savyasachin, still sits in the most austere tapasya, living only upon air.

Yudhishtira hears that Arjuna performs penance so fierce that none else has done before him. His mind controlled, his vows unfaltering, sworn to perfect mowna, Pritha's son Dhananjaya, through his tapasya, blazes forth like Dharma Deva himself in his embodied form.

O King, the Pandava hears that his precious brother sits in such a terrible penance in the great jungle, and grieves for him. His heart burning with sorrow, the eldest son of Pandu seeks consolation in that deep vana from the Brahmanas there, men of diverse and profound knowledge."

CANTO 80

TIRTHA-YATRA PARVA

Janamejaya said, "Holy one, after my great-grandfather Partha left the forest of Kamyaka, what did the sons of Pandu do? It seems to me that mighty ambidextrous bowman, vanquisher of armies, was their refuge, as Vishnu of the Devas. How did my heroic grandsires pass their time in the forest, without the company of that hero who was like Indra himself in prowess, and who never turned his back in battle?"

Vaisampayana said, "After Arjuna of unbaffled prowess leaves Kamyaka, the sons of Pandu, child, are filled with sorrow. The cheerless Pandavas are like pearls unstrung from their string, or birds shorn of their wings. Without that Kshatriya of the white horses, that forest is like the Chaitraratha vana without Kubera.

O Janamejaya, those Purushavyaghras continue to live in that forest, in sorrow. Those mighty Kshatriyas kill many kinds of sacrificial animals for their Brahmanas, with arrows purified with mantras. Daily they hunt those wild beasts and offer them to the Brahmanas after sanctifying them.

O King, those bulls among men continue to live in that vana, their hearts empty of all cheer after Dhananjaya's departure. Panchali, in particular, misses her third husband.

She says to the anxious Yudhishtira, 'Without Arjuna, who with two arms rivals the thousand-armed Arjuna of old, this forest has not beauty in my eyes. Without him, whenever I look, this earth seems forlorn. Even this vana with its blossoming trees and so full of marvels, holds no delight as it did before, without Arjuna.

Without him who is like a mass of blue clouds, who has the prowess of an infuriated elephant, and whose eyes are like the leaves of the lotus, ah, this Kamyaka does not seem beautiful in the least. I think of Savyasachin, the twang of whose bow is like thunder, and all that I feel is sorrow, O King!'

Hearing her, Bhimasena says, 'Blessed one of the slender waist, your words are like nectar to me. Without him, whose mighty arms adorned with golden bracelets, like a pair of five-headed snakes, are long and powerful as iron maces, round and marked by the abrasions of bowstrings, whose hands wield a bow and a sword and other weapons, without that tiger among men the sky itself seems to be without the sun.

Without that mighty-armed one, relying on whom the Panchalas and the Kauravas fear not the hosts of the Devas themselves, without that lustrous Kshatriya relying on whose arms we consider all our enemies already dead and the earth conquered, without our Phalguna I find no moment's peace in this Kamyaka vana.

Wherever I turn my gaze, the ten directions also seem to be empty!'

When Bhima finishes, Nakula, his voice choking with tears, says, 'What pleasure can we find here without him of whose extraordinary deeds on the field of battle even the gods speak, that greatest of warriors? Without him, who went north and vanquished hundreds of great Gandharva chieftains, and who having taken numberless magnificent horses of the Tittiri and Kalmasha breeds, all endowed with the speed of the wind, and gifted them in love to his brother, the king, during the

Rajasuya Yagna; without that beloved and luminous warrior, that terrible bowman born after Bhima, without that Kshatriya equal to a god, I have no wish to remain any longer in this Kamyaka aranya.'

After Nakula's lamentations, Sahadeva says, 'He vanquished mighty warriors in battle, won wealth and virgins and brought them unto the king on the occasion of the great Rajasuya. That immeasurably splendid Kshatriya singe-handedly vanquished all the Yadavas assembled together, and then took Subhadra for himself with Krishna's consent. He invaded Drupada's kingdom and gave Acharya Drona his dakshina. Ah, seeing his bed of grass empty in this asrama, my heart is breaking.

Bhaarata, Parantapa, I would prefer to leave this forest, for without Arjuna, there can be no trace of joy here.'"

CANTO 81

TIRTHA-YATRA PARVA CONTINUED

Vaisampayana said, "Yudhishtira's dejection deepens on hearing what his brothers and Panchali say, all of them distraught over the absence of Arjuna. Just then he sees the Devarishi Narada, ablaze with Brahmic beauty, like a fire flaming up at being fed sacrificial libations. Seeing Narada come, Raja Yudhishtira and his brothers stand up and duly worship the illustrious one. Himself blessed with great tejas, the handsome king of the Kurus shines forth like the God of a hundred sacrifices surrounded by the Devas. In obedience to the dictates of dharma, Yagnaseni follows her lords, the sons of Pritha, like Savitri follows the Vedas, or the rays of the Sun the peak of Meru.

Accepting their worship, Narada comforts Dharma's son. The Rishi says to Dharmaraja Yudhishtira, 'Tell me, O foremost of virtuous men, what it is you want and what I can do for you.'

Yudhishtira and his borthers bow reverently to Narada, whom the Devas worship, and Dharma's son, with folded hands, says, 'Lord, most blessed one, whom all the worlds worship, when you are pleased with me, I regard all my wishes as already fulfilled. If, O Sinless, my brothers and

I deserve your favour, I beg you, answer the question, the doubt, which is in my mind, O best of Munis. Tell me in detail what punya belongs to the man who travels the earth to visit the sacred waters and the shrines that are upon her.'

Narada says, 'O King, listen carefully to what the intelligent Bhishma heard from Pulastya. Once, that best of men, Bhishma, while keeping the Pitriya vrata, lived in the company of Munis in the auspicious and sacred tapovana near the source of the Ganga, where Devarishis, Gandharvas and the Devas themselves come.

Living there, the splendid Bhishma gratified the Pitrs, the Devas and the Rishis with oblations, according to the rites inculcated in the scriptures. One day, while he sat doing silent japa, he saw Pulastya, best of Rishis, altogether marvellous in appearance. Seeing that austere Sage, blazing with beauty, Bhishma was filled with great delight and wonder. O Bhaarata, Bhishma worshipped the blessed Rishi according to the rites of the Veda.

Purifying himself and with rapt attention, he approached that best of Brahmarishis, with the Arghya on his head. And uttering his name aloud, he said, "O you of excellent vows, be blessed! I am Bhishma, your slave. At the sight of you, I am set free from all my sins."

Saying this, Bhishma stood in silence and with joined hands. Seeing Bhishma, that greatest of the Kurus, reduced and emaciated by the observance of vows and the study of the Vedas, the Muni was filled with joy.'

CANTO 82

TĪRTHA-YATRA PARVA CONTINUED

'Pulastya said, "O you of excellent vows, I am very pleased with your humility, your self-control, and your truth, blessed one, knower of dharma. Sinless one, it is the punya which you have acquired through your devotions to your ancestors that has pleased me and, O child, given you sight of my person.

Bhishma, my sight penetrates all things. Tell me what I can do for you. Anagha, Kurusthama, I will give you whatever you ask for."

Bhishma said, "O most blessed one, when you, whom the three worlds worship are pleased with me and I have seen you with my eyes, I think of myself as being already crowned with success. Yet, if I have deserved your favour, most virtuous and holy one, allow me to tell you some religious doubts I have in regard to the tirthas, and dispel them for me.

Tell me in detail about the tirthas. O you who are like a Deva, what is the punya of a man who goes round the earth visiting the sacred tirthas and shrines? O answer me this with certainty."

Pulastya said, "O son, listen with attention, I will tell you about the punya which is attached to the tirthas and which is the refuge of the

Rishis. He whose hands and feet and mind and knowledge and asceticism and deeds are under wholesome control, enjoys the fruit of the tirthas. He who has ceased to accept gifts, he that is contented, he that is free from pride enjoys the fruits of the tirthas. He that is without sin, he that acts without desire, he that eats light, he that has his senses under control, he that is free from every sin, enjoys the fruits of tirthas.

O King, he that is free from anger, he who cleaves to truth, he that is firm in his vows, he that regards all creatures as his own self, enjoys the fruit of the tirthas. In the Vedas, the Rishis have declared in due order the sacrifices and also their fruits, here and hereafter truly. O lord of the earth, those yagnas cannot be accomplished by him that is poor, for those sacrifices require diverse materials and offerings in large measures. These, therefore, can be performed by kings or sometimes by other men of prosperity and wealth.

However, O lord of men, best of warriors, let me now declare to you that rite which men without wealth, without allies, singly, without wife and children, and destitute of means, can accomplish, whose punya is equal to the sacred fruit of sacrifices. O Bharatottama, visiting the sacred tirthas, which constitute one of the high mysteries of the Rishis, is superior even to sacrifices.

He is a poor man who goes to a tirtha without fasting for three nights, without giving gold as alms, without distributing kine. Why, not by the performance of the Agnishtoma and other sacrifices distinguished by large gifts, does a man acquire the punya which visiting a tirtha confers.

In the world of men, there is that tirtha of the God of gods, celebrated throughout the three worlds by the name Pushkara. One that journeys there becomes equal to Brahma. O noble son of the Kurus, during the three sandhyas – dawn, noon and dusk – there is the presence of a hundred thousand million of tirthas in Pushkara. The Adityas, the Vasus, the Rudras, the Sadhyas, the Maruts, the Gandharvas, and the Apsaras are always present in Pushkara. It was there, O King, that the Devas, the Daityas and Brahmarishis performed tapasya and gained vast punya, and attained godhood.

Men of self-control are purified of their sins by merely thinking of Pushkara, and find high regard in heaven. Rajan, the illustrious Pitamaha, who has the Lotus for his throne, once dwelt with great joy in this tirtha. Having of old acquired great punya, it was in Pushkara that the Devas and the Rishis found moksha.

The wise say that one who is devoted to the worship of the Devas and the Pitrs, and bathes in this tirtha, gains punya which is equal to ten times that of the Aswamedha Yagna. Having gone to the forest of Pushkara, he that feeds even one Brahmana becomes happy here and hereafter, O Bhishma, for that single act. He who lives on vegetables, roots and fruits, may, with pious regard and without disrespect, give even such fare to a Brahmana, and he will gain the punya of a horse-sacrifice.

Illustrious Brahmanas, Kshatriyas, Vaisyas or Sudras that bathe in Pushkara are set free from rebirth. In particular, that man who visits Pushkara on the full moon of the month of Kartika acquires everlasting regions in Brahmaloka. O Bhaarata, he who remembers Pushkara with folded hands, morning and evening, as good as bathes in every tirtha.

Man or woman, one's every sin since being born is destroyed as soon as one bathes in Pushkara. As Madhusudana, the slayer of Madhu, is the first among all the gods, so is Pushkara, the foremost of all tirthas. He who lives a pure life, regulated by vratas, for twelve years in Pushkara gains the merit of all the sacrifices, and goes to the abode of Brahma. The punya of one who performs the Agnihotra for full one hundred years is equal to that of him who spends the single month of Kartika in Pushkara.

There are three white hillocks and three springs known from the remotest times which, we do not know why, go by the name of Pushkara. It is difficult to go to Pushkara; it is difficult to do tapasya at Pushkara; it is difficult to give alms in Pushkara; and it is difficult to live in Pushkara.

Having stayed twelve nights at Pushkara, with regulated diet, and vows, and having walked in pradakshina around the place, one should then go to Jambumarga. He that travels to Jambumarga, where the

Devas, the Rishis and the Pitrs go, acquires the punya of the Aswamedha and the fruition of all his wishes. The man who remains there for five nights has his soul cleansed from all sins. He never sinks into hell, but acquires lofty success.

Leaving Jambumarga, one should journey to Tandulikasrama. He who visits this tirtha never devolves into Naraka but rises into Brahmaloka. He that goes to the lake of Agastya and, fasting for three nights, worships the Pitrs and the Devas, acquires the merits of the Agnishtoma. He who subsists there on fruit or vegetables gains the condition known as Kaumara, lasting youth.

Next, the pilgrim should take himself to the beautiful asrama of Kanva, which is worshipped by the whole world. That sacred forest has existed, Bharatarishabha, from the most ancient times. As soon as a man enters it, he is freed from all his sins. He who controls what he eats and observes vratas, while worshipping the ancestors and god there, obtains the fruit of a sacrifice which can bestow all desires.

Having circumambulated this asrama, the pilgrim must then go to the place where Yayati fell from heaven. He who comes to this place gains the merit of a horse-sacrifice.

Next, one must journey to Mahakala, with senses; bathing there in the tirtha called Koti, one gains the punya of another Aswamedha. Next, a virtuous man should go to the tirtha of Sthanu, the husband of Uma, the sacred place known through the three worlds as Bhadravata. The man who visits Bhadravata has a vision of Isana and gains the punya of making a gift of a thousand holy cows. Through the grace of Mahadeva, he acquires the state of Ganapatya, blessed with peace, prosperity and great auspiciousness.

He that then comes to the Narmada, the river celebrated throughout the three worlds, and offers oblations of water to the manes and the gods, acquires the punya of an Aswamedha.

He who keeps bramacharya and goes into the Southern Ocean, his senses subdued, gains the fruit of the Agnishtoma yagna and ascends into Swarga.

Food and senses controlled, he who journeys to Charmanwati, also gains the merit of the Agnishtoma, at the command of Rantideva. One must next go, O virtuous lord of Kshtariyas, to Arbuda, the son of Himavat, where there was a hole right through the earth in days of yore. Here there is the asrama of Vasistha, renowned through the three worlds. Spending one night here, one gains the punya of giving a gift of a thousand cows.

Kshatriyavyaghra, the brahmacharin who bathes in the tirtha called Pinga obtains the merit of having made a gift of a thousand Kapila cows. One must go next, O King, to that excellent tirtha called Prabhasa. There Agni Hutasana is always present in his own person. He, the friend of Pavana, O hero, is the mouth of all the gods. The man who, with his souls subdued and sanctified, bathes at that tirtha finds punya greater than even that of the Agnishtoma or Atiratra sacrifices.

Journeying next to the place where the Saraswati mingles with the sea, one obtains the fruit of the gift of a thousand kine and heaven also besides, O Bharatarishabha, blazing forth for all time like Agni himself. His mind and heart subdued, he who bathes in the tirtha of the King of waters, and offers oblations of water to the manes and the gods, remaining there for three nights, blazes forth like the Moon, and also gets the punya of the Aswamedha.

The pilgrim must continue, Bharatasreshta, to the tirtha known as Varadana, where Durvasa gave Vishnu a boon. A man by bathing in Varadana obtains the fruit of a thousand kine. Next, he should procceds to Dwaravati, where by bathing in Pindaraka he can gain an abundant gift of gold. Blessed one, wonderful to tell, to this day in that tirtha, coins with the mark of the lotus, and lotuses also with the mark of the trident, are seen, O Kshatriyavijaya! Bull among men, the presence of Mahadeva is there.

Then, O Bhaarata, arriving at the place where the Sindhu flows into the sea, one should with subdued soul, bathe in that tirtha of Varuna. Bathing there and giving oblations of water to the Pitrs, the Rishis, and the Devas one acquires the realm of Varuna, and blazes forth in effulgence. Men of wisdom say that by worshipping the god known as Shankukarneswara a man acquires ten times the merit of the horse-sacrifice.

Bharatarishabha, having walked round that tirtha, one should go on to Drimi, another tirtha celebrated throughout the three worlds. This tirtha cleanses from every sin, and it is here that the gods, including Brahma, worship Maheswara. Having bathed there and worshipped Rudra, surrounded by the other gods, one is freed from all sins since birth. It was there, O best of men, that Drimi was adored by the Devas. Bathing there, Purushottama, one surely gains the fruit of the horse-sacrifice, for O you of great intelligence, after killing the Daityas and Danavas, Vishnu the creator of the universe went there to purify himself.

Virtuous, the pilgrim goes next to Vasudhara adored by all. The moment one arrives at that tirtha, one acquires the fruit of the horse-sacrifice. Kurusthama, by bathing there with subdued soul and rapt attention, and giving oblations of water to the Devas and Pitrs, one ascends into Vishnuloka and is adored there.

In that tirtha, O Bharatarishabha, there is a sacred lake of the Vasus. By bathing there and drinking its water, a man becomes honoured by the Vasus.

There is a famed tirtha of the name Sindhuttama, which destroys every sin. By bathing there, one gains gold in plenitude. By going in a state of purity to Bhadratunga, one gains Brahmaloka and a condition of great blessedness.

Then there is the tirtha of the Kumarika of Indra, much resorted to by the Siddhas. O best of men, bathing there, a pilgrim obtains Indraloka. In Kumarika there is another tirtha called Renuka, which also the Siddhas go to. A Brahmana who bathes there becomes as lustrous as the Moon.

Journeying next, senses subdued and food regulated, to the tirtha called the Panchananda, one obtains the fruit of the five sacrifices that have been mentioned one after another in the scriptures. Then one should go to the excellent realm of Bhima. Best of the Bhaaratas, bathing in the tirtha there, which is called Yoni, a man, in his next birth, becomes the son of a goddess, wearing earrings adorned with pearls, and also gains the punya of making a gift of a hundred thousand cows.

Going next to Srikunda, celebrated through the three worlds, and worshipping the Pitamaha, one obtains the fruit of the gift of a thousand kine. After this, one should go to the excellent tirtha called Vimala, where to this day fish of golden and silver hues can be seen. Bathing there, one quickly acquires the region of Vasava, where one's soul being cleansed of every sin, one attains a high state of blessedness.

O Bhaarata, going next to Vitasta and offering oblations of water to the manes and the gods, a man is purified of all his sins, gains the fruit of the Vajapeya sacrifice and a high state of blessedness. That sin-destroying tirtha known as Vitasta is in the country of the Kasmiras and is the abode of the Naga Takshaka.

One should next proceed to Badava famed throughout the three worlds. Bathing there with due rites in the evening, one should offer rice boiled in butter and milk, according to the best of his might, to the deity of seven flames. Men of wisdom say that a gift made here in honour of the Pitrs, becomes inexhaustible.

The Rishis, the Pitrs, the Devas, the Gandharvas, several tribes of Apsaras, the Guhyakas, the Kinnaras, the Yakshas, the Siddhas, the Vidhyadharas, the Rakshasas, Daityas, Rudras, and Brahma himself, with their senses subdued, performed tapasya for a thousand years at Badava in order to move Vishnu to grace.

They cooked rice in milk and butter and gratified Kesava with oblations, each offered with seven Riks at which, the gratified Kesava conferred on them the eight-fold attributes called Aiswarya and other objects that they desired. Having bestowed these, that God disappeared from their sight like lightning in the clouds. And it is for this, O Bhaarata, that that tirtha became known as Saptacharu, and if one offers Charu there to the seven flamed god, one obtains punya superior to that of the gift of a hundred thousand cows, to that of a hundred Rajasuya sacrifices, as also of a hundred Aswamedhas.

Leaving Badava, the pilgrim travels to Raudrapada, and seeing Mahadeva there, obtains the merit of the Aswamedha. Then, soul subdued, observing brahmacharya, he goes to Manimata, and staying there for one night, acquires the merit of the Agnishtoma.

One should then go to Devika celebrated throughout the world. It was there, O Bharatarishabha, that, as I have heard, the Brahmanas first sprang into existence. This is also the realm of the Trisulin, a place famed everywhere. Having bathed in Devika and worshipped Maheswara by offering him, to the best of one's means, rice boiled in milk and butter, a man obtains the merit of a sacrifice that can fulfil every desire.

There also is another tirtha of Rudra's, Kamakhya, which is much resorted to by the gods. Bathing there, a man swiftly finds success. By touching the waters of Yajana, Brahmavaluka, and Pushpamba, one becomes free from sorrow in the afterlife. The learned have said that the sacred tirtha of Devika, resort of the Devas and the Rishis, is five Yojanas in length and half a Yojana in breadth.

The pilgrim next, in due order, journeys to Dirghasatra. There the gods with Brahma at their head, the Siddhas, and the greatest Rishis, with regulated vows and the chanting and acceptance of the initiatory pledge, perform the long-extending sacrifice. By going only to Dirghasatra, O Parantapa, one gains punya which is superior to that of the Rajasuya or the Aswamedha.

Senses restrained, diet controlled, one should next go to Vinasana, where the Saraswati disappearing on the breast of Meru, reappears at Chamasa, Shivodbheda and Nagodbheda. Bathing in Chamasodbheda, one gets the punya of the Agnishtoma sacrifice. Bathing in Shivodbheda, one acquires the merit of the gift of a thousand kine. And bathing in Nagodbheda, one gains the realm of the Nagas.

One should go on to the well-nigh inaccessible tirtha of Shasayana, where the cranes, O Bhaarata, disappearing in the forms of sasas, reappear every year in the month of Kartika, and bathe in the Sarsawati. Bathing there, O tiger among men, one shines forth like the Moon, and obtains the merit of the gift of a thousand kine.

Next the pilgrim must go to Kumarakoti, with subdued senses, and bathing there, worship the gods and the manes. By doing this, he gains the punya of the gift of ten thousand kine, and raises all his ancestors into higher realms.

After this, virtuous one, proceed with subdued soul to Rudrakoti, where in olden days ten million Munis gathered. Filled with great joy at the prospect of beholding Mahadeva, the Rishis each cried, 'I will be the first to see the God!' And, in order to prevent disputes amongst those Rishis, the Lord of Yoga multiplied himself into ten million forms and appeared simultaneously before every Sage, so every one cried, 'I have seen Him first!'

Gratified with the deep devotion of those self-controlled Munis, Mahadeva granted them a boon, saying, *'From this day your dharma shall grow'* 'O tiger among men, he that bathes, with a pure mind, in Rudrakoti obtains the merit of the horse-sacrifice and delivers his ancestors.

One should next go to that most sacred and famed confluence where the Saraswati enters the sea. There, the Devas with Brahma at their head, and Rishis with a wealth of asceticism, repair to adore Kesava, on the fourteenth day of the lighted fortnight of the month of Chaitra. Bathing there, O tiger among men, one obtains the merit of giving away an abundance of gold; and his soul cleansed from every sin, he ascends into Brahmaloka. It is here, O Kshatriya, that the Rishis have performed numberless yagnas. A pilgrimage to this place confers the punya of giving away a thousand holy cows."

CANTO 83

TIRTHA-YATRA PARVA CONTINUED

Pulastya said, "One should next travel to the adored Kurukshetra, the sight of which can free any creature at all from all sins. Why, a man who says 'I will live in Kurukshetra', constantly, is set free from his sins. The very dust of Kurukshetra, blown by the wind, leads a sinful man to a blessed course in life and the afterlife.

They that dwell in Kurukshetra, which lies to the south of the Saraswati and to the north of the Drishadwati, are said to dwell in heaven. O greatest of Kshatriyas, one should remain there for a month. There, lord of earth, the gods with Brahma at their head, the Rishis, the Siddhas, the Charanas, the Gandharvas, the Apsaras, the Yakshas and the Nagas, come often, O Bhaarata, to the most holy Brahmakshetra.

The sins of one who merely wishes fervently to visit Kurukshetra are all destroyed, and he finally goes into the world of Brahma. Kurunandana, by visiting Kurukshetra in a pious frame of mind, one obtains the fruit of the Rajasuya and Aswamedha Yagnas.

Next, the tirthayatri salutes the Yaksha Mankanaka, Kubera's mighty dwarapalaka, and gains the punya of giving away a thousand kine.

After this, one should repair to the excellent realm of Vishnu, where Hari is always present. Bathing there and bowing down to Hari, the Creator of the three worlds, one obtains the fruit of the Aswamedha and goes to the abode of Vishnu. One should next go to Pariplava, that tirtha celebrated across the three worlds, and bathing there, O Bhaarata, one finds punya that is greater than that of the Agnishtoma and the Atiratra sacrifices.

Journeying next to the tirtha called Prithivi, one gets the fruit of a gift of a thousand kine. The pilgrim should next travel to Shalukini and bathing there in the Dasaswamedha one gains the punya the merit of ten horse-sacrifices. Going on to Sarpadevi, most excellent tirtha of the Nagas, one obtains the merit of the Agnishtoma Yagna and attains to the realm of the Nagas.

After this, the pilgrim goes on to Tarantuka, the gate-keeper, and staying there for one night he obtains the merit of giving away a thousand sacred cows. On he goes, with subdued senses and his food regulated, to Panchananda and bathing in the tirtha there, called Koti, one gains the fruit of the horse-sacrifice.

Proceeding to the tirtha of the twin Aswins, he gets great personal beauty. Virtuous one, one should next go to the fine tirtha called Varaha, where Vishnu once stood in the form of a boar. Bathing there, O best of men, one gains the merit of the horse-sacrifice.

One should next repair to the tirtha called Soma in Jayanti. Bathing there one acquires the merit of the Rajasuya sacrifice. By bathing in Ekahamsa, a man obtains the punya of giving away a thousand cows. A pilgrim who goes to Kritasaucha gains the lotus-eyed Lord Vishnu and perfect purity of soul.

After this, he should go on to Munjavata, a place sacred to the illuminous Sthanu. Remaining there without eating for one night, he acquires the condition of Ganapatya. Then there is the celebrated tirtha Yakshini, bathing at which a man attains the fruition of all his desires. Bharatarishabha, that tirtha is regarded as the gateway of Kurukshetra. His mind absorbed in dhyana, the pilgrim should walk around it. Equal to the

Pushkaras, it was created by the high-souled Rama, the son of Jamadagni. Bathing there and worshipping the ancestors and the gods, one gains the punya of the horse-sacrifice and becomes successful in everything.

Next, the rapt pilgrim goes on the Ramahrada. There, as we have heard, the heroic Rama of resplendent energy exterminated the Kshatriyas with his might, dug five lakes and filled them, O tiger among men, with the blood of his victims. And having filled those lakes with Kshatriya blood, Rama offered oblations of blood to his sires and grandsires.

Gratified, those Rishis then addressed Rama, 'O Rama, Rama, O you of great good fortune, we are pleased with you, O you of the Bhrigu race, for this your regard for the Pitrs, and for your prowess, O exalted one! Be blessed, and ask for the boons of your choice. What is it that you want, O you of great splendour?'

Rama folded his hands to the manes in the sky, and said, 'If you are pleased with me and I deserve your favour, O Pitrs, let me have the joy of doing tapasya again. Let me also, through your power, be freed from the sin of wrath I have committed of exterminating the Kshatriya race. Also let these my lakes become tirthas celebrated the world over.'

Gratified, joyful to hear him, the Pitrs answered him, 'Let your tapasya increase because of the regard for the Pitrs. You have exterminated the Kshatriyas in wrath. You are already free from that sin for they perished from their own crimes. Have no doubt, these lakes of yours shall become tirthas. And if anyone bathed in these lakes, offering tarpana to the manes, they will grant him his desire in this world, however difficult it might be, and also eternal heaven.'

Having granted him these boons, the Pitrs joyfully saluted Rama of the Bhrigus and vanished. It was thus that the lakes of the illustrious Rama became sacred.

Keeping Brahmacharya and observing sacred vows, one should bathe in the lakes of Rama. Bathing there and worshipping Rama, one obtains the merit of a gift of gold in abundance.

The pilgrim next takes himself, O Kurunandana, to Vamsamulaka, and by bathing there uplifts and exalts all his race. Going after this to the tirtha Kayasodhana, and bathing there, he purifies his body, and ascends to the realm of unrivalled grace.

He next repairs to that tirtha, celebrated across the three worlds, called Lokodwara, where once Vishnu of great prowess created the worlds. Arriving at that tirtha, which is adored by the three worlds, and bathing there one earns many lofty worlds for oneself.

Mind subdued, he goes next to the tirtha known as Sri; bathing there, worshipping the gods and manes, he acquires great felicity. Sworn to Brahmacharya, absorbed in dhyana, he should next take himself to Kapila tirtha. Bathing there and worshipping one's own ancestors and the Devas, a man earns the fruit of the gift of a thousand Kapila cows.

Repairing next to the tirtha called Surya and bathing there, heart quietened and worshipping the Pitrs and the Devas, fasting all the while, he gains the punya of the Agnishtoma sacrifice and goes finally to the Suryaloka, realm of the Sun.

The pilgrim travels next to Gobhavana and bathing there obtains the merit of the gift of a thousand kine. O son of the Kurus, he next jounreys to the tirtha called Shankhini and bathing in the Devi-tirtha that is there, gains awesome prowess.

O Kshatriya, he should go next then to the tirtha called Tarandaka situated in the Saraswati and belonging to the lustrous chief of the Yakshas who is one of the gate-keepers of Kubera. Bathing there, he gains the punya of the Agnishtoma Yagna.

Virtuous Kuru, one should next go to the tirtha called Brahmavarta. Bathing in Brahmavarta, one ascends to the abode of Brahma. After this, he seeks the sacred tirtha Sutirtha. Here, the Pitrs are ever-present along with the Devas. One should bathe here and worship the manes and the gods. By so doing, one acquires the punya of the horse-sacrifice and goes into the realm of the Pitrs. This is why the Sutirtha in Ambumati is regarded as being so auspicious.

And, Bharatottama, bathing in the Kasiswara tirtha, a man is set free from every disease and is adored in Brahmaloka. There, in that tirtha, is another called Matri; one who bathes in the Matri tirtha has many children and finds great fortune.

The pilgrim next goes, in self-restraint, to the tirtha called Sitavana, whose punya has been observed to be rare and such as hardly any other owns. He who merely goes there becomes holy. O Bhaarata, by offering his hair in that tirtha, the pilgrim acquires great sanctity. In that tirtha, is another called Swavillomapaha, where, O tiger among men, learned Brahmanas go to obtain profound satisfaction by bathing in its waters. Offering their hair in this tirtha, too, good Brahmanas acquire holiness through pranayama and attain a lofty spiritual state.

In that tirtha is also another called Dasaswamedhika, by bathing in which too an exalted spiritual condition can be attained.

One should next proceed to the famed tirtha called Manusha where, once, a herd of black antelope wounded by a hunter's arrows, plunged into its waters, and they were transformed into human beings. Bathing in that tirtha, while observing continence and with one's mind focused in dhyana, a man is freed from all his sins and is worshipped in heaven.

A krosa to the east of Manusha is the renowned river Apaga that the Siddhas resort to. The man who offers syamaka grain here, in honour of the gods and the manes acquires great religious merit; if one Brahmana is fed here, it is equal to feeding ten million Brahmanas. Having bathed in that tirtha and worshipped the Devas and the Pitrs, and staying there for one night, a man gains the merit of the Agnishtoma.

Then, O Bhaarata, the pilgrim should go to that auspicious tirtha of Brahma, known as Brahmodumbara. Bathing in the tank of the seven Rishis which is there, O bull among men, with his diet and mind restrained, as also in the tirtha Kedara of the great-souled Kapila, and beholding Brahma who is there, the pilgrim's soul is purified of every sin and he goes to the abode of Brahma.

Also, by burning his sins through performing tapasya at the almost inaccessible Kedara tirtha of Kapila, he acquires the siddhi of being able to vanish at will.

The pilgrim continues his journey and goes to the renowned tirtha called Saraka, and seeing Mahadeva there on the fourteenth day of the dark fortnight, he gets everything he might wish for and also goes to heaven. O son of the Kuru race, in Saraka and Rudrakoti and in the well and the lakes that are there, thirty million tirthas are present.

In that place is another tirtha called Ilaspada. After bathing there and worshipping the gods and the ancestors, one will never sink into hell but gain the merit of the Vajapeya Yagna.

Repairing next to Kindana and Kinjapya, the pilgrim gains the punya of giving away boundless charity as also an infinite recitation of prayers. Once he journeys to the Kalasi tirtha, and bathing there devoutly, his senses under control, he gains the fruit of the Agnishtoma.

To the east of Saraka, is an auspicious tirtha, Ambajanma, of the Mahatman Narada. He that bathes there, O Bhaarata, finds, after dying, many unrivalled realms of glory, at the command of Narada Muni.

Next, on the tenth day of the lighted fortnight, the pilgrim should go to the tirtha called Pundarika. Bathing there, he gains the merit of the Pundarika Yagna. After this, he must go to the tirtha called Trivishtapa, famed through the three worlds. In that tirtha flows the sacred and sin-destroying river Vaitarani. Bathing there and adoring the god known by the mark of the bull who holds the trident in his hand, the pilgrim's soul is washed of every sin and he attains to the highest state.

Then, he proceeds to the excellent Phalakivana. In this holiest tirtha the Devas performed a tapasya of many thousand years. One should then go on to the Dhrishadwati. Bathing there and worshipping the gods, one obtains, O Bhaarata, punya which is superior to that of both the Agnishtoma and the Atiratra sacrifices.

Bathing in that Sarvadeva tirtha, a man acquires the merit of giving away a thousand cows. Bathing next in the Panikhata tirtha and worshipping all the gods, a man finds punya superior to that of both the Agnishtoma and the Atiratra sacrifices, besides acquiring that of the Rajasuya Yagna; and finally, he attains the realm of the highest Rishis.

Dharmatma, after this, one must visit the Misraka tirtha. There, O tiger among kings, as I have heard, the great-souled Vyasa, for the sake of the Brahmanas, has mingled all the tirthas. He, therefore, that bathes in Misraka bathes in all the tirthas.

Mind and senses restrained, the yatri goes next to the tirtha Vyasavana. Bathing in the sacred waters of Manojava there, he gains the punya of the gift of a thousand cows. He goes on to the Devitirtha which is in Madhuvati; whoever bathes here and worships the manes and the gods receives the spiritual merit of a gift of a thousand cows, through the grace of the Goddess.

He who then bathes at the confluence of the Kausiki and the Dhrishadwati is freed from all his sins. He proceeds to Vyasasthali where Vyasa of great intelligence, burning with grief for his son, had resolved to cast off his body but was put in good heart again by the gods. Here the pilgrim gains the merit of the making a gift of a thousand kine.

Journeying on to the sacred well called Kindatta, he who casts a measure of sesame into it is freed from all his debts and finds success. Bathing in the tirtha called Vedi, one obtains the merit of making a gift of a thousand cows. There are two other celebrated tirthas called Ahas and Sudina. Bathing there, Purushavyaghra, one goes to the realm of the Sun.

The pilgrim continues to the tirtha called Mrigadhuma that is celebrated throughout the three worlds. Here he bathes in the Ganga, worships Mahadeva, and obtains the punya of the Aswamedha Yagna. Bathing next in the Devitirtha there he obtains the merit of the gift of a thousand sacred cows.

He goes on to Vamanaka, also celebrated across the three worlds. Bathing there in Vishnupada and worshipping Vamana, his soul is purified from every sin, and he goes to the abode of Vishnu.

Bathing next in Kulampuna, one sanctifies one's race. Going after this to the Pavana-hrada, that great tirtha of the Marutas, and bathing there, O tiger among men, one becomes adored in the realm of the

Wind-god. Bathing in the Amara-hrada and worshipping Indra with devotion, the pilgrim becomes adored in Devaloka and he will sit in a scintillating vimana and course through the sky in the company of the immortals.

Best of great men, bathing next with due rites in the tirtha called Sali surya, of Salihotra, he acquires the punya of the gift of a thousand kine. Bhaaratottama, there is another tirtha called Srikunja in the Saraswati. Bathing there, one gains the merit of the Agnishtoma sacrifice.

The pilgrim goes next to Naimishakunja. In days of yore, the Rishis who performed tapasya in the Naimisha vana took the vows of pilgrimage and went to Kurukshetra. There, on the banks of the Saraswati a tapovana was created, which served as a resting place for them and which pleased them greatly. Bathing in the Saraswati in that sacred grove, one obtains the merit of the Agnishtoma sacrifice.

O Virtuous, one should go after this to the excellent Kanya tirtha. Bathing there one obtains the merit of the gift of a thousand kine. Then, on to the tirtha of Brahma. Bathing here, a person of the inferior varnas becomes a Brahmana, and if he is already a Brahmana, his soul is purified of every sin, and he attains moksha.

After this, the pilgrim journeys to the auspicious Soma tirtha, bathing at which place, he gains the world of Soma. The yatri now proceeds to the tirtha called Saptasaraswata, where the renowned Rishi Mankanaka found ascetic success. As I have heard, in olden days, Mankanaka cut his hand with a pointed blade of Kusa grass, upon which, from his wound flowed not blood but vegetable sap. Seeing this, his eyes wide with wonder, the Sage began to dance. And as the Rishi danced, all the mobile and immobile creatures, overwhelmed by his power, began to dance with him.

Then, the Devas with Brahma at their head, and Rishis of vast tapasya said to Mahadeva, 'Lord, you must stop the Sage from dancing.'

His heart full of joy, Siva went to the dancing Rishi and said, 'Maharishi, most virtuous one, why do you dance? O bull among Munis, what can be the reason for this great joy?'

The Rishi answered, 'O best of Brahmanas, I am an ascetic who treads the path of dharma. Do you not see that vegetable sap flows from the wound in my hand? This fills me with great joy and I dance.'

To the Rishi blinded by emotion, the God laughingly said, 'O Brahmana, I do not wonder at this. Look at me!'

Mahadeva made a cut on his own thumb with the nail of his forefinger, and lo, from the wound there came ashes white as snow. Seeing this, the Muni became ashamed and fell at Siva's feet, and believing that there was nothing better and greater than the God Rudra, he began to hymn him: 'O Trisulin, you are the refuge of the Devas and the Asuras, of, indeed, the universe. You have created the three worlds with all their beings, mobile and unmoving. It is you again that swallow everything at the end of the Yuga. Not the gods themselves can know you, far less me. O sinless one, the Devas with Brahma at their head are all revealed in you. You are all, the Creator himself and the Ordainer of the worlds. It is by your grace that all the gods sport without anxiety or fear.

Devadeva, God of gods, grant me your grace, so that my tapasya may not diminish.'

The God replied, 'Brahmana, let your tapasya increase a thousandfold through my grace. Great Muni, I will dwell with you in this your asrama. Those who bathe here in Saptasaraswata, and worship me, will attain everything here and hereafter. And without doubt they shall all attain finally to the realm of Saraswata.'

With that, Mahadeva vanished.

After visiting Saraswata, one should travel on to Ausanasa, also famed throughout the three worlds. There, Bhaarata, the gods with Brahma before them, and Rishis endowed with the wealth of asceticism, and the illustrious Kartikeya, are always present during the two twilights and midday, impelled by the desire to do good to Bhargava.

In that tirtha is another called Kapalamochana, which cleanses one from every sin. O tiger among men, bathing there the taint of all one's sins vanish.

The pilgrim should then proceed to the tirtha called Agni. Bathing there, Purusharishabha, one obtains the worlds of Agni and raises his very race. There in that tirtha is another, O lord of the Bhaaratas, that belongs to Viswamitra. Bathing there, best of men, one gains the status of a true Brahmana.

Purushavyaghra, the pilgrim, his body pure and his mind subdued, goes on to Brahmayoni, and bathing there at the abode of Brahma, he sanctifies his race for seven generations before and after.

Next, he travels to another tirtha renowned through the worlds, Prithudaka, which belongs to Kartikeya. He bathes there, worshipping the Devas and the Pitrs. Whatever evil any man or woman has committed, knowingly or otherwise, is destroyed by a bath in that sacred tirtha, which also confers the punya of an Aswamedha and Swarga, as well. The learned say that Kurukshetra is holy; holier than Kurukshetra is the Saraswati; holier than the Saraswati are all the tirthas together, and that holier than all the tirthas together is Prithudaka.

He who casts off his body at Prithudaka, while chanting holy mantras, becomes an immortal. Sanatkumara and the high-souled Vyasa have sung, and it is in the Vedas also, that one should indeed go to Prithudaka, with soul subdued. O son of the Kurus, there is no tirtha which is superior to Prithudaka. Without doubt, that tirtha is purifying, holy and sin-destroying. The most sinful man who bathes in Prithudaka goes to heaven.

O best of the Bhaaratas, in that tirtha is another called Madhustrava; bathing there, one acquires the merit of giving away a thousand cows.

After this, the pilgrim must proceed to the calebrated and sacred tirtha where the Saraswati unites with the Aruna. Bathing there, after fasting for three nights, one is cleansed of even the sin of killing a Brahmana, and obtains punya that is superior to that of either the Agnishtoma or Atiratra sacrifice, and redeems his race to the seventh generation, up and down.

In that tritha is another called Ardhakila. From compassion for the Brahmanas, Darbhi created that tirtha in days of old. Without doubt, by vows, by investiture of the sacred thread, by fasts, by rites and by mantras, one becomes a Brahmana. However, Bharatarishabha, wise men of old have observed that even a man who is without ritual and mantras becomes learned and blessed with the punya of vratas – merely by bathing at Ardhakila.

Darbhi also brought the four oceans there. Best of men, he that bathes there never meets distress again and also gains the punya of giving away four thousand cows.

The tirtha-yatri goes on to Satasahastraka, next to which is another sacred tirtha called Sahasraka. Both are renowned, and bathing in them, one obtains the merit of giving away a thousand kine. Fasts and gifts here multiply a thousandfold.

Then, on he must go the wonderful tirtha Renuka, bathe there and worship the Pitrs and the Devas. By this, cleansed of every sin, he receives the merit of the Agnishtoma sacrifice. Bathing next in the tirtha called Vimochana, with passions and senses under control, he is cleansed from all the sins which accrue from accepting gifts.

Senses controlled and observing Bramacharya, he must then go to the forest of Panchavati. A sojourn there brings great virtue and he becomes adored in all the realms of the good and godly.

After this, one should travel to the tirtha of Varuna called Taijasa, blazing with its own effulgence. In that tirtha the lord of Yoga, Sthanu himself dwells, the bull his mount. He that stays there finds success by worshipping the God of gods. It was here that the Devas, with Brahma at their head, and Rishis endowed with the wealth of asceticism, installed Guha as the Senapati of the celestials.

To the east of that tirtha is another, which is called Kuru tirtha. With senses controlled and keeping brahmacharya, he that bathes in Kuru tirtha is cleansed of all his sins and gains Brahmaloka.

He must go next to Swargadwara. Staying there, the pilgrim finds the merit of the Agnishtoma sacrifice and goes to the abode of Brahma.

After this, he must take himself to the the tirtha called Anaraha. Bathing there, he will never meet again with distress, for there Brahma himself and the other gods with Narayana at their head are always present, O tiger among men. O royal son of the race of Kuru, the wife of Rudra is also present there. Beholding the Goddess, one never meets with any sorrow thereafter. In that tirtha is also an image of Visweswara, the lord of Uma; seeing the God of gods there, one is cleansed of all one's sins. Also, seeing the idol of Narayana, from whose navel the Lotus sprang, the tirthayatri blazes forth, O Parantapa, and goes to the abode of Vishnu.

Bull among men, he that bathes in the tirtha of all the gods is redeemed from all his sins and shines like the Moon.

The pilgrim goes next to Swastipura. By walking in pradakshina around that place, one gains the punya of giving away a thousand holy cows. Arriving next at the tirtha called Pavana, one should offer oblations to the Pitrs and the Devas; with this, he gets, O Bhaarata, the merit of the Agnishtoma sacrifice.

Near Pavana is Ganga-hrada, and another tirtha, O Bhaarata, called Kupa. Thirty million tirthas are present in that Kupa. Bathing there, a person finds heaven. Bathing also in the Ganga-hrada and adoring Maheswara, one finds the condition of Ganapatya and redeems his race.

One should next travel to Sthanuvata, celebrated all over the three worlds. Bathing there, also, one finds heaven. The pilgrim goes on to Badaripachana, the asrama of Vasishtha. Having fasted there for three nights, one should eat the badari fruit. He that lives on badari for twelve years, and he that fasts at that tirtha for three nights acquires punya which is eternal.

Journeying then at Indramarga, and fasting there for a day and night, the pilgrim becomes adored in the realm of Indra. Going on to the Ekaratra tirtha, he who spends a single night there, with vratas and with perfect truth, becomes adored in Brahmaloka. One should next go to the asrama of Aditya, that lustrous god who is a mass of effulgence. Bathing in that tirtha famed through three worlds, and worshipping the god of light, one goes to the realm of Aditya and saves his own race.

The pilgrim then goes on to bathe in the Soma tirtha and without any doubt finds the realm of Soma for himself.

Next, he must visit the most sacred tirtha of the illustrious Dadhicha, that sanctifying tirtha which is celebrated all over the world. It was here that Angiras of the Saraswatas, that ocean of tapasya, was born. Bathing in that tirtha, one gains the punya of the Aswamedha, and without doubt, also the realm of Saraswati.

With senses subdued observing brahmacharya, the pilgrim goes on Kanyasrama. Staying there for three nights, with subdued senses and a regulated diet, he acquires a hundred Apsaras, and also goes to Brahma's realm.

O Virtuous, he continues his yatra, now to the tirtha called Sannihati. Living there, the gods with Brahma at their head, and Rishis endowed with the wealth of asceticism earn great punya. Bathing in the Saraswati during a solar eclipse, one gains the merit of a hundred Aswamedhas, and any sacrifice that one might perform there produces merit that is eternal. Whatever tirthas exist on earth or in the firmament, all the rivers, lakes, pools, springs, tanks large and small, and places sacred to particular gods all come, O tiger among men, month after month, and mingle with Sannihati! It is because all the other tirthas are united together here, that this tirtha is so named. Bathing here and drinking of its water, one becomes adored in heaven.

Listen to the punya acquired by a mortal who performs a Sraddha there on the day of the new moon during a solar eclipse, after bathing in this tirtha. He gains the punya of one who assiduously and thoroughly performs a thousand Aswamedhas. Whatever sins a man or woman commits are, beyond doubt, all destroyed as soon as one bathes in that tirtha. Bathing here one also ascends to the abode of Brahma in the lotus-coloured vimana.

Bathing next in Koti-tirtha, after having worshipped the Yaksha dwarapalaka Machakruka, one gains the merit of giving away a bounty of gold.

Best of the Bhaaratas, near this is a tirtha called Ganga-hrada. Mind subdued, keeping brahmacharya, and bathing here, a pilgrim acquires punya which is greater than that of the Rajasuya and the Aswamedha Yagnas.

The Naimisha tirtha confers its fruit on earth; Pushkara confers punya in the realms of the firmament; Kurukshetra, however, confers felicity in all the three worlds. Even the dust of Kurukshetra, carried by the wind, leads sinful men to a highly blessed state. They that live in Kurukshetra, which lies to the north of the Drishadwati and to the south of the Saraswati, really reside in heaven.

'I will go to Kurukshetra. I will dwell in Kurukshetra,' he that utters these words even once, becomes cleansed of all sin. Sacred Kurukshetra, worshipped by Brahmarishis, is regarded as the Vedi, the sacrificial altar of the Devas. Mortals that dwell there have nothing to grieve for at any time. That which lies between Tarantuka and Arantuka and the lakes of Rama and Machakruka is Kurukshetra. It is also called Samanta-panchaka and is said to be the northern sacrificial altar of the Grandsire."

TIRTHA-YATRA PARVA CONTINUED

Pulastya said, "Then, O great Kshatriya, one should journey on to the excellent tirtha of Dharma, where the illustrious god of justice once performed an austere tapasya. And it is for this that he made the place a sacred tirtha which would be known after his own name. Bathing there, a virtuous man with his mind concentrated in dhyana certainly sanctifies his family to the seventh generation.

Next, the pilgrim goes to the wonderful Jnanapavana. Staying there, he acquires the merit of the Agnishtoma, and goes to Muniloka, the realm of the Munis.

Then, he must travel to the Saugandhika-vana. There the Devas dwell, with Brahma at their head, Rishis with a wealth of asceticism, the Siddhas, the Charanas, the Gandharvas, the Kinnaras and the Nagas. As soon as he enters these woods, he is cleansed of all his sins.

After this, he goes on to visit the stream of the Devi Saraswati, known here as the Devi Plaksha. There he must bathe in the water issuing from an anthill, worship the manes and the gods, thereby gaining the punya of the Aswamedha. At a distance of six throws of a heavy stick from the anthill, there is a rare tirtha called Isanadhyushita. The Puranas say, Purushavyaghra, that bathing here a man obtains the merit of giving away a thousand Kapila cows, and also of the Aswamedha Yagna.

Journeying next to Sugandha and Satakumbha and Pancha-yagna, a man becomes adored in heaven. He must visit another tirtha there called Trisulakhata, bathe and set himself to worship the Pitrs and the Devas. Doing so, without doubt, he finds, after his death, the condition of Ganapatya.

The pilgrim travels on to the glorious tirtha of the Devi known through the three worlds as Sakambhari. There, for a thousand celestial years, she of the fervent vow, had subsisted, month after month, only upon herbs. Drawn by their reverence for the Goddess, many Rishis of great tapasya came there, O Bhaarata, and she entertained them with herbs; it is for this that they named her Sakambhari. Bhaarata, the man who comes to Sakambhari, observing brahmacharya and rapt in dhyana, and passes three nights there in purity, eating only herbs, obtains, at the will of the Goddess, the punya of one who lives on just herbs for twelve years.

From there he goes on to the tirtha called Suvarna, famed through the three worlds, where in days of old Vishnu paid his adorations to Rudra for his grace, and obtained many boons difficult of acquisition even by the gods. And, O Bhaarata, the gratified destroyer of Tripura said, 'Krishna, you will be much beloved in the world, and the foremost of everything in the universe.' Worshipping the God having the bull for his mark, in that place, the tirthayatri gains the punya of the Aswamedha and also the state of Ganapatya.

After this, he goes on to the tirtha of Dhumavati. Fasting there for three nights, he has his every wish fulfilled. In the southern part of this tirtha of the Goddess, there is another tirtha called Rathavarta. With a devout heart and senses controlled one should visit this sacred place, and, through the grace of Mahadeva, attain a lofty condition of grace.

After circumambulating this tirtha, Bharatarishabha, the pilgrim continues his pilgrimage going to the tirtha named Dhara, which, O you of great wisdom, washes away every sin. Bathing there, tiger among men, a man is freed from every sorrow.

Bowing to the Great Mountain Himavat, the pilgrim now takes himself to the source of the Ganga, which is beyond doubt the very gateway to heaven. There, his mind fixed in dhyana, he bathes in the tirtha called Koti, thereby gaining the punya of the Pundarika sacrifice; and he delivers all his race. Spending one night there, one acquires the merit of giving away a thousand cows.

By offering oblations of water to the gods and the manes at Saptaganga, Triganga and Sakravarta, all of which are here, one becomes adored in the realms of the virtuous.

Bathing next at Kanakhala, and fasting there for three nights, a man reaps the punya of the horse-sacrifice and goes to heaven.

After this, O lord of men, the pilgrim should repair to Kapilavata. Fasting for one night there, he acquires the merit of giving away a thousand cows. This tirtha of the illustrious Kapila, king of the Nagas, is celebrated, O best of Kurus, over all the worlds. Bathing at the Nagatirtha, one gains the merit of giving away a thousand Kapila kine.

After this the pilgrim journeys to the most excellent tirtha of Santanu, called Lalitaka. Bathing there, one never sinks into distress thereafter. The man who bathes at the confluence of the Ganga and the Yamuna obtains the punya of ten horse-sacrifices, and also redeems his race.

Next, the pilgrim should go to Sugandha, celebrated over the world. Here, cleansed of every sin, he becomes adored in the abode of Brahma. Then, on to Rudravarta, where bathing, one ascends to heaven. Bathing at the confluence of the Ganga and the Saraswati, a man finds the merit of the Aswamedha and also heaven.

Going on to Bhadrakarneswara and worshipping the gods, the pilgrim ensures that he will never be in distress again and will be loved in heaven. Then, lord of men, he goes to the Kubjamraka tirtha, and gains the merit of giving away a thousand cows, and swarga also.

From there he journeys to the Arundhativata, observing brahmacharya and his mind fixed in dhyana. Bathing there in Samudraka and fasting for three nights, he acquires the punya of the Aswamedha, that of giving away a thousand cows, and also redeems his entire clan.

One should next go to Brahmavarta, soul concentrated and locked in brahmacharya vratas. By this, one obtains the merit of the horse-sacrifice, and goes to the world of Soma.

The man who goes on to the Yamuna-prabhava, the source of the Yamuna, and bathes there, finds the punya of the Aswamedha and is worshipped in swarga. Arriving after this at Darbisankramana, a tirtha worshipped in the three worlds, a person acquires the merit of the horse-sacrifice and goes to heaven.

Repairing next to Sindhu-prabhava, he source of the Sindhu, which is worshipped by Siddhas and Gandharvas, and staying there for five nights, one obtains the merit of giving away an abundance of gold. Going next to the almost inaccessible Vedi tirtha, the pilgrim finds the punya of the Aswamedha and ascends into heaven.

Then, O Bhaarata, one should proceed to Rishikulya and Vasishtha. By visiting the latter, all varnas attain to Brahmanahood. Bathing at Rishikulya, while living a month eating just herbs, and worshipping the gods and manes, one is cleansed of all one's sins, and obtains the realm of the Rishis. Going next to Bhrigutunga, a pilgrim acquires the merit of the horse-sacrifice.

Going on to Virapramoksha, one is freed from every sin. Travelling then to the tirtha of Krittika and Magha, one, O Bhaarata, gains punya superior to that of the Agnishtoma and Atiratra sacrifices. The man who goes to the most excellent tirtha called Vidya and bathes there in the evening, becomes a master of every kind of knowledge.

Next, the pilgrim must stay for one night at Mahasrama, capable of destroying every sin; and eat only a single meal. By this, he gains many auspicious realms, and delivers ten preceding and ten succeeding generations of his race.

Dwelling next for a month in Mahalaya, and fasting there for three nights, one's soul is purged of all sin, and one acquires the merit of giving away gold in abundance. Proceeding to Vetasika, worshipped by the Grandsire, the tirtha-yatri obtains the merit of the Aswamedha and the state of Usanas.

He goes on to the tirtha Sundarika, worshipped by the Siddhas, and obtains radiant personal beauty, as witnessed by the ancients. Proceeding to Brahmani, with subdued senses and observing the brahmacharya vrata, a person rises into Brahmaloka in a lotus-hued chariot.

The yatri journeys next to the sacred Naimisha, worshipped by the Siddhas, where Brahma dwells with the Devas. Just the intention of visiting Naimisha, destroys half one's sins; by entering it, one is cleansed of all one's sins. The pilgrim of subdued senses should stay in Naimisha for a month; for, O Bhaarata, all the tirthas of the earth are present in Naimisha. Bathing there, with restrained senses and regulated fare, one obtains the merit of the cow-sacrifice, and also sanctifies his race for seven generations, before and after himself. The wise have always said that he who renounces his life at Naimisha by fasting, enjoys bliss in the heavenly regions, for Naimisha is ever sacred and most holy.

Travelling next to Gangodbheda and fasting there for three nights, a man obtains the merit of the Vajapeya sacrifice, and becomes like Brahma himself. Journeying to the Saraswati, one should offer oblations to the Devas and the Pitrs; with this, the pilgrim will surely enjoy bliss in the regions called Saraswata.

After, he wends his way to Bahuda, with soul subdued and keeping the brahmacharya vrata. Staying there for one night, one becomes beloved in heaven, and also gains the punya of the Devasatra sacrifice. On then he must go to Kshiravati, frequented by the most holy men. By worshipping the gods and the manes there, he acquires the punya of the Vajapeya.

Travelling next to Vimalasoka, mind subdued and keeping brahmacharya, and remaining there for one night, one is adored in heaven.

After this, he must go the exalted Gopratara in the Sarayu, where Sri Rama, with all his attendants and animals, abandoned his body, and ascended to heaven through the power of this tirtha. Bathing in that tirtha, O Bhaarata, through Rama's grace and by virtue of his own karma, one is washed of one's every sin and becomes adored in heaven.

Going next, O son of the Kurus, to the Rama-tirtha on the Gomati, and bathing there, one gains the merit of the Aswamedha, and also sanctifies his race. There, Bharatarishabha, is another tirtha called Satasahastrika. Bathing in it, with senses restrained and fasting, a person reaps the merit of giving away a thousand sacred cows.

Now he should go to the unrivalled tirtha called Bhartristhana, where he finds the merit of the Aswamedha. Bathing next in the tirtha called Koti, and worshipping Kartikeya, a man reaps the punya of giving away a thousand kine, and acquires great energy.

Going next to Varanasi, and worshipping the God having the bull for his mark, after a bath in the Kapilahrada, the pilgrim obtains the merit of the Rajasuya Yagna.

Journeying then to Avimukta, and seeing there the God of gods, he is instantly cleansed of even the sin of killing a Brahmana. By giving up one's life there, one attains moksha.

Arriving next at the rare tirtha Markandeya, celebrated over the world and situated on the Ganga, a person obtains the merit of Agnishtoma sacrifice, and delivers his race. On next to Gaya, with subdued senses and observing brahmacharya, one obtains the punya of the horse-sacrifice and also redeems his race. In that tirtha is the Akshaya-vata, celebrated throughout the three worlds. Whatever is offered here to the Pitrs is said to become inexhaustible. Bathing there in the Mahanadi, and offering oblations to the gods and the manes, a man acquires eternal regions, and also saves his race.

Then the pilgrim travels to Brahmasara in the forest of Dharma, and passing one night there, he attains Brahmaloka. In that lake, Brahma raised a sacrificial pillar; by walking round this stamba, a man acquires the punya of the Vajapeya sacrifice.

After this, mighty Kshatriya, the tirtha-yatri should go to Denuka, famed the world over. Staying there for one night and giving away sesame and cows, one's soul is cleansed of every sin, and one ascends into the world of Soma. Here, of yore, the cow Kapila ranged over the mountains, with her calf. O Bhaarata, her great hoof-prints and her young ones can be seen in that place even today. By bathing in those hoof-prints, whatever sin a man may have incurred is washed away.

Then should one go to Gridhravata, consecrated to the trident-bearing God. Approaching the Deity having the bull for his mark, the pilgrim should rub himself with ashes. If a Brahmana, he gains the merit of observing the twelve-year vow and if he belongs to any of the other varnas, he is freed from all his sins.

After this, on to the Udyanta mountains, which resound with great and mysterious songs. There, Bharatarishabha, you can still see the the footprints of Savitri. The Brahmana of rigid vows who says his morning, noon and evening prayers here, for a day, finds the punya of performing that service for twelve years.

The famous Yonidwara is in this place; going there one is set free from the pain of rebirth. The person who stays at Gaya during both the dark and lighted fortnights, certainly sanctifies his own race, up and down, to the seventh generation. One should wish for many sons so that at least one of them might go to Gaya, or celebrate the horse-sacrifice, or offer a Nila bull.

Then, the pilgrim should proceed to Phalgu, where he acquires the punya of the Aswamedha, and finds great success. After this, the pilgrim, his mind quietened, should travel to Dharmaprastha. There, O foremost of Kshatriya, Dharma dwells for ever. Drinking of the water of a well, which is there, and purifying one's self with a bath, he who offers oblations to the Devas and the Pitrs is cleansed of all his sins and ascends into swarga.

In that tirtha is the hermitage of the great Rishi Matanga of the perfectly restrained soul. By entering that beautiful asrama, which can soothe fatigue and sorrow, one earns the merit of the Gavamayana sacrifice, and by touching the image of Dharma, which is there, one obtains the fruit of the horse-sacrifice.

One should next go, O Kshatriya, to the excellent Brahmasthana. Approaching Brahma, that bull among male beings, who is present there, one acquires the merit of the Rajasuya and Aswamedha Yagnas.

The pilgrim should then repair to Rajagriha. Bathing there, one lives as happily as the Rishi Kakshivan. Purifying himself, the pilgrim should partake here of the offerings daily made to the Yakshini. By this, one is freed even from the sin of killing a Brahmana, through the Yakshini's grace.

Going on to Maninaga, one finds the punya of giving away a thousand kine. O Bhaarata, he that eats anything at all offered at the tirtha of Maninaga, becomes immune to the venom of the most deadly serpents. Staying there for one night, one is cleansed of one's sins.

Then should the pilgrim continue to the favourite forest of the Brahmarshi Gautama. There, bathing in the lake of Ahalya, he attains to an exalted slate. After this, seeing the image of Sri, he acquires great prosperity. There in that tirtha is a well famed through the trilokas. Bathing in it, one acquires the merit of the Aswamedha. Here is also a well sacred to the Rajarishi Janaka, a well that the gods worship. Bathing in this well, one rises into Vishnuloka.

Then should one repair to Vinasana that destroys every sin. By going there, one acquires the punya of a Vajapeya sacrifice, and also gains Somaloka. Travelling next to Gandaki, which is created by the waters of every tirtha, a person acquires the merit of the Vajapeya, and ascends into Suryaloka.

The pilgrim journeys next to the Visala, river celebrated across the three worlds, and gains the merit of the Agnishtoma and also rises into Swarga. After this, virtuous one, he goes to the tapovana of Rishis called Adhivanga, and finds great happiness amongst the Guhyakas.

Continuing to the river Kampana, visited by the Siddhas, one obtains the merit of the Pundarika sacrifice, and also ascends into heaven. Arriving then, O lord of earth, at the stream called Maheswari, one acquires the punya of the horse-sacrifice and also redeems his own race.

Journeying after this to the realm of the Devas, the pilgrim earns freedom from misfortune and also the merit of the horse-sacrifice. Next, he must go to Somapada, with subdued soul and keeping brahmacharya. Bathing in Maheswarapada there, one reaps the merit of the Aswamedha. In that tirtha, O Bharatarishabha, it is well known that ten millions of tirthas exist together.

Once a fiendish Asura, in the shape of a tortoise, attempted to carry it away, but the mighty Vishnu recovered it from him. There in that tirtha one should perform ablutions, for by doing this one acquires the punya of the Pundarika sacrifice and ascends into Vishnuloka besides.

Then, O best of kings, one should proceed to the Narayana tirtha, where, O Bhaarata, Narayana is always present and dwells for ever. The Devas with Brahma at their head, Rishis endowed with the wealth of asceticism, the Adityas, the Vasus, and the Rudras, all adore Janardana in that tirtha, and Vishnu of wonderful deeds has come to be known as Salagrama. Approaching eternal Vishnu, Lord of the three worlds, giver of boons, one obtains the merit of the horse-sacrifice, and goes to Vishnuloka.

In that place is a sacred well, capable of destroying every sin; the four seas are ever present in that well. He that bathes in it will be free from misfortune. Beholding the image of the boon-giving, eternal, and fierce Mahadeva who is also there, the pilgrim glows like the moon emerging from behind a cloud.

Bathing then in Jatismara, with a pure mind and subdued senses, one acquires, without doubt, the recollections of his past life. Going on to Maheswarapura, and worshipping the God having the bull for his mark, fasting the while, one gets the fruition of all one's desires.

Journeying, after this, to Vamana, which destroys every sin, and beholding the Lord Hari, the pilgrim is set free from all misfortune. He goes on to the asrama of Kusika that can remove every sin. Going then to the river Kausika, which cleanses even great sins, mahapaapas, one should bathe in it. By this one obtains the merit of the Rajasuya Yagna.

Next, best of Kshatriyas, he should go to the sacred Champaka forest. By spending one night there, he will acquire the merit of giving away a thousand cows. Arriving next at Jyeshtila, tirtha of rare worth, and passing one night there, one reaps the fruit of the gift of a thousand cows. Seeing the image of Visweswara of great splendour there, with his consort the Devi, a person obtains, O bull among men, the world of Mitra-Varuna. By fasting there for three nights, a man acquires the merit of the Agnishtoma.

By visiting Kanya-samvedya, with senses restrained and fasting, the pilgrim gains the region of Manu, the lord of creation. Rishis of stern vows have said that he that gives away rice or makes any gift at the tirtha called Kanya, renders such a gift eternal.

Arriving next at Nischira, celebrated through the three worlds, he gains the merit of the horse-sacrifice and goes to Vishnuloka. Those that give daana at the confluence of Nischira, ascend into blessed Brahmaloka. In that tirtha is the asrama of Vasishtha, known in the three lokas; bathing there, one obtains the merit of the Vajapeya.

Going on to Devakuta, to which Devarishis resort, one acquires the punya of the Aswamedha, and also delivers his race. After this, the tirtha-yatri should go to the lake of the Muni Kausika, where Kausika's son, Viswamitra, found grace. Bathing there, a man acquires the merit of the Vajapeya. O Kshatriya, at Kausika, the pilgrim should spend one month and reap the punya of an Aswamedha Yagna.

He that lives in that best of tirthas, Maha-hrada, enjoys immunity from misfortune, and also gains the merit of giving away gold in abundance. Next, seeing Kartikeya who dwells at Virasrama a man surely reaps the fruit of the horse-sacrifice. Proceeding to Agnidhara, celebrated across the three worlds, and after a bath there, beholding the eternal and boon-giving Vishnu, that god of gods, the pilgrim acquires the punya of the Agnishtoma.

Journeying on to the pool of Brahma, near the mountains with peaks of snow, and bathing in it, a man gets the merit of the Agnishtoma. Falling from the Grandsire's pool, is that world-sanctifying stream, celebrated through the three worlds, called Kumara-Dhara. Bathing there, one has all his purposes fulfilled. Fasting in that tirtha for three days, one is cleansed even of the sin of slaying a Brahmana.

The pilgrim should go on the peak of the great Goddess Gauri, also renowned across the three worlds. Climbing it, O best of men, one should approach Stana-Kunda. By touching the waters of Stana-Kunda, a person gains the merit of the Vajapeya sacrifice. Bathing in that and worshipping the Devas and Pitrs, one acquires the merit of the horse-sacrifice and also rises into Indraloka.

Arriving next at the well of Tamraruna, frequented by the gods, one acquires, O lord of men, the merit which attaches to human sacrifice. Bathing next at the confluence of the Kalika with the Kausiki and the Aruna, and fasting there for three nights, a man of learning is cleansed of all his sins.

Going on to the Urvasi tirtha, and then to Somasrama, a wise man, by bathing next at Kumbhakarnasrama, becometh loved through the world. The ancients knew that by touching the waters of Kokamukha, while observing steady vows and bramacharya, a man revives the memory of his former life.

The pilgrim goes quickly next to the river Nanda, where a regenerate man becomes free from all his sins and, soul controlled, rises into Indraloka. Then, on he goes to the island called Rishabha, where cranes die, and bathing in the Saraswati he blazes forth in heaven.

Continuing to the tirtha Auddalaka, frequented by Munis, and bathing there, one is cleansed of all one's sins. Repairing next to the sacred tirtha Dharma, where Brahmarishis come, one acquires the merit of the Vajapeya and becomes respected in Swargaloka.

Proceeding to Champa and bathing in the Bhagirathi, he who goes to Dandaparna, finds the punya of giving away a thousand kine. After this, he must go on to sacred Lalitika, graced by the presence of the virtuous. By this the tirtha-yatri acquires the merit of the Rajasuya sacrifice and is regarded in heaven."

CANTO 85

TIRTHA-YATRA PARVA CONTINUED

Pulastya said, "Arriving next at the excellent Samvedya tirtha in the evening, and touching its waters, the pilgrim surely gains knowldge and wisdom. Created a tirtha in days of old by Rama's power, at Lauhitya one obtains the merit of giving away a bounty of gold.

Then, on to the river Karatoya; and fasting there for three nights, a man acquires the merit of the horse-sacrifice.

This is the injunction of the Creator himself. It has been said by the wisest, O Kshatriya, that if a person goes to the place where the Ganga mingles with the sea, he reaps merit which is ten times that of the Aswamedha Yagna. Crossing over to the opposite bank of the Ganga, he that bathes there, having spent three nights in the place, is cleansed of all his sins.

The pilgrim must next go to the Vaitarani capable of destroying every sin. Arriving after this at the tirtha named Viraja one he like the moon, and sanctifying his race, rescues it and is himself purified of all his sins. He that bathes in Viraja further reaps the merit of giving away a thousand cows.

Living in purity at the confluence of the Sona and the Jyotirathi, and offering oblations of water to the gods and the manes, a man reaps the merit of the Agnishtoma sacrifice. Touching the waters of the Vamsagulma, constituting the sources of both the Sona and the Narmada, one obtains the punya of the Aswamedha.

Travelling on to the tirtha called Rishabha in Kosala, O lord of men, and fasting there for three nights, one earns the merit of the Vajapeya sacrifice, and of the gift of a thousand kine, and also delivers his race. Arriving at Kosala, a man should bathe in the tirtha named Kala, and by this he surely obtains the merit of giving away one and ten sacred bulls.

By bathing in Pushpavati and fasting there for three nights, one sanctifies one's own race, besides earning the merit of the gift of a thousand cows. O foremost of the Bhaaratas, by bathing in the tirtha called Badarika, one obtains long life, and also goes to heaven.

Arriving next at Champa, and bathing in the Bhagirathi, and seeing Danda one earns the punya of giving away a thousand kine. Then the pilgrim should go to the sacred Lapetika, graced by the presence of the pious; there he reaps the punya of the Vajapeya and also becomes regarded by the gods.

Proceeding next to the mountain Mahendra, where Jamadagnya lived, and bathing in Rama's tirtha, a person acquires the merit of the horse-sacrifice. Here is Matanga's tirtha, Kedara, O son of the Kurus; bathing in it, a man gains the merit of giving away a thousand kine.

Going on to the mountain Sri, he who touches the waters of the stream there, worshipping the God who has the bull for his mark, obtains the merit of the horse-sacrifice. On the mountain Sri the effulgent Mahadeva dwells in joy with the Goddess, as also does Brahma with the other gods. By bathing in the lake of Beva, with purity and mind restrained, one gets the merit of the horse-sacrifice, and also attains the highest success.

Proceeding next to the mountain Rishabha in Pandya, worshipped by the gods, he finds the merit of the Vajapeya and rejoices in heaven.

After this, he must go to the river Kaveri, frequented by Apsaras. Bathing there, he gains the merit of giving away a thousand cows.

After this he must touch the waters of the tirtha called Kanya on the shores of the sea, and be cleansed of every sin.

Going next to Gokarna, celebrated across the three worlds, which is situated in the midst of the deep, and is reverenced by all the lokas, and where the gods headed by Brahma, and Rishis endowed with the wealth of asceticism, and Bhutas and Yakshas and Pisachas, and Kinnaras and the great Nagas, and Siddhas and Charanas and Gandharvas, and men and Pannagas, and Rivers, Seas and Mountains worship the lord of Uma, one should worship Isana, fasting there for three nights. By this, one acquires the merit of the horse-sacrifice, and the state of Ganapatya. By staying there for twelve nights, one's soul is cleansed of all sin.

One should go to the tirtha known as Gayatri, renowned across the worlds. Staying there for three nights, one acquires the merit of giving away a thousand cows. A strange phenomenon is seen to occur there, O lord of men. If a Brahmana, whether born of a Brahmani or any other woman, recites the Gayatri there, the recitation becomes rhythmic and musical, while, O Kshatriya, one who is not a Brahmana cannot chant it adequately at all.

Going next to the well nigh inaccessible tank of the Brahmana Rishi Samvarta, one acquires personal beauty and prosperity. Repairing next to Vena, he that offers oblations of water to the gods and the manes, gains a chariot drawn by peacocks and cranes.

Going next to the Godavari, ever frequented by the Siddhas, one earns the merit of the cow-sacrifice, and goes to the wondrous realm of Vasuki. Bathing next at the confluence of the Vena, one obtains the merit of the Vajapeya sacrifice.

Bathing next at the confluence of Varada, one acquires the punya of giving away a thousand kine. Arriving next at Brahmasthana, he that stays there for three nights acquires the merit of giving away a thousand kine, and also ascends into swarga.

Coming next to Kusaplavana, with a subdued mind and keeping brahmacharya, and staying there for three nights, he that bathes in that tirtha obtains the merit of the Aswamedha. Bathing next at the romantic Deva-hrada, fed by the waters of the Krishna-Vena, and also in the Jatismara-hrada, one regains the memory of one's former life. It was here that Indra celebrated a hundred sacrifices and ascended to heaven. By visiting only this tirtha, one acquires the punya of the Agnishtoma.

Bathing next in the Sarvadeva-hrada, the pilgrim obtains the merit of giving away a thousand sacred cows.

Going on to the most holy tank Payoshni, best of waters, he that offers oblations of water to the gods and the manes acquires the merit of the gift of a thousand kine. Arriving next at the sacred forest of Dandaka, a person should bathe in the waters there, and immediately gain the punya of giving away a thousand cows.

Journeying next to the asrama of Sarabhanga and that of the illustrious Suka, one acquires immunity from all misfortune, besides sanctifying his race. Then should one travel to Surparaka, where Jamadagni's son lived of old. Bathing in that tirtha of Rama, one acquires the merit of giving away gold in abundance.

Bathing next in the Saptagodavara, with senses subdued and food regulated, one earns great merit, and also goes to Devaloka.

Going on to Devahrada, a man obtains the merit of the Devasatra sacrifice. After this, the pilgrim should journey to the forest of Tungaka, in self-restraint and keeping bramacharya. It was here that, in olden days, the Muni Saraswata taught the Vedas to other ascetics. When the Vedas had been lost, in consequence of the Munis having forgotten them, Angirasa's son, seated at his ease upon the upper garments of the other Munis, duly spread out, pronounced the sacred syllable AUM, and at this the Sages again remembered all that they had learnt before.

It was there that the Rishis and the Devas Varuna, Agni, Prajapati, Narayana who is also called Hari, Mahadeva and the lustrous Pitamaha of great splendour, appointed the resplendent Bhrigu to officiate at a sacrifice. Gratifying Agni with libations of ghee, poured according to the law of ritual, the illustrious Bhrigu performed the Agnidhana sacrifice for all those Rishis, after which both they and the gods went away to their respective homes, one after another.

One who enters the forest of Tungaka, male or female, is cleansed of every sin. In that tirtha, O Kshatriya, one should remain for a month, with senses and food controlled; by this, one ascends into Brahmaloka, and also delivers one's race. Arriving next at Medhavika, one should offer oblations of water to the gods and the manes, and so acquire the merit of the Agnishtoma sacrifice, and also memory and intellect.

In that tirtha is the mountain famed the world over, called Kalanjara. Bathing in the unwordly lake that is there, one acquires the merit of giving away a thousand kine. He who, after a bath, offers oblations on the Kalanjara mountain is, without doubt, regarded in heaven.

Going on to the river Mandakini, which can destroy every sin, and which flows on that best of mountains, Chitrakuta, he that bathes there and worships the gods and the manes, receives the merit of the horse-sacrifice and attains to an exalted state.

After this, virtuous one, the pilgrim should visit the excellent tirtha Bhartristhana, where Kartikeya, Senapati of the Devas, is ever present; by going to just this tirtha a man finds success.

Bathing next at the tirtha called Koti, he earns the merit of giving away a thousand cows. Having walked around Koti, he must go on to Jyeshtasthana. Looking at the image of Mahadeva there, the tirtha-yatri shines like the moon. There is a renowned well in that place, Bharatarishabha, in which are the four seas. He that bathes there, and with mind subdued, worships the gods and the ancestors, is cleansed of all his sins and attains to an exalted state.

Then, one should journey to the great Sringaverapura, where once Dasaratha's son Rama crossed the Ganga. Bathing in that tirtha, Mahabaho, one is exorcised of all one's sins. Bathing with subdued senses in the Ganga, while observing brahmacharya, one is washed of every sin, and also receives the punya of the Vajapeya.

After this, the pilgrim goes on to Mayuravata, consecrated to Mahadeva of awesome intelligence. Seeing the image of the God there, bowing down to him and walking around the place in pradakshina, one acquires the condition of Ganapatya. Bathing in Ganga at that tirtha, all one's sins are washed away.

Then, O Kshatriya, one should go on to Prayaga, whose praises have been sung by Rishis and where the gods dwell with Brahma at their head, the cardinal directions with their presiding deities, the Lokapalas, the Siddhas, the Pitrs adored by the worlds, the Maharishis – Sanatkumara and others, stainless Brahmarshis – Angiras and others, the Nagas, the Suparnas, the Siddhas, the Rivers, the Seas, the Gandharvas, the Apsaras, and the Lord Hari with Prajapati.

In that tirtha are three fiery caverns between which the Ganga, that foremost of tirthas, rushes. There in that place the world-purifying daughter of the Sun, Yamuna, celebrated across the three worlds, unites with the Ganga. The country between the Ganga and the Yamuna is regarded as the yoni, mons veneris, of the world, and Prayaga as the foremost point of that.

The tirthas Prayaga, Pratishtana, Kambala, Aswatara and Bhogavati are the sacrificial altars of the Creator. In those places, O Kshatriyottama, the Vedas and the Yagnas, in embodied forms, and the Rishis blessed with the wealth of asceticism, adore Brahma, and there the gods and kings of the world also celebrate their sacrifices. The learned however, say that of all these tirthas Prayaga is the most sacred, in fact, the foremost of all tirthas in the three worlds.

By going to that tirtha, by singing its praises, or by taking a little earth from it, one is purified of every sin. He who bathes in that confluence, celebrated the world over, acquires all the punya of the Rajasuya and the Aswamedha Yagnas. The gods themselves worship this tirtha.

If a man gives ever so little here, it increases, O Bhaarata, a thousandfold. Child, do not let the texts of the Veda, nor the opinions of men turn your mind from the desire to die at Prayaga. O son of the

Kurus, the wise say that six hundred million and ten thousand tirthas exist at Prayaga. Bathing in the confluence of Ganga and Yamuna, one obtains the merit that attaches to the four kinds of knowledge and the merits also of those that are founded in the truth.

At Prayaga is the excellent tirtha of Vasuki, called Bhogavati. He that bathes in it, obtains the merit of the Aswamedha. There in the Ganga is also the tirtha famed throughout the three worlds, called Hamsaprapatana, which confers the merit of ten Aswamedhas.

O Kurunandana, wherever a person bathes in the Ganga, he earns merit equal to that of a trip to Kurukshetra. An exception, however, is made in regard of Kanakhala, while the punya attaching to Prayaga is the greatest. Having committed a hundred sins, he that bathes in the Ganga, has all his sins washed away by the waters, even as fuel is consumed by fire.

It has been said that in the Satya-yuga all the tirthas were sacred; in the Treta, Pushkara alone was holy; in Dwapara, Kurukshetra; and in the Kali-yuga, the Ganga alone is sacred. In Pushkara, one should practise austerities; in Mahalaya, one should perform charity; in the Malaya mountains, one should ascend the funeral pyre; and in Bhrigutunga, one should renounce one's body by forgoing food.

Bathing in Pushkara, in Kurukshetra, in the Ganga and in the confluence of the Ganga and the Yamuna, one sanctifies seven generations of one's race up and down. He that recites the name of the Ganga is purified; he that sees her, receives prosperity; while he that bathes in her and drinks of her waters sanctifies seven generations of his race, above and below himself.

As long as one's bones lie touching the waters of the Ganga, so long does one live regarded in heaven, even as one lives in heaven in consequence of the merit he earns by pious pilgrimages to all the sacred tirthas and other holy places. There is no tirtha like the Ganga, there is no god like Kesava, and there are none superior to Brahmanas – this has been said even by Brahma, the Grandsire.

The land through which the Ganga flows must be regarded as a sacred asrama, and any place on the banks of the Ganga should be regarded as one favourable to the attainment of ascetic success.

One should narrate this description of the tirthas only to the regenerate, to those that are pious, to one's son and friends and disciples and dependents. This narrative, without a rival is blessed and holy and leads to heaven. Sacred, enlivening and sanctifying, it bestows merit and high worth. Destructive of every sin, it is a mystery that the great Rishis cherish with care. By reciting it in the midst of Brahmanas, one is cleansed of every sin, and ascends to heaven.

Truly, this description of the tirthas is auspicious and heaven-giving and sacred indeed; ever blessed as it is, it destroys one's enemies; foremost of all accounts, it sharpens the intellect. By reading this narrative the sonless obtains sons, the destitute obtains riches, the Kshatriya conquers the whole world, the Vaisya comes by great wealth, the Sudra has all his desires fulfilled, and the Brahmana crosses the ocean of samsara.

Purifying himself, he that listens daily to the merits of the different tirthas, recollects the incidents of many previous births and rejoices in heaven. Of the tirthas that have been named here, some are easily accessible, while others are difficult of access. But he who is inspired with the desire of beholding all the tirthas, should visit them even in imagination.

Wanting to obtain punya, the Vasus, the Sadhyas, the Adityas, the Maruts, the Aswins, and the Rishis equal to the Devas, all bathed in these tirthas. O Kuru, observe the vows I have explained, and with subdued senses, visit these tirthas, increasing your punya. Because of their pure senses, their belief in God, and their knowledge of the Vedas, pious men are able to visit these holy tirthas.

O Kauravya, he who does not observe vows, he whose mind is not conrolled, he that is impure, he that is a thief, and he that is of crooked mind, does not bathe in any tirthas. You always keep dharma, and are of pure character. By your virtue, you have always gratified your father, your grand-father, and great-grand-fathers, and the gods with Brahma at their head, and the Rishis also.

O Bhishma, who resembles Vasava, you will attain to the world of the Vasus, and also find eternal fame on earth!'"

"Narada continues, 'With this, the illustrious Rishi Pulastya, well-pleased, bid Bhishma farewell and vanished before his eyes. And Bhishma, O tiger among men, well knowing the import of the Shastras, wandered over the world at the behest of Pulastya. Bhishma ended his great pilgrimage to all these tirthas, which destroy every sin, at Prayaga.

The man that ranges the earth in accordance with these injunctions, obtains the highest fruit of a hundred horse-sacrifices and earns salvation thereafter. O son of Pritha, you will acquire punya consisting of the eight attributes, even as Bhishma, foremost of the Kurus, did of yore. And since you will lead these ascetics to those tirthas, your merit will be much greater.

These tirthas are infested by Rakshasas, and no one but you, O Kauravya, can go to them. He who rises early and recites this narrative by the Devarishis on the subject of the tirthas becomes free from all sins. Those best of Rishis, Valmiki, and Kasyapa, and Atreya, and Kundajatara, and Viswamitra, and Gautama, and Asita, and Devala, and Markandeya, and Galava, and Bharadwaja, and Vasishtha, and the Muni Uddalaka, and Saunaka with his son, and Vyasa, best of Sages, and Durvasas, foremost of Munis, and Jabali of great austerities – all these lustrous Rishis, endowed with the wealth of tapasya, are waiting for you. Mighty king, meet with these by undertaking a tirtha-yatra to all the tirthas.

A great Rishi of immeasurable tejas, Lomasa, will come to you. Follow him, and me, and visit the tirthas one by one. By this, you will acquire great fame, even like King Mahabhisha! O tiger among kings, even as the virtuous Yayati and King Pururava, you blaze forth with your own virtue. Like King Bhagiratha and the illustrious Rama, you shine among kings even as the Sun himself. And you are, Maharajan, celebrated in the world even as Manu or Ikshvaku, or the famed Puru or Vainya!

As in days of yore, the slayer of Vritra, after burning all his enemies, ruled the three worlds, his mind freed from anxiety, so will you rule your people, after killing all your enemies. And, O you of eyes like lotus leaves, having conquered the earth according to the customs of your varna, you will have renown by your dharma, fame even like Kartaviryarjuna.'"

Vaisampayana continued, "O great King Janamejaya, having comforted and advised the monarch thus, the illustrious Rishi Narada bids him farewell and vanishes before Yudhishtira's eyes. And the virtuous Yudhishtira, reflecting upon what Narada Muni said, begins to describe to his Brahmanas and Rishis the great spiritual merit attaching to the tirthas."

CANTO 86

Tirtha-yatra Parva Continued

Vaisampayana continued, "Having ascertained the opinion of his brothers, and of the intelligent Narada, Yudhishtira says to Dhaumya, who was even like the Pitamaha himself, 'I have sent Purushavyaghra Jishnu away to acquire the Devastras. Arjuna, whose prowess can never be baffled, whose arms are long and his intelligence immeasurable – that hero of immense ability and a master of weapons, who is like the peerless Vasudeva himself, is devoted to me.

O Brahmana, I know both Krishna and Arjuna, those destroyers of enemies, endowed with untold prowess, even as the puissant Vyasa knows them. I know Vasudeva and Dhananjaya to be none else than Vishnu himself, possessed of the six gunas. And this is what Narada also knows, for he has always spoken so to me. I also know the two to be the Rishis Nara and Narayana.

I have sent Arjuna on this mission, knowing that he will accomplish it. Not inferior to Indra and entirely capable, I have sent that son of a god to meet the king of the Devas and to receive astras from him.

Bhishma and Drona are Atirathas. Kripa and the son of Drona are invincible; Dhritarashtra's son has made these mighty warriors the commanders of his army. All of them are versed in the Vedas, they are heroic, and possess of the knowledge of every weapon. Endowed with great strength, they always want to face Arjuna in battle.

And the Sutaputra Karna is also a mighty warrior, a master of celestial astras. As far as the swiftness of his missiles is concerned, he owns the strength of Vayu. Himself a fire, his arrows are like great tongues of flame; the sound his left hand cased in leather makes, when he looses these shafts, are like those flames crackling. The dust of the battlefield is the smoke of the fire. Spurred on by the son of Dhritarashtra, even as the wind urges agni, Karna is like the all-consuming apocalypse at the end of the Yuga, which Death himself sends. He will consume my troops like straw.

Only that awesome thunderhead called Arjuna, helped along by Krishna like a powerful wind, with devastras its fierce lightning, the white steeds the rows of white cranes coursing below it, and the unbearable Gandiva the rainbow ahead, can extinguish the conflagration that is Karna with arrowy showers loosed with unflagging consistency.

I have no doubt that that conqueror of hostile cities, Vibhatsu, will acquire all the celestial astras, with their awesome might and energy, from Indra himself. I believe that Arjuna by himself is equal to all the great heroes that oppose us; otherwise, we could never hope to vanquish them.

We shall see Arjuna, Parantapa, entirely armed with devastras, for once he undertakes a task he never droops under its weight.

However, without him here in the Kamyaka, Draupadi and we can find no peace. So, tell us of some other vana, which is sacred and full of delight, where game and fruit abound, where pious Munis live in tapasya, and where we can pass our days waiting as eagerly for mighty Arjuna as the Chataka birds do the gathering of rainclouds. Tell us of some asramas; tell us where we can find lakes and streams and beautiful mountains.

O Brahmana, I cannot stay on in this Kamyaka without Arjuna. All of us want to leave and go elsewhere.'"

CANTO 87

TIRTHA-YATRA PARVA CONTINUED

Vaisampayana said, "Seeing the Pandavas so anxious and dejected, Dhaumya, who resembles Brihaspati, comforts them, 'Bharatarishabha, sinless one, listen to me and I will tell you about some sacred asramas and lands and tirthas and mountains of which the great Brahmanas approve. Listen to me, yourself, your brothers and Drupada's daughter, and you will find relief from your sorrow. Son of Pandu, by merely hearing of these places, you will acquire punya; by visiting them, you will gain merit a hundred times greater, O best of men!

First, O King, I will, as far as I recall, speak of the beautiful eastern country, much adored by Rajarishis. In that direction, O Bhaarata lies a place called Naimisha which is regarded by the Devas. There, in that land, are several sacred tirthas belonging to the gods. There, too, flows the sacred and beautiful Gomati, worshipped by Devarishis; and there, as well, stands the sacrificial stake of Surya.

In that quarter is also that best of hills, Gaya, sacred and much regarded by royal Sages. On that hill, is the auspicious lake called

Brahmasara, which is adored by celestial Rishis. The ancients say that one should wish for many sons, so that at least one among them might visit Gaya, perform the Aswamedha or give away a Nila bull, and thereby deliver ten generations of his clan, up and down.

There, O Yudhishtira, is a great river and a particularly auspicious spot called Gayasira. In Gayasira is a nyagrodha, a banyan tree, which the Brahmanas call the Eternal banyan: for, food that is offered there to the Pitrs becomes eternal, O Mahatman! The great river that flows by the tree is known by the name of Phalgu, and its waters are most sacred.

Bharatarishabha, in that place is also the Kausiki, whose basin abounds in various fruit and roots, and where Viswamitra, his wealth his tapasya, acquired Brahmanahood.

Towards that direction also is the sacred Ganga, on whose banks Bhagiratha performed many sacrifices with profuse gifts to Brahmanas.

They say that in the country of Panchala there is a forest called Utpala, where Viswamitra of Kausika's race performed sacrifices with his son, and where, seeing the relics of Viswamitra's superhuman power, Rama, the son of Jamadagni, recited the praises of his ancestry. At Kamyaka, Kausika's son once quaffed the Soma rasa with Indra. Then, abandoning the Kshatriya varna, he said, "I am a Brahmana!"

In that quarter, O hero, is the sacred confluence of Ganga and Yamuna, which is celebrated the world over. Holy and sin-destroying, that tirtha is much reverenced by the Rishis. It is here that the soul of all things, Brahma the Grandsire, in olden days, performed his sacrifice; and it is for this, O lord of the Bhaaratas, that the place has come to be called Prayaga.

In this direction, O foremost among kings, lies the beautiful asrama of Agastya, and the forest called Tapasa, which many Rishis adorn. And there also is the great tirtha called Hiranyabindu on the Kalanjara hills, and that best of mountains called Agastya, which is sacred and auspicious.

In that quarter, O scion of the Kurus, is the mountain called Mahendra, sacred to the illustrious Rama of the Bhrigus. There, Kaunteya, the Grandsire performed sacrifices of yore. There, O Yudhishtira, the sacred Bhagiratha enters a lake and there also, O King, is that holy river, the punya-giving Brahmasara, on whose banks live men whose sins have been washed away, whose very sight bestows great grace.

In that direction, also, lies the high-souled Matanga's fine asrama, Kedara, which is holy and auspicious and renowned through the world. There is also the mountain called Kundoda, so delightful and abounding in fruit and roots and waters, where Nala, king of the Nishadhas, slaked his thirst and rested for a while.

In that quarter, also, is the delighlful Deva-vana, graced by ascetics; there, too, are the rivers Bahuda and Nanda on the mountain's crest. Mighty king, I have described to you all the tirthas and other sacred places in the eastern quarter.

Hear now of the tirthas, and rivers and mountains and holy places in the other three quarters.'"

CANTO 88

TIRTHA-YATRA PARVA CONTINUED

"Dhaumya continues, 'Listen, O Bhaarata, and I will now tell you about the holy tirthas of the south. In that quarter flows the sacred and auspicious Godavari, full of crystalline water, abounding in tapovanas and frequented by ascetics.

In the south also are the rivers Vena and Bhimarathi, both of which destroy sin and fear, and their banks abounding in birds and deer, and graced with the hermitages of Munis. In that part, too, O Bharatarishabha, is the tirtha of the Rajarishi Nriga – the river Payoshni, enchanting and brimfull of water and visited by Brahmanas. There the lustrous Markandeya, of lofty ascetic merit sang the praises, in verse, of King Nriga's line.

We have heard what happened to King Nriga while performing a yagna at the auspicious Varaha tirtha on the Payoshni. Indra became intoxicated by drinking the Soma rasa during the sacrifice, and the Brahmanas, with the gifts they received. The water of the Payoshni, taken up in a vessel or flowing along the ground, or as spray blown by the wind, can cleanse a person from whatever sins he may commit until the the day of his death.

Higher than heaven itself, and pure, and created and given by the Trisulin, in that tirtha is an image of Mahadeva, seeing which a mortal attains to Sivaloka. Placing on a scale Ganga and the other rivers with their waters on one side, and on the other the Payoshni, in my opinion the latter would outweigh all the other tirthas in terms of punya.

Then, O Bharatottama, upon the mountain called Varuna-strotasa is the sacred and auspicious vana Mathara, with its plenitude of fruit and roots, and containing a sacrificial stake. In the land north of the Praveni, and around the holy asrama of Kanva, are many tapovanas of Rishis.

And, O child, in the tirtha called Surparaka are two sacrificial platforms of the illustrious Jamadagni, known as Pashana and Punaschandra. And, O son of Kunti, in that place is the tirtha Asoka, also with an abundance of hermits' tapovanas.

And, O Yudhishtira, in the country of the Pandyas are the tirthas named Agastya and Varuna. Bull among men, there, amongst the Pandyas, is the tirtha called the Kumaris.

Listen, O son of Kunti, I will now describe Tamraparni. In that asrama, the Devas, impelled by the desire of obtaining salvation, performed tapasya. In that country, also, is the lake of Gokarna, celebrated across the three worlds, which is full of cool, pure water, and which is sacred, auspicious, and can bestow great punya. That lake is extremely difficult of access to men of unpurified hearts and souls.

Near that tirtha is the sacred asrama of Agastya's disciple, the mountain Devasabha, which abounds in trees and grass, and fruit and roots. And there also is the Vaidurya mountain, delightful, replete with gemstones and which bestows great spiritual merit. There on that mountain is the hermitage of Agastya, rich with fruit and roots and water.

Lord of men, I will now describe the tirthas, asramas, and holy rivers and lakes that belong to the Surashtra country. O Yudhishtira, the Brahmanas say that on the sea-coast is the Chamasodbheda, and also Prabhasa, that tirtha which is highly regarded by the gods. There also is the tirtha called Pindaraka, frequented by ascetics and which can bestow great punya.

In that region is a mighty hill named Ujjayanta, which is conducive to quick success, about which Devarishi Narada of great intelligence has composed an ancient sloka. By performing tapasya on the sacred hill of Ujjayanta in Surashtra, which abounds in birds and animals, a person becomes honoured in heaven.

Dwaravati is also in this region, producing great merit, where Madhusudana dwells, who is the Ancient One, in embodied form, and the Sanatana Dharma. Brahmanas versed in the Vedas, and men who know the Atma Vidya say that the illustrious Krishna is eternal Virtue. Govinda is said to be the purest of all pure things, the most righteous of the righteous and the most auspicious of the auspicious.

In all the three worlds, He of eyes like lotus-leaves is the God of gods, and is eternal. He is the pure soul and the Life of life, the Supreme Brahman and the lord of all. That slayer of Madhu, Hari of inconceivable soul, dwells in Dwaravati!'

CANTO 89

TIRTHA-YATRA PARVA CONTINUED

Dhaumya continues, 'O Bhaarata, I will describe to you the holy tirthas, which lie in the west, in the land of the Anartas. There, in a westward course the sacred river Narmada flows, graced by priyangu and mango trees, and garlanded with thickets of bamboo. All the tirthas and sacred spots, and rivers and woods and foremost of mountains that are in the three worlds, all the gods with the Grandsire, along with the Siddhas, the Rishis and the Charanas, Kurusthama, always come to bathe in the sacred waters of the Narmada.

And I have heard that the holy asrama of the Muni Visravas once stood there, and that there was born the Lord of treasures, Kubera, who has men for his vahanas. There also is that best of hills, the sacred and auspicious Vaidurya peak with abundant trees that are evergreen and always graced with flowers and fruit. Lord of the earth, on the top of that mountain is a sacred tank laden with full-blown lotus, to which the Devas and the Gandharvas come. Many are the wonders, O mighty King, that can be seen on that holy mountain, which is like heaven itself and which is visited by celestial Rishis.

There, O subduer of hostile cities, is the sacred river called Viswamitra, which belongs to the Rajarishi of that name and which teems, O Rajan, with tirthas. It was on the banks of this river that Yayati, the son of Nahusha, fell from heaven among the virtuous, and also obtained once more the eternal regions of the righteous.

In this region also are the famed lake called Punya, the mountain called Mainaka, and that other mountain Asita, rich with fruit and roots. And here also is the sacred hermitage of Kakshasena, and O Yudhishtira, the asrama of Chyavana, also, which is famed in every country, O son of Pandu. In that place, O noble one, men attain to moksha without performing severe austerities.

Here, also, Maharajan, is the land called Jambumarga, inhabited by birds and deer, where Sages of self-restraint dwell, O foremost of those that have subdued their senses.

Next, lie the exceedingly sacred Ketumala and Medhya, always graced by Munis, and, O lord of earth, Gangadwara, and the renowned vana of Saindhava, most holy, where the regenerate ones dwell. Here also is the celebrated lake of Brahma, called Pushkara, the favourite abode of the Vaikanasas, and Siddhas and Rishis.

Moved by the desire of having its protection, the Creator sang this verse at Pushkara, O lord of the Kurus and most virtuous of men – If a person of pure soul ever imagines a pilgrimage to the Pushkara, he is purged of all his sins and rejoices in heaven!'

CANTO 90

TIRTHA-YATRA PARVA CONTINUED

Dhaumya continues, 'O tiger among kings, I will now describe the tirthas and sacred places that lie in the north. Do you, O exalted one, listen to me attentively. By hearing this narration, O Kshatriya, one acquires a reverential frame of mind, which is conducive to great good.

In those parts, flows the most sacred Saraswati, abounding in tirthas and her banks easy of descent. There, also, O son of Pandu, is the impetuous ocean-going Yamuna, and the tirtha called Plakshavatarana, which bestows high merit and prosperity. It was there that the Brahmanas bathed after having performed the Saraswata Yagna.

Sinless one, in the famed celestial tirtha called Agni-siras, which generates great punya, the King Sahadeva once performed a sacrifice, after measuring out the sacrificial ground by a throw of the Samya. It is for this reason, Yudhishtira, that Indra sang the praises of Sahadeva in verses, which are still current in this world, and recited by the Dvijas – *On the Yamuna Sahadeva worshipped the sacrificial fire, with gifts in a hundred thousands to Brahmanas.*

There, too, the illustrious king, the imperial Bharata, performed thirty-five horse-sacrifices.

O child, I have heard that Sarabhanga once used to fully gratify the desires of the Brahmanas. In this region is his celebrated asrama, which produces great merit. In that region also, O son of Pritha, is the river Saraswati, which is ever worshipped by the gods, where, in elder days, the Balakhilyas, O great king, performed sacrifices.

In the northern region, also, O Yudhishtira, is the renowned river Drishadwati, which bestows great punya. Then, O chief of men, are Nyagrodhakhya, and Panchalya, and Punyaka and Dalbhyaghosha, and Dalbhya, which are, O son of Kunti, the sacred resort in this world of illustrious Anantayasas of excellent vows and great energy, and which are celebrated over the three worlds.

Here, too, O lord of men, the illustrious Etavarna and Avavarana, versed in the Vedas, learned in Vedic lore, and proficient in the knowlegde of Vedic rites, performed sacrifices of great merit, O king of the Bhaaratas.

Here in the north, is also Visakhayupa to which, in days of yore, came the Devas with Varuna and Indra, and performed tapasya. And that is why the place is so eminently sacred.

Here, also, is Palasaka, where the great and lustrous and most blessed Rishi Jamadagni performed sacrifices, and all the great rivers, in their embodied forms, each bringing their own holy waters, stood surrounding that best of sages. And there also, O king, Viswavasu, Agni himself, at seeing that Mahatman's initiation, sang this sloka – *The rivers, coming to the illustrious Jamadagni, who was sacrificing to the gods, gratified the Brahmanas with offerings of honey.*

O Yudhishtira, the place where Ganga rushes past, cleaving that king of mountains, which is frequented by Gandharvas and Yakshas and Rakshasas and Apsaras, and inhabited by hunters, and Kinnaras, is called Gangadwara. Sanatkumara regards that place visited by Brahmarshis, as also the tirtha Kanakhala that is near it, as being sacred.

There, as well, is the mountain named Puru to which great Rishis come, and where Pururavas was born, and Bhrigu performed tapasya, for which that asrama has become known as the peak Bhrigutunga.

Near that peak is the sacred and extensive Badari, most auspicious asrama, famed over the three worlds, of Him, O Bharatarishabha, who is the Present, the Past and the Future, who is called Narayana and Lord Vishnu, who is eternal and the best of male beings, and who is pre-eminently illustrious.

Near Badari, the cool current of Ganga was once warm, and the banks there were covered with golden sands. There the Devas and Rishis of high fortune and great effulgence, approach the divine Lord Narayana, always, and worship him. All the universe, with all its tirthas and other holy places, is there where the divine and eternal Narayana, the Supreme soul, dwells, for he is Punya, he is the Parabrahman; he is the tirtha, he is the asrama; he is the First, he is the foremost of gods, and he is the great Lord of all creatures. He is eternal, he is the great Creator, and he is the highest state of blessedness.

Learned men, versed in the scriptures, attain to great happiness by knowing him.

In that place are the Devarishis, the Siddhas, and, indeed, all the Rishis, where the slayer of Madhu dwells, that primeval Deity and mighty Yogin. Let no doubt enter your heart that this place is the first of all sacred places.

These, O lord of the earth, are the tirthas and other sacred places in the world. These are all visited by the Vasus, the Sadhyas, the Adityas, the Marutas, the Aswins and the illustrious Rishis who resemble the celestials themselves. By journeying, O son of Kunti, to those places, with your Brahmanas and ascetics, and with your blessed brothers, you will be set free from fear!' says Dhaumya."

TIRTHA-YATRA PARVA CONTINUED

Vaisampayana continued, "O son of the Kurus, even as Dhaumya speaks, Rishi Lomasa of great tejas arrives there; and Yudhishtira, with his followers and his Brahmanas sits around that most righteous Sage, even as the celestials in heaven do around Indra. And having received him with reverence, Dharmaraja Yudhishtira enquires after the reason of his arrival, and the object of his wanderings.

Well-pleased with his welcome, the illustrious Muni replies in sweet words which delight the Pandavas, 'Travelling at will, O Kaunteya, over all the realms, I came to Indra's abode and saw the lord of the Devas there. There, I saw your heroic brother, who can wield the bow with both hands, seated on the same throne with Sakra. Seeing Partha in the lofty place, I was greatly astonished, O tiger among men.

Indra then said to me, "Go, Lomasa, to the sons of Pandu." At his behest, as also that of the noble Arjuna, I have come swiftly here to you, wanting to see you and your younger brothers. Child, I will relate something that will please you greatly, O son of Pandu. Listen to it, O king, with Krishnaa and the Rishis that are with you.

Bharatarishabha, Partha has got that peerless weapon from Rudra for which you sent him on his journey. That fierce astra, the Brahmasira, which arose after the Amrita, and which Rudra once gained through stern tapasya. Arjuna now has that astra, along with the mantras to loose and withdraw it, and the rites for expiation and revival.

Yudhishtira, Arjuna of immeasurable prowess has also acquired Vajras and Dandas and other celestial weapons from Yama and Kubera and Varuna and Indra. He has also learnt music, both vocal and instrumental, thoroughly, and dancing and the art of the proper recitation of the Sama, from Vishwavasu's son. And having thus acquired weapons and mastered the Gandharva Veda, your third brother lives happily in Devaloka.

Listen now Yudhishtira to the message of Indra. He commanded me, "You will go to the world of men. O best of Brahmanas, tell Yudhishtira that I said, 'Your brother Arjuna will soon return to you, having acquired the astras and also having accomplished a great deed for the Devas, which they themselves cannot accomplish. Meanwhile, devote yourself to sannyasa, along with your brothers. There is nothing superior to asceticism, and it is through sannyasa that a person achieves great results.

And, O Bharatarishabha, I well know that Karna is endowed with great ardour and energy and strength and prowess, all incapable of being baffled. Well do I know that, skilled in fierce battle, he has no rival in war; that he is a mighty bowman, a hero who is a master of great weapons and cased in the best mail. Well do I know that that lofty son of Aditya resembles Siva's son Kartikeya himself.

I also well know the awesome natural prowess of the broad-shouldered Arjuna. In battle, Karna is not even a sixteenth part of Pritha's son. And as for the fear of Karna which is in your heart, O Parantapa, I will dispel that when Savyasachin leaves Devaloka.

As for your intention, Kshatriya, to set out on a pilgrimage to the tirthas, Maharishi Lomasa will speak to you about that. And whatever that regenerate Sage says to you about the great merits of sannyasa and the tirthas, you must receive with respect and not otherwise,' said the Lord Indra," Lomasa says.

CANTO 92

TIRTHA-YATRA PARVA CONTINUED

Lomasa continues, "Listen now, O Yudhishtira, to what Dhananjaya said – 'Cause my brother Yudhishtira to attend to the practice of dharma, which leads to prosperity. Blessed with the wealth of asceticism, you are conversant with the highest dharma, with ascetic austerities of every kind, with the eternal duties of kings blessed with prosperity, and the high and sanctifying merit that men obtain from the tirthas. Persuade my brothers, the sons of Pandu, to acquire the punya attaching to the tirthas. With all your soul persuade the king to visit the tirthas and to give away kine.'

This is what Arjuna said to me. Indeed he also said, 'Protected by you, let Yudhishtira visit all the tirthas. You must also protect him from Rakshasas, watch over him in inaccessible regions and upon rugged mountain breasts. And as Dadhichi protected Indra, and Angiras protected the Sun, so must you, O Dvijottama, protect the sons of Kunti from demons. Along the way are many Rakshasas, big as mountain-cliffs, but with your protection, these will not be able to approach the sons of Kunti.'

Obeying the command of Indra and the request of Arjuna, and also protecting you from all danger, I will come with you on your pilgrimage. I have visited the tirthas twice before, O Kuru, and with you I will go to them a third time.

O Yudhishtira, Manu and other Rajarishis of great deeds journeyed to the tirthas. Indeed, a tirtha-yatra can dispel all fear. They that are crooked-minded, who do not have their minds under control, who are ignorant and perverse, do not, O Kauravya, bathe in tirthas. But you are ever virtuous and conversant with dharma and firm in keeping your promises. You will certainly free yourself from samsara, for, O Pandava, you are even like King Bhagiratha, or Gaya, or Yayati, or any one, O son of Kunti, that is like them."

Yudhishtira replies, 'I am so overwhelmed with delight, O Brahmana, that I cannot find words to answer you. Who can be more fortunate than he who is remembered even by the lord of the Devas? Who can be more fortunate than he who has been favoured with your company, who has Dhananjaya for a brother, and who is thought of by Vasava himself?

As for what you say, illustrious one, about a tirtha yatra, my mind had already been made up at what Dhaumya said to me. O Brahmana, I will set out at whatever hour you may be pleased to appoint, on the pilgrimage. This is my firm resolve!'

Lomasa then says to Yudhishtira, who has made up his mind to go on the yatra, 'O mighty king, be light in your retinue, for so you will travel more easily.'

Yudhishtira then says, 'Let those mendicants and Brahmanas and Yogis that cannot bear hunger and thirst, the fatigues of travel and toil, and the severity of winter, desist from coming with us. Let those Brahmanas also not come that live on sweetmeats, and they also that desire cooked food that is sucked or drunk, as well as meat. And let those also remain behind that are dependent on cooks.

Let those citizens that have followed me from loyalty, and whom I have hitherto suppported, go back to King Dhritarashtra. He will give them succour and allowances. If, however, that king refuses to grant them proper allowances, the king of the Panchalas will, for my satisfaction and welfare, surely maintain them.'

And now, though stricken with grief, the citizens and the prinicipal Brahmanas and Yatis set out for Hastinapura, and out of affection for Dharmaraja Yudhishtira, the royal son of Ambika receives them properly, and gratifies them with proper allowances.

And the royal son of Kunti, with only a small band of Brahmanas, stays for three nights in Kamyaka, consoled by Lomasa."

CANTO 93

TIRTHA-YATRA PARVA CONTINUED

Vaisampayana said, "The Brahmanas, who have been living with him in the forest, see the son of Kunti about to set out on his tirtha yatra, approach him, O King, and say, 'You are about to set out on your journey to the sacred tirthas, along with your brothers and the Rishi Lomasa. O King, O son of Pandu, take us with you, for without you we will never be able to visit them at any time. Surrounded by dangers and difficult of access, they are infested by beasts of prey.

Those tirthas, O lord of men, are inaccessible to small bands of men. Greatest among bowmen, your brothers are always valiant; and with your protection, we also wish to visit the sacred places. Help us also, O lord of the earth, to acquire the punya of the tirthas. Protected by your valour, let us, as well, be cleansed of all our sins by visiting the sacred fords and bathing in their waters.

Bathing in the tirthas, O Bhaarata, you will certainly gain the realms so difficult of acquisition, which only Kartavirya and Ashtaka, the Rajarishi Lomapada and the imperial and heroic Bharata earned for themselves. Rajan, we want to behold Prabhasa and the other tirthas,

Mahendra and the other mountains, Ganga and the other rivers, and Plaksha and the other giant trees.

If, O lord of men, you have any regard for Brahmanas, do our bidding; you will surely gain prosperity from this. Mahabaho, the tirthas swarm with Rakshasas that ever obstruct ascetic penances. It falls to you to protect us from them. Watched over by Lomasa and taking us with you, go to all the tirthas of which Dhaumya and the wise Narada spoke, as also to all those of which the celestial Lomasa, blessed with great ascetic wealth, told; and by this, be cleansed of all your sins.'

Thus addressed respectfully by them, the king, that bull amongst the sons of Pandu, surrounded by his heroic brothers led by Bhima, with tears of joy in his eyes, says to all those ascetics, 'Let it be so.'

So, at Lomasa's behest and Dhaumya's urging, that best of the Pandavas, his soul perfectly restrained, resolves to set out, along with his brothers and Draupadi of faultless features. Just then, the blessed Vyasa, as also Parvata and Narada, all of lofty wisdom, come to Kamyaka to meet the son of Pandu. Seeing them, Yudhishtira worships them with proper rites.

Thus worshipped by the king, those blessed ones say, 'O Yudhishtira, O Bhima, and you twins, banish all evil thoughts from your minds. Purify your hearts and then set out for the tirthas. The Brahmanas have said that the observance of regulations for the body are called earthly vows, while efforts to purify the heart, so that it may be free from evil thoughts, are called spiritual vows.

O King, the mind that is free from all evil thoughts is most pure. Purifying yourselves, therefore, harbouring only friendly feelings for all, go and see the tirthas. Observing earthly vows with your bodies and purifying your minds through spiritual vows, obtain all the fruit, as told to you, of pilgrimages.'

Saying, 'So be it,' the Pandavas, with Krishnaa, had those celestial and human Rishis perform the customary propitiatory rituals. And having worshipped the feet of Lomasa and Dwaipayana and Narada and the divine Rishi Parvata, and accompanied by Dhaumya as also the ascetics that had been living with them in the forest, the Pandavas set out on the day following the full moon of Agrahayana in which the constellation Pushya is ascending.

Dressed in bark and hides, and with matted locks on their heads, they are all cased in impenetrable mail and armed with swords. And, O Janamejaya, the heroic sons of Pandu, with quivers and arrows and scimitars and other weapons, and accompanied by Indrasena and other attendants, with fourteen and one chariots, a number of cooks and servants of other classes, set out with their faces turned towards the east!"

CANTO 94

Tirtha-yatra Parva Continued

"Yudhishtira says, 'O best of Devarishis, I do not think that I am without merit. Yet I am afflicted with so much sorrow that there never was a king like me. I think, however, that my enemies have no good in them, nor even any dharma. Then why, O Lomasa, do they prosper in this world?'

Lomasa says, 'Do not grieve, O son of Pritha, that sinful men often do prosper as a consequence of the sins they commit. A man may be seen to prosper by his sins, obtain good therefrom and vanquish his enemies. However, destruction overtakes him to his very roots.

O King, I have seen many Daityas and Danavas prosper through sin but I have also seen doom overtake them. O exalted one, I have seen all this in the Krita Yuga.

The Devas practised dharma, while the Asuras abandoned it. The gods visited the tirthas, while the demons did not. And at first the sinful Asuras were possessed by pride; pride begot vanity and vanity begot wrath. And from wrath there arose every kind of evil propensity, and from these sprang shamelessness. And in consequence of shamelessness, good conduct disappeared from amongst them; and because they had become shameless and devoid of virtue and good conduct and virtuous vratas, forgiveness and prosperity and morality forsook them in no time.

And then, O King, prosperity sought the Devas, while adversity found the Asuras; and when the Daityas and the Danavas, deprived of good sense by pride, were possessed by adversity, Kali also sought to possess them. And, O son of Kunti, overwhelmed by pride, and destitute of rites and sacrifices, and devoid of reason and feeling, and their hearts full of vanity, destruction soon overtook them. Covered with infamy, the Daityas were quickly exterminated.

However, the Devas, who were virtuous in their practices, going to the seas, the rivers, the lakes and the holy spots, cleansed themselves of all sins, O son of Pandu, through ascetic penances and sacrifices and gifts and blessings, and found prosperity. And because the gods always performed sacrifices and holy deeds abandoning every practice that was evil, and visited the tirthas, they acquired great good fortune.

Be guided by this, O King; and you also, with your brothers, bathe in the tirthas, for then you will regain prosperity once more. This is the eternal road. As King Nriga and Sibi and Ausinara and Bhagiratha and Vasumanas and Gaya and Puru and Pururavas performed tapasya and, visiting the tirthas, touched sacred waters and saw illustrious Rishis, gained fame and sanctity and merit and wealth, so will you find fortune that is great. And as Ikshvaku with his sons, friends and followers, as Muchukunda and Mandhatri and King Marutta, as the Devas, through the power of asceticism and the Devarishis also, all gained fame, so will you also find great celebrity. The son of Dhritarashtra, on the other hand, enslaved by sin and ignorance, will, without doubt, soon be destroyed like the Daityas.'"

CANTO 95

Tirtha-yatra Parva Continued

Vaisampayana said, "The heroic sons of Pandu, accompanied by their followers, travelling from place to place, at last arrive at Naimisha. O King, reaching the Gomati, the Pandavas bathe in the sacred tirtha of that river, and having performed their ablutions there, they give away, O Bhaarata, both kine and wealth. Repeatedly offering oblations of water to the Devas, the Pitrs, and the Brahmanas, in the tirthas called Kanya, Aswa, and Gaya, and staying in Kalakoti and the Vishaprastha hills, the Pandavas then come to Bahuda and perform their ablutions in that stream.

Going next, O lord of earth, to the sacrificial realm of the gods known as Prayaga, they bathe in the confluence of Ganga and Yamuna and living there, perform tapasya of great merit. And bathing in that tirtha, the Pandavas, of firm vratas, cleanse themselves of every sin.

The sons of Pandu, accompanied by those Brahmanas, travel next to the tirtha called Vedi, sacred to the Creator and adored by ascetics. Staying there for some time and gratifying the Brahmanas with the fruit and roots of the wilderness and with ghee, those Kshatriyas begin to perform ascetic penances of deep punya.

They next journey to Mahidhara consecrated by the great Rajarishi Gaya of unrivalled splendour. In that land is the mountain called Gayasira, as well as the enchanting river Mahanadi, her fine banks graced by thickets of bamboo. On that divine mountain of holy peaks is another tirtha, the Brahmsaras, adored by ascetics. On the banks of that lake, of old, Dharma Deva, eternal god of justice himself dwelt, and it was there that the illustrious Rishi Agastya went to see that deity.

From that lake, all those sacred rivers arise, and in that tirtha, Mahadeva, wielder of the Pinaka, is present for ever.

Arriving there, the Pandavas keep the vrata called Chaturmasya, observing all the rites of the great sacrifice called Rishiyajna. There that mighty tree called the Eternal Banyan stands; any sacrifice performed there produces merit that is eternal. In that sacrificial dais of the gods producing eternal punya, the Pandavas begin to fast with concentrated souls. And there, Brahmanas, by hundreds, endowed with the wealth of asceticism, come to them; these Brahmanas also all perform the Chaturmasya sacrifice according to the rites prescribed by the Rishis.

In that tirtha, those Brahmanas old in knowledge and ascetic merit and masters of the Vedas, become the court of the lustrous sons of Pandu, and they discourse upon various subject of sacred import. And it was in that place that the wise and holy Shamata, who leads a life of celibacy, speaks to them, O King, of Gaya, the son of Amurtaraya.

Shamata says, 'Gaya, the son of Amurttaraya, was one of the greatest of all Rajarishis. Listen to me, O Bhaarata, I will tell of his deeds of dharma. It was here, O King, that Gaya performed many sacrifices distinguished by the vast quantities of food he distributed and the profuse gifts he gave. Those yagnas had hundres of thousands of hills of cooked rice, lakes of clarified butter and rivers of curds, in many hundreds, and streams of rich curries, in thousands.

Day after day, these were prepared and given to all comers, while, over and above this, Brahmanas and others, O king, received more food that was clean and pure. During the conclusion of every sacrifice, when gifts were dedicated to the Brahmanas, the chanting of the Vedas reached the heavens. And so loud, indeed, was the sound of the Vedic mantras that nothing else, O Bhaarata, could be heard, for these sacred sounds filled the earth, the points of the horizon, the sky and heaven itself.

Such were the wonders that people observed on those occasions. Gratified with the excellent food and drink that the illustrious Gaya provided, men, O Bharatarishabha, went about singing these verses:

At Gaya's great sacrifice, who is there today, amongst creatures, that still wants to eat anymore? There are yet twenty-five mountains of food there after everyone has been fed! What Rajarishi Gaya of untold splendour has achieved in his sacrifice has never been achieved by men before, nor will be by any in the future. The gods have been so surfeited by Gaya with clarified butter that they are unable to take anything that anybody else offers. As sand grains on earth, as stars in the firmament, as raindrops showered by clouds cannot ever be counted by anyone, so, too, can no one count the gifts given during Gaya's sacrifice!

O son of the Kurus, many times did King Gaya perform such yagnas here, by the side of this Brahmasaras!"

CANTO 96

TIRTHA-YATRA PARVA CONTINUED

Vaisampayana said, "After this, the royal son of Kunti, who always gave profusely to Brahmanas, goes to the asrama of Agastya and takes up his abode in Durjaya. It is here that that best of speakers, King Yudhishtira asks Lomasa why Agastya slew Vatapi in this place. And the king also enquires after the extent of that man-killing Daitya's prowess, and the reason, also, why the illustrious Agastya's wrath was stirred against that Asura.

So questioned, Lomasa says, 'O son of the Kurus, there was in the city called Manimati, in days of yore, a Daitya named Ilvala, whose younger brother was Vatapi. One day that son of Diti said to a Brahmana endowed with ascetic merit, "Holy one, grant me a son equal unto Indra."

The Brahmana, however, did not grant the Asura a son like Indra. At this, the Asura was inflamed with wrath, and from that day, O king, the Asura Ilvala became a killer of Brahmanas. And blessed with the power of maya, the angry Asura would transform his brother into a ram. And Vatapi, who could also assume any form at will, would assume the shape of a ram; and the flesh of that ram, after being properly cooked, was offered to Brahmanas as food. And after they ate, they were killed, for whoever Ilvala summoned with his voice would come back to Ilvala, re-embodied, even if he had gone to the land of Yama, and show himself to Ilvala.

So, tranforming Vatapi into a ram and properly cooking his flesh and feeding Brahmanas therewith, he would summon Vatapi. And the mighty Asura Vatapi, that enemy of Brahmanas, endowed with great strength and the power of illusion, upon hearing, O king, the loud voice of Ilvala calling, would tear open the belly of the Brahmana and come out chortling! So it was that the evil Daitya Ilvala, having fed unsuspecting Brahmanas, frequently took their lives.

Meanwhile, the illustrious Agastya saw his departed ancestors hanging in a pit with their heads downwards. He asked them, "What is the matter with you?"

Those Brahmavadins replied, "We are your manes, and it is to have offspring that we hang in this pit. Agastya, if you can beget a good son, we can be saved from this hell and you will also find the blessed state of having a child."

Blessed with great energy and observant of truth and dharma, Agastya replied, "O Pitrs, I will accomplish your desire. Let this anxiety of yours be dispelled."

And the lustrous Rishi then began to think of perpetuating his race. But he did not see a wife worthy of him, from whom he himself could take birth in the form of a son. Then he took every part considered most beautiful from many who possessed these individually, and created an exquisite woman.

That Muni, endowed with great ascetic merit, gave that girl created for himeslf to the king of the Vidharbhas who was then performing tapasya to have children. Through Agastya's power, the lovely girl he had created was born into Vidarbha's royal line and, beautiful as effulgent lightning, she grew day by day. And as soon as that lord of earth—the king of the Vidarbhas—saw her ushered into life, he joyfully gave the news, O Bhaarata, to the Brahmanas. The Brahmanas blessed the girl and they named her Lopamudra.

Possessed of great beauty, she began to grow as quickly as a lotus in the water or the flame of a fire. And when she attained puberty, a hundred virgins decked in ornaments and a hundred maids waited in obedience upon her; she shone in their midst, brilliant as she was, like Rohini in the firmament amidst an inferior multitude of stars. And possessed as she was of good conduct and excellent manners, none dared ask for her hand even when she attained puberty, through fear of her father, the king of the Vidharbhas.

Lopamudra, devoted to truth, surpassing even the Apsaras in beauty, gratified her father and relatives with her deportment. Seeing his daughter turn into a young woman, her father began to think, "To whom should I give this daughter of mine?"'

CANTO 97

TIRTHA-YATRA PARVA CONTINUED

Lomasa continues, 'When Agastya thought that that girl was competent for domesticity, he approached the king of the Vidharbhas, and said, "I ask you, O king, to give me your daughter Lopamudra."

The king swooned; yet, though unwilling to give the Muni his daughter, he dared not refuse. Going to his queen, he said, "This Rishi has great power. If angered, he may consume me with the fire of his curse. O you of the sweet face, tell me what you wish."

His queen did not say a word. Lopamudra saw them both distraught and came to them. She said, "O king, do not grieve on my account. Give me away to Agastya, and, O father, save yourself."

So, the king gave Lopamudra to the illustrious Agastya with due rites. When she was his wife, Agastya said to Lopamudra, "Cast away these costly robes and ornaments."

At the word of her lord, that large-eyed young woman, of thighs tapering as the stem of the plantain tree, put aside her fine and costly robes, and she dressed herself in rags and tree-bark and deer-skin, and became her husband's equal in vrata and karma.

Going then to Gangadwara that best of Rishis began to practise the severest penances along with his dutiful and helpful wife. Lopamudra, herself well pleased, began to serve her lord from the deep respect that she bore him. The lofty Agastya also began to show great love for his wife.

After a considerable time, O king, the Rishi one day saw Lopamudra, blazing in ascetic splendour, come up after the bath, in her season. And pleased with the girl, for her services, her purity, and self control, as also with her grace and beauty, he called her to him for marital intercourse.

However, the girl, folding her hands, said bashfully but lovingly to the Rishi, "The husband, without doubt, weds the wife for offspring. But, O Muni, I beg you show me the same love which I bear for you. O Dvija, it becomes you to approach me on a bed like the one I had in the palace of my father. I also want you to be decked in garlands of flowers and other ornaments, and that I should come to you adorned in the celestial ornaments that I like.

Otherwise, I cannot come to you, dressed in these rags dyed in red. Nor, O regenerate Rishi, is it sinful to wear ornaments on such an occasion."

Agastya replied, "O blessed girl, you of the slender waist, I do not have wealth like what your father has, Lopamudra!"

She said, "You who have the wealth of tapasya can certainly fetch anything that exists in the world of men, in a moment, by your power."

Agastya said, "It is even as you say, but that would exhaust my punya. O bid me do what may not make me lose my ascetic merit."

Lopamudra then said, "O Muni, my season will not last long, but I do not wish to come to you otherwise, nor do I wish to diminsh your punya in any way. You must do as I wish, without injuring your virtue."

Agastya then said, "O blessed one, if this is your resolve, upon which you have set your heart, I will go out in quest of wealth. Meanwhile, you stay here, as it pleases you.'"

CANTO 98

TIRTHA-YATRA PARVA CONTINUED

Lomasa continues, 'Agastya went to King Srutarvana who was regarded as richer than other kings, to beg for wealth. And that monarch, learning of the arrival of the pot-born Rishi on the frontiers of his kingdoms, went out with his ministers and received the holy one reverentially. The king duly offered the Sage arghya, submissively and with folded hands and then enquired after the reason for the Rishi's coming.

And Agastya answered, "Lord of the earth, know that I have come to you for wealth. Give me what you can afford and without doing injury to anyone."

The king, then, told the Rishi how his income and his expenditure were equal, adding, "Learned one, take from my possessions the wealth you please."

Seeing however that the king's income and what he spent were equal, the Sage thought that if he took anything, he would deprive someone by what he did. So, taking Srutarvan with him, the Rishi went to Bhadhnaswa, who, hearing of their arrival on his frontiers, went forth to receive them. 'Bhadhnaswa also offered them the arghya and padya, water to wash their feet. Then, with their leave, he asked after the reason for their coming.

Agastya said, "Lord of the earth, know that we have come to you for wealth. Give us what you can, while doing no injury to any of your subjects."

That king informed them of how his income and his expenditure, also, were equal, and said, "Knowing this, take whatever you want."

The Rishi, who saw all things with equal eyes, thought that if he took anything under the circumstances, what he did would injure all creatures. Agastya and Srutarvan, with King Bhadhnaswa then went to Purokutsa's son, Trasadasyu, of enormous wealth. The high-souled Trasadasyu learnt of their arrival on the border of kingdom, went out and received them with reverence. And that best of kings, in Ikshvaku's line, having worshipped all of them duly, asked why they had come.

And Agastya said, "Lord of earth, know that we have all come to you for wealth. Give us what you can, while doing no creature any harm."

That monarch then, also, told them how his income and his expenses were equal, and added, "Knowing this, take what you wish."

However, seeing how that king's expenses were equal to his income, the Rishi, who saw all things with equal eyes, thought that if he took anything, he would harm all creatures.

Now, Rajan, those kings looked at one another, and together said to the Rishi, "O Brahmana, there is a Danava called Ilvala, who of all beings on earth has the most wealth. Let us go together to him today and beg wealth of him."

This suggestion, O king, of begging wealth of Ilvala appeared to them to be proper; and all of them went together to Ilvala.'

TIRTHA-YATRA PARVA CONTINUED

Lomasa says, 'When Ilvala learnt that those kings along with the Maharishi had arrived on the confines of his domain, he went out with his ministers and worshipped them duly. And that prince of Asuras received them hospitably, entertaining them, O son of the Kuru race, with well cooked meat, which was that of his brother Vatapi, transformed into a ram.

When those Rajarishis saw the mighty Asura Vatapi, who had changed into a ram, thus cooked for them, they became disconsolate and were almost senseless with grief and fear.

But Agastya , best of Rishis, said to those royal sages, "Do not worry, I will eat the Asura."

And the mighty Rishi sat himself down on an excellent chair, and the prince of Asuras, Ilvala, began to serve the food, smiling. Agastya ate up all of the meat of the ram which Vatapi had turned into. When the meal was over, Ilvala began to call out to his brother. But only a great belch of air issued from the belly of Agastya, with a sound, O child, as loud as the rumbling of clouds.

Repeatedly, Ilvala called, "Come out, O Vatapi!"

Then that best of Munis, Agastya, burst out laughing, and said, "How can he come out, I have digested him?"

Ilvala was stricken, and folding his hands, along with his ministers, said, "What have you come here for? What can I do for you?"

Smiling, Agastya replied, "We know, O Asura, that you have great power and great wealth, as well. I have great need of wealth and these kings cannot give it to me, being needy themselves. Give us what you can, without depriving anyone."

Ilvala saluted the Rishi and said, "Say what I should give, and I will."

Agastya said, "O great Asura, give each of these kings ten thousand cows and as many gold coins; and to me give twice as much, as well as a golden chariot and a pair of horses fleet as thought. Why, if you look even now you will find that your chariot has become made of gold."

At which, O son of Kunti, Ilvala made enquiries and learnt that the car he intended to give away was really a golden one. His heart sad, the Daitya then gave away much wealth and that ratha, to which two steeds called Virava and Surava were yoked. Those steeds, O Bhaarata, took the kings and Agastya and all that wealth to the Sage's asrama, in the twinkling of an eye. Taking Agastya's leave, the Rajarishis went away to their respective cities.

Agastya, using the wealth of the Asura, did all that Lopamudra wanted. And Lopamudra said, "Most illustrious one, you have given me everything I wanted. Now beget a son on me, a child of immense tejas."

And Agastya replied, "Blessed and beautiful one, you have pleased me greatly with your conduct. Listen now to what I have to say with regard to your offspring. Would you have a thousand sons, or a hundred sons each equal to ten, or ten sons equal each to a hundred, or only one son who may vanquish a thousand?"

Lopamudra answered, "Let me have one son equal to a thousand! One good and wise son is preferable to many evil ones."

Saying, "So be it," that pious Muni took his chaste wife to himself, and after she had conceived, he retired into the forest. After Agastya Muni had gone away, the foetus grew inside Lopamudra for seven years. At the end of seven years, from her womb there issued the wise and learned Dridasyu, blazing, O Bhaarata, in his own splendour. He came forth auspiciously, as if chanting the Vedas, with the Upanishads and the Angas.

Endowed with great energy while yet a child, he would carry loads of sacrificial fuel into his father's asrama, and so he was called Idhmavaha – the bearer of sacrificial wood.

When Agastya saw his son, with such virtue, he was greatly pleased. So it was, O Bhaarata, that Agastya begot a splendid son, as a result of which his ancestors, O king, gained the realms they desired. And it is from that line that this place has become known in the world as Agastyasrama.

Indeed, Rajan, this is the asrama of great beauty, of the Rishi Agastya who consumed Vatapi of the race of Prahlada. The sacred Bhagirathi, adored by Devas and Gandharvas, gently flows by this hermitage like a breeze-shaken pennon in the sky. Yonder also she flows over craggy crests, descending lower and lower, and looks like an affrighted she-snake lying along the hilly slopes. Issuing out of the matted locks of Mahadeva, she passes along through the southern country nurturing it like a mother; and ultimately flows into the ocean as if she were his favourite bride.

Bathe as you like in this sacred river, you son of Pandu! And behold there, O Yudhishtira, the tirtha of Bhrigu that is celebrated throughout the three worlds and adored, O King, by Maharishis. Bathing there, Rama, of Bhrigu's race, regained his might, which had been taken from him by Dasaratha's son. Bathing here, O son of Pandu, with your brothers and Krishnaa, you will certainly regain that power of yours, which has been taken by Duryodhana, even as Parasurama regained his, which Dasaratha's son took from him during their hostile encounter.'

At this, Yudhishtira bathes there with his brothers and Krishnaa, and offers oblations of water, O Bhaarata, to the Devas and the Pitrs.

And, O bull among men, after Yudhishtira has bathed in that tirtha, his body blazes forth in brighter effulgence, and he becomes invincible to all his enemies.

The Pandava asks Lomasa, 'Illustrious one, why were Rama's energy and might taken away? And how did he regain them? Mahatman, I beg you, tell me everything.'

Lomasa says, 'Listen, O king, to the tale of Dasaratha's son Rama and Rama of Bhrigu's line, of great intelligence. To kill Ravana, O king, Vishnu incarnated himself as the son of Dasaratha. We saw Dasaratha's son in Ayodhya after he was born. It was then that Rama of Bhrigu's line, the son of Richika by Renuka, heard of Dasaratha's son Rama, of immaculate purity, and impelled by curiosity, he went to Ayodhya, taking with him the divine bow which had been the scourge of the Kshatriyas, to test the prowess of Dasaratha's son.

Hearing that Rama of Bhrigu's race had arrived at the borders of his dominion, Dasaratha sent his own son Rama to receive the great one with reverence. Seeing Dasaratha's son approach and stand before him with his weapons, Rama of Bhrigu's line said challengingly, sneeringly, to him, "O king, O lofty one, if you can, with all your might, string this bow, which in my hands became the instrument of the destruction of the race of Kshatriyas."

Dasaratha's son answered, "Illustrious one, it does not behove you to insult me like this. I do not lack the virtues of the Kshatriya varna, and the descendants of Ikshvaku, in particular, never boast of their prowess."

Rama of Bhrigu's line replied, "Be done with clever talk and take this bow!"

At this, Rama the son of Dasaratha, angered, took that celestial bow from the hands of Rama of Bhrigu's, that weapon which had killed the greatest Kshatriyas. And, O Bhaarata, the mighty prince smilingly strung that bow, effortlessly, and with its twang loud as thunder, terrified all creatures.

Dasaratha's son Rama said to Parasurama Bhargava, "Here, I have strung this bow. What else, O Brahmana, shall I do for you?"

Jamadagni's son Rama handed Dasaratha's Rama a heavenly arrow, and said, "Fit this to the bow-string and draw it to your ear, O Kshatriya!"

Dasaratha's son blazed up in wrath and said, "I have listened to whatever you said and even forgiven you; O Bhargava, you are full of vanity. Through Brahma's grace you have got prowess superior to that of the Kshatriyas, and it is for this that you insult me. But behold me now in my pristine form – I give you sight."

Then Rama, the Bhargava, saw in the body of Dasaratha's son the Adityas with the Vasus, the Rudras, the Sadhyas with the Marutas, the Pitrs, Hutasana, the stellar constellations and the planets, the Gandharvas, the Rakshasas, the Yakshas, the Rivers, the tirthas, those eternal Brahmarishis called the Balakhilyas, the Devarishis, the Seas and Mountains, the Vedas with the Upanishads and Vashats and the sacrifices, the Samans in their living form, the Science of weapons, O Bhaarata, and the Clouds with rain and lightning, O Yudhishtira!

And lustrous Vishnu then loosed that arrow, and the earth was filled with sounds of thunder, and burning meteors began to flash through the sky; and showers of dust and rain fell upon the earth; and whirlwinds and frightful reverberations convulsed everything, and the earth herself began to quake.

And shot by the hand of Rama, that shaft, confounding the other Rama, came back blazing into Rama's hands. Bhargava, who had fainted, regaining consciousness, now bowed to Rama –that manifestation of Vishnu's power. Then, commanded by Vishnu, he went away to the mountains of Mahendra, and then onwards that great ascetic began to live there, in terror and shame.

When a year passed, the Pitrs, seeing Rama there, bereft of all vitality, his pride quelled, and sunk in affliction, said to him, "O son, having approached Vishnu, you did not behave properly towards him. He deserves worship for ever and reverence in the three worlds. Go, O child, to the sacred river Vadhusara. Bathing in all the tirthas of that stream, you will regain your vigour. There in that river is the tirtha

Diptoda where your grandsire Bhrigu, O Rama, performed great tapasya in the Krita Yuga."

Rama, O son of Kunti, did as the Pitrs asked, and at this tirtha, he regained the powers he had lost. This, O Pandava, was what befell the great Rama in days of yore, after he met Vishnu incarnate as Dasaratha's son.'

TIRTHA-YATRA PARVA CONTINUED

Yudhishtira says, 'Dvijottama, I want to listen again in detail to the achievements of Agastya Rishi, of awesome glory.'

Lomasa says, 'Listen then, O king, to the excellent and wonderful and extraordinary story of Agastya, as also about the prowess of that Rishi of immeasurable tejas.

In the Krita Yuga there were some tribes of fierce Danavas that were invincible in battle, and they were called the Kalakeyas and possessed dreadful prowess. Vandinng together under Vritra and arming themselves with diverse weapons they hunted the Devas with Indra at their head, in all directions.

The gods decided that Vritra must be killed, and went with Indra to Brahma. Seeing them standing before him with folded hands, Parameshti addressed them all, saying, "I know everything, O Devas, and why you have come. I will tell you how you can kill Vritra.

There is a high-souled and great Rishi called Dadhicha. Go, all together, and seek a boon from him. He will become pleased, and that virtuous Rishi will grant you the boon. If you want victory, go and say to him: *For the good of the three worlds, give us your bones.*

Renouncing his body, he will give you his bones. With these bones of his, make a fierce and powerful weapon, which will be called Vajra, with six sides, and a terrible roar, and capable of destroying even the most powerful enemies. With that weapon, Indra of a a hundred sacrifices shall kill Vritra.

This is all I have to say; see you do as I have told you, quickly."

Taking his leave, the gods came away, and with Narayana at their head went to Dadhicha's asrama, which stood on the banks of the Saraswati, in an entwinement of many diverse trees and vines. The hermitage resounded with the hum of bees as if they were reciting Samans; it echoed with the melodious songs of the male Kokila and the Chakora. Bison and boar and deer and chamaras wandered there at their pleasure, free from the fear of tigers in this holy place; and tuskers with the juice of rut trickling down from rent temples, plunged in the stream, sported with she-elephants and made all the place resound with their trumpeting.

The place also echoed with the roars of lions and tigers, while at times those grisly monarchs of the forest could be seen lying stretched in caves and glens, adorning them with their presence. Such was the asrama of Dadhicha, like a bit of heaven, which the gods entered. And there they saw Dadhicha looking like the Sun himself in splendour and ablaze with grace like the Grandsire himself.

The Devas prostrated at the feet the Rishi, and bowing low before him, begged the boon that Brahma had told them to.

Well pleased, Dadhicha said to those greatest of gods, "Devas I will do anything for your good, even give up this body of mine."

Saying this, that greatest of men, his soul under perfect restraint, suddenly renounced his life. The gods then took the bones of the deceased Rishi as they had been directed to. Glad at heart, the Devas went to Tvashtri, the celestial Artificer, and told him about the way in which they could defeat the Asuras.

Tvashtri was filled with joy, and, with great attention and care, he fashioned the awesome weapon called the Vajra. And having made it, he said happily to Indra, "Great One, make ashes of the terrible enemy with this ayudha; and having slain him, rule all the domains of swarga in joy, with all who follow you."

Purandara took the Vajra from Tvashtri's hand, joyfully and with proper reverence.'

TIRTHA-YATRA PARVA CONTINUED

Lomasa says, 'Armed with the Vajra, and with the mighty Deva host behind him, Indra confronted Vritra, who was then ruling all of Swarga and Bhumi, heaven and earth. Kalakeyas, of immense bodies, guarded Vritra on every side, with upraised weapons and resembling great mountains with towering peaks.

The battle between the Devas and the Danavas lasted for a short while and was, O lord of the Bhaaratas, terrific in the extreme, appalling the three worlds. Thunderous was the clash of swords and scimitars, wielded by heroic hands. Heads that had been severed fell down from the sky onto the earth like fruits of the palmyra falling onto the ground, when loosened from their stalks.

Armed with iron-mounted bludgeons and cased in golden mail, the Kalakeyas ran against the gods, like moving mountains afire. And unable to stand the shock of that ferocious and haughty host, the Devas broke ranks and fled in fear. Purandara of a thousand eyes saw his gods flying in terror and Vritra growing in boldness, and Indra was dejected.

Now, terrified himself by the Kalakeyas, Indra, king of the Devas, sought refuge with Narayana, the Supreme One. Seeing Indra so distraught, eternal Vishnu infused the Deva with a part of his own infinite prowess; and when the Devas saw that Vishnu now protected Sakra, each of them also transferred a portion of his prowess to Indra.

The taintless Brahmarishis also imparted their mystic energies to the lord of the celestials. Indra was mightier than ever, and when Vritra learnt that the Deva king was infused with powers of others, he sent forth some terrific roars. At these, the earth, the directions, the firmament, heaven, and the mountains, all began to tremble.

Hearing this awful sound, Indra was filled with fear and, wanting to kill the Asura quickly, cast, O king, the mighty Vajra at the Demon. Struck by Indra's Vajra, the great Asura, decked in gold and garlands fell headlong, like the great mountain Mandara hurled of old by Vishnu's hands; and although the prince of Daityas was slain, yet Indra ran in panic from the field, and took shelter in a lake, thinking the Vajra had not killed Vritra.

However, the Devas and the Maharishis were filled with joy, and all of them began to joyously sing Indra's praises. Mustering their forces again, the gods began to slaughter the demons, now dispirited at the death of their leader. The Danavas fled into the depths of the sea; and having entered the fathomless deep teeming with fish and crocodiles, the Asuras assembled together and arrogantly began to conspire to destroy the three worlds.

Those among them that were deemed wise suggested different courses of action, each according to his judgment. In course of time, however, the dreadful resolution those sons of Diti arrived at was that they should, first of all, compass the destruction of all men of knowledge and ascetic virtue: for, the worlds are all supported by tapasya.

Therefore, they said, "Lose no time in wiping out dhyana and yagnas. Kill all those on earth who have ascetic virtues, those who know the ways of karma and dharma, and especially those that have knowledge of Brahman; for when these are dead, the very universe will be destroyed."

Arriving at this decision to destroy the universe, the Danavas were pleased. They made the ocean—that realm of Varuna—with waves high as hills, their fortress, from which to make their attacks.'

CANTO 102

TIRTHA-YATRA PARVA CONTINUED

Lomasa says, 'The Kalakeyas began to put their plan to destroy the universe in motion. During the darkness of night, the angry Daityas would issue from the Sea and devour all the Munis they found in wooded asramas and other sacred places.

In Vasishta's asrama, the evil ones ate a hundred and eighty Brahmanas, besides nine other ascetics. Going on to Chyavana's hermitage, home to many Brahmacharis, they devoured another hundred Brahmanas who lived on just fruit and roots.

While these depredations continued through the nights, they returned to safety under the sea by day. In Bharadwaja's asrama, they killed a score of Brahmanas of subdued souls, Brahmacharis who lived just on air and water. So, the Kalakeyas, intoxicated with power and their lives nearly run out, invaded every Rishi's asrama, one by one, during the hours of darknes, and slaughtered numberless holy Brahmanas.

And, O best of men, though they continued with these savage attacks, killing so many Sages in their asramas, no one could find them, or where they hid. Every morning dead bodies of fragile Munis were found, many of them without flesh and without blood, without marrow, without entrails, and with limbs torn from one another; here and there, bones were heaped like conch shells.

And the earth was strewn with the contents of broken sacrificial jars and shattered ladles for pouring libations of clarified butter and with the ruins of sacred fires once kept burning with care by the ascetics.

And the universe, afflicted with terror of the Kalakeyas, and without the Vedas being chanted or vashats or sacrificial festivals or religious rites, was dreary and without any joy. O king, when men began to perish in this way, the survivors, taken with fear, fled for their lives in all directions; some fled to caverns and some hid behind mountain-streams and springs, while others just died of fear.

But some that were brave and mighty bowmen, spiritedly, cheerfully, went out and took great pains to track the Danavas to their lair; however, they did not find them because the demons hid beneath the sea. The valiant bowmen returned to their homes, at least satisfied that they had searched.

And, O lord of men, while the universe was being destroyed, and when sacrificial festivals and religious rites had all ceased, the gods became deeply perturbed. Gathering together around Indra, they held council; and then going to the exalted and un-born Narayana—that unvanquished God of Vaikunta—the celestials sought his protection.

Bowing to Madhusudana, the Devas said, "O Lord, you are the creator, the protector, and the destroyer of ourselves, as well as of the universe. It is you who have created this universe with its mobile and immobile creatures. O lotus-eyed one, in days of old, you took the form of the Varaha and raised the sunken earth out of the Sea, to benefit all beings.

Purushottama, you assumed the form of the Narasimha, and, in ancient times, killed the mighty Asura Hiranyakasipu; taking the form of the Vamana, you subdued the invincible Bali, and thrust him down into Patala. Lord, it was you who killed the evil Jambha, who was a matchless bowman and who always desecrated and obstructed sacrifices.

Achievements like these, beyond count, belong to you. O slayer of Madhu, we are taken with terror and have only you for our refuge. Devadeva, protect the worlds, the gods, and Sakra also, from this terrible fear."

CANTO 103

Tirtha-yatra Parva Continued

The Devas said, "Through your grace everything is born and the four kind of beings increase. And being created, they worship the dwellers of heaven with offerings made to the gods and the manes of departed fathers.

So, protected by you and free from troubles, they live depending on one another, and increase. Now this peril has befallen the people. We do not know who is killing the Brahmanas during the night. But if the Brahmanas are destroyed, the earth itself will cease to exist, and if the earth comes to an end, heaven also will cease to exist.

Mahabaho, O lord of the universe, we beg you to save all the worlds!"

Vishnu said, "Devas, I know the reason why these Brahmanas die; I will tell of it, listen to me with calm minds. There exists a savage and ferocious host of demons called Kalakeyas. Led by Vritra, these were devastating the very universe.

When the thousand-eyed Indra slew Vritra, to save their lives these Kalakeyas submerged themselves in Vaurna's domain, the ocean. Making the ocean deeps, which abound with sharks and crocodiles, their refuge, they come out at nights, and kill the holy sages, with a view to ending the worlds.

But they cannot be killed, since they have made the sea deeps their sanctuary. Think of some way to dry up the ocean, and I say to you – who but Agastya can achieve this thing? Without drying up the sea, you have no way to attack these Asuras.'

The gods listened to Vishnu, then sought leave from Brahma, who lives in the best of all lokas, and then went to the hermitage of Agastya. They saw the high-souled Agastya, the son of Varuna, of resplendent mien, waited upon by sages, even as Brahma is by gods.

Approaching that son of Mitra and Varuna in his asrama, that magnanimous and unswerving one, who looked like an embodiment of pious karma heaped together, they glorified him by reciting his deeds.

The deities said, "You were once the refuge of the gods when Nahusha oppressed them. Thorn of the world that he was, he was cast down from his throne in swarga – from the celestial realms.

Vindhya, foremost of mountains, suddenly began to increase his height, due to an angry competition with the Sun, but you commanded him to stop and he could not refuse you and stopped growing.

And when darkness covered the world, the created were all threatened by death, but having gained you for a protector, they found utmost security. Whenever peril besets us, you are always our refuge; this is why we have come to ask a boon from you, and we know that you always grant any boon for which you are asked.'"

CANTO 104

Tirtha-yatra Parva Continued

Yudhishtira says, 'O Maharishi, I am eager to know in detail how Vindhya became so incensed that he began to grow.'

Lomasa says, 'Between his rising and setting, the Sun used to revolve around that monarch of mountains – the great Meru of golden lustre. Seeing this, the Mountain Vindhya said to Surya, "As you go every day round Meru and honour him with your pradakshinas, do the same to me, O maker of light!"

The Sun replied to the great mountain, "I do not honour Meru by my own will. Those who have made this universe have assigned my path to me."

Wrathful in a moment, the Vindhya mountain suddenly began to increase his size, for, O Parantapa, he wanted to obstruct the paths of the Sun and the Moon. All the Devas assembled and came to Vindhya, that mighty king of mountains, and tried to dissuade him from this. But he paid no heed to their entreaties.

Then the gods went to the Sage in his asrama, at his tapasaya, the very best and most powerful of those who are devoted to dharma, and told Agastya Muni what had happened.

The Devas said, "This king of hills, Vindhya, has yielded to anger and stops the paths of the Sun and the Moon, and also the course of the stars. O best of Brahmanas! O most gifted one! None but you can make him desist; we beg you, make him stop."

Hearing what the Devas said, the Brahmana came to the mountain; and, with his wife, he said to the Vindhya, "O best of mountains, give me a path, for I need to go south for a purpose of mine. Until my return, wait for me; and when I have come back grow on as much as you please!"

Parantapa, having made this compact with Vindhya, Varuna's son has not, until today, returned from the southern region. So it is that, by Agastya's power, the Vindhya has not grown any further.

Now, O king, listen to how the Devas killed the Kalakeyas, after getting their boon from Agastya Muni.

Having heard what the gods said, Agastya, the son of Mitra and Varuna, said, "Why have you come here? What boon do you want from me?"

The Devas replied, "O Magnanimous, we beg you to drink up the ocean and drain it, for then we shall be able to kill the Kalakeyas, and all their allies."

The Sage said, "So be it. I will do what you wish, and that will bring great happiness to all men."

Saying this, O virtuous one, Agastya went to the ocean, lord of rivers, and with him went Rishis of great tapasya, and the Devas as well. And Manavas and Nagas, Gandharvas, Yakshas and Kinnaras followed the awesome Sages, wanting to witness the event of wonder.

Together they came to the sea, which roared, dancing with its waves, leaping in the wind, and laughing with masses of froth, and gushing into caves on the shore, the ocean thronging with all kinds of sharks, and flocks of diverse birds above and upon his waters.

The Devas, along with Agastya and the Gandharvas and huge Nagas and most gifted Munis, approached the immense waters.'

CANTO 105

TIRTHA-YATRA PARVA CONTINUED

Lomasa says, 'Varuna's son, that blessed saint spoke to the assembled gods, and the sages, "I am going to drink up the ocean, abode of the god of waters. You be ready with whatever preparations you need to make."

With these few words, the unswerving son of Mitra and Varuna, now full of wrath, began to drink up the sea, while all the worlds watched. Indra and the Devas were awestruck and began to give praise to mighty Agastya:

"O you are our protector, and Providence itself for men, why, the very creator of the worlds. By your grace, possibly, the universe with its gods might be saved."

Glorified by the Devas, while the musical instruments of Gandharvas played all around, and while celestial blossoms were showered upon him, the great Agastya drained the vast ocean and it was dry!

Seeing the ocean rendered devoid of water, the host of gods rejoiced; taking up diverse weapons of celestial forge, they fell to slaughtering the demons. Assailed by the Devas of untold strength and speed, who came roaring at them, the Asuras could not stand before the heaven dwellers, O Bhaarata! Only for a moment, did the demons last before the onslaught of the gods, and return battle.

Moreover, the evil ones had already been consumed by the tapasya shakti of the greatest Rishis; the Devas quickly massacred the Kalakeyas. Decked with brooches of gold, wearing ear-rings and armlets, the demons, when slain, looked beautiful indeed, like palasa trees in full crimson bloom.

Then, O best of men, a few of the Kalakeyas who remained alive rent the goddess Earth, and took refuge at the bottom of the Patalas.

When they saw that the demons were slain, the gods gave praise to the mighty sage:

"O Mahabaho, through your grace, all men have found a great blessing, and the ruthless Kalakeyas have been killed by your power, O creator of beings! Now, mighty-armed, fill the ocean again, give up once more the waters that you drained."

The blessed and mighty saint replied, "I have digested that water, so if you wish to fill the ocean again, you must think of some other expedient."

Great king, the assembled gods were struck with both wonder and sadness. Now, after bowing to the Maharishi and saying farewell to one another, they all went away to their respective homes.

The Devas, with Vishnu, came to Brahma; they consulted again now about how to fill the empty sea. They stood with folded hands, and forlorn.'

CANTO 106

TIRTHA-YATRA PARVA CONTINUED

Lomasa says, 'Brahma Pitamaha said, "Go, O Devas, where your pleasure may lead you, or your desire takes you! It will take a long course of time for the ocean to resume its original state; the occasion will be furnished by the ancestors of the great king Bhagiratha."

Hearing what the Pitamaha said, all those main gods went to their homes, and would bide their time until the day when the ocean was filled again.'

Yudhishtira says, 'What was that occasion, O Muni? And how did Bhagiratha's ancestors furnish it? And how was the ocean filled again through Bhagiratha's efforts? O Sage, who deem your tapasya as your only treasure, O Brahmana, I want to hear the achievements of that king, in detail, from you.'

Thus addressed by the magnanimous and virtuous king, Lomasa, best of Brahmanas, narrates the achievements of the high-souled king, Sagara.

Lomasa says, 'Into the clan of the Ikshvakus, was born a ruler of the earth named Sagara, endowed with beauty and strength. And that king was sonless, O Bhaarata! He brought havoc through the tribes of the Haihayas and the Talajanghas, all of Kshatriya kind under his rule, and then reigned over his own kingdom.

And, O most praiseworthy of the scions of Bhaarata, O chief of the Bhaarata race, Sagara had two wives, proud of their beauty and of their youth – one a princess of the Vidarbhas, and the other of the royal line of Sibi.

Best of kings, Sagara and his wives went to Mount Kailasa, and sat in severe tapasya in order to have a son. Practising rigid penance, and locked in Yoga, Sagara had a vision of three-eyed Siva, who made ashes of the Tripura, who is the eternal one, the bestower of blessings to all beings, the Great Sovereign, who wields the bow Pinaka, with the Trisula in his hand, in whom infinite peace resides, the lord of all those that are fierce, who can assume any form; and who is the Lord of the goddess Uma.

Mahabaho, as soon as Sagara saw that God, the giver of boons, he and his two queens fell at Siva's feet, and offered him a prayer to have a son.

Well pleased, Siva said to that most just king and his wives, "Lord of men, considering the moment at which you have offered your prayer to me, sixty thousand sons, valiant and exceedingly proud, will be born in one of your two wives. But they will all perish together.

In the other wife, a single brave son will be born, who will perpetuate your race."

Having said this to him, the God Rudra vanished, and king Sagara came home with his queens, all of them delighted with what had transpired. And, O best of men, there, the two lotus-eyed queens—the princess of Vidarbha and the princess of Sibi— soon became pregnant.

When her time came, the princess of Vidarbha brought forth something shaped like a gourd while the princess of Sibi gave birth to a boy as beautiful as a god. Sagara decided to throw away the gourd, when he heard an asariri speak gravely from the sky, "O King, do not be hasty, you must not become guilty of abandoning your sons! Take the seeds out from the gourd and let them be preserved with care in steaming vessels partly filled with ghrita. Then thou will get, O scion of Bharata's race, sixty thousand sons.

King of men, Mahadeva Siva has decreed that your sons are to be born in this fashion, so do not turn your mind away from what must be.'"

CANTO 107

Tirtha-yatra Parva Continued

Lomasa says, 'Most righteous king, when he heard the voice speak from the sky, he believed what it said and did as it asked. Sagara took each seed from the gourd, separately, and immersed it in a vat of ghee. Intent on the survival of his sons, he provided a nurse for every receptacle.

Then, after a long time, there arose sixty thousand immeasurably strong and powerful sons from those vessels of ghee, sons born to the Rajarishi Sagara through Siva's grace.

And they were terrible and their deeds were ruthless. They could fly and range through the sky, and being as many as they were, they were unafraid of anyone, including the gods. They would chase even the Devas, the Gandharvas, and the Rakshasas and all the born, for they were mighty and addicted to fighting.

Harassed by the dull-headed sons of Sagara, all men and the gods with them went to Brahma, as their refuge.

The Grandsire of all beings said to them, "Go your way, Devas, and take these mortal men with you, for very soon the sons of

Sagara will find death for all their sins, and a terrible end will they find."

The Devas and the Manavas bade farewell to the Pitamaha, and went back to where they had come from. Then, O Bhaarata, when many days had passed, the mighty king Sagara took the consecration for performing the rites of a horse-sacrifice, an Aswamedha yagna.

Protected by his ferocious sons, the king's sacrificial horse ranged across the earth; when it reached the sea, waterless and frightful to behold, although the horse was guarded with very great care it suddenly vanished from where it stood.

Sagara's sons thought that fine steed had been stolen; they returned to their father and told him how it had disappeared.

He said to them, "Go and look for the horse in all the cardinal points."

Great king, at their father's command, his sons began their quest for the horse in all the cardinal points and throughout the surface of the earth. But even all together, those sixty thousand could not find the horse, nor the one who had stolen it.

Returning home, they stood with folded hands before their father, and said, "O Protector of men! O ruler of the earth! O king! At your command, we combed all this world, with all its hills and its forests, with its seas, and its woods, and its islands, with its rivulets and rivers and caves. But we did not find either the horse, or the thief who stole it."

Sagara was insensate with anger, and stirred by destiny, too, he said to them in wrath, "Go again and seek the horse and never return until you find it!"

Again obedient to their father's command, his sons, those awesome Kshatriyas, once more searched the earth and they found a cleft upon her surface, upon the dried up sea-bed. The sons of Sagara began to excavate it.

Exerting themselves to the utmost, with spades and pickaxes they dug the bed of the sea. At their violent excavation, Varuna's abode writhed in agony, and Asuras, Nagas, Rakshasas and all living beings began to cry out in distress, while Sagara's sixty thousand sons slaughtered them.

Hundreds of thousands of living creatures could be seen with severed heads and trunks and with their skins and bones and joints rent asunder and broken.

They went on digging up the ocean, abode of Varuna, and a vast amount of time went by but they still did not find the horse. Then, lord of earth, towards the north-eastern region of the sea, the incensed sons of Sagara dug down as far as Patala, and there they saw the animal, roaming about as it pleased.

And they saw the magnificent Kapila, looking like a perfect mass of splendour. Seeing him shining even as the fire does with flames and seeing the horse, as well, they became flushed with joy. Having been sent by fate, and after their fervid exertions, they paid Kapila Muni no heed but ran forward to seize the horse.

Maharajan, Kapila, most righteous of saints, whom the great sages name Kapila Vasudeva, assumed a fiery look, and the mighty saint loosed flames at Sagara's sons, and burnt them to ashes.

Narada, of vast tapasya, saw Sagara's sons reduced to ashes and he came to that king and told him what had happened. When Sagara heard the terrible news from the Rishi's lips, he was plunged in grief for an hour, until he recalled what Siva had said.

Sending for his grandson Ansuman, the son of Asamanjas, he said, "Because of me, my sixty thousand sons of measureless strength encountered Kapila's wrath and have met their death. My pure child, taintless Ansuman, I have also forsaken your father for the sake of my Rajadharma and for the weal of my people."'

Yudhishtira says, 'O Muni, whose only wealth is your tapasya, tell me why Sagara, foremost of kings, abandoned his own son, endowed with valour – something so diffcult for other men to do.'

Lomasa says, 'A son was born to Sagara, by the princess of Sibi, and he was called Asamanjas. The prince would seize the weaker children of the townspeople and throw them into the river. Outraged, and stricken by grief and fear, the townsmen met together, and came, hands folded before Sagara, and implored him, "Great king, you protect us from invasions by hostile enemies. Now you must protect us from the peril of Asamanjas."

Hearing the fearful news of his son's doings, the king fell sad and silent for almost an hour, and then he said to his ministers, "Let my son Asamanjas be driven out of our city from this day. If you wish to please me, do it quickly!"

And, O King, the ministers did what he asked without delay. So did the great Sagara banish his son for the welfare of his people. Now listen in full to what Sagara said to his grandson Ansuman of the powerful bow.

Sagara said, "O my child, my heart is broken from having banished your father and now from having sent your uncles to their deaths. Besides, I have not recovered the horse for my sacrifice.

My grandson, grief tears at me and my mind is confounded that I cannot complete my Aswamedha yagna. Your must fetch the horse back and deliver me from hell."

Ansuman went with sorrow to the place where the earth had been excavated; he went down by the same tunnel beneath the dry sea bed, and saw the illustrious Kapila and the horse. Seeing the ancient Sage, most righteous of his kind, who looked like a mass of light, the prince bowed touching his head to the ground, and told the Rishi why he had come.

Maharajan, Kapila was pleased with Ansuman, and told him to ask for a boon. Ansuman first asked to have the horse back for the sacrifice, and then he prayed for the purification of his uncles.

The mighty Kapila said, "I will grant you all that you desire, stainless prince. May good fortune be with you! In you I see forbearance, truth, and righteousness. By you Sagara shall have his wishes fulfilled; you are truly a grandson to your sire. Through your goodness, the sons of Sagara will find redemption and heaven.

Your son's son will find Mahadeva Siva's grace so your ancestors might be purified of their sin. He will perform a great tapasya that will bring the river of three streams down into this world – the Ganga, O lord of men!

May good fortune be yours! Here, take this sacrificial horse with you and complete the Aswamedha yagna of the great Sagara."

Ansuman took the horse with him, and returned to mighty king Sagara's yagnashala. He prostrated at the feet of the high-souled Sagara, who sniffed the top of his head lovingly; Ansuman told him everything, all that he had seen and heard, and all about the death of Sagara's sons. He also announced that he had brought back the horse.

When Sagara heard all this, he no longer grieved on account of his dead sons. He praised and honoured Ansuman, and completed his sacrifice. When this was done, all the Devas greeted him with honour, and Sagara made the sea, where Varuna dwells, his son.

The lotus-eyed Sagara ruled his kingdom for a great length of time, and then he set his grandson Ansuman upon his throne, laden with responsibility, and ascended into Swarga.

Like his grandsire, the virtuous Ansuman ruled over the world with dharma, as far as the edge of the sea, following in the footsteps of his father's father. His son was named Dilipa, versed in virtue. Finally, Ansuman gave his throne to Dilipa and he also left this world.

When Dilipa learnt of the awful fate that had overtaken his forefathers, he grieved and thought of the means to redeem their souls. That king of men did his utmost to bring the Ganga down into the world, but he did not succeed.

A son was born to him, and known by the name of Bhagiratha, who was beautiful, and devoted to a virtuous life, and truthful, and free from all malice. Dilipa made his son the king, and took to vanaprastha himself. And, O best of all the scions of Bhaarata's race, Dilipa devoted himself to a long tapasya, at the end of which he, too, rose from the forest into heaven.'

CANTO 108

TIRTHA-YATRA PARVA CONTINUED

Lomasa says, 'Bhagiratha, of the mighty bow, Maharatha, lord of all he surveyed, became the delight of the eyes and the soul of the world. He, the Mahabaho, learnt how his ancestors had met an awful end from Kapila, and how they had been unable to attain the realm of the gods.

With a sorrowful heart, he made over his kingly duties to his minister, and, O lord of men, he went to the Himalayas, mountains of snow, to sit in tapasya, and by leading the most austere life, to gain the favour of the Devi Ganga.

He saw Himavana, adorned with peaks of diverse forms, full of bright minerals, strewn on all sides with raindrops from clouds resting upon the breeze; beautiful with rivers and groves and rocky spurs, looking like so many palaces in a city, attended upon by lions and tigers that had hidden themselves in its caves; and also inhabited by birds of myriad species, uttering diverse sounds – bhringarajas, and ganders, and datyuhas, and water-cocks, and peacocks and birds with a hundred feathers, and jivanjivakas, and blackbirds, and chakoras with black-cornered eyes, and the koyals that love their young.

He saw the mountain abounding in lotus plants that grew in enchanted lakes. And kraunchas, cranes, rendered it charming with their sounds; and Kinnaras and Apsaras sat upon its stone slabs.

And the Diggajas, the elephants of the cardinal points, had marked the trees growing there with their tusks; and Vidyadharas frequented the mountain, which was replete with treasures of jewels, as it was infested by serpents with glowing tongues and virulent venom.

In places the mountain seemed to be made of gold, while in others it was silver, and yet other peaks were like massifs of kohl. So was the snowy mountain where the king now found himself.

There, that best of men sat in a fierce tapasya. For one thousand years, he sustained himself on just water, fruit and roots. When a thousand years of the Devas passed, the great Devi, the divine river Ganga, manifested herself before him, embodied and shimmering.

Ganga said, "Great king, what do you want from me? What boon must I bestow upon you? I will do what you ask."

Bhagiratha replied to Himalaya's daughter, "Grantress of boons, O great River, when my father's fathers went in search of their sire's sacrificial horse, Kapila sent them to the land of Yama; in an instant, those sixty thousand perished.

Since then, there has been no place for them in Swarga. O great river, as long as you do not wet their ashes with your water, they will not find moksha. Blessed Devi, I beg you, redeem my ancestors, Sagara's sons, lead them into heaven. I am here to beg you to save their souls."

Ganga, the goddess whom the worlds worship, was pleased to hear what Bhagiratha said, and she said to him, "Great King, I am prepared to do what you ask. But when I descend from the sky to the earth, the force of my fall will be impossible to bear.

Protector of men, in the three worlds none but Siva, greatest of Gods, the Lord Nilakanta whose throat is sable blue, can break my falling into the world.

Mahabahao, with tapasya gain the grace of the Lord Siva, river of boons. He will bear my descent upon his head; he will fulfil your desire, and save your sires, O King."

Maharaja Bhagiratha went to Mount Kailasa and undertook a great penace, and after a long tapasya, he gained the grace of Lord Siva, worker of blessings. Protector of men, that king secured from Mahadeva a boon that the Ganga might fall safely upon his head, and flow into the world.'

CANTO 109

TIRTHA-YATRA PARVA CONTINUED

Lomasa sayas, 'The blessed Siva listened to Bhagiratha's petition, and, also, in order to fulfil the wishes of the dwellers in Swarga, said, "Tathastu! So be it, O guardian of men, O Mighty-armed. For your sake I will contain the descent of the pure and blessed and divine river of heaven, O King!"

Saying this, The Lord came to the snowy mountain, surrounded by his ganas, of awful mien, who bore uplifted weapons of diverse forms. Standing there, he said to Bhagiratha, most praiseworthy of men, " Mahabaho, you pray to the river who is the daughter of the king of mountains. I will contain her when she falls down from Swarga."

Reassured by Siva, Bhagiratha made obeisance with utmost devotion, and directed his thoughts again towards Ganga. Seeing that Mahadeva stood to receive her fall, Ganga flashed down suddenly in a pure and crystal torrent from the sky, and the Devas, the Maharishis, the Gandharvas, the Nagas, and the Yakshas, assembled there as witnesses.

Down from the sky came the snow mountain, Himavan's daughter; her whirlpools raged and she teemed with fish and sharks. O King, directing her course towards the sea, she separated herself into three streams; and her water was strewn with piles of froth, which seemed like so many rows of white ganders.

Sinuous and twisting, at times, at others stumbling, as it were; covered in foam as with a robe; she came down like a woman drunk. Elsewhere, by virtue of the roar of her waters, she gave vent to loud sounds.

Thus assuming many different aspects, when she fell from the sky, she reached the surface of the earth, and said to Bhagiratha, "Great King, show me the path I must take! Lord of the earth, for your sake I have come down into the world."

Bhagiratha made a course towards where the dead sons of mighty Sagara lay, so that the sacred waters might drench their ashes. Having borne and contained the fall of Ganga, Siva, saluted by all men, went back to Kailasa, best of mountains, accompanied by the Devas.

With Ganga following him, Bhagiratha reached the sea; and the sea, the abode of Varuna, was quickly filled! The king adopted Ganga as his own daughter, and at that spot offered libations of water, tarpana, to the manes of his ancestors; thus was his heart's wish fulfilled.

At your asking me, I have narrated the whole story of how Ganga, running in three streams, was brought down to the earth to fill the sea; how the mighty Sage drained the sea for a particular reason, and how Vatapi, slayer of Brahmanas, was destroyed by Agastya.'"

CANTO 110

TIRTHA-YATRA PARVA CONTINUED

Vaisampayana said, "O lord of the Bhaaratas, next the son of Kunti goes leisurely to the two rivers Nanda and Aparananda, which have the virtue of destroying the dread of sin. Reaching a great mountain Hemakuta, he sees many strange and inconceivable sights there. When their party merely speak among themselves, clouds rumble into the sky and a thousand volleys of stones fall, so they cannot climb the mountain.

Here the winds blow incessantly, and the heavens forever lash down rain; they also hear the chanting of the Veda, yet they see nobody. In the evening and in the morning they see the blessed fire that carries offerings to the gods, and there sharp insects sting them to interrupt their tapasya.

An unaccountable sadness overtakes the soul, and men fall sick. Seeing all these uncanny phenomena, Yudhishtira asks Lomasa what they are and what causes them.

Lomasa says, "Parantapa, Rajan, I will tell you about this as we heard it of old; listen carefully to what I say.

Upon this peak of Rishabha, there was once a Rishi of that name, who lived for hundreds of years. He was devoted to penance and was also wrathful. When some men came and spoke to him, interrupting his dhyana, he said in anger to the mountain, "If any man speaks in this place, cast stones at him and summon the winds to prevent him from making any sound."

This was what the sage said; and so, in this place, as soon as a man utters any words, he is forbidden by a roaring cloud. Rajan, in anger he also forbade other deeds in this place, that Maharishi.

Yudhishtira, tradition has it that, when of old, the Devas came to the Nanda, suddenly a number of men arrived there to look at the gods. However, the Devas, at whose head Indra stood, did not want to be seen; and so they rendered this spot inaccessible, by raising obstructions in the form of mountains. From that day, O Kaunteya, men could not cast their eyes, at any time, upon what looked like this mountain, far less climb it.

No one who has not led an austere life can see this mountain, or ascend it.

Therefore, O son of Kunti, keep your tongue under control. Here, at that time, all those gods performed the most sacred yagnas. O Bhaarata, even to this day the marks of those sacrifices can be seen. This grass here has the form of the sacred kusa grass; the ground here seems to be covered by the sacred grass; and, O lord of men, so many of these trees here look as if they are ideal for tying up yagnapasus.

O Bhaarata, the Devas and the Rishis still dwell here and one can see their sacred agni burning in the morning and in the evening. If one bathes here, one's sins are immediately destroyed, Kaunteya! So, best of the Kurus, you and your younger brothers, perform your ablutions here.

Having bathed in the Nanda, you must journey to river Kausiki, to the place where Viswamitra performed his great tapasya."

Yudhishtira, and all that are with him, bathe in that river, and then go on to the Kausiki, crystalline, her waters cool and delightful.

Lomasa says, "This is the pure and divine Kausiki. Lord of the Bhaaratas, here is the enchanting asrama of Viswamitra; and there is the hermitage of the mighty-souled Kasyapa, whose son was Rishyasringa, devoted to tapasya, his passions under control. Through the rigours of his penance he forced Indra to pour down his rain during a drought, for the Deva, slayer of Bala and Vritra, was in dread of Rishyasringa's penance.

That powerful son of Kasyapa was born of a hind. He worked a great marvel in the kingdom of Lomapada; and when the rains brought forth crops in his lands, Lomapada gave his daughter Santa in marriage to Rishyasringa, even as the Sun gave away his daughter Savitri."

Yudhishtira says, "How was Kasyapa's son, Rishyasringa, born of a hind? And how was he endowed with such holiness, being the offspring of a sinful sexual union? Why did Indra fear this Rishi, so he poured down his rain during a time of drought?

Tell us about the beauty of the princess Santa, pure in life, she who captivated his heart when he had turned himself into a stag? And since the Rajarishi Lomapada was as virtuous as he is known to have been, why was it that over his lands, Indra, scourge of Paka, withheld rain?

Most holy one, I beg you, relate all this to me in detail, exactly as it happened, for I want to know everything about Rishyasringa's life."

Lomasa says, 'Listen to how Rishyasringa, of dreaded name, was born as the son of Kasyapa Muni's son Vibhandaka, A Brahmana Rishi who had evolved through tapasya, of unfailing seed, who was learned and bright like the Lord of beings. And the father was honoured, and the son was possessed of a mighty spirit, and, though a boy, he was respected by old men.

Vibhandaka went to a great lake and devoted himself to the practice of austerities. He who was like a Deva performed a long penance. One day, while he was washing his mouth in the water, he saw the Apsara Urvasi, at which he ejaculated his seed.

Rajan, a hind was drinking from the lake and she lapped up his seed, floating on the water, and at once she became pregnant. That hind was, in fact, a Devaputri, and Brahma had once told her, "You will be a hind; and while you have that form, you will give birth to a Rishi; then you will be free."

As fate would have it, and as the word of the creator can never prove untrue, that female deer bore Vibhandaka's son, a mighty sage, Rishyasringa.

Rishyasringa, devoted to tapasya, always passed his days in the forest, and there was a horn on his head and for this he came to be known as Rishyasringa. Apart from his father, he had never seen any other man; and so, his life was entirely absorbed in brahmacharya.

During this same time, there was a king of the land of Anga known as Lomapada, who was a friend of Dasaratha. We have heard that, from his love of pleasure, he had been guilty of telling a lie to a Brahmana; and for that Lomapada was shunned by all men of the priestly varna, and he had no priest to perform his religious rites.

And Indra of a thousand eyes abruptly withdrew the rains from his kingdom and his people suffered. He asked a number of Brahmanas, devoted to austerities, of cultivated minds, "How will the heavens send us rain? Think of some expedient."

Each of them gave their view, and among them, the best, said to the king, "King of kings, the Brahmanas are angry with you, so you must do something to appease them. Send for Rishyasringa, the Muni's son, who lives in the forest and knows nothing of women, who is the epitome of simplicity.

O King, if he whose tapasya is so great, shows himself in your kingdom, I have no doubt that the rain will also come."

Lomapada made atonement for his sins, and he went away. When the Brahmanas had been pacified, he returned and his people were glad. The king of Anga convened a meeting of his ministers, men who were expert at giving counsel, and he sought their counsel to devise a plan to fetch Rishyasringa into his lands.

Finally, with the advice of those men versed in all branches of knowledge, very proficient in worldly matters, he settled on a plan. He sent for a number of courtesans, women of the town, all clever.

When they came, Lomapada said to them, "Lovely ones, you must find a way to entice Rishyasringa into my kingdom."

Those women, on the one hand afraid of the king's wrath and on the other dreading a curse from the Rishi, were alarmed and declared the business to be beyond their power.

However, one among them, a seasoned and forward woman, said to the king, "Maharajan, I will try to fetch him whose wealth consists solely of tapasya, into your lands. However, there are some things I will need to put my plan into action. If you can give me these, I might be able to bring Rishyasringa here."

The king gave an order that all that she might ask for should be procured. He also gave her a good deal of wealth and jewels of various kinds. Then, Lord of the earth, taking a number of young and beautiful women with her, she went to the forest.'

TIRTHA-YATRA PARVA CONTINUED

Lomasa says, 'O Bhaarata, she prepared a floating hermitage, both because the king had ordered so, and also because it exactly accorded with her plan. Delightful it was, the floating asrama, with artificial trees adorned with various flowers and fruit, with diverse shrubs and creepers, and it provided delicious fruit. It truly looked as if it had been created by magic.

She moored this great craft very near from the hermitage of Kasyapa's grandson, then sent emissaries to survey the places that that Rishi habitually frequented. Then she saw her opportunity, and sent forth her daughter, also a courtesan and of smart sense. That clever woman went to the vicinity of the Rishis's hermitage, and she saw Rishyasringa.

Approaching him, she said, "Muni, I hope that all is well with you and the other tapasvins. I trust that you have a plentiful store of fruit and roots and that you take delight in this hermitage.

I have come to visit you, and I hope the tapasya of the Rishis waxes, daily. I trust your father's spirit has not slackened and that he is well pleased with you. O Rishyasringa, I hope that you pursue the studies that are appropriate for you!"

Rishyasringa said, "You shine with lustre, as if you were made of light; and I say you are worthy of worship. I will give you padya to wash you feet and such fruit and roots that you might like, for this is what my dharma says.

This darbhasana is made of kusa grass and covered with a black deer-skin to make it comfotable. Sit upon it, O Brahmana who resembles a Deva, and tell me where is your asrama. And what is this vrata called, which you now seem to be observing?"

The courtesan said, "O son of Kasyapa, my asrama is on the other side of yonder hill; it covers three yojanas and is full of delight. There, it is my faith not to receive obeisance or to touch water to wash my feet. I am not worthy of being worshipped by men like you, rather I must make my obeisance to you.

O Brahmana, this is the vrata that I must observe – to clasp you in my arms!"

Rishyasringa said, "Let me give you ripe fruits, gallnuts, myrobalans, karushas, ingudas from sandy soil, and figs. Be pleased to taste them and find some pleasure."

She, however, flung aside all those pure things he offered and instead gave him unclean things to eat, but deliciously prepared and fine to look at; and the innocent Rishyasringa found them most agreeable.

She gave him the most fragrant garlands, exquisite and shimmering garments to wear, and fine drink; they talked and laughed and played together. In his sight she played with a ball, sinuously, and seemed like a creeping plant broken in two, her lissom body.

Repeatedly she touched his body with her own, and clasped him in her arms. She took flowering twigs from sala, asoka and tilaka trees. Drunk, assuming a bashful look, she continued tempting Rishyasringa; and when she saw that she had touched his heart, she pressed his body with her own, again and again, and with sidelong, seductive glances, slowly wandered away, saying that she was going to make offerings to the fire.

When she left him, Rishyasringa was frantic with desire, and could think of nothing else but her. His mind turned constantly to her and felt empty. He began to sigh and seemed to be in great distress.

At that moment, Kasyapa's son Vibhandaka, whose eyes were tawny like a lion's, whose body was covered with hair down to the tips of his nails, who was devoted to Brahmana dharma, whose life was pure and spent in dhyana, came and saw his son sitting alone, pensive and sad, obviously distraught, and sighing again and again with upturned eyes.

Vibhandaka said to Rishyasringa, "My child, why are you not chopping firewood for the agni. I hope that you have offered havis, the burnt offering, today? I hope you have polished the sacrificial ladles and spoons and brought the calf to the milch cow whose milk gives us all we need to make our sacrificial offerings to the fire?

Surely, you are not yourself, my son. You are pensive, why, you seem to be terribly disturbed. Why are you so sad today? Who has come here this day?"

CANTO 112

TIRTHA-YATRA PARVA CONTINUED

Rishyasringa said, "A Brahmachari with a mass of jata on his head came here today. He was neither short nor tall. He had a spirited look, a golden complexion, and eyes large as lotuses; and he was shining and graceful as a god.

Rich was his beauty, alight like the sun; and he was exceedingly fair, ah his eyes graceful and black. His twisted hair was blue-black and neat and long and fragrant and tied up with strings of gold. A beautiful ornament glittered at his throat, like lightning in the sky.

And under the throat he had two balls of flesh without a single hair upon them, and oh an exceedingly beautiful form, with such a slender waist and a deep navel; and the skin upon his chest was smooth. A golden string shone from under his cloth, just like this waist-string of mine.

There was something on his feet of a wonderful shape which gave forth a lovely tinkling. His wrists, likewise, bore a pair of ornaments that made a similar sound and looked just like these prayer beads. And when he walked, his ornaments sounded like delighted ganders upon a sheet of water.

He wore garments of wonderful make upon his person; these clothes I wear are by no means beautiful like those. His face was was also so wonderful to behold; and his voice was modulated to gladden the heart, just as his speech was as sweet as the song of the koyal; while I listened to him, I felt stirred in my inmost heart.

As a forest in spring is most graceful when swept by a breeze, even so, my father, that fragrant sage is most beautiful when the air fans him. His mass of hair is neatly tied and is slick againt his head and brow, divided evenly by a parting.

His eyes seemed to be covered with chakravaka birds of exceptionally beautiful forms. In his right hand he held a wonderful round fruit, which falls to the ground and again leaps up to the sky, in the strangest way; and he beats it and turns himself round and whirls: like a tree moved by the breeze.

When I looked at him, O father, he seemed to be a son of the Devas, and my joy was extreme, and my pleasure unbounded. He clasped my body, seized my matted hair, and bent me down, and mingling his mouth with my own, uttered a delightful sound I have never heard.

He does not care for padya or the fruit I offered him, and said to me that this was his vrata. But he gave me many fruit, and these we have do not match those nearly for taste. They have no rind nor any stone within them, like these.

That noble-formed one gave me water of such flavour that I have never drunk before; it was exquisite and having drunk it, I felt uncanny pleasure; why, the ground seemed to move under my feet.

These redolent garlands, entwined with silken threads, belong to him. And he, bright with fervent piety, scattered these garlands here, then went back to his own asrama. His going has saddened my heart; and my body seems to burn all over.

My desire is to go to him as soon as I can, and to have him walk about here every day. O father, let me go to him this very moment.

Ah, what tapasya does he practise? As he, that pious one, is performing tapasya, I want to go and live with him, and share his penances. My heart yearns for his unusual mode of practising austerities; my soul will be in torment if I cannot see him."

TIRTHA-YATRA PARVA CONTINUED

Vibhandaka said, "My child, these are Rakshasas, who walk about in wonderful forms. Their strength is unrivalled and their beauty great, and they always strive to obstruct the practice of true austerities. They assume lovely forms and try to seduce by various means.

Those fierce beings hurled the Rishis, the dwellers in the forest, down from blessed regions won through their piety. And the Muni who has control over his soul, and who wants to gain the realms where the righteous go, must have nothing to do with them.

They are vile creatures, who obstruct tapasya and delight in that, and a Rishi should never look at them.

O my son, those were drinks unworthy to be drunk; they were spirits that sinners consume. And these garlands, bright and fragrant and of many hues, are not intended for sannyasis."

Having thus forbidden his son, saying that those were evil demons, Vibhandaka went in quest of her. When, after a three days' search he could not find her, he returned to his asrama.

In the meanwhile, when Rishyasringa went out to gather fruit, the courtesan returned to tempt him.

And as soon as Rishyasringa saw her, he was ecstatic and ran to her, crying, "Let us go to your asrama before my father returns!"

Rajan, those courtesans made Rishyasringa board their floating hermitage. As soon as he was aboard, they unmoored the vessel and cast off. With a myriad of pleasures they kept him engaged and delighted, until they arrived in the kingdom of Anga.

Then, leaving the floating vessel, of dazzling white, upon the water, they fetched the innocent Rishi, Vibhandaka's son, to the king Lomapada, who kept him in his antahpura, among his women. Suddenly, the heavens opened and it poured over the kingdom, why, the very world seemed to become flooded with water.

His fervent wish fulfilled, Lomapada bestowed his daughter Santa on Rishyasringa in marriage.

With a view to appease the wrath of his father, he ordered kine to be placed, and fields to be ploughed, by the road that Vibhandaka would take to come to his son. He also set stout cowherds along the route, with a plenitude of cattle, and ordered them:

"When the Maharishi Vibhandaka asks you about his son, you must fold your hands and say to him that all these cattle, all these fields belong to his son, and that you yourselves are his slaves, ready to obey his every wish."

Now, having gathered roots and fruit, the Rishi Vibhandaka, whose temper was fierce, returned to his hermitage, and looked for his son; not finding him, he became fiercely angry. He was beside himself with fury and he suspected king Lomapada's hand in what had befallen Rishyasringa.

He set out for the city of Champa, having made up his mind to burn the king, his city, and his whole kingdom. On the way, he was tired and hungry, when he reached the cleverly placed and opulent cowherd settlements, rich with cattle. He felt honoured at the way in which the cowherds welcomed and feted him; and he spent that night in a manner befitting a king.

Having partaken of their great hospitality, he asked them, "To whom, O cowherds, do you belong?"

They surrounded him and said, "All this wealth has been provided for your son."

Vibhandaka continued his journey, and along his way he was similarly honoured, frequently. Finally, arriving, he saw Rishyasringa, his son, who looked like the god Indra in heaven. He also saw his daughter-in-law, Santa, looking like lightning springing from a cloud. Having seen everything provided for Rishyasringa, as well as the exquisite princess Santa, Vibhandaka was appeased.

Rajan, he expressed his satisfaction with Lomapada. The Maharishi, whose powers rivalled those of Surya and Agni, said to Rishyasringa, "As soon as a son is born to you, and having done all that this king wants from you, you must return immediately to the forest."

Rishyasringa did exactly as his father said, and he returned to Vibhandaka's asrama. Rajan, Santa obediently waited upon him, as in the firmament Rohini waits upon the Moon, or as the fortunate Arundhati waits upon Vasishta, or as Lopamudra waits upon Agastya. Just as Damayanti was an obedient wife to Nala, or as Sachi is to the god who wields the thunderbolt, or as Indrasena, Narayana's daughter, was always obedient to Mudgala, so did Santa wait lovingly upon Rishyasringa, while he lived in the forest.

This is the holy hermitage that was Rishyasringa's; ennobling the great lake here, it bears holy fame. Perform your ablutions here and have your desire fulfilled. And having purified thyself, direct your course towards other holy tirthas.'"

CANTO 114

TIRTHA-YATRA PARVA CONTINUED

Vaisampayana said, "Then, O Janamejaya, the son of Pandu sets out from the river Kausiki and journeys in succession to all the sacred shrines; and he comes to the sea where the river Ganga flows into it. There, at the nave of five hundred rivers, he performs the holy ceremony of an ablution.

Then, O ruler of the earth, accompanied by his brothers, the valiant Kshatriya goes along the shore towards the land where the Kalinga tribes dwell.

Lomasa says, 'This is the land, Kaunteya, where the Kalinga tribes live. The river Vaitarani passes through it, upon the banks of which river Dharma Deva performed a tapasya, having first placed himself under the protection of the celestials.

This is the northern bank, with its charmed mountain, inhabited by Rishis, ideal for the performance of religious rites, and frequented by Brahmanas. This place rivals the path by which a virtuous man, fit for heaven, repairs to Devaloka. Here, in days of yore, other sages worshipped the Gods with austerities.

It was here, O King, that the Lord Rudra seized the sacrificial beast and cried, "This is my share!" Bharatottama, when Siva carried away the yagnapasu, the Devas said to him, "Do not covet the property of others, flouting the laws of dharma."

They eulogised the Lord Rudra, and pleased him with the offering of a sacrifice, and honoured him duly. Thereupon he gave up the beast, and left by the path trodden by the gods.

Hear what happened to Rudra, O Yudhishtira! Influenced by their dread of him, the Devas forevermore set apart the best of all shares of their offerings, what was fresh and not stale for him.

Whoever performs ablutions at this spot, while reciting this ancient story, will see, with his mortal eyes, the path that leads to Devaloka.'

All the sons of Pandu and the daughter of Drupada—all of whom were the favoured by fate—descend to the river Vaitarani, and offer libations in the names of their fathers.

Yudhishtira says, 'O Lomasa, how great must be the force of a pious deed! Having bathed here, I feel as if I am no more in the world of men! Maharishi, I see all the worlds! And I hear the holy Munis of the forest chanting the Veda.'

Lomasa says, 'Yudhishtira, the place from where the chanting comes is three hundred thousand yojanas from here. Lord of men, be quiet and utter no word. This is the divine forest of the Swayambhuva, which has now come to our view. There Viswakarma, whose name is dreaded, performed a yagna.

During that mighty sacrifice, the Self-existent One made a gift of this entire earth, with all its hilly and forest tracts, to Kasyapa, by way of dakshina, for serving as a priest. As soon as Bhumi Devi was given away, she became sad, and spoke in anger to that great lord, the ruler of the worlds.

"O Mahadeva, it is unworthy of you to give me away to an ordinary mortal, and this daana of yours will come to nothing. For I mean to plunge down into the bottom of Patala!"

When the blessed Rishi Kasyapa saw the goddess Earth despondent and angry, he performed a propitiatory ritual to appease her. Pandava, Bhumi Devi was pleased with his worship and she rose again from within the waters, and showed herself in the form of a sacred altar.

This, O king, is the place which distinctly manifests the form of a vedi. Walk over it, and thou will gain valour and strength. Rajan, this is the very altar which reaches as far as the sea, and rests itself upon its bosom.

May good fortune be yours; climb here and by yourself walk out into the sea, while I perform the ritual to averting all evil from you. For, as soon as it receives a mortal's touch, this vedi at once enters into the sea.

Salutation to the God who protects the universe! Salutation to You that are beyond the universe! O Lord of gods, vouchsafe your presence in this sea.

Pandava, you must swiftly climb the vedi, while chanting this mantra: "The god of fire, and the sun, and the organ of generation, and water, and goddess and the seed of Vishnu, and the navel of nectar. The god of fire is the organ that generated the ocean; the earth is your body; Vishnu deposited the seed that caused your being and you are the navel of nectar!"

Chant these words aloud, Pandava, and plunge into the sea even as you do so. Otherwise, O best of Kunti's son, this lord of waters of divine birth, this most auspicious of all waters of the earth, must not be touched, not even with the tip of a blade of sacred grass.'

When the ritual for averting evil has been completed, Yudhishtira enters the sea, and having done everything that the Rishi had asked of him, repairs to the foothill of the Mahendra mountain, and spends the night in that place."

TIRTHA-YATRA PARVA CONTINUED

Vaisampayana said, "The king of the earth spends a single night there, and, with his brothers, pays the highest homage to the Rishis. And Lomasa acquaints him with the names of all of them – the Bhrigus, the Angiras, the Vasishtas, and the Kasyapas.

And the Rajarishi visits them all and makes obeisance to them, with folded hands.

And then he asks the valiant Akritavrana, who is a follower of Parasurama, 'When will the worshipful Parasurama show himself to the Rishis here? I, too, wish to have a darshana of the Bhargava.'

Akritavrana says, 'Rama already knows about your coming here, for his soul spontaneously knows all things. He is in every way well-pleased with you, and he will show himself readily to you.

The Rishis who perform tapasya here are allowed to see him on the fourteenth and the eighth day of the lunar month. When this night ends, tomorrow, the fourteenth day of this moon will begin; and you shall see him, clad in a sable deerskin, and wearing his hair in a mass of jata.'

Yudhishtira says, 'You have long been a follower of the mighty Rama, Jamadagni's son; you must have been an eye-witness to all his awesome deeds of yore.

I beg you, tell me how Rama vanquished all the Kshatriyas on the field of battle, and tell me also what the original cause of the conflict was.'

Akritavrana says, 'Bhaarata, gladly, I will narrate that great tale to you, the legend of the the godlike deeds of Rama, the son of Jamadagni, who belongs to the race of Bhrigu.

I will also relate the achievements of the great king of the Haihaya tribe; his name was Arjuna, and Parasurama killed him. He, O Pandava, was endowed with a thousand arms; and through the grace of Dattatreya he also had a golden, heavenly vimana.

His sway extended over all the worlds, and his vimana could go anywhere at his very thought. Become invincible with the boon, he went everywhere in that vimana, and rode rough over the Devas, Yakshas and Rishis, wherever he pleased; he tyrannised all the created.

Finally, the Devas and the Rishis of austere tapasya went together to Vishnu, slayer of demons, God of gods, of inexorable prowess, and said to him, "Blessed and revered Lord, if creation is to be saved, you must kill Kartaviryarjuna."

The mighty king of the Haihayas, riding his vimana, rudely affronted Indra, while that Deva was alone with his queen Sachi. At this, O Bhaarata, the Lord Vishnu consulted with Indra with a view to killing Kartavirya's son Arjuna.

Indra told Vishnu all about Arjuna's depredations and sins, and the God whom the worlds worship went to the enchanted Badari forest, which was his own chosen tapovana.

At this very time, there lived on the earth a mighty sovereign, monarch in the land of Kanyakubja, a king with a vast army. His name was Gadhi and his fame resounded through the world. He, however, retired into the forest, becoming a vanaprastha.

While he lived in the vana, a daughter was born to him, as beautiful as an Apsara was she. And Richika, the son of Bhrigu, asked for her to be his wife.

Gadhi said to that Brahmana, who led a most austere life, "We have a family custom in our race, founded by our most ancient ancestors – know, O Brahmanottama, that he who wishes to marry a princess of our clan must offer a dowry of a thousand fleet horses, whose colour must be brown and every one of which must have a single sable ear.

But, son of Bhrigu, a reverend Muni like you cannot be asked to make the same offering, neither can I refuse to give my daughter to an exalted and holy one like you."

Richika said, "I will give you a thousand fleet steeds, brown in hue and each one with a single black ear; give me your daughter."

Richaka went to Varuna and said, "Give me a thousand swift horses, brown in colour, and each with one black ear. I want them as the dowry for my marriage."

Varuna gave him a thousand steeds. These steeds had issued out of the river Ganga; and so the place has been named Aswatirtha.

In the city of Kanyakubja, the daughter of Gadhi, the princess Satyavati was given in marriage; and the gods themselves were in the bride's party. Thus, Richaka, best of Brahmanas, procured a thousand horses, and saw the dwellers of heaven and won a wife. And he enjoyed the girl of the slender waist, and gratified all the desire that he ever had.

When the marriage had been celebrated, O king, his father Bhrigu came on a visit to see him and his wife; and he was glad to see his son. The husband and wife together paid their respects to him, who was worshipped by all the gods. Bhrigu sat, and they stood near him with folded hands, waiting to do his bidding.

Maharishi Bhrigu, glad at heart, said to his daughter-in-law, "Lovely child, ask me for a boon, I will give you anything you want."

And she asked that a son might be born to both herself and her mother. And he granted her wish.

Bhrigu said, "During the days that your season lasts, you and your mother must bathe, observing the vrata to bear a son. Then you must both separately embrace two different trees — she a peepal tree, and you a fig tree.

Dutiful child, here are two pots of payasa, rice and milk, which I have prepared with great care. I have combed the universe to find the medicaments that I have blended into this payasa. With great care must you both drink this."

Saying this, he vanished. However, the two women interchanged not only the vessels of payasa that he gave them but also the trees that they embraced. After many days, the Sage appeared again, and he already knew, through his mystic vision, what had happened.

The mighty Bhrigu said to Satyavati, his daughter-in-law, "Dharmaputri, you ate the wrong pot of payasa and you embraced the wrong tree. It was your mother who deluded you. You will have a son who, though born a Brahmana, will have the character and nature of a Kshatriya. Your mother will have a Kshatriya son who will live the life of a Brahmana, and great shall be his power and he will walk the path trodden by the righteous."

She begged repeatedly, "O let my son not be so but my grandson!"

And, O Pandava, Bhrigu replied, "Tathastu, so be it!" and he was pleased to grant her wish.

On the expected day, she gave birth to a son, who was called Jamadagni, endowed with both splendour and grace. As he grew in years and in strength, he excelled all the other Sages in his knowledge of the Vaidik lore. Bhaarata, he rivalled the Sun in lustre and the entire astra shastra, the martial science, and the fourfold Devastra gyana came to him spontaneously, with no instruction.'

CANTO 116

TIRTHA-YATRA PARVA CONTINUED

Akritavrana says, 'Jamadagni devoted himself to the study of the Veda and the practice of tapasya, and became famous for his great austerities. He pursued a deep and systematic course of study and gained mastery over the entire Veda.

Then, O king, he went to Prasenajit and sought the hand of Renuka in marriage. That king happily gave the Sage his daughter, and having got Renuka for his wife, the Bhrigunandana, delight of Bhrigu's race, began living with her in his asrama; now, he performed tapasya and she helped and looked after him.

Four boys were born to her, Rama the fifth. Although the youngest, he was superior to all his brothers.

One day, when her sons had gone into the forest to gather fruit, the pure and austere Renuka went to bathe in the river. While bathing, she happened to see the king of Martikavataka, who was known as Chitraratha. This Kshatriya, wearing a lotus wreath upon his chest, was sporting with his wives in the water.

Seeing his magnificent form, Renuka was touched by desire that she could not contain, and she sinned in thought in the very river and was polluted. She returned to the hermitage, trembling in her heart. Her husband instantly saw the condition she was in, and seeing that the lustre of chastity had abandoned his wife, he cried out in anguish and anger.

At that very moment, the eldest of Jamadagni's sons, Rumanvan arrived there; and then, Sushena, and then, Vasu, and Viswavasu also. One by one, the Maharishi ordered them to kill their mother. However, they could not find the heart to do so; they stood silent. He cursed them in anger, and they lost their reason, and became like senseless things, dull as inanimate objects, and in conduct like beasts and birds.

Now, Rama arrived in the asrama, last of all. The mighty-armed Jamadagni, of great austerities, said to him, "Kill this evil mother of yours, without compunction, O my son."

Rama immediately took up an axe and cut off his mother's head. The wrath of Mahatama Jamadagni was appeased; and well-pleased, he said, "My child, knower of dharma, you have done this most difficult thing at my bidding. Ask me for whatever your heart wishes for and I will give you everything you want."

At which, Rama asked that his mother be restored to life, and that he himself not be haunted by the remembrance of his savage deed and that he might not be affected by any sin, and that his brothers might recover their former condition, and that he might be unrivalled on the field of battle, and have a long life.

Bhaarata, Jamadagni of awesome tapasya granted all those wishes of Rama.

Then, one day, when the Sage's sons had all gone out again, the valiant son of Kartavirya, the lord of the country near the shore of the sea, came to Jamadagni's hermitage. The Sage's wife received him hospitably. However, intoxicated with a Kshatriya warrior's pride, he was not pleased with the reception given to him, and forcibly seized and carried off the foremost among the cows whose milk supplied the sacral butter, heedless of its loud lowing.

He wantonly tore down the great trees of the forest. When Rama came home, his father told him all that had happened. When Rama saw how the cow lowed for its calf, anger arose in his heart and he rushed towards Kartavirya's son, whose last moments had drawn near.

Then Bhargava, scourge of the Kshatriyas, put forth his valour on the field of battle, and with flat-tipped, sharp arrows loosed from a beautiful bow, cut away Kartaviryarjuna's thousand arms, which were as massive as great door bolts. Touched by the hand of death, Kartavirya's son died at Rama's hands.

Their wrath stirred against Rama, Arjuna's kinsmen rushed at Jamadagni in his hermitage, while Rama was still away. They slew him there; for although his strength was great, he was at tapasya and would not fight. Helplessly, repeatedly, he cried out Rama's name in a piteous voice.

And, O Yudhishtira, the sons of Kartavirya shot Jamadagni dead with their arrows, and left the asrama. When they had gone, and when Jamadagni had breathed his last, Rama Bhrigunandana returned to the hermitage, bearing fuel for the sacred agni in his arms, and saw his father lying slain. He was stricken and railed against the grievous fate that had caused this tragedy.'

CANTO 117

TIRTHA-YATRA PARVA CONTINUED

Rama cried, "The blame is mine, O father, that the wretched sons of Kartavirya have shot you dead with arrows, like a stag in the woods. O father, you were always virtuous and never swerved from the path of dharma, nor harmed any living creature. How did Fate bring you such a vile death?

What an awful sin they have committed, who have killed you with hundreds of arrows, although you were an old man and performing tapasya and would not fight them! With what face will those shameless ones speak of this deed of theirs to their friends and servants? That they have murdered an unassisted and unresisting holy man?"

O King, thus Rama of great penance wailed, piteously, and then, at last, performed the obsequies for his dead sire. Rama, conqueror of hostile cities, cremated his father on a pyre, and vowed, O scion of Bharata, to annihilate the very race of Kshatriyas.

Of awesome strength, with the valour of a great warrior, and comparable to the god of death himself, he took up his weapon in wrath, went forth and singlehandedly put Kartavirya's sons to death. In three encounters, he struck down all the Kshatriya followers of Kartavirya's sons.

And seven times, that powerful one exterminated the warrior tribes of the earth. In the land called Samanta-panchaka, he made five lakes of their blood.

There the mightiest scion of Bhrigu's race offered tarpana to his ancestors, and Richika appeared to him in a visible form, and spoke words of counsel to him; after this, Jamadagni's son performed a mighty sacrifice and gratified the king of the Devas, and gifted the Earth to the ministering priests.

Lord of men, he raised a golden altar there, ten vyamas in breadth and nine in height, and gifted that vedi to the great Kasyapa. At Kasyapa's bidding, the Brahmanas divided the altar into a number of shares, and so they became known as as the Khandavayanas, the share takers.

The exterminator of the Kshattriyas bestowed the earth upon Mahatma Kasyapa, then engaged himself in an atikatora tapasya. He now dwells upon this Mahendra, monarch of hills.

So it was that there were hostilities between Rama and all the Kshatriyas of the world; and killing them, Rama conquered all the earth,' says Akritavrana.

Then on the fourteenth day of the moon, at the appointed hour, the mighty-souled Rama shows himself to those Brahmanas and also to the virtuous Yudhishtira and his younger brothers. And, O king of kings, the Pandavas worship Rama, and also all the other Dvijas. After worshipping Jamadagni's son and receiving words of praise from him, at Parasurama's behest, Yudhishtira spends the night on the Mahendra Parvata, and then sets out on his journey towards the southern lands."

CANTO 118

TIRTHA-YATRA PARVA CONTINUED

Vaisampayana said, "The great king pursues his journey, and at different places on the sea shore he visits all the auspicious tirthas to which Brahmanas went. And O son of Parikshit, Yudhishtira bathes in them all, and his brothers with him.

Later, they come to a sacred river, holiest of them. There, also, the king performs his ablutions and offers libations to his ancestors and the gods, and distributes riches to the leaders of the dvijas.

Next he comes to the Godavari, river that falls directly into the sea. There he is freed from his sins. He reaches the sea in the Dravida land, and visits the holy tirtha bearing Agastya's name, which is exceedingly sacred and exceptionally pure. The valiant king visits the feminine tirthas, of the crocodiles who were Apsaras; here he listens to the story of Arjuna's feat, which no other mortal man could have performed.

Here, the Pandava is praised by the highest men among all Brahmanas, and Yudhishtira experiences the greatest delight. And, O Lokarakshaka, along with Krishnaa, Pandu's son bathes in those tirthas, and lauding Arjuna's valour, spends some delightful time there.

Yudhishtira gives away thousands of cows at those tirthas on the coast of the sea; and with his brothers tells, with pleasure, of how Arjuna had made a gift of kine here. Rajan, one after another, they visit those holy places, both on the coast and many other sacred spots, as well, fulfiling their hearts' desire, until they come to that holiest tirtha known as Surparaka.

Crossing over a stretch of the sea coast, they arrive at a forest celebrated over the world. Here the Devas had performed tapasya in the elder days, and so had the great Rajarishis of dharma undertaken yagnas. Here, Yudhishtira, of long and mighty arms, sees the celebrated altar of Richaka's son, who had been the greatest of archers.

And the vedi is surrounded by hosts of ascetics, altar fit to be worshipped by men of dharma. The king sees the holy, and beautiful, and delightful shrines of all the Devas and of the Vasus, and of the Maruts and of the Aswin twins, the celestial physicians, and of Yama, son of Surya, and of Kubera, the lord of riches, and of Indra, and of Vishnu, and of Brahma and of Siva, and of Soma the Moon, and of Surya, author of day, and of Varuna, lord of waters, and of the host of Sadhyas, and of the Pitrs, and of Rudra together with all his ganas, and of Saraswati, the goddess of learning, and of the host of Siddhas, and of many other immortal holy gods besides.

In all those shrines the king observes various vratas, and gives away countless gemstones. He bathes in all the tirthas, then returns to Surparaka, from where, with his brothers, he crosses to Prabhasa, whose fame great Brahmanas have spread throughout the world.

There Yudhishtira, of the large reddish eyes, bathes with his brothers and offers libations to the Pitrs and the Devas, as do Krishnaa and all the Brahmanas travelling with them, and Lomasa as well. For twelve days he subsists upon air and water, and performs ablutions during those days and their nights, surrounding himself with kindled fires.

Thus that greatest of all virtuous men engages himself in asceticism, while word reaches Balarama and Krishna in Dwaraka of Yudhishtira's severe penance, and those two lords of all the Vrishnis, bring a large complement of soldiers with them, and come to meet the Pandava of the race of Ajamidha.

When the Vrishnis see the sons of Pandu lying upon the ground, their bodies covered in dirt, when they see the daughter of Drupada in a piteous condition, their grief is great and they cannot stop themselves from breaking out into loud lamentation.

Now the king, whose courage is such that no misfortune can ever prevail over his heart, rises and lovingly meets Rama and Krishna and Krishna's son Samba, and the grandson of Sini and other Vrishnis, and pays his respects to them, suitably. In return, they also honour him and all the sons of Pritha, who in turn honour them.

And they seat themselves around Yudhishtira, as the Devas sit around Indra, O king! He describes the machinations of his enemies to them, and how he has spent his years in the forest, and how Arjuna has gone to Indra's realm to acquire the Devastras; he is joyful in their company and relates all this with a light and glad heart.

And they are happy to learn all this news from him; but when they see the Pandavas so emaciated, the majestic and kindly Vrishnis cannot stanch their tears, gushing from their eyes for the anguish they feel."

TIRTHA-YATRA PARVA CONTINUED

Janamejaya said, "O you of ascetic wealth, when the sons of Pandu and the Vrishnis reach holy Prabhasa, what do they do and what conversation do they have between them? For all of them were such Mahatmans, and held each other in high esteem."

Vaisampayana said, "When the Vrishnis arrive in holy Prabhasa, the sacred landing on the coast of the sea, they surround the sons of Pandu and wait upon them.

Then, Balarama, whose complexion is as fair as the milk of the cow, the kunda flower, the moon, silver and the lotus root, Balarama who wears a vanamala and whose weapon is the ploughshare, speaks to the lotus-eyed Panchali, 'Krishnaa, I do not see that the practice of dharma leads to any good or that sin fetches evil upon the sinners, for I see the godly Yudhishtira in this miserable condition, with matted hair, a vanaprastha, and wearing valkala; while Duryodhana rules the earth, and the ground does not open to swallow him.

It would seem that a life of viciousness is more rewarding than a virtuous one. All ordinary men wonder that the sinner Duryodhana flourishes while the righteous Yudhishtira Dharmaputra, who cleaves to justice, is always honest and liberal has been robbed of his throne.

Why, this son of Pritha would give up his kingdom and his pleasure but would not swerve from the path of dharma. How do Bhishma and Kripa and the Brahmana Drona and the old king Dhritarashtra live happily after banishing the sons of Pandu into exile? Ah, fie on the sinful lords of Bharata's race!

What will Dhritarashtra say to the Pitrs of his noble line when the wretch meets them in the next world? He has cast his sinless sons from their throne; how can he ever claim that he is not guilty of the worst crime?

At this time he does not see with his mind's eye that he has acted blindly, and truly gone blind in the sight of the kings of the earth. It is because he has banished Kunti's son from his kingdom! I have no doubt that, when he with his sons perpetrated this inhuman act, Vichitravirya's son saw the dread smasana where bodies are burnt with flowering trees of a golden hue.

Surely, when these stooped towards him, the evil dead with great crimson, staring eyes, he must have heeded their vicious counsel, since he so fearlessly sent Yudhishtira to the forest, even while this son of Pandu had all his weapons with him and his brothers, as well.

This Bhima here, whose voracious appetite is like that of a wolf, can decimate a formidable army just with the strength of his arms and bearing no weapon. The forces on the battlefield were unmanned just to hear his war-cry. And now this mighty one suffers from hunger and thirst, and is emaciated with toilsome journeys.

But when he takes up his arrows and other weapons, and meets his enemies on the field, he will remember the suffering of his wretched forest-life, and kill them to the last man – of this I have no doubt.

Throughout the whole world no one can boast of strength and prowess equal to his. Alas, his great body is denuded by the cold, and heat and the winds. But when he stands up to fight, he will not spare a single enemy.

This mighty Kshatriya is inexorable when he rides a chariot — this Vrikodara single-handedly conquered all the rulers of the east, together with ther armies; and he returned from those wars uninjured. And that same Bhima, clad miserably in the bark of trees, now leads a sorry life in the vana.

This powerful Sahadeva vanquished all the kings of the south; those lords of men who amassed on the sea coast – look at him now in tapasavesham, an anchorite's dress. Valiant Nakula singe-handedly vanquished the kings of the west; and he now roams the jungles, subsisting on fruit and roots, with a matted mass of jata on the head, and his body covered with dirt.

This daughter of a king who is a maharatha, rose from the flames during a sacrifice. She has always known a life of luxury and happiness; how does she now endure this sorry existence in a forest?

And rhe son of the god of virtue—dharma which stands at the head of the three purusharthas—and the son of the wind god and the son of the lord of the Devas, and these two sons of the Aswini Kumaras – how do they live in the forest? deprived of all comforts?

When Dharmaputra was beaten at dice, and when he, his wife, his brothers and his followers were all driven into exile, and Duryodhana began to flourish, why did the very earth not perish with all her mountains?"

CANTO 120

TIRTHA-YATRA PARVA CONTINUED

Satyaki says, "Rama, this is not the time to lament. Although Yudhishtira does not say a single word, we must do what the time and occasion demand. Those who have others to look after their welfare do not need to undertake anything themselves; others do their work, as Saibya and the rest did for Yayati.

So, too, Rama, those who have friends, patrons who, of their own accord, fight their causes meet with no trials, as if they are helpless. How is it that when the sons of Pritha have Balarama and Krishna for friends and patrons, as well as Samba and Pradyumna and myself—we who can protect the three worlds—how is it then that Yudhishtira lives in the forest with his brothers?

Even today our army of Dasarhas, fully armed and wearing chequered mail, should march on Hastinapura, and the Vrishnis should send Dhritarashtra's sons and their allies to Yamaloka. If roused, Krishna by himself, Krishna who wields the bow made of horn, could subdue all the world. Krishna, I ask you to kill Dhritarashtra's son, with all his men, even as Indra did Vritra.

Pritha's son Arjuna is my brother, and my friend, and my guru; he is like another Krishna. It is for this that men wish for a worthy son, and that a guru seeks a pupil who would never contradict him. It is for this that the time has come for that best of all tasks, difficult to perform.

I will baffle Duryodhana's volleys of weapons with my archery. I will overpower them all on the field of battle. In my wrath, I will strike him down with my fine shafts that are no less that snakes, poison and fire. And with the keen edge of my sword, I will cut his head from his trunk, on the battlefield.

After this, I will kill his followers, and annihilate all of Kuru's race. O son of Rohini, let the followers of Bhima look at me with joy in their hearts, when I wield my weapons on the field of war, when I slay all their best warriors, just as fire consumes the worlds like bales of straw, when time ends.

Kripa and Drona and Vikarna and Karna will not stand against Pradyumna's fierce arrows. And I know the power of Arjuna's son – he is like the son of Krishna in battle. Let Samba punish Duhsasana; let him kill Duhsasana and his charioteer and destroy his ratha, for on the field of battle Jamabavati's son is irresistible and nothing can withstand him. Why, when he was a mere boy he routed the Asura Sambara's army; he slew Asvachakra, whose thighs were like pillars, and whose muscular arms were of great length.

Who can even approach Samba's chariot? Even as all mortals that are born do not escape death, so, too, whoever meets Samba on the battlefield will die.

As for Krishna, he will burn up the enemy troops with his astras of fire; he will kill the maharathas Bhishma and Drona, and Somadatta surrounded by all his sons. Who or what is there in all the world, including the gods, that Krishna cannot vanquish in battle when he takes up arms?

Then let Aniruddha also take up his bow and sword, and let him cover the earth with Dhritarashtra's sons, their heads hewn from their trunks, even as a sacrificial vedi is strewn with blades of kusa grass.

And Gada and Ulmuka, and Bahuka and Bhanu and Nitha and the young Nishatha, so valiant in battle, and Sarana, and Charudeshna, inexorable in war — let them all perform feats that befit their race.

Let the united army of the Satwatas and Suras, together with the best warriors of the Vrishnis, the Bhojas, and the Andhakas slay the sons of Dhritarashtra upon the field of war, and swell their great fame throughout the world.

Then let Abhimanyu rule the world as long as this best of virtuous men, Yudhishtira, is away fulfilling the vow that he swore during the game of dice. Afterward that time expires, he will rule the world again, unchallenged, for we would have slain all his enemies already. No son of Dhritarashtra will remain on earth, neither the Sutaputra.

This is the vital mission before us, which we must accomplish without delay."

Krishna says, "O scion of the race of Madhu, what you say is true and we accept and honour your words, always valiant one! But this bull of the Kurus would never accept sovereignty of the earth, unless it were won by the prowess of his own arms. Neither for the sake of pleasure, nor from fear, nor from greed would Yudhishtira ever renounce Kshatriya dharma; and nor would these two heroes, the maharathas Bhima and Arjuna; nor the twins, and neither Drupada's daughter Krishnaa.

Vrikodara and Dhananjaya have no equals or rivals in battle throughout the word. And why will this king not rule the whole world when he has Madri's twin sons to fight for him?

The noble king of Panchala, together with the Kekaya king, and we ourselves shall put forth our might, and at that time the enemies of Yudhisthira shall be annihilated."

Yudhishtira says, "It is not strange that you should say this, Satyaki! However, to me dharma must be the first consideration, above that of sovereign power.

But only Krishna knows what I am, just as I alone know who he truly is. Scion of Madhu, most valiant of Sini's race, when Krishna knows that the time for war has come, he, Kesava of the beautiful hair, will also help vanquish Suyodhana.

But today let the Dasarha heroes go back; they are my patrons and the greatest of all men, who have visited me here. O you of immeasurable strength, never fall away from the path of dharma, and I will see you again and that shall be a joyful occasion."

Then, after exchanging mutual greetings and paying obeisance to their elders, and having embraced the youthful, the Yadavas and the Pandavas part. The Yadus return to their home, and the Pandavas continue their tirthayatra.

Leaving Krishna, Yudhishtira, accompanied by his brothers and servants, and also by Lomasa, goes to the sacred river Payoshni, with its fine landing-ford that had been built by the king of Vidarbha. The Pandavas begin living on the banks of the Payoshni, whose waters are mixed with Soma rasa.

There, Yudhishtira is greeted with praise and affection by very many Brahmanas, who are delighted to see him in that place.

TIRTHA-YATRA PARVA CONTINUED

Lomasa says, "Rajan, King Nriga performed a sacrifice here, he gratified Indra Purandara with the offering of Soma rasa. Indra was refreshed and very pleased. Here, Indra and the Devas and the protectors of all born beings celebrated Mahayagnas of diverse kinds, and gave abundant wealth to the ministering priests.

Here King Amurtarayasa, lord of the earth, gratified Indra Vajradhari, also with Soma rasa, when that king performed seven aswamedha yagnas. All things which in other sacrifices are made of wood and earth, were made of gold in those seven horse sacrifices.

And he himself fashioned for all the rites seven sets of stakes, the rings for the sacrificial stambas, the pots, the ladles, utensils, and spoons. On top of each sacrificial stake, seven rings were fastened, and, O Yudhishtira, Indra and the Devas themselves erected the stakes of shining gold which had been prepared for that king's sacred rites.

In all the magnificent yagnas of Gaya, protector of the earth, he delighted Indra by giving him Soma rasa to drink, and the ministering priests were gratified with the untold wealth the king gave them. As no one can count the sand-grains of the earth, or the stars in the sky, or rain-drops when it rains, so, too, the wealth Gaya gave away was beyond calculation, it was past anything given before, even during the seven aswamedhas.

And Viswakarman created golden images of Saraswati, Goddess of speech, and Gaya gave these away to the Brahmanas who attended his sacrifice, coming from all the directions and cardinal points.

Lord of men, when King Gaya, Mahatman, performed his sacrifices, he erected sacrificial mounds at so many different places that but little space was left upon the surface of the earth. Bhaarata, through this Mahayagna, Gaya attained Devaloka, Indra's realm.

Whoever bathes in the river Payoshni goes to the realms which Gaya attained, so, Rajadhiraja, prince of dharma, you and your brothers must bathe in this river; and, O protector of the earth, you will be freed from all sin."

Purushottama, Yudhishtira and his brothers perform ablutions in the river Payoshni, after which they journey on to the hill of sapphires and the great river Narmada, where Lomasa names all the sacred tirthas for the Pandava and all the holy shrines of the Devas, as they visit each of these, one after the other, at their leisure.

At each of them, Brahmanas by thousands receive gifts from Yudhishtira.

Lomasa says, "Kaunteya, he who visits the Vaidurya Parvata, the sapphire mountain, and immerses his body in the river Narmada, attains the lokas of the Devas and the Rajarishis. This is the cusp of the Dwapara and the Kali yugas; this is the time when a man rids himself of all his sins.

This is where Saryati performed sacrificial rites, at which Indra appeared and drank Soma rasa, along with the Aswini Kumaras. And here Bhrigu's son of great tapasya became angry with Mahendra, and the mighty Chyavana paralysed Indra, and gained the princess Sukanya for his wife."

Yudhishtira says, "How did Chyavana paralyse the Deva of the six gunas, the scourge of Paka? Why did the Maharishi become angry with Indra? And how, O Brahmana, did Chyavana enable the Aswini Kumaras to drink the Soma rasa? I beg you, tell me about all this exactly as it happened."

CANTO 122

TIRTHA-YATRA PARVA CONTINUED

Lomasa says, "A son was born to the Maharishi Bhrigu, and he was called Chyavana. He was respelendent and sat in tapasya on the banks of the lake you see there. Pandava, Chyavana of great tejas sat in the posture called Vira; he sat quiet and still as a post, for a very long time, in the same place.

An anthill covered him, and creepers the hillock. Swarms of ants enveloped him, and he looked just like a mound of earth, but he continued his tapasya, lost to the world.

When a long time passed, King Saryati came to this fine lake for his amusement. With him, came four thousand women, his wives all, O Bhaarata! Also with him came his only daughter, Sukanya of the beautiful brows.

She wore jewels fit for the Apsaras, was surrounded by her sakhis, and while wandering here, came to the anthill inside which Bhrigu's son sat in dhyana. She looked around her, enchanted by the beauty of the place, the grand and lofty trees.

Ah, she was exquisite and in the prime of her youth. She was playful and began to break the twigs of the forest trees bearing blossoms. Bhrigu's son of awesome intelligence saw her roaming about bright like a streak of lightning, now having left her maids behind, and wearing just a single cloth and her ornaments.

The Muni was stricken with desire, and he called out to her in a low voice, but she did not hear him. Then she saw his eyes shining through the anthill, and not knowing what they were, and becoming curious, she pierced those eyes with a twig of thorns. From that searing pain of being blinded Chyavana in anger cursed Saryati and his party — freezing their bowels! Unable to answer the calls of nature, the men suffered direly.

Seeing their agony, the knowing king asked, "Who has offended the illustrious son of Bhrigu? He is old and always at tapasya, and he is wrathful. Tell me quickly if you know who has wronged him."

His soldiers replied, "We do not know who has wronged the Rishi. We ask you to inquire into this thing."

At which, using both menace and conciliation, Saryati asked his advisors and friends about what had happened, but they did not know anything either.

When Sukanya saw the distress of the army and her father aggrieved, she said, "Roving in the forest, I lighted upon this anthill and saw something shining inside it. Taking it for glowworms, I pierced the anthill with thorns."

Saryati immediately came to the anthill, and there he saw Bhrigu's son, old both in years and tapasya. With folded hands, the lord of the earth begged the Sage, "My daughter did this atrocious thing in ignorance and youth, it becomes you to forgive her."

Bhrigu's son Chyavana said, "Full of pride, she pierced my eyes. O King, I will forgive you only on one condition — that you give me your beautiful, ignorant and arrogant daughter for my wife."

Saryati never paused but bestowed Sukanya on Mahatama Chyavana. Now the holy one was pleased with the king and withdrew his curse. Having won the Rishi's grace, the king went home to his city, with his troops.

Having become the Muni's wife, the lovely Sukanya quickly proved herself to be dutiful – in tending to his needs, in keeping vows and practising austerities herself, in observing dharma. She was graceful, guileless and she worshipped her husband Chyanava, she looked after his guests, whenever they came, and she kept the sacred fire burning."

CANTO 123

TIRTHA-YATRA PARVA CONTINUED

Lomasa says, "One day the Aswin twins saw Sukanya, when she had just finished bathing and she was naked. They approached her, who was as beautiful as the daughter of the king of the Devas, and they said, 'You of the shapely thighs, whose daughter are you? And what are you doing in this forest? Auspicious, most graceful one, tell us who you ae."

She replied shyly, "I am Saryati's daughter, and Chyavana's wife."

At which, the Aswins smiled, "Why, most fortunate one, has your father given you to a man who is near death? Ah, timid girl, you shine like lightning in this jungle. Why, not in Devaloka have we seen the likes of you. Even wearing no ornament and neither any costly garment, you light up this vana!

Still, faultless limbs, you cannot be as beautiful here as you would decked in every ornament and wearing gorgeous apparel. Why, exquisite one, do you serve a decrepit old husband, who is incapable of satisfying you or even maintaining you, O luminous smiles? Divine beauty, leave

Chyavana and take one of us for your husband. You must not lay waste your youth."

Sukanya replied, "I am devoted to my husband, do not think for a moment that I would betray him."

They said to her, we are the Aswins, the legendary physicians of heaven. We will make your lord as young and handsome as ourselves, but then you must choose one among us to be your lord. Swear you will do this and having sworn go and fetch your husband here."

Rajan, Sukanya went and told Bhrigu's son what the Aswin Kumaras proposed. Chyavana Muni said to her, "Do as they ask."

She went back with him to the Aswins and said, "Do what you said."

They said, "Let your husband enter into this lake."

Chyavana, who wanted beauty and youth, quickly walked into the water. The twin Aswins also, O king, sank into the sheet of water. Next moment, all three emerged with surpassingly beautiful forms, and young, and wearing burnished earrings. But all three looked exactly alike, indistinguishable from one another.

They said to Sukanya, "Fortunate one, choose one of us to be your lord, whichever of us takes your fancy."

Finding all three of them identical, she deliberated; and at last her heart discovered who her husband was, and she chose him for her lord.

Having become young and radiantly handsome, and his wife having chosen him, as well, Chyavana of geat tejas was pleased and said to the Aswini Kumaras, those nose-born twins*, "You have given me youth and beauty, and I will make you drink Soma rasa in the very presence of Indra. This I solemnly swear."

The Aswins were delighted and flew up into Devaloka. Chyavana and Sukanya passed their days in fine joy, even like a Deva and his wife.'

CANTO 124

TIRTHA-YATRA PARVA CONTINUED

Lomasa says, 'Now the news came to Saryati that Chyavana had been turned into a youth. Well pleased, he went with his troops to the hermitage of the son of Bhrigu. And he saw Chyavana and Sukanya, like Devas' children, and his joy and that of his wife were as great as if the king had conquered the whole world.

The Sage received the king and queen with honour. Saryati sat next to the Rishi, and entered into a happy and auspicious conversation with him.

Bhrigu's son said, "O King, perform a yagna at which I shall be the priest. Procure everything that we need for the sacrifice."

At which, Saryati was overjoyed and expressed whole-hearted approval. On an auspicious day, Saryati ordered a most excellent sacrificial shrine to be erected, provided with all that was needed for the yagna.

Chyavana, the son of Bhrigu, was the king's priest; and listen to the wonderful events which unfolded there. Chyavana took up some Soma rasa to offer it to the Aswini Kumaras, who are physicians to the Devas.

Even as the Rishi was doing this, Indra declared, "These Aswins have no right to receive an offering of the Soma rasa. They are the physicians to the Devas in heaven – their vocation does not permit them to drink the Soma."

Chyavana said, "These two are of mighty enterprise, possessed of mighty souls, and endowed with uncommon beauty and grace. Besides, Indra, they have given me eternal beauty, even as of a Deva. Why should you and the other Devas have a right to drink the Soma juice, and not they?

Lord of the Devas, Puranadara, know that the Aswins are also Devas!"

At this, Indra said, "These two practise the healing arts, they are but servants; assuming different forms at their pleasure they roam the world of mortal beings. How can they justly claim the juice of the Soma?"

Indra spoke these words again and again, but setting him at naught, Bhrigu's son still took up the offering he meant to make. As he was about to offer a sizeable portion of Soma rasa to the Aswins, Indra said, "If you offer the Soma to the Awins, I will burn you with my thunderbolt!"

But Chyavana only gave Indra a smile and took a a goodly portion of Soma rasa to offer it to the Aswins. Indra began to cast the dreadful Vajra as the Sage, but found his arm frozen by Bhrigu's son.

Chyavana continued to chant mantras and made his offerings into the sacred fire. Through the Rishi's tapasakti, an evil spirit, an immense and mighty demon called Mada sprang forth from the flames. So great was he that neither the Devas nor the Asuras could measure his body.

His mouth was terrifying, chasmal, with rows of razor sharp teeth; one of his jaws rested on earth while the other stretched up into heaven. Four fangs he had, each a hundred yojanas, while his other teeth were ten yojanas each and like the towers of a palace, all pointed and sharp as spears.

The demon's arms were like hills, both of equal bulk, stretching ten thousand yojanas each. His two eyes resembled the sun and the moon;

and the fire of his face rivalled the conflagration at the dissolution of the universe.

He licked his lips with his tongue like a gash of lightning, without pause; his maw gaped wide, his gaze was frightful, and it seemed that he meant to swallow the every earth.

This demon rushed at Indra of a thousand yagnas, and he meant to devour that Deva. The world rang with the terrifying roars of the Asura."

TIRTHA-YATRA PARVA CONTINUED

Lomasa says, "When Indra saw the Asura Mada, looking like Yama himself, rushing at him, jaws agape, certainly meaning to devour him, while the Deva's arms remained frozen, that god could only lick the corners of his mouth in terror.

Frightened past endurance, Indra cried to Chyavana, "O Bhargava, O Brahmana, I swear to you in the name of truth itself that from today the Aswini Kumaras shall partake of the Soma rasa! Be merciful to me, for I can never forswear myself.

May your yagna be fruitful; these Aswins shall drink Soma rasa from now because you, most holy one, have entitled them to it. O Bhargava, I did all this to spread the renown of your powers, my purpose being to provide an occasion for their display. My other object was to spread the fame of Sukanya's father Saryati.

So be merciful to me."

Mahatama Chyavana's wrath was quickly appeased and he freed Indra from the spell that held the Deva frozen. As for the Asura Mada, whose name means intoxication, the Rishi divided the demon and put his spirit into drink, into women, into gambling, into field sport.

Having lessened Mada, Chyavana now gratified Indra with a draught of Soma and helped Saryati worship the entire host of Devas, and now the Aswins with them, equally, thereby truly covering the earth with the fame of that king. His yagna complete, Bhrigu's son, best among those blessed with speech, passed his days happily in the forest, in the company of Sukanya, his loving wife.

This is his lake, shining before you, O Yudhishtira, and echoing with the voices of birds. Here you and your brothers must offer tarpana to your Pitrs and to the Devas.

Sovereign of the earth, scion of Bharata, you must go to Sikataksha, as well, then to the Saindhava vana, where you will find a number of small rivers and lakes. You must touch the waters of all these, while chanting mantras to Lord Siva; and so you will find success in every endeavour of yours.

For this is the conjunction, of two yugas, the Dwapara and the Kali. It is a time, O Kaunteya, in which a man's every sin can be destroyed.

Perform ablutions here, for this place can take all his sins from a man. And yonder is the Archika hill, where men of evolved souls live; fruit of all seasons grow here perennially and the streams run always full.

Why, this is a place fit for the Devas and indeed they have erected various holy images of diverse forms, which you see. Look, Yudhishtira, here the gods built the bathing tank of the Moon.

Rishis dwell here on every side, in the forest, as do the Balakhilyas and the Pavakas, who live just on air. Here are three peaks and three springs; you can walk around them in pradakshina, one by one; then you may bathe at your leisure.

Santanu, and Sunaka, the sovereign of men, and both Nara and Narayana attained everlasting realms from this place. Here the gods constantly come, as also the manes, together with the greatest sages.

All of them have performed tapasya upon this Archika Parvata. Sacrifice to them, Yudhishtira; here the Devas and the Rishis eat payasa.

And here is the Yamuna, her spring exhaustless; here Krishna sat in tapasya. O Pandava, you who drag the dead bodies of your enemies across the ground, the twins, Bhimasena, Panchali and all of us will come with you to the river.

Lord of men, this is the holy spring that belongs to Indra. Here Varuna Deva also rose up, and here they sat with faith, in dhyana. This sacred hill welcomes kindly and honest folk. This is Yamuna of renown, frequented by hosts of mighty sages, and the setting for diverse religious rituals; she is most holy and destroys the fear of sin.

Here Mandhata himself, of the mighty bow, performed yagnas to the gods; and so did Somaka, the son of Sahadeva, and a most munificent giver of gifts."

CANTO 126

TIRTHA-YATRA PARVA CONTINUED

Yudhishtira says, "Great Brahmana, how was that tiger among kings, Mandhata, Yuvanaswa's son, born, that best of monarchs, celebrated across the three worlds? And how did he of unmeasured lustre attain the very pinnacle of regal power, since all the three worlds were as much under his subjection as they are under that of Vishnu of mighty soul?

I am eager to hear all about the life and achievements of that Rajarishi. I would also like to hear how he was named Mandhata, he whose lustre rivalled that of Indra himself. Tell me also how he was born, for you are a master of narration."

Lomasa says, "Listen attentively, Rajan, to how the name of Mandhata, of the great soul, came to be celebrated throughout all the worlds. Yuvanaswa, ruler of the earth, was born into Ikshvaku's race. That protector of the world performed many sacrifices, noted for their magnificent gifts.

A thousand times, that most virtuous of men performed the Aswamedha yagna. He also performed other sacrifices of the highest order, wherein he gave abundant daana. But that saintly king had no son; and he of mighty soul and rigid vows made over the duties of the state to his ministers, and went away to dwell in the forest.

There, he undertook a stern tapasya during which, once, he kept a fast. Pangs of hunger tormented him and his very soul seemed parched with thirst. In this state, he came to the asrama of Bhrigu. That same night, king of kings, the Maharishi who was the joy of Bhrigu's race had overseen a sacrifice devoted to a son being born to Saudyumni.

In the place where the rituals had been performed stood a great urn filled with holy water, consecrated with mantras; and that water was imbued with the virtue that when Saudyumni's wife drank it she would give birth to a godlike son. Those great Sages had left the blessed water on the altar and had gone to sleep, for they were exhausted after the nightlong ritual.

As Yuvanaswa passed by them, his mouth was dry, and he was in the grip of an agony of thirst; ah, he was desperate for a drink of water. The king entered that hermitage and asked for water, but his voice was feeble with weakness, and coming from an arid throat the sound he made was like the inarticulate cry of a bird. Nobody heard him.

Then the king saw the jar full of water and he ran to it, and drank deeply, thirstily, emptying the vessel. The water was cool and appeased his thirst. Then, the Rishis there awoke and found that the jar of water had been disturbed from its place and it was empty.

They gathered together and asked who had drunk the water, at which Yuvanaswa confessed that it had been he. The revered son of Bhrigu said to him, 'It was not right. This water was infused with an occult siddhi and had been placed there so that a son could be born to you. I invested the water with the power of my tapasya.

Mighty Rajarishi, you would have had a son of great strength and valour, why a prince who could have despatched even Indra to Yamaloka. So much power had I infused into this water, and now look what you have done.

It is impossible to undo what has been done, and surely what you did was fate's own fiat. Great king, you were thirsty and you drank the water consecrated by my mantras of power and blessed with the punya of my tapasya; there is only one course ahead – you must bring forth the splendid child I have described from your own body!

We will perform a sacrifice to that end, of wonderful effect, and brave as you are, you will bring forth a son as great as Indra. Nor will you experience any pain of labour.'

When a hundred years passed, a son brilliant as Surya burst out from the king's left side, and he was mighty indeed; and neither did Yuvanaswa die, which was also strange.

Indra came to visit the child and the Devas asked great Indra, 'What will this boy suck to feed?'

Indra put his own forefinger into the child's mouth and the Vajradhari said, 'Mandhata – me he shall suckle on.'

The dwellers of heaven and Indra as well named the boy Mandhata. He tasted Indra's forefinger and grew instantly to be thirteen yojanas, and he was incomparably powerful. Rajan, the prince acquired all sacred knowledge, all the Shastras, along with the holy science of arms, just through the power of his thought and intuition, unassisted.

That same day, the renowned bow Ajagava and a host of arrows made of horn, an impenetrable coat of armour, all these came magically into his possession! Indra himself set Mandhata on the throne and that king conquered the three worlds, always with dharma, even as Vishnu did with his three strides.

Mandhata's chariot was inexorable on its course through the world; and the greatest jewels came of their own accord into that Rajarishi's keep.

Lord of the earth, this is Mandhata's land; it abounds in wealth. Here he performed a number of diverse yagnas, during which vast bounties were given to the officiating priests.

Mandhata of immense power and measureless lustre erected sacred shrines, performed countless deeds of untold piety, and he attained the honour of sitting by Indra's side.

That wise king of dharma sent forth his command and just by its virtue conquered the earth, together with the sea—source of gems—and all the cities of the world. The yagnashalas that he made covered the very face of Bhumi, on all sides.

That great sovereign gave ten thousand padmas* of cows to Brahmanas. Once, there came a drought of twelve years and Mandhata made it rain over the parched earth, while Indra could not prevent it but only stared.

Mandhata slew the powerful Gandhara king, born into the House of the Moon, who was dreadful like a thundercloud full of lightning and who wounded Mandhata sore with arrows.

Rajan, he led a virtuous and austere life and with his untold might protected the worlds from all evil, and nurtured the four varnas equally. This is where, lustrous like the Sun, he sacrificed to God. Look at the place – here it is, in the very midst of the field of the Kurus, holiest of holies!

Master of the world, I have told you how Mandhata was born, extraordinarily, and also about his magnificent life."

Yudhishtira immediately asks Lomasa fresh questions, now about Somaka.

CANTO 127

TIRTHA-YATRA PARVA CONTINUED

Yudhishtira says, "O best of masters, how strong and powerful was King Somaka? I want to hear a detailed account of his might and his deeds."

Lomasa says, "Yudhishtira, Somaka was a most virtuous king. He had a hundred wives, all chaste and noble, but he did not have a son by any of them, for a long, long time.

Then one day, when he had become old, a son was born to him, and called Jantu. All day long, the prince's hundred mothers would sit around their child, every one giving him whatever he wanted or whatever they thought would please him.

One day, an ant stung the boy on his leg and he screamed. His mothers were so distressed that they stood around him and set up a chorus of cries of their own — a tumult of shrieks.

That great outcry reached the ears of the king, where he sat in his court among his ministers, with his family priest at his side. He sent forth to discover what had caused the agitation. A royal guard brought him the news of how his son had been bitten by an ant.

Somaka rose and, with his ministers, hurried to the antahpura, and there he tenderly comforted his child, Parantapa.

When the prince grew quiet, the king came out from his harem and sat again in his sabha with his family priest and his council of ministers.

Somaka said sombrely, 'Fie on having a single son! I had rather been a sonless man, for if one thinks of how vulnerable to sickness all men are, to have just one son is only a trouble and a heartache.

O Brahmana, I married a hundred wives so that I might have many sons. But they gave me none, until at last this single boy was born, this prince Jantu.

What grief can be greater than this? Dvijottama, I have grown old and so have my wives; yet, this child is like our very prana, our life-breath. But, tell me now, is there any yagna, performing which one can get a hundred sons? Tell me if the sacrifice is great or small, easy to perform or difficult.'

The family priest, the kulaguru, said, 'There is indeed a yagna by which a man may get a hundred sons. If you can perform it, O Somaka, I will explain it to you.'

Somaka said, 'Whether it be a good or an evil rite, take it that I have already performed the yagna for a hundred sons. Explain it to me.'

The Brahmana said, 'I will begin a yagna and at it you must sacrifice your son Jantu. Then, very soon, you will have a hundred splendid sons. When Jantu's fat is offered into the fire to the gods, the queens must inhale the smoke of the burning flesh and they will bring forth a hundred radiant princes, brave and powerful. Why, and Jantu himself will be born again, of himself, svaymbhuva, and upon his back there will be a golden mark.'

TIRTHA-YATRA PARVA CONTINUED

Somaka said, 'Brahmana, do whatever you must. I want to have many sons and I will do as you say.'

The priest commenced the sacrifice at which Jantu was to be the offering. But the hundred wailing mothers snatched at their son and tried to save him.

'Ah, we are lost!' they cried, and held the boy's right arms, but the priest snatched him back, while the queens screamed like female ospreys. The Brahmana killed Jantu and offered his flesh as havis, the burnt offering into the sacred agni.

Kurunandana, while the prince's fat burned, the agonised mothers whiffed its smell and fell in a swoon all together. At once, all those women became pregnant, and when ten months passed they delivered a hundred sons to Somaka.

Lord of the earth, Jantu was also born again, to his own mother, and he was the eldest of the hundred princes and the most beloved of all his mothers; not so their own sons. And upon his back there was the mark of gold, and of those hundred sons he was the superior one.

Somaka's kulaguru left this world after a time, and so did that king. After they died, Somaka saw his priest being tortured with fire in a dreadful hell.

Somaka asked him, 'Why are you being roasted in this naraka?

In searing pain, the priest gasped, 'This is my punishment for performing that sacrifice for you.'

Rajarishi Somaka said to Dharmaraja, who punishes dead sinners, 'Lord, free my priest. I am to blame for the torment he suffers; burn me in the fire instead.'

Dharmaraja replied, 'No one can suffer for another's sins or enjoy the fruit of anyone else's good deeds. Look, here is the fruit of all the punya you have done.'

Somaka said, 'Without this, I have no wish to go to the blessed realms. I want to remain with this man, either in heaven or here in hell, for I have done what he has and we should share an identical fate.'

Dharmaraja said, 'O King, if this is what you want, then taste the fruit of his sin for the same time that he does. After that you will find the realms of heaven.'

That lotus-eyed king did exactly that, and when his sins were paid for he and his kulaguru were set free together. Fond as Somaka was of his priest, he shared all the fruit of his punya, his great good deeds, with the Brahmana.

This is his enchanting asrama, which is so lovely before your eyes. Anyone who spends six nights here, with his passions controlled, will attain the blessed realms of heaven. King of kings, let us rid ourselves of all excitations, and spend six nights in this sacred place!"

TIRTHA-YATRA PARVA CONTINUED

Lomasa says, 'O King, in this place Narayana himself performed a sacrifice of old, the yagna called Ishtikrita, which lasted a thousand years.

Nabhaga's son Ambarisha sacrificed near the Yamuna river; and he gave away ten padmas of gold coins to the attendant priests; and he attained the final felicity through sacrifices and austerities.

Kaunteya, this is the place Nahusha's son, Yayati, lord of all the world, man of dharma, his power measureless, performed his sacrifice. He was as mighty as Indra and performed his yagna here. Look how the ground is strewn with fire pits of diverse kinds, and how the earth seems to subside here under the weight of Yayati's pieties.

Look, here is the Sami tree, which has just one leaf, and look at this sparkling lake. Why, behold all these lakes of Parasurama, and the asrama of Narayana. Rajan, here is the path that Richaka's son of untold tejas trod, who ranged over the world, and practised rites of yoga in the river Raupya.

Kurunandana, listen to what a Pisachi, who wore pestles for her ornaments, said to a Brahmana woman, as I once sat here chanting the timeless lineages.

Having eaten curd in Yugandhara, and stayed in Achutasthala, and also bathed in Bhutalaya, you must remain here with your brothers. Having passed one night here, if you stay another, what happens during the night will be very different from the events of the day, O most righteous of Bharata's race.

We will spend tonight here; this is the threshold of Kurukshetra, field of the Kurus. In this very place did Nahusha's son Yayati perform a yagna and gave gifts of a bounty of gemstones. Indra was pleased with those sacred rites.

This is a most auspicious tirtha along the Yamuna, called Plakshava-tarana, the descent of the banyan tree. Evolved men call it the entrance to Swarga. Here the greatest Rishis performed the sacrificial rites of the Saraswata king, using the sacrificial stake for their pestle, and when the sacrifice ended they performed their ablutions in the river.

Rajan, King Bharata undertook his sacrifice here, sending forth the sacrificial horse for his Aswamedha yagna, the animal which would be sacrificed. Through dharma that king won sovereignty over the earth by righteousness. The horses that he sent forth, many times, were mottled with black.

Purushvyaghra, it was here that Samvarta, greatest among Rishis, helped Marutta perform his renowned yagnas.

Bathing in this tirtha one can see into all the worlds, and is purified of all one's sins. Therefore, you, too, must bathe here, Yudhishtira.'

Yudhishtira, best of Pandu's sons, bathes there with his brothers while the mighty Munis chant his praises.

Yudhishtira says to Lomasa, 'O Rishi whose power is dharma, bathing here I see all the worlds! Ah, from here I see Arjuna, who rides the white charger!'

Lomasa says, 'Mahabaho, the greatest Rishis see all realms even so! This is holy Saraswati, thronged by those that regard her as their sole refuge. You have bathed here and you shall be free of all your sins.

Kaunteya, the Devarishis performed sacrifices for the Saswata king here, as did the Rishis and Rajarishis. This is the Vedi of Brahma Prajapati, extending five yojanas on every side. And this is the field of the magnificent Kurus, who always undertake great yagnas.'

CANTO 130

TIRTHA-YATRA PARVA CONTINUED

Lomasa says, 'Bhaarata, if any of the mortals breathes their last here, they find Swarga. Thousands upon thousands of men come to this place to die. Daksha pronounced a blessing on this place, while he performed his yagna here, saying, "Whoever dies in this place will win a place in Swarga."

Look at this beautiful and sacred Saraswati full of crystalline water; and here, lord of men, is Vinasana, where the Saraswati disappeared. Here is the gate of the kingdom of the Nishadas and it is from hatred for them that the Saraswati entered into the earth, so that the Nishadas might not see her.

Here, too, is the sacred land of Chamasodbheda, where the Saraswati became visible to them again. And here she is joined by other sacred rivers flowing seawards. Parantapa, here is the sacred Sindhu – where Lopamudra accepted the Maharishi Agastya for her lord; and, you of sunlike lustre, here is the holy tirtha Prabhasa, which Indra favours and which removes all sins.

Yonder is Vishnupada, and here is the sacred river Vipasa. Grieftsricken at the death of his sons, Maharishi Vasistha bound himsef hand and foot and cast himself into this river. But he rose out of the waters and was unfettered.

Look, O king, with your brothers, at the sacred land of Kasmira, frequented by holy sages. Here, O scion of Bharata, is the place where Agni Deva and Maharishi Kasyapa conferred; and also Nahusha's son and the sages of the north.

Yonder, Kshatriya, is the gateway to the Manasa-sarovara, where Sri Rama opened a gap in the mountain with his astra. And there is the renowned realm of Vatikhashanda, which, although adjacent to the gate of Videha, lies to its north.

There is something else very remarkable about this place— that on the waning of every yuga, the Lord Siva, who can assume any form at will, can be seen here with Uma and his ganas.

In the holy lake, also, those wanting the weal of their familes worship Siva Pinakin with sacrifices during the month of Chaitra. Devoted folk, their passions restrained, who bathe in the Manasa-sarovara are freed from their sins, and attain the holy realms.

And here is the tirtha called Ujjanaka, where the Maharishi Vasistha, his wife Arundhati and also the Muni Yavakri found peace.

Yonder is the lake Kusava, where the lotuses called Kusesaya grow; and here also is the sacred hermitage of Rukmini, where she attained mukti, after conquering that evil passion, anger.

I think, O prince, that you have heard something about that mountain of meditation, Bhrigutunga; look, that is the lofty peak. And there is Vitasta, the sacred stream that absolves men from all sins; its water is cool and limpid, and used mainly by the great sages.

Kshatriya, behold the holy rivers Jala and Upajala, on either side of the Yamuna. By performing a sacrifice here, king Usinara surpassed Indra himself in greatness; wanting to test Usinara's merit and also wanting to bestow boons on him, Indra and Agni came to his yagnashala.

Indra took the form of a hawk, and Agni that of a pigeon, and they flew to the king. In apparent fear of the hawk, the pigeon fell upon the king's thigh, seeking his protection.'

CANTO 131

TIRTHA-YATRA PARVA CONTINUED

'The hawk said, "The kings of the earth all say that you are a righteous sovereign. Why, O Kshatriya, have you stooped to this adharma? I am afflicted with hunger, do not keep me from my prey which God has given me to be my food. You think that you serve dharma by this, while, in fact, you forsake it."

The king said, "Best of avians, this pigeon is terrified of you and for its life. It has flown to me to escape you, and to beg for its life. How do you not see that my highest dharma is to give it my protection?

It trembles in fear and I would surely find sin if I abandon it. He that slays a Brahmana, he that slaughters a cow—the common mother of all the worlds—and he that forsakes one seeking protection are equally sinful."

The hawk replied, "O King, all beings live through food, which nourishes and sustains them. A man can live long even after relinquishing what is dearest to him, but he cannot live without food.

If you deprive me of my food, my life will leave this body and find realms where such troubles are unknown. But at my death, pious king, my mate and children will also surely perish, and by protecting this single pigeon, you will take many lives.

The virtue that stands in the way of another virtue is certainly no virtue at all, but in reality is sin. O King, whose prowess consists of truth, only the dharma which does not conflict with a greater dharma is worthy of being called dharma. Compare the conflicting costs in lives; you should not do what you mean to. Take the course of the lesser evil."

The king said, "O best of birds, you speak words fraught with wisdom, and I suspect that you are Suparna, monarch of birds. I have no hesitation in declaring that you are fully conversant with the ways of dharma. You disclose wonders about dharma so that I must believe there is nothing that you do not know about it.

So, then, how can you say that abandoning a creature that seeks my protection is dharma? Sky ranger, you are in quest of food; surely, you can assuage your hunger with some other food, more copious than this pigeon. I am willing to procure any kind of food for you, which is even more to your taste, even if it be an ox, or a boar, or a deer, or a buffalo."

There hawk said, "Great king, I have have no wish to eat a boar or an ox or any other animal; they are not my natural prey. So, O bull among Kshatriyas, give me this pigeon that heaven has ordained to be my meal today, for, that hawks will eat pigeons is the law of nature. Do not cling to a plantain tree for support, O king; it is not strong enough to support you."

The king said, " Sky rover, I will give you this rich kingdom of my race, or anything else you want; anything other than this pigeon, which has flown to me for my protection. Ah, tell me what I should do to save this bird because I do not mean to give him to you under any circumstance."

The hawk said, "Rajan, if you have such love for this pigeon, then cut off some of your own flesh and weigh it upon a scale until it equals the pigeon's weight. And when it does, give me that flesh and I will be satisfied."

The king said, "I will do so gladly and consider this a favour to me."

The Rajarishi Usinara cut off some of his flesh and weighed it in a balance against the pigeon. He found the pigeon heavier and cut off another piece of his flesh, and still the bird weighed more. Portion after portion of his flesh he cut and added but the scale remained tilted on the side of the bird.

At last there was no flesh left upon Usinara's body and he mounted the scale himself.

Now the hawk said, "King of dharma, I am Indra and the pigeon is Agni, who bears the havis to the gods. We came to your yagnashala to test your merit. You cut all the flesh from your body and your glory shall be resplendent, and will surpass that of all others in the world.

As long as men speak of you, your glory will endure and you will dwell in Swarga, in the holiest realms."

Saying this to the king, Indra flew up into Devaloka. And, after having filled heaven and earth with the punya of his great and pious deeds, Usinara also ascended into heaven in a radiant form.

Look, O King, at the asrama of that noblest-hearted sovereign. Here the Devas and Maharishis come, along with the purest Brahmanas.'

TIRTHA-YATRA PARVA CONTINUED

Lomasa says, 'And look here, lord of men, at the holy asrama of Uddalaka's son Swetaketu, whose fame as an expert in the sacred mantras is spread across earth. Coconut trees grace this hermitage. Here Swetaketu saw the Goddess Saraswati in her human shape, and said to her, "Bless me with the gift of speech!"

In that yuga, Swetaketu, the son of Uddalaka, and Ashtavakra, the son of Kahoda, who were uncle and nephew, were the greatest masters of the sacred lore. Those two Brahmanas, of matchless tejas, went to King Janaka's yagnasala and bested Vandin in a debate.

Kaunteya, you and your brothers worship the holy asrama of him whose grandson was Ashtavakra, who, even as a child, drowned Vandin in a river, after having vanquished him in a metaphysical debate.'

Yudhishtira says, 'Tell me, O Lomasa, all about the power of this man, who vanquished Vandin. Why was he born as Ashtavakra, crooked in eight parts of his body?'

Lomasa says, 'The Rishi Uddalaka had a disciple named Kahoda, of subdued passions, and entirely devoted to the service of his guru, who had studied long. The Brahmana had served his master for many years, and recognising his service, his preceptor gave him his own daughter, Sujata, in marriage, as well as a mastery over the Shastras.

And she conceived a child, radiant as fire.

One night, while his father was reading the scriptures aloud, the child spoke from his mother's womb, "Father, you have been reading all night but it seems to me that not everything you recite is correct. Through your study, I have become versed in the Shastras and the Vedas, and their Angas. I say to you that what comes from your mouth is inaccurate."

Insulted in the presence of his disciples, the Maharishi cursed the child in the womb in anger, "Because you speak even from the womb, you shall be crooked in eight parts of your body!"

The child was born crooked, and he was known as Ashtavakra. Now, he had an uncle named Swetaketu who was the same age as himself.

Anxious about the child growing in her, one day Sujata said to her impoverished husband, "Maharishi, the tenth month of my pregnancy is near. You have nothing to sustain us once our child is born."

Kahoda Muni went to King Janaka for wealth. In that Rajarishi's court, Vandin, master of dialectics, defeated Kahoda in a debate and drowned him in a river. Hearing of this, Uddalaka said to his daughter Sujata, "You must keep this secret from Ashtavakra."

She did so, and when Ashtavakra was born, he heard nothing about the matter; and he regarded Uddalaka as his father and Swetaketu as his brother. One day, when Ashtavakra was in his twelfth year, Swetaketu saw him sitting in Uddalaka's lap and pulled him roughly down.

Ashtavakra began to cry and Swetaketu said, "It isn't your father's lap!"

Ashtavakra was devastated. He went home and asked his mother, "Where is my father?"

Sujata was stricken by his question and she was also afraid that he might curse her; she told him what had happened.

At night Ashtavakra said to his uncle Swetaketu, "Let us go to the sacrifice of King Janaka, where we might see many wonderful things. We will listen to the debate between the Brahmanas and partake of excellent food. Our knowledge will increase. The recitation of the sacred Vedas is sweet to hear and is fraught with blessings."

Uncle and nephew went to Janaka's splendid sacrifice. Upon being turned away from the entrance to the yagnasala, Ashtavakra spoke to the great king inside.'

CANTO 133

TIRTHA-YATRA PARVA CONTINUED

'Ashtavakra said, "Where no Brahmana is encountered, the right of way belongs to the blind, the deaf, the women, carriers of burden, and the king. But when a Brahmana is on the way, the path belongs to him alone."

King Janaka said, "I give you the right to enter; go in by whichever entrance you choose. No fire, be it ever so small, is to be slighted. Even Indra bows to the Brahmanas."

Ashtavakra said, "Ruler of men, we have come to witness your sacrifice and our curiosity is great. Besides we have come here as guests, sadasyas; we want your permission to enter. And, O son of Indradyumna, we have come to meet King Janaka and to speak to him. But your gatekeeper obstructs us and for this our anger burns us like fever."

The gatekeeper said, "We carry out the orders of Vandin. Listen to what I have to say. Boys are not allowed to enter here, only learned old Brahmanas."

Ashtavakra said. "If this is the condition, dwarapalaka, that the door is open only to those that are old, then we have a right to enter. We are old and we have observed sacred vratas and possess energy which comes from the Vedas. We have served our elders and subdued our passions, and have mastered the scriptures.

It is said that even boys are not to be slighted, for a fire, small though it be, burns on being touched."

The gatekeeper replied, "Young Brahmana, I consider you a boy. But if you are a gyani, then recite, if you know it, the mantra that demonstrates the existence of the Supreme Being, the hymn adored by the Devarishis, which, although composed of one letter, is yet multifarious. Make no vain boast, learned men are really very rare."

Ashtavakra said, "True growth cannot be inferred from the mere development of the body, even as the growth of the knots of the Salmali tree cannot signify its age. That tree is full-grown, which although slender and short, bears fruits, while the tree, however large, which does not bear fruit, is not mature."

The gatekeeper said, "Boys receive instruction from the old and in time they also grow old. Knowledge certainly cannot be attained in a short time. Why, then, being a child, do you talk like an old man?"

Ashtavakra said, "One is not old because his head is grey. But the gods regard him as old who, although a child in years, is yet possessed of knowledge. The sages have not laid down that a man's merit consists in years, or grey hair, or wealth, or friends. To us, he is great who is versed in the Vedas.

I have come here, O gatekeeper, to see Vandin in the sabha. Go and inform King Janaka, who has a garland of lotuses around his neck that I am here. Today you will see me enter into dispute with all the learned men, and defeat Vandin in a debate. And when the rest have been silenced, the Brahmanas of mature learning and the king also, with his principal priests, shall bear witness to the superior or the inferior quality of my attainments."

The dwarapalaka said, "You are just ten; how can you hope to enter this yagnasala? Only great scholars can go in here. But I will try to let you in, and you yourself also try."

Then Ashtavakra said to the king, "O Janaka, best of your race, you are the greatest sovereign and all power reposes in you. In times of old, King Yayati was the celebrator of sacrifices, and in this yuga you.

We have heard that the learned Vandin bests the most expert debators and then has your loyal servats drown them. Hearing this, I have come to these Brahmanas, to expound the doctrine of the unity of the Brahman.

Where is Vandin? Tell me so that I can face him, and eclipse him even as the sun does the stars."

Janaka said, "Brahmana, you hope to defeat Vandin without knowing his power of speech. None who knows his powers will dare say what you do. The greatsest masters of the Veda have faced and been vanquished by him; you only say what you do because you do not know how mighty he is.

So many Brahmanas have wilted before him even as the stars before the sun. Countless scholars, arrogant of their learning, merely saw Vandin and lost all their pride. They left my sabha, shamed, without uttering a word."

Ashtavakra said, "Vandin has never debated against a man like me; only so does he look upon himself as a lion, and goes about roaring like one. But meeting me today he will fall dead, even like a cart whose wheels have come loose on a highway."

The king said, "Only he is a truly learned man who understands the significance of the thing that has thirty divisions, twelve parts, twenty-four joints, and three hundred and sixty spokes."

Ashtavakra said, "May that ever-moving wheel that has twenty-four joints, six naves, twelve peripheries, and sixty spokes protect you!"[1]

The king said, "Who amongst the gods bears those two which go together like two mares yoked to a chariot, and sweep like one hawk, and to what also do they give birth?"

---

[1] This wheel is the wheel of Time—i.e., measured according to the solar, lunar and astral revolutions. The significance of Ashtavakra's reply is: May the meritorious deeds performed at proper times during the revolution of this wheel of Time protect you.

Ashtavakra said, "May God, O king, forfend the presence of these two[1] in your house; yes, even in the house of your enemies. He who appears, having the wind for his charioteer,[2] begets them, and they also produce him."

Thereupon the king said, "What does not close its eyes even while sleeping; what is it that does not move, even when born; what is it that has no heart; and what increases even in its own speed?"

Ashtavakra said, "It is a fish[3] that does not shut its eye-lids while sleeping; and it is an a egg[4] that does not move when born; it is stone[5] that hath no heart; and it is a river[6] that increases in its own speed."

The king said, "It seems, O Tejasvin, that you are no human being. I do not consider you a boy, but a matured man; there is no other man who can compare with you in the art of speech. I therefore give you admittance. There is Vandin." '

---

[1] Thunder and lightning or misery and death.
[2] The male being that is ever conscious.
[3] Cloud or the mind.
[4] The mundane egg.
[5] The soul that has renounced connection with the body.
[6] The heart of a *Yogi*.

CANTO 134

Tirtha-yatra Parva Continued

'Ashtavakra said, "O king, O leader of fierce legions, in this assembly of monarchs of unrivalled power who have met together, I cannot recognise Vandin, master of the controversialists. But I am searching for him, even as one does for a swan on a vast expanse of water.

O Vandin, you regard yourself as the foremost of debators; yet, when you debate against me you will hardly flow like the current of a river. I am like a fire in full flame. Be silent before me, Vandin! Do not awaken a sleeping tiger. Know that you will not escape unstung, after trampling on the head of a venomous snake licking the corners of its mouth with its tongue. That weak man who, in pride of strength, attempts to strike a blow at a mountain, only gets his hands and nails broken, but no wound is left on the mountain itself.

As the other mountains are inferior to the Mainaka, and as calves are inferior to the ox, so are all other kings of the earth inferior to the lord of Mithila. And as Indra is the foremost of Devas, and as the Ganga is the best of rivers, so you alone are, O king, the greatest of monarchs. O king, have Vandin brought into my presence."

O Yudhishtira, when Vandin stood forth, Ashtavakra thundered at him in wrath, "You answer my questions, and I will answer yours!"

Vandin said, "Only one fire blazes forth in various shapes; only one sun illumines this whole world; only one hero, Indra, the lord of the Devas, destroys all enemies; and only one Yama is the sole lord of the Pitrs."[1]

Ashtavakra said, "The two friends, Indra and Agni, ever move together; the two Devarishis are Narada and Parvata; the twins are the Aswini kumaras; two is the number of the wheels of a chariot; and it is as a couple that husband and wife live together, as ordained by God."[2]

Vandin said, "Three kinds of born beings are produced by acts; the three Vedas together perform the Vajapeya; at three different times, the Adhwaryas commence sacrificial rites; three is the number of worlds; and three also are the divine lights."[3]

Ashtavakra said, "Four are the Asramas of the Brahmanas; the four varnas perform sacrifices; four are the cardinal points; four is the number of letters; and four also, as is ever known, are the legs of a cow."[4]

---

[1] Ashtavakra comes to Janaka's sacrifice with the object of proving the unity of the Supreme Being. Vandin avails himself of various System of Philosophy to combat his opponent. The iterative form of the dialogue is unique in being that of enigmas, and the latent meaning is in a queer way hidden under the appearance of puerile and heterogeneous combinations of things.

Vandin opens the debate by saying that as the number of each of these is one, so one only intellect is the lord, leader and guide of the senses.

[2] There is a Vedic revelation that two birds live together on a tree as friends—one of these eats the fruits and the other looks at the former. From this it is manifest that these two are the lords, leaders and guides of the senses. That there is a second faculty besides the intellect is also proved by the fact that in sleep when the intellect is inactive that faculty continues in action, for if it were not so we could not remember having slept, nor connect the state after awaking with that preceding sleep. Accordingly by citing the number two Ashtavakra asserts that besides intellect there is another faculty—conciousness, and that these two are jointly the lords, leaders and guides of the senses and that they act together as Indra and Agni, etc.

[3] By citing the number three Vandin means to say that as it is deeds that produce the three kinds of born beings, etc., so deeds are supreme and that everything else be it intellect alone, or intellect and conciousness together is subservient to Karma.

[4] Ashtavakra here advances the thesis that even if Karma be supreme, still when the Fourth or Supreme Being (Turiya) becomes manifest to the soul, it stands in no further need to act or perform any karma.

Vandin said, "Five is the number of fires; five are the feet of the metre called Punki; five are the sacrifices; five locks, it is said in the Vedas, are on the heads of the Apsaras; and five sacred rivers are known in the world."[1]

Ashtavakra said, "Some assert that six cows are given while first lighting the sacred fire; six are the seasons belonging to the wheel of time; six is the number of the senses; six stars constitute the constellation Kirtika; and six, it is found in all the Vedas, is the number of the Sadyaska sacrifice."[2]

Vandin said, "Seven is the number of the domesticated animals; seven are the wild animals; seven metres are used in completing a sacrifice; seven are the Rishis; there are seven forms of paying homage in the world; and seven, it is known, are the strings of the Vina."

Ashtavakra said, "Eight are the bags containing a hundred fold; eight are the legs of the Sarabha, which preys upon lions; eight Vasus, as we hear, are amongst the Devas; and eight are the angles of the yupastamba in all sacrificial rites."[3]

Vandin said, "Nine is the number of the mantras used in kindling the fire in sacrifices to the Pitrs; nine are the appointed functions in the processes of creation; nine letters compose the foot of the metre, Brihati; and nine is also always the number of the figures in calculation."[4]

---

[1] By bringing in the quinquennial series, Vandin wants to assert that the five senses are competent to cognise their respective objects and that besides these senses and their objects there is neither any other sense to perceive nor any other object of perception. He also cites the authority of the Veda according to which the Apsaras (or consciousnesses) have five locks on their heads—i.e., five objects of perception.

[2] Vandin admits the existence of the six senses but says that the soul experiences happiness and misery through those as well as through the intellect.

[3] Ashtavakra advances an eighth element, namely, the knowledge of these.

[4] Each of the three qualities (existence, foulness and ignorance) of prakriti (the passive or material cause of the world) mixing with each of the three corresponding qualities of pradhana (the active or spiritual cause of the world) in various proportions produces the mundane order of things. Thus is proved the eternity of prakriti or nature and so, also, established the doctrine of duality.

Ashtavakra said, "Ten are the cardinal points, entering into the cognition of men in this world; ten times hundred make up a thousand; ten is the number of months of a woman's gestation; and ten are the teachers of true knowledge, and ten, the haters thereof, and ten again are those capable of learning it."[1]

Vandin said, "Eleven are the objects that beings can enjoy; eleven is the number of the yupas; eleven are the changes of the natural state of those that have life; and eleven are the Rudras among the gods in heaven."[2]

Ashtavakra said, "Twelve months compose the year; of twelve consists a foot of the metre Jagati; twelve are the minor sacrifices; and twelve, according to the learned, is the number of the Adityas."[3]

Vandin said, "Unaffected by happiness and misery, the Paramatman does exist, but His existence is not susceptible of being proved, nor can the ignorant ever perceive Him. Men attain that condition through these twelve – virtue, truth, self-restraint, penance, good-will, modesty, forgiveness, freedom from envy, sacrifice, charity, concentration and control over the senses.

The thirteenth lunar day is considered the most auspicious; thirteen islands exist on earth."[4]

---

[1] Prakriti does not really create. It is the Supreme Being who through the medium of illusion in contact with the ten organs (the five locomotive organs and the five organs of sense) makes manifest the System of things. Prakriti therefore has no real existence—her existence is only apparent in the real existence of the soul.

[2] Yupas (stakes) mean here, feelings, etc., which keep men bound to the world. Rudras are those who makes others cry.

[3] Vandin means to say that the soul is not essentially free from the fetters of happiness and misery arising from the eleven objects of perception. In this world all men are subject to happiness and misery. We also hear that there are Rudras in heaven.

[4] According to some, endeavours to attain emancipation can be successful not in this world but in the world of Brahma. Others say that to that end a special yoga is necessary. By bringing forward the objects numbering thirteen, Vandin advances the opinion that, virtue, etc., are not sufficient to attain moksha but that a suitable time and place are also essential.

Saying this much, Vandin stopped; he could not go on. Ashtavakra completed the sloka, "Thirteen sacrifices are presided over by Kesi; and thirteen are devoured by Atichhandas, the longer metres, of the Veda."[1]

And seeing Ashtavakra speaking and the Suta's son silent and pensive, and with his head hung down, the assembly broke into a loud uproar. Delighted, the Brahmanas at king Janaka's splendid sacrifice rose as a man, and, with folded hands, paid Ashtavakra homage."

Ashtavakra said, "Before today, this man would best all Brahmanas in debate and cast them into water. Let Vandin meet the same fate today. Seize him and drown him in water!"

Vandin said, "O Janaka, I am the son of King Varuna. Simultaneously with your sacrifice, there also began another twelve years' yagna. It was to that sacrifice that I despatched the principal Brahmanas; they have gone to witness Varuna's sacrifice.

Look! There they are returning. I pay homage to the worshipful Ashtavakra, by whose grace today I shall join him who begot me."

Ashtavakra said, "Defeating the Brahmanas either with straight debate or sophistry, Vandin had cast them into the waters of the sea. That Vedic truth which he had suppressed by false arguments I rescued by dint of my intellect today.

Now let honest men judge. As Agni, who knoweth the character of both the good and the bad, leaves the bodies of those whose designs are honest, untouched by his heat, and is thus partial to them, so, too, good men judge the assertions of boys, and are favourably disposed towards them.

O Janaka, you listen to me as if you have been stupefied by eating the fruit of the Sleshmataki tree; as if flattery has robbed you of your

---

[1] Ashtavakra concludes by citing the same number thirteen. The soul, which is essentially unaffected, becomes subject to happiness and misery through the thirteen: the ten organs of locomotion and sense, and intellect, mind and egoism. But Atichhanadas, i.e., those that have surmounted ignorance, namely, the twelve, virtue, etc., destroy those thirteen and that is emancipation.

good sense; and this seems why, although my words pierce as hooks do an elephant, you do not heed them."

Janaka said, "Listening to you, I find your words extraordinary, more than merely human. Your form is also superhuman. You have vanquished Vandin in debate and I put him at your disposal."

Ashtavakra said, "O king, Vandin remaining alive will serve no purpose of mine. If Varuna really is his father, let Vandin be drowned in the sea."

Vandin said, "I am King Varuna's son. I have no fear of being drowned. Even at this moment, Ashtavakra shall see his long-lost sire, Kahoda."

Then all the dead Brahmanas appeared before Janaka, after having been duly worshipped by the magnanimous Varuna.

Kahoda said, "It is for this, O Janaka, that men pray for sons, by performing deeds of punya. That in which I failed has been achieved by my son. Weak persons may have sons endowed with strength; fools can have intelligent sons; and the illiterate may have learned sons."

Vandin said, "It is with your sharpened axe, O monarch, that even Yama severs the heads of foes. May prosperity attend upon you! In this sacrifice of King Janaka, the principal hymns of the Uktha rites are being chanted, and the Soma rasa is also being amply quaffed. And the gods themselves come to accept their sacred shares of the sacrifice, with joyful hearts."

When the dead Brahmanas rose up, their splendour enhanced, Vandin took his leave of King Janaka and entered into the waters of the sea.

Then Ashtavakra worshipped his father, and he himself was worshipped by the Brahmanas. And thus having defeated the Suta's son, Ashtavakra returned to his own fine hermitage, and his uncle with him.

Then, in the presence of his mother, his father said to him, "Hurry, son, and enter this river, Samanga."

Ashtavakra did so, and as he submerged himself beneath the water all his crooked limbs were instantly made straight. And from that day that river is called Samanga and she became invested with the virtue of purifying. He that bathes in her is set free from his sins.

Therefore, O Yudhishtira, do you, with your brothers and wife, enter the river and perform your ablutions in her. Kaunteya, scion of the race of Ajamidha, we will remain here with the Brahmanas, and you will perform other deeds of punya with me, for you are bent upon doing good.'

CANTO 135

TIRTHA-YATRA PARVA CONTINUED

Lomasa says, 'Here, of yore this Samanga was called Madhuvila, and yonder is Kardamila, the bathing place of Bharata. When misery struck Sachi's lord, after he killed Vritra, Indra bathed in this Samanga and was freed from his sin.

Here, Purusharishabha, is where the Mainaka mountain sank his roots into the earth, and so it is called Vinasana.

Once, it was here that Aditi cooked her offering of sacred food to the Brahman, so that she might have sons. Climb this lofty hill, O you bulls among men, and put an end to your inglorious, untellable sorrow.

Here before you, O king, is the Kanakhala mountain range, a favourite resort of sages. Yonder is the mighty Ganga. In ancient times, the Rishi Sanatkumara found mukti by performing ablutions here in this river.

You will also be freed from all your sins, son of Kunti, if you and your brothers touch the waters of this lake called Punya, and this mountain Bhrigutunga and also the waters of these two rivers, called Ushniganga.

Look, here is the asrama of the Rishi Sthulasiras; here renounce your anger and sense of self-importance. And there, Pandava, is Raibhya's beautiful asrama, where Bharadwaja's son, Yavakrita, profound in Vedic lore, perished.'

Yudhishtira says, 'How did the mighty Yavakrita, son of Bharadwaja, acquire profundity in the Vedas? And how also did he perish? I am eager to hear all this, just as it happened. I find great delight in listening to the deeds of such godlike men.'

Lomasa says, 'Bharadwaja and Raibhya were two friends. And they lived here, ever taking the greatest pleasure in each other's company. Raibhya had two sons, named Arvavasu and Paravasu, while Bharadwaja had an only son, named Yavakrita. Raibhya and his two sons were versed in the Vedas, while Bharadwaja practised tapasya. But, O Bhaarata, from their boyhood, the friendship that existed between these two was unequalled.

Sinless, the highspirited Yavakrita found that brahmanas slighted his father, who practised asceticism, while they revered Raibhya and his sons; Yavakrita was overwhelmed with sorrow, and became sorely aggrieved. He embarked upon severe austerities, in order to obtain knowledge of the Vedas.

He exposed his body to fire. He made Indra anxious with his terrific penance.

Indra went to him and said, "Why, O sage, do you sit in such a dreadful tapasya?"

Yavakrita said, "O you whom the Devas adore, I sit in penance to gain such gyana of the Vedas as no Brahmana has ever had before. O conqueror of Paka, my tapasya is to have the Vedas manifest themselves in me; why, I mean to acquire every manner of knowledge through my tapasya.

Lord, learnt through gurus, the Vedas take a long time to be known. I perfom my austerities to have them in a short while."

Indra said, "Brahmana, the path you tread is not the proper way. Why do you want to destroy yourself? Go and learn from the lips of a preceptor."

Saying this, Sakra went away and Yavakrita of immeasurable energy fell once more to his tapasya. O king, I have heard that by continuing his stern penance he greatly agitated Indra, who came again to that Maharishi and forbade him, saying, "You strive so that the Veda manifests both in yourself and in your father; but your exertions can never be fruitful, nor is this tapasya of yours well-advised."

Yavakrita said, "Lord of the Devas, if you do not give me what I want, I will perform even more stringent tapasya. Indra, if you do not grant me what I want, I will cut off my limbs and offer them as a sacrifice into a blazing fire."

Indra realised how determined the sage was and decided to use some guile to dissuade him. Indra assumed the guise of an ascetic Brahmana, hundreds of years old, and infirm, and suffering from consumption. And he fell to throwing up a dam with sand, at the very place along the Bhagirathi to which Yavakrita used to come to bathe.

Unceasingly, Sakra began to fill the Ganga with sand, and he attracted Yavakrita's attention. When that bull among the sages saw Indra earnestly building his dam, he broke into laughter, and said, 'What are you doing, O Brahmana, and what is your object? Why do you undertake this mighty endeavour for no good reason?"

Indra said, "My child, I am trying to dam the Ganga so that there may be a commodious passage across the water. People experience considerable difficulty in crossing and recrossing the river by boat."

Yavakrita said, "O you of ascetic wealth, you cannot dam this mighty current. O Brahmana, desist from what is impracticable, and take up something that you can achieve."

Indra said, "Rishi, I have imposed this weighty task upon myself just as you have undertaken your tapasya, which can never be fruitful, in order to know the Vedas."

Yavakrita said, "If, Lord of the Devas, my penance is doomed to fail, be pleased to grant me something that I can achieve. Bless me with boons by which I can excel other men."

Indra said, "The Vedas will be manifest in you, and in your father as well; and all your other desires will also be fulfilled. Return home, Yavakrita."

Having thus got the object of his desire, Yavakrita came to his father and said, "Father, the Vedas will be manifest in you as well as myself, and I have obtained boons whereby we shall excel against all men."

Bharadwaja said, "O my son, because you have obtained the objects of your desire, you will become proud. And when you are puffed up with pride and have also become uncharitable, destruction will soon overtake you.

There is a tale that the gods themselves tell. In ancient times, there lived a sage named Baladhi, possessed of great energy. And in grief over the death of a child, he practised the severest penance to have a child that would be immortal; and he got a son even as he desired. But though they were favourably disposed towards him, the gods did not yet make his son immortal.

They said, 'No mortal can be deathless, without some condition by which he can die.'

Baladhi said, 'O Devas, these mountains have always existed and are invincible; let their destruction be the condition of my son's death.'

Baladhi's son was called Medhavi, and he was highly irascible. When he learnt of the only way in which he could die, he grew haughty and began to insult the sages of the earth. And he ranged over the world, doing mischief to the Munis.

One day, he met the Maharishi Dhanushaksha of immense tejas and the arrogant Medhavi insulted him. The Rishi cursed him, 'Be you ashes!'

But Medhavi was not reduced to ashes. Then Dhanushaksha had a vast herd of buffaloes shatter the mountain, which stood as the condition of Medhavi's immortality. The young man instantly died.

Taking his son's corpse in his arms, Medhavi's father began to bewail his fate. Now listen, my child, to what the Rishis, who were masters of the Vedas, chanted when they found the sage mourning: *Never can a mortal overcome what Fate ordains. Lo! Dhanushaksha shattered even the mountain with a herd of buffaloes.*

So do young ascetics, who are puffed up with the pride of the boons they have received, swiftly perish. You do not want to be one of them.

This Raibhya, O my son, is possessed of great tejas, and his two sons are like him. Therefore, be vigilant – never approach him. My child, Raibhya is a Maharishi of short temper; if angered, he can do you harm.

Yavakrita said, "I will do as you say. Do not be anxious, father, for Raibhya deserves my reverence even as you do.'

Yet, after placating his father with sweet words, Yavakrita, fearing nothing and nobody, began to take his delight in wantonly offending other munis.'"

CANTO 136

TIRTHA-YATRA PARVA CONTINUED

Lomasa says, 'One day in the month of Chaitra, while wandering fearlessly, Yavakrita approached the asrama of Raibhya. In that beautiful hermitage, adorned with trees rich with flowers, he saw the daughter-in-law of Raibhya, sauntering about like a Kinnara woman.

Smitten by swift passion, deprived of his good sense, Yavakrita said shamelessly to the bashful young woman, "Be mine!"

At which, knowing his nature, and afraid of a curse, and also thinking of Raibhya's power, she said to him, "I will, wait for me here", promising him everything and, tying him up with vines, sweetly, she went back into her dwelling.

When Raibhya returned to his asrama, he found his daughter-in-law, Paravasu's wife, in tears. Consoling her with soft words, he asked what was the cause of her grief.

Thereupon, the beautiful girl told him what Yavakrita had said to her, and also how she had adroitly kept him at bay.

Raibhya's mind flared up in wrath. He tore off a matted lock of his jata, and with holy mantras offered it to the sacred fire. At this, a woman who resembled his daughter-in-law in every particular, sprang out of the flames.

The Rishi plucked out another dreadlock from his head, and again offered it to the fire. Now a terrible demon leapt forth from the flames, his eyes fiery.

The two said to Raibhya, "What shall we do?"

The angry sage said to them, "Go and kill Yavakrita."

They said, "We shall!" and flew to do as he bid them.

Using her charms, the lovely woman spirit took Yavakrita's sacred water-pot from him. Then, spear upraised, the demon flew at Yavakrita, when he had been deprived of his water-pot and rendered unclean.

Yavakrita jumped up and fled towards a tank. He found it empty of water and flew towards all the rivers, but found them dry too. Threatened repeatedly by the Rakshasa with his spear, the terrified Yavakrita tried to enter his father's Agnihotrasala. But there a blind Sudra seized and prevented him.

Now the demon cast his spear at Yavakrita and struck him through the heart, and Yavakrita fell dead. After killing Yavakrita, the Rakshasa went back to Raibhya, and with the permission of that sage, began to live with the female spirit.'

CANTO 137

TIRTHA-YATRA PARVA CONTINUED

Lomasa says, 'Kaunteya, Bharadwaja returned to his hermitage after performing the nitya karma of the day and having collected wood for the sacred fire of sacrifice. But since his son had been slain, the sacrificial flames that came to welcome him every day, did not come forth to greet the Rishi.

Seeing this change in the Agnihotra, the Mahamuni asked the blind Sudra, "Why, O Sudra, do the fires not rejoice at sight of me? You, also, do not welcome me gladly, as you usually do.

Is all well in my asrama? I hope my son of little sense did not go to Raibhya. Answer me quickly, Sudra, my heart misgives me."

The Sudra said, "Your foolish son did go to the Rishi Raibhya, and that is why he lies dead on the ground, slain by a mighty demon. Attacked by the Rakshasa holding a spear, he tried to force his way into this room, and I barred his way.

Then, wanting holy water while he was unclean and stood hopeless, he was slain by the Rakshasa."

Bharadwaja, griefstricken, took his dead son in his arms and began to lament. He cried, "O my son, you did tapasya for the weal of all Brahmanas, so that the Vedas, which had not been studied by any Brahmana at all, might become manifest in you.

You were always kindly and reverent towards any Brahmana, why towards all creatures.* But, alas, you did lapse into arrogance and rudeness. O my son, I warned you never to go to Raibhya's arama, but even there you went like Yama himself.

Evil is that man, who, knowing that I am an old man, and also that Yavakrita was my only son, gave way to wrath and killed my child. My son, without you, the most precious thing in the world, I will give up my life as well.

Yes, in grief at the death of my child I renounce my life; but this I say, that Raibhya's eldest son will soon kill him, although he be innocent.

Blessed are those to whom children have never been born, for they lead a happpy life, without having to experience this dreadful grief. Who in this world can be more vile than they, who made senseless with sorrow at the death of a child, curse even their dearest friend? Finding my son dead I cursed my dearest friend.

Ah, which other man in this world has ever suffered such misfortune!"

After lamenting long, Bharadwaja cremated his son and then consigned himself to a full-blazing fire.'

CANTO 138

TIRTHA-YATRA PARVA CONTINUED

Lomasa says, 'At this very time, the mighty king Brihadyumna, of great fortune, who was the Yajamana of Raibhya, began a sacrifice. The two sons of Raibhya, Arvavasu and Paravasu, were engaged by that wise sovereign to assist him in the performance of the yagna.

Kaunteya, with their father's leave, the two went to the sacrifice, while Raibhya remained in their asrama, with Paravasu's wife. One day, wanting to see his wife, Paravasu returned home alone. He met his father in the vana, wrapped in the skin of a black antelope. The night was far advanced and dark; Paravasu, blinded by drowsiness in that deep forest, mistook his father for a wild stag, and fearing for his own safety, killed his father.

Then, after performing the funeral rites for his father, he returned to the sacrifice and said to his brother, "You will never be able to perform this task unassisted. And I have killed our father, mistaking him for a deer. My brother, keep a vrata of expiation for the sin of killing a Brahmana, and I, O Muni, shall complete the yagna by myself."

Arvavasu said, "Do then fulfil this sacrifice of the gifted Brihadyumna; and for you, bringing my senses under perfect control, I will observe the vow to expiate the sin of a Brahmahatya."

Having kept the vrata for that sin, the Muni Arvavasu came back to the sacrifice. Seeing his brother, Paravasu, in a voice choked with malice, cried to Brihadyumna, "O king, see that this slayer of a Brahmana does not enter your yagna, or even look upon it. Even by a glance, the killer of a Brahmana can harm you immeasurably."

The king ordered his attendants to turn Arvavasu out. As they drove him out the king's men repeatedly cursed Arvavasu, crying, "Brahmana killer!"

More than once Arvavasu protested, "It is not I that have killed a Brahmana!"

He said he had not kept the vrata for his own sake, but to free his brother from the sin that Paravasu had committed.

Having said this in anger, and being reprimanded by the attendants, the Brahmana sage of austere penance retired silently into the forest. There he sat in fierce tapasya, worshipping the Sun. The Surya mantra was revealed to him, and then Agni Deva, immortal god who has the first share of the havis from any yagna, appeared, embodied, to the Rishi.

The Devas were well pleased with Arvavasu for what he had done; they had him made chief priest at Brihadyumna's sacrifice, and Paravasu dismissed from it.

Agni and the other celestials bestowed boons on Arvavasu, without his asking. He prayed that his father might be restored to life. He prayed that his brother might be absolved from his sin; that his father might have no recollection of his having been slain; that Bharadwaja and Yavakrita might both be restored to life; and that the solar revelation would find celebrity on earth.

The god said, "Tathastu, so be it," and conferred other boons on him also. Yudhishtira, all those who had died were restored to life.

Yavakrita now said to Agni and the other deities, "I gained a knowledge of all the Vedas, and also performed tapasya. How, then, did Raibhya manage to kill me as he did, O best of the gods?"

The Devas said, "Yavakrita, never again do what you did. You could be killed because you acquired the Vedas without studying them and without learning from a guru. But Raibhya bore many trials, he satisfied his preceptor with his conduct, and gained the Vedas through great exertion and in a long time."

Having said this to Yavakrita, and having given life back to the dead, the Devas with Indra at their head ascended into heaven.

Look, Yudhishtira, here is the sacred asrama of that sage, with trees that bear flowers and fruit in all seasons. O tiger among kings, by staying here for a while you will be exorcised of all your sins.'

CANTO 139

TIRTHA-YATRA PARVA CONTINUED

Lomasa says, 'O Bhaarata, O king, now you have crossed the mountains Usirabija, Mainaka and Sweta, as well as the Kala hills, and look, O son of Kunti, O Bharatarishabha, here before you flow the seven Gangas!

This is a most pure and holy place. Here Agni blazes forth without pause. No son of Manu can see this wonder. So, Pandava, concentrate your mind in dhyana so that you can behold all these tirthas.

Now you will see the playground of the gods, marked with their footprints. Since we have passed the mountain Kala, we will now cilmb Mandara, the white mountain, inhabited by the Yakshas, by Manibhadra, and Kubera, lord of the Yakshas.

Rajan, here eighty thousand fleet Gandharvas, and four times as many Kimpurushas and Yakshas of various shapes and forms, holding various weapons, attend upon Manibhadra, king of the Yakshas. Great indeed is their power in this realm, and their swiftness is like the very wind.

Why, they can unseat Indra himself from his throne. Protected by them, and also watched over by the Rakshasas, these mountains are inaccessible. Therefore, son of Pritha, fix your mind in dhyana for, besides these, Kubera dwells here with his ministers and his Rakshasa kindred. We will have to encounter them, so muster your energies.

O king, the mountain Kailasa is six yojanas high; upon it grows a gigantic nyagrodha tree. Kaunteya, numberless Devas and Yakshas and Rakshasas and Kinnaras and Nagas and Suparnas and Gandharvas pass this way, going towards Kubera's palace. With my protection, as well as the might of Bhimasena, and also the virtue of your own asceticism and self-command, today you must mingle with them.

May Lord Varuna and Yama, conqueror of battles, and Ganga, and Yamuna, and this mountain, and the Maruts and the twin Aswins, and all rivers and lakes, vouchsafe your safety. And, O effulgent one, may you be safe from all the Devas and the Asuras, and the Vasus.

Devi Ganga, I hear your roar from this golden mountain, sacred to Indra. O Goddess of high fortune, in these mountains, protect this king, worshipped by all of the race of Ajamidha. O daughter of Himalaya, this king is about to enter into this realm; do you confer your protection upon him.'

Having invoked the protection of the river, Lomasa says to Yudhishtira, 'Be careful.'

Yudhishtira says to his brothers, 'I have never seen Lomasa so anxious, so watch carefully over Krishnaa, and do not be careless. Lomasa knows this place is surely difficult of access. Therefore, observe utmost purity here.'

He now says particularly to his brother Bhima, of vast prowess, 'Bhimasena, watch intently over Draupadi. Whether Arjuna be near or away, in times of danger she always seeks only your protection.'

Then Yudhishtira goes to Nakula and Sahadeva, and after lovingly sniffing the tops of their heads, and embracing them, he says with tears in his eyes, 'Do not be afraid, yet go cautiously in this place.'

CANTO 140

Tirtha-yatra Parva Continued

Yudhishtira says, 'Vrikodara, there are mighty and powerful invisible spirits in this place. We shall, however, pass safely through it with the punya of tapasya and Agnihotra sacrifices. So, Kaunteya, restrain your hunger and thirst by collecting your energies, and also, O Bhima, keep both your strength and your wits at the ready.

You heard what Rishi Lomasa said about Mount Kailasa; so think how Krishnaa will pass this place. Or, mighty Bhima of the large eyes, return from here, taking Sahadeva with you, and all our charioteers, cooks, servants, chariots, horses, and our Brahmanas worn out with travel; while Nakula and I, together with Muni Lomasa of great tapasya go on, subsisting on the lightest fare and observing vows.

You await my return at the source of the Ganga, protecting Draupadi till I come back.'

Bhima replies, 'Bhaarata, although this blessed princess has been sorely afflicted by toil and sorrow, yet she travels on easily in the hope of seeing Arjuna of the white steeds. Your grief also is great at not seeing the noble Arjuna, who never flees a battle.

It goes without saying that your sorrow will only increase if you do not see me, Sahadeva and Krishnaa, as well.

It is best that the Brahmanas turn back, with our servants, charioteers, cooks, and whoever else you command. I will never leave you in these wild and inaccessible mountain realms, infested by Rakshasas.

And, O tiger among men, this princess of great fortune, always devoted to her lords, does not want to turn back without you. Sahadeva is ever devoted to you; he too will never turn back, I know him well.

Rajan, we are all eager to see Arjuna, and so we will all go on together. If we cannot pass over this mountain in our chariots, because it abounds in defiles, we will go on foot. Do not worry, O King, I will carry Panchali wherever she cannot walk.

This is what I have decided, so do not be anxious or distracted. Over impassable places, I will also carry our tender-bodied heroes, the twins, the delight of their mother, wherever they cannot walk."

Yudhishtira says, 'May your strength increase, O Bhima, for what you say, that you will carry the illustrious Panchali and these twins. Bless you! No man is as brave as you are. May your strength, fame, merit and reputation increase! O long-armed one, since you offer to carry Krishnaa and the twins, exhaustion and defeat will never be yours.'

Now the enchanting Krishnaa says with a smile, 'O Bhaarata, I will be able to go, so do not be anxious on my account.'

Lomasa says, 'Access to the Mountain Gandhamadana can only be gained through asceticism. So, Kaunteya, we must all do tapasya; and then, O King, Nakula, Sahadeva, Bhimasena, you and I will all see Arjuna Swetavahana.'

Thus speaking together, journeying on, they see with delight the great domains of Subahu, situated on the Himalayas, abounding in horses and elephants, densely inhabited by the Kiratas and the Tanganas, crowded by hundreds of Pulindas, frequented by the Devas, and rife with wonders.

King Subahu, the lord of the Pulindas, receives them joyfully at the frontier of his realms, paying them proper respect. Being received with honour, and dwelling in comfort in that place, they set out for the Himalaya, when the sun shines brightly in the sky.

They entrust the care of all their servants—Indrasena and the others, and the cooks and the stewards, and Draupadi's accoutrements, and everything else⊠those Maharathas, the mighty scions of the Kurus, and Krishnaa with them, go forth from that land, cautiously, all of them glad at heart at the prospect of seeing Arjuna.

Yudhishtira says, 'Bhimasena, Panchali, and you twins, listen to me. The karma done in previous births does not perish, but surely produces its fruit, sooner or later. Look how even we have become rangers of the wilderness!

Exhausted and distressed as we are, we have to support one another, and pass through well-nigh impassable places, so that we might see Arjuna. Kshatriya, I do not see Dhananjaya beside me and this burns me even as fire does a heap of cotton.

I live in the forest with my younger brothers, anxious to see Arjuna again. This thought, as also the memory of the grave insult to Yagnaseni, consumes me.

O Vrikodara, I do not see the invincible Partha of the great bow and incomparable energy, who is younger than you and older than Nakula. For this, Bhima, I am miserable.

Just to see my Arjuna again, I have been wandering to various tirthas for five years, passing through charmed jungles, passing lovely lakes; yet I do not see him. For this, Vrikodara, I am miserable.

I do not see the long-armed Gudakesa, of the dark blue skin, and the lion's gait. For this, Vrikodara, I am miserable. I do not see that Kurusthama, master of weapons, most skilful in battle, and matchless among bowmen. For this, Vrikodara, I am miserable.

I am distraught because I do not see Pritha's son Dhananjaya, born under the nakshatra Phalguni, who goes amongst his enemies even like Yama during the Pralaya; Partha who has the prowess of an elephant in musth, with the juice of rut trickling down its temples; Arjuna of the leonine shoulders; not inferior to Sakra himself in strength and energy;

elder in years to the twins; of white steeds; unrivalled in heroism; invincible; and wielding an awesome bow. For this, O Vrikodara, I am miserable.

And he is always of a forgiving temper, even when insulted by the meanest man; and he confers benefit and protection to the righteous; but to a perfidious one who tries to do him harm with treachery, Dhananjaya is like virulent poison, be not the one Sakra himself.

And the mighty Vibhatsu of immeasurable soul and strength shows mercy and extends protection even to a foe, when fallen. He is the refuge of us all and he crushes his enemies in battle. He owns the power to garner any treasure whatever, and he ministers to our happiness.

It was through his prowess that I owned measureless precious jewels of myriad kinds, which now Suyodhana has usurped. It was through his might, O Kshatriya, that I owned the palatial Mayaa Sabha, embellished with every manner of gemstone, and celebrated throughout the three worlds.

Pandava, in prowess Phalguni is like Krishna, and in battle he is invincible and unrivalled, even like Kartavirya. Alas, I do not see him, Bhima, Arjuna who in strength is like Krishna and Balarama!

In strength of arms and spirit, he is like Purandara himself; in swiftness, he is like the wind; in grace, like the moon, and in wrath he is like eternal Yama.

Mahabaho, to see that warlike Purushavyaghra, tiger among men, we will go to Gandhamadana, where the hermitage of Nara and Narayana is, beneath the celebrated nyagrodha tree, the asrama inhabited by Yakshas.

We will see that best of mountains, and by doing stern tapasya, we shall walk to Kubera's beautiful lake guarded by Rakshasas. That place cannot be reached by chariots or carts, Vrikodara, and neither can cruel, greedy or irascible men ever go there, Bhaarata.

Bhima, in order to see Arjuna, there shall we journey, in a company, with Brahmanas of strict vows, girding on our swords, and wielding our bows. Only those who are impure meet with flies, mosquitoes, tigers, lions, and reptiles, but never the pure.

Therefore, controlling our diet, and restraining our senses, we shall go to the Gandhamadana, to see Arjuna Dhananjaya.'

CANTO 141

TIRTHA-YATRA PARVA CONTINUED

Lomasa says, 'Pandavas, you have seen many a mountain, and river and town and forest and beautiful tirtha; you have touched their sacral waters with your hands.

Now this way leads to the celestial Mount Mandara; therefore be you attentive and composed. You will now climb to the dwelling place of Devas and Devarishis of great punya. Here, O King, there flows the mighty and lovely river Alakananda, of holy water adored by hosts of celestial ones and sages, and we will trace its source to the great nyagrodha tree.

High-souled Vaihayasas, Balakhilyas and Gandharvas of mighty spirits frequent this holiest asrama. Those unmatched singers of the Sama hymns, the Rishis Marichi, Pulaha, Bhrigu and Angiras chanted them here.

Here the king of the Devas performs his nitya puja, along with the Maruts; and the Sadhyas and the Aswins attend on him. The Sun, the Moon and all the luminaries with the planets come to this river, alternately by day and by night.

Most fortunate king, Mahadeva, protector of the world, the Bull his emblem, received the descent of the Ganga from the sky here, where now her source is.

My children, approach this Goddess of the six attributes and bow down before her with your minds concentrated in dhyana.'

Having listened to the Maharishi Lomasa, the sons of Pandu reverentially worship the Ganga, who flows through the firmament. And after having adored her, the pious Pandavas resume their journey, accompanied by the sages.

And in a while, those best of men behold at a distance a white massif of vast proportions, even like Meru, and stretching on all sides.

Knowing the question in the hearts of Pandu's sons, Lomasa master of speech, says, 'Listen, O sons of Pandu! Purushottamas, what you see before you, vast as a mountain and beautiful as the cliffs of Kailasa, is a mound of the bones of the mighty Daitya Naraka. Being heaped, they resemble a mountain!

The Daitya was slain by that Paramatman, the eternal Lord Vishnu, to help Indra, king of the Devas.

Wanting to usurp Indra's posotion, Narakasura, of the mighty mind, acquired knowledge of the Vedas and performed a dread tapasya, which lasted ten thousand years. And through this penance, as also by the force and might of his arms he became invincible and forever harassed Indra.

Anagha, Sinless, knowing the might of the Demon and his great penance, Indra became agitated and fear overwhelmed him. In his heart he thought fervently of Vishnu, the eternal One. At which, the gracious Lord of the universe, who is present everywhere, appeared and stood before Indra.

The Devas and Rishis began to sing hymns to Narayana, and to propitiate him with prayers. In his presence even Agni of the six attributes and of blazing beauty was overpowered by his effulgence, and was shorn of radiance.

Seeing Mahavishnu before him, the king of the Devas, the Vajradhari bowed his head low and told Narayana what the source of his fear was.

Vishnu said, "I know, O Sakra, that your fear is from Naraka, lord of the Daityas. He aims for your throne through his tapasya. And so, to please you, I will sever his soul from his body, despite his great tapasya. King of the Devas, wait a moment."

Vishnu then struck Naraka with a blow of his hand; the Asura fell to the ground even like the lord of mountains struck by cosmic thunder. So he died, and his bones gathered in this place.

Another miracle of Vishnu's is also manifest in this place. Once, when all the Earth was lost, having sunk into Patala, Narayana assumed the form of the Varaha, a Boar with a single tusk, and raised her up.'

Yudhishtira says, 'Worshipful one, tell me in detail how Vishnu, Devadeva, raised up the earth which had sunk a hundred yojanas. How was Bhumi Devi, of lofty fortune, support of all created things, who dispenses blessings and brings forth all manner of grain, rendered stable?

Through whose power had she sunk a hundred yojanas? And how did the Paramatman come to rescue her with this great exploit? Dvijottama, you certainly know all about what transpired and I want to hear it all from you.'

Lomasa says, 'Yudhishtira, listen to that tale at length.

My child, in ancient days, there came a time of dread in the Krita Yuga, when the eternal and primeval Deity assumed the dharma of Yama; and when the God of gods began to do the work of Yama, not a creature died, while the births were as usual.

Birds and beasts and kine, and sheep, and deer and all kinds of carnivores multiplied, Parantapa, and the race of humans also swelled in tide, in millions.

My son, when the population multiplied to a frightening extent, the Earth, oppressed with her intolerable burden, sank a hundred yojanas. Agony lanced through all her limbs, and barely conscious from the vast pressure upon her, Bhumi Devi in great distress sought the protection of the Lord Narayana, the foremost of the gods.

The Earth said, "It is through your grace, O possessor of the six attributes, that I was able to remain so long in my position. But now I have been overcome with burden which I cannot sustain any longer.

Most adorable One, relieve me of my burden. I seek your protection, Lord, give me your favour."

Hearing her, the eternal Lord, possessor of the six attributes, Vishnu, said calmly, his words distinct in their every syllable, "Do not fear, O afflicted Bhumi devi, bearer of all treasures. I will relieve you of your burden."

Thus consoling Bhumi, who has the mountains for her earrings, and then sending her away, Vishnu suddenly turned into a refulgent boar with one tusk. Striking terror with his glowing red eyes and his blazing lustre smoking, fuming, he began to grow amazingly.

Kshatriya, then bearing the Earth upon his single radiant tusk, that Being who pervades the Vedas raised her up a hundred yojanas. And while she was being so raised, there was a terrific agitation and all the Devas, and all the Rishis of great tapasya became distraught.

Heaven, and the sky, and the earth, as well, were filled with exclamations of alarm and neither the gods nor men could find any peace. Then countless celestials and sages went to Brahma, who sat blazing with his own lustre.

Approaching Brahma, the lord of every celestial, and the witness of the deeds of all beings, they said to him with folded hands, "Devadeva, all the created are agitated and every being, mobile and immobile, are distraught.

Lord of the Devas, even the oceans are fraught and this whole world has sunk a hundred yojanas. What is the cause of this ferment in the universe? We are bewildered and dismayed; we beg you tell us what is happening."

Brahma replied, "Devas, do not be afraid of the Asuras, in any matter or place. Listen, O celestials, to the reason for all this commotion. The illustrious One, who is omnipresent, eternal and the never-pershiing Soul is responsible for this agitation.

The Paramatman Vishnu has raised up Bhumi, who was submerged a hundred yojanas; the great disturbance is in consequence of the Earth being lifted up. Know this and dispel your doubts."

The Devas said, "Where is that Being who joyfully raises up the Earth? O you who possess the six attributes, tell us where this is happening, so we might go to that place."

Brahma said, "Go, and may good befall you! You will find him resting in the gardens of Nandana. Look, there is the glorious and worshipful Garuda.

After having raised up the Earth, the God from whom the world became manifest, flames forth in the shape of a boar, even like the all-consuming apocalypse during the pralaya. Upon his breast the Srivatsa shines. Go and behold that Being who knows no decay."

Setting Brahma, the Grandsire, at their head the Devas came to that infinite Soul, and having sung his praises, bade him farewell, and went back to where they had come from,' says Lomasa.

Having heard this story, all the Pandavas go with all haste towards the place to which Lomasa pointed."

CANTO 142

Tirtha-yatra Parva Continued

Vaisampayana said, "O King, those foremost of bowmen, of immeasurable prowess, holding bows strung tightly, carrying quivers brimful of arrows, wearing fingerlets made of iguana-skin, and their swords at their sides, go, with Panchali, towards the Gandhamadana, also taking with them the best of their Brahmanas.

On their way, they see lakes and rivers and mountains and forests, and trees of wide-spreading shade upon mountain summits; and places abounding in trees bearing flowers and fruit in all seasons, and frequented by Devas and Rishis.

Restraining their senses within the inner self, subsisting on fruit and roots, the heroes pass through rugged realms, craggy and difficult of passage, seeing diverse and numerous birds and beasts as they go.

Thus those high-souled ones enter the mountain of Rishis, Siddhas and Devas, of Gandharvas, Kinnaras and Apsaras. And, O lord of men, as those mighty Kshatriyas first set foot upon Gandhamadana, a violent wind blows there, bringing a torrent of rain with it. Great clouds of dust, bearing dry leaves, rise up, and all on a sudden cover earth, air and the firmament.

When the heavens are obscured by dust nothing can be seen, and neither can the Pandavas speak to one another. Eyes full of darkness and stung by the wind that carries rock particles, they cannot see one another.

Trees split open, cracking in the gale; towering trees crash down to the ground with force of the wind.

Dismayed by the storm, they think, 'Are the heavens falling down or is this mountain and the very earth cracking open?'

Terrified by the storm, they grope in the pitch darkness with arms outstretched, and shelter under trees, inside large anthills, and in caves.

Holding his bow and supporting Krishnaa, the mighty Bhimasena stands under a tree; Yudhishtira Dharmaraja, with Dhaumya, scurries into some heavy woods; Sahedeva, carrying the sacred fire, takes shelter under a huge rock. Nakula, with Lomasa and the other Brahmanas of great tapasya stand trembling, each one under a tree.

Then when the wind abates and the dust subsides, the sky opens and down comes a cascade of rain. The heavens shake with shocking batteries of thunder, each like Indra's Vajra being cast; and quick-flashing lightning begins to play gracefully through the clouds. Without pause it rains, and everything is a solid sheet of water, until rivers of hurtling water rush all around, foam-crested and turbid with mud. These roaring cataracts uproot the greatest trees and plunge them down the mountain like twigs.

As suddenly as it began, the storm ceases, and when the wind is still and the air is clear, each of them comes out cautiously from their places of hiding, and they met together again.

Again, those Kshatriyas and their party set foot upon Mount Gandhamadana."

CANTO 143

TIRTHA-YATRA PARVA CONTINUED

Vaisampayana said, "When the noble sons of Pandu have gone a mere two yojanas, Draupadi, unaccustomed to walking for long, cannot go on. She is weary, Panchala's most delicate daughter, and faint, and the storm has also terrified her.

The black-eyed Krishnaa supports herself with her graceful arms on her thighs, clenched together, for just a moment, before she collapses trembling onto the ground. Seeing her fall like a severed vine, Nakula runs forward and supports her.

The distrait Nakula cries, 'O King, Panchali has fallen down from tiredness. Tend to her, O Bhaarata. She deserves no such misery and has borne long hardship; she is exhausted from our journey. Comfort her, O mighty king.'

Hearing Nakula, Yudhishtira, and Bhima and Sahadeva, as well, rush to Panchali in alarm. They see her pale and drained, and, taking her onto his lap, Yudhishtira laments, 'Ah, accustomed to ease, used to sleeping in luxurious chambers, on beds spread over with fine sheets, how does this beautiful one lie on rough, bare ground now?

Alas! Only because of me, the soft feet and the lotus-like face of she who deserves all the finest things in life are callused pale. O what have I done!

Fool that I am, being addicted to dice, I have been wandering in forests full of wild beasts, taking Krishnaa with me. Her father King Drupada gave this doe-eyed one to me, trusting that his blessed child would be happy by having the Pandavas for her husbands. But because I am a wretch, today she lies on the rough earth, exhausted with every hardship, sorrow and wearying travel.'

As Yudhishtira Dharmaraja laments, Dhaumya and all the other principal Brahmanas come to him, and begin to console him and to honour him with their blessings.

They recite mantras to keep Rakshasas away and also perform some holy rites to restore Panchali's health and spirits. At this, and also at being stroked soothingly by her husbands' palms, as well as by a cool, moist breeze, she slowly recovers consciousness.

The sons of Pritha now lay her down upon a deerskin, and make her rest. Taking her red-soled feet, bearing auspicious marks, the twins begin to press them gently with their hands scarred by bowstrings. Yudhishtira, foremost of the Kurus, also comforts her.

Dharmaraja says to Bhima, 'Bhima, before us lie so many rough and rugged mountains, full of ice and snow, inaccessible. How, long-armed one, will Krishnaa pass over these?'

Bhima says, 'Rajan, I will carry you, our princess, and these Purusharishabhas the twins; so do not be anxious. Or, Anagha, at your command, with your leave, Hidimba's son, the mighty Ghatotkacha, who is as strong as I am and can fly through the sky, will carry us all to our destination.'

With Yudhishtira's permission, Bhima thinks of his Rakshasa son; and in an instant, the pious Ghatotkacha appears, salutes the Pandavas and the Brahmanas, and stands before them with folded hands. And they also caress him of the mighty arms.

Ghatotkacha says to his father, Bhimasena of dreadful prowess, 'You thought of me and I came at once to serve you. Command me, O long-armed, and I will do whatever you wish.'

Hearing this, Bhimasena hugs the Rakshasa to his breast.

CANTO 144

TIRTHA-YATRA PARVA CONTINUED

Yudhishtira says, 'Bhima, let this mighty and heroic Rakshasa lord, your son, devoted to us, truthful and conversant with dharma, carry his mother Draupadi without delay. Owner of dreadful prowess, depending on the strength of your arms, I will reach the Gandhamadana unhurt, with Panchala's daughter.'

Hearing his brother, that Purushavyaghra Bhimasena commands his son Ghatotkacha Parantapa, 'Invincible son of Hidimba, this mother of yours is exhausted. You are strong and can go wherever you wish. So, sky-ranger, do you carry her.

May good fortune attend upon you! Carry her on your shoulders, and go with us, flying not too high so that she is not frightened.'

Ghatotkacha says, 'Single-handed, I can bear Yudhishtira Dharmaraja, and Dhaumya, and Krishnaa, and the twins. Then what wonder that today I will carry them, where there are others to help me? And, O sinless one, hundreds of other valiant Rakshasas, all of whom can fly, and assume any shape they wish, will together carry you all, and all the Brahmanas.'

Saying this, Ghatotkacha picks up Krishnaa, and the other Rakshasas, the Pandavas, while by virtue of his inherent power, Lomasa of incomparable effulgence moves along the path of the Siddhas, even like a second Sun. And at the command of the lord of the Rakshasas, the other Rakshasas of terrific strength bear all the other Brahmanas.

Flying above enchanted forests, they fly towards the gigantic Nyagrodha tree. Going at great speed, borne by the Rakshasas, the Kshatriyas pass over long distances as if over a few steps.

On their way they see below them lands crowded with Mlechha tribes, rich with mines of diverse gems. They see hills glittering with precious metals, where Vidyadharas throng, and Vanaras and Kinnaras and Kimpurushas and Gandharvas, and full of peacocks, and chamaras, and monkeys, and rurus, and bears, and gavayas, and bison, latticed with networks of rillets, full of countless species of bird and beast, handsome with lordly elephants, the birds all full of rapture in their trees.

Passing over many lands and kingdoms, including that of the Uttarakurus, they see that foremost of mountains, the Kailasa, replete with all wonders, and beside it, they behold the hermitage of Nara and Narayana, with unearthly trees bearing flowers and fruit in all seasons.

They also see the exquisite and mighty Nyagrodha, of the round trunk, fresh and so alive, its shade wide and deep, its foliage thick, soft and sleek; full of health; its boughs gigantic and wide-spreading and of incomparable lustre; and bearing full, delicious and holy fruit, dripping nectar.

And this celestial tree is visited by hosts of mighty sages, and its branches teem with birds maddened by spirits; it grows in a grove where no mosquito or fly comes, a spot abundant with fruit, roots and sprakling water, covered in velvet green grasses, where Devas and Gandharvas come.

Its trunk is smooth, cool, its bark delicate and lovely. Reaching that ancestral tree, along with the Brahmanarishabhas, those mahatmans alight from the shoulders of the Rakshasas, and they see the charmed, most holy asrama of Nara-Narayana, where no sorrow comes, nor the rays of the Sun; where no hunger, thirst, heat or cold venture; where all grief melts away; where hosts of Maharishis throng; which hermitage is adorned by the grace of the Vedas, Saman, Rik, and Yajus; asrama inaccessible to men who have no devotion; asrama beautiful with offerings, and homas; and most sacred; and well-swept and fragrant; and shining all around with offerings of celestial blossoms; and spread over with altars of sacrificial fire, and holy women and water-pots and urns of holy waters and baskets, this refuge of all beings; and echoing with the chanting of the Vedas; and heavenly and most worthy of being dwelt in; where all tiredness disappears; and splendent and full of incomprehensible grace; and majestic, divine.

The Maharishis who live in that asrama subsist on fruit and roots, their senses perfectly restrained; they wear black deer-skins; they are effulgent like the Sun and Agni; their souls have been made great through tapasya and they are intent on mukti, while they lead the lives of Vanaprasthas, in communion with the Paramatman; and constantly the sound of Vedic hymns fill that place.

Then, having purified himself, and restraining his senses, Dharmaputra Yudhishtira of great tejas, together with his brothers, approaches those Rishis. And knowing him, for they are all blessed with supernatural knowledge, all the great sages receive him joyfully.

And those Munis, chanters of the Veda, themselves like fire, bless Yudhishtira; they give him holy water and flowers and roots. And Yudhishtira Dharmaraja receives these with reverence and joy.

Now, O sinless one, Pandu's son, along with Krishnaa and his brothers, and thousands of Brahmanas versed in the Vedas and the Vendangas, enters that most sacred asrama, which is like the abode of Sukra himself, and which pleases the mind with scents of heaven, which resembles heaven itself, so beautiful is it.

There Yudhishtira sees the hermitage of Nara and Narayana, made enchanting by the Bhagirathi and worshipped by the Devas and the Devarishis. Seeing that hermitage where Brahmarshis dwell, where fruits dripping ambrosia grow all around, the Pandavas are filled with rare delight.

Having reached that place, those high-souled Kshatriyas begin living with the Brahmanas. There they see the holy lake Vinda, and the mountain Mainaka, of golden summits, where so many species of birds live, and those magnanimous ones live there happily.

The sons of Pandu and Krishnaa delight in ranging through charmed woods and forests, bright with flowers of every season; exquisite on every side with trees bearing full-blown blossoms, and bending with the weight of fruits, and with countless male kokilas among their glossy leaves; and growing thickly and their shade cool and lovely to behold.

They delight in coming upon diverse lakes of limpid water, shimmering with lotuses and lilies. And there, O lord, the balmy mountain breeze blows, bearing the purest fragrances, gladdeing their hearts.

And hard by the gigantic nyagrodha, the mighty sons of Kunti see the Bhagirathi falling down, crystalline, cool, bearing fresh lotuses, softly over a gentle descent of steps made of ruby and coral, and graced on both sides with celestial trees and her waters strewn with celestial flowers, and enchanting the mind and heart.

In that place, frequented by Deva and Rishi, and so hard of access, they make themselves pure and offer oblations to the manes, the gods and the great sages in the sacred waters of the Bhagirathi.

Thus those bulls among men, the heroic Kurupraviravas, begin to dwell there with the Brahmanas, making their offerings and practising dhyana. The Purushavyaghras feel particularly joyful to watch the various amusements of Draupadi."

CANTO 145

Tirtha-yatra Parva Continued

Vaisampayana said, "There, in purity, those tigers among men remain for six nights, waiting to see Arjuna.

One day, a gust of wind blows from the north-east bringing a heavenly lotus of a thousand petals, effulgent as the Sun. Panchali sees that bloom of unearthly fragrance, brought by the wind and left on the ground; she picks it up and is enraptured.

She cries to Bhimasena, 'Look, Bhima, this unearthly flower has the quintessential source of all redolence within it! Parantapa, it makes my heart soar in joy.

I will give this bloom to Yudhishtira Dharmaraja, so you must fetch some more for me, so that I can take them to our asrama in the Kamyaka. If, O Pandava, you do love me, bring me many, many of these wondrous flowers.'

Saying this, that chaste queen of the beautiful glances approaches Yudhishtira with the flower. Bhima Purusharishabha, mightiest of all men, sets out to satisfy her wish; intent upon bringing her the flowers, he goes swiftly, facing the wind, in the direction from which the flower had come.

With his bow and mace inlaid with gold, with his arrows like venomous serpents, he goes forth like an angry lion or an elephant in rut; and all creatures on his way gaze at him with the powerful bow and arrows.

He felt no exhaustion, no languor, no fear or confusion, as that son of Vayu and Pritha. Up the peak he climbs, with the strength of his arms, to please Draupadi. That slayer of his foes ranges that finest mountain covered with trees and creepers, its ground black rock; and frequented by Kinnaras; and with all manner of mineral, plant, beast, and birds of various hues; and appearing like an upraised arm of the Earth adorned with an entire set of ornaments.

His eyes fixed on the slopes of Gandhamadana, fragrant mountain, various thoughts swirling through his mind, his ears thrilling with the sweet songs of male kokilas and the ubiqitous hum black bees, and his eyes enchanted by the vivid colours of the profusion of flowers of all seasons, he of unmatched prowess goes along even like an elephant in musth ranging mad through a forest.

And fanned by the fresh breeze of the Gandhamadana, bearing the scents of myriad blossoms and cooling like a father's touch, Bhima goes along sniffing the bright and perfumed air. The hairs on his body stand on end with delight, as he surveys all of that mountain for the flowers for which he has come, Gandhmadana home to Yakshas and Gandharvas and Devas and Brahmarshis.

Brushed by the leaves of Saptachchada tree, besmeared with fresh red, black and white minerals, he looks as if decorated with lines of holy unguenta drawn by uncanny fingers. With clouds stretching away at its sides, the mountain seems as if it were dancing with outspread wings; with its spring and streams flowing and sparkling, it seems to be decked with necklaces of pearls.

Upon its slopes are romantic caves and groves and waterfalls; brilliant peacocks dance to the chiming of the anklets and bangles of Apsaras; the mountain's jagged surfaces have been worn smooth by the tusks of the Diggajas; with the rivers cascading down, Gandhamadana looks as if its clothes are being loosened.

Cheerfully, playfully, that graceful son of the wind-god hies on, forcing his way through countless intertwined creepers. Great stags gaze curiously at him, with lush grass in their mouths; never having known fear before, they do not flee.

Determined to fulfil the wish of his love, Pandu's mighty and youthful son, stalwart and of splendour like that of gold, his body strong as a lion's, crashing along like a maddened elephant, and with the force of an elephant in rut, and his eyes coppery like those of a musth-stirred elephant, and able to stop the charge of a maddened elephant, ranges the enchanting Gandhamadana with his beautiful and extraordinary eyes upraised – presenting a most novel and unusual spectacle.

The wives of Yakshas and Gandharvas sitting invisible beside their lords, stare at him, turning their faces as he storms past. Intent upon gratifying Draupadi exiled into the forest, as he traverses wondrous Gandhamada, Bhima remembers all the grief and pain that Duryodhana has inflicted upon them.

Bhima thinks, 'What will Yudhishtira do now, with Arjuna not returned from Devaloka and with me here looking for Draupadi's flowers? Surely, out of love and uncertainty about their prowess he will not send Nakula and Sahadeva to look for us. Ah, how can I find these flowers quickly?'

Worried, his mind and eyes fixed to the mountains lovely slopes, that tiger among men goes along as swiftly as the lord of birds, as the wind, with Draupadi's wish his provender, making the earth tremble with his tread, he goes like the wind, even like a hurricane at the equinox; and frightening herds of elephants and prides of lions and lone tigers, and deer; and uprooting and smashing great trees and tearing up plants and creepers, he goes like some wild tusker, climbing higher and higher towards the summit of a mountain, and now roaring fiercely even like a cloud full of thunder.

Awakened by Bhima's dreadful roaring, tigers come out of their dens, while other rangers of the forest hide. The coursers of the skies spring up from their perches and wheel into the air. Deer herds run away in panic; mighty lions awake from their slumber and forsake their caves. Huge bison stand and stare. Terrified elephants, along with their mates, flee that forest and lumber away to more open spaces below.

And the boars and the deer and the lions and the bison and the tigers and the jackals and the gavayas of the forest wood all together set up a dismal outcry of fear; and geese, and gallinules ? and ducks and karandavas and plavas and parrots and kokilas and herons all fly frantically in every direction.

Some haughty elephants, goaded by their mates, as also some enraged lions fly at Bhimasena, but in their hearts they are afraid and they rush at him spraying urine and dung, and trumpeting and roaring only to embolden themselves.

The wind-god's lustrous and graceful son, the mighty Pandava, promptly begins to kill them all, why he hefts one elephant and swinging it through the air kills another with it; he does the same with some lions; while others he despatches with mere slaps!

At being struck by Bhima, all the elephants, lions, tigers and leopards that come yelp and scream in terror, and discharge more dung and urine. Quickly, he kills them all, those that do not flee, and the majestic and awesomely strong son of Pandu enters the jungle, now roaring and shouting aloud himself, making the forest echo.

Then that long-armed one sees upon the slopes of the Gandhamadana a beautiful and extraordinary grove of plantain trees, spreading over some yojanas. Like some crazed lion, he rushes towards it trampling countless plants on his way. That strongest of men begins to tear up the plaintain trees, each as tall as many palmyras, and flings them all around him like so many blades of grass. All the while his shouts and yells resound through the forest.

Forging on, he encounters countless beasts of gigantic size, and stags, and monkeys, and lions, and bison, and great fish in the streams; with the cries of these, and the roars of Bhima, even animals and birds in the remotest parts of the jungle all tremble and cry out.

At their cries, a great flock of waterfowl suddenly rise up into the sky on wet wings. Seeing these, that bull of the Bhaaratas now goes towards them, and he sees a great and lovely lake, rippled by soft breezes, fanned by the golden leaves of the plantain tree which grew upon its banks.

Immediately plunging into the water, abounding in lotuses and lilies, Bhima begins to sport lustily just like an elephant in rut. Having thus pleased himself for a long while, the bright one climbs out again, to make his way deeper into the thick jungle.

Filling his great lungs he blows a thunderous blast on his conch; striking his arms with his hands, the mighty Bhima makes all the points of heaven reverberate. Filled by the sounds of the shell, and by the shouts of Bhimasena, and also with the reports of his striking his own arms, the caves of the mountain seem as if they are roaring.

Hearing him smite his arms like thunderclaps, the lions asleep inside those caves howl like terrified cats. Frightened by the lions, the elephants of this deeper forest set up an awful trumpeting, which also echoes upon the mountain.

Hearing those sounds, and also knowing that this was Bhimasena his brother, the Vanara Hanuman, greatest of monkeys, wanting to meet and to bless Bhima, lays himself across the Pandava's path. Not wanting Bhima to go on, Hanuman lies squarely across the narrow way, flanked by plantain trees, obstructing it to keep Bhima safe.

So that Bhima does not face curse or defeat by entering the plantain forest, Hanuman lays his huge body down; he begins to yawn, and lashes the earth with his great tail first, raising it even like a stambha raised to Indra, and that sound is thunder. All around, the maintain caves echo those great reports, like a cow lowing.

As the tail lashes and the mountain quakes, it also begins to crumble on every side; the reverberations drown the trumpeting of frightened elephants and spread across every slope of Gandhamadana.

Bhima hears the sounds and the fine hairs on his body stand on end; he begins to range through that plantain wood in search of the source of the crashes. Upon a raised rocky base, he sees Hanuman, whose body is as brilliant as a streak of lightning and difficult to even look at; his fur is coppery, like the lightning-flash; the whiplashes of his tail are like lightning; the Vanara's waist seems slender for his shoulders are so vast; his neck his thick and short.

Long hairs cover his tail, which is a little bent at the end, and raised like some flag. Bhima sees Hanuman's coppery face, and his tongue between small lips, his ears red, his eyes bright and brisk, and his white sharp teeth.

Hanuman's head glows like the full moon ashine; his mane is tousled wild around it, like a pile of asoka flowers. Amidst the golden plantain trees, that effulgent one lies like some blazing fire, his body radiant, at times looking around him with eyes red as if with wine.

The most intelligent Bhima sees that mighty Vanara chieftain lying like the Himalaya, obstructing the path of heaven. Seeing him alone in that mighty forest, the dauntless Bhima approaches him with rapid strides, and gives a loud shout like thunder.

Birds and beasts are alarmed by that shout and scatter, but the great Hanuman only half opens his eyes, and looks at Bhima with disregard, through his eyes red as if with intoxication.

Then, with a smile, Hanuman says, "I was sleeping sweetly. Why have you awakened me? You have reason, surely, and you must show kindness to all creatures. We belong to the animals and are ignorant of dharma, but possessing reason, men show kindness towards creatures. Then why does a reasonable man like you do things which contaminate body, speech and heart, alike, and destroy virtue?

You do not know what dharma is and neither have you taken the counsel of the wise. Is it that from ignorance, and childishness, that you kill the animals?

Say, who are you, and for what have you come to this forest devoid of humans? And, O foremost of men, tell me also, where you are going today. You cannot go any further, for the hills ahead are inaccessible.

Shura, save the passage gained through tapasya there is no path to that place. This is the path of the celestials; mortals can never go this way. Out of kindness, O hero, I dissuade you. Listen to me, you cannot go on from this place, so desist.

Lord of men, you are welcome here in every way; so rest here and partake of fruits and roots, sweet as amrita and do not go on and have yourself killed for no reason.'

CANTO 146

TIRTHA-YATRA PARVA CONTINUED

Vaisampayana said, "O Parantapa, hearing what the wise Vanara says, Bhima asks, 'Who are you? And why have you assumed the form of a monkey? It is a Kshatriya—one of the varna next to the Brahmanas—that asks you; and he belongs to the Kuruvamsa and the House of the Moon, and was borne by Kunti in her womb, and is one of the sons of Pandu, and is the offspring of Vayu, and is known by the name of Bhimasena.'

Hanuman smiles to listen to the Kurupravira; that Vayuputra says to the other Vayuputra, his brother Bhimasena, 'I am a Vanara, and I will not allow you the passage that you desire. It is best that you return; do not go on to meet your death.'

Bhimasena replies, 'O Vanara, arise and let me pass; do not come to grief at my hands.'

Hanuman says, 'I have not the strength to arise; I am ill and suffering. If you must go on, step over me and do so.'

Bhima says, 'The Nirguna Paramatman pervades every body. I cannot disrespect Him that is knowable only by gyana. So, I will not step over you. If I had not known Him from whom all creatures manifest, I would have leapt over you and even the mountain, even as Hanuman once leapt across the ocean.'

At which, Hanuman says, 'Who is this Hanuman, who leapt across the ocean? Best of men, tell me about him if you can.'

Bhima replies, 'He is even my brother, excellent with every perfection, and endowed with intelligence and strength of both mind and body. He is the most illustrious lord of monkeys, renowned in the Ramayana; and for Rama's queen, that lord of the Vanaras crossed the ocean of over a hundred yojanas with a single leap.

That mighty one is my brother. I am his equal in energy, strength, and prowess, and also in battle. And I can chasten you, monkey; so get up. Either give me passage or witness my might today. If you do not listen to me, I will send you to halls of Yama.'

Realising that Bhima is intoxicated with his own strength, and full of pride of the might of his arms, Hanuman chides him in his heart, and says, 'Relent, sinless one. I am so old and weary that I do not have the strength to get up. Take pity on me; move my tail aside and pass.'

Bhima, proud and by now angry, believes Hanuman and thinks, 'I will seize the weakling monkey by his tail and send him to Yamaloka!'

With a mocking smile, he takes hold of the tail with his left hand; but he cannot move that monkey's tail. Bhima seizes the tail, straight and stiff like a stambha erected for Indra, with both hands; he still cannot shift it at all.

Quickly, the Panadava's brows are knit, his face wrinkled with effort, his eyes roll in their sockets, but he cannot budge the Vanara's tail.

Defeated, Bhimasena returns to the old monkey's side, and stands crestfallen and ashamed. Folding his hands, bowing low, Bhima says in a faltering voice, 'Relent, O Vanarottama, forgive me for the harsh words I spoke to you! Are you a Siddha, a Deva, a Gandharva, or a Guhyaka? I ask you out of curiosity. If it is not a secret and if I may hear it, tell me who you are that have assumed the shape of monkey, O long-armed. I ask you even as a disciple his master, and I, O Anagha, seek your protection!'

Hanuman says, 'O Parantapa, I will satisfy your curiosity fully, and tell you all that you want to know. Listen, O son of Pandu!

Lotus-eyed one, I was begotten by Vayu Deva, life of the world, upon the wife of Kesari. I am a Vanara and my name is Hanuman. All the greatest monkey-kings, and monkey-chieftains once used to wait upon Surya's son Sugriva and Indra's son Vali. Scourge of your enemies, Sugriva and I were friends even as the wind and fire.

Driven out from their kingdom by his brother Vali, Sugriva lived for a long time on Rishyamukha, and I with him. And the mighty son of Dasaratha, the heroic Rama, who is Vishnu's own self in human form, was born into the world.

His great bow in his hand, and his wife and his brother with him, Rama, greatest among archers, began to dwell in the Dandaka vana, to preserve his father's dharma.

From Janasthana, in that forest, the awesome Rakshasa King, the evil Ravana carried Rama's queen away, deceiving, O sinless one, that Purushottama through the agency of a demon, Maricha, who assumed the form of a golden deer marked with gem-like spots.'

CANTO 147

TIRTHA-YATRA PARVA CONTINUED

Hanuman continues, 'After his wife was carried away, Rama, scion of the Raghuvamsa, with his brother Lakshmana, searched for his queen on that mountain, and there met Sugriva, lord of the Vanaras. He made a pact of friendship with the noble Sugriva; Rama slew Vali and installed Sugriva as king of the Vanaras.

Having the kingdom, Sugriva sent forth his monkeys, hundreds and thousands of them, in search of Sita. I, too, with numberless monkeys, set out towards the south in quest of Sita, O Mahabaho.

On our quest, a mighty vulture called Sampati informed us that Sita was in the palace of Ravana. Then, to serve Rama, I leapt across the ocean of a hundred yojanas, the abode of sharks and crocodiles.

In Lanka, I saw in Ravana's palace the daughter of king Janaka, Sita, like the daughter of a Deva. I spoke with Vaidehi, Rama's beloved, and then I burnt Lanka with its towers and ramparts and lofty gates, and proclaimed my name there, and then I returned to Bharatavarsha.

I told Rama everything, and that lotus-eyed immediately set out to rescue his wife. He created a bridge across the ocean for his army of monkeys and we crossed over it. In Lanka, Rama slew the Rakshasas in battle; he killed Ravana, oppressor of the worlds, and all his demons. Having slain the king of the Rakshasas, his brother, his sons and other kin, Rama crowned the pious and kindly Rakshasa lord Vibhishana as king.

Rama recovered his wife, even like the lost Vaidik revelation. Then Raghu's scion and his devoted Sita returned to Ayodhya, inaccessible to enemies; and that lord of men was crowned and began to rule from there.

Then, I asked a boon of the lotus-eyed Rama, saying, "Parantapa, Rama, let me live for as long as the story of your deeds is told in the world!"

Rama said, "So be it."

Bhima, through the grace of Sita, also, in this place I have everything I need or want, every rare luxury, as do all that dwell in this place. Rama reigned for ten thousand and ten hundred years; and then he ascended to his own abode. Ever since, Apsaras and Gandharvas delight me here, singing the pure and mighty deeds of that hero.

Sinless one, Kurunandana, this path is impassable to mortals. For this, O Bhaarata, and also to ensure that noone vanquishes you, or curses you, have I obstructed your passage to this path that the immortals tread. For the celestials, this is one of the paths to heaven; mortals cannot pass this way.

But the lake in search of which you have come lies in that direction.'"

CANTO 148

TIRTHA-YATRA PARVA CONTINUED

Vaisampayana continued, "The powerful Bhimasena Mahabaho bows lovingly, and with a cheerful heart, to his brother Hanuman, the Vanara lord, and says in the mildest voice, 'Noone is more fortunate than I am, now that I have seen my elder brother! Fortune has been so kind to me, and I cannot express my delight.'

But now I have a wish that I pray you will fulfil. Shura, I want to see that incomparable form you had when you leapt across the ocean full of sharks and crocodiles, ocean of a hundred yojanas. If you show me that form I will be satisfied, I will believe everything that you have said.'

The mighty Vanara replies with a smile, 'No one today can see that form of mine, not you or anyone else. In that yuga, all things were different, not as they are today, dwindled.

In the Krita yuga, the state of things was one; and in the Treta, another; and in the Dwapara, still another. Diminution is sweeping through this age; and I do not have that form now. Why, the earth, rivers, plants, and rocks, and Siddhas, Devas and Devarishis conform to Time, according to the yugas.

Therefore, do not wish to see my old form, O Kurupravira. I am bound by the nature of this age; time is irresistible.'

Bhimasena says, 'Tell me about the duration of the different yugas, and of the varied manners and customs and of dharma, kama and artha, and of karma, of tejas, and of life and death in the different yugas.'

Hanuman says, 'Child, that yuga is called Krita when the one eternal religion existed, the Sanatana Dharma. In that best of yugas, everyone owned spiritual perfection and, therefore, there was no need for religious deed or rituals. Dharma knew no deterioration, and neither did anyone die. For this, that yuga is called Krita, the perfect.

But in time the Krita yuga has come to be considered as an inferior one. In the Krita, there were neither Devas nor Asuras, nor Gandharvas, nor Yakshas, nor Rakshasas, nor Nagas.

There was no commerce, no buying and selling. And the Sama, the Rik, and the Yajus did not exist. And there was no manual labour. All the necessaries of life were obtained merely by being thought of, and the only punya lay in renouncing the world.

During that yuga, there was neither disease nor decay of the senses. There was neither malice nor pride, nor hypocrisy, nor discord, nor ill-will, nor cunning, nor fear, nor misery, nor envy, nor covetousness.

And for this, that prime refuge of Yogis, the Supreme Brahman, was attainable to all. Narayana, wearing a white complexion, was the soul of all creatures. In the Krita Yuga, the distinctive characteristics of Brahmanas, Kshatriyas, Vaisyas and Sudras were natural and these always adhered to their respective dharmas.

Brahman was the sole refuge, and their manners and customs were naturally adapted to the attainment of Brahman; and the objects of their knowledge was the sole Brahman, and all their karma also had reference to Brahman. In this way, all the varnas attained punya.

One uniform Soul was the object of their meditation; and there was only one mantra, the Pranava, AUM, and there was one law. And although they had different natures, all of them followed a single Veda; and they had one dharma, one religion.

And according to the divisions of time, they lived the four asramas, without any desires, and so they attained moksha. The dharma which comprises of identifying the Atman with the Brahman is the sign of the Krita Yuga.

In the Krita Yuga, the dharma of the four varnas is universal, entire; thus the Krita Yuga is devoid of the three gunas.

Now listen to the character of the Treta Yuga. In this age, sacrifices are introduced, and dharma decreases by a fourth part. And Narayana, who is the Soul of all creatures, assumes a red colour. And men practise truth, and devote themselves to religion and religious rites; sacrifices and various religious observances come into existence.

In the Treta Yuga, people begin to devise means for the attainment of objects, for possession; and they attain it through karma and dana. However, they never deviate from dharma, and they are devoted to asceticism and to the giving of gifts.

The four varnas adhere to their respective swadharmas, and perform rituals. Such are the men of the Treta Yuga.

In the Dwapara Yuga, the Sanatana Dharma decreases by one half. Now Narayana wears yellow; and the Veda becomes divided into four parts. Now some men retain the knowledge of the four Vedas, and some of three Vedas, and some of one Veda, while others do not even know even the Riks.

Upon the Shastras becoming so divided, karma multiplies. And largely influenced by passion, men still engage in tapasya and dana. But from their incapacity to study the entire Veda, it becomes divided into several parts; and in consequence of the intellect having decreased, few are established in truth.

And when people fall away from the truth, they become subject to myriad diseases; and then lust and natural calamities ensue. Afflicted by these, some men perform penance, while others celebrate sacrifices, yagnas, wishing to enjoy the good things of life, or to attain heaven.

Upon the coming of the Dwapara Yuga, men become degenerate, in consequence of their impiety.

O son of Kunti, in the Kali Yuga only a quarter of dharma survives. And in the beginning of this iron age, Narayana wears a black hue. And the Vedas and the Shastras, and dharma, and yagans, and every religious observance, all these fall into disuse.

Then Iti[1] reigns, and disease, and lassitude, and anger and deformities, and natural calamities, and anguish, and fear of scarcity. As the yugas wane, dharma dwindles, and all creatures degenerate. As creatures degenerate, their natures deteriorate.

The religious rites performed at the waning of the yugas produce contrary effects. And even those that live for several yugas conform to these changes.

Parantapa, as for curiosity to know me, I say this —why should a wise person be eager to know a superfluous thing? O long-armed, I have told you in full what you asked me regarding the nature of the different yugas.

May good fortune befall you! Now return from where you came.'

---

[1]Iti: six pernicious things for crops: excessive rain, drought, vermin, locusts, birds, and a neighbouring hostile king.

CANTO 149

TIRTHA-YATRA PARVA CONTINUED

Bhimasena says, 'I will not leave without seeing your olden form. If I have found favour with you, show me your pristine self.'

With a smile, the Vanara shows Bhima the form in which he, Hanuman, once leapt across the sea. Wanting to gratify his brother, Hanuman assumes a gigantic body of immeasurable effulgence; the Vanara stands there, covering all the plantain grove, and as lofty as the Vindhya.

Great as a mountain, with coppery eyes and sharp teeth, and a face marked by a dreadful frown, Hanuman stands covering all that grove and lashing his long tail. Bhima sees that gigantic form of his brother, and his hair stands on end in wonder.

Seeing the great monkey ablaze like the Sun, like golden Meru, splendent as the sky, Bhima cannot look upon him and shuts his eyes.

Smiling again, Hanuman says to his brother, 'Anagha, you are able to see my form to this extent. But I can grow on for as long as I wish. Bhima, amidst enemies, my size increases through its own tejas.'

Seeing that wondrous and dreadful body of Hanuman, like the Vindhya mountain, Bhima Vayuputra is bewildered.

Folding his hands, the Pandava says to Hanuman, 'Lord, I have seen the immense dimensions of your body. Awesome one, I beg you make yourself small again, for I cannot look at you, like the sun risen, of measureless power, irrepressible, and resembling the Mountain Mainaka.

O Hero, great is the wonder in my heart today that with you by his side Rama himself needed to encounter Ravana. With your might, you could have annihilated Lanka and all its warriors in an instant, all its horses, elephants and chariots.

Surely, O Vayuputra, there is nothing that you cannot achieve; and in battle, I am certain that Ravana, together with all his Rakshasas, was no match for you, by yourself.'

Hanuman replies in affectionate words, solemnly spoken, 'Mahabaho, O Bhaarata, it is as you say; Bhimasena, that worst of Rakshasas was no match for me. But if I had slain Ravana—that thorn of the worlds—the glory of Raghu's son would have been obscured; and it is for this that I left him alive.

By killing that lord of the Rakshasas and his demons, and bringing back Sita unto his own city, Rama established his fame among men.

Now, O wise one, since you are intent on the welfare of your brothers, and protected by Vayu, travel on a fortunate and auspicious path. Kurusthama, this path will lead you to the Saugandhika forest.

You will see Kubera's gardens, guarded by Yakshas and Rakshasas. Do not pluck the flowers there, for the gods deserve reverence, especially from mortals. Only if they are worshipped with offerings, and homas, and salutations, and the recitation of mantras, do the Devas confer their favour upon men.

So, do not, my child, be rash; do not deviate from your svadharma. Be faithful to your duty, understanding what the highest dharma is. Without knowing your duty and serving the old, even great ones like Brihaspati cannot understand artha and dharma.

One should ascertain with discrimination that circumstance in which vice goes under the name of virtue, and virtue under the name of vice – circumstances in which men who are without intelligence become perplexed.

From religious observances merit ensues; and in merit are the Vedas founded; and from the Vedas, sacrifices come into being; and through sacrifice the gods are established. The Devas are maintained by yagnas prescribed by the Vedas and the Shastras; while men maintain themselves by following the ordinances of Brihaspati and Sukra; and also by these avocations, by which the world is maintained – serving for wages; receiving taxes; merchandise; agriculture and tending kine and sheep.

The world subsists through profession. The study of the three Vedas and agriculture and trade and government constitutes, say the Rishis, the professions of the twice-born; and each varna maintains itself by following the profession prescribed for it. And when these callings are properly pursued, the world itself is maintained with ease.

However, if the people do not lead righteous lives, the world becomes lawless, in consequence of the lack of Vedic merit and government. If the people do not follow their prescribed vocations, they perish; but by regularly following the three professions, they bring about dharma.

The dharma of Brahmanas consists in the knowledge of the soul; and the hue of only that varna is universally the same. The celebration of sacrifices, and study and bestowal of gifts are well-known to be the three duties common to all the orders.

Officiating at sacrifices, teaching and the acceptance of gifts are the duties of a Brahmana. To rule is the dharma of the Kshatriya; and to tend cattle, that of the Vaisya; while to serve the twice-born varnas is said to be the duty of the Sudra.

The Sudras cannot beg alms, or perform homas, or keep vratas; and they must dwell in the homes of their masters.

Your vocation, O son of Kunti, is that of the Kshatriya, which is to protect. Perform your svadharma, with humility and restraining your senses. That king alone can rule who takes the counsel of experienced men, and is helped by honest, intelligent and learned ministers; a king who is addicted to vices meets with defeat.

Only when the king justly punishes and confers favours is order secure in the world. Therefore, it is needful to ascertain, through spies, the nature of a hostile country, its fortified places and the allied forces of the enemy, and their prosperity and decay and the way in which they retain the adhesion of the powers they have drawn to their side.

Spies are among the important instruments of the king; and tact, diplomacy, prowess, chastisement, favour and cleverness lead to success. And success is to be attained through these, either in separation, or combined – namely, conciliation, gifts, sowing dissensions, chastisement, and might.

And, O Bhaarata, politics has for its root diplomacy; and diplomacy is also the main qualification of spies. Politics, if well judged, confers success. Therefore, in matters of polity the counsel of Brahmanas should be taken.

In secret affairs, these should not be consulted – namely, a woman, a fool, a boy, a covetous person, a mean-minded individual, and one that betrays signs of insanity. Wise men only should be consulted, and affairs are to be despatched through officers that are able.

Policy must be executed through persons that are friendly; but fools should be excluded from all affairs. In matters religious, pious men; and in matters of gain, wise men; and in guarding families, eunuchs; and in all crooked affairs, crooked men must be employed. The dharma or adharma of the resolve of an enemy, as also his strength or weakness, must be gauged through one's own as well as hostile spies.

Favour should be shown to honest persons who have prudently sought protection; but lawless and disobedient individuals should be punished. And when the king justly punishes and shows favour, the dignity of the law is well maintained, O son of Pritha.

These are the hard duties of kings, difficult to comprehend. Observe them with equanimity, even as they are prescribed for your Kshatriya varna.

Brahmanas attain Swarga through punya, mortifying the senses, and sacrifice. Vaisyas attain felicity through gifts, hospitality, and religious deeds. Kshatriyas attain the celestial regions by protecting and chastising their subjects, without being influenced by lust, malice, avarice or anger. If kings justly punish their subjects, they go to the place where men of dharma go.'"

CANTO 150

TIRTHA-YATRA PARVA CONTINUED

Vaisampayana said, "Now, contracting that immense body, which he had assumed at will, Hanuman puts his arms around Bhima and embraces him. Bhaarata, at his brother's embrace, Bhima's fatigue vanishes and new strength courses through his body. Stronger than he has ever been before, Bhima is certain that now there is no man who can match him for strength.

With tears of love in his eyes, and his voice choking, Hanuman says to Bhima, 'Kshatriya, return to your abode, and remember me incidentally in your talk! But, best of Kurus, do not tell anyone that I live here. O you of great strength, the most excellent of the wives of the Devas and Gandharvas come to this place, and the time of their arrival is near.

My eyes have been blessed that they have seen you. And, O Bhima, having embraced you, a man, a Manava, I have been reminded so much of Raghu's son, Rama, who was Vishnu himself, who was the delight of the heart of this very world. He was like the Sun that made the lotus face of Sita bloom; he was the Sun who dispelled the darkness which was Ravana.

Therefore, heroic Kaunteya, let your meeting with me not be fruitless. As my brother, ask me for a boon. If you wish, I can go to Varanavrata, even now, and kill all Dhritarashtra's insignificant sons. Or if you like I can raze that entire city with rocks; I can bind Duryodhana and bring him before you today, mighty one.'

Listening to that Mahatman, Bhima replies happily, 'Vanarottama, I will think that you have already done all this! May every good fortune befall you, Mahabaho. But what I ask of you is this — be well pleased with me. Mighty one, upon your having become our protector, the Pandavas have found help. Even through your prowess, we will conquer all our enemies.'

Hanuman says to Bhimasena, 'From brotherly love, I will do good to you by diving into the army of your enemies armed with arrows and spears. And, O Kshatriya, when you roar like a lion, I will lend force to your roars.

I will set myself on the flagstaff of Arjuna's chariot and give fierce yells that will terrifry your enemies, so that you can kill them easily.'

Saying this to the Pandava, and also pointing the way ahead, Hanuman vanishes before Bhima's eyes."

CANTO 151

Tirtha-yatra Parva Continued

Vaisampayana said, "When that greatest of Vanaras has gone, Bhima treads the path across the mighty Gandhamadana. And as he goes along, he thinks of Hanuman's vast body and splendour unrivalled on earth, and also of the greatness and dignity of Dasaratha's son Rama.

Going on in quest of the place of the saugandhikas, Bhima sees enchanting forests, groves, rivers, and lakes whose banks are graced with trees, blossom-laden, and woods of countless flowers and colours.

Bhaarata, he sees herds of wild elephants smeared with mud, resembling massed thunderheads. Graceful Bhima lopes ahead with speed, seeing among the trees around him deer of quick glances, with their mates, and long tufts of grass in their mouths.

Fearless because of his strength, as if invited by the breeze-shaken trees of the forest always fragrant with flowers, bearing delicate coppery twigs, Bhimasena plunges into mountain realms inhabited by bison, bear and leopard.

And on his way, he passes lotus-lakes over which maddened black bees swarm; on those waters it seemed as if the lotus buds were hands reverently folded to him. His provender for his journey is what Draupadi said, and Bhima speeds on, his mind and his gaze fixed upon the slopes of the mountain abloom.

When the Sun passes his zenith, Bhima sees a mighty river in the deer-filled jungle, a river full of fresh golden lotuses, a river crowded with Hamsa and Karandava, and graced with Chakravakas, river which looks like a garland of fresh lotuses put on by the mountain.

In this river, that mighty Kshatriya found banks after banks of Saugandhika lotuses, effulgent as the rising Sun, and absolutely delightful. Seeing the flowers Bhima thinks that he has attained his objective, and in his heart he thinks of Panchali and presents himself before her in his thought, his beloved Krishnaa worn out by their exile."

CANTO 152

TIRTHA-YATRA PARVA CONTINUED

Vaisampayana said, "In that place, Bheema sees, near the Kailasa massif, that beautiful lotus lake surrounded by lovely woods, and guarded by Rakshasas. He sees that it is fed by waterfalls next to the abode of Kubera. Great flowering trees shade its banks, and green water-lily pads cover its surface.

This unearthly lake is filled with golden lotuses, and swarms with diverse birds; its shallows are crystalline, with no mud at all. This lake is a wonder of the world, health-giving and enchanting. Kunti's son sees that the ambrosial water is cool, lucid, bright and fresh; the Pandava drinks thirstily, profusely, from it.

The lake is covered over with celestial Saugandhika lotuses, and other golden lotuses with stalks of sapphire. Swayed by swans and Karandavas brushing past them, the lotuses scatter fresh glimmering pollen.

This lake is where the great-souled Kubera, king of the Yakshas, comes to sport; the Gandharvas, the Apsaras and the Devas hold it in high regard; Devarishis, Yakshas, Kimpurushas, Rakshasas and Kinnaras frequent it. And it is well-protected indeed by Kubera.

Feverish delight sweeps over Bhima as soon as he lays eyes on those waters. Thousands of Rakshasas called Krodhavasas, armed with every kind of weapon, guard that lake, by the command of their lord Kubera.

Bhima of awesome prowess, wearing deerskin, golden armlets, his sword strapped to his side, plunges fearlessly ahead to gather the Saugandhikas.

The Rakshasas see him and shout to one another, 'Let us ask why this man has come here, wearing deerskin and carrying weapons!'

They approach the lustrous Vrikodara of mighty arms and ask, 'Who are you? Answer us! We see you wearing a hermit's garb yet bearing weapons. Intelligent one, tell us why you have come here.'

CANTO 153

TIRTHA-YATRA PARVA CONTINUED

Bhima says, 'I am the son of Pandu, and next by birth to Yudhishtira Dharmaraja, and my name is Bhimasena. Rakshasas, I came with my brothers to the Nyagrodha which is called Visala. There, Panchali saw a most excellent Saugandhika, which, of a certainty, was borne thence by the wind from this lake. She wishes to have the flowers in some abundance. Know, Rakshasas, that I have come to fulfil the wish of my wife of faultless features; I have come here to gather flowers for her.'

At which, the Rakshasas say, 'Purushottama, this place is dear to Kubera; he comes to sport here. Mortal men cannot enjoy this place. Vrikodara, the Devarishis and the Devas ask Kubera's leave before they drink this water or swim in it. Pandava, the Gandharvas and the Apsaras also come to please themselves in this lake.

The wicked man who, disregarding the lord of treasures, seeks to enjoy himself here surely meets his death. With no regard for Kubera you seek to take away the Saugandhikas from here by force. How then do you claim to be the brother of Yudhishtira Dharmaraja?

First, seek the permission of the lord of Yakshas, only then drink and pluck the lotuses. If you do not do this, you will not be able to have even a single Saugandhika.'

Bhimasena says, 'Rakshasas, I do not see the lord of wealth here. And even if I did see that Lokapala I would not beg him, for Kshatriyas never beg. This is the eternal dharma, and I have no intention of abandoning Kshatriya dharma.

Moreover, this lotus lake has been formed from the waterfalls of the mountain; it has not been excavated in the palace of Kubera. And so, it belongs as much to every creature as it does to Kubera Vaisravana. Who goes to beg another for such a thing?'

With this, the impatient Bhima wades into the lotus lake.

The Rakshasas, forbid him, crying, 'Desist!' and abuse him roundly from every side. Bhima ignores them, and continues wading into the water.

Their eyes rolling in anger, they arms upraised, they rush at him, roaring variously, 'Seize him! Bind him! Hew him! We will cook this Bhima and eat him!'

Bhima raises his great mace, inlaid with golden plates and like the mace of Yama himself, and turning back to face them, roars, 'Stay!'

Brandishing lances and axes, and other weapons, they run at him. The dreadful Krodhavasas surround Bhima. But he is Kunti's son begotten by Vayu, and he is mighty beyond reckoning and heroic, the slayer of his foes, and always devoted to dharma and satya, no one can vanquish him.

Swiftly, the great Bhima crushes those Rakshasas, beginning with their leader, breaking their arms, killing more than a hundred on the banks of that lake. When they see how strong he is, and that they cannot resist him, the rest of those powerful Rakshasas run in all directions, in bands, so many of them pierced and bleeding.

They fly through the air towards Mount Kailasa. Having beaten his enemy, even as Indra did the armies of the Daityas and Danavas, Bhima plunges into the lake again and begins to gather the golden lotuses as he pleases.

And as he drinks the waters, like nectar, his energy and strength surge back, and he falls to plucking and gathering the fragrant Saugandhikas.

Meanwhile, the Krodhavasas, driven away and terrified by Bhima's onslaught, flee to Kubera, Lord of treasures, and tell him everything that transpired at the lake and especially about Bhima's might.

The Deva smiles, then says, 'I already know what you have told me. Let Bhima take as many lotuses as he likes for Krishnaa.'

Those Rakshasas return to the Pandava and see him alone, enjoying himself in the lake of lotuses."

CANTO 154

TIRTHA-YATRA PARVA CONTINUED

Vaisampayana said, "Bhima gathers the rare, unearthly and fresh flowers as he pleases, in abundance.

Now a high and violent wind begins to blow, blowing up sand and earth, and portending battle. Ominous meteors fall from the sky, and thunder echoes everywhere. Enveloped in darkness, the Sun grows pale, his rays being obscured.

At Bhima displaying his prowess, dreadful explosions ring through the sky; the earth trembles, and dust falls in showers. The cardinal points of the heavens grow red, and beasts and birds begin to cry out in shrill tones.

All things are enfolded in darkness, and indistinguishable; other evil omens appear there. Yudhishtira Dharmaputra sees the strange phenomena, and says, 'Someone means to attack us. Arm yourselves Pandavas, and may good fortune befall you! From what I see, I believe that the time has come for us to show our strength.'

The king looks around and does not see Bhima. He turns to Panchali and the twins, 'Panchali, has Bhima gone to perform some great feat, or has he done so already? These omens surely portend some grave danger; they foretell a great battle.'

To allay his anxiety, Krishnaa of the sweet smile says, 'Rajan, I showed the Saugandhika which the wind blew here to Bhima. I said to him that if he could find more for me he should bring back as many as he could. Pandava, he must have gone looking for the golden lotuses for my sake. He must have gone north-east.'

Hearing her, Yudhishtira says to the twins, 'Let us follow Vrikodara's path. Let the Rakshasas carry those Brahmanas who are tired and weak. Ghatotkacha, you carry Krishnaa.

I am convinced that Bhima has gone into the jungle, for it is long since he has been gone. He travels as swiftly as the wind, or as Vinata's son, and he will even leap into the sky and alight at his will. Rakshasas, we will follow him through your prowess. He will not do any wrong to the Siddhas in the forest, who are versed in the Vedas.'

Saying, 'So be it,' Hidimba's son and the other Rakshasas, who know the lotus lake of Kubera, set out cheerfully with Lomasa, carrying the Pandavas, and many of the Brahmanas.

Soon arriving at the lake, they see it covered with Saugandhika and other lotuses and surrounded by ethereal woods. On its shores they see the noble and fierce Bhima, as also the slaughtered Yakshas of large eyes, with their bodies, arms and thighs smashed, and their heads crushed.

Upon seeing Bhima standing there like an angry lion, his eyes staring, biting his lip, his mace upraised in both hands, even like Yama at the Mahapralaya, Yudhishtira Dharmaraja runs to his brother and embraces him repeatedly.

Gently Yudhishtira says, 'Kaunteya, what have you done? Ah, may good fortune be with you, but if you love me and wish my welfare never again be so rash, nor offend the Devas!'

Now those godlike ones all begin to sport in those waters and to pluck the Saugandhikas as they please. Suddenly, the immense guardians of the gardens, with rocks for their weapons, arrive there.

Seeing Yudhishtira Dharmaraja, Maharishi Lomasa, Nakula, Sahadeva and the other great Brahmanas, those guardian Rakshasas bow down low in humility.

Yudhishtira pacifies them, and they are gratified. Thus, with Kubera's knowledge, for a short time, those Kurusthamas dwell there in those gardens upon the slopes of the Gandhamadana, waiting for Arjuna," said Vaisampayana to Raja Janamejaya.

End of Vana Parva (Part 1)